Advances in Political Economy

Norman Schofield • Gonzalo Caballero •
Daniel Kselman
Editors

Advances in Political Economy

Institutions, Modelling and Empirical Analysis

Springer

Editors
Prof. Norman Schofield
Center in Political Economy
Washington University in St. Louis
Saint Louis, MO, USA

Assoc. Prof. Gonzalo Caballero
Faculty of Economics
University of Vigo
Vigo, Spain

Daniel Kselman, PhD.
Centro de Estudios Avanzados
en Ciencias Sociales
Juan March Institute
Madrid, Spain

ISBN 978-3-642-35238-6 ISBN 978-3-642-35239-3 (eBook)
DOI 10.1007/978-3-642-35239-3
Springer Heidelberg New York Dordrecht London

Library of Congress Control Number: 2013933596

Printed on acid-free paper

Springer is part of Springer Science+Business Media (www.springer.com)

Introduction

Political Economy is both a growing field and a moving target. The concept 'political economy' remains something of an open signifier, alternatively used to describe a methodological approach in political analysis, grounded in the application of formal and quantitative methods to the study of politics; or one of any number substantive areas in the contemporary social sciences. In economics, new institutional economics (Williamson 1985, North 1990) has established the fundamental importance of history- and polity-specific governance structures in sustaining economic markets. Comparative research has investigated the effect of democratic institutions and processes on economic policy and outcomes, research given perhaps its most comprehensive statement in Persson and Tabellini (2000) and Drazen (2001), which have constituted the so-called "macroeconomics side" of political economy (Merlo 2006). Development economists increasingly recognize that, absent sound governance institutions, standard macroeconomic prescriptions for economic growth and stability often fail to bear fruit (Rodrik 2007). Economists have also recently joined political scientists in examining the role of economic factors in explaining democratic transitions and the evolution of political regimes (Acemoglu and Robinson 2000, 2006). Dewan and Shepsle (2008) have emphasized that in recent years some of the best theoretical work on the political economy of political institutions and processes has begun surfacing in the political science mainstream, and they consider that this is a result of economists coming more firmly to the conclusion that modeling governments and politicians is central to their own enterprise.

Moving to political science, work on the *modernization hypothesis*, motivated by the consistently high cross-national correlation between democratic consolidation and economic development, has also recognized the role of economic factors in determining the evolution of political regimes (Moore 1965; Przeworski et al. 2000). Furthermore, comparative political science in many ways beat economics to the punch in recognizing the role that political institutions play in determining the economic trajectories of developing and still industrializing economies (Haggard and Kaufmann 1990). Economic class structures, and their embodiment in labor unions and professional organizations, have occupied an important place in comparative politics research on the economic institutions of advanced industrial societies

(Hall and Soskice 2001). Studies of voter behavior have identified both the role that conjuntural economic factors play in informing voter choice and the relationship between voters' professional context and their preferences for redistribution. As already mentioned, the label political-economy also refers more loosely to the application of formal and game theoretic methods first developed by economists to the study of political phenomena, including legislative bargaining (Shepsle 1979; Krehbiel 1998), government coalition formation (Laver and Schofield 1990; Laver and Shepsle 1996), and campaign position-taking (Cox 1987, 1990; Schofield 2006). In this sense, the effect of economics has been felt more strongly in contemporary political science than any other social science (Miller 1997).

As evidenced by this brief, and necessarily incomplete, literature review, political economy is a concept with fairly flexible boundaries, encompassing research from a wide variety of fields and approaches. For example, Weingast and Wittman (2008) viewed political economy as the methodology of economics applied to the analysis of political behavior and institutions, but they assumed that it is not a single approach because it consists of a family of approaches. Previously, two views had been distinguished in the new political economy, and both have contributed to the advance of the understanding of modern political economy: on the one hand, Hamiltonian political economy has been interested in economic patterns and performance, but it considers that political institutions and political choices are relevant explaining factors; on the other hand, Madisonian political economy has assumed that the economic approach is central in political analysis, quite apart from economic content (Shepsle 1999). Rather than an explicit "field" or "discipline" in and of itself, the notion of political economy represents rather a growing awareness in both political science and economics that their respective contributions to our understanding of society are intelligible only in mutual conversation. It is one thing for scholars in both disciplines to recognize the interdependence of their subject matters; it is another to create professional fora in which practitioners of these two disciplines come together. The current volume results from the latest in a series of conferences designed to engender a closer collaboration between economists and political scientists. Its contributions represent a broad spectrum of research, and its contributors a diverse group of scholars from diverse academic traditions in political economy. Nonetheless, as a group we share a commitment to mutually beneficial interdisciplinary collaboration, such it has been shown in previous efforts (Schofield and Caballero 2011).

These conferences took place in April and May of 2012. The first was held at the Juan March Institute in Madrid, Spain, and was entitled *Contemporary Applications of the Spatial Model*. Ever since Downs' seminal work (1957), the spatial model has been a workhorse in formal political theory. While its core content addresses how parties choose the relative extremism or moderation of campaign positions, its results have also been used in studies of economic policy and redistribution (Meltzer and Richard 1978; Persson and Tabellini 2000). The Madrid conference brought together a group of leading scholars working on contemporary applications of the spatial paradigm, including theoretical contributions on spatial consequences of primary elections and the spatial consequences of vote buying; and empirical contributions on the measurement of parties actual policy positions, the extent to which voters accurately perceive such positions, and how these perceptions are moulded by voters' ideological predispositions.

The second conference was held in Baiona, Spain, and supported by the Erenea Research Group at the University of Vigo, and the Center in Political Economy at Washington University in Saint Louis. This conference was in fact the second installment of the *International Conference on Political Economy and Institutions* (ICOPEAI); and like the first, which was held in June 2010, it brought together political scientists and economists from many countries. The spatial model featured prominently in Baiona as well; but to this agenda was added a variety of papers on political transitions, democratic performance and human capital formation, social networks, and new institutional economics, and voting.

There was substantial overlap in the participants at both conferences, allowing for a fruitful extended dialogue that, along with an internal peer-review process, has improved the content of the volume's contributions.

The editors thank the University of Vigo, the Juan March Institute, and the Center in Political Economy, Washington University in Saint Louis for the support they provided. In addition, an earlier version of Chap. 4 was presented at the conference on the Political Economy of Democratic Institutions, organised by Lauretta Frederking at the University of Portland, June 2009. We thank Lauretta and the University of Portland for organising this earlier conference.

We have decided to structure the volume in three sections, each dealing with a particular emphasis in political economic research: Institutions, Modelling, and Empirical Analysis.

Each chapter in this book went through a review process before publication. These chapters deal with theoretical and empirical issues over the behavior of institutions and the operation of democratic elections.

Saint Louis, USA — Norman Schofield
Vigo, Spain — Gonzalo Caballero
Madrid, Spain — Daniel Kselman

Further Reading on Political Economy

Acemoglu D (2008) Oligarchic versus democratic societies. J Eur Econ Assoc 6:1–44

Acemoglu D, Robinson J (2000) Why did the West extend the franchise? Growth, inequality and democracy in historical perspective. Q J Econ 115:1167–1199

Acemoglu D, Robinson J (2006) Economic origins of dictatorship and democracy. Cambridge University Press, Cambridge

Acemoglu D, Robinson J (2012) Why nations fail. Profile, New York

Acemoglu D, Johnson S, Robinson J (2001) The colonial origins of comparative development. Am Econ Rev 91:1369–1401

Acemoglu D, Johnson S, Robinson J (2002) Reversal of fortune. Q J Econ 118: 1231–1294

Acemoglu D, Johnson S, Robinson J (2004) Institutions as the fundamental cause of long run growth. NBER, Washington

Acemoglu D, Johnson S, Robinson J (2005) The rise of Europe: Atlantic trade, institutional change, and economic growth. Am Econ Rev 95:546–579

Acemoglu D, Johnson S, Robinson J, Yared P (2008) Income and democracy. Am Econ Rev 98:808–842

Acemoglu D, Johnson S, Robinson J, Yared P (2009) Reevaluating the modernization hypothesis. J Monet Econ 56:1043–1058

Boix C (2003) Democracy and redistribution. Cambridge University Press, Cambridge

Buchanan JM, Tullock G (1962) The calculus of consent: logical foundations of constitutional democracy. University of Michigan Press, Ann Arbor

Bunce V, Wolchik S (2010) Democracy and authoritarianism in the post communist world. Cambridge University Press, Cambridge

Coase RH (1984) The new institutional economics. J Inst Theor Econ 140:229–231

Clark G (2007) A farewell to alms. Princeton University Press, Princeton

Collier P (2007) The bottom billion. Oxford University Press, Oxford

Cox GW (1987) Electoral equilibria under alternative voting institutions. Am J Polit Sci 31:82–108

Cox GW (1990) Centripetal and centrifugal incentives in electoral systems. Am J Polit Sci 34:903–935

Dewan T, Shepsle K (2008) Recent economic perspectives on political economy, Part I. Br J Polit Sci 38:363–382.

Downs A (1957) An economic theory of democracy. Harper Collins, New York

Drazen A (2001) Political economy in macroeconomics. Princeton University Press, Princeton

Easterly W (2007) Globalization, poverty and all that: factor endowment versus productivity views. In: Harrison A (ed) Globalization and poverty. Chicago University Press, Chicago

Eggertsson T (1990) Economic behaviour and institutions. Cambridge University Press, Cambridge

Epstein D, Bates R, Goldstone J, Kristensen I, O'Halloran S (2006) Democratic transitions. Am J Polit Sci 50:551–568

Greif A (2006) Institutions and the path to modern economy. Cambridge University Press, Cambridge

Haggard SM, Kaufmann RR (1992) The politics of adjustment. Princeton University Press, Princeton

Hall PA, Soskice D (eds) (2001) Varieties of capitalism. Oxford University Press, Oxford

Jones CI, Romer P (2010) The Kaldor facts: ideas, institutions, population and human capital. Am Econ J Macroecon 2:224–245

Kingston C, Caballero G (2009) Comparing theories of institutional change. J Inst Econ 5(2):151–180

Kitschelt H, Mansfeldova Z, Markowski R, Tóka G et al (1999) Post-communist party system. Cambridge University Press, Cambridge

Kornai J, Eggleston K (2001). Welfare, choice, and solidarity in transition: reforming the health sector in Eastern Europe. Cambridge University Press, Cambridge

Krehbiel (1998) Pivotal politics. A theory of U.S. lawmaking. University of Chicago Press, Chicago.

Laver M, Schofield N (1990) Multiparty government. The politics of coalition in Europe. University of Michigan Press, Ann Arbor

Laver M, Shepsle KA (1996) Making and breaking governments: cabinets and legislatures in parliamentary democracies. Cambridge University Press, Cambridge

Libecap GD (1989) Contracting for property rights. Cambridge University Press, Cambridge

Meltzer AH, Richard SF (1978) Why government grows (and grows) in a democracy. Public Interest 52:111–18

Menard C, Shirley MM (eds) (2005) Handbook of new institutional economics. Springer, Berlin

Merlo A (2006) Wither political economy? Theories, facts and issues. In: Blundell R, Newey W, Persson T (eds) Advances in economics and econometrics. Theory and applications. Cambridge University Press, Cambridge, pp 381–421

Miller GJ (1997) The impact of economics on contemporary political science, J Econ Lit XXXV:1173–1204

Mokyr J (2010) The enlightened economy: an economic history of Britain 1700–1850. Yale University Press, New Haven

Moore B (1965) Social origins of dictatorship and democracy: lord and peasant in the making of the modern world. Beacon Press, Boston

North DC (1990) Institutions, institutional change and economic performance. Cambridge University Press, Cambridge

North DC (2005) Understanding the process of economic change. Princeton University Press, Princeton

North DC, Wallis JJ, Weingast BR (2009) Violence and social orders: a conceptual framework for interpreting recorded human history. Cambridge University Press, Cambridge

Ostrom E (1990) Governing the commons. Cambridge University Press, Cambridge

Ostrom E (2005) Understanding institutional diversity. Princeton University Press, Princeton

Persson T, Tabellini G (2000) Political economics: explaining economic policy. MIT Press, Cambridge

Persson T, Tabellini G (2003) The economic effect of constitutions. MIT Press, Cambridge

Przeworski A (1991) Democracy and the market: political and economic reforms in Eastern Europe and Latin America. Cambridge University Press, Cambridge

Przeworski A (2006) Democracy and economic development. In: Mansfield E, Sisson R (eds) Political science and the public interest. Ohio State University Press, Columbus

Przeworski A, Alvarez ME, Cheibub JA, Limongi F (2000) Democracy and development: political institutions and well-being in the world, 1950–1990. Cambridge University Press, Cambridge

Rawls J (1971) A theory of justice. Harvard University Press, Cambridge

Rodrik D (2007) One economics, many recipes. Globalization, institutions and economic growth. Princeton University Press, Princeton

Schofield N (2006) Architects of political change: constitutional quandaries and social choice theory. Cambridge University Press, Cambridge

Schofield N (2007) The mean voter theorem: necessary and sufficient conditions for convergent equilibrium. Rev Econ Stud 74:965–980

Schofield N (2009) The political economy of democracy and tyranny. Oldenbourg, Munich.

Schofield N, Caballero G (eds) (2011) Political economy of institutions, democracy and voting. Springer, Berlin.

Schofield N, Gallego M (2011) Leadership or chaos. Springer, Berlin

Schofield N, Gallego M, Jeon J (2011a) Leaders, voters and activists in elections in the Great Britain 2005 and 2010. Elect Stud 30(3):484–496

Schofield N, Gallego M, Ozdemir U, Zakharov A (2011b) Competition for popular support: a valence model of elections in Turkey. Soc Choice Welf 36(3–4):451–482

Serra G (2011) Why primaries? The party's trade-off between policy and valence. J Theor Polit 23(1):21–51

Shepsle KA (1979) Institutional arrangements and equilibrium in multidimensional voting models. Am J Polit Sci 23:23–57

Shepsle K (1999) The political economy of state reform. Political to the core. Braz J Pol Econ 19:39–58

Sokoloff KL, Engerman SL (2000) Institutions, factor endowments and the paths of development in the new world. J Econ Perspect 14:217–232

Weingast BR, Wittman DA (2008) The reach of political economy. In: Weingast BR, Wittman DA (eds) The Oxford handbook of political economy. Oxford University Press, Oxford, pp 3–25

Williamson OE (1985) The economic institutions of capitalism: firms, markets, relational contracting. The Free Press, New York

Williamson OE (2000) The new institutional economics: taking stock, looking ahead. J Econ Lit 38:595–613

Contents

Contributors

James Adams Department of Political Science, University of California, Davis, Davis, CA, USA

Luz Marina Arias CEACS, Juan March Institute, Madrid, Spain

Xosé Carlos Arias Faculty of Economics, University of Vigo, Vigo, Spain

Walter Borges Division of Liberal Arts and Life Sciences, University of North Texas-Dallas, Dallas, TX, USA

Thomas L. Brunell School of Economic, Political and Policy Sciences, University of Texas at Dallas, Richardson, TX, USA

Gonzalo Caballero Faculty of Economics, University of Vigo, Vigo, Spain

Ernesto Calvo Government and Politics, University of Maryland, College Park, MD, USA

Kiyoung Chang Government and Politics, University of Maryland, College Park, MD, USA

Harold D. Clarke School of Economic, Political and Policy Sciences, University of Texas at Dallas, Richardson, TX, USA; Department of Government, University of Essex, Colchester, UK

Leandro De Magalhães Department of Economics, University of Bristol, Bristol, UK

Betul Demirkaya Center in Political Economy, Washington University in Saint Louis, Saint Louis, MO, USA

Jon X. Eguia Department of Politics, New York University, New York, NY, USA

Bernard Grofman Department of Political Science and Center for the Study of Democracy, University of California, Irvine, Irvine, CA, USA

Timothy Hellwig Department of Political Science, Indiana University, Bloomington, IN, USA

Jee Seon Jeon Center in Political Economy, Washington University in Saint Louis, Saint Louis, MO, USA

Daniel Kselman Center for Advanced Studies in the Social Sciences, Juan March Institute, Madrid, Spain

Dean Lacy Department of Government, Dartmouth College, Hanover, NH, USA

Kevin McAlister Center in Political Economy, Washington University in Saint Louis, Saint Louis, MO, USA

Samuel Merrill Department of Mathematics and Computer Science, Wilkes University, Wilkes-Barre, PA, USA

Katja Michalak Department of Public Management and Governance, Zeppelin University, Friedrichshafen, Germany

Emerson M.S. Niou Department of Political Science, Duke University, Durham, NC, USA

John W. Patty Center in Political Economy, Washington University in Saint Louis, Saint Louis, MO, USA

Gerald Pech Department of Economics, KIMEP University, Almaty, Republic of Kazakhstan

Elizabeth Maggie Penn Center in Political Economy, Washington University in Saint Louis, Saint Louis, MO, USA

Arturas Rozenas ISM University of Management and Economics, Vilnius, Lithuania

David Sanders Department of Government, University of Essex, Colchester, UK

Keith E. Schnakenberg Center in Political Economy, Washington University in Saint Louis, Saint Louis, MO, USA

Evan Schnidman Cambridge, MA, USA

Norman Schofield Weidenbaum Center, Washington University in St. Louis, St. Louis, MO, USA

Gilles Serra Department of Political Science, Center for Economics Research and Teaching (CIDE), Mexico City, Mexico

Olga Shvetsova Department of Political Science, Binghamton University, Binghamton, NY, USA

Katri K. Sieberg Department of North American Studies, University of Tampere, Tampereen Yliopisto, Finland

Marianne C. Stewart School of Economic, Political and Policy Sciences, University of Texas at Dallas, Richardson, TX, USA

Fernando Toboso Faculty of Economics, Departamento de Economía Aplicada, University of Valencia, Valencia, Spain

Paul Whiteley Department of Government, University of Essex, Colchester, UK

Part I
Institutions

Transaction Cost Politics in the Map of the New Institutionalism

Gonzalo Caballero and Xosé Carlos Arias

1 Introduction

During the mid-eighties, Matthews (1986) affirmed in his presidential address to the Royal Economic Society that the economics of institutions had become one of the liveliest areas in economics. Two years prior to that, March and Olsen (1984) stated "a new institutionalism has appeared in political science" and that "it is far from coherent or consistent; it is not completely legitimate; but neither can it be entirely ignored". Although sociology had been less responsive than political science, this was quickly changing, and the new institutionalism also became incorporated into sociology (Brinton and Nee 1998).

There has been a considerable and notable increase in research on institutions since then. The different social sciences have begun to assume that "institutions matter" and that they can be analyzed and therefore there has been an ongoing research effort both at the theoretical and applied levels on the subject of notion, role and change of institutions. The New Institutional Economics (NIE) has been developed in economics, based on the contributions of authors such as Ronald Coase, Douglass North, Oliver Williamson and Elinor Ostrom. In as far as political science is concerned, the literature of the new institutionalism includes political scientists such as Guy Peters, Johan Olsen, Peter Hall, Kenneth Shepsle and Barry Weingast. The new institutionalism in sociology is part of this emerging paradigm in the social

An initial version of this paper was presented at the Annual Meeting of the Public Choice Society (USA, 2009). This renewed version was presented in a specialized workshop at the European School for New Institutional Economics (Cargese, France, 2011) and the Second International Conference on Political Economy and Institutions, ICOPEAI (Baiona, Spain, 2012).

G. Caballero (✉) · X.C. Arias
Faculty of Economics, University of Vigo, Campus As Lagoas-Marcosende, 36310 Vigo, Spain
e-mail: gcaballero@uvigo.es

X.C. Arias
e-mail: xcarias@uvigo.es

N. Schofield et al. (eds.), *Advances in Political Economy*,
DOI 10.1007/978-3-642-35239-3_1, © Springer-Verlag Berlin Heidelberg 2013

sciences, and it includes the contributions of authors such as Paul Dimaggio, Walter Powell and Victor Nee, among others.

Thus, the "return of institutions" has become unquestionable in social sciences, and the focus on institutions as a key concept in social sciences has given rise to a variety of new institutionalist approaches (Nee 2005). This has provided a strong impetus to political economy based on new theoretical foundations thereby boosting interdisciplinary relations among the social sciences (Schofield and Caballero 2011). This modern political economy of institutions has included relevant advances in issues such as the effect of extractive political and economic institutions (Acemoglu and Robinson 2011), the modeling of the authoritarian regimes (Schofield and Levinson 2008), the study of social order (Schofield 2010) and the utilization of a higher dimensional policy space in the analysis of different political situations (Schofield et al. 2011), among others.

The different institutional arrangements have systematic effects on policy-making (North and Weingast 1989; Haggard and McCubbins 2001). But if we want to have a deeper understanding of the relationships between institutions and policy, we should view public policies as the outcome of political transactions made over time (Spiller and Tommasi 2007). Political life is characterized by exchanges, agreements and transactions, which frequently are only an attempt, therefore transaction analysis is a fundamental step for studying political interaction and institutions of governance.

The notion of transaction costs was the key concept that the NIE used to understand how institutions affected efficiency in economy. Coase (1937, 1960) and North (1990a) enabled the justification of the importance of institutions and organizations for the economic mainstream and furthermore, the notion of transaction costs surpassed the limits of economic relationships (Caballero 2001). "Modifying the standard rational choice model by incorporating transaction cost theory into it can substantially increase the explanatory power of the model" of political markets (North 1990b, p. 355). In this manner, the new transactional institutionalism has dealt with the study of political institutions and processes through the Transaction Cost Politics research program (TCP) carried out over the past twenty years (Weingast and Marshall 1988; North 1990b; Dixit 1996, 2003; Epstein and O'Halloran 1999; Williamson 1999; Spiller and Tommasi 2003, 2007).

TCP uses political transaction as the unit of analysis, and explains the evolution of political relationships in their condition as transactions and contracts, thereby highlighting the relevance of institutions in political markets, which are characterized by incomplete political rights, imperfect enforcement of agreements, bounded rationality, imperfect information, subjective mental models on the part of the actors and high transaction costs. If the presence of transaction costs decisively affects economic exchange then their relevance is even greater for the functioning of political markets. This is so not only for political transactions carried out between citizens and politicians, which both North (1990b) and Dixit (1996, 1998) emphasized, but also for those in which all participants are politicians, as dealt with by Weingast and Marshall (1988), Epstein and O'Halloran (1999) and Spiller and Tommasi (2007). In this sense, TCP allow us to make more sense out of the political markets we observe.

Transaction Cost Politics (TCP), besides considering the contract as an analysis unit, also studies the enforcement mechanism of contracts, compares the different *governance* structures and adopts the bounded rationality supposition (Epstein and O'Halloran 1999). A first approach to the theoretical bases of TCP is characterized by the following proposals: (1) The application of the transactional approach to the political field leads us to consider political interaction as a set of (implicit or explicit) contractual relations. In this sense, public policies are the outcome of transactions among policy-makers. (2) Institutions are the rules of the political game, and they determine the incentive structure of the agents, and therefore institutions affect public policy *outputs*. (3) Organizational structures of governance are quite relevant when explaining the relations between institutions and outcomes. (4) Transaction costs tend to be higher in the political field than in the economic one and therefore the design of an efficient institutional structure becomes more complex in the political world. (5) In recent times, we are witnessing the progressive vision of public policies as a result of a series of inter-temporal political transactions. (6) TCP provides a central role to the notion of credible commitment, which justifies the importance of *reputational capital* and the organizational formulae of the State.

This chapter reviews and analyzes the approach of Transaction Cost Politics as a new transactional institutionalism in political economy. Moreover, the paper places TCP within the current panorama of new institutionalism and studies the theoretical foundations and the main contributions of TCP up to the present day. When reviewing the literature, we specify the most relevant contends of the main contributions, and for the rest of references, we only mention its arguments. The main goal of the paper is searching the theoretical sources of TCP, and relates it with other approaches, both close and rivals. TCP is a positive approach of political analysis, and this paper shows the analytical characteristics of TCP in a comparative way.

Section 2 presents several approaches of new institutionalism within the social sciences. Section 3 presents the two approaches of new institutionalism that formed the fundamental basis on which Transaction Cost Politics (TCP) was constructed: Rational-Choice Institutionalism (RCI) and the New Institutional Economics (NIE). Section 4 studies the fundamental arguments and contributions of Transaction Cost Politics. Section 5 shows why transaction costs are so high in political markets. Section 6 analyzes the governance of political transactions in Congress as a case-study from TCP. Section 7 compares the TCP approach with that of Constitutional Political Economy. The conclusions are outlined at the end of the chapter.

2 New Institutionalism: An Overview into the Social Sciences

2.1 Definitions of Institutions

During the last two decades of the 20th century, institutions have reopened an agenda for research into the social sciences based on renewed theories. The new institutionalism has emerged in economics, sociology and political science, and has led to sizeable progress on how institutions are understood. Nevertheless, there is no unique definition of institutions, and several different views of institutions can be presented. For example, Acemoglu and Robinson (2007) distinguish the efficient institutions view, the social conflict view, the ideology view and the incidental institutions view. According to Kingston and Caballero (2009), we should introduce at least the "institutions-as-rules" approach and the "institutions-as-equilibria" approach. Greif and Kingston (2011) extended that perspective: the institutions-as-rules approach focuses on a theory of how the "rules of the game" in a society are selected, while the "institutions-as-equilibria" approach emphasizes the importance of a theory of motivation and thereby endogenizes the "enforcement of the rules".

According to the Northian approach, institutions are the rules of the game, that is to say, the humanly devised constraints that structure political, economic and social interaction. Institutions consist of formal rules, informal rules and enforcement mechanisms, and they provide the incentive structure of an economy. This approach assumes a specific reference to transaction cost theory. "In order to lower the costs of exchange, it was necessary to devise a set of institutional arrangements that would allow for exchange over space and time", and institutions "reduce uncertainty by creating a stable structure of exchange" (North 1990b, p. 359). Institutions determine the level of efficiency of political markets and the level of efficiency "is measured by how well the market approximates a zero transaction cost results" (North 1990b, p. 360).

Following the institutions-as-rules approach, March and Olsen (1989) state that institutions are "collections of interrelated rules and routines that define appropriate actions in terms of relations between roles and situations". Peters (1999, p. 18) further adds four key characteristics to the concept of political institution: (A) An institution constitutes a structural feature of the society and/or polity. (B) An institution shows some stability over time. (C) An institution must affect individual behavior. (D) There should be some sense of shared values and meaning among members of the institution.

The institutions-as-equilibrium approach defines institutions as equilibrium solutions of a game. Historical and Comparative Institutional Analysis (Greif 1998; Aoki et al. 2001) assumed this view of institutions, although recent theoretical developments in institutional analysis by Avner Greif (2006, p. 39) consider "institutions as systems of interrelated rules, beliefs, norms, and organizations, each of which is a man-made, nonphysical social factor", and this definition "encompasses many of the multiple definitions of the terms institutions used in economics, political science and sociology".

2.2 Institutional Approaches

The study of institutions can be carried out using several approaches. The new institutionalism—that has been developed on new theoretical bases during the last two decades of the 20th century—can be distinguished from the old institutional traditions in economics, political science and sociology, although there are several connection points.

(a) The original institutionalism in economics (Thorstein Veblen, John Commons, Clarence Ayres) rejected the foundations of neoclassical analysis and adopted the methods of holism analysis. The contributions of such old institutionalists was marked by an anti-formalist nature, a tendency to argue in holistic terms and a "collectivist and behavioristic framework", as well as their rejection to the individualist welfare criterion and their tendency towards a certain economic interventionism (Rutherford 1994). It was centered on distributive consequences of the many institutional structures and devised its theories and analysis based on the conceptualization of power.
(b) The old institutionalism tradition in political science was made up of a set of multi-approach heterogeneous contributions and assumed certain general characteristics such as legalism, structuralism, holism, historicism and normative analysis (Peters 1999).
(c) The earlier sociological institutionalism pioneered by Talcott Parsons (1937) assumed the existence of institutions, but it did not emphasize institutional analysis. Just as Nee (1998, p. 5) points out the tradition of comparative institutional analysis established in the classical and modern periods of sociology, provides an appropriate foundation for the new institutional approach in sociology, where Weber (1922—*Economy and Society*) is probably the best example of the traditional sociological approach to comparative institutional analysis.

On the other hand, New Institutionalism in the social sciences assumes the choice-theoretic tradition and generally presumes purposive action on the part of individuals, who act with incomplete information, inaccurate mental models and costly transactions (Nee 1998). It tends to move towards methodological individualism, the conceptualization of voluntary exchange and the study of the effects of alternative institutional frameworks on efficiency. In this manner, "new institutionalism" appears to be more formalistic, individualistic and reductionist, it is orientated to rational choice and "economizing models", and it shows a less-interventionist character (Rutherford 1994).

In economics, Coase (1984) sustained that "if modern institutionalists had any antecedent, then we should not be looking for these in their immediate predecessors". NIE therefore did not arise from the old institutionalism but was created thanks to a set of contributions that highlighted the relevance of institutional and organizational aspects, and these contributions arose from different scientific areas such as Property Rights Analysis, the New Economic History, the New Industrial Organization, Transaction Cost Economics, Comparative Economic Systems, and Law and Economics (Eggertsson 1990). The analytical framework of the NIE is a modification of neoclassical theory, and it preserves the basic assumptions of scarcity and competence, as well as the analytical tools of microeconomic theory, however, it modifies the assumption of rationality and further adds a time dimension (North 1994).

Nevertheless, the idea of a serious rift between the old and new institutionalist economists has been modified in recent times. For example, North (1994, 2005), Greif (2006) and Ostrom (2007) surpassed the limits of the methodological individualism and the hypothesis of rationality, going beyond the bounded rationality.

In this sense, Groenewegen et al. (1995) found some bridges between new and old institutionalism via the North's contributions, and Hodgson (1998) pointed out the evolution of the new institutionalist project towards a possible convergence with the thinking of the old economic institutionalism. In spite of the considerable concern among new economic institutionalists to differentiate themselves sharply from the old American institutionalism, some aspects of the new institutionalism are connecting back to the old institutionalism in recent years (Rutherford 2001).

Simultaneously with the consolidation of the New Institutional Economics, Hall and Taylor (1996) stated that during the eighties and nineties of the 20th century, there existed three approaches in political science and sociology, each of which called itself a "new institutionalism" as a reaction to the behavioral perspectives, these being:

(1) Historical Institutionalism developed in response to the group theories of polities and structural functionalism, and it defines institutions as formal and informal procedures, routines, norms and conventions embedded in the organizational structure of the polity. This approach emphasizes the relevance of early decisions throughout political history: the initial political decisions determine the course of politics and consequently of any posterior political decision (Thelen and Steinmo 1992; Thelen 1999; Pierson 2000; Pierson and Skocpol 2002). This implies that there exists a "path dependence" which generates an institutional inertia, which results in the persistence of initial decisions made by government. Historical institutionalism, whose term was coined by Theda Skocpol, has Peter Hall (1986) as one of its principal precursors, however it was Steinmo, Thelen and Pierson who provided some of the main contributions to this approach.

(2) Rational choice institutionalism (RCI) arose from the study of the American congressional behavior and it received some inputs from the "new economics of organization". This approach perceives institutions as a system of rules and incentives for behavior within which individuals try to maximize their benefit and therefore RCI sustains that behavior is a function of rules and incentives. Four of its features are as follows: (A) It employs a model of rationality when it tries to explain human behavior. (B) It tends to see politics as a series of collective action dilemmas. (C) It emphasizes the role of strategic interaction in the determination of political outcomes. (D) With respect to the origin of institutions, RCI explains the existence of the institution by reference to the value provided by those functions to the actors affected by the institutions.

(3) Sociological institutionalism has been developed in sociology, especially in organization theory. It considered that many of the institutional forms and procedures were not adopted to gain efficiency, but instead should be considered as culturally-specific-practices. This type of institutionalism, to which Hall and Taylor (1996) incorporate the contribution of March and Olsen (1984), can be characterized in the following manner: (A) Sociological institutionalists define institutions much more broadly than political scientists do, and their definition includes a set of elements such as symbol systems, cognitive scripts and moral templates. (B) It emphasizes the highly-interactive and mutually-constitutive

nature of the relationship between institutions and individual actions. (C) In as far as the origin and change of institutions is concerned, institutions can adopt a new institutionalist practice because it enhances the social legitimacy of the organization and its participants.

A more complete map of new institutionalism in social sciences has been presented using eight approaches (Peters 1999): Normative Institutionalism, Rational Choice Institutionalism, Historical Institutionalism, Empirical Institutionalism, New Institutional Economics, Sociological Institutionalism, Interest Representation Institutionalism and International Institutionalism. Although some of the classification criterions are not clear and could be discussed or adapted, this extended map is quite useful for understanding the diversity, pluralism and complexity of the new institutionalism in social sciences.

In that map, the sociological institutionalism indicated by Hall and Taylor (1996) is divided into two approaches namely, a normative institutionalism and a truly sociological institutionalism. (A) Normative institutionalism highlights the central role assigned to norms and values within organizations for understanding how institutions function and their influence on the behavior of individuals (March and Olsen 1984, 1989). Institutions mold their own participants and supply meaning systems for those participating in politics, and therefore this approach renounces the exogeneity of preferences. (B) There has been a strong institutional analysis tradition in sociological research right from the time of classical authors such as Weber or Durkheim. Such tradition has been maintained in areas like historical sociology and organizational sociology and we can distinguish between an old and a new institutional school of thought in sociology, based on the irrational sources of institutions, the conception of relations between the institution and its environment and the molding role of politics. The new approach in sociology should be construed as an individualization process of societies.

Moreover, another approach, empirical institutionalism in politics, has been added in the map due to its lack of theoretical approach and because it emphasizes a set of traditional empirical institutional issues. This approach empirically studies certain institutional differences and their effects, and furthermore indicates that government structure conditions the politics and decisions of governments. Empirical institutionalism has been centered on the study of a group of applied issues, such as the differences between presidential and parliamentary government, the case of the "divided government", the legislative institutionalization or the independence of central banks. Some of these contributions are descriptive and nearer to the old traditionalist approach (for examples, the contributions of Woodrow Wilson), but others imply a more advanced empirical analysis (Peters 1999).

Finally, pointing out the aim of the study, two other institutionalist approaches have been incorporated in the map. On the one hand, Interest Representation Institutionalism analyzes the structure of such "institutionalized relationships" between State and society, assuming that there are many relations in politics that are conceptualized as being less formal and highly institutionalized, such as Kickert et al. (1997) show. The interest representation institutionalism is especially centered on the analysis of the actions of political parties and interest groups. On the other hand, the approach of International Institutionalism conceives international politics along institutional lines and highlights the role of structure when explaining the behavior of States. International institutionalism perceives regimes as international level institutions, since they generate stability and predictability, shape the behavior of States and promote a set of values. One of the relevant research lines in international institutionalism has been led by Keohoane and Nye (1977).

In this sense, the views of Hall and Taylor (1996) and Peters (1999) on institutionalism are different but compatible, and we should complete the overview with the incorporation of the NIE. In order to integrate TCP within the new institutionalism, we need to first perform a detailed analysis of RCI and the NIE.

3 Rational Choice-Institutionalism and New Institutional Economics

3.1 Rational Choice Institutionalism

The program of Public Choice was the principal development of rational choice for studying politics after the Second World War. Sometime later, academic tradition of rational choice gave rise to a set of tasks that assumed the importance of institutions in political life and included political institutions into the research agenda of rational choice theory. We can therefore use the concept of RCI (Shepsle 1986, 2006; Hall and Taylor 1996; Weingast 1996, 2002; Peters 1999).

RCI emerged from the rational choice approaches that assumed methodological individualism, and it inherits the importance of basing political activity on human behavior theories that explain the nature of individuals. As against other approaches, such as normative institutionalism, which do not provide a specific theory for human behavior, rational-choice is characterized for presenting a clear and explicit model of individual behavior. However, even though Rational Choice did not attend to institutions in a relevant manner during its early stages, it did end up generating theoretical developments which incorporated the role of political institutions. In this sense, some authors have used the expression "actor-centered institutionalism" to indicate the important role bestowed to individuals by the RCI (Peters 1999).

Rational choice theory has provided a distinctive set of approaches to the study of institutions, institutional choice and long-term durability of institutions (Weingast 1996, p. 167). This approach provides a systematic treatment of institutions through the importation of the micro-foundations of institutional analysis from rational choice theory. Institutions are conceived as a set of rules and incentives that restrict the choice possibilities of political agents, who seek to maximize their preferences within such an institutional framework. According to Kiser and Ostrom (1982), institutions are rules that individuals use to determine what and who is included in decision-making situations, how the information is structured, what measures can be taken and in what sequence, and how individual actions are integrated into collective decisions. In this manner, RCI sets out the role of institutions in political activity as a means of containing the uncertainty of action and political results.

RCI considers political institutions as structures of voluntary cooperation that resolve collective action problems and benefit all concerned. Therefore, the way to resolve collective action problems through cooperation can be found in formal or informal institutions, and this permits opportunistic individuals looking for personal gains to obtain mutual benefits.

Individuals observe that institutional rules also limit the choice possibilities of competitors, and realize that rules benefit the entire group of individuals. Shepsle (1986) states that any cooperation that is too costly at the individual agent level is facilitated at the institutional level. In this manner, institutions appear as ex-ante agreements to facilitate cooperation structures, as claimed by Weingast (2002), when he affirms that we need institutions to obtain gains from cooperation.

RCI assumes the following three features: (1) Rational individuals that maximize personal utility are the central actors in the political process. (2) RCI has been concerned with the problem of stability of results and the problem of control of public bureaucracy. (3) Institutions are formed on a tabula rasa (Peters 1999).

Weingast (1996) points out four characteristic features of RCI: (A) This approach provides an explicit and systematic methodology for studying the effects of institutions, which are modeled as constraints on action. (B) The methodology is explicitly comparative, through models that compare distinct institutional constraints with their corresponding implications in behavior and outcomes and through the analysis of how behavior and outcomes change as the underlying conditions change. Moreover, this approach affords comparisons of the behavior and outcomes under related institutions within a given country and of the effects of similar institutions across countries. (C) The study of endogenous institutions yields a distinctive theory about their stability, form and survival. (D) The approach provides the micro-foundations for macro-political phenomena such as revolutions and critical election.

Two separate levels of analysis can be distinguished in the RCI (Shepsle 1986, 2006; Weingast 1996), namely; (a) A level considers institutions as fixed and exogenous, i.e., analyzes that study the effects of institutions; (b) the other level studies institutions as endogenous variables, that is to say, why institutions take particular forms (Weingast 1996).

In as far as Weingast's (1996) first level of analysis is concerned, we have to point out that work has been done on almost all democratic institutions such as constitutions, the legislative body, the executive body, bureaucracy, the courts of justice and the elections. The analysis is centered on how institutions influence results and we can verify that micro level details have a great influence on results.

With respect to Weingast's (1996) second level of analysis, it covers questions such as why institutions take one form instead of another, and why institutions are altered in some circumstances but not others. The rules of the game are provided by the players themselves; and these tend to be simple rules. Institutional arrangements are focal and may induce coordination around them (Shepsle 2006). A model of institutional stability must allow institutions to be altered by specific actors and it must show why these actors have no incentives to do so (self-enforcing institutions) (Weingast 1996).

Institutionalists of rational choice highlight the role of institutions in strategic interaction between actors and in determination of political results (Hall and Taylor

1996). However, this institutionalism does not explain the details of how institutions are created, although it recognizes the possibility that the creation of institutions is a rational action of actors who are interested in the creation of those institutions. This approach, in any case, has a functionalist content (Peters 1999) and concludes a sense of "goodness" of institutions (Moe 2005).

3.2 New Institutional Economics

Price theory enables us to respond to some economic matters but not to others that require a richer theoretical body. NIE does not try to replace price theory but tries to "put it in a setting that will make it vastly more fruitful" (Coase 1999b), which implies the incorporation of institutional issues. As indicated by Arrow (1987), the NIE movement consists of answering new questions that traditionally were not framed in economic mainstream.

NIE accepts orthodox neoclassical assumptions of scarcity and competition, but it rejects the neoclassical assumption of perfect information and instrumental rationality, and it considers a theoretical framework with incomplete property rights, positive transaction costs and institutions, and assumes a world where the passage of time matters (North 1994).

The theoretical framework of the New Institutional Economics combines the *coasean* notion of transaction costs with the *northian* notion of institutions, such that institutions are a medium for reducing transaction costs and obtaining a greater efficiency in economic performance. On the one hand, Coase (1937) generated a microanalytical approach of organizations which gave rise to "transaction cost economics" (Williamson 1975, 1985, 1996); while on the other hand, Coase (1960) generated a macroanalytical approach that studied the relations between institutions and economic performance, as well as institutional change processes (North 1990a). NIE incorporates both approaches, which are mutually inter-related, that is to say, NIE studies institutions and how institutions interact with organizational arrangements within economy (Menard and Shirley 2005; Ostrom 1990, 2007).

Property rights are one's ability to exercise choices over a good. Individuals will carry out transactions, i.e., they will carry out property rights transfers, which will produce transaction costs. We can define transactions costs as the resources used to maintain and transfer property rights (Allen 1991), that is to say, "transaction costs arise when individuals try to acquire new ownership rights, defend their assets against transgressions and theft, and project their resources against opportunistic behavior in exchange relationships" (Eggertsson 2005, p. 27). Transaction costs are the sum of costs required to perform the "transaction function". The carrying out of transactions can be understood as a contracting problem, such that transaction costs are those which are derived from the signing *ex-ante* of a contract and of its *ex-post* control and compliance (Eggertsson 1990).

In a world with zero transaction costs, the parties concerned would carry out all the transactions that would result in social efficiency gains. However, as against this hypothetical world where negotiation does not cost anything, economic markets are characterized by the presence of positive transaction costs, and therefore no transaction is carried out whenever such costs surpass the expected gains from such transaction. The readjustment of rights will only go ahead whenever the value of production from such transactions is greater than the costs implied in producing the same (Coase 1960).

The level of transaction costs will depend on the characteristic traits of each specific transaction as well as on the nature of the institutional environment in which the transaction is being carried out. In this sense, every society will have its own "rules of the game", which will determine the cost of carrying out transactions (North 1990a).

Understanding the relationship between institutions and economic performance requires the study of human decision-making. NIE considers that the orthodox rationality approach of human behavior is defective because: (a) individual motivations are not limited to maximizing wealth or utility: altruism and individual's self limitations also influence behavior; (b) individuals subjectively process incomplete information of the world around them: there is need to distinguish between reality and perception (North 1990a). NIE defends that individuals act with incomplete information and models that have been subjectively deduced, and assume the model of bounded rationality, by conceiving the individual as intentionally rational but only in a limited way (Williamson 2000).

Along these lines, North (1994, p. 362) states that "history demonstrates that ideas, ideologies, myths, dogmas, and prejudices matter, and an understanding of the way they evolve is necessary". In order to understand the behavior of individuals in decision-making within an uncertainty context, NIE considers the subjective mental models of individuals as key factors. Such mental models will be closely linked with institutions. "Mental models are the internal representations that individual cognitive systems create to interpret the environment; institutions are the external (to the mind) mechanisms individuals create to structure and order the environment" (Denzau and North 1994, p. 4).

Together with the study of mental models and human behavior, NIE assumes the importance of the passage of time to create institutions. Institutional change is characterized by increasing returns and imperfect markets with high transaction costs. In this theoretical framework, path dependence is reinforced by the externalities of the institutional matrix, by the processes of social learning and by the creation of the *shared mental models* on which individuals make decisions. Path dependence is one way of bridging the choice gap and binding the evolution of a society over time (North 1990a).

In this manner, the institutional framework not only determines the current economic results but also delimits the set of opportunities that affect our future situation. We can adopt an efficiency view when analyzing evolution of institutions, according to which relative prices are the source of institutional change, however, NIE sustains that the existence of transaction costs provokes the agents to not always coincide towards the search for a greater efficiency.

The NIE argues that the processes of institutional change are normally incremental due to the increasing returns of institutional change: (A) Institutional change is an incremental process that is heavily weighted in favor of policies that are broadly consistent with the basic institutional framework. (B) Institutional change is characterized by a slow evolution of formal and informal limitations. (C) Individual and specific changes in formal and informal institutions can change history but will find it difficult to reverse the course of history (North 1990a, 1990b).

Positive economic analysis conclusions cannot be exported from one economy to another in the case of economies with positive transaction costs, mental models and institutional changes: "you get a different answer for every country and every historical situation... there is no one way better economic system because everything depends on the society you are in" (Coase 1999a, p. 5).

The NIE is a research program that continually evolves, and recent new institutional contributions incorporate relevant advances and interesting questions on institutions. Eggertsson (2005) presents a general framework to reflect on institutional failure, social technology and institutional policy. North (2005) explores the relationships among cognitive science, institutions and economic change. Acemoglu and Johnson (2005) conclude that property rights institutions have a first-order effect on long-run economic growth and investment, while contracting institutions appear to matter for financial intermediation. Acemoglu and Robinson (2008) construct a model of simultaneous change and persistence in institutions where the main idea is that equilibrium economic institutions are a result of the exercise of de jure and de facto political power. Recently, North et al. (2009) propose the theoretical foundations for understanding violence and social order in human history.

4 Transaction Cost Politics

Transaction Cost Politics has emerged as an application of the theoretical approach of the New Institutional Economics to political analysis from a *madisonian* point of view in political economy (Shepsle 1999). Understanding the foundations of TCP implies a look to Rational-Choice Institutionalism and, especially, to the New Institutional Economics:

(A) Rational-Choice Institutionalism was interested in political markets and institutions, understood political institutions as a cooperation structure and assumed a model of rationality for political behavior. According to Rational-Choice Institutionalism, TCP focuses on political institutions, and indicates that "political institutions constitute ex ante co-operation agreements among politicians" (North 1990b, p. 359). Furthermore, TCP coincides with Rational-Choice Institutionalism when it defends the assumption of a rationality model for economic behavior, which implies a big difference from other institutionalists traditions such as normative institutionalism or the old approaches. However, the TCP rationality model is not found in Rational-Choice Institutionalism, and Rational-Choice Institutionalism forgot the main role of transaction costs and history, and therefore we should look to the NIE.

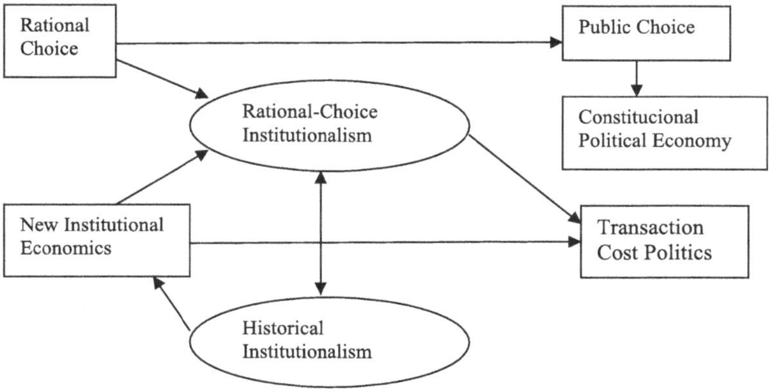

Fig. 1 Transaction Cost Politics

(B) NIE points out that the economic world is characterized by positive transaction costs and institutions. It rejects instrumental rationality by assuming the implications of bounded rationality and considers that the passage of time matters. TCP assumes these three NIE foundations when studying political transactions and institutions. "A transaction cost theory of politics is built on the assumptions of costly information, of subjective models on the part of the actors to explain their environment, and of imperfect enforcement of agreements" (North 1990b, p. 355). Moreover, TCP is interested in explaining the differential performance of polities over time, and therefore elaborates a theoretical framework where history matters.

TCP is different from RCI because TCP assumes three characteristic foundations of the NIE (bounded rationality, a transactional approach, passage of time matters). Figure 1 shows how the extension of Rational Choice theory towards political analysis allowed the emergence of Public Choice, with CPE as its main continuation, whereas the extension of the NIE towards political analysis allowed the appearance of TCP. In this sense, TCP—as an extension of the NIE—surpassed the theoretical framework of RCI in the same way that the NIE surpassed the (instrumental) rational choice approach. On the one hand, there is no direct relationship between CPE and TCP in Fig. 1 because their theoretical foundations have different origins, and on the other hand, historical institutionalism is shown as an antecedent of NIE and RCI but it has not a direct influence over TCP (the influence is indirect via NIE and RCI). Finally, we should point out that other institutionalisms, such as empirical, normative or sociological institutionalism, have not had influence on the emergence of TCP, and their references have not been incorporated in the background of TCP. Even these institutionalisms have not a fruitful dialogue with TCP nowadays.

While transactional analysis had been applied to economic and organizational interactions by a relevant tradition of literature, the approach of TCP focuses on political transactions and he considers that "public policy is a sometimes explicit, sometimes implicit agreement (or transaction) among policy makers" (Spiller and

Tommasi 2007, p. 3). In this sense, we should point out the distinction between TCP and politics of transaction costs: TCP is an analysis of diverse political processes based on the existence of positive transaction costs and the governance solutions that actors come up with in order to deal with them, whereas politics of transaction costs in its original sense would be a direct application of economic policy that takes into account the effects of positive transaction costs.

TCP assumes methodological individualism and studies political transactions from a microanalytical perspective that tries to rigorously tackle positive political analysis. TCP sustains that political institutions matter, that they can be analyzed and that their effect is to economize transaction costs. TCP likewise construes political activity as a dynamic process in evolution, which is incomplete and imperfect and which takes place in "real time", in history (Dixit 1996, 1998).

In the pre-coasean neoclassical world where transaction costs are zero, political activity would correspond to a simple assignment of rights that would permit efficiency through transfer of rights from owners who value them less to those that value them more (no "Pareto improvement" would stay unexecuted) (North 1990b). This situation allows us to derive a macro version of Coase's theorem according to which economic growth is not affected by the type of government of a country as long as transaction costs are zero (Eggertsson 1990). But we can go a step further in the reasoning process and conclude that in such an ideal world, the political process would not matter, since an efficient plan would always be achieved (Dixit 1996).

TCP uses political transaction as the unit of analysis and explains the evolution of political relationships as transactions and contracts. It highlights the relevance of institutions in political markets characterized by incomplete political rights, imperfect enforcement of agreements, bounded rationality, imperfect information, subjective mental models on the part of the actors and high transaction costs. The institutional structure of polity acts as a set of rules that structures incentives, determines the volume of transaction costs and biases political output.

The NIE has focused most of its efforts in demonstrating that passage of time and history matter. North (1990a) defended the relevance of path dependence in economic analysis, and the notion of path dependence has been integrated too into the organizational studies. These features are also verified for political analysis and were thus assumed by TCP (North 1990b; Dixit 1996). Therefore, such a transactional approach also assumes the importance of history and path, which in turn facilitates a greater contact with arguments of historical institutionalism. Really, historical institutionalism has exercised influence on TCP through the foundations of NIE. Literature furthermore has recently indicated the relationship between historic institutionalism and the RCI. There are authors of historic institutionalism such as Steinmo, Thelen and Longstreth, who appreciated the approaches of rational choice and moreover Katznelson and Weingast (2005) have recently indicated that historic institutionalism and RCI have many aspects in common and detect that there are points of intersection and overlap between the agendas of both institutional approaches. Furthermore, and through its connection with RCI, the TCP program has points that overlap with historic institutionalism, especially regarding the way institutions shape incentives and preferences of actors.

The other principal effort made by NIE has been to escape from strict rationality models in order to highlight the importance of cultural and cognitive factors such as beliefs, ideology and myths. In this way, the instrumental rationality approach of RCI meant that "the actors either have correct models by which to interpret the world around them or receive information feedback that will lead them to revise and correct their initially incorrect theories" (North 1990b, p. 356). Nevertheless, the NIE and TCP reject instrumental rationality and assume bounded rationality. North's (1990b, 1994) proposal includes the idea that individuals make decisions based on subjective models, which had already been presented by Weingast (1996) as one of the challenges of RCI. In this manner, transactional institutionalism surpasses the suppositions of RCI.

This opens the possibility of indicating that history and ideology matter in order to understand politics. The novelty of this perspective is that it is justified through an institutionalism that had initially strictly assumed the following two foundations: methodological individualism and rational approach.

Regarding the main contributions of TCP, we should point out that North (1990b) and Dixit (1996, 1998) are the two fundamental contributors who provided the theoretical bases for the program, while Weingast and Marshall (1988) and North (1989) formed the two relevant precedents. An important contribution to TCP from political science has been Epstein and O'Halloran (1999), which applied the transactional perspective to the delegation of powers. It included a review of the theory of TCP, and it showed several differences and similarities between economic and political interaction. Taking some lessons from the theory of the firm, Epstein and O'Halloran analyzed the hold-up problem in political transactions.

The approach of TCP is useful for organization studies. Public bureaucracy, delegation to independent agents and political parties are three relevant issues on which TCP has significantly contributed. Firstly, TCP assumes that the adequate institutions of governance will depend on the characteristics of each type of transactions. Then, all models of governance (markets, hybrids, firms, regulation, public bureaucracy, . . .) should be considered if we want to determine the best organizational structure that minimizes transaction costs so much as possible. For example, public bureaucracy is well suited to some transactions, such as the "sovereign transactions" of which foreign affairs is an example, and poorly suited to others (Williamson 1999). In this way, TCP incorporates several efforts to study governance structures and institutional design in the public sector (Estache and Martimort 1999; Gallego-Calderón 1999; Ruiter 2005). Secondly, delegation of power to independent agents—such as the central banks or supranational institutions like the European Commission—is best understood as a means of reducing political transaction costs (Majone 2001). In fact, there are empirical studies that show that in the process of the autonomization of government organizations, strictly economic aspects are less relevant than factors as bounded rationality, opportunism and social institutions (Ter Bogt 2003). Thirdly, some contributions of TCP have tried to advance towards a transaction cost theory of political parties. Jones and Hudson (1998, 2001) explored how political parties reduce voters' information costs and they argue that if voters reduce transaction costs by relying on party signal, politicians have an incentive to maintain party reputation. Other topics in TCP have been the design of budgeting institutions (Patashnik 1996), the countries' international institutional choices and the hierarchy in international politics (Weber 1997), the institutional design relying on separation of powers among specialized agents (Laffont and Martimort 1998) and the governance of the relationship between private investors and governments (Henisz and Zelner 2004).

5 High Transaction Costs in Political Exchange

The peculiar nature and intensity of transaction costs in political transactions convert them into an irreplaceable concept when we try to get a better understanding of politics. Several considerations are essential for understanding the relevance and characteristics of political transaction costs, and some of the most important ones must be emphasized.

Firstly, property rights are subject to strong constraints within political interactions: they are not safe nor do agents possess them in an unlimited manner. While economic competence takes place on property rights that are normally safe, political competition includes the fight for authority and this means change of rights. Therefore, politics revolves around a set of less safe rules.

Secondly, contracting parties are many and cannot be perfectly identified in many cases of political transactions. This happens especially when one of the parties is a multiple subject; furthermore, many political contracts are neither explicit nor formal and rest on verbal and even tacit agreements. Moreover, political transactions affect many agents due to the wide presence of spillover effects that enable interpretation of interaction between political agents in terms of a "common agency" relationship with multiple principals (Dixit 1996). Furthermore, the structure of agency-relation amongst political actors tends to be especially complex: an example can be the vertical agency-relation that is configured by the chain "electorate-parliament-government-bureaucracy", and yet another example can be the governance of territorial distribution of power.

Thirdly, there are huge informational problems in political transactions. The world of politics is opaque, unclear and it is difficult to observe and measure the different factors of political performance, such as the objects of political transaction (Pierson 2000). In this sense, political markets lack a measurement formula like the price system in economic markets. Even if they were explicit, political contracts clearly respond to an incomplete contract prototype, containing vague and interpretable terms. This implies that the ex-post power relations matters exceedingly: the possession of the residual rights of control is key when, for example, an uncontracted eventuality occurs. Moreover, ex-post control rights may exert strong influence over ex-ante contractual arrangements (Epstein and O'Halloran 1999). Moreover, situations of asymmetric information are particularly relevant in political transactions and the subjective models of the actors increase the amount of transaction costs even more in political markets (therefore different ideologies affect political exchange).

Fourthly, the problem of collective action characterizes a wide range of political transactions. The collective nature of politics makes the consequences of my action depend highly on actions of others, such that the relationship between effort and effect becomes quite unclear and informational problems are augmented (Pierson 2000). Moreover, the short-term horizon of political actors, who are interested in the electoral logic, contrasts with the nature of those political decisions whose implications only play out in the long run. While the economic marketplace possesses some strong mechanisms for lengthening time horizons (such as property rights and capital markets), there are no analogous mechanisms that are equally effective in politics (Pierson 2000).

Fifthly, regarding the passage of time, the choice and evolution forces in political markets are slower and weaker than in economic markets, leading to a lower efficiency and a less intense choice of organizations (Dixit 1996). That is to say, the corrective and learning mechanisms are less effective in political scenarios characterized by a path with increasing returns. Political institutions tend to establish a bias towards *status quo* which hampers change and adaptation to new situations, and there exists an institutional density that incorporates constraints based on authority. In this sense, the structure of power can hamper exchange (Pierson 2000), and the carrying out of institutional adjustments to reduce transaction costs. To the above, we must add the difficulties of designing institutions that achieve a high influence of incentives in the political process (Dixit 1996), and the incentive structures in politics are significantly weaker than those in economic markets (Vanhuysse 2002).

Sixthly, regarding the enforcement mechanisms, political action promises are a fundamental exchange unit in political contracts but such promises are typically not subject to a compliance mechanism (*third party enforcement*) and limited commitment possibilities constrain the political process. Since public policies are not spot transactions, cooperation requires striking and enforcing intertemporal political agreements, that is, agreements that should be enforced over time. The intertemporal nature of political exchanges increases transaction costs (Spiller and Tommasi 2007). This is the case of those contracts whose bills are not simultaneously considered for a vote, and the case of those with non-contemporaneous benefit flows, such as the next section will show. Moreover, public policies with more complex transaction characteristics will require more institutional safeguards to make them effective over time (Spiller and Tommasi 2007), because as Ostrom (2004) has concluded, "rules without enforcement are but words on paper".

Based on these characteristics, among others, transaction costs tend to be systematically higher in political markets than in economic ones (North 1990b; Dixit 1996; Caballero and Arias 2003). Several case studies show that political transactions are very complicated due to the impact of high political transaction costs, such as for example Sorensen (2006) evaluated when he studied local governments consolidations in Norway. Moreover, high transaction costs issues tend to gravitate to polity from the economy (North 1990b) and political transaction costs sometimes are increased intentionally; political actors manipulate them strategically to achieve personal objectives. In this way, politically relevant transaction costs are also to a great extent endogenously determined through self-interested use of government mechanisms. There are several ways of political transaction-cost manipulation (using informational costs, costs of negotiation, agreement or enforcement), and there are some specific conditions under which officeholders are predicted to act via manipulation of political transaction costs (Twight 1994). In this sense, for example, there is empirical evidence that shows that the enacting coalition manipulates political transaction costs in designing US administrative agencies (Wood and Bohte 2004).

In a very relevant applied work, Spiller and Tommasi (2003, 2007) have studied the institutional foundations of public policy in Argentina from TCP and they identified some key features that do not promote intertemporal political transactions in the country: "a legislature uninterested in legislative activities, a bureaucracy with no long-term objectives, a judiciary that has often been aligned with the executive, a federal system that grants provinces little incentives for fiscal responsibility, and an executive with excessive leeway for unilateral moves". The institutional framework of each country is the key factor to make political transactions difficult or easier, and the number of players, time horizons and enforcement technologies are some of the key institutional determinants (Scartascini 2007). In this sense, the framework of Spiller and Tommasi (2007) has been extended to explain the workings of democratic institutions and political actors (Scarstacini et al. 2010). Finally, Dixit (2003) expounds that transactions costs are higher in less-developed countries, where the success of policy reform will depend on the ability to alter or adapt institutions in the desired direction and where credibly commitment to good policies without rent-seeking is difficult (Murshed 2001).

Therefore, high transaction costs in political markets imply that inefficient policies and institution can be prevalent (Acemoglu 2003). Studying the institutions of governance that structure political processes in each society is fundamental. We need to know in each scenario how political institutions and historical inheritances lead to the interrelated political behaviors that characterize the policy-making process (Spiller and Tommasi 2007).

6 A Case-Study: The Governance of Political Transactions in Congress

A case study can be useful to show the possibilities of the approach of TPC on political transactions and institutions. This section introduces the case of legislative transaction and governance as a case analysis of TCP.

Political agreement among legislators is necessary to pass bills in Congress. Legislators look for exchange and cooperation to pass those projects in which they are interested. Pre-transactional analysis was focused on vote-trading or logrolling in the tradition that was initiated by Buchanan and Tullock. But the logrolling tradition was "too simple to solve fundamental problems in legislative exchange" (North 1990b). In fact, legislative exchange has high transaction costs due to non-contemporaneous benefit flows and non-simultaneous exchanges. It implies that, firstly, differential patterns of benefit flows can inhibit trading and, secondly, many potential legislative trades concern bills that do not come up for a vote simultaneously. The explicit market form of exchange does not resolve these problems of enforceability of legislative transactions (Weingast and Marshall 1988). It is necessary to establish an institutional structure of governance that allows the agreement among congressmen and the industrial organization of Congress should try to make legislative exchanges easier. In this sense, "political institutions constitute ex-ante agreements about cooperation among politicians" (North 1990b).

Weingast and Marshall (1988) analyzed how the Committee System of the US Congress had relatively low transaction costs. Under this system, a legislator of committee A can cede his intention to influence the selection of jurisdiction of committee B. In return the members of committee B may waive their right so as not to influence the proposals of the jurisdiction of A. The "institutionalization of rights on the agenda control" substitutes the explicit market exchange mechanism. Legislators seek a seat on those committees which are more highly valued for them, instead of trading votes. The restrictive access to the agenda constitutes a mechanism by which each committee can avoid declining the agreements ex-post. Having a position in a committee is a type of property right mechanism that reduces transaction costs and favors independent negotiations among congressmen regardless of their party affiliation.

Legislative behavior and the organization of legislative institutions are affected by political and electoral rules. It is important to distinguish between "party-centered electoral rules" and "candidate-centered electoral rules", since it is key for the incentives of congressmen. Moreover, the institutional structure of committees is relevant for the structure of property rights of individual congressmen. Electoral rules and committee systems are two of the main institutional determinants of political property rights in legislative organization, and they determine the structure of governance of legislative organization.

While the American Congress represents a prototype model of Congress in which congressmen have strong property rights that facilitate the legislative transaction (candidate-based electoral politics, powerful committees with individual property rights), recently the industrial organization of the Spanish Congress has been characterized by party-based electoral politics, weak committees and the power of national leaders of each political party (Caballero 2011). In this sense, different models of institutional governance are presented to facilitate political transactions. The industrial organizational model of the Spanish Congress does not grant property rights to the individual deputies for their committee seats, and the head of each parliamentary group has the property rights on committees.

In this way, legislative transactions and agreements are carried out via a hierarchical system in the Spanish model. As long as the executive and the majority of the legislature represent the same political preferences, the role of the Congress is clearly reduced. On the other hand, the system of property rights regarding the US committees reduces the high transaction costs of legislative exchange, being that the United States Congress establishes a system of committees that allow transactions between congressmen in order to achieve majorities that permit changing the *status quo*. Therefore, political parties (hierarchy) in the Spanish case and committees (decentralized system) in the American case appear as key factors in the different models of governance that facilitates decision making and transacting. Each institutional structure has different implications for policy-making (Caballero 2011).

7 Constitutional Political Economy and Transaction Cost Politics

Previously to NIE and TCP, the instrumental rationality approach constituted the main research program on madisonian political analysis from economics. Public Choice and Constitutional Political Economy (CPE) implied a rational approach to politics. Comparing CPE and TCP will show some of the characteristics of the new institutional approach with more clarity.

The Public Choice research program has been developed over half a century. Its hard core can be summarized by three presuppositions: methodological individualism, rational choice and politics-as-exchange. According to Buchanan (1966), such exchange approach is especially useful at the level of constitutional political choices, when the interests of individuals and groups are not clearly identifiable and "the great game of politics" is configured as a positive sum game. The study of this type of choice gave rise to the principal development within Public Choice: CPE.

CPE studies the efficiency of constitutional rules in their positive and normative dimension. Starting from *statu quo,* CPE indicates how the veil of uncertainty in constitutional decisions generates a cooperative attitude towards consensus, and concludes the convenience of the unanimity rule for making this type of decisions (the "*rules over rules*" system is studied).

The main contribution of Buchanan and Tullock (1962) was to impose a two-level framework on analyzes of collective action, by categorically distinguishing the level of ordinary-politics from the level of constitutional politics (Buchanan 2003). This book meant the start of the CPE, which was founded on the same methodological postulates as Public Choice. CPE studies constitutional order of democratic societies to research into the effects of such order and offer possible improvements to the same.

CPE defends a contractarian framework, both for political analysis as well as for economic theory. However, the application and analytical extension of this contractarian approach turned out to be limited: on the one hand, it was unable to expand as a methodological fundament in the economics mainstream; and on the other hand, the transactional analysis in political studies of the CPE was short and was centered on specific issues (for example around *logrolling,* or around the study of the cost of reaching constitutional agreements). On the other hand, TCP assumed the contractual or transactional approach, initially for economic analysis, and such approach was later expanded from economics to political theory. Transaction is converted into a par excellence unit for political analysis in TCP.

A notable difference between CPE and TCP resides in the human behavior model which they assume. The orthodox CPE adopts the model of substantive rationality (which has been inherited from neoclassical economy), while TCP incorporates the model of bounded rationality (which is characteristic of NIE). These suppositions are key to understand why a greater economicism emanates from CPE that is not quite patent in TCP because TCP integrates economic and political logics on more flexible human behavioral approaches.

The theoretical framework of constitutionalists indicates that constitutional decisions are carried out behind a veil of uncertainty, thereby permitting the analysis of "the great game of politics" such as that of a positive sum game. This framework links constitutions with the notion of rule and confers a key role to constitution to understand the operation and results of economy and politics ("the constitution determines everything"), thereby making any political action irrelevant whenever it is not carried out in the constitutional decision level.

According to the TCP theoretical approach, the agents involved for making constitutional decisions will act strategically despite information problems. Dixit (1996) states that such agents are not behind a "rawlsian" veil of ignorance. Therefore, constitutions are elaborated-rules wherein not everything is a "justice criterion" but where negotiation power structure and the interests of several groups and agents also exert their influence. Furthermore, constitution is just one more element within the complex institutional framework of a society, and this framework integrates formal and informal institutions. According to TCP, constitutions are perceived as incomplete contracts due to their incapacity to foresee all future contingencies, due to the complexity of specifying rules even for foreseen contingencies and due to the difficulty to objectively observe and verify contingencies. Thus, constitutions leave many contractual terms open for future specification and one can gauge the weight of political acts, especially when some of them have long-lasting effects. In this manner, TCP defends that the distinction between rules and political acts is more a matter of level than type and furthermore that the path of institutional evolution is made up of constitutional rules and past political acts (Dixit 1996).

Works carried out within the TCP program highlight the relevance of transaction costs in political exchanges, thereby permitting us to explain the difficulties entailed in achieving a cooperative solution that leads to optimal efficiency. On the other hand, CPE does not stress the central role of transaction costs for political analysis and, in any case, it assumed a static and simplistic view of political transaction that did not incorporate elements such as intertemporality.

TCP assumes a theoretical perspective that incorporates the importance of the historic dimension in political studies and assumes the challenge of delving into cognitive matters. In this manner, history and ideologies matter in order to understand political actions. However, CPE assumes a non-historic and non-ideological perspective in positive analysis, and is reinforced in normative-philosophical theoretical developments.

8 Conclusion

North (1990b) and Dixit (1996) provided the two founding contributions to TCP. Since then, the TCP research program has indicated the importance of transaction costs in political markets and has studied how political institutions determine the volume of transaction costs and political outcome. In this manner, political institutions become the object of study from a transaction point of view and the map of the new institutionalism in social sciences must incorporate TCP as one of its approaches.

TCP is a transactional institutionalism that studies political institutions with its own approach, and has very few common elements with the institutional approaches of normative institutionalism, empirical institutionalism, sociological institutionalism, interest-representation institutionalism and international institutionalism. On the contrary, the appearance, content and development of TCP was possible based on the institutionalist advances of the programs of RCI, NIE and historical institutionalism.

TCP coincides with RCI because both are interested in political markets and institutions, both understand political institutions as a cooperative structure and assume a model of rationality for political behavior. However, TCP is different from RCI because TCP assumes three characteristic foundations of NIE (bounded rationality, a transactional approach, passage of time matters). In this sense, TCP constitutes an extension of NIE towards an analysis of politics from a *madisonian* perspective (Shepsle 1999).

Historical institutionalism has had an important indirect influence on the TCP approach. The main influence was through NIE, which understood the importance of history for institutional analysis but eliminated any historic determinism doses and established an institutional theory based on the fundament of individual choices. This historical perspective of NIE was exported to political analysis by TCP. Likewise, there were considerable points of intersection and overlap between historical and rational choice institutionalism, and in this sense, there was an overlap with the historical institutionalist content when TCP was in contact with RCI.

TCP thus appears as a true and intrinsically institutional research program that occupies its niche in the new institutionalism map of social sciences. This program is centered on positive analysis and concludes the importance of comparative analysis in order to understand the role of the different institutions on political transactions and outcomes.

As a conclusion, we should point out some strengths, weaknesses and challenges of TCP. Three relevant strengths of TCP are the following ones: (a) political transactions are considered as the unit of analysis; (b) political transactions costs can explain the existence of inefficient institutions, therefore the governance structure matters; (c) this approach incorporates bounded rationality into the analysis. Among the weakness of TCP, three issues should be considered: (a) TCP lacks a general theory of political institutions, and possibly this general theory does not exist; (b) TCP is an approach whose contents are slightly diffuse and the limits of the approach are not always well-defined (for example, North's shared mental models goes beyond bounded rationality); (c) power and coercion are very important factor in political life but TCP has not adequately incorporated the role of coercion in political transactions (Nye 1997; Moe 2005). In any case, these three weak points of TCP are present too in the NIE.

Finally, three challenges for the future are presented: (a) TCP needs more empirical work: case-studies, institutional comparative analysis, econometrical work and experimental techniques are useful in a TCP that assumes methodological pluralism. (b) There should be more and more dialogue and exchange between the several types of institutionalisms. In this sense, Shepsle (2006) sustains that the differences between some types of institutionalisms are fewer than in the past. In order to understand the notion, role and change of institutions, we need to assess and integrate contributions coming from the different institutional approaches. (c) Transcending disciplinary institutionalism implies too that a multidisciplinary profile in social sciences is convenient when we are interested in institutions. In this sense, Coase (1999b, p. 4) defended the convenience of linking economic science with other subjects to convert it into hard science: "We have to take account of the effects of the legal system, the political system, etc., and if my impression is correct, their theories often have a stronger empirical base than is usual in economics". North (1999) works on the hypothesis of the marriage of political and economic theory and Bates (2010) points out the relevance of politics for the new institutionalism. Coase (1999b, p. 5) likewise highlighted how "hybrid subjects are often astonishingly fertile" in science as against the scientific disciplines that remain too pure, and proposed transactional analysis as a hybrid subject prototype. The several institutionalisms should simultaneously assume a multidisciplinary vocation in social sciences.

The transactional approach born in economic analysis managed to tackle the study of politics through TCP. The search for a theory of institutions based on individual choice favors reconciliation among the different social sciences (North 1990a). According to North (1999, p. 315), "What Coase started with transaction cost approach, is well on its way to being a foundation for restructuring social science theory in general, not just political theory or economic theory". In this sense, there is a road to the New Institutional Social Sciences.

References

Acemoglu D (2003) Why not a political Coase theorem? Social conflict, commitment and politics. J Comp Econ 31(4):620–652

Acemoglu D, Johnson S (2005) Unbundling institutions. J Polit Econ 113(5):949–995

Acemoglu D, Robinson JA (2007) Lecture notes for political economy of institutions and development. MIT Press, Cambridge

Acemoglu D, Robinson JA (2008) Persistence of power, elites and institutions. Am Econ Rev 98(1):267–293

Acemoglu D, Robinson J (2011) Why nations fail: the origins of power, prosperity and poverty. Crown Publishers, New York

Allen DW (1991) What are transaction costs? Res Law Econ 14:1–18

Aoki M et al (2001) Comparative institutional analysis. MIT Press, Cambridge

Arrow KJ (1987) Reflections on the essays. In: Feiwel G (ed) Arrow and the foundations of the theory of economic policy. New York University Press, New York, pp 727–734

Bates R (2010) The new institutionalism. In: The legacy and work of Douglass North, conference, CNISS, Washington University, St. Louis

Brinton M, Nee V (1998) The new institutionalism in sociology. Russell Sage Foundation, Thousand Oaks
Buchanan JM (1966) An individualistic theory of political process. In: Buchanan J (1987): Economics. Between predictive theory and moral philosophy. Texas University Press, Austin
Buchanan JM (2003) Public choice: the origins and development of a research program. Center for the study of public choice, George Mason University
Buchanan JM, Tullock G (1962) The calculus of consent. Logical foundations of constitutional democracy. University of Michigan Press, Ann Arbor
Caballero G (2001) La nueva economía institucional. Sistema 156:59–86
Caballero G (2011) Institutional foundations, committee system and amateur legislators in the governance of the Spanish Congress: an institutional comparative perspective (USA, Argentina, Spain). In: Schofield N, Caballero G (eds) Political economy of institutions, democracy and voting. Springer, Heidelberg
Caballero G, Arias XC (2003) Una reorientación teórica de la economía política: el análisis político de costes de transacción. Rev Esp Cienc Política 8:131–164
Coase RH (1937) The nature of the firm. Economica 4:386–405
Coase RH (1960) The problem of social cost. J Law Econ 3(1):1–44
Coase RH (1984) The new institutional economics. J Inst Theor Econ 140(1):229–231
Coase RH (1999a) An interview with Ronald Coase. ISNIE Newslett 2(1):3–10
Coase RH (1999b) The task of the society. ISNIE Newslett 2(2):1–6
Denzau AT, North DC (1994) Shared mental models: ideologies and institutions. Kyklos 47:3–31
Dixit A (1996) The making of economic policy: a transaction-cost politics perspective. MIT Press, Cambridge
Dixit AK (1998) Transaction cost politics and economic policy: a framework and a case study. In: Baldassarri M (ed) Institutions and economic organization in the advanced economies. St. Martin's, New York
Dixit AK (2003) Some lessons from transaction-cost politics for less-developed countries. Econ Polit 15(2):107–133
Eggertsson T (1990) Economic behaviour and institutions. Cambridge University Press, Cambridge
Eggertsson T (2005) Imperfect institutions. University of Michigan Press, Ann Arbor
Epstein D, O'Halloran S (1999) Delegating powers. A transaction cost politics approach to policy making under separate powers. Cambridge University Press, Cambridge
Estache A, Martimort D (1999) Politics, transaction costs and the design of regulatory institutions. World Bank Policy Research
Gallego-Calderón R (1999) Institutional design in the public sector: the role of political transaction costs. ECPR Joint Session, Mannheim
Greif A (1998) Historical and comparative institutional analysis. Am Econ Rev 88(2):80–84
Greif A (2006) Institutions and the path to the modern economy. Cambridge University Press, Cambridge
Greif A, Kingston C (2011) Institutions: rules or equilibria. In: Schofield N, Caballero G (eds) Political economy of institutions, democracy and voting. Springer, Heidelberg
Groenewegen J et al (1995) On integrating new and old institutionalism: Douglass C. North building bridges. J Econ Issues 29(2):467–476
Haggard S, McCubbins MD (2001) Political institutions and the determinants of public policy. In: Haggard S, McCubbins MD (eds) Presidents, parliaments and policy. Cambridge University Press, Cambridge
Hall PA (1986) Governing the economy: the politics of State intervention in Britain and France. Oxford University Press, London
Hall PA, Taylor R (1996) Political science and the three new institutionalism. Polit Stud XLIV:936–957
Henisz WJ, Zelner BA (2004) Explicating political hazards and safeguards: a transaction cost politics approach. Ind Corp Change 13(6):901–915
Hodgson GM (1998) The approach of institutional economics. J Econ Lit XXXVI:166–192

Jones P, Hudson J (1998) The role of political parties: an analysis based on transactions costs. Public Choice 94:175–189

Jones P, Hudson J (2001) Political parties, political integrity and public policy: a transactions costs approach. Polit Stud 49:70–88

Katznelson I, Weingast BR (2005) Intersections between historical and rational choice institucionalism. In: Katznelson I, Weingast BR (eds) Preferences and situations: points of intersection between historical and rational choice institutionalism. Russell Sage, New York

Keohoane RO, Nye JS (1977) Power and interdependence: world politics in transition, Little, Brown, Boston

Kickert WJM, Klijn EH, Koppenjan JFM (1997) Managing complex networks: strategies for the public sector. Sage, London

Kingston C, Caballero G (2009) Comparing theories of institutional change. J Inst Econ 5(2):151–180

Kiser L, Ostrom E (1982) The three worlds of action: a metatheoretical synthesis of institutional approaches. Ostrom E (ed) Strategies of political inquiry. Sage, Thousand Oaks

Laffont JJ, Martimort D (1998) Transaction costs, institutional design and the separation of powers. Eur Econ Rev 42:673–684

Majone G (2001) Nonmajoritarian institutions and the limits of democratic governance: a political transaction-cost approach. J Inst Theor Econ 157:57–78

March JG, Olsen JP (1984) The new institutionalism: organizational factors in political life. Am Polit Sci Rev 78:738–749

March JG, Olsen JP (1989) Rediscovering institutions. Free Press, New York

Matthews RCO (1986) The economics of institutions and the sources of economic growth. Econ J 96:903–918

Menard C, Shirley M (2005) Handbook of new institutional economics. Springer, Dordrecht

Moe TM (2005) Power and political institutions. Perspect Politics 3(2):215–233

Murshed SM (2001) Transaction cost politics, institutions for commitment and rent-seeking, Discussion paper 125. WIDER. United Nations University

Nee V (1998) Sources of the new institutionalism. In: Brinton M, Nee V (eds) The new institutionalism in sociology. Russell Sage Foundation, Thousand Oaks

Nee V (2005) The new institutionalism in economics and sociology. In: Smelser N, Swedberg R (eds) Handbook for economic sociology. Princeton University Press, Princeton

North DC (1989) A transaction cost approach to the historical development of polities and economies. J Inst Theor Econ 145:661–668

North DC (1990a) Institutions, institutional change and economic performance. Cambridge University Press, Cambridge

North DC (1990b) A transaction cost theory of politics. J Theor Polit 2(4):355–367

North DC (1994) Economic performance through time. Am Econ Rev 84(3):359–368

North DC (1999) In anticipation of the marriage of political and economic theory. In: Alt J, Levi M, Ostrom E (eds) Competition and cooperation. Russell Sage Foundation, New York

North DC (2005) Understanding the process of economic change. Princeton University Press, Princeton

North DC, Weingast BR (1989) Constitutions and commitment: the evolution of institutions governing public choice in seventeenth-century England. J Econ Hist 49(4):803–832

North DC, Wallis JJ, Weingast BR (2009) Violence and social orders: a conceptual framework for interpreting recorded human history. Cambridge University Press, Cambridge

Nye JV (1997) Thinking about the state: property rights, trade, and changing contractual arrangements in a world with coercion. In: Drobak J, Nye J (eds) The frontiers of the new institutional economics. Academic Press, San Diego

Ostrom E (1990) Governing the commons. The evolution of institutions of collective action. Cambridge University Press, Cambridge

Ostrom E (2004) Rules without enforcement are but words on paper. IHDP Update 2:8–10

Ostrom E (2007) Challenges and growth: the development of the interdisciplinary field of institutional analysis. J Inst Theor Econ 3(3):239–264

Parsons T (1937) The structure of social action. McGraw-Hill, New York
Patashnik E (1996) The contractual natural of budgeting: a transaction cost perspective on the design of budgeting institutions. Policy Sci 29:189–212
Peters G (1999) Institutional theory in political science: the new institutionalism. Routledge, London
Pierson P (2000) Path dependence, increasing returns and the study of politics. Am Polit Sci Rev 94:251–267
Pierson P, Skocpol T (2002) Historical institutionalism in contemporary political science. In: Katznelson I, Milner (eds) Political science: the state of the discipline. Norton, New York
Ruiter DWP (2005) Is transaction cost economics applicable to public governance? Eur J Law Econ 20:287–303
Rutherford M (1994) Institutions in economics. Cambridge University Press, Cambridge
Rutherford M (2001) Institutional economics: then and now. J Econ Perspect 15(3):173–194
Scartascini C (2007) The institutional determinants of political transactions. W.P. 580, Inter-American Development Bank, Washington
Scartascini C, Stein E, Tommasi M (2010) Political institutions, actors, and arenas in Latin American policymaking. In: Scartascini C, Stein E, Tommasi M (eds) How democracy works. Inter-American Development Bank, Washington
Schofield N (2010) Social orders. Soc Choice Welf 34:503–536
Schofield N, Caballero G (2011) Political economy of institutions, democracy and voting. Springer, Berlin
Schofield N Gallego M et al (2011) Leadership or chaos: the heart and soul of politics. Springer, Heidelberg
Schofield N, Levinson M (2008) Modeling authoritarian regimes. Polit Philos Econ 7(3):243–283
Shepsle KA (1986) Institutional equilibrium and equilibrium institutions. In: Weisberg HF (ed) Political science: the science of politics. Agathon, New York
Shepsle K (1999) The political economy of state reform. Political to the core. Rev Econ Polit-Braz J Polit Econ 19:39–58
Shepsle KA (2006) Rational choice institutionalism. In: Binder S, Rhodes R, Rockman B (eds) Oxford handbook of political institutions. Oxford University Press, London
Sorensen RJ (2006) Local government consolidations: the impact of political transaction costs. Public Choice 127:75–95
Spiller PT, Tommasi M (2003) The institutional foundations of public policy: a transactions approach with applications to Argentina. J Law Econ Organ 19(2):281–306
Spiller PT, Tommasi M (2007) The institutional foundations of public policy in Argentina. A transaction cost approach. Cambridge University Press, Cambridge
Ter Bogt H (2003) A transaction cost approach to the autonomization of government organizations: a political transaction cost framework confronted with six cases of autonomization in the Netherlands. Eur J Law Econ 16:149–186
Thelen K (1999) Historical institutionalism in comparative politics. Annu Rev Pol Sci 2:369–404
Thelen K, Steinmo S (1992) Historical institutionalism in comparative politics. Steinmo S et al (eds) Structural politics: historical institutionalism in comparative analysis. Cambridge University Press, Cambridge
Twight C (1994) Political transaction-cost manipulation. An integrating theory. J Theor Polit 6(2):189–216
Vanhuysse P (2002) Efficiency in politics: competing economic approaches. Polit Stud 50:136–149
Weber K (1997) Hierarchy amidst anarchy: a transaction costs approach to international security cooperation. Int Stud Q 41:321–340
Weingast BR (1996) Political institutions: rational choice perspectives. In: Goodin RE, Klingemann HD (eds) A new handbook of political science. Oxford University Press, London
Weingast BR (2002) Rational choice institutionalism. In: Katznelson I, Milner HV (eds) Political science. The state of the discipline. Norton, New York

Weingast BR, Marshall WJ (1988) The industrial organization of congress; or, why legislatures, like firms, are not organized as markets. J Polit Econ 96(1):132–163
Williamson OE (1975) Markets and hierarchies: analysis and antitrust implications. Free Press, New York
Williamson OE (1985) The economics institutions of capitalism: firms, markets, relational contracting. Free Press, New York
Williamson OE (1996) Revisiting legal realism: the law, economics, and organization perspective. Ind Corp Change 5(2):383–420
Williamson OE (1999) Public and private bureaucracies: a transaction cost economics perspective. J Law Econ Organ 15(1):306–342
Williamson OE (2000) The new institutional economics: taking stock, looking ahead. J Econ Lit 38:595–613
Wood BD, Bohte J (2004) Political transaction costs and the politics of administrative design. J Polit 66(1):176–202

Political Transitions in Ancient Greece and Medieval Italy: An Analytic Narrative

Leandro De Magalhães

Keywords Political transitions · Wars · Ancient Greece · Athens · Venice · Genoa · Democracy · Republic

1 Introduction

Models of political transitions to democracy or on the extension of the suffrage have tended to focus on the 19th and 20th centuries (Acemoglu and Robinson 2001; Lizzeri and Persico 2004; Llavador and Oxoby 2005), disputes over redistribution, and over the provision of economic public goods, such as infrastructure. These issues are relevant for the period intended in these papers. But as we go back in history, the defining public good is defence, and the contention policy issues seem to be whether to go to war and which wars to fight.

De Magalhães and Giovannoni (2012) propose a model where wars play a key role in explaining political transitions. They model the bargaining game that may bring an absolutist ruler to hand over power to an assembly of citizens (the commercial elite in the paper). Wars determine both the policy available to the players (whether to go to war and which wars to fight), and their threat points (what happens to the players when a war is lost). In De Magalhães and Giovannoni (2012) the focus is on the English case and the Glorious Revolution of 1688. The objective of this paper is to provide an analytic narrative to test whether the model in De Magalhães and Giovannoni (2012) is relevant to the understanding of political transitions in Ancient Athens, Medieval Venice, and Genoa.[1]

Literature on the historical emergence of inclusive institutions has focused on the economic changes that made it easier for rule by parliament to emerge. Bates and Lien (1985), for example, formalize the idea that the tax elasticity of a sector increases its bargaining power. They show that the most elastic sector will be taxed

[1] For a detailed description of the method of analytic narrative see Arias (2012).

L. De Magalhães (✉)
Department of Economics, University of Bristol, 8 Woodland Road, Bristol BS8 1TN, UK
e-mail: leandro.magalhaes@bristol.ac.uk

N. Schofield et al. (eds.), *Advances in Political Economy*,
DOI 10.1007/978-3-642-35239-3_2,

less and that the equilibrium policy will be closest to the preferred policy position of the most elastic sector. As the economy becomes more dependent on trade and manufacture and less on agriculture, we should observe a transfer of power to the commercial classes. A similar argument is made in Levy (1988), where stable institutions must include a form of quasi-voluntary financial contribution to the state. Fleck and Hanssen (2006) focus on ancient Greece to show that the extension of political powers may be necessary to provide the right economic incentives when effort is not observable.

Bates and Lien (1985), Levy (1988), and Fleck and Hanssen (2006) describe how a particular economic environment makes it easier for a transition to occur. As we will see below, their broad predictions of the joint rise of commercial wealth and democracy (or rule by parliament) holds true for both ancient Greece and Medieval Italy, but to understand the transitions themselves we need to look at the role of war.

Extensive literature has focused on how the threat of war drove the formation of the state and helped states build capacity (see Tilly (1990), Hoffman and Rosenthal (2000), Besley and Persson (2009), Gennaioli and Voth (2011), Boix et al. (2011), and Arias (2012)). In these papers, a war is a common threat and the defence of the country is a common-interest public good. The objective of these papers is to explain institutional changes such as the size of the states, investments in financial capacity on a judicial system, or on a centralizing bureaucracy. The institutional change we are interested in here is a transition to rule by assembly and considerable constraints on the executive (we will call such a regime a democracy or rule by assembly, council, or parliament).

The model in De Magalhães and Giovannoni (2012) builds on Acemoglu and Robinson (2001), where the handing-over of power is a commitment device to ensure higher redistribution for the poor in the future. High redistribution is necessary to prevent the poor from acting on their threat of revolution. Contrary to Acemoglu and Robinson (2001), De Magalhães and Giovannoni (2012) focus on wars. The ruler will be unable to commit to going to the wars preferred by the commercial elites in the future. Handing over power to an assembly (where the commercial elite plays the leading role) solves this commitment problem and buys the financial assistance of the commercial elites during a defensive war, when the ruler is at risk.

Wars are introduced in De Magalhães and Giovannoni (2012) by building on Jackson and Morelli (2007), where wars have different risk-reward ratios for rulers and citizens. De Magalhães and Giovannoni (2012) allow for different types of war. Some wars, called misaligned, have an intrinsic bias: the ruler receives an ego-rent from winning, but this brings little economic return to both the ruler and to the commercial elite. Alternatively, aligned wars are also available: both the commercial elite and the ruler receive high economic returns if an aligned war is won, but there are no ego-rents involved. A key example of misaligned wars are costly dynastic wars that benefit the ruler and his kin, but not the commercial elite. Examples of aligned wars are commercial wars that expand the markets for the commercial elite's products.

De Magalhães and Giovannoni (2012) show that for an absolutist ruler to hand over power to an assembly, there must be a credible threat that the sitting ruler will be replaced if the war is lost. The commercial elite must prefer the alternative invading ruler to their sitting ruler. This condition is satisfied, for example, if the invading ruler is better at winning wars (maybe because of alliances with other foreign powers). The commercial elite may then prefer to withhold financial assistance to the sitting ruler on a defensive war against the stronger contender. If they do so, they increase the probability of a transition to either rule under the stronger contender, or to self rule as the sitting ruler may be willing to hand-over power in return for their assistance. Therefore, one of the predictions of the model is that transitions should occur in countries of intermediate military strength (if they were hegemonic there would be no credible threat to the ruler). De Magalhães and Giovannoni (2012) also show that transitions to rule by parliament are likely to be preceded by a period of unstable absolutist rule, which is characterized by a ruler who goes on dynastic wars and defensive wars without the assistance of the commercial elite.

We will also confront the evidence in ancient Greece and medieval Italy with Ticchi and Vindigni (2009), where the threat of war helps the elite make a credible commitment—in the form of democratization—to the citizen-soldiers, who demand redistribution in return for exerting effort during wars. As we will see, their model seems particularly relevant for the first steps of representative government in Greece, where the Army and later the Navy was manned by the citizens. For Venice and Genoa this also played a role, but the main constraint seems to have been the financing of the fleet.

In summary, we will go through historical examples of transitions to rule by assembly and check what role, if any, was played by wars. Did the transitions take place during a period of strong foreign threat? Is there evidence that the aristocracy and the merchants had diverging opinions on foreign policy; that the merchants withheld resources from their ruler; or that the merchants preferred a foreign ruler to the sitting ruler? By trying to answer these questions, we should be able to gauge the relevance of the model in De Magalhães and Giovannoni (2012) in understanding the political transitions in ancient Greece and medieval Italy.

2 Political Transitions in Ancient Greece

Before looking into the political reforms of Athens in detail, let's briefly discuss the evidence from general trends towards democratic government in ancient Greece. There seems to be a clear link between economic activity, in particular trade, and democracy. This evidence supports the predictions of models such as Bates and Lien (1985), Levy (1988), and De Magalhães and Giovannoni (2012).

Specific to ancient Greece, Fleck and Hanssen (2006) show how democracy can mitigate a time inconsistency problem. Workers and property owners must input unobservable effort to plant and maintain olive trees in the Athenian hills that only bear fruit years later. The time inconsistency problem arises because the aristocracy cannot commit ex ante not to expropriate the fruits of the laborers' investment. The hand-over of power to the producers is a way to mitigate this problem. Democracy is therefore more likely to arise the greater the gains from solving this time inconsistency problem are.

The Athenian example contrasts with Sparta according to Fleck and Hanssen (2006). Sparta's vast plains were ideal for growing grain. Not only is the effort exerted by the workers in grain production more easily observable, but also the time inconsistency is of a smaller scale. There was little economic gain for the Spartan elite in handing over power to grain producers.

Fleck and Hanssen (2006) extend their analysis to other cities and find support for their model. Cities with dry soil unsuitable for grains, such as Argos, achieved moderate democracy, whereas cities with richer soils, such as Corinth and Thebes, were oligarchies.

In De Magalhães and Giovannoni (2012) one of the key variables is the relative importance of commercial wealth (versus land). Raaflaub and Wallace (2007, p. 43) discuss how there is evidence that some archaic cities—in the period before 480BC—had democratic constitutions. These are: Achaea (coast of mainland Greece), Croton (Sicily), Acragas (Sicily), Ambracia (coast of mainland Greece), Argos (next to coast on mainland Greece), Chios (coastal island facing Izmir), Cyrene (coast of Lybia), Heraclea Pontica (coast of Turkey), Megara (coast near Athens), Naxos (Greek island), and Syracuse (Sicily). It is interesting to note that all these are coastal cities and off-shots from Greece. They would have invariably been highly dependent on trade.

The other important consideration is that a form of government with some degree of representativeness appeared even in Sparta, away from the coast and surrounded by high quality soil for grain production. Neither the models of Fleck and Hanssen (2006) or De Magalhães and Giovannoni (2012) explain these institutional changes. These changes are better understood in the context of the model of Ticchi and Vindigni (2009), where power is granted to the citizen-soldiers in order to guarantee their effort during war.

The advances in warfare practice that led to Hoplite regiments manned by small landowners (those who could afford the weapons and the time off from their farms) created some sense of equality in Sparta and in the rest of Greece (see (Raaflaub and Wallace 2007, p. 37)). In Sparta this took the form of the set of laws called the Great Rhetra, laid down sometime in the 9th century. It established the two hereditary Kings of Sparta, a council of 28 Elders, and that a full Assembly should have final decision on state matters. It also divided the population into villages and tribes, which made military organization into phalanxes easier. Eventually, the two kings gave themselves veto power 'if the assembly spoke crookedly'.[2] Besides this veto power, the militarization of all aspects of life, potentially also voting, suggests that Sparta was not a fully fledged Democracy.[3]

[2]See Raaflaub and Wallace (2007, p. 39) for more details and primary sources.

[3]See Raaflaub and Wallace (2007, p. 34).

Within the interpretation of De Magalhães and Giovannoni (2012) the lack of democratic institutions in Sparta could be due not only to the lack of trade, but also to Sparta becoming hegemonic—at least on land. There seems to have been few credible threats to the rule of the Spartan elite. Without such a threat there was no incentive for the elite to hand over power.

2.1 Athens

The transition to democracy in Athens has, by most accounts, consisted of three steps: Solon's reforms in 594, Kleisthene's reforms in 508, and Ephialte-Perikles' reforms in 462–450.

2.1.1 Solon, 594BC

The main innovation of Solon's reform in 594 was to change how status had been defined in Athenian society (and therefore a place in public life). Status was no longer determined by belonging to a hereditary aristocracy, but was linked instead to wealth, which was measured by the amount of agricultural output, and on the capacity to either keep a horse, a span of oxen, or neither.[4] Solon's reforms also included an Assembly of 400 (100 from each of the four Ionic tribes) with limited powers. Participation in the Assembly was probably restricted to the top land-owning classes, as were the offices of the nine Archons (the executive offices). Solon also codified civil and criminal law.

The reforms of Solon (unlike the later reforms) do not seem directly motivated by a foreign threat, but are described as the result of socio-economic strife within Athens. Osborne (2009, p. 211) describes Solon's world as "a world of bitter conflict between the elite". Moreover, Osborne (2009, p. 213) goes on to describe how the economy of Athens was changing rapidly during that time. Athenian fine pottery and amphorae (used to transport olive oil and wine) had been found all over the Mediterranean from around 700 onwards. According to Osborne (2009) this new trade related wealth generated competition within the elite, and possibly between the elite and the poor, as trade created an incentive to maximize agricultural production. The interpretation of Solon's institutional reforms seem closely related to the political-economy model proposed by Fleck and Hanssen (2006).

2.1.2 Kleisthenes, 508BC

Kleisthenes's reforms in 508 extended the assembly to 500, reorganized the four old Ionic tribes in Attica (the region surrounding Athens) into ten new tribes and,

[4]See Hansen (1991, p. 30). for further details and primary sources.

most importantly, extended political rights to those who could afford to be part of a hoplite regiment (each of the ten tribes had to supply one regiment). Political rights were also extended to all the demes (villages) of Attica and were no longer confined to Athens itself. Kleisthenes also introduced the law of ostracism, which allowed Athenians to vote for important political figures to leave the city for a certain period of time without losing title or property.[5] In 501, a board of ten Generals was introduced. These Generals commanded the Army jointly with the Polemarch (one of the nine Archons).[6] The Generals were elected by popular vote and the post could be held repeatedly—contrary to most other public offices. The Generals yielded great influence over Athenian policy. Both Themistocle and Cimon would hold the post of Polemarch within the nine Archons in the early 5th century and Perikles would be elected General repeatedly later in the 5th century.

The reforms of Kleisthenes were directly linked to foreign threats and both models in De Magalhães and Giovannoni (2012) and Ticchi and Vindigni (2009) help us understand this transition.

Athens was under the rule of the tyrant Peisistratos and his son Hippias from 561 until 510. Sparta attacked Athens in 511 and lost to Hippias (who made use of Thessalian mercenary support to defend Athens). Sparta attacked again and was able to capture Hippias' children; in exchange for the hostages Hippias went in exile in Sigeion.[7] Osborne (2009) suggests that Sparta's motives were part of a deliberate policy to increases its influence beyond the Peloponnese. The wealth and size of Athens would be an important addition to Sparta's network of allies against Argos (a rival city-state).[8] In the past, Sparta had generated allies by delivering cities from their unpopular tyrants.[9]

With the tyrant Hippias in exile Athenian factions fought for power. Isagoras, who favored an alliance with Sparta, was elected Archon. Kleisthenes, who was defeated, tried to gather popular support by proposing the political reforms described above. Sparta invaded Athens again to support Isagoras and forcing Kleisthenes into exile. The Athenian people rioted and were able to defeat Isagoras and the Spartan forces. Kleisthenes's reforms were subsequently implemented.[10]

Kleisthenes's reforms had important military consequences. The newly formed Assembly of the 500 gave a clear say in foreign policy to the hoplite classes all over Attica. This new power was immediately put into use with Kleisthenes himself ostracized for supporting an alliance with Persia.[11] The organization of Attica in

---

[5] See Hansen (1991, p. 35) for further details and primary sources.

[6] See Hansen (1991, pp. 34–35) for more details and primary sources.

[7] See Osborne (2009, p. 277) for more details and primary sources. See also Hansen (1991, p. 36).

[8] See Osborne (2009, p. 275).

[9] Athenian stories about the fall of Hippias either omit Spartan intervention or mention that the intervention was due to the oracle of Delphi, see Osborne (2009, p. 277) for more details and primary sources.

[10] See Osborne (2009, p. 278) for more details and primary sources. See also Ober (2007).

[11] See Fornara and Samons (1991, p. 56) for more details and primary sources.

ten tribes and 139 demes strengthened and modernized the Athenian army, reducing their dependence on mercenaries.[12] The power of the people over foreign affairs would increase even further with the creation of an elected board of generals in the year 501.

Kleisthenes's reforms handed over power from the elite to the Athenian citizens needed to both finance and man the Hoplite regiments. It is noteworthy that the tyrants were not able to summon the Athenians themselves to fight against Sparta, but had to rely on mercenaries to defend their rule. The Spartan attack on Athens can be interpreted, in the context of De Magalhães and Giovannoni (2012), as a defensive war where the Athenians (the commercial elite in the model) chose not to help defend their ruler. Instead, their aim was to trigger a political transition, which eventually took place.

The Athenian army had parallels with the mass armies of the early 20th century, in that citizen-soldiers must exert unobservable effort in war. In Ticchi and Vindigni (2009), external threats make an equilibrium possible, where the elite hands over power (which guarantees redistribution) and the citizens exert effort during a war. This is another way to understand the extension of political rights in the late 6th century.

The threat to Athens remained high, not only were the Persians intent on conquering Greece, but the exiled tyrant Hippias seemed to be in alliance with the Persians.[13] The new Athenian army defeated the Persians at Marathon in 490. The threat persisted as Aigina (a prosperous island rivaling Athens in commerce)[14] sided with Persia. Themistocles as Archon persuaded the Assembly to pay for the harbor of Peiraieus to be fortified, and later to use the revenue from a recent silver strike to pay for 100 triremes to be added to the Athenian Navy. In 480, Athens led the victory in a naval battle against Persia at Salamis. In 478, the Dealian league was created solidifying Athenian naval supremacy in the Aegean.[15] This turn to the sea is important to understand the further developments of the Athenian democratic reforms. It is also important to notice that the decision to invest the silver windfall on the Navy was approved by the Assembly. The alternative would have been to pay each Athenian a lump sum transfer. The investment on the Navy was a deliberate move to strength Athenian naval power and a deliberate choice of foreign policy.

The political consequences of this turn to the sea were clear as 100 trimeres implied organizing almost 20,000 men to row them.[16] Most of these men would have to come from the property-less class, the Thetes. Both models in De Magalhães and Giovannoni (2012) and (in particular) Ticchi and Vindigni (2009) would predict that political powers would be extended to the Thetes and that is what eventually happened under Ephialtes and Perikles.

---

[12]See Osborne (2009, p. 279).

[13]See Hansen (1991) for more details and primary sources.

[14]See Osborne (2009, p. 308).

[15]See Hansen (1991, p. 36).

[16]See Osborne (2009, p. 310).

2.1.3 Ephialtes, 462BC

In 461/2 Ephialtes proposed a reform to transfer power from the Areopagos—the main judiciary body and a bastion of the land owning aristocracy—to other institutions more representative of the Demos (mostly the Assembly). Opposers of these reforms included the Aristocracy and Cimon, an Archon and General of the Athenian Navy. The reform was passed while Cimon was away with a large Hoplite contingent to help Sparta suppress a Helot revolt. The conditions under which the reform was approved shows that a dispute over foreign policy was a key issue: those that proposed the political reforms were also against the willingness of Cimon to assist the Spartans. The other key element is that due to a large regiment of Hoplites being away, the Assembly was tilted towards the poorest citizens.[17] The reforms resulted in bitter dispute with Cimon ostracized as he tried to reverse the reforms, and Ephialtes eventually assassinated. Raaflaub (2007, p. 122) explains these democratizing reforms and the support for a prominent Athenian naval role as a result of the empowerment of the Thetes, who were essential for the Navy, and who therefore benefited directly from Empire. Perikles's reforms followed soon after and allowed the Thetes to take a more active part in public life, as they started to be paid for it.

With Empire, Athens became the center of a large network of Mediterranean trade. Within Athens commerce was financed by maritime loans and a strong commercial elite emerged.[18] The financing of the Navy was considerably different from that of financing a Hoplite regiment. An important component in financing the Navy was a liturgy (a rotating tax) that required the wealthiest citizens to pay for, maintain, and command (or hire another to command) a trireme for one year (in some cases rich individuals would pool together for this purpose).[19] Of course, such systems were prone to free-riding problems, and tax avoidance was common. Christ (1990) describes in detail the extent of the tax avoidance problem and the attempted solutions.

For the wealthiest individuals in society to quasi-voluntarily finance Athenian foreign policy, we should expect that the Athenian political system gave the commercial elite some degree of control over foreign policy. Indeed, up to and including Perikles, the main political leaders in Athens were part of the Aristocracy. After Perikles they were often of lower birth, but still considerably wealthy. Hansen (1991, p. 39) gives the following examples: tannery-owner Kleon, lamp-manufacturer Hyperbolos, and lyre-maker Kleophon. This evidence suggests that we can interpret the political transition of Ephialtes within the model of De Magalhães and Giovannoni (2012). Ephialtes (himself an aristocrat) reduces the power of the Areopagos, the last bastion of the Aristocracy intent on alliance with Sparta. The transfer of power increases the relative weight of those who finance the Navy, and Athens goes

[17]See Raaflaub (2007, p. 113) for details and primary sources.

[18]See Raaflaub (2007, p. 118) and Millet (1983) for details and primary sources.

[19]See Hansen (1991, p. 110) for more details and primary sources.

on to pursue a policy of maritime hegemony and conflict with Sparta. Kyriaziz and Zouboulakis (2004) also argue that the rise of influence of the commercial class is linked to the financial needs of the Athenian Navy.

In summary, the political transition to democracy in Athens had a clear role in creating incentives for individuals to both participate and put effort into war as described in Ticchi and Vindigni (2009). However, as the Athenian Navy becomes the main military instrument and Athens' wealth starts to depend more and more on commerce, the model of De Magalhães and Giovannoni (2012) seems more appropriate to understand the consolidation of Athenian democracy and its stability until the Macedonian conquest. The commercial elite was indispensable in financing Athenian defences, and under constant foreign threats (Persia and Sparta) were able to gain and yield power to further their commercial interests.

3 Political Transitions in Medieval Venice and Genoa

3.1 Venice

There are two important dates in the Venetian transition from elected monarchy (with some degree of heredity) to a Republican system with considerable checks and balances on the executive: 1032 and 1172. The events around 1032 illustrate how the dodgeship came close to becoming a hereditary monarchy, but there were no clear institutional changes in 1032. The key political reform took place 1172, when the dodge was constrained to abide by the decisions of his council.

Venice began its history under control of the Byzantine Empire. The first rulers in the area were Byzantine officials appointed by the Emperor in Constantinople (Lane (1973), Norwich (2003)). By the 8th century, Venice was electing their ruler in a general assembly (the *concio* or *Arengo*) most likely dominated by the powerful families.

With time, powerful dodges were able to raise their sons to rule together with their fathers, setting them for succession. With the Orsoleo family, Venice came close to becoming a hereditary monarchy. Pietro Orsoleo II was a very successful ruler and was able to marry his eldest son to the niece of the Byzantine Emperors. With the premature death of his eldest son in 1005, Pietro raised his third son, Otto, to the dodgeship and retired. Otto was made a dodge at 16 and married the daughter of King Stephen of Hungary. In 1017, Otto placed two brothers in the two most important religious positions in Venice, as Patriarch of Grado, and as Bishop of Torcello. Due to further contentious religious and political appointments, Otto was ousted and sent to exile in Constantinople in 1024. King Stephen swiftly attacked and conquered Venetians cities along the Adriatic. The Byzantine Emperor withdrew trading privileges granted to Venice that formed the backbone of Venetian wealth.[20] With such external pressure, the interim dodge

[20]For a description of the self enforcing institutions that promoted trade in Venice in this period see Gonzáles de Lara (2011).

Centranico abdicated. Otto was called back, but died before his return to Venice. An obscure member of the Orseolo family tried to seize the dodgeship but was ousted.[21]

The first important reform in Venice came as a response to the Orseolo family's attempt to establish hereditary rule in Venice. The Venetians chose as their next dodge Domenico Flabanico in 1032, a wealthy silk-merchant with no link to the old powerful families of Venice. According Norwich (2003) there was no clear reform in Venetian law then. Existing law already called for elections and described the positions of councillors as a counterbalance to the dodge. There was a change in what was acceptable behavior for a ruler, specially regarding nepotism. By choosing a dodge with no dynastic pretensions the Venetians were sending a clear signal that they did not favor a hereditary monarchy. From 1032 onwards, Norwich (2003) notes that no fathers passed the dodgeship to their sons. The executive power of the dodgeship, however, remained intact, and the dodge continued to rule as an elected monarch.

Even with this aversion to a hereditary monarchy by 1172, Lane (1973) remarks that the dodgeship had been held by members of the Michiel family for sixty-two out of the last seventy-six years. The change in the law that would consolidate the constraints on the executive came in 1172 and would be linked to external threats and to the financing of the Venetian Navy.

Norwich (2003, Chap. 8) describes how, in 1171, relations between Byzamtium and Venice were at the point of break-down. The Emperor blamed the Venetians for an attack on the Genoese at Galata (the Genoese settlement opposite Constantinople) and had all Venetian citizens and property confiscated in Constantinople and other ports of the Empire.

Dodge Vitale II Michiel led the war preparation under strenuous financial conditions. Norwich (2003, Chap. 8) mentions that all the revenues of the state for at least a decade had already been pledged for previous debts. Dodge Vitale ordered a forced loan: every citizen with means had to contribute, and all able men were expected to man the Navy. With the fleet already at sea, the Byzantine Emperor asked a Venetian embassy to go to Constantinople and work out a peace plan. Dodge Vitale accepted what turned out to be a ploy by the Emperor to gain time. During the wait, the Plague spread in the fleet; and Vitale was forced to return to Venice in humilation. Not only did Vitale loose men and ships (that had to be burnt) to the Plague, but he also brought the Plague to the city. He was ousted and murdered in the streets.

Before immediately electing a new dodge, the Venetians decided to impose political reforms. They were now at war with both the eastern and western Roman Empires, in dire straits financially, and had a Navy in difficulties. The institutions that followed were designed to constrain the power of the dodge, whose unconstrained power was blamed for the position Venice found herself in. A Great Council of 480 was to be nominated by the neighborhoods of Venice to hold office

[21] For more details see Norwich (2003, Chap. 5).

for one year and thereafter nominate the chief officials of the state, including the dodge (until then officially elected by the Arengo, and comprising all citizens of Venice). Instead of nominating the dodge directly, the Great Council nominated 11 electors to choose the dodge and present their choice to the people as a done deal (see Norwich (2003, Chap. 9) for details and Lane (1973, pp. 95–101)). The other reform was to increase the number of councillors from two to six. The councillors were also given power to restrain the dodge. The Senate gained power in foreign affairs. Norwich (2003) interprets the effect of these reforms to 'weaken both the apex and the base of the administrative pyramid while strengthening its center'.

The choice of the next dodge clearly reflected a change in power towards the financiers of the Republic. Dodge Sebastiano Ziani was one of the wealthiest men in Venice. According to Norwich (2003, Chap. 9), Ziani suspended payment on the new government bonds (from the forced loans to finance the Navy). It seems there was little resentment, which demonstrates a willingness of the creditors (Venetians themselves) to finance the State under the new dodge. Venice also immediately sued for peace with Byzantium, who refused to accept the terms, so that the consolidation of the new regime was done under considerable foreign threat at a point when Venice was militarily weakened.

The political reform in Venice of 1172 can be best understood in light of the model in De Magalhães and Giovannoni (2012). These reforms seem to be designed to transfer power to the financiers of the state, the wealthy merchants, and away from the old quasi-nobility, and the populace. During a period of high external threat and dire financial straights, the power over foreign policy was entrenched in the hands of those who could afford to finance the defence of the state. Once in power, they would decide over foreign policy with their interests in mind, and not with the objective of setting up a hereditary monarchy, or of antagonizing the foreign powers essential for the wealth of the state.

3.2 Genoa

Genoa has no clear historically accepted date for a transition to rule by council or parliament. The best candidates are the rise of Gugliemo Boccanegra as Captain of the People in 1257 and Simone Boccanegra as the first Dodge of Genoa in 1339. In between Genoa was ruled by podestas, foreign rulers, and the aristocracy. None of these forms of government proved stable.

Throughout its history, Genoa is well known for internal strife that would regularly escalate into civil war between different noble families (clans). Since power never consolidated with any of the key clans, the families agreed by 1190 (under the influence of the Holy Roman Emperor) to be ruled by a Podesta, a foreigner who would rule Genoa with a mandate of one year.[22]

---

[22] See Epstein (1996, p. 88) for more details and Greif (2006) for a game theoretic analysis of the podestaria.

Besides the conflict between different noble families, there was also a conflict between the noble families and the people, in particular what Epstein (1996, p. 206) called the *popolo grasso*, the rich merchants who were not part of the nobility. Epstein (1996, p. 137) describes the events of 1257: after a crash in the economy a popular revolt elected Gugliemo Boccanegra as Captain of the People and a new council of 32 Anziani. The new regime's policies were geared towards 'the people who put him in office, the middling traders and master artisans, not the poor or the traditional elite' (Epstein 1996, p. 138). Interestingly, one of the financial reforms of Boccanegra was aimed at preventing the default on state debt and led to the creation of a 'precautions markets for public securities' to finance the Genoese state (p. 147). Gugliemo Boccanegra was to stay in office for five years before he fell (probably due to a coup by some of the nobles).

In 1339, after a period under foreign rule by Robert Anjou, King of Naples, and a period of unstable rule by the old nobility, the people revolted and created a new position of Dodge electing Simone Boccanegra (grandnephew of Gugliemo).[23] Again, this was the rule of the merchant classes and not of the nobles. Epstein (1996, p. 205) notes that we have details for 16 of the 22 ducal councillors: none is a noble; and there are 'two drapers, three butchers, a shield maker, and a master of the wool guild' of those that identified themselves by profession. The new governor strengthened Genoese defences and again had to consolidate public debt without repudiating any old debt. By 1340, a new fleet was out to Pera for commercial ventures. Epstein (1996, p. 207) notes that these policies reflected a 'turning away from civil war to the more congenial task of making money'. Simone Boccanegra was also to fall by 1344 under the imminent attack of an alliance made up of nobles who had been excluded from power.[24]

Another characteristic of Genoa was that it was repeatedly ruled by foreigners. Not because they were conquered, but by choice. The podesta is the key example, but Henry VII ruled in 1311, the King of Naples from 1331–1335, and later France and then Milan.

The events in Genoa highlight two important aspects of the model in De Magalhães and Giovannoni (2012). The first is the clear conflict between the nobility's dynastic concerns and attempts to impose aristocratic rule versus the merchant classes interests in a stable government with stable finances and following commercial objectives abroad. De Magalhães and Giovannoni (2012) model this conflict with the choice of a misaligned (dynastic) war versus an aligned (commercial) war. The second aspect is the will of the merchant classes to support foreign rule. A necessary condition for political transitions in De Magalhães and Giovannoni (2012) is a credible outside threat, someone ready to replace the current monarch (or aristocratic families in the case of Genoa). For the threat to be credible it must be that the commercial elite prefer a foreigner to their sitting ruler. This seems to have been the case repeatedly in Genoa.

---

[23] See Epstein (1996, p. 204).

[24] See Epstein (1996, p. 208).

Why was there no stable transition to rule by assembly in Genoa? Within the logic of De Magalhães and Giovannoni (2012), there seems to have been no clear moment when the country faced a hostile foreign threat and financial difficulties (as Venice did in 1172). An alternative explanation is to recognize a shortcoming in the model in De Magalhães and Giovannoni (2012) where the aristocracy is modeled as a single ruler. It seems clear that a divided aristocracy with competing dynastic objectives played a key role in preventing a stable form of government from appearing in Genoa.

4 Final Remarks

A picture emerges of different driving forces for political transitions. One driving force is the creation of representative institutions as a response to economic conditions: either in order to help solve a time inconsistency problem in the economy—olive oil production in Athens, and international trade in Athens, Venice, and Genoa—or due to a relative growth in importance of the economic sectors with high tax elasticity. The papers of Bates and Lien (1985), Levy (1988), Fleck and Hanssen (2006), and De Magalhães and Giovannoni (2012) predict that representative governments are more likely to arise where trade flourished. The evidence seems to support this prediction. The cities in the ancient and medieval worlds that developed representative institutions with considerable constraints on the executive were the leading trading cities of those times. Moreover, they seem to have had little choice but to turn to the sea. As Fleck and Hanssen (2006) notes, ancient city-states like Athens had insufficient and inadequate soil for grain production; this was also true for Venice and Genoa.

Political transition may also come as a solution to a problem of how to motivate an army manned by the state's own citizens. This motive seems to have been key for the creation of the Great Rhetra in Sparta, and also for the political inclusion of the Hoplites and later of the landless class (the Thetes) in Athens. Similar forces must have played a role in how the populace was given a voice to chose their dodges, both in Venice and later in Genoa. The model that best helps us understand these driving forces is Ticchi and Vindigni (2009).

A transition may also come about as an established aristocratic elite chooses to hand over power either to the people or to the commercial elite, so that the state can raise enough funds to defend itself against a foreign threat. This seems a plausible interpretation of events in Athens, in which members of the aristocracy (Kleisthenes, Ephialtes, and Perikles) proposed the institutional reforms discussed above. In Venice, the powerful families proposed the institutional changes of 1172 and in both key moments (1032 and 1172) chose dodges who were wealthy merchants of lower birth. The model that best explains this aspect of political transition is De Magalhães and Giovannoni (2012).

We also found evidence to support two aspects of political transitions that are specific to the model of De Magalhães and Giovannoni (2012). The first is that a transition to rule by parliament should be preceded by an unstable period where the ruler goes to war without the support of the citizens or the merchants. The Tyrant of Athens, Hippias, for example, had to rely on mercenaries to defend the city against Sparta. Later, Cimon's assistance to Sparta in containing a Helot revolt was a contentious foreign policy move opposed by Ephialtes and his supporters. In Venice, the Dodge Vitale II Michiel followed policies that put Venice's key commercial interests in both the Byzantine and the Western empire in jeopardy. The dodge had to eventually resort to forced loans in order to fund the Navy against Byzantium.

The second aspect is that the model in De Magalhães and Giovannoni (2012) predicts that we should observe political transitions only in states of intermediate military strength. This is because there must be a credible external threat. Athens faced clear threats from both Persia and Sparta (to whom it would eventually lose the Peloponnesian war), and Venice was under direct threat from both Byzantium and from the western Roman Empire when the power of the dodge was constrained in 1172.

Finally, Genoa provided an example that showed the limitations of the model in De Magalhães and Giovannoni (2012). An important aspect of the Genoese political system was internal strife between different clans with dynastic interests. Genoese leaders never consolidated power in the way that the tyrants of Athens or the dodges of Venice were able to. This could suggest that the centralization of power (as described in Tilly (1990), Hoffman and Rosenthal (2000), Besley and Persson (2009), Gennaioli and Voth (2011), and Arias (2012)) may be an important and counter-intuitive step towards constraining the executive through rule by parliament. Centralized power may have to be established before it can be handed-over.

References

Acemoglu D, Robinson JA (2001) A theory of political transitions. Am Econ Rev 91(4):938–963

Arias LM (2012) Building fiscal capacity in colonial Mexico: from fragmentation to centralization. Working paper, Juan March Institute, Madrid

Bates RH, Lien D (1985) A note on taxation, development and representative government. Social science working paper 567, Caltech

Besley T, Persson T (2009) The origins of state capacity: property rights, taxation, and politics. Am Econ Rev 99(4):1218–1244

Boix C, Codenotti B, Giovanni R (2011) War, wealth and the formation of states. In: Political economy of institutions, democracy and voting. Springer, Heidelberg, pp 45–74

Christ MR (1990) Liturgy avoidance and antidosis in classical Athens. Trans Am Philol Assoc 120:147–169

De Magalhães L, Giovannoni F (2012) War financing and the transition from absolutism to rule by parliament. Mimeo, Bristol University

Epstein SA (1996) Genoa and the genoese. University of North Carolina Press, Chapel Hill, pp 958–1528

Fleck RK, Hanssen FA (2006) The origins of democracy: a model with application to ancient Greece. J Law Econ 49(1):115–146

Fornara CW, Samons LJ II (1991) Athens from Cleisthnes to Pericles. University of California Press, Berkeley

Gennaioli N, Voth H-J (2011) State capacity and military conflict. Working paper, CREI-Barcelona

Gonzáles de Lara Y (2011) Self-enforcing, public-order institutions for contract enforcement: litigation, regulation, and limited government in Venice, 1050–1350. In: Political economy of institutions, democracy and voting. Springer, Heidelberg, pp 95–115
Greif A (2006) Institutions and the path to the modern economy. Cambridge University Press, New York
Hansen MH (1991) The Athenian democracy in the age of Demosthenes: structure, principles and ideology. Blackwell, Oxford
Hoffman PT, Rosenthal J-L (2000) Divided we fall: the political economy of warfare and taxation. Caltech working paper
Jackson M, Morelli M (2007) Political bias and war. Am Econ Rev 97(4):1353–1372
Kyriaziz NC, Zouboulakis MS (2004) Democracy, sea power and institutional change: an economic analysis of the Athenian naval law. Eur J Law Econ 17:117–132
Lane FC (1973) Venice a maritime republic. The Johns Hopkins University Press, Baltimore
Levy M (1988) Of rule and revenue. University of California Press, Berkeley
Lizzeri A, Persico N (2004) Why did the elites extend the suffrage? Democracy and the scope of government, with an application to Britain's "Age of reform". Q J Econ 119(2):707–765
Llavador H, Oxoby RJ (2005) Partisan competition, growth, and the franchise. Q J Econ 120(3):1155–1189
Millet P (1983) Maritime loans and the structure of credit in fourth-century Athens. In: Trade in the ancient economy. Chatoo & Windus – The Hogarth Press, London, pp 36–52
Norwich JJ (2003) A history of Venice. Penguin, London
Ober J (2007) 'I besieged that man'. In: Origins of democracy in ancient Greece. University of California Press, London, pp 83–104. Chapter 4
Osborne R (2009) Greece in the making 1200–479 BC, 2nd edn. Routledge, London
Raaflaub KA (2007) The breakthrough of demokratia in mid-fifth-century Athens. In: Origins of democracy in ancient Greece. University of California Press, London, pp 105–154. Chapter 5
Raaflaub KA, Wallace RW (2007) "People's power" and egalitarian trends in archaic Greece. In: Origins of democracy in ancient Greece. University of California Press, London, pp 22–48. Chapter 2
Ticchi D, Vindigni A (2009) War and endogenous democracy. Working paper, IMT Lucca
Tilly C (1990) Coercion, capital, and European states. Blackwell, Oxford

A Collective-Action Theory of Fiscal-Military State Building

Luz Marina Arias

> *Where benefits are not earmarked, 'somebody else should pay' is always a powerful motivation in tax policy.* Alt (1983, p. 194)

The emergence of the fiscal-military state in the eighteenth century granted the central government new and unprecedented roles. In England, fiscal collection was increasingly centralized and put in the hands of a new and efficient fiscal bureaucracy, an army was created, and the navy acquired world-renown reputation (O'Brien 1988 and Brewer 1989). Tax proceeds as a percentage of national income rose from 3.5 percent in the 1670s to over 12 percent by the end of the eighteenth century.[1] Even though parallel attempts at fiscal modernization in Spain met with limited success until the early nineteenth century, in colonial Mexico public officials succeeded at strengthening the central administration with fiscal bureaucrats and a proficient accounting system. Mean growth for the Mexico City Treasury averaged almost 60 percent in each of the decades between 1770 and 1800.[2] Other European states followed in the late eighteenth and early nineteenth centuries.

Prior to this transition, most monarchs depended to a large extent on economic and local elites for the collection of tax revenue and defense. Fiscal capacity was

[1] O'Brien (1988, Table 2).

[2] Klein (1985, 566–574).

I am grateful to an anonymous referee, David Baron, B. Douglas Bernheim, Paul David, Alberto Díaz-Cayeros, Marc Dincecco, Rafael Dobado, Avner Greif, Luis Jáuregui, Yadira Gonzalez de Lara, Steve Haber, Margaret Levi, Carlos Marichal, Romans Pancs, Alvin Rabushka, Gavin Wright, and the participants at the II International Conference on Political Economy and Institutions in Baiona, the Social Science and History Workshop at Stanford University, and the Workshop on Endogenous Institutions and Political Conflict at UC Berkeley's Center on Institutions and Governance. This work would have not been possible without the financial support from the Stanford Institute for Economic Policy Research, the John M. Olin Program in Law and Economics, Stanford Law School, and the Center on Democracy, Development, and the Rule of Law (CDDRL) at Stanford University.

L.M. Arias (✉)
CEACS, Juan March Institute, C/Castello 77, Madrid 28006, Spain
e-mail: larias@march.es

N. Schofield et al. (eds.), *Advances in Political Economy*,
DOI 10.1007/978-3-642-35239-3_3,

fragmented. The central ruler invested minimally in monitoring and enforcement capacities to collect taxes. Treasuries and fiscal institutions at the national level functioned primarily as recipients of the monies collected by the local elites. Provincial authorities or economic actors organized in corporations—such as aristocrats, merchants or ecclesiasts—were responsible for the collection and dispatch of taxes. Rulers negotiated monetary transfers and loans with these elites and corporations, and granted them exemptions and other privileges in return.[3] For instance, in France the provincial Estates, the assembly of the clergy, and tax farmers had tax authority and transferred funds to the Crown.[4] The Spanish crown protected the merchant guild from foreign competition in the colonies, provided them with defense in the form of convoys, and had a contract with them for the collection of the *alcabala* (sales) tax in colonial Mexico.[5]

The fiscal-military state, then, implied losses of fiscal and other privileges for different elites. Why did fiscally and politically powerful elites allow the ruler to increase fiscal centralization and build-up militarily? To the extent that a ruler lacked the ability to unilaterally increase revenue to provide an army or to strengthen fiscal administration, the compliance of at least a fraction of the elites was necessary. Indeed, all across early modern Europe "provinces, estates, ecclesiastical domains, privileged cities, and corporations, as well as noble families [...] and city states, maintained privileges and defences against the imposition of more modern, centralized, universal, equitable, and potentially more productive systems of taxation and finance."[6]

Explanations for fiscal centralization emphasize the need to increase military establishments as the major impetus for the growth of European states' administrative apparatuses. There are two approaches in the literature. One approach highlights the role of military conflicts.[7] Military conflicts facilitate fiscal reform because wars unify a diverse population (Huntington 1968; Herbst 2000; and Kiser and Kane 2001), or the benefits of taxation become more salient to citizens (Levi 1988; and Besley and Persson 2009) or capital investors (Mann 1988). Explanations in the second approach underscore the need to constrain rulers upon granting them higher fiscal revenues. The establishment of political institutions of representation, like a parliament, increases fiscal cooperation by making commitments on public expenditures credible (North and Weingast 1989; Hoffman and Norberg 1994; and Dincecco et al. 2011).[8]

---

[3] See, for instance, O'Brien (2011, 421–423), Brewer (1989), and Levi (1988).

[4] Rosenthal (1998, 68).

[5] Marichal (2007, 76–77) and Smith (1948).

[6] O'Brien (2011, 432). See also Bonney (1999) and Storrs (2009).

[7] See for instance Weber (1922), Skocpol (1979), Tilly (1990, 1993), Bonney (1995), and Brewer and Hellmuth (1999). For a synthesis, see Campbell (1993) and O'Brien (2011).

[8] A number of studies have expanded this argument and included qualifications. See for instance Stasavage (2002, 2003), and Cox (2011). Ertman (1997) maintains that it is the timing of representative institution-building relative to the onset of wars what explains the variation in fiscal capacity centralization.

Both of these approaches contribute to our understanding of the growth of the fiscal-military state. Military conflicts provide a window for monarchs and governments to negotiate fiscal centralization by making salient the benefits of taxation. The second approach highlights, however, that increases in the benefits of taxation may not translate in fiscal cooperation because of commitment problems. A ruler with more fiscal and coercive powers may have incentives to expropriate elites or renege on its debts.[9] Some monarchs, however, succeeded at increasing fiscal centralization with no institutions of representation in place. The evidence in Dincecco (2011, 27) shows that in many European states fiscal centralization came before the formation of parliaments. Marichal (2007, 51) highlights that colonial Spanish America lacked representative assemblies yet Spanish officials successfully implementated fiscal and military reforms in some regions in the eighteenth century.

In this chapter, I underscore the collective action problem present in fragmented fiscal regimes that impeded the cooperation of the elites with the contribution of men and resources for the defense of the territory. As such, the chapter emphasizes a commitment problem among the fiscally powerful elites, rather than between the elites and the ruler, in the process of fiscal-military state formation.[10] In fragmented regimes, the ruler's fiscal income rested on earmarking benefits to elites. In the face of a threat of military conflict, fiscal fragmentation then led to a collective action problem: each elite group had incentives to free ride on the contributions of others, thereby contributing less than the socially optimal amount to military protection. The elites and the ruler were stuck in a low-contribution and low-public-good-provision equilibrium. I argue that fiscal centralization provided an institutional framework that allowed elites to commit to contribute to military protection by ensuring others were contributing as well.[11]

That collective action problems are inherent to fiscally fragmented states has been well documented. Ertman (1999, 50) notes about the Estates in Germany that: "the structure of the assemblies, divided as they were into separate *curiae* of élite groups each with their own distinct privileges, tended to inhibit cooperation among the *curiae* and lead the nobility, clergy, and the towns to focus on the defense of their narrow group rights." Bates and Lien (1985, 57) quote from Henneman (1971) that "fiscal jealousies led towns to make subsidy grants conditional upon similar grants from other towns" in France. Summerhill (2008, 224–225) notes that because rulers bargained separately with each group, fiscal fragmentation led to free riding and lower fiscal revenues.[12]

---

[9]Further, in times of war, the ruler may discount the future more than other citizens (Levi 1988).

[10]Many scholars have emphasized the role of collective action and free-rider problems in preventing the compliance of actors with welfare-enhancing cooperation. See, for instance, Olson (1993), Greif (2006) and Greif et al. (1994).

[11]Emerson (1983) provides a similar insight regarding state formation at an earlier stage in Baltistan. Greif (1998, 2006) also highlights the importance of military threats and the need for elite cooperation in shaping the internal organization of the state.

[12]See also Levi (1988, 56–57).

I provide a game-theoretic framework to analyze the conditions under which corporate and local elites gain by surrendering to a central government their power to levy taxes.[13] The analysis shows that an increase in the probability of a threat of external invasion or internal unrest is more likely to cause fiscal centralization when the elites are more dependent on the ruler for future economic rents, and when the prospects of economic activity are higher. To the extent that the stakes from military protection are aligned between the elites and the ruler, and the elites lack alternative ways to commit to cooperate for defense, the elites acquiesce to fiscal capacity centralization.[14]

Historical evidence from the increases in fiscal centralization and military build up in seventeenth century England and eighteenth century colonial Mexico provides support for the implications of the theoretical argument. The evidence highlights the importance of the Civil War for England and the Seven Years' War for colonial Mexico, and the lack of standing armies in both regions, in aligning the benefit from military protection between the elites and the ruler.

I present the formal argument in Sect. 1. Section 2 confronts the theoretical argument with evidence from English and colonial Mexican history. The final section concludes with a discussion of the implications and further avenues for research.

1 Formal Model

This section provides a theoretical framework to explain why fiscal-military state building is more likely when the probability of a threat of unrest or invasion increases. The focus is on the conditions under which corporate and local elites have incentives to surrender their power to levy taxes to a central government.

1.1 The Game

A central government, henceforth referred to as a ruler, R, interacts with n economic corporations, indexed by $i = 1, \dots, n$. These corporations are composed of agents that are able to make agreements binding on all their members.[15]

[13] This theoretical framework is built on the history of eighteenth-century colonial Mexico. Arias (2012) provides a detailed historical analysis of the successful increase in fiscal centralization and military reorganization in colonial Mexico after the Seven Years' War.

[14] Besley and Persson (2009) and Besley and Persson (2011) study the joint development of fiscal capacity and market-supporting institutions. They also emphasize the salience of a public good for increases in fiscal capacity. Their analysis, however, does not incorporate the role of a powerful elite in blocking fiscal changes. In their comparative study of state finance in Britain and France, Hoffman and Rosenthal (1997) and Rosenthal (1998) illustrate the importance of the difference in preferences for war between crown and elite when fiscal power is decentralized. They do not seek to explain transitions between fiscal regimes but only the impact of regimes on the number of wars fought.

[15] Historically, the corporations were represented by local authorities (e.g. majors) or heads of economic corporations or guilds (e.g. aristocrats, merchants or ecclesiasts). Many scholars have

The ruler is threatened with an invasion (or unrest) with probability θ. A public good (G)—military defense—is necessary to defeat the invaders (or the unruly). In order to provide military defense, the ruler depends on the contributions of the corporations because initially fiscal capacity is fragmented. That is, the ruler depends on the corporations for the enforcement and collection of fiscal monies. The corporations levy taxes and transfer some of the proceeds to the ruler.

The ruler is able to enforce bilateral contracts with the individual corporations, and by means of these private contracts the corporations transfer part of their fiscal proceeds to the ruler. Each bilateral contract is observed only by the parties to the contract. A contract with corporation i specifies the amount $x_i \geq 0$ of good i that the ruler provides to corporation i in exchange for a payment $\tau_i \geq 0$.[16] Let $(x, \tau) = ((x_1, \tau_1), \ldots, (x_n, \tau_n))$ be the profile of the ruler's unilateral offers to each corporation.

Under fragmented capacity, the corporations make contributions to the public good, $g_i \geq 0$, that result in a level of the public good $G = f(g)$, where $g = (g_1, \ldots, g_n)$, f is (strictly) increasing in g and $f_{g_i g_j} > 0$ for $i \neq j$. These contributions are voluntary because the ruler is unable to enforce them under fragmented fiscal capacity.

The ruler can propose to the corporations an increase in fiscal centralization, whereby the corporations surrender to the ruler the power to levy taxes. The increase costs F to the ruler. Under centralization, the ruler publicly announces and enforces uniform tax payments $t \geq 0$ from each i.

1.1.1 Timing

There are two periods. In the first period, all players observe θ. The ruler then chooses whether to propose an increase in fiscal centralization or to keep fiscal capacity fragmented.[17] If proposing an increase in fiscal centralization, the ruler proposes a policy profile $\{t, x, G\}$ consisting of tax payments, a vector of private goods, and a level of the public good. If not proposing centralization, the ruler proposes a "fragmented" policy profile $\{\tau, x, g\}$, which includes a vector of payments, private goods, and contributions to the public good. Each corporation accepts or rejects the policy profile proposed by the ruler.

In the second period, if the ruler proposed an increase in fiscal centralization and at least $\bar{n} \leq n$ corporations accept, the ruler invests in a fiscal-military state

---

stressed the importance of corporate forms in the development of tax systems. For instance, Strayer (1970), Henneman (1971), Prestwich (1972), Bates and Lien (1985), and Levi (1988).

[16] Examples of publicly provided private goods include royal monopolies (e.g. exclusive access to trade between specific regions), value added to commodities (e.g. mint silver coins), or the provision of local defense (convoys for merchants, fleets for miners). The collection of specific taxes by corporations also guaranteed loans between rulers and the lending corporations.

[17] Historical evidence supports giving the ruler agenda-setting power. Monarchs and public officials typically played an important role in coordinating economic elites and raising the elite's awareness about the need to negotiate fiscal-military building.

and implements the policy agreed to in the first period.[18] If less than $\bar{n}$ corporations accept, fiscal capacity remains fragmented, the ruler proposes a "fragmented" policy profile $\{\tau, x, g\}$, and the corporations accept or reject the ruler's proposal. If the ruler did not propose an increase in fiscal centralization, the ruler implements the "fragmented" policy profile agreed to in the first period.

1.1.2 Payoffs

A corporation's payoff depends on the amounts of the private good, x_i, and the public good, G, and on (exogenous) overall economic activity, $\bar{y}$. Some corporations benefit more from military protection than others. A corporation is vulnerable to the threat (of an invasion or unrest) to the extent that the corporation depends on the survival of the ruler for future rents and protection. Let $\alpha_i \geq 0$ parametrize the degree to which corporation i benefits from the public good (G). A higher α_i implies greater dependence on the ruler and therefore a higher benefit from G.[19] The (expected) payoff of each corporation (when fiscal capacity is fragmented) is:

$$u_i^F(x_i, G) = v(x_i, \bar{y}) + \theta\alpha_i y\big(f(g_i, g_{-i}), \bar{y}\big) - g_i - \tau_i - e_i.$$

where v and y are the values of the private and public goods, respectively, at a given level of economic activity, θ is the probability of a threat, τ_i is corporation i's payment to the ruler, and $e_i > 0$ is corporation i's cost to collect taxes.[20] The function v is increasing and concave in x and $\bar{y}$, $v_{x_i\bar{y}} > 0$ for all i, and $v(0, \bar{y}) = 0$. Accordingly, y is increasing and concave in G and $\bar{y}$, $y_{G\bar{y}} > 0$, and $y(0, \bar{y}) = 0$. Recall that $G = f(g_i, g_{-i})$, where g_i is corporation i's contribution to G. Each corporation's payoff is a function of its individual exchange with the ruler if $\theta = 0$. If, by contrast, $\theta > 0$, the corporation's payoff is also a function of the public good. The more a corporation depends on the ruler for economic rents (α_i), the higher the benefit from the public good.[21] Finally, for any θ, an increase in economic activity increases the payoff of each corporation.

---

[18]This framework does not explicitly incorporate the ruler's commitment problem regarding t. Once a ruler invests in centralization, the ruler could renege on the agreement in period 1 and forcibly collect tax payments higher than those agreed to (see e.g. North and Weingast 1989). If fiscal capacity is fragmented, this commitment problem between the corporations and the ruler is not an issue. Reputation ensures commitment from both corporations and ruler because exchanges under fragmented capacity rely on private contracts. A threat of reversion to fragmentation from the elite may not be credible, however, after the ruler has increased fiscal centralization. I discuss the commitment problem between ruler and corporations in the conclusion.

[19]For instance, some corporations may be able to keep their economic rents even in the case of a British takeover of Spanish colonial territory, say, or they may have their own defense against internal uprisings.

[20]This cost captures the effort to assess, collect, enforce, and dispatch taxes locally.

[21]The ruler and the corporations could also differ in their perception of the probability of a threat (θ). This can be incorporated in the parameter α_i.

If corporation i rejects the ruler's fragmented policy proposal, $x_i = 0$ and corporation i receives payoff $u_0 = v(0, \bar{y}) + \theta\alpha_i y(f(0, g_{-i}), \bar{y})$, where g_{-i} denotes the contributions of all other corporations given that corporation i is not contributing. There are positive externalities on those that do not contribute to building an army because f is increasing in g_{-i} for all i. That is, if $\theta > 0$, all groups with $\alpha_i > 0$ benefit and cannot be excluded from the military protection.[22]

When fiscal centralization is implemented, the (expected) payoff of each corporation is:

$$u_i^C(x_i, G) = v(x_i, \bar{y}) + \theta\alpha_i y(G, \bar{y}) - t,$$

where t is corporation i's tax payment. (Recall the ruler sets $t_i = t$ for all i when centralizing tax collection.) Because the ruler collects and enforces taxes under fiscal centralization, $e_i = 0$ for all i.

The ruler's payoff is the revenue obtained from corporations' payments. Let $c(x, G)$ be the cost of providing private and public goods in both fiscal regimes. Assume c is increasing and convex in x and G, and $c_{x_i x_j} = 0$ and $c_{x_i G} = 0$ for all i. Then, the ruler's payoffs under fragmented and centralized fiscal capacities are, respectively:

$$u_R^F(x, G) = \sum_{i=1}^{n}(\tau_i + g_i) - c(x, G),$$

$$u_R^C(x, G) = nt - c(x, G) - F.$$

1.2 Equilibrium

I solve for the pure-strategy subgame-perfect Nash equilibria (SPNE) of the game preferred by the ruler.[23] By backward induction, I first study the choice of payments and private and public goods proposed by the ruler under fiscal fragmentation.

If fiscal capacity is fragmented, corporation i accepts policy profile $\{x_i, \tau_i, G\}$ if and only if:

$$v(x_i, \bar{y}) + \theta\alpha_i y\big(f(g_i, g_{-i}), \bar{y}\big) - g_i - \tau_i - e_i \geq \theta\alpha_i y\big(f(0, g_{-i}), \bar{y}\big). \quad (1)$$

[22] This non-exclusion assumption distinguishes defensive warfare from predatory warfare. The former is a pure public good, whereas the latter is a private good. The spoils of a war can be promised to only some groups, while others are excluded. For more on the distinction between defensive and predatory warfare see Emerson (1983).

[23] I assume the corporations accept the ruler's proposal when indifferent. This allows me to rule out trivial equilibria. Also, the ruler makes a take-it-or-leave-it offer and so extracts all of the surplus from the corporations. Giving a higher share of the surplus to the corporations makes a transition to centralization more likely as long as the corporations receiving a large share of the surplus benefit from the public good (high α_i).

In the SPNE, the participation constraint in (1) binds for all i. Otherwise, the ruler would be able to increase his payoff by increasing the payment for some corporations. By solving for τ_i from each i's binding participation constraint, we obtain the equilibrium payment $\hat{\tau}_i$ for each corporation. Substituting each $\hat{\tau}_i$ in the ruler's objective function, the ruler's set of profit-maximizing policies is:

$$(\hat{x}, \hat{G}) \in \arg\max_{x,g\in\mathbb{R}^n} \sum_{i=1}^{n} v(x_i, \bar{y}) + \sum_{i=1}^{n} \theta\alpha_i\big[y\big(f(g_i, g_{-i}), \bar{y}\big) - y\big(f(0, g_{-i}), \bar{y}\big)\big]$$
$$-\sum_{i=1}^{n} e_i - c(x, G). \tag{2}$$

Solving we obtain the unique $\hat{x}$ and $\hat{g}$ the ruler proposes to the corporations under fragmented fiscal capacity. Notice that the equilibrium amount of private goods is the same for all corporations because the choice of x is independent from α_i and g. The proposal $\hat{x}$ is also equal to the socially optimal amount x^* such that $x^* \in \arg\max_{x\in\mathbb{R}^n} \sum_{i=1}^{n} v(x_i, \bar{y}) - c(x, G)$.

Lemma 1 *The equilibrium level of public good provision under fragmented fiscal capacity is lower than the socially optimal*: $\hat{G} < G^*$.

Proof The socially optimal level of public good provision solves:

$$G^* \in \arg\max_{g\in\mathbb{R}^n} \sum_{i=1}^{n} \theta\alpha_i y\big(f(g_i, g_{-i}), \bar{y}\big) - c(x, G). \tag{3}$$

The first order conditions: $\theta \sum_i \alpha_i \partial y/\partial G \cdot \partial f/\partial g_i = \partial c/\partial G \cdot \partial f/\partial g_i$ for $i = 1, \dots, n$, characterize G^*. From (2), the first order conditions: $\theta \sum_i \alpha_i \partial y/\partial G \cdot \partial f/\partial g_i - \theta \sum_{j\neq i} \alpha_j \partial y/\partial G \cdot \partial f/\partial g_i = \partial c/\partial G \cdot \partial f/\partial g_i$ for $i = 1, \dots, n$, characterize $\hat{G}$. The result follows because f is increasing in g. (The solution is interior because of the assumptions on y and c.) □

Under fragmented fiscal capacity, each corporation has incentives to transfer resources to the ruler only to the extent that it receives x_i. The corporations free ride on others in their contributions to the public good, and the ruler has no means of enforcing these contributions. Internalizing the lower contribution of each corporation, the ruler's choice of G is lower than the socially optimal.

Lemma 1 allows us to define the social cost due to free riding as the increase in the aggregate value from public good provision if the corporations were able to commit to pay: $Y(G^*, \bar{y}) - Y(\hat{G}, \bar{y}) > 0$, where $Y(G, \bar{y}) = \sum_{i=1}^{n} y(G, \bar{y}) = ny(G, \bar{y})$. If the groups were able to coordinate and police themselves to commit to pay, there would be no cost from the free riding problem. The difference $Y(G^*, \bar{y}) - Y(\hat{G}, \bar{y})$ increases when the groups interact only with the ruler and are unable to solve the collective action problem among themselves.

1.3 Investment in fiscal centralization

First, notice that when fiscal capacity is centralized the ruler maximizes fiscal transfers by choosing the socially optimal amount G^*. Each corporation faces the following participation constraint when the ruler proposes centralization:

$$v(x_i, \bar{y}) + \theta\alpha_i y(G, \bar{y}) - t \geq v(\hat{x}_i, \bar{y}) + \theta\alpha_i y\big(f(\hat{g}), \bar{y}\big) - \hat{g}_i - \hat{\tau}_i - e_i. \qquad (4)$$

The right hand side of (4) is constant and given by the equilibrium policy profile $\{\hat{\tau}, \hat{x}, \hat{g}\}$. The corporations can refuse centralization and force the ruler to keep fiscal capacity fragmented. Summing over n and solving for t, we obtain $nt \leq \sum_i [v(x_i, \bar{y}) + \theta\alpha_i y(G, \bar{y})] - C$, where C is a constant. It follows that $u_R^C(x, G) \leq \sum_i [v(x_i, \bar{y}) + \theta\alpha_i y(G, \bar{y})] - C - c(x, G) - F$. Therefore, the ruler sets the maximum upper bound on net fiscal transfers by choosing G^* as defined in (3).

Two conditions must hold for fiscal centralization to occur. First, the participation constraint in (4) must hold for at least $\bar{n}$ corporations. The corporations can refuse centralization and the ruler has no credible threat but to preserve fiscal fragmentation. Second, the ruler's payoff must be higher under centralization than under fragmentation. If the ruler's payoff given the tax payment necessary to obtain compliance from $\bar{n}$ corporations is less than the payoff from $\{\hat{\tau}, \hat{x}, \hat{g}\}$, the ruler does not propose centralization.

Substituting in (4) for $(\hat{\tau}_i, \hat{x}_i, \hat{g})$ and solving for t we obtain the maximum tax payment that each corporation is willing to pay in exchange for the optimal level of the public good:

$$t_i^M \leq v(x_i, \bar{y}) + \theta\alpha_i\big[y\big(G^*, \bar{y}\big) - y\big(f(0, g_{-i}), \bar{y}\big)\big], \quad \text{for } i = 1, \ldots, n. \qquad (5)$$

A couple remarks about this maximum tax payment are in order. First, the ruler obtains higher maximum payments from those corporations who benefit more from the public good (α_i). Second, the ruler can obtain compliance from corporation i at a tax payment higher than the maximum in (5) by compensating with private goods (a higher x_i) or if the prospects of economic activity increase.

I first obtain the SPNE assuming the ruler can collect corporation-specific tax payments and provides the socially optimal amount of private goods x^*. The constraints in (5) bind for all i, otherwise the ruler would be able to increase his payoff by increasing the tax payment for some corporations. Let $t_i^* \equiv v(x_i, \bar{y}) + \theta\alpha_i[y(G^*, \bar{y}) - y(f(0, g_{-i}), \bar{y})]$ be the binding constraint in (5) for i. The following proposition gives the condition under which policy profile $\{t^*, x^*, G^*\}$ is an equilibrium for $\bar{n} = n$, where $t^* = (t_1^*, \ldots, t_n^*)$.

Proposition 1 *At the SPNE, the ruler proposes policy profile $\{t^*, x^*, G^*\}$, all corporations accept and the ruler increases fiscal centralization if the probability of a threat is such that*:

$$\theta \geq \frac{F + c(x^*, G^*) - [\sum_i e_i + c(x^*, \hat{G})]}{[Y(G^*, \bar{y}) - Y(\hat{G}, \bar{y})] \sum_i \alpha_i / n}. \qquad (6)$$

Proof The ruler proposes a transition if and only if $\sum_i t_i^* - c(x^*, G^*) - F \geq u_R^F(\hat{\tau}, \hat{x}, \hat{G})$. Substituting in for t_i^* and $\hat{\tau}_i$, and solving for θ gives condition (6). Note that by Lemma 1 and since y is increasing, $Y(G^*, \bar{y}) - Y(\hat{G}, \bar{y}) > 0$. □

Condition (6) shows that an increase in fiscal centralization depends on the cost increase to the ruler from providing the optimal amount of public good and on the corporations' overall gain from overcoming free riding, relative to the probability of a threat. Notice that the lower the average corporation's dependence on the ruler ($\sum_i \alpha_i/n$), the higher the probability of a threat needs to be for the ruler to propose centralization. That is, fiscal centralization occurs for smaller values of the probability of a threat, the smaller the divergence between the corporations' and the ruler's benefit from military protection. Also, centralization occurs for smaller values of θ if the prospects of economic activity ($\bar{y}$) increase, because the stakes of all parties increase. If condition (6) does not hold, the ruler proposes a fragmented policy profile and fiscal capacity remains fragmented.

The tax policy $t^* = (t_1^*, \ldots, t_n^*)$ is not an equilibrium strategy if $\bar{n} < n$.[24] For $\bar{n} < n$, the ruler optimizes by setting a tax policy such that constraint (5) binds for exactly $\bar{n}$ corporations. Under fiscal centralization, the ruler can use its monitoring and enforcing capacity to oblige the remaining $n - \bar{n}$ corporations to pay a tax rate higher than their maximum tax rate. I derive below the SPNE when the ruler sets a uniform tax payment for all corporations under centralization and $\bar{n} < n$.

Definition 1 For some t proposed by the ruler, corporation i is **pivotal** if $t_i^* \geq t$ and $m(i) + 1 = \bar{n}$, where $m(i) \equiv \#\{j | t_j^* > t_i^*\}$ is the number of corporations whose maximum payment exceeds i's maximum payment.

When proposing centralization, the ruler maximizes his payoff and ensures compliance from $\bar{n}$ corporations by proposing the tax payment of the pivotal corporation for a given (x, G). Let corporation p, with corresponding t_p^*, be the pivotal corporation when the ruler proposes (x^*, G^*).[25] The following result gives the condition under which the policy profile $\{t_p^*, x^*, G^*\}$ yields centralization in equilibrium. I assume a corporation accepts if indifferent.

Proposition 2 *At the SPNE, $\bar{n}$ corporations accept policy profile $\{t_p^*, x^*, G^*\}$ and the ruler invests in a centralized fiscal administration if the probability of a threat of invasion or unrest is such that:*

$$\theta \geq \frac{F + c(x^*, G^*) - [\sum_i e_i + c(x^*, \hat{G})]}{\alpha_p Y(G^*, \bar{y}) - Y(\hat{G}, \bar{y})[\sum_i \alpha_i/n]}. \tag{7}$$

[24] It is an equilibrium for $\bar{n} < n$, trivially, if all corporations are identical ($\alpha_i = \alpha$ for all i).

[25] From condition (4), the ruler maximizes by choosing the socially optimal level of private good.

Proof The ruler proposes a transition if and only if $nt_p^* \geq u_R^F(\hat{\tau}, \hat{x}, \hat{G})$. Substituting in for t_p^* and $\hat{\tau}_i$, and solving for θ gives condition (7). □

The gain from providing the optimal amount of military protection is now weighted by the vulnerability to a threat of each corporation relative to that of the pivotal corporation. If the pivotal corporation has a degree of vulnerability higher than the average, the transition to centralization occurs for a lower probability of the threat than in Proposition 1, all else constant.[26] However, if the pivotal corporation has a lower benefit from the public good than the average corporation, the condition in Proposition 2 does not hold and the ruler does not propose centralization even though it is socially optimal. This occurs because the ruler endures a loss in fiscal revenue from requesting a uniform transfer rather than discriminating across corporations according to their benefit from the public good.

1.4 Implications

Both Propositions 1 and 2 highlight the main implication from the analysis. An increase in the probability of a threat is more likely to cause an increase in fiscal centralization and military build-up, the higher the corporations' stakes on the survival of the ruler for their economic future. The higher the corporations' dependence on the ruler for future rents, the higher is the benefit from the provision of the optimal military protection, and the more that the corporations are willing to transfer under centralization. Also, all else equal, a higher level of economic activity facilitates centralization by increasing the maximum a corporation is willing to pay under centralization and by increasing the social gain from overcoming free riding. A fiscal regime may therefore remain fragmented because the alignment between the benefits to the ruler and the corporate elites from military protection is small, or the ruler's cost of investing in centralization is too high.

Proposition 2 shows in addition that if the ruler is unable to collect corporation-specific payments (and is thus unable to extract all the corporations' benefits from the public good), an increase in fiscal centralization depends on the size of the 'accepting' coalition ($\bar{n}$). In particular, we may not observe centralization when it is socially optimal, if the pivotal corporation has a lower benefit from the public good than the average corporation.

Finally, a couple remarks about the theoretical framework are in order. First, the analysis emphasizes that unless the ruler has the support of some of the corporations, the increase in fiscal centralization and military build up are not feasible. The

[26] This can be seen clearly by rewriting the denominator in condition (7) as follows and comparing it with the denominator in condition (6):

$$\alpha_p Y(G^*, \bar{y}) - Y(\hat{G}, \bar{y}) \sum_i \frac{\alpha_i}{n} = \left[Y(G^*, \bar{y}) - Y(\hat{G}, \bar{y})\right] \sum_i \frac{\alpha_i}{n} - Y(G^*, \bar{y}) \sum_i \frac{\alpha_i - \alpha_p}{n}.$$

corporations can refuse centralization and the ruler has no credible threat except to preserve fiscal fragmentation. If, however, the ruler has alternative or external sources of revenue to finance an army or impose centralization, negotiation with the corporations may not play such an important role.

Second, the setup implicitly assumes the ruler has the authority and the ability to propose and implement centralization. For the results to hold, the ruler must have legal authority and the corporations must believe the ruler can credibly monitor and enforce tax collection. Lacking a central actor with legal authority or the credible ability to monitor and sanction, an increase in the probability of internal or external threat will not lead to an increase in fiscal centralization.

2 Historical Evidence

To provide support for the theoretical argument, this section discusses historical evidence from the transition to a fiscal-military state in seventeenth-century England and eighteenth-century colonial Mexico.[27] I organize the evidence around the two main factors highlighted by the theoretical analysis leading to a fiscal-military reform: (1) military vulnerability and the alignment between the corporate elites' and the ruler's benefit from military protection, and (2) the need for rulers to negotiate with the corporate elites to obtain their compliance. Section 2.1 presents evidence for England while Sect. 2.2 discusses the evidence for colonial Mexico.

The cases of England and Mexico are pertinent because they allow us to isolate the public good nature of military protection. When an army is created with predatory goals and the spoils of war exclusively assigned to specific groups, military protection confounds both a private and a public good nature. The objectives (at least initially) of the build up of a fiscal-military state in seventeenth-century England and eighteenth-century Mexico were defensive. The historical evidence below shows that they both lacked armies and had enjoyed relatively long periods of no military involvement prior to the increase in the probability of a threat.

Also, the cases of England and colonial Mexico corroborate the importance of a ruler or central government with the credible authority and ability to implement the fiscal-military reforms. Brewer (1989) notes the importance of the British crown's recognized authority and infrastructure in the administration of justice for their success in building a fiscal-military state. In colonial Mexico, the wars of independence

[27] Many scholars have documented the important changes in fiscal administration and enforcement, and in military capacity, that colonial Mexico and England underwent in the second half of the eighteenth century and the mid-seventeenth century, respectively. For colonial Mexico's fiscal, administrative, and financial reforms, see for instance Fonseca and Urrutia (1791), Brading (1973, 1987), Elliott (1987), Klein (1998), Jáuregui (1999), Coatsworth (1990), Knight (2002), Stein and Stein (2003), and Marichal (2007). Regarding colonial Mexico's military reorganization, see McAlister (1953), Gutiérrez-Santos (1961), Fisher (1982), Marichal and Souto Mantecón (1994), Kuethe (1986), Archer (1981, 1978) and Elliott (2006). The main sources for England are O'Brien (1988, 2011), Brewer (1989) and Brewer and Hellmuth (1999).

(1810–1821) and resulting political instability provide an example of the importance of legal authority. The internal and external threats faced by the elites in different regions in the aftermath of independence from Spain did not lead to centralization. It took almost fifty years for the region to stabilize its newly minted state. Centeno (2002) argues that this was a result of the authority void left by the Spanish crown: no group was superior to the rest.

2.1 England

In contrast to other European nations, England lacked a standing army from the late fifteenth to the late seventeenth centuries. Its landed aristocrats were also effectively demilitarized; by the 1640s "four out of five aristocrats had no military experience at all" (Brewer 1989, 12). This was partly a result of England's non-involvement with major international conflicts during that time-period. According to Brewer (1989, 12), "England was sheltered not just by her insular position but by the scale of war in early modern Europe." The large increase in army sizes and number of troops deployed made an invasion of England complicated, and an English invasion of the continent difficult. English naval power only began to be established in the second half of the seventeenth century. Castilian and French fleets managed to seize and sack various English ports during the Hundred Years war. Further, prior to the seventeenth century, the navy depended heavily on private support and armed merchantmen ships.[28]

The Civil War (1642–1651) marked a turning point for the need to secure the state against domestic rivalries. An interregnum of civil warfare and challenges to hierarchy created the conditions for a watershed in England's fiscal and military history. Importantly, the succession of events "forged a political consensus among England's wealthy elites for an altogether stronger and more centralized state, above all to maintain order and political stability, but also to afford greater protection for the economy's growing commercial interests overseas" (O'Brien 2011, 426). The threat of internal political stability together with the lack of military protection provided the conditions for an alignment of the executive's and the elite's benefit from creating a standing army and strengthening the navy.

The important role played by Parliament in fiscal matters gives evidence of the need to negotiate and obtain cooperation from the wealthy elites. Parliament decided on the selection of the levels and types of taxes, the rules for their assessment and collection, and had control over the state departments in charge of implementing those rules.[29] In fact, the landed elites set the terms for cooperation by initially avoiding direct taxes on land. It was not until 1799 that Pitt managed to introduce

[28]This paragraph summarizes Brewer (1989, 8–13).

[29]Horowitz (1977) and O'Brien (2011).

Britain's first income tax.[30] "Only the armies of Revolutionary France and the probable collapse of public credit prompted the political classes to accept [direct taxation]" (O'Brien 1988, 22).

In sum, English fiscal history shows the importance of a threat of internal unrest (evident after the Civil war) in increasing fiscal centralization. By aligning the benefit from military protection for a majority of the wealthy elites and monarch, a transition out of a low-contribution and low-public-good-provision was possible. Also, the role played by parliament attests to the need to negotiate with the elites and to the importance of centralized and public fiscal policies to ensure every elite group that others were cooperating and contributing with the forging of a fiscal-military state.

2.2 Colonial Mexico

The Spanish crown faced practically no internal or external challenges in its American territories during its first 200 years of colonial rule.[31] The crown did not need to incur in major expenses to defend its colonial territory and relied only on minimal forces at the ports and borders for the protection of the Spanish American empire.[32] The vulnerable position of colonial Mexico is evidenced by the efforts to garner a field army in 1762 in the port of Veracruz, on the coast of the Gulf of Mexico.[33] This port was the point of entry and exit for all European trade with New Spain, and therefore one of the most guarded locations in colonial Mexico. In 1760, the port and fortress were guarded by around 1,000 men.[34] The port of Veracruz was vulnerable to attack just before the end of the Seven Years' War. The Viceroy Marqués de Cruillas spent 3,398,471 pesos of extraordinary funds to ready the fortifications and mobilize a force of 8,500 men in and around Veracruz.[35] This was a force eight times the size of the previous force. Notwithstanding, according to the Viceroy, a much larger force was necessary to ensure the security of the kingdom.[36]

The lack of military protection in conjunction with the Seven Years' War (1756–1763) identify a watershed in colonial Mexican history. The Seven Years' War

[30] O'Brien (1988).

[31] Arias (2012) provides a thorough historical analysis of colonial Mexico supporting the theoretical argument presented here.

[32] McAlister (1953, 2).

[33] Colonial Mexico was part of New Spain, one of the Spanish viceroyalties in colonial Spanish America. After the conquest, the Spanish crown divided the territory in two viceroyalties, New Spain and Peru, comprising roughly contemporary Mexico and Peru, respectively. In the 18th century, two more viceroyalties were created: New Granada and Río de la Plata. The viceregal governments functioned as a link between the crown in Spain and its subjects in America. Even so, colonial corporations and powerful individuals negotiated directly with the government in Madrid.

[34] McAlister (1953, 2–3).

[35] Archer (1981, 315).

[36] McAlister (1953, 7).

changed the balance of power within colonial territory among the European powers.[37] In 1756, France declared war on Great Britain. This was the beginning of the French-Indian War, as the conflict was known to the colonists. The war was a struggle for primacy between Britain and France. For the first time in European history, battles occurred in colonial territory.[38] There were battles in India, North America, the Caribbean isles, the Philippines, and coastal Africa, and Europe. By the autumn of 1760, all French territory in mainland America was in British hands. An agreement made in August 1761 between the Bourbon kings of Spain and France, the Family Compact, brought Spain into the war. In August of 1762, the British Royal Navy captured Havana, Cuba, and Manila in the Philippines. The war ended following the Treaty of Paris on February 10, 1763, with a victory for Great Britain, who emerged as the dominant European power.

The military defeats suffered by Spain during the Seven Years' War highlighted the need to secure Spanish colonial possessions against British attack. Also, because of the demographic recovery of the Indian population in the first half of the eighteenth century, many provinces in colonial Mexico saw internal unrest increase to new levels.[39] The Seven Years' War, together with the increased Indian unrest, marked the fiscal centralization and military reorganization undertaken by royal officials in the second half of the eighteenth century.

A growing body of scholarship demonstrates that centralization was pursued through bargaining, compromise, and political contestation between crown officials and the main elites and local authorities.[40] There were few military or police forces in the Spanish colonies that the crown could rely upon for a top-down imposition, at least in the initial stages of reform. Furthermore, because net transfers were always positive from the Americas to Spain, the fiscal-military transition could not have been financed with continental monies.[41]

Reform was more successful in the regions where the elites' network of privilege and patronage relied on the existence of the Spanish monarch and were more affected by the British threat. In the imperial capitals Mexico and Peru, and in Veracruz, Cuba and coastal regions of Panama and Colombia the crown's officials transformed the state administration into a more highly structured apparatus, increased fiscal revenues by means of a larger and more efficient fiscal bureaucracy, and renovated military establishments to a larger extent than in other regions.[42]

Failed attempts to implement fiscal reform earlier in the colonial period also attest to the importance of the Seven Years' War. In 1626 the Count-Duke of Olivares attempted a fiscal reform through the creation of the Union of Arms with the

---

[37] See, for instance, Bonney (2004) and Elliott (2006).

[38] Elliott (2006, 292). The conflict in North American soil began in 1754, two years before the formal outbreak of war in Europe.

[39] Fisher (1982, 219).

[40] Kuethe and Inglis (1985, 122–123). See also Paquette (2007).

[41] See Irigoin and Grafe (2008) and Marichal and Souto Mantecón (1994).

[42] Marichal (2007, 48–80), Kuethe and Inglis (1985), Brading (1971, 1987).

goal of sharing the burdens of defense in mainland Europe between the Spanish kingdoms and the Spanish American colonies. A fixed annual contribution was demanded from every part of the empire. Colonial territory, however, was not subject to territorial threats and the colonial elites resisted the fiscal reforms. Only temporary increases to trade tax rates took effect.[43]

The evidence of negotiation with the elites, and earlier failed attempts to increase fiscal centralization, provide evidence for the inability to implement reform in colonial Mexico lacking an alignment between the fate of the crown and that of the local and corporate elites regarding the provision of military protection.

3 Conclusion

This chapter contributes to the literature by providing a complementary mechanism for why threats of external invasion or internal unrest can lead to increases in fiscal centralization. Fragmented fiscal capacity leads to free riding in the face of a threat. Fiscal centralization provides an institutional framework that allows elites to commit to contribute to military protection by ensuring others also contribute. The analysis shows that, even if there is agreement on the need to provide military protection, it is not until a majority of the fiscally powerful have stakes on the survival of the ruler for their economic future (and so their benefit from military protection aligns with that of the ruler) that they can agree to the centralization of fiscal capacity.

The analysis here highlights two issues that suggest avenues for future research. First, the theoretical argument assumes the ruler can commit to implement the policy profile agreed to before the increase in centralization. Once a ruler invests in fiscal centralization, the ruler could renege on the policy agreement and unilaterally increase future taxes or default on its debts.[44] Reputation, however, limits the ruler's incentives to renege on his agreements. If the future is sufficiently important, the ruler has a reputation to maintain. Scholars have argued, however, that in some cases reputation may not be enough to limit rulers, and that more elaborate institutional arrangements may be required (e.g. institutions of representation).[45]

My analysis complements this literature on the need to constrain the ruler by emphasizing another commitment problem—that between the elites resulting from free

---

[43]Elliott (1986, 246–274).

[44]Notice that fiscal fragmentation serves as a commitment devise for the ruler to pay its debts. By granting the corporation/debtor the right to directly collect certain taxes, rulers were able to obtain payments in advance and guarantee the service of interest and repayment. The major legal form used for this transaction in Spain and its colonies were the *asientos*. *Asientos* were contracts between the Crown and a private corporation or individual through which the latter promised to pay an amount to the Crown in exchange for the right to make use of the revenues resulting from a specific royal tax. See Domínguez Ortiz (1960), Conklin (1998), and Alvarez-Nogal and Chamley (2011). For the case of England, see Brewer (1989, 93).

[45]See for example North and Weingast (1989), Greif et al. (1994), and Bullow and Rogoff (1989).

riding under fragmented fiscal capacity. The results suggest that guaranteeing credibility from the ruler may not be enough. If the benefit from overcoming free riding is not sufficiently large, both the ruler and the corporations prefer fragmented capacity. The results also suggests that institutions of representation are not necessary, at least in the initial stages of fiscal centralization, to the extent that the corporate elites' and the ruler's benefits from military protection are aligned in response to a threat. The case of colonial Mexico corroborates that institutions of representation are not necessary for the elites to agree to fiscal centralization. Future research needs to study more carefully the timing between centralization and representation and the links between the two commitment problems mentioned.

Second, the theoretical argument does not incorporate dynamics to explain whether the investments in fiscal capacity are irreversible. Why should we not observe a reduction in fiscal centralization once the threat disappears? Incorporating the complementarity between the creation of a standing army and a fiscal administration with monitoring and enforcement capabilities, could make an increase in fiscal centralization difficult to reverse. In addition, the sunk-cost nature of the investment in fiscal centralization can lead to irreversibility after the threat disappears, all else constant.

Both the theoretical argument and the evidence from England and colonial Mexico emphasize the defensive, public-good aspect of military protection in leading to an increase in fiscal centralization. In so doing, the analysis here may tell us something about the evolution of fiscal capacity at other times and places. For a state relying on fragmented fiscal capacity to increase fiscal centralization, a sufficiently large shock jointly affecting the income of both the central government and the relevant fiscal actors is necessary. Two conditions are key: that the shock creates a collective action problem among the key actors, and that those actors believe the ruler can credibly monitor and enforce tax collection. The new fiscal regime allows for the coordination of policies and the enforcement of contributions.

References

Alt JE (1983) The evolution of tax structures. Public Choice 41:181–222

Alvarez-Nogal C, Chamley C (2011) Debt policy under constraints between Phillip II, the Cortes and Genoese bankers. WP in economic history, Univ. Carlos III de Madrid 11-06

Archer CI (1978) The army in bourbon Mexico, 1760–1810. Univeristy of New Mexico Press, Albuquerque

Archer CI (1981) Bourbon finances and military policy in New Spain, 1759–1812. Americas 37(3):315–350

Arias LM (2012) Building fiscal capacity in colonial Mexico: from fragmentation to centralization. Working paper

Bates RH, Lien D-HD (1985) A note on taxation, development, and representative government. Polit Soc 14(53):53–70

Besley T, Persson T (2009) The origins of state capacity: property rights, taxation, and politics. Am Econ Rev 99(4):1218–1244

Besley T, Persson T (2011) Pillars of prosperity: the political economics of development clusters. Princeton University Press, Princeton

Bonney R (ed) (1995) Economic systems and state finance. Clarendon, Oxford
Bonney R (ed) (1999) The rise of the fiscal state in Europe c. 1200–1800. Oxford University Press, Oxford
Bonney R (2004) Towards the comparative fiscal history of Britain and France during the long eighteenth century. In: Prados L (ed) Exceptionalism and industrialization: Britain and its European rivals, 1688–1815. Cambridge University Press, Cambridge
Brading DA (1971) Miners and merchants in bourbon Mexico 1763–1810. Cambridge University Press, Cambridge
Brading DA (1973) Government and elite in late colonial Mexico. Hisp Am Hist Rev 53(3):389–414
Brading DA (1987) Bourbon Mexico and its American empire. In: Bethell L (ed) Colonial Spanish America. Cambridge University Press, Cambridge
Brewer J (1989) The sinews of power. Hutchinson, London
Brewer J, Hellmuth E (eds) (1999) Rethinking leviathan: the eighteenth century state in Britain and Germany. Oxford University Press, Oxford
Bullow J, Rogoff K (1989) A constant recontracting model of sovereign debt. J Polit Econ 97:155–178
Campbell JL (1993) The state and fiscal sociology. Annu Rev Sociol 19:163–185
Centeno MA (2002) Blood and debt: war and the nation-state in Latin America. Pennsylvania University Press, Pennsylvania
Coatsworth J (1990) Los orígenes del atraso. Alianza Mexicana, México
Conklin J (1998) The theory of sovereign debt and Spain under Philip II. J Polit Econ 106(3):483–513
Cox G (2011) War, moral hazard, and ministerial responsibility. J Econ Hist 71(1):133–161
Dincecco M (2011) Political transformations and public finances. Europe, 1650–1913. Cambridge University Press, Cambridge
Dincecco M, Federico G, Vindigni A (2011) Warfare, taxation, and political change: evidence from the Italian Risorgimento. J Econ Hist 71(4):887–914
Domínguez Ortiz A (1960) Política y Hacienda de Felipe IV. Derecho Financiero, Madrid
Elliott JH (1986) The count-duke of olivares: the statesman in an age of decline. Yale University Press, New Haven
Elliott JH (1987) Colonial Spanish America. In: Bethell L (ed) Spain and America before 1700. Cambridge University Press, Cambridge
Elliott JH (2006) Empires of the Atlantic world: Britain and Spain in America, 1492–1830. Yale University Press, Cambridge
Emerson RM (1983) Charismatic kinship: A study of state-formation and authority in Baltistan. Polit Soc 12(4):413–444
Ertman T (1997) Birth of the leviathan: building states and regimes in medieval and early modern Europe. Cambridge University Press, Cambridge
Ertman T (1999) Variation in early modern state structure. In: Brewer J, Hellmuth E (eds) Rethinking leviathan: the eighteenth century state in Britain and Germany. Oxford University Press, Oxford
Fisher J (1982) Soldiers, society, and politics in Spanish America, 1750–1821. Lat Am Res Rev 17(1):217–222
Fonseca F, Urrutia C (1791) Historia general de la real hacienda, 1845–1853 edn. Impr. por V. G. Torres, Mexico
Greif A (1998) Self-enforcing political systems and economic growth: late medieval Genoa. In: Bates R, Greif A, Levi M, Rosenthal JL, Weingast BR (eds) Analytic narratives. Princeton University Press, Princeton
Greif A (2006) Institutions and the path to the modern economy: lessons from medieval trade. Cambridge University Press, Cambridge
Greif A, Milgrom P, Weingast BR (1994) Coordination, commitment, and enforcement: the case of the merchant guild. J Polit Econ 102(4):745–776
Gutiérrez-Santos D (1961) Historia Militar de México, 1325–1810. Ediciones Ateneo, México

Henneman JB (1971) Royal taxation in fourteenth century France: the development of war financing 1322–1356. Princeton University Press, Princeton
Herbst J (2000) States and power in Africa: comparative lessons in authority and control. Princeton University Press, Princeton
Hoffman P, Norberg K (eds) (1994) Fiscal crises, liberty, and representative government 1450–1789. Stanford University Press, Stanford
Hoffman P, Rosenthal JqL (1997) The political economy of warfare and taxation in early modern Europe: historical lessons for economic development. In: Drobak JN, Nye JV (eds) The frontiers of the new institutional economics. Academic Press, San Diego
Horowitz H (1977) Parliament, policy and politics in the reign of William III. Manchester University Press, Manchester
Huntington S (1968) Political order in changing societies. Yale University Press, New Haven
Irigoin MA, Grafe R (2008) Bargaining for absolutism: a Spanish path to nation-state and Empire Building. Hisp Am Hist Rev 88(2):173–209
Jáuregui L (1999) La Real Hacienda de Nueva España. Su administración en la época de los intendentes: 1786–1821. UNAM, México
Kiser E, Kane J (2001) Revolution and state structure: the bureaucratization of tax administration in early modern England and France. Am J Sociol 107(1):183–223
Klein HS (1985) La economía de la nueva españa, 1680–1809: un análisis a partir de las cajas reales. Hist Mex 34(4):561–609
Klein HS (1998) The American finances of the Spanish empire: royal income and expenditures in colonial Mexico, Peru, and Bolivia, 1680–1809. University of New Mexico Press, Albuquerque
Knight A (2002) Mexico: the colonial era. Cambridge University Press, New York
Kuethe AJ (1986) Cuba, 1783–1815: crown, military and society. University of Tennessee Press, Knoxville
Kuethe AJ, Inglis GD (1985) Absolutism and enlightened reform: Charles III, the establishment of the alcabala, and commercial reorganization in Cuba. Past Present 109:118–143
Levi M (1988) Of rule and revenue. University of California Press, Berkeley
Mann M (1988) State and society, 1130–1815: an analysis of English state finances. In: Mann M (ed) States, war, and capitalism. Basil Blackwell, New York, pp 73–123
Marichal C (2007) Bankruptcy of empire: Mexican silver and the wars between Spain, Britain and France, 1760–1810. Cambridge University Press, Cambridge
Marichal C, Souto Mantecón M (1994) Silver and situados: New Spain and the financing of the Spanish empire in the Caribbean in the eighteenth century. Hisp Am Hist Rev 74:587–613
McAlister LN (1953) The reorganization of the army of New Spain, 1763–1766. Hisp Am Hist Rev 33(1):1–32
North DC, Weingast BR (1989) Constitutions and commitment: the evolution of institutions governing public choice in seventeenth-century England. J Econ Hist 34:72–96
O'Brien PK (1988) The political economy of British taxation, 1660–1815. Econ Hist Rev 41(1):1–32
O'Brien PK (2011) The nature and historical evolution of an exceptional fiscal state and its possible significance for the precocious commercialization and industrialization of the British economy from Cromwell to Nelson. Econ Hist Rev 64(2):408–446
Olson M (1993) Dictatorship, democracy, and development. Am Polit Sci Rev 87(3):567–576
Paquette GB (2007) State-civil society cooperation and conflict in the Spanish empire: the intellectual and political activities of the ultramarine *Consulados* and economic societies, c. 1780–1810. J Lat Am Stud 39:263–298
Prestwich M (1972) War, politics, and finance under Edward I. Rowman & Littlefield, Totowa
Rosenthal JqL (1998) The political economy of absolutism reconsidered. In: Bates R, Greif A, Levi M, Rosenthal JL, Weingast B (eds) Analytic narratives. Princeton University Press, Princeton
Skocpol T (1979) States and social revolutions. Cambridge University Press, Cambridge
Smith RS (1948) Sales taxes in New Spain, 1575–1770. Hisp Am Hist Rev 28:2–37
Stasavage D (2002) Credible commitment in early modern Europe: North and Weingast revisited. J Law Econ Organ 18(1):155–186

Stasavage D (2003) Public debt and the birth of the democratic state: France and Great Britain, 1688–1789. Cambridge University Press, Cambridge

Stein SJ, Stein BH (2003) Apogee of empire. Spain and New Spain in the age of Charles III, 1759–1789. John Hopkins University Press, Baltimore

Storrs C (ed) (2009) The fiscal-military state in eighteenth century Europe: essays in honour of P.G.M. Dickson. Ashgate, Farnham

Strayer JR (1970) On the medieval origins of the modern state. Princeton University Press, Princeton

Summerhill WR (2008) Fiscal bargains, political institutions, and economic performance. Hisp Am Hist Rev 88(2):219–233

Tilly C (1990) Coercion capital and European states, AD 990–1992. Blackwell, Cambridge

Tilly C (1993) European revolutions. Basic Blackwell, Oxford

Weber M (1922) Economy and society, 1968 edn. Bedminster, New York

Stable Constitutions in Political Transition

Katja Michalak and Gerald Pech

1 Introduction

This paper develops a spatial model where an autocrat selects a status quo constitution. This constitution may or may not be accepted by a succeeding elected constitutional assembly as a blue print for negotiations on constitutional reform. A constitution defines as legitimate a status quo point in policy space with policy dimensions redistribution and social policy. Moreover, it guarantees property rights and provides a policy rule of how the status quo point can be modified. We model constitutional design and reform as a dynamic game. As the first mover, the autocrat is free in selecting the status quo point. If accepted by the succeeding assembly, it becomes the default outcome when the assembly enters negotiations over constitutional reform which take the form of changing the status quo policy. In the absence of a prior constitution or after a rejection of the prior constitution, the assembly enters free negotiations on a new constitution.

More recently, constitutional succession has become an issue in many Arab countries where autocratic regimes were succeeded by freely elected governments. When the White House called for Husni Mubarak, then president of Egypt, to step down, the question immediately arose whether the rules of succession would apply as laid out in the Egyptian constitution or whether the constitution had to be suspended to negotiate a transition between the old regime and the opposition (see Brown 2011). After Mubarak eventually resigned, the interim military government, i.e. the

We wish to thank Keith Schnakenberg and Norman Schofield for helpful comments.

K. Michalak (✉)
Department of Public Management and Governance, Zeppelin University,
Am Seemooser Horn 20, 88045 Friedrichshafen, Germany
e-mail: katja.michalak@zu.de

G. Pech
Department of Economics, KIMEP University, Abay 2, 050010 Almaty, Republic of Kazakhstan
e-mail: gp@geraldpech.net

N. Schofield et al. (eds.), *Advances in Political Economy*, 67
DOI 10.1007/978-3-642-35239-3_4, © Springer-Verlag Berlin Heidelberg 2013

Supreme Council of the Armed Forces, adopted a provisional constitution which contained significant amendments and aimed at paving the way to parliamentary elections.[1] The elected parliament set out on what proved to be a bumpy road towards negotiations over a new constitution.

Of these events, two facts stand out: On the one hand, the Mubarak constitution turned out to be not acceptable to all parties involved in the transition process. Therefore, on the face of it the Egyptian case is one of discontinuity of the existing authoritarian constitution. On the other hand, the leadership of the military, which had significant bargaining power in the transition process, was widely seen to be able to hold on to their privileges and property interests.[2] These two observations suggest that the Egyptian transition is an ambivalent case where the formal constitution handed down by the autocrat lacked perseverance yet the property order established under the constitution was kept in place.

Moreover, whilst this paper looks into the possibility for an autocratic regime to select a constitution which is accepted as a blue print by its successors, the Supreme Council of the Armed Forces faced a rather similar choice problem when drafting the amendments of the provisional constitution.[3] In principle, our framework should lend itself to analyzing constitutional choice in this slightly different context. Whilst it is still too early to judge the outcome of this constitution project, at the time of finalizing this paper it appeared as if the army was revoking its support for the constitutional reform process in the face of a legislature dominated by Islamist parties.[4]

Chile, as the second example which we look at, is a clear example of successful constitutional succession.[5] In 1980, the Chilean military junta adopted a constitution which subsequently not only governed the internal workings of the junta and imposed constraints on its exercise of power, but which set the rules by which the transition to democracy finally took place: In 1988, Pinochet stood for election, thereby sticking by the letter of the constitution. Following electoral defeat, the Chilean parties of the right and the center negotiated constitutional amendments which were adopted as part of a reformed constitution by plebiscite in 1989. The amendments included restrictions on presidential powers, the lowering of the quorum for changing non vital parts of the constitution, admittance of parties of the left, and a modification of the relative voting power of civilians versus the military on the national security council. In large parts, the constitution of 1980 remains in place today.

There are clear differences but also similarities between Egypt and Chile: Chile has a long and recent history of constitutionalism. The Chilean constitution was a

---

[1] For details of the process see Brown and Dunnes (2011).

[2] Egypt's freedom, Financial Times, 20 May 2012.

[3] Other classification schemes agree on the ambiguity of the Egyptian case: In the framework of Munck and Leff (1997) the Egyptian transition can be classified as one of defeat of the old order. Yet if one considers the military as part of this order, one could equally argue that the transition can be classified as a pact.

[4] Egypt court orders parliament dissolved, Financial Times, 15 June 2012.

[5] For an overview see Barros (2002) and Montes and Vial (2005).

binding constraint on the dealings of the junta (see Barros 2002). Most significantly, transition took place because the regime, after some hesitation, obeyed the letter of the constitution. In Egypt, on the other hand, the transition of power was brought about by street protests. Common to both countries is the influence exercised by parties and organizations associated with the old regime during the transition period. In Egypt this was mainly the military which served as a power broker during the revolution whilst in Chile these were the parties of the right which bargained in the shadow of power which was projected by the military.

In this paper, we see a preexisting constitution as a natural focal point in the transition process which can serve both as a reference but also as a reversion point for constitutional reform. The reform process in which a society attempts to newly arrange its social compact creates many uncertainties. The negotiating parties may end up in a game of attrition where each tries to secure concessions from the other parties involved in the process. The attempt of constitutional reform may end in open conflict if the participation constraint of one of the players is not satisfied. For those reasons, the elected successor parties which are interested in changing the constitution may yet agree on the preexisting constitution as a default outcome in order to insure against the risks otherwise involved in negotiating a new constitution.

If the autocrat expects a succeeding constitutional assembly to use a preexisting constitution in that way, it creates an avenue through which the autocrat, in writing a constitution, can influence the power play after his demise. In this paper we assume that the interest group of the property owning class can exert sufficient influence on the autocrat to make him write a constitution on their behalf.

We show, first of all, that constitutions exist which are stable in the transition process. Whether or not the autocrat strictly prefers to hand down a constitution depends on who he expects to bargain over constitutional reform. If the autocrat expects that the future constitutional assembly is dominated by parties which favor redistribution, he does not want to bind himself by the constitution. If not a single party dominates the constitutional assembly and the middle class opposes redistribution or it is expected to forge a coalition with the right dominate, stable constitutions exist which are in the interest of the autocrat. Here, our model provides a theoretical underpinning for the frequently stated idea that a middle-class which is interested in maintaining property rights is a prerequisite for constitutional stability.[6]

Moreover, we show that if the autocrat can hand down a constitution immediately before his demise, he may choose to write a stationary constitution, i.e. a constitution which he predicts to be accepted by a succeeding constitutional assembly without further amendment. Only if the autocrat expects that he will have to abide by the constitution himself for some time, he will compromise on the stationarity property. We also argue that, theoretically, a succeeding assembly will elect the prior constitution as default bargaining outcome, irrespective of what it says. Hereby, cases are possible where a preexisting constitution is accepted in the reform process even when it has hardly constrained the autocrat and is significantly amended in the reform process.

[6]See e.g. Ordeshook (1997), Easterly (2001).

1.1 Related Literature

Looking at the selection of rules in general and the constitution in particular in terms of manipulating strategic situations to achieve desirable outcomes was advanced by Riker (1986) with his analysis of the events leading to the adoption of the American constitution.[7] Our paper models constitutional choice in terms of the strategic selection of a status quo point in a spatial model. This places our model in a strand of literature which derives equilibria of the political game which are predicated on previous choices such as the move of an agenda setter or the selection of institutions. Tsebelis (2002), for example, shows how institutions determine the set of veto players within a spatial policy framework and thus shape policy outcomes.[8] Whilst constitutional norms typically provide general rules for policy selection rather than making policy choices more directly, the selection of institutions together with the legitimization of a status quo policy has implications for policy outcomes. In the case of Chile and Egypt, one can argue that choices over political institutions were often clearly aimed at preventing or promoting particular policy outcomes.[9]

In our framework, a constitution provides a focal point which enables agents to coordinate on Pareto-better outcomes compared to outcomes achieved in the absence of a constitution. A different way of understanding constitutions as coordination devices—understood as "red-lines" the crossing of which agents accept as triggers for coordinated action—has been introduced by Weingast (1997). Other approaches focus on the role of constitutions as commitment devices by which a government can credibly pledge to uphold property rights (North and Weingast 1989) or an autocrat to give legally enshrined guarantees to his followers (Myerson 2008). Moreover, Grossman (2002) gives conditions under which it is possible to design constitutions with self-enforcing properties—i.e. where agents abide by constitutional processes—when facing the alternative of descending into conflict. Pech (2009) and Naqvi et al. (2012) focus on self-enforcing properties of constitutions which contain the rule of law as a mechanism. Another strand of literature looks at constitutions in terms of the properties and desirability of the voting rules it provides.[10] Finally, in an accompanying paper, Michalak and Pech (2012) provide a full equilibrium analysis which extends and applies the present framework to the

[7]See also Riker (1996). Schofield (2002) elaborates on this logic and applies it to the evolution of the American constitution.

[8]In a more general setting one may ask how the historical and/or constitutional choice of rules determines the selection of rules which at later stages emerge from the political game. See Barbera and Jackson (2004) and Lagunoff (2007).

[9]In the case of Chile, parties of the left were not admitted under the Pinochet constitution but they were admitted under the reform constitution, provided they were not antisystem. The decision of the Supreme Council of the Armed Forces to dissolve a parliament dominated by the Muslim brotherhood was a move which interfered with the institutional set-up of post-revolutionary Egypt but was mainly aimed at preventing parliament from selecting policies which were against the interests of the military rulers.

[10]See, for example, Gersbach (2004) and Barbera and Jackson (2006).

Chilean transition process. That paper, in more detail, focuses on the significance of middle class wealth for constitutional stability.

1.2 Outline of the Paper

Section 2 sets up the model. Section 2.1 presents negotiations in the absence of a prior constitution or after its rejection. Section 2.2 details bargaining on constitutional reform in the presence of a prior constitution. Section 2.3 derives optimal constitutions for the autocrat. Section 3 analyses the static constitutional choice problem of the autocrat. Section 4 extends our results to a dynamic setting. Section 5 discusses applications to different experiences of political transition and derives conclusions from our framework.

2 The Model

A constitution is a pair (t, x), representing a country's basic choices[11] on redistribution—associated with a tax rate t—and social policy x which may be measured along a scale representing liberalism versus authoritarianism, secularism versus a greater role for religion in public life or the relative importance of the social solidarity principle versus the free market principle.[12] The policy space $\Im$ is $T \times X = [0, 1] \times \Re$.

There are three socio-economic groups, the clientele of the autocrat, R, the middle class, M, and the working class, L. We do not explicitly model the military as a player. In the Chilean case the junta emerged from within the military. Therefore, one can identify the military in the aftermath of transition as a lingering aspect of the junta and closely associate it with the autocrat's clientele. In Egypt, autocratic government and military were organizationally separate but the military leadership shared interests with the possessing class and can, for the purposes of our model, be associated with the clientele of the autocrat. In both cases we can see some harmony of interest between the military and what we modelled as the autocrat's clientele. The military is a particularly powerful player when the option of freely negotiating the constitution degenerates into conflict. In this case, we expect the cost of free negotiations to be especially high to everyone, but the more powerful the military, the more limited will the possibility of achieving redistribution in the case of conflict be.

Furthermore, we assume that the autocrat perfectly internalizes the preferences of his clientele. For this assumption to be reasonable, either the clientele must be able to offer a perfect incentive contract to the autocrat, by which it offers support

[11] We do not discuss in this model rules governing post constitutional choices such as electoral rules. Stability properties of electoral rules are discussed, for example, in Barbera and Jackson (2004).

[12] Kitschelt (1996) finds that the majority of policy choices can be subsumed under a distributional/communitarian dimension.

in exchange for favorable constitutional rules or, alternatively, the autocrat "sells" those advantages to his clientele in exchange for support.

For simplicity, we assume that all groups have the same size when calculating the effects of different redistributive policies. Gross incomes of representatives of each group are $w_R > w_M > w_L$. The utility function of a citizen belonging to class i is $u_i = \alpha_i v_i(x) + w_i^n$ where w_i^n is citizen i's net income after taxes and transfers and where $v_i = -|x - x_i|^2$ captures the loss associated with realizations on the social policy scale where x_i, $i = L, M, R$ represents the bliss point of group i. We assume that $x_M < x_L$, $x_R \neq x_M$ and x_L yet $\alpha_R = 0$. In order to uniquely assign bargaining outcomes when R and M agree on t, we assume that R's income motive is overwhelming yet for two allocations where the income realization is the same, R strictly prefers the allocation where x is closer to x_R.[13]

The net income distribution is obtained from taxing income available for redistribution at a tax rate $t \in [0, 1]$. Proceeds from the tax finance a lump sum transfer which is evenly distributed among members of the three groups.[14] Thereby we impose equality in transfers and rule out the possibility of one socio-economic class enriching itself at the expense of some other class. This assumption is less problematic when we construct outcomes for the case of free negotiations over the constitution: The reversion wealth level which we associate with this scenario may be thought of as the level of wealth which agents expect to be able to defend or appropriate in a situation of conflict. Yet for the case where the assembly bargains over constitutional reform, we must specify the set of admissible choices. In restricting the bargaining space to choices of t and x, we effectively assume that accepting the prior constitution as a template for negotiations implies acceptance of the property rights which were defined under that constitution. Once the property order is accepted in principal, redistribution of property can only be achieved through general rules, i.e. general taxes.[15]

Inserting our assumption on feasible tax policies into the utility function for group i and denoting average income for redistribution $\overline{w}$, we obtain

$$u_i(t, x) = \alpha v_i(x) + (1 - t)w_i + t\overline{w}.$$

In all societies we know of, average income exceeds the income of the median citizen. This observation leaves the political theorist struggling for an explanation

[13]We effectively assume that R has lexicographic preferences where the utility function—with some abuse of notation—captures the net income part only.

[14]Assigning the choice of a tax policy to the constitutional stage appears to be counterfactual at first sight, because tax policies are normally determined by simple tax laws. However, it turns out that for some bargaining scenarios such as freely bargaining the constitution, the choice reduces to selecting either a tax rate of 1 or a tax rate of zero. The proper way of thinking of such an extreme choice is the election of the economic order of a country. Such a choice is clearly on a constitutional level.

[15]Such acceptance does not in general rule out that individual cases of "unfair" enrichment under the old regime are tried in court but it provides assurances to the vast majority of beneficiaries of the old system that expropriative measures by the new regime will not affect their property alone but would have to simultaneously affect the property of the middle class as well.

of the fact that in democratic societies we should have majorities in favor of expropriation when we hardly observe expropriating tax policies in practice. In order to allow for the possibility of a political equilibrium with non expropriating taxation for empirically relevant income distributions we make the assumption that only a share $(1-\gamma)$ of w_R is actually available for redistribution. If w_R consists mainly of productive capital, agency problems involved in its nationalization are likely to reduce its value. In practice, γ is likely to depend on the kind of industry in which the capital is deployed. If the capital is mostly invested in the natural resources sector, γ is likely to be low. We assume $(1-\gamma)w_R > w_M$ and define average income available for distribution as $\overline{w} = \frac{(1-\gamma)w_R + w_M + w_L}{3}$. As $\overline{w} > w_L$, the left always favors redistribution.

2.1 Freely Negotiating a New Constitution

We assume that in the absence of a default constitution, the outcome of the constitutional reform process can only be predicted with some uncertainty. That is, independently of how precisely the constitutional process unfolds, from an ex ante point of view the expectations over the final outcome take the form of a lottery $\ell = \{(x, t, \pi(x, t))\}$ with probability weights $\pi(x, t) < 1$ for all (x, t). The continuation pay off of each player $i = R, M, L$ when entering the constitutional reform process in the absence of a default constitution is $Eu_i(\ell)$. Throughout the paper we maintain that at any point a player who is dissatisfied with the outcome of the constitutional reform process can reject this outcome and revert to freely negotiating a constitution, ensuring for himself a default outcome of $u_i^0 = Eu_i(\ell)$. Such an assumption is compatible with scenarios where the draft reform constitution requires, formally or factually, widespread support in a referendum or where the free negotiation process takes the form of open conflict and such conflict can be precipitated by any party. We define (x^0, t^0) as the expected value of x and t for this lottery. From concavity of v and linearity of u in t it follows that $Eu_i(\ell) < u_i(x^0, t^0)$ for all i, a result which we use in the proof of Lemma 2 where we show that the set of outcomes which are generally acceptable over freely negotiating the constitution is non empty and contain, in particular, the policy point where the expected values of x and t are offered. More formally, we define the set I of outcomes which are preferred by all players to the lottery of freely negotiating x and t, ℓ:

Definition 1 I is the set out feasible outcomes which are weakly preferred by all players to freely negotiating the constitution with associated lottery ℓ, i.e. $I = \{x, t \mid (x, t) \succsim_i \ell \text{ and } (x, t) \in \Im\}$, $i = L, M, R$.

Note that I has a closed graph. In what follows, we focus on the case where $1 > t^0 > 0$. The case where $t^0 = 0$ is trivial: R can enforce its preferred outcome in terms of income realization and the incentives for writing a constitution would be minimal. The case $t^0 = 1$ corresponds to a situation where L can enforce its preferred outcome in the transition and R can do nothing about it. Again, incentives for writing a constitution would be minimal. In the intermediate range, the following lemma holds:

Lemma 2 *For* $1 > t^0 > 0$, *the set* I *is non empty and convex.*

Proof By concavity of v, at least the point x^0, t^0 must be in I. Because v is strictly concave, I is not vanishingly small, i.e. there is $\varepsilon > 0$ such that L strictly prefers to get $(x^0, t^0 - \varepsilon)$ with certainty over a lottery with expected outcome x^0, t^0. As M and R also prefer this point, it must be in I. By convexity of preferences and $\Im$, I is also convex. □

Ignoring the trivial case $t^0 = 0$, the result of Lemma 2 only hinges on the assertion that expectations over the outcome from freely negotiating the constitution take the form of a lottery ℓ which is common knowledge to all players. One possible way of consistently modelling a bargaining game which provides such a lottery is to assume that each party is given a chance to implement its preferred outcome with a probability P^j.[16] In the case where this opportunity arises, rationality dictates that the party imposes its preferred policy point. Thus, if L wins, the policy realization (t, x) is $(1, x^L)$, if M wins, the policy realization is $(1, x^M)$ for $w_M \leq \overline{w}$ and $(0, x^M)$ for $w_M > \overline{w}$ and if R wins, the policy realization is $(0, x^R)$. Thus, for party i, expected utility from freely negotiating the constitution is

$$V_i^0 = P^R v^i(x^R) + P^M v^i(x^M) + P^L v^i(x^L) + (1 - P^L)w^i + P^L\overline{w} \quad \text{if } w_M > \overline{w}, \tag{1}$$

$$V_i^0 = P^R v^i(x^R) + P^M v^i(x^M) + P^L v^i(x^L) + P^R w^i + (1 - P^R)\overline{w} \quad \text{if } w_M \leq \overline{w}, \quad \text{for } i = L, M, R. \tag{2}$$

We can modify pay offs by admitting a conflict cost K_i which is incurred if free negotiations take the form of open conflict. Without changing any of the results of this paper we may extend the model to cover the case where players form a priori-coalitions before entering conflict. For example, L and M may form a coalition against R and expect to realize a point on their contract curve if they win. Note that our model does not attempt to explain conflict but instead uses a conflict scenario to rationalize a settlement in the shadow of conflict.

2.2 Negotiating a Constitution in the Presence of c

Suppose a constitution c specifying a tax/policy combination (t, x) has been handed down by the autocrat. Moreover, suppose that a pre-determined set of players negotiates over constitutional reform or de-novo design of the constitution. This set of

[16]For other specifications, see Michalak and Pech (2012).

bargainers is determined exogenously to the model. In what follows we focus on the case where two parties bargain. Sections 3.1 and 3.2 discuss in greater detail special applications of the two party bargaining game. Section 3.3 gives an overview of the remaining cases. The different cases where one party is in a position to impose the constitution or all three parties bargain over constitutional reform are straightforward extensions of the two-party bargaining model.[17]

Once the pre-determined bargainers accept c rather than reverting to freely negotiating the constitution, c serves as the default outcome which prevails if the bargainers are unable to find an agreement on the reform constitutional draft. Recall, however, that any group in society still has the option to revert at any time to the non cooperative outcome.

We think of the bargaining procedure as taking the simplest form of a two player random proposer game where the proposer makes a take-it-or-leave-it offer to the other player. Let $\Gamma_{ij}(c)$ be a correspondence which assigns to each choice of c as possible outcomes for the bargaining game between i and j, the equilibrium proposals submitted by i as a proposer, $P_{i\to j}$, and submitted by j as a proposer, $P_{j\to i}$. Naturally, $i, j \in \{R, M, L\}$ and $i \neq j$. Note that $P_{i\to j}$ and $P_{j\to i}$ might be set valued although they turn out to be singular in our application. All our results hold under the assumption that the ex ante probability of making a proposal is strictly positive for each player in a coalition which is a mild assumption as it only requires to exclude the case where agents are predicted to have no bargaining power at all when they enter the coalition which bargains over constitutional reform.

If $c \in I$, $u_j(c)$ is the default utility which player j realizes when a proposal is rejected. Hence, each player i, when making a reform proposal to j, chooses for $P_{i\to j}$ a pair $(x, t) \in I$ which maximizes $u_i(x, t)$ subject to $u_j(x, t) \geq u_j(c)$. If $c \notin I$, rejecting a proposal results in implementing an outcome c which will ultimately be vetoed by at least one player. Hence, a rejection of a proposal when the default constitution is $c \notin I$ results in every agent realizing his or her continuation pay off from descending into conflict, V^0. By this device, players who stand to benefit from bargaining in the constitutional reform process have incentives to accept even constitutions outside of I. Yet, as the following lemma shows, in the static model with two players bargaining, the autocrat will choose a constitution in I whenever he has a strict preference over constitutions in I.

Lemma 3 *If there are two bargainers and the autocrat uniquely prefers a constitution $c^* \in I$, this constitution is strictly preferred over any constitution not in I.*

Proof By construction of $\Gamma(c)$, any $c \in I$ is strictly preferred to the default outcome at least by the players involved in constitutional bargaining. If $c \notin I$, a proposal can-

[17]We do not explicitly model elections but rather assume that the representatives of each group can secure support of their clientele. Relative strength of representation and voting rule in the assembly determine the set of effective coalitions in the assembly. Moreover, given the set of effective coalitions—which is non empty because the grand coalition always is effective—there is a clear prediction which coalition forms, independently of the default constitution. See Michalak and Pech (2012) for endogenous coalition formation.

not be rejected against c without precipitating conflict. With $c \notin I$, $\Gamma_{ij}(c)$ assigns i's and j's ideal points in I. For i and j a lottery on $\Gamma_{ij}(c)$ with non zero weights must strictly dominate the alternative of realizing the default outcome from conflict with certainty and rationality commands that they accept c. Note that by construction of $\Gamma_{ij}(c)$, $c \notin I$ does not constrain the proposer other than by requiring him or her to choose a proposal in I. Yet it constrains the responder in rejecting a proposal. If there uniquely exists a constitution $c^* \in I$ which is preferred by the autocrat when the choice of c is restricted to be in I, the autocrat must wish to constrain at least one proposer to select not the proposer's ideal point in I because he cannot agree with the outcome proposed by both proposers.[18] Hence, a constitution which does not constrain proposals, i.e. any constitution not in I, is strictly dominated by the constitution $c^* \in I$ which does. □

This lemma extends to the case where only one party dominates the reform process. The dominant party strictly prefers the constitution over its default outcome and the other parties at least weakly prefer a constitution over their default outcome. It also extends to the case of unanimity where all c in I are at least weakly preferred by all parties over the default outcome. In the remainder of the paper we consider I as the choice set of the autocrat and obtain unique optimal choices in the cases of Propositions 5 and 6. Using the lemma, we can conclude that these constitutions are also strictly preferred over constitutions which are not in I.[19] Proposition 7 considers a case where L dominates the constitutional assembly and no optimal constitutional choice exists in I. In this case, the autocrat may choose a constitution $c \notin I$. Yet for this case we find that the autocrat always ends up with his default outcome, hence the autocrat is not only indifferent with respect to which constitution to write but he is also indifferent between writing and not writing a constitution.

2.3 Optimal Constitutions

The way the bargaining game is set up, given c the two bargainers have incentives to realize a point on their contract curve or, if this violates $(x, t) \in I$ to realize a point on the boundary of I. The following proposition characterizes (strictly) optimal constitutions of the static game as stationary constitutions, i.e. constitutions which are not amended in the bargaining process:

Proposition 4 *When the autocrat can directly propose a constitution without incurring a cost, for any constitution c which is not stationary, i.e. for which $\Gamma(c) \neq c$, there exists a stationary constitution which is at least as good for the autocrat as c.*

---

[18]Recall that $x_R \neq x_M$, so even if M and R bargain and agree on t, they still disagree over x.

[19]In the case of Proposition 6 where L bargains with an M party in favor of redistribution the autocrat has a unique preference of $c \in I$ but the preference is only in terms of policy realization and, hence, of a second order magnitude.

Proof Define the Pareto-set $B_{ij}(c)$ for the bargainers i and j given the default constitution c. First suppose that $B_{ij}(c) \subset I$. In that case, proposals coincide with points on the contract curve, i.e. $P_{i\to j}$ maximizes u_i given $u_j(c)$ and $P_{j\to i}$ maximizes u_j given $u_i(c)$. If one proposal P includes a lower value of t than the other, the autocrat is better off by selecting this proposal P instead of c. Setting $c = P$ guarantees that each proposer has to propose c when this is the default outcome. If the proposals $P_{i\to j}$ and $P_{j\to i}$ include the same value of t, the autocrat is as well off if he selects either $P_{i\to j}$ or $P_{j\to i}$ instead of c.

Next suppose that $B_{ij}(c) \cap I \subsetneq B_{ij}(c)$. In that case, the constraint that the proposal has to be in I may be binding. Yet a proposal P maximizes the proposer's utility given that it is in $B_{ij}(c) \cap I$. Note that $B_{ij}(c) \cap I$ is convex. When L or M is proposal maker, preferences of the proposal maker are strictly convex and the optimal proposal is uniquely defined. If this point is selected as default, the constitution is stationary. If R makes a proposal the binding segment of the boundary of I is strictly convex unless it coincides with the $t = 0$-line.[20] In either case, R has a unique proposal which, if selected as default results in a stationary constitution[21] and we are left with three possibilities: a) In point P constraint $B_{ij}(c)$ is binding and I is not. This coincides with the case where $B_{ij}(c) \subset I$. b) Constraint I is binding and $B_{ij}(c)$ is not. In that case, with P the proposer realizes the highest utility in I. If the autocrat selects $c = P$, either proposer must propose point c when it is the default outcome. c) Both constraints are binding. This case coincides with case b). □

This proposition allows us to focus on stationary constitutions when looking for optimal constitutions for the autocrat when discussing the static constitutional choice problem. In the dynamic constitutional choice problem, the autocrat incurs a cost when committing to a constitution and, as shown in the proof of Proposition 9, Proposition 4 does not apply.

3 Static Constitutional Choice

In this section we derive the optimal constitutional choice for the autocrat if he believes that his demise is imminent. As we know from Lemma 3, any default constitution c will be accepted by the bargainers. Yet only if the constitution is in the set I, will it actually impact on the successor's decision other than by requiring them to propose amendments only in I. Hence we are going to focus on the autocrat's constitutional choice as the problem of picking a constitution from within the set I.

[20] To see that R's proposal is unique when the $t = 0$ line is binding, recall that by our assumption that R's preferences are lexicographic, R's preferred point on the $t = 0$-line is uniquely determined. Hence, the optimal constitutional choice coincides with this point.

[21] To see that the point $c = (0, x^R)$ is stationary when selected as default in the case where $t = 0$ is the constraint on R's proposal, observe that R as a responder will reject any proposal which does not coincide with c.

Finally, from Proposition 4 we know that we can focus on stationary constitutions, i.e. constitutions which the predecessors accept with no amendment.

3.1 M and L Negotiate on Constitutional Reform

Suppose it is known that after transition M and L negotiate over constitutional reform and suppose in particular that this is known to the autocrat when he writes the status quo constitution. From the perspective of the autocrat's clientele, the case where R is excluded as negotiator represents a worst case scenario. So it is not implausible that, when writing the constitution, the autocrat focuses on that scenario in order to provide insurance against its consequences.

During the Egyptian revolution it was widely expected that it was ultimately up to the street protesters and the Muslim brotherhood to negotiate the future constitutional compact. If we identify the Muslim brotherhood with its welfare goals as the L party and the street protesters with their middle class ambitions as the M party,[22] we can explore the possible impact which the choices of an initial agenda setter—be it Mubarak or the military—would have had on the outcomes which the other two groups could have obtained.

3.1.1 Case $w_M > \overline{w}$

Initially we suppose that the lower boundary of the set I intersects the vertical part of the contract curve between L and M. That the contract curve is a vertical line for $0 < t < 1$ is demonstrated in the appendix. In that case, the autocrat wants to choose c^* such that c^* coincides with the intersection of the lower boundary of I and the contract curve in Fig. 1. To see the latter point, suppose that the autocrat picks a constitution at a point such as z which also is on the boundary of I and corresponds to a lower tax t. As the boundary of I coincides with l^0, M must realize a lower indifference curve m_z. If L proposes, she will propose a higher tax at the point where the contract curve intersects with m_z. This comes with a higher tax rate. If M proposes, she will propose the point where l^0 intersects with the contract curve. Here the tax rate is the same as with c^*. Hence, as long as L proposes with positive probability, it is better to select c^* in the point where l^0 intersects with the contract curve.

We can exclude the case where the lower boundary of I intersects with the upper horizontal part of the contract curve (i.e. where $t = 1$) because this would imply $t^0 = 1$. So consider the case where the lower boundary of I intersects with the lower horizontal part of the contract curve (i.e. where $t = 0$). In that case, the autocrat may select any point on the horizontal part of the contract curve and he will choose to

22 See Sect. 5 for a more detailed discussion of these claims.

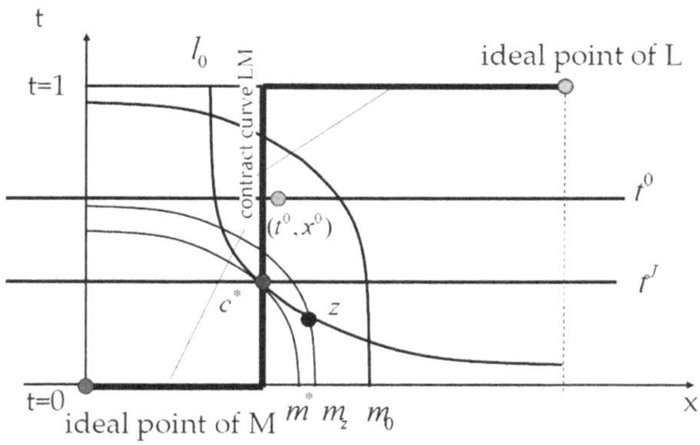

Fig. 1 Optimum constitution when L is expected to negotiate with M over reform and $w_M > \overline{w}$

select $x \in [x^M, x^L]$ as close as possible to x^R. The two negotiators will necessarily propose the default outcome c to each other. Naturally, also in the case where the optimal constitution involves $t^* = 0$, writing the constitution offers positive monetary value to the autocrat because $t^0 > 0$.

Proposition 5 *In the static model with L and M as bargainers and $w_M > \overline{w}$, the autocrat strictly prefers handing down a constitution. The monetary value of handing down a constitution is strictly positive.*

Proof See discussion above. □

3.1.2 Case $w_M \leq \overline{w}$

Next suppose that M has less than average effective wealth and, therefore, agrees with L on the ideal tax rate of $t = 1$. In that case which is illustrated in Fig. 2, negotiations between L and M will result in the maximum level of redistribution which does not violate R's participation constraint, i.e. the tax rate is $t = t^0$, independently of the status quo constitution. To R, who lexicographically prefers wealth, the monetary value of writing a constitution is zero yet he would still like to write a constitution in order to satisfy his policy preference with ideal point x^R. If writing a constitution is costly in terms of wealth, the autocrat prefers not to write a constitution.

Proposition 6 *In the static model with L and M as bargainers and $w_M \leq \overline{w}$, a constitution affects only policy but does not affect post transition wealth. Hence the monetary value of writing a constitution to the autocrat is zero.*

Proof See discussion above. □

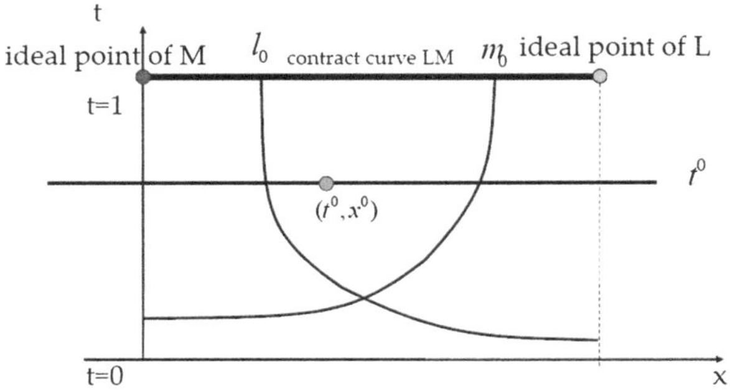

Fig. 2 A constitution which guarantees a positive monetary value to R does not exist when L is expected to negotiate with M over reform and $w_M \leq \overline{w}$

3.2 R and M Negotiate on Constitutional Reform

In this section we assume that R and M are predicted to negotiate on constitutional reform. This was effectively the bargaining set up in the Chilean transition with the PN of the right and the moderate concertación negotiating transition. The "Pinochet" constitution had banned left-wing parties from political participation and their admission was one element of constitutional reform which emerged from the negotiations. It is, therefore, possible to argue that the authors of the "Pinochet" constitution had believed that any successor government was not going to include parties of the left.

3.2.1 Case $w_M > \overline{w}$

In this case there is harmony between M and R on their redistributive goals. Yet L's participation constraint has to be satisfied. Without further constraints, M would choose her ideal point in I which is not the point with the lowest tax rate but a point on the contract curve with L. By strategically choosing the status quo constitution c^* to coincide with point in I where t is minimal, R can ensure a better outcome for himself: If M proposes against c^*, she has to offer $t \leq t^*$ to R, so it must propose c^* itself. And if R proposes, he wants to propose c^* as well. Therefore, equilibrium c^* is a stationary constitution.

It is easy to see in Fig. 3 that a point such as z is not an optimal choice for a status quo constitution: When R proposes he needs to offer M the point z again because there the tax rate is lowest given that M must obtain m_z and L must obtain l^0. When M proposes, she needs to offer the point z as well. Thus, z is also a stationary constitution but it is not optimal for the autocrat.

Note that if L's power to enforce outcomes in the conflict scenario is weak, I may include the $t = 0$ axis. In that case, R and M will always agree on a tax rate of zero. The monetary value of writing a constitution is strictly positive, as the reversion outcome in the absence of a constitution involves $t^0 > 0$.

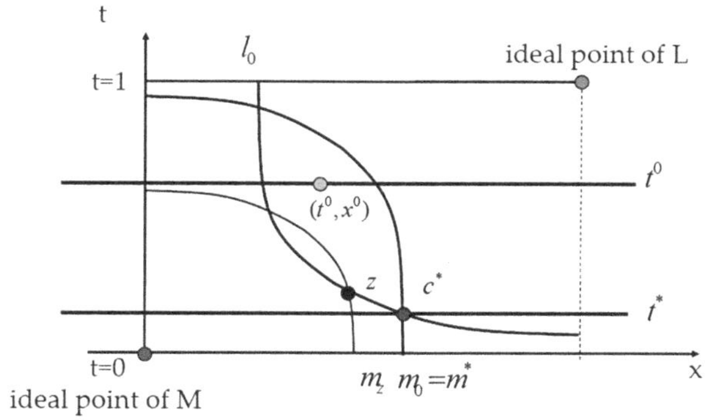

Fig. 3 Optimal constitution when M is expected to negotiate with R over reform and $w_M > \overline{w}$

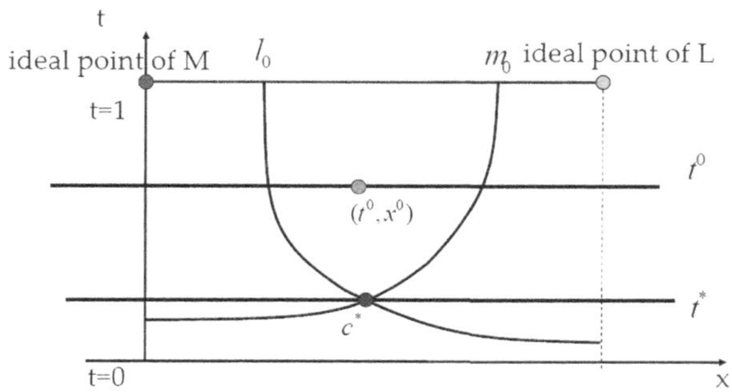

Fig. 4 Optimal constitution when M is expected to negotiate with R over reform and $w_M \leq \overline{w}$

3.2.2 Case $w_M \leq \overline{w}$

Finally consider the case where M has below average effective wealth and negotiates with R. In that case, it is straightforward that R selects the status quo constitution c^* by choosing the point in I where the tax rate gets minimal. This case is illustrated in Fig. 4. Again, it is easy to check that this constitution is stationary. Moreover, the constitution has monetary value to the autocrat because I is not vanishing by Lemma 2 and, hence, $t^* < t^0$.

3.3 Other Cases

For the case of negotiations between R and L, the choice of a constitution follows the same pattern as in the case of negotiations between R and M: If the middle class has more than average effective wealth, c^* is chosen in the point in I where the tax rate gets minimal (see Fig. 3). If M has less than effective average wealth, c^* is again chosen in the point in I where the tax rate gets minimal (see Fig. 4).

The same holds if a proposal in the constitutional bargaining game needs approval of all three players. In that case, any selection of $c \in I$ leaves no proposer with another possibility than proposing c. Hence, the autocrat selects his preferred point in I, as in the case where R and M negotiate with each other.

To complete our exposition, suppose that one party is sufficient to carry through constitutional reform. Majority rule may put one party in such a position even when the other parties can prevent her from realizing her ideal point in the conflict scenario. If the preexistence of a constitution c is necessary to prevent descent into conflict, such a constitution would at least be weakly acceptable as a template to all players and it would be strictly preferred by the player who stands to gain from the reform process. Moreover, if the dominant party selects a reform constitution within the constitutional process, it will propose its preferred point in I. The question for the autocrat of whether to write a constitution now reduces to whether the dominant party will select $t < t^0$ in the constitutional process. This is obviously the case when either M is predicted to be dominant and fulfills $w_M < \overline{w}$ or when R is dominant. Hence, in those cases writing a constitution creates positive monetary value for the autocrat. On the other hand, if L is predicted to be dominant, it offers M and R their reversion value which puts them in no better place than with open conflict. Hence, incentives for writing a constitution would completely vanish. The same applies to the case where M with $w_M > \overline{w}$ is dominant. The following proposition summarizes our results:

Proposition 7 *With negotiations between M and R or between L and R or with all three players, writing a constitution always has positive monetary value for the autocrat. If there is one dominant party in the constitutional reform process, writing a constitution only has positive monetary value for the autocrat in the cases where R is dominant or an M party opposed to redistribution is dominant. If L or an M party in favor of redistribution is predicted to be dominant, the autocrat is indifferent between writing and not writing a constitution.*

4 A Model of Intertemporal Constitutional Choice

The previous section has introduced a static model of constitutional choice where the autocrat can choose the default constitution for his successors without incurring any cost such as being bound by the constitution himself. In practice, it is likely to be a condition for a constitution to be acceptable that it actually has been adhered to for some time before the regime's demise. In addition, the autocrat may not know the precise date of his demise and, therefore, will want to write and implement the constitution at a time when the probability that he will be in his post for another day is still greater than zero. On the other hand, the consequences of successfully handing down a constitution might be felt for a long time. Therefore, we think it is reasonable to assume that the autocrat will attach non zero weights to the cost which he incurs by not realizing his preferred policy outcome $(0, x^R)$ during the time for which he has to abide by the constitution himself and to the gains his constituency realizes during the time when his successors deliver a preferred policy outcome.

We assume, that depending on the expected length of time in both states and the discount rate of the autocrat, these weights assume the values $(1-\delta)$ and δ. Even though $(1-\delta)$, which increases with the time in office, may itself depend on the choice of the autocrat's constitution, we ignore the possibility of such endogeneity. If the autocrat hands down a constitution, he choose the constitution (t, x) which gives him the highest total benefit, i.e. he maximizes

$$V_R(t, x) = (1-\delta)u_R(t, x) + \delta u_R\bigl(\Gamma(t, x)\bigr).$$

If he does not hand down a constitution, his total pay off is

$$V_R(\emptyset) = (1-\delta)u^R(0, x_R) + \delta u_R^0.$$

By selecting a constitution $c' \notin I$ which is not binding during his term in office, the autocrat can realize the same pay off as with no constitution in the initial period and a pay off $u_R(\Gamma(c')) \geq u_R^0$ in the second period. The latter relationship follows because the successors want to choose a reform constitution $(t, x) \in I$.[23]

In all cases, where the monetary value from writing a constitution in the static model is strictly positive, there must exist a constitution which the autocrat strictly prefers writing if the weight of the future is sufficiently great:

Proposition 8 *If the weight of the future, δ, in the autocrat's objective function is sufficiently great, there is a binding constitution which the autocrat strictly prefers to hand down in all cases where there is a positive monetary value to writing the constitution in the static model.*

Proof The autocrat can always choose to hand down the statically optimal constitution. For that constitution, the cost of commitment $u_R(x^*, t^*) - u_R(0, x_R)$ is finite and the benefit of commitment is strictly positive, i.e. $u_R(x^*, t^*) - u_R(\Gamma(c' \notin I)) > 0$ if, as we have claimed, there is a positive monetary value to writing the constitution. □

In all cases where there is no positive monetary value to writing a constitution the autocrat would only consider writing a constitution which is non binding during his term of office. This scenario comprises the cases where $w_M \leq \overline{w}$ and L is dominant or bargains with M bargain and the case where L or an M party in favor of redistribution is dominant in the succeeding assembly.

Finally, even when choosing a binding constitution, the autocrat may not necessarily want to choose the stationary, statically optimal constitution. At least in those case where the statically optimal constitution does not involve choosing the point in I where t gets minimal, i.e. in the case where L is expected to negotiate with an M party opposed to redistribution, the autocrat faces a trade off between loosening the constraint during his term in office and creating stronger incentives for a low tax regime after his demise:

[23] See the proof of Lemma 3.

Proposition 9 *In the case where L negotiates with M and* $w_M > \overline{w}$ *there exists a critical weight* δ^* *such that if* δ *falls below that weight, the autocrat compromises on the statically optimal constitution.*

Proof Let p^M be the probability that M proposes in the bargaining process. If the autocrat chooses the statically optimal constitution c^*, M proposes c^* and L proposes c^*. Now suppose that the autocrat chooses a constitution with a slightly smaller tax rate such as z in Fig. 1. In that case, M continues to propose c^*, so the autocrat gets t^* with a weight of $p^M\delta$. If L proposes, she proposes $t'|(t', x')$ in the intersection of m_z and the contract curve. $t' > t^*$, hence the outcome is worse for R and it is weighted with $(1 - p^M)\delta$. However, $t^z < t^*$, hence by choosing z, the autocrat realizes a better outcome with a weight $(1 - \delta)$. Hence, for $\delta \to 0$, c^* results in a higher value of V_R and for $\delta \to 1$, z results in a higher value of V_R. □

Obviously, for very small δ, the autocrat may not want to hand down a constitution. Therefore, the critical weight δ^* only becomes relevant if the distance between t^0 and the statically optimal constitution c^* is sufficiently large to induce the autocrat to write a constitution given δ^*. The following proposition generalizes this insight on the desirability of writing a constitution:

Proposition 10 *The greater the power of R in the transition scenario and, hence, the smaller* t^0*, the less value writing a constitution has.*

Proof In all cases where there is a monetary value of writing the constitution, the dynamically optimal constitutional choice c is independent of t^0. Hence, R's benefit of writing a constitution, $u_R(\Gamma(c)) - u_R(t^0)$ is increasing in t^0, i.e. the smaller t^0, the smaller the benefit. Finally, $u_R(\Gamma(c)) \leq u_R(t^0)$, hence the benefit must vanish as $t^0 \to 0$. □

5 Application to Different Experiences of Political Transition

From our analysis two hypotheses emerge.

1. If an autocrat expects that his own clientele will have influence on a succeeding constitutional assembly, he generally has incentives to write a constitution, although those incentives vanish if he expects that parties opposing redistribution will be able to impose their preferred policy without the left being able to object.
2. If an autocrat expects that his own clientele will have no influence on a succeeding constitutional assembly, he only has strong incentives to write a constitution if he expects that the middle class prefers a low redistribution policy.

In the case of the Chilean constitutional project, it seems plausible that the conditions for constitution writing in hypothesis 1—negotiations between the right and the middle class under a sufficiently strong perceived threat by the left—have been met or were believed to be met by the autocrat. That the left would not in a formal sense be involved in negotiations over a successor constitution was plausible from the point of view of the old regime because it did its utmost to keep it outside the political process. As it turned out, a substantial part of the left also objected to accept the constitution as a vehicle towards political reform.[24] If one accepts that one rationale of the Pinochet regime for embarking on the constitutional project was to build a bulwark against communism, as suggested by Montes and Vial (2005), the possibility of a left-wing threat must have been on the mind of the authors of the constitution. Protest movements such as the one led by copper miners in 1983 (see Collier and Sater 1996) and the so-called "protesta" movement which involved members of privileged, middle and working class (see O'Donnell and Schmitter 1986) must have reminded the junta of such a lingering threat.

An interesting question which remains is which the influence of middle class wealth has been in the case of Chile's successful constitutional transition. The moderation which the parties of the concertación showed in the transition process suggests that redistribution was not on the mind of the middle class which it represented. In an accompanying paper we discuss the relationship between middle class wealth and stable transition in the Chilean case in greater depth (Michalak and Pech 2012).

It is more difficult to see to which case the Egyptian transition corresponds. The Muslim brotherhood, with its social welfare goals probably best fits the description of leftist in the context of our model. On the other hand, the often secular groups which started the street protests voiced aspirations which are more compatible with a middle-class mind set with an emphasis on improvement of opportunities rather than the redistribution of existing wealth. Moreover, Egypt's Gini coefficient is lower than Chile's and the wooing of the presidential candidate of the right for the voters of this "middle class" further supports the view that Egypt best fits the case of a country with a middle class opposed to redistribution. This would give the autocrat strong incentives to write a constitution provided that he expects that the constitutional reform process takes the form of multiparty bargaining. If, on the other hand, the expectation is that the Muslim brotherhood plays a dominant role in the constitutional reform process, there is no value at all to writing a constitution.

Therefore, the prediction of our model critically depends on the prior about the bargaining strength of the different players in negotiating constitutional reform. In the case where the Muslim brotherhood is expected to be dominant, we predict that no constitution will be handed down. In the case where multiparty bargaining is expected to take place, we predict a constitution will be handed down which might be significantly amended in the bargaining process. Moreover, there are reasons why the monetary value of constitution writing may be low even when the expectation is multiparty bargaining: The autocrat may predict the military to be a strong player with significant power to enforce a high default outcome in any transition process or he may predict a long time horizon of his rule. In these cases he would have been reluctant to chose a constitution which binds his own actions. Finally, it is unclear

[24] For a dissenting view see Tapia (1987).

how to interpret the fact that the constitution was formally revoked even by those players who would have stood to benefit to the extent that they expected to have a share in future bargaining over reform. An orthodox interpretation of this fact would be to say that non compliant constitutional practice during the autocracy turned out to be a bar to acceptability. However, our model suggests a second interpretation which is more in line with the observation that the property order established under the constitution was kept in place. This observation would correspond to the case of stable constitutional transition but with major amendments.

We lack observations where constitutional succession was tried in the face of a middle class supporting redistribution. On the other hand, our model predicts that such cases would be rare to observe. What our model highlights, though, is the importance of established property rights as an element of constitutional arrangements which the autocrat wants to protect. This may shed a light on the failure of stable constitutional transition in the case of former communist countries. This was not completely for the lack of trying because at least in the case of Poland we observe a transition through pact between the old and incoming power (see Munck and Leff 1997). However, in the case where a new constitution has to legitimize an emerging property order, the stakes are quite different from the cases discussed in this paper. Indeed, it will be more important for emerging property owners—often members of the former nomenclature—to secure their share in the emerging property rights before they can think about securing those property rights within a constitutional compact.

6 Further Discussion

The main lesson which emerges from the model and the preceding discussion is that handing down a constitutional compact offers benefits to the autocrat's clientele in almost all cases where multiparty bargaining is expected during the transition process: If a constitution is accepted by its successors, it provides insurance against being excluded from transition bargaining as long as the middle class is opposed to redistribution and improves the bargaining position of the clientele relative to representatives of other classes. There is no such benefit if during transition one party is able to impose its preferred outcome. This suggests that there are economic and political conditions which facilitate successful constitutional transition. If the middle class is sufficiently wealthy to oppose redistribution, it serves as a natural proxy for the autocrat's clientele during the transition process. Furthermore, only if society is sufficiently heterogeneous such that there are different groups with diverging interests which find it necessary to reach compromise in the transition process is there a role to play for any inherited constitutional template. The latter point suggests that transitions such as in Poland or in South Africa where Solidarnocz and the ANC emerged as main players were less open to be manipulated by autocratic constitutional choice than the transitions discussed in this paper.

Appendix

In this appendix we show that in the case where L and M bargain and $w_M > \overline{w}$ the contract curve is vertical for $0 < t < 1$. For convenience, we define the income gap of each group relative to average available income as $\Delta_M = w_M - \overline{w} \lesseqgtr 0$, $\Delta_L = w_L - \overline{w} < 0$ and $\Delta_R = (1-\gamma)w_R - w > 0$.

For $0 < t < 1$, M's proposal $P^{M \to L} = (t', x')$ given $c = (t^*, x^*)$ solves the constrained optimization problem

$$\max\left[v_M(x) + (1-t)w_M + t\overline{w}\right] \quad \text{s.t. } v_L(x) + (1-t)w_L - t\overline{w} \geq u\left(t^*, x^*\right).$$

Writing $\mu(x') = \frac{\frac{\partial v_M(x')}{\partial x}}{\frac{\partial v_L(x')}{\partial x}} \leq 0$, the first order conditions for an interior solution of this problem, x' satisfies

$$\mu\left(x'\right) = \frac{\Delta_M}{\Delta_L} \tag{3}$$

and the tax rate is determined as the residual satisfying

$$t' = \frac{v_L(x^*) - v_L(x')}{(-1)\Delta_L} + t^*. \tag{4}$$

At x^M, $\mu(x^{M \to L}) = 0$ and at x^L, $\mu(x^{M \to L}) \to -\infty$. By continuity of μ, a solution x' satisfying the first order conditions uniquely exists with $x' \in [x^M, x^L)$. As $\frac{\partial v_M(x')}{\partial x} = -2|x' - x_M|$ and $\frac{\partial v_L(x')}{\partial x} = 2|x' - x_L|$, x' only depends on the ratio $\frac{\Delta_M}{\Delta_L}$. By construction, x' is the policy level which is Pareto-optimal for L and M. Call this policy realization x^e. It is easy to show that L, when proposing to M selects the same policy x^e.

The optimal proposal can be interpreted as follows: x^e is the policy which would maximize the joint pay off for L and M given that transfers between M and L can only be achieved through the linear tax system: $\frac{\Delta_M}{\Delta_L}$ is the rate at which M's income is converted into L's income as the tax rate increases. Note that a transfer rate of greater than -1 signifies an involuntary contribution of R.[25] If the ratio is $-1/2$, it costs half a unit of M's income to increase L's income by one unit. μ is the rate at which M's utility from consuming x increases per unit of utility decrease by L. In an optimum, M's gain has to be equal to M's cost of compensating L at an admissible tax rate $t \in (0, 1)$.[26]

[25]One can show that the ratio is greater than -1 if $\frac{w^L + w^M}{2} < (w^M - w^L)$, i.e. if M's wealth exceeds L's wealth by more than average wealth, where the latter is calculated looking at M and L only. To demonstrate this point, note that $\frac{\Delta^M}{\Delta^L}$ can be written as $\frac{w^M + (w^M - w^L) - w^R}{w^L - (w^M - w^L) - w^R}$.

[26]If $\Delta^M / \Delta^L = -1$, we obtain the familiar policy choice rule of selecting x half way between the bliss points, see e.g. Baron and Diermeier (2001).

References

Barbera S, Jackson MO (2004) Choosing how to choose: self-stable majority rules and constitutions. Q J Econ 119:1011–1048
Barbera S, Jackson MO (2006) On the weights of nations: assigning voting weights in a heterogeneous union. J Polit Econ 114:317–339
Baron DP, Diermeier D (2001) Elections, governments, and parliaments in proportional representation systems. Q J Econ 932–967
Barros R (2002) Constitutionalism and dictatorship. Pinochet, the Junta, and the 1980 constitution. Cambridge University Press, Cambridge
Brown N (2011) The Egyptian constitution's rulebook for change, foreign policy. http://mideast.foreignpolicy.com/posts/2011/02/03/the_egyptian_constitution_s_rulebook_for_change. Accessed 3 February 2011
Brown N, Dunnes M (2011) Egypt's draft constitutional amendments answer some questions and raise others. Carnegie Endowment for International Peace, 4 March 2011
Collier S, Sater WF (1996) The history of Chile 1808–1994. Cambridge University Press, Cambridge
Easterly W (2001) Middle class consensus and economic development. J Econ Growth 6:317–335
Egypt's freedom. Financial Times, 20 May 2012
Egypt court orders parliament dissolved. Financial Times, 15 June 2012
Gersbach H (2004) Why one person one vote? Soc Choice Welf 23:449–464
Grossman HJ (2002) Constitution or conflict? NBER working paper 8733
Kitschelt H (1996) The transformation of European social democracy. Cambridge University Press, Cambridge
Lagunoff R (2007) Dynamic stability and reform of political institutions. Games Econ Behav 67:569–583
Michalak M, Pech G (2012) Strategic constitutional choice in an autocracy: the 1980 constitution in Chile
Montes J Esteban, Vial T (2005) The constitution building process in Chile: the authoritarian roots of a stable democracy. International Institute for Democracy and Electoral Assistance, Stockholm
Munck GL, Leff CS (1997) Modes of transition and democratization: South America and Eastern Europe in comparative perspective. Comp Polit 29:343–362
Myerson R (2008) The autocrat's credibility problem and foundations of the constitutional state. Am Polit Sci Rev 102:125–139
Naqvi N, Neumärker KJB, Pech G (2012) The rule of law and sustainability of the constitution. CEN working paper 02-2012, Freiburg
North DC, Weingast B (1989) Constitutions and commitment: the evolution of institutions governing public choice in seventeenth century England. J Econ Hist 49:803–832
Ordeshook P (1997) Constitutions for new democracies. Reflections of turmoil or agents of stability? Public Choice 90:55–72
O'Donnell G, Schmitter PC (1986) Transitions from authoritarian rule. Tentative conclusions about uncertain democracies. John Hopkins University Press, Baltimore
Pech G (2009) Rationality and the legal order. In: Boylan T, Gekker R (eds) Economics, rational choice and normative philosophy. Routledge series frontiers of political economy
Przeworski A, Wallerstein M (1988) Structural dependence of the state on capital. Am Polit Sci Rev 82:12–29
Riker W (1986) The art of political manipulation. Yale University Press, Newhaven
Riker W (1996) The strategy of rhetoric. Yale University Press, Newhaven
Schofield N (2002) Evolution of the constitution. Br J Polit Sci 32:1–20
Tapia J (1987) Sobre el uso de la 'legalidad' de la dictatura. Cauce 113(22 June):22–29

Tsebelis G (2002) Veto players: how political institutions work. Princeton University Press, Princeton
Weingast B (1997) The political foundations of democracy and the rule of law. Am Polit Sci Rev 91:245–263

Quandaries of Gridlock and Leadership in US Electoral Politics

Evan Schnidman and Norman Schofield

1 Introduction

The United States currently faces a number of severe political economic quandaries. First is the economic quandary of debt. From 1993 to 2001, the US public debt to GDP ratio fell from 49 % to 33 % but has since risen to about 100 %. Entitlements, due to the aging "baby boom generation" will, in all likelihood, increase this ratio even more. The transformation to the global economy coupled with the internet revolution has changed the international structure of comparative advantage and has had a dramatic effect on employment possibilities and on income and wealth distribution. China, India and Brazil are growing rapidly, and China's propensity to save, coupled with its manipulated currency has contributed to the US current account deficit, as well as facilitated the level of US public debt. The resulting uncertainties have induced violent swings in global stock markets. In the background is the fear of the effects of global warming or "weirding" and concerns about how to deal with the US appetite for oil.[1]

Many people now fear that we face a repetition of the 1930's. While the "Great Depression" may have started with the market collapse of 1929, it was the failure of the largest Austrian bank, Kreditanstalt, in 1931 that triggered the sequence of bank

[1]Too many books to name have addressed these quandaries, but we can mention Galbraith (2008), Reich (2010), Milanovic (2010), Friedman and Mandelbaum (2011), Harvey (2011), Lessig (2011), Rachman (2011), Sachs (2011), Steyn (2011), Buchanan (2011), Noah (2012), Stiglitz (2012), Smith (2012).

E. Schnidman (✉)
11 Vandine Street #2, Cambridge, MA 02141, USA
e-mail: evan.schnidman@gmail.com

N. Schofield
Weidenbaum Center, Washington University in St. Louis, Seigle Hall, Campus Box 1027, One Brookings Drive, St. Louis, MO 63130-4899, USA
e-mail: schofield.norman@gmail.com

N. Schofield et al. (eds.), *Advances in Political Economy*,
DOI 10.1007/978-3-642-35239-3_5,

failures in Europe and the US, coupled with the Smoot-Hawley Tariff Act earlier in June 1930, that led to the enormous contraction of world trade and deepening of the crisis.[2]

As Keynes (1936: 380) made clear

> at the cost of the enlargement of the functions of government [to involve] the task of adjusting to one another, the propensity to consume, and the inducement to invest

the liberty and efficiency of the world economy could be preserved and enhanced.

From Roosevelt's inauguration on March 3 until June 16, 1933, he pushed through the beginnings of the New Deal, including the Emergency Banking Act, the Economy and Beer-Wine Revenue Act (finishing Prohibition, and providing much needed government revenue), the Agricultural Adjustment Act (to deal with over production, but also with an amendment that essentially took the dollar off the gold standard), and the National Industrial Recovery Act (although Title I of the Act was deemed unconstitutional by the Supreme Court on May 27, 1935). The CCC (Civilian Conservation Corps), the FERA (Federal Emergency Authority), the TVA (Tennessee Valley Authority), the NIRA (National Industrial Recovery Administration), the PWA (Public Works Administration) and the AAA (Agricultural Adjustment Administration) were all created to attempt to deal with unemployment, partly through public works. In June 16, 1933, the Glass–Steagall Act had established the Federal Deposit Insurance Corporation (FDIC) in the United States and introduced banking reforms, some of which were designed to control speculation. Regulation Q allowed the Federal Reserve to regulate interest rates in savings accounts. Although these policy moves predated Keynes's book, they were consistent with some of Keynes's earlier ideas (Keynes 1930a,b, 1933). Keynes himself had written to the President in 1933 to praise him as a "trustee of the social system" and met with him later in May 1934. Keynes later wrote to Roosevelt in 1938 recommending public ownership of the utilities, nationalization of the railroads and subsidies for housing.

The severe economic downturn in 1937, caused partly by attempts to balance the budget, led to a Republican gain of 81 seats in the House and 6 seats in the Senate in the 1938 election. The Fair Labor Standards Act (FLSA) of June 25, 1938, just prior to the election, was the last of the New Deal legislation. In a presentiment of the 1960's, Roosevelt also faced opposition from southern Democrats and had to give way on an anti-lynching bill. As Kennedy (1999: 343) notes,

> Roosevelt judged and the six week filibuster confirmed [that a frontal assault on the South's racial system] would irretrievably alienate the white southern establishment beyond repair and indefinitely deadlock the Congress.

However, the various efforts, prior to 1938, to regulate the economy eventually paid off in a significant increase in real US GDP as well developments in new

[2]See also the work by Fisher (1933) on debt deflation as a fundamental cause of the depression.

technologies and large increases in factor productivity (Field 2003; Allen 1994). These productivity increases may have been due to the ability of large corporations to increase output even when reducing labor input. Livingston (2011) provides a good argument that the New Deal had reversed the earlier pattern of increasing income inequality and reanimated consumer led growth. (If this argument is correct, then it suggests a way out of the consequences of the current Great Recession.)

The period from the collapse of democracy in Europe in the 1930's to the end of World War II led to major works of political economy by Von Mises (1940), Schumpeter (1942), Von Hayek (1944) and Popper (1945) that are still being debated today.

Fearful of another collapse, by the close of World War II, Keynes was arguing for a clearing Union, with assets of the order of $500 billion in current terms. After the death of Roosevelt in April 1945, however, the US pursued a strategy that might be termed "hegemonic internationalism," triggering European recovery by providing liquidity through the Marshall Plan.

By 1960, however, it had become obvious that there was an imbalance in the demand and supply of international liquidity.[3] Efforts were made in 1964–1968 to maintain stability through the creation of special drawing rights but by the Smithsonian agreement of December 1971, the post war Bretton Woods system was dismantled. In 1977, the McCracken report suggested that inflation was gathering pace in the OECD countries because of the so-called "political business cycle" and the continuing US payments deficit.[4] The commodity boom that followed led to the formation of OPEC and a price rise from about $1.80/barrel to $11.65 in January 1974. The chaos of the 1970's forms the background to the dramatic changes implemented after the presidential election of Reagan in November 1980 and the election of the Conservative Party in the UK under Margaret Thatcher in 1979. For these two leaders, government was the problem. Inflation was eventually stripped from the US and UK and economic growth began. From 1982 to 1988, and the election of G. Bush, US GDP grew at about 3 %/annum, but the trade deficit also grew, to about $115 billion. With the collapse of the Soviet Union in 1989, the US became the world hegemon. Globalization, coupled with democratization and capitalization gathered speed. From Clinton's election in 1992 to 2000, US GDP/capita grew at about 3.5 % while the trade deficit grew to $376 billion.

During Clinton's second administration, the provisions of the Glass Steagall Act (prohibiting a bank holding company from owning other financial companies) were repealed on November 12, 1999, by the Financial Services Modernization Act, also called the Gramm–Leach–Bliley Act, named after its co-sponsors Phil Gramm (R, Texas), Jim Leach (R, Iowa), and Thomas J. Bliley, Jr. (R, Virginia).[5] This ended the regulatory regime that had been put in place during the New Deal.

---

[3]See Triffin (1960).

[4]In 1970 the US had a trade surplus of $2.2 billion but by 1977 this was a deficit of $27 billion.

[5]See Morgenson and Rosner (2011) for discussion, as well as the account by Clinton (2011) of these events.

Globalization has meant that 2 billion people have joined the world's labor force since 1989. It is no surprise that this labor shock has meant that global inequality has decreased but that income inequality in all developed economies has increased. Deregulation in the US has contributed to the expansion of global trade and investment, but has also meant that the global market became unstable. In 2006 the US balance of payments deficit reached $750 billion, while its trade deficit with China reached $130 billion for the first six months of 2011. As a result, China currently has foreign exchange reserves of $3.2 trillion and holds about $1 trillion in US Treasury and government agency bonds.[6] Japan also has about $800 billion. Cheap money led to a significant increase in household debt in the US, rising from about 65 % of GDP in 1995 to 100 % of GDP in 2009.

In a deregulated world, and in a context of moral hazard, financial institutions competed for profits, speculating in risky assets, particularly derivatives based on the housing market. The presumption that the market could regulate itself proved unfounded, just as Minsky (1986) has argued. This imbalance can lead to the kind of instability that Keynes feared.

> If I may be allowed to appropriate the term speculation for the activity of forecasting the psychology of the market, and the term enterprise for the activity of forecasting the prospective yield of assets over their whole life, it is by no means always the case that speculation predominates over enterprise. As the organization of investment markets improves, the risk of the predominance of speculation does, however, increase... Speculators may do no harm as bubbles on a steady stream of enterprise. But the position is serious when enterprise becomes the bubble on a whirlpool of speculation. (Keynes 1936: 158–159)

Lehman Brothers did file for bankruptcy on September 15, 2008, and the bubble burst. The market crash has left the US with a public debt of about $15 trillion. US household net worth fell from about $70 trillion in 2007 to about $50 trillion in 2009.[7] Even in the year from June 2010 to 2011 house values fell by $1 trillion, and about 15 million homeowners find themselves owing more than their homes are worth.

The contagion spread to Europe, where the debt overhang meant that many states found themselves at risk of default. The EU was forced to put together the European Financial Stability Fund (EFSF) rescue package of € 750 billion, able to issue bonds for up to € 440 billion for support to Euro member states in difficulty, including Greece, Italy, Ireland, Greece, Spain and Portugal.[8] European banks were also at risk, holding over $2 trillion in risky sovereign debt.

---

[6] Alpert et al. (2011) note that China saves about 50 % of GDP, invests about 15 % and consumes only about 35 %.

[7] Alpert et al. (2011).

[8] The European levels of total public debt/GDP currently are: Greece 166 %, Italy 121 %, Ireland 109 %, Portugal 106 %, Belgium 96 %, Germany 83 %, France 87 %, Britain 80 %, Spain 56 %.

A number of EU governments have fallen because of opposition to the austerity measures imposed by the European Union, in order to deal with the debt crisis. First, the Irish Parliament was dissolved on February 1, 2011, and an election held on February 26. From 78 seats in 2007, the governing party, Fianna Fail, only took 25, and Enda Kenny of the opposition party, Fine Gael, became Taoiseach (Prime Minister) of Ireland on 9 March.

In the 2011 general election in Finland, the Center Party, led by Prime Minister, Mari Kiviniemi, lost 16 of the 51 seats that they had held, while the True Finns party gained 34 seats. The center-right National Coalition Party, under Jyrki Katainen, became the largest party for the first time. After long and difficult negotiations, Katainen was elected Prime Minister by the Finnish Parliament on 22 June 2011, leading a coalition of six parties (National Coalition, Social Democrats, Left Alliance, Greens, Swedish People's Party and Christian Democrats).

Then the Prime Minister of Portugal, Jose Socrates, of the Socialist Party, resigned on March 23, and the caretaker government obtained a bailout of $116 billion on May 3, 2011. In the election of June 5, the center right Social Democrats, under Pedro Passos Coelho, took 39 % of the vote to 28 % for Socialists and 12 % for the Popular Party. Coelho will lead a coalition with the Popular Party, and promised further austerity measures to deal with the crisis.

Lars Løkke Rasmussen, leader of the center-right liberal party, Venstre, lost his position as Prime Minister of Denmark in the September 2011 parliamentary election. He remained in office as head of a caretaker government until his successor, Helle Thorning-Schmidt, was appointed on 3 October 2011.

Iveta Radičová was the leader of the Slovak Democratic and Christian Union—Democratic Party, and Prime Minister of Slovakia from 8 July 2010 as the head of a four-party center-right coalition government. Radičová lost a vote of confidence in the parliament on 11–12 October, 2011, leading to the fall of her government. An early election will be held on 10 March, 2012.

On November 5, 2011, the Greek Prime Minister, George Papandreou, agreed to step down to make way for a unity government, and on November 10, Lucas Papademos became interim prime minister. In the election of May 6 2012, both major parties, PASOK, the center left party, only won 41 seats with 14 % of the vote, while the center right, New Democracy took 108 seats with 18 % of the vote. These reverses were seen as a rejection of the austerity measures, imposed by the EU. Of greater importance was the defeat of Nicolas Sarkozy in the second round of the French Presidential election, also on May 6 by the socialist candidate Francois Hollande.

On November 12, 2011 the Italian Prime Minister, Silvio Berlusconi, had resigned after Parliament approved a number of measures to reduce the deficit. Italy's president then asked Mario Monti, a former European Commissioner, to form a government.

José Luis Rodríguez Zapatero, the leader of the Spanish Socialist Workers' Party (PSOE), was elected for terms as Prime Minister of Spain in the 2004 and 2008 general elections. In the election of November 20, 2011, the conservative People's party (PP) led by Mariano Rajoy won 186 of the 350 seats in parliament, with a 44 % vote and a mandate to carry out further austerity measures.

Even Belgium found itself in difficulty, with a debt to GDP ratio of 96 %, No coalition government had been able to form after the election of June 2010, because of conflicts between Flanders and Wallonia. Eventually on December 1, 2011, the downgrading of Belgium's sovereign debt forced a coalition of six parties to reach a tentative agreement to form a government under the Socialist Party leader, Elio Di Rupo.

In fact the first political effects of the debt crisis were the fall of the Labor government in the United Kingdom in May 2010 and the defeat of the Republican administration in the US in November 2008. The Conservative government in the UK dealt with its debt problem by an intervention of the order of 13 % of GDP by the Bank of England. In the US the intervention by the Federal Reserve has been of order 11 % of GDP. In contrast the EU intervention has been limited to about 2 % of EU GDP, which is why the euro debt crisis continues to destabilize bond markets.

The complex web of the global economic crisis has created a great deal of uncertainty in the market as well as in the political systems of both Europe and the United States. In Europe there is much debate whether the eurozone can be sustained, though on December 9, 2011, twenty-six of the twenty-seven member states (all but the UK) agreed to a deepening of the EU. However, the election defeats in Greece and France in May may have changed the emphasis on the fiscal austerity strategy of German Chancellor Angela Merkel. Muddling matters further is the rising debt default threat in Italy and Spain which has created continued market unrest and political ambivalence.

In the United States, this uncertainty coupled with decades of rising income and wealth inequality has resulted in increased political volatility and partisan strife. The indebted EU polities have electoral systems based on proportional representation, and as a result, government requires coalition agreement. Indeed the formal model (Schofield 2007) underlying this paper suggests that, under proportional representation, smallparties will generally adopt positions far from the center. This political polarization sustains fragmentation and governmental instability. In contrast the theory we use here suggests that "first past the post" or plurality electoral system of the US generates a strong convergent electoral effect on political candidates, similar to the *Downsian median voter result* (Downs 1957). We discuss recent events since the 2008 presidential election, and argue that candidates do not adopt centrist policies. Instead, money has played an increasingly important role in recent elections. Because of the two dimensionality of the policy space, activists have been able to exert a *centrifugal* force on the policy positions of the parties. As a result US politics is now characterized by legislative *gridlock*. Indeed the increase in partisan rancor resulting from the need to deal with federal debt of over $14 trillion has highlighted the extreme lack of convergence in US partisan politics. The remainder of this paper seeks to explain this centrifugal tendency in the 2008 and 2010 election cycles in the United States.

2 Activist Politics

2.1 The Logic of the Argument

Wise government should be able to address the quandaries described above. Madison's logic in Federalist X (Madison [1787] 1999) was that a Republic could exhibit a "probability of a fit choice", suggesting that voters would make their choices on the basis of judgements rather than simply interests.

In this paper we argue that the US polity is currently unable to make wise decisions due to a structural defect that Jefferson feared could occur in the US. Jefferson followed the arguments of Henry St. John, Viscount Bolingbroke, that the noble constitution of England had been destroyed by the crass commercialization and corruption of the Whig ascendency in the 1720s. Jefferson believed that the opening of Hamilton's First Bank of America in 1791 would also allow capital to corrupt. He fought and won the election of 1800 to preserve the "Empire of Liberty".[9] We can put this conflict in the more general context of rival philosophical systems of belief, as suggested by Israel (2012), who has pointed out that the modern period since 1700 witnessed a conflict between a "Radical" Enlightenment espoused by Bolingbroke, Condorcet, Jefferson and Paine, in support of reason and equality and opposed to monarchy and hierarchical hegemony, and the compromising "Moderate" Enlightenment of Hamilton and Burke. The importance of the social dimension in US politics, as discussed below, suggests that this conflict is as important as ever.[10]

In the early 20th century both Teddy Roosevelt and Woodrow Wilson had contested the 1912 presidential election as Progressives, opposed to the power of commercial interests and the increasing economic inequality that had resulted (Gould 2008). Indeed Chace (2004) suggests that the difference between Roosevelt and Wilson was that Wilson espoused a Jeffersonian belief in liberty and competition (through free trade etc.) while Roosevelt believed in a Hamiltonian acceptance, but regulation, of industrial capitalism.

The thesis of this paper is that just as in 1800, in 1912 and in 1932, the US faces a quandary that is essentially constitutional and involves the interrelationship between the polity and the economy. There are a number of components to the current quandary:

(i) The election of L.B. Johnson in 1964 was the beginnings of a new "political realignment" that involved the social dimension of civil rights as well as the usual economic dimension involving taxes and the like.[11] We use factor analysis to

[9] Kramnick (1990, 1992). See also Lind (2012) for the continuing conflict between the Jeffersonian and Hamiltonian visions of the development of the USA political economy. Lind gives a detailed account of the logic of using resources generated by tariff protection to induce infrastructural improvements such as railways and canals, facilitating the industrial development of the Northern states.

[10] See also the recent books by Crick (1995), Hitchens (2007), Dawkins (2011).

[11] See Caro (2012) for a discussion of how LBJ was able to force through the civil rights legislation in 1964 against Southern Democrat opposition in Congress. The gridlock in Congress in 1964

construct these two dimensions. The social axis involves attitudes to African Americans, abortion, civil right for gays, traditional values and equality. The economic axis involves government services, size of government, health care, a preference for the market over government and a belief that welfare expenditure should be decreased. As Putnam and Campbell (2010) have shown, religiosity of voters is related to many of the beliefs that characterize the social axis. The second axis has become more important over time, and we use the term *social activists* for activists on this axis. The principal consequence of this realignment has been the gain of the South by the Republican Party. Indeed, Reagan won the 1980 Presidential election as a result. The Republicans also gained both Houses of Congress in 1994.[12] The change in the regulatory regime that has occurred in the last 30 years is a consequence of this realignment.

(ii) Although the social axis has become electorally more important, economic growth before the bursting of the balloon has increased the ability of those with economic assets to influence elections. We term these *economic activists*. Increasing income and wealth inequality has contributed to the enhanced power of these activists. Indeed, an arms race between the parties has also increased activist power. At the same time, the significant benefits that have accrued to economic activists have led to a radicalization of economic activist preferences. By this we mean that their preferences, in comparison to the distribution of electoral preferences, have become more extreme.[13]

The Supreme Court decision, *Citizens United v. Federal Election Commission*, on January 21, 2010, removed many restrictions on the money that could raised for political campaign and in essence deregulated elections. This means that activists previous constrained to providing small amounts of cash and/or volunteer time are now able to provide large sums of money to pay for large media buys and thousands of man-hours of electoral activism.

(iii) The existence of two political dimensions has meant that it is possible for winning coalitions to be constructed that combine both axes. In particular, the Republicans have benefited from a coalition of conservative economic and conservative social activists. This has led to dramatic differences in the pattern of voter characteristics in states that tend to vote Democrat in contrast to those who tend to vote Republican.[14]

(iv) Models of elections are typically based on voter preferences alone. Recent studies of US elections (Clarke et al. 2009, 2011) have emphasized the electoral perception of the character traits of candidates. Such perceptions can be influenced

over this issue combined with partisan conflict over the budget has some similarity to the current gridlock in Congress, discussed in this paper.

[12]See Schofield et al. (2003), Miller and Schofield (2003), Schofield (2007) and Schofield and Miller (2007) for a discussion of this realignment. See also Micklethwaite and Wooldridge (2004) for a discussion of the changes in ideology and electoral support for the Republican party in this period.

[13]See Abramowitz and Saunders (2005) and Abramowitz (2010).

[14]Abramowitz and Saunders (2005), Gelman (2009).

by the media, and in turn therefore by the money that candidates spend. We suggest this provides the logic for the arms race between candidates.

(v) Acemoglu and Robinson (2008) have discussed the ability of elites to exert de facto power in order to collect economic rents thus inducing inefficiencies in the political economy. Earlier work by Olson (1982) also focused on the ability of interest groups, such as labor, to exert undue influence because of the nature of the democratic machinery. The model that we propose suggests that the de facto elite power is a result of a kind of rent seeking that occurs in the context of a political prisoners' dilemma.

(vi) The influence of money and the polarization within Congress suggests that at the heart of the political quandary is a need to reconsider the constitutional separation of powers in the US.[15]

In the rest of the paper we consider models of US Presidential elections for 2000 to 2008, and then discuss the details of the contest between Obama and Congress over the last three years in order to gauge the validity of the above argument.

2.2 Modeling Elections

As we have noted, the formal literature on electoral competition has tended to focus on preferences rather than judgements. Models of two-party competition have typically been based on the assumption that parties or candidates adopt positions in order to win, and has inferred that parties will converge to the electoral *median*, under deterministic voting in one dimension (Downs 1957; Hotelling 1929), or to the electoral mean in stochastic models.[16] These models of political convergence at least imply that political choice lead to a moderate or centrist outcome. On the contrary, there is extensive evidence that politics has become *polarized* with the two major parties far removed from one another.[17]

In this paper we consider a theory of political choice which accounts for polarization in terms of activist influence. To do this, we first offer evidence that the political space is at least two dimensional. The nature of this policy space can be inferred for recent elections from voter surveys. For example, Fig. 1 presents an estimate of the distribution of voter preferences (or preferred positions) in the US presidential election of 2004.[18] The first-left right dimension represents preferences

---

[15]Posner and Vermeule (2011).

[16]See the earlier work by Enelow and Hinich (1989), Erikson and Romero (1990) and more recent work by Duggan (2006), and Patty et al. (2009).

[17]See the works by Fiorina et al. (2005), Fiorina and Abrams (2009) and McCarty et al. (2006) on polarization in the electorate and Layman et al. (2010) on polarization among activists.

[18]This figure is based on factor analysis of the American National Election Study (ANES) for 2004. In the next section we give more details on the factor model that we used for the 2004 and 2008 Presidential elections.

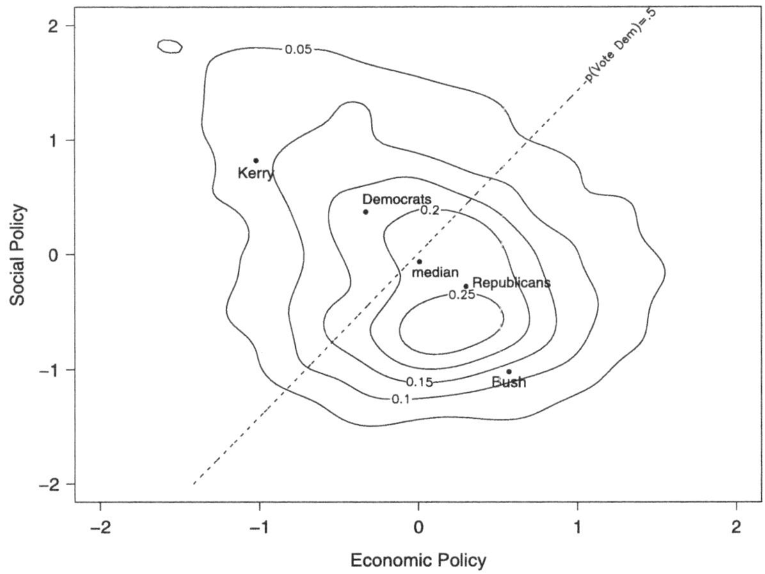

Fig. 1 Electoral distribution and candidate positions in the United States in 2004

(or attitudes) towards government expenditure and taxes and can be interpreted as a *economic* axis.[19] The second north-south or *social* dimension reflects attitudes on social policy, particularly civil rights, as well as voter opinions about abortion etc.[20] Figure 1 also shows estimates of the positions of the two presidential candidates.

Because the political space is two-dimensional, parties in the United States must be coalitions of opposed interests. Figure 1 also shows a *partisan cleavage line* obtained from a simple logit model of the 2004 Presidential election. This cleavage line joins the preferred points of voters who, according to the logit model, would choose the candidates with equal probability of one half. The logit model gives

$$\rho_{dem} == \frac{\exp(a + bx_i + cy_i)}{1 + \exp(a + bx_i + cy_i)} \tag{1}$$

with $(a, b, c) = (-0.2, 1.34, -0.93)$. Setting $\rho_{dem} = \frac{1}{2}$ we obtain the equation

$$y = 1.44x - 0.21. \tag{2}$$

This equation almost passes through the point $(0, -0.21)$ and suggests that the Democrat candidate, Kerry, had a slight advantage over the Republican candidate,

[19]The economic axis is defined so that voters who believe in the free market and that spending on welfare programs should be decreased are located on the right of this x-axis.

[20]The social axis is defined so that voters who support civil rights for gays and believe that abortion should be readily available are located to the north of this y-axis.

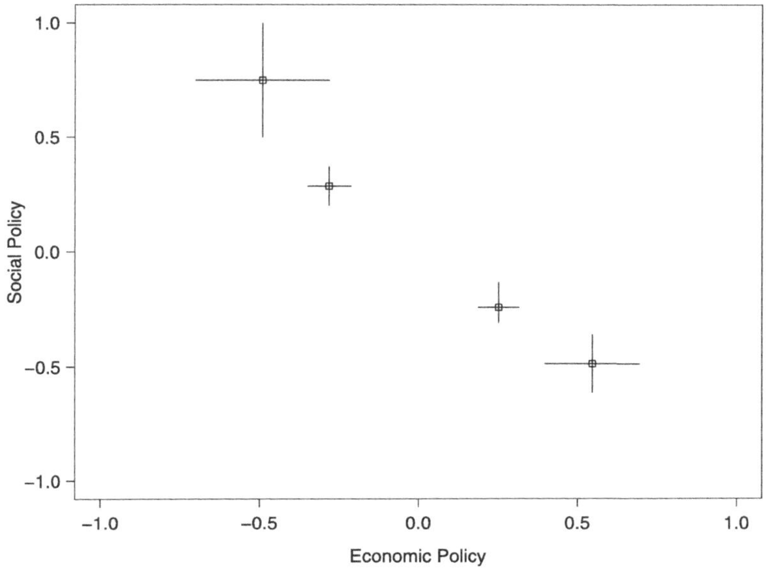

Fig. 2 Comparison of mean partisan and activist positions for Democrat and Republican voters in 2004 (error bars are larger for the mean activist positions)

Bush. This *partisan cleavage line* separates respondents who tend to vote Democrat, and generally are located in the upper left quadrant, from those who tend to vote Republican, in the lower right quadrant.

Figure 2 shows the mean positions of Democratic and Republican Party voters and activists.[21] Figure 2 suggests that though the Republican party contains both socially conservative and socially liberal groups, almost all Republican activists are located in the lower right of the policy space. In opposition, all the Democrat party activists tend to be located in the upper left of the policy space. The mean activist estimates are

$$\begin{bmatrix} Act:2004 & \text{Rep} & \text{Dem} \\ x & 0.55 & -0.49 \\ y & -0.48 & +0.75 \end{bmatrix}. \tag{3}$$

The two dimensionality of the political space is corroborated by work in social psychology that finds that there are in essence four "quadrants" to morality: Liberal secularists (upper left), the religious left (lower left), Libertarians (upper right) and social conservatives (lower right). The social psychological literature defines the

[21]The figure shows the standard error bars for these estimates, with larger error bars for activist estimates.

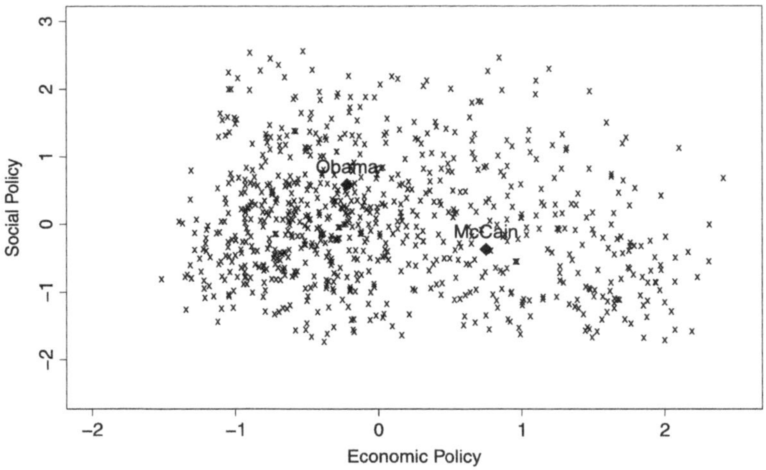

Fig. 3 Distribution of voter ideal points and candidate position in 2008

left hand domain in terms of an emphasis on justice while the right hand domain is defined in terms of authority.[22]

An analysis for the 2000 contest between Gore and Bush gives a similar result with a partisan cleavage line given by

$$y = 1.87x - 0.34. \tag{4}$$

Figures 3 and 4 show the distribution of voter and activist preferred positions for the 2008 election. For this election, the *partisan cleavage line* is given by the equation

$$y = 0.82x - 0.4, \tag{5}$$

which passes through the point (0, −0.4). This cleavage line suggests the greater advantage of the Democrat candidate, Obama, over McCain. Notice that the cleavage lines from 2000 to 2004 to 2008 had rotated slightly, in a clockwise direction, suggesting that the social axis had become increasingly important.

[22]More precisely, Graham et al. (2009) use factor analysis on five moral traits, including "compassion", "fairness", "loyalty", "authority" and "purity". These define the four moral clusters. Mondak et al. (2010) uses regression analysis to explore the effects of personality traits such as "openness", "conscientiousness", "extraversion", "agreeableness" and "emotional stability" on political choice. Using the 2006 Congressional Election Study (CES) he shows that "openness" and "conscientiousness" are correlated with liberal/conservative ideology respectively. Moreover, "openness" is associated with agreement with legalized abortion and weakly associated with opposition to Federal income tax cuts. This analysis is suggestive of a correlation between the two dimensional trait space and the two dimensional policy space.

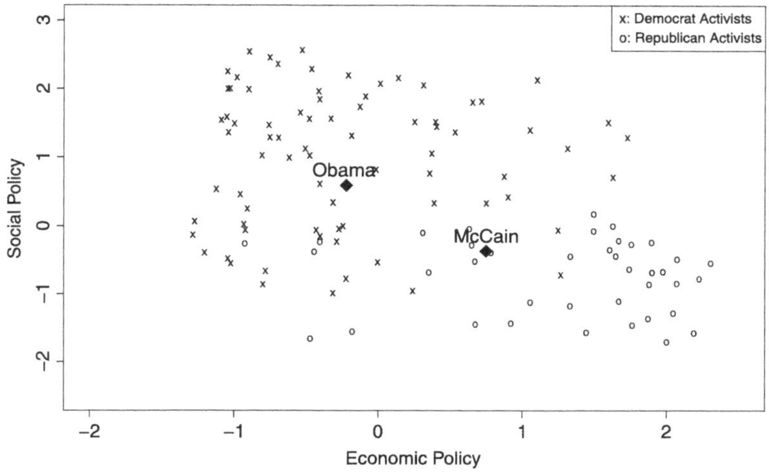

Fig. 4 Distribution of activist ideal points and candidate positions in 2008

Table 1 Factor loadings for economic and social policy

Question	Economic policy	Social policy
Less Government services	0.53	0.12
Oppose Universal health care	0.51	0.22
Oppose Bigger Government	0.50	0.14
Prefer Market to Government	0.56	
Decrease Welfare spending	0.24	
Less government	0.65	
Worry more about Equality	0.14	0.37
Tax Companies Equally	0.28	0.10
Support Abortion		0.55
Decrease Immigration	0.12	0.25
Civil right for gays		0.60
Disagree Traditional values		0.53
Gun access	0.36	
Support Afr. Amer	0.14	0.45
Conservative v Liberal	0.30	0.60
Eigenvalue	1.93	1.83

Table 1 gives the two dimensional factor model based on the ANES 2008 Survey, while Tables 2 and 3 give the results of the estimates of mean positions of voters, activists and the candidates in 2008.

Table 2 Descriptive data for the 2008 presidential election

	Economic policy			Social policy			n
	Mean	s.e.	95 % C.I	Mean	s.e.	95 % C.I	
Activists							
Democrats	−0.20	0.09	[−0.38, −0.02]	1.14	0.11	[0.92, 1.37]	80
Republicans	1.41	0.13	[1.66, 1.16]	−0.82	0.09	[−0.99, −0.65]	40
Non-activists							
Democrats	−0.17	0.03	[−0.24, −0.11]	0.36	0.04	[0.29, 0.44]	449
Republicans	0.72	0.06	[0.60, 0.84]	−0.56	0.05	[−0.65, −0.46]	219
							788

Table 3 Obama and McCain electorally perceived positions

Question	Obama	McCain
Estimated position on economic policy	−0.22	0.59
Estimated position on social policy	0.75	−0.37

The mean activist estimates are

$$\begin{bmatrix} Act:2008 & Rep & Dem \\ x & 1.41 & -0.20 \\ y & -0.82 & +1.14 \end{bmatrix}. \tag{6}$$

A comparison of (3) and (5) provides some evidence that activist average positions have become more extreme between 2004 and 2008. One way to check this inference is to compare (3) and (5) in terms of the electoral standard deviations obtained from the factor models for the two elections.[23] Using $(\sigma_x, \sigma_y) = (0.76, 0.76), (0.9, 0.91)$ for 2004 and 2008 respectively, this correction gives

$$\begin{bmatrix} Act:2004 & Rep & Dem \\ x/sd & 0.72 & -0.64 \\ y/sd & -0.63 & +0.99 \end{bmatrix}, \quad \begin{bmatrix} Act:2008 & Rep & Dem \\ x/sd & 1.56 & -0.22 \\ y/sd & -0.91 & +1.26 \end{bmatrix}. \tag{7}$$

The correction suggests that Republican activists have, on average, become much more radical in their preferences in both axes relative to the average distribution of electoral preferences. In contrast, Democrat Party activists have on average, become more moderate on the economic axis, and more radical on the social axis.

[23]Details of the 2008 factor model is given in the next section.

Performing the same calculation for non-activists for the parties we find:

$$\begin{bmatrix} 2004 & \text{Rep} & \text{Dem} \\ x & 0.30 & -0.33 \\ y & -0.28 & +0.37 \end{bmatrix}, \quad \begin{bmatrix} 2008 & \text{Rep} & \text{Dem} \\ x & +0.72 & -0.17 \\ y & -0.56 & +0.36 \end{bmatrix}, \tag{8}$$

$$\begin{bmatrix} 2004 & \text{Rep} & \text{Dem} \\ x/sd & 0.40 & -0.43 \\ y/sd & -0.37 & +0.49 \end{bmatrix}, \quad \begin{bmatrix} 2008 & \text{Rep} & \text{Dem} \\ x/sd & 0.80 & -0.19 \\ y/sd & -0.62 & +0.40 \end{bmatrix}. \tag{9}$$

Average voter positions for the two parties have therefore shifted somewhat towards the two opposed quadrants, but not as much as the activist mean positions. The increasing dominance of "Tea Party" social conservatives in the Republican Party, and indeed the fact that the Congressional Republican positions in the recent election of 2010 appeared to be fairly "radical" in the lower right quadrant of the political space, caused some prominent Republicans to consider a change of party allegiance to the Democrats. Shifts in the activist coalitions for the two parties thus cause a transformation of the *partisan cleavage line*.

This phenomenon appears to be a fundamental aspect of US politics: as activists on the "trailing edge"[24] of the cleavage line change party allegiance, then the positions of the two parties shift. This can be interpreted as a clockwise rotation in the political space.

We argue that the fundamental changes in voter choice result not only from changes in the distribution of electoral preferences, but from the shifts in electoral perceptions about the competence and character traits of the political candidates.[25] These perceptions are influenced by the resources that the candidates command. In turn, these changes in perceptions are the consequence of the shifting pattern of activist support for the candidates. The essence of the underlying model is that it attempts to endogenize the resources available to candidates by modeling the contracts they can make with their supporting activists. The activists must solve their own optimization problem by estimating the benefit they receive from their contributions and deciding what resources to make available to their chosen candidate.

In recent years, the importance of activist contributions has increased, and this has enhanced the influence of activist groups.[26] The empirical and formal models

---

[24]These would, on the one hand, be cosmopolitan, socially liberal but economically conservative Republicans (in the upper right quadrant) or on the other hand, populist, socially conservative but economically leftist Democrats (in the lower left quadrant).

[25]Below we present an empirical model that links electoral perceptions to candidate character traits such as moral, caring, knowledgeable, strong, honest, intelligent, optimistic.

[26]Indeed, Herrera et al. (2008) observe that spending by parties in federal campaigns went from 58 million dollars in 1976 to over 1 billion in 2004 in nominal terms. The Center for Responsive Politics estimates that election spending, including candidate spending, went from about $3.5 billion in 2000 to $4.6 billion in 2004 to $5.3 billion in 2008.

that we discuss here provide a reason why electoral politics has become so polarized in the United States. This model of activist polarization accounts for the "disappearing center" in politics (Gelman 2009) and the paradox that poor states seemingly tend to vote Republican while rich states tend to vote Democrat (Abramowitz 2010).[27]

Moreover, this polarization appears to have benefited the wealthy in society and may well account for the increase in inequality in income and wealth distribution that has occurred over the last decade (Hacker and Pierson 2006, 2010; Pierson and Skocpol 2007).

Essentially there is an arms race between candidates over these resources due to a feedback mechanism between politics and economics. As the outcome of the election becomes more important, activists become increasingly aware that the resources they provide have become crucial to election victories, and they become more demanding of their chosen candidates. Because of the offer of resources, candidates are forced to move to more radical positions, and polarization in candidate positions increases, even though there may be little change in the degree of polarization of the electorate.

Over the long run we see two forces at work. First, the continuing "circumferential" realignment induced by a slow rotation of the partisan cleavage line, as activists switch party allegiance. Secondly, a "radial" polarization that occurs at times of political quandary, caused by economic downturn or shocks to the global political economy, inducing a change in the distribution of voter preferred points.

In the next section we present an outline of the model that we use. In Sect. 3 we discuss the effect of the 2008 election followed by Sect. 4 where we discuss the midterm election of 2010 and the ensuing conflict between the Presidency and Republican groups in Congress. The last section makes some brief comments about the viability of the constitutional balance between executive and legislature in the United States.

3 An Outline of the Model

In the standard spatial model, only candidate *positions* matter to voters. However, as Stokes (1963, 1992) has emphasized, the non-policy evaluations, or *valences*, of candidates by the electorate are equally important. In empirical models, a party's *valence* is usually assumed to be independent of the party's position, and adds to the statistical significance of the model. In general, valence reflects the overall degree to which the party is perceived to have shown itself able to govern effectively in the past, or is likely to be able to govern well in the future (Penn 2009).

[27]The recent 2011 census stated that the poorest state was Mississippi, followed by Arkansas, Tennessee, West Virginia, Louisiana, Montana, South Carolina, Kentucky, Alabama and North Carolina. All these are Republican strongholds.

Over the last decade a new literature has developed that considers deterministic or probabilistic voting models including valence or bias towards one or other of the candidates.[28]

Recent work has developed an empirical and formal stochastic electoral model based on multinomial conditional logit methods (MNL). In this model, each political candidate, j, was characterized by an *intrinsic or exogenous valence*, λ_j. This model can be considered to be Downsian, since it was based on a pure spatial model, where the estimates of valence were obtained from the intercepts of the model. It was possible to obtain the conditions for existence of "a local Nash equilibrium" (LNE) under vote maximization for a parallel formal model using the same stochastic assumptions as the MNL empirical model. A LNE is simply a vector of candidate positions with the property that no candidate make a small unilateral move and yet increase utility (or vote share).[29]

The *mean voter theorem* asserts that all candidates should converge to the electoral origin.[30] Empirical analyses of the 2004 and 2008 US presidential elections that are mentioned in this paper have corroborated the earlier work by Enelow and Hinich (1989) and shown, by simulation on the basis of the MNL models, that presidential candidates should move close to the electoral origin. However, the empirical work resulting in Figs. 1–4 also suggests that presidential candidates do not in fact adopt positions close to the electoral center.

This paper offers a more general model of elections that, we suggest, accounts for the difference between the estimates of equilibrium positions and actual candidate positions. The model is based on the assumption that there are various additional kinds of valence. The first is referred to as *activist valence*. When party, or candidate j adopts a policy position z_j, in the policy space, X, then the *activist valence* of the party is denoted $\mu_j(z_j)$. Implicitly we adopt a model originally due to Aldrich (1983). In this model, activists provide crucial resources of time and money to their chosen party, and these resources are dependent on the party position.[31] Each candidate then uses these resources to enhance his image before the electorate, thus affecting his overall valence. In the empirical model we can also estimate two additional aspects of valence which we call *trait valence*[32] and *sociodemographic valence*.[33]

---

[28]Adams (2001), Ansolabehere et al. (2001), Aragones and Palfrey (2002), Banks and Duggan (2005), Groseclose (2001) and McKelvey and Patty (2006).

[29]A Nash equilibrium (NE) is a vector of candidate positions so that no candidate has a unilateral incentive to deviate so as to increase vote share. Thus any NE must be a LNE.

[30]The electoral origin is the mean of the distribution of voter preferred points.

[31]For convenience, it is assumed that $\mu_j(z_j)$ is only dependent on z_j, and not on z_k, $k \neq j$, but this is not a crucial assumption.

[32]See Clarke et al. (2011) and Sanders et al. (2011) for empirical analyses using the voters' perceptions of candidate character *traits*.

[33]Sociodemographic valence refers to the propensity of members of various groups to highly regard one or the other of the candidates.

Table 4 Factor loadings for candidate traits scores 2008

Question	Obama traits	McCain traits
Obama Moral	0.72	−0.01
Obama Caring	0.71	−0.18
Obama Knowledgeable	0.61	−0.07
Obama Strong	0.69	−0.13
Obama Honest	0.68	−0.09
Obama Intelligent	0.61	0.08
Obama Optimistic	0.55	0.00
McCain Moral	−0.09	0.67
McCain Cares	−0.17	0.63
McCain Knowledgeable	−0.02	0.65
McCain Strong	−0.10	0.70
McCain Honest	−0.03	0.63
McCain Intelligent	0.11	0.68
McCain Optimistic	−0.07	0.57
Eigenvalue	3.07	3.00

We assume voter utility is given by the equation

$$\begin{aligned} u_{ij}(x_i, z_j) &= \lambda_j + \mu_j(z_j) + (\theta_j \centerdot \eta_i) + (\alpha_j \centerdot \tau_i) - \beta\|x_i - z_j\|^2 + \epsilon_j \\ &= u^*_{ij}(x_i, z_j) + \epsilon_j. \end{aligned}$$

Here $u^*_{ij}(x_i, z_j)$ is the observable component of utility. The constant term, λ_j, is the *intrinsic or exogenous valence* of party j. The function $\mu_j(z_j)$ is the component of valence generated by activist contributions to candidate j. The term β is a positive constant, called the *spatial parameter*, giving the importance of policy difference defined in terms of a metric induced from the Euclidean norm, $\|\cdot\|$, on X. The vector $\epsilon = (\epsilon_1, \dots, \epsilon_j, \dots, \epsilon_p)$ is the stochastic error, whose multivariate cumulative distribution is the Type 1 extreme value distribution, denoted by Ψ. The terms $(\theta_j \centerdot \eta_i)$ are individual specific scalars giving the influence of sociodemographic characteristics of the voter on vote choice. Similarly the terms $(\alpha_j \centerdot \tau_i)$ model the influence on voter choice of the voter's perceptions of the character traits of the candidates. The term $\mu_j(z_j)$, is j's activist support function. We suggest that we can indirectly estimate $\mu_j(z_j)$ by modeling the election.

The ANES 2008 gave individual perceptions of the character traits of the candidates, in terms of "moral", "caring", "knowledgeable", "strong" and "honest". We performed a factor analysis of these perceptions as shown in Table 4.

ANES 2008 also gave socio-demographic characteristics of respondents by the gender, ethnicity, education, income and class. Table 5 shows the result of the logit models of the electoral response: (1) is a pure spatial, (2) is a spatial model with traits, (3) is a spatial model with socio-demographics while (4) is a full model with

Table 5 Spatial logit models for USA 2008[a]

Variable	(1) Spatial	(2) Sp. & traits	(3) Sp. & Dem.	(4) Full
McCain valence λ	-0.84^{***}	-1.08^{***}	-2.60^{**}	-3.58^{***}
	(7.6)	(8.3)	(2.8)	(3.4)
Spatial β	0.85^{***}	0.78^{***}	0.86^{***}	0.83^{***}
	(14.1)	(10.1)	(12.3)	(10.3)
McCain traits		1.30^{***}		1.36^{***}
		(7.6)		(7.15)
Obama traits		-1.02^{***}		-1.16^{***}
		(6.8)		(6.44)
Age			–0.01	–0.01
			(1.0)	(1.0)
Gender (F)			0.29	0.44
			(1.26)	(0.26)
African American			-4.16^{***}	-3.79^{***}
			(3.78)	(3.08)
Hispanic			–0.55	–0.23
			(1.34)	(0.51)
Education			0.15^{*}	0.22^{***}
			(2.5)	(3.66)
Income			0.03	0.01
			(1.5)	(0.50)
Working Class			-0.54^{*}	-0.70^{**}
			(2.25)	(2.59)
South			0.36	–0.02
			(1.5)	(0.07)
Observations	788			
log likelihood (LL)	–299	–243	–250	–207
AIC	601	494	521	438
BIC	611	513	567	494

$^{*}prob < 0.05$ $^{**}prob < 0.01$ $^{***}prob < 0.001$
[a]Baseline Obama

socio-demographics and traits. Using Table 5 (Model 4) we can estimate vote maximizing equilibria for the model and compare this to the positions of the candidates.

In the theoretical model just proposed, activist valence is affected by party position. As party j's activist support, $\mu_j(z_j)$, increases due to increased contributions to the party in contrast to the support $\mu_k(z_k)$ received by party k, then (in the model) all voters become more likely to support party j over party k.

The problem for each party is that activists are likely to be more extreme than the typical voter. By choosing a policy position to maximize activist support, the party will lose centrist voters. The party must therefore determine the "optimal marginal condition" to maximize vote share. Theoretical results give this as a (first order) *balance condition*. Moreover, because activist support is denominated in terms of time and money, it is reasonable to suppose that the activist function will exhibit decreasing returns. When these activist functions are sufficiently concave, then the vote maximizing model will exhibit a Nash equilibrium.[34]

It is intrinsic to the model that voters evaluate candidates not only in terms of the voters' preferences over intended policies, but also in terms of electoral judgements about the quality of the candidates. These judgements are in turn influenced by the resources that the candidates can raise from their activist supporters.

Grossman and Helpman (1996), in their game theoretic model of activists, consider two distinct motives for interest groups:

> Contributors with an *electoral motive* intend to promote the electoral prospects of preferred candidates, [while] those with an *influence motive* aim to influence the politicians' policy pronouncements.

In the activist model the term $\mu_j(z_j)$ influences every voter and thus contributes to the electoral motive for candidate j. In addition, the candidate must choose a position to balance the electoral and activist support, and thus change the position adopted. This change provides the logic of activist influence.

We argue that the influence of activists on the two candidates can be characterized in terms of activist gradients.

Because each candidate is supported by multiple activists, we extend the activist model by considering a family of potential activists, $\{A_j\}$ for each candidate, j, where each $k \in A_j$ is endowed with a utility function, U_k, which depends on candidate j's position z_j, and the preferred position of the activist. The resources allocated to j by k are denoted $R_{jk}(U_k(z_j))$. Let $\mu_{jk}(R_{jk}(U_k(z_j)))$ denote the effect that activist k has on voters' utility. Note that the activist valence function for j is the same for all voters. With multiple activists, the *total activist valence function* for candidate j is the linear combination $\mu_j(z_j) = \sum_{k\in A_j} \mu_{jk}(R_{jk}(U_k(z_j)))$.

Bargains between the activists supporting candidate j then gives a *contract set* of activist support for candidate j, and this contract set can be used formally to determine the *balance locus*, or set of optimal positions for each candidate. This balance locus can then be used to analyze the pre-election contracts between each candidate and the family of activist support groups. Below we define the balance condition, and argue that suggests that the aggregate activist gradients for each of the two candidates point into opposite quadrants of the policy space.

Consider now the situation where these contracts have been agreed, and each candidate is committed to a set of feasible contracts as outlined in Grossman and Helpman (1996). Suppose further that the activists have provided their resources. Then at the time of the election the effect of this support is incorporated into the empirical estimates of the various exogenous, socio-demographic and trait valences.

[34] A Nash equilibrium is a vector of candidate positions so that no candidate has a unilateral incentive to deviate so as to increase vote share.

Consequently, when we estimate these valences we also estimate the aggregate activist influence. The estimated positions of the candidates can then be regarded as incorporating policy preferences of the activists.

Electoral models where candidates have policy positions, as proposed by Wittman (1977), Calvert (1985), Duggan and Fey (2005), and Duggan (2006) implicitly assume that candidates would be willing to accept defeat because of an adherence to particular policy positions. We argue that it is more plausible that the estimated positions of the candidates are the result of maximizing candidate utility functions that balance the electoral consequences of position-taking with the necessity of obtaining activist resources to contest the election. This calculation requires an estimate of the degree to which these resources will influence the perceptions that the electorate has of the various valences associated with the model.

A recent literature on elections has focused on the effects of campaign expenditure on US election results.[35] Herrera et al. (2008) suggest that electoral volatility forces candidates to spend more, while Ashworth and Bueno de Mesquita (2009) suppose that candidates buy valence so as to increase their election chances. Meirowitz (2008) notes that "candidates and parties spending this money thought that it would influence the election outcome. Downsian models of competition cannot explain how candidates choose spending campaign levels or what factors influence these decision." Meirowitz proxies the choice of expenditure in terms of candidate choice of effort, but his model does not explicitly deal with an endogenous budget constraint.

To apply the above model, suppose there are two dimensions of policy, one economic, and one social. These can be found by factor analysis of survey data as indicated above.

As Fig. 5 indicates, we can represent the conflicting interests or bargains between the two activist groups of supporters for the Republican Party, located at R and C, by a "contract curve." This represents the set of policies that these two groups would prefer their candidate to adopt. It can be shown that this contract curve is a *catenary* whose curvature is determined by the eccentricity of the utility functions of the activist groups. We call this the *Republican contract curve*. The Democrat activist groups may be described by a similar contract curve. (This is the simplest case with just two activist groups for each candidate. This idea can be generalized to many activist groups.)

The first order condition for the candidate positions (z^*_{dem}, z^*_{rep}) to be a Nash equilibrium in the vote share maximizing game is that the party positions satisfy a *balance equation*. This means that, for each party, $j = dem$ or rep, there is a weighted electoral mean for party j, given by the expression

$$z_j^{el} = \sum_i \varpi_{ij} x_i .$$

[35]See Coate (2004) for example. An earlier paper by Groseclose and Snyder (1996) looked at vote buying, but in the legislature.

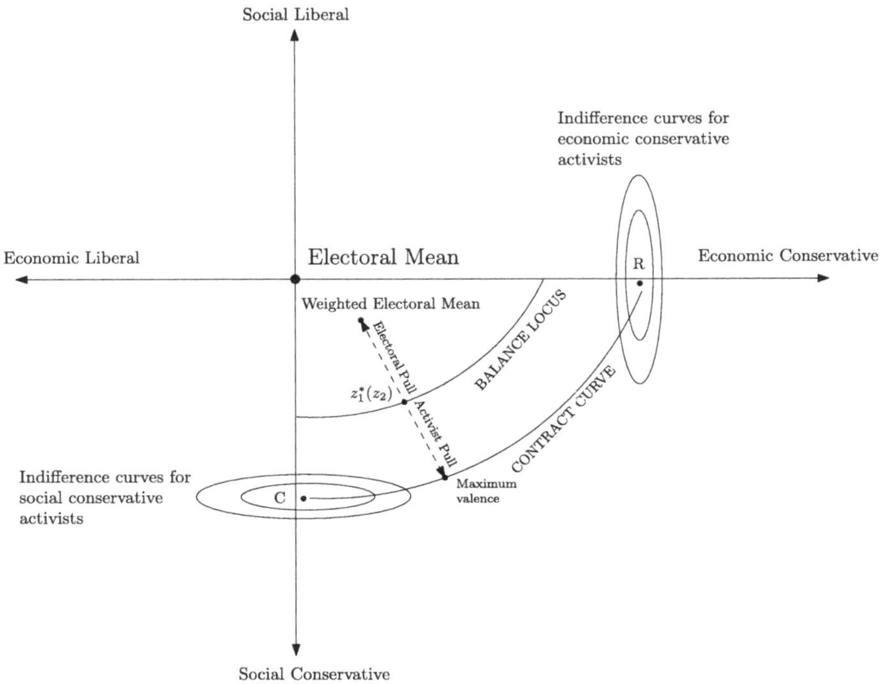

Fig. 5 Optimal Republican position

This is determined by the set of voter preferred points $\{x_i\}$. The coefficients $\{\varpi_{ij}\}$ for candidate j will depend on the position of the other candidate, k. The *balance equation* for each j is then given by:

$$\left[z_j^{el} - z_j^*\right] + \frac{1}{2\beta}\left[\frac{d\mu_j}{dz_j}\bigg|_z\right] = 0.$$

Here we call $[z_j^{el} - z_j^*]$ the *electoral gradient for party j*, since in the absence of activist resources, the equilibrium condition would be given by the condition

$$\left[z_j^{el} - z_j^*\right] = 0.$$

The second term in this expression is called the *activist gradient for party j*. We suggest that this first order condition will guarantee that the vector $\mathbf{z}^* = (z^*_{dem}, z^*_{rep})$ will then be a *pure strategy Nash equilibrium of the vote maximizing political contest*.

In the model for the 2008 election given in Table 5, we used a simulation procedure and found that the equilibrium for the model (4) in Table 5 was given by the vector

$$\mathbf{z}^{el} = \begin{bmatrix} & McCain & Obama \\ x & +0.13 & +0.10 \\ y & -0.12 & -0.07 \end{bmatrix}.$$

However, as discussed above, and shown in Table 3, the estimated candidate positions were given by

$$\mathbf{z}^{*} = \begin{bmatrix} & McCain & Obama \\ x & 0.59 & -0.22 \\ y & -0.37 & +0.75 \end{bmatrix}.$$

Assuming that $\mathbf{z}^*$ reflects the influence of activists, then we obtain an estimate of the activist gradient of

$$\begin{aligned} \frac{1}{2\beta}\left[\frac{d\mu}{d\mathbf{z}}\right] &= \mathbf{z}^* - \mathbf{z}^{el} \\ &= \begin{bmatrix} & McCain & Obama \\ x & 0.59 & -0.22 \\ y & -0.37 & +0.75 \end{bmatrix} - \begin{bmatrix} & McCain & Obama \\ x & +0.13 & +0.10 \\ y & -0.12 & -0.07 \end{bmatrix} \\ &= \begin{bmatrix} & McCain & Obama \\ x & +0.46 & -0.32 \\ y & -0.25 & +0.82 \end{bmatrix}. \end{aligned}$$

The activist mean positions are

$$\mathbf{z}^{act} = \begin{bmatrix} & \text{Rep} & \text{Dem} \\ x & 1.41 & -0.20 \\ y & -0.82 & +1.14 \end{bmatrix}.$$

This suggests that activists pull Republican candidates to the lower right quadrant of the policy space, while Democrat activists pull the Democrat candidate to the upper left of the policy space.

Similar conclusions can be made about Congressional elections. In the following sections we discuss the conflicts that ensue between a Democratic President and Congress.

4 Post 2008 Election

Despite Democratic majorities in both houses of Congress the precise policy outcomes from President Obama's administration were still initially dependent on the degree to which Republicans in the Senate blocked Democratic policies through the use of the filibuster. Early in his administration some of Obama's policy initiatives successfully passed through Congress but only after navigating Republican opposition in the Senate. For example, on January 15, 2009, the Senate voted 52 against and 42 in support of Obama's economic recovery program. On February 6, 2009 an agreement was reached in the Senate to reduce the size of the stimulus bill to $780 billion, in return for the support of three Republican senators. On February 9 the Senate did indeed vote by the required majority of 61 to halt discussion of the stimulus bill, thus blocking a filibuster. A compromise bill of $787 billion, including some tax cuts, was agreed upon by both the House and Senate within a few days; the bill passed the House with 245 Democrats voting in favor and 183 Republicans voting against while the Senate passed it with just 60 votes. The bill was immediately signed by President Obama.

As Obama commented afterwards:

> Now I have to say that given that [the Republicans] were running the show for a pretty long time prior to me getting there, and that their theory was tested pretty thoroughly and its landed us in the situation where we've got over a trillion dollars' worth of debt and the biggest economic crisis since the Great Depression, I think I have a better argument in terms of economic thinking.

On February 26, 2009 Obama proposed a 10 year budget that revised the priorities of the past, with an estimated budget deficit for 2009 at $1.75 trillion (over 12 % of GDP). It included promises to address global warming and to reverse the trend of growing inequality. The $3.6 trillion Federal budget proposal passed the House on April 2, 2009 by 233 to 196, with even "blue dog" conservative Democrats supporting it, but no Republicans.

Obama's social policies even received a modicum of success; on January 22, 2009 a bill against pay discrimination passed the Senate 61 to 36. The House also gave final approval on February 4, by a vote of 290 to 135, to a bill extending health insurance to millions of low-income children. Forty Republicans voted for the bill, and 2 Democrats voted against it. When the bill was signed by President Obama, it was seen as the first of many steps to guarantee health coverage for all Americans but it was not clear that the battle over broader healthcare legislation would take most of 2009.

Obama gained another important victory when the Senate confirmed Sonia Sotomayor as Supreme Court Justice on August 6, 2009, by a vote of 68 to 31. She is the first Hispanic and the third woman to serve on the Court. Similarly, Obama nominated another woman, Elena Kagan, to the high court and she was confirmed almost exactly one year after Sotomayor on August 7, 2010 by a vote of 63 to 37. Though adding two left-leaning female justices to the court has increased the number of women on the Supreme Court to an all time high of 3, it has not fundamentally changed the ideological makeup of the current court which still regularly splits 5 to 4 in favor of more right-leaning rulings.

In October, 2009, one group identifying as populist Republicans, the "Tea Party" activists opposed Obama's policies on health care so much that they began lining up against the centrist Governor Charlie Crist in the GOP Senate primary. Ultimately, Crist was forced to become an Independent and a Tea Party darling, Marco Rubio, was nominated as the GOP candidate for the Florida Senate seat (and ultimately won the seat, beating Crist handily). Similarly, on November 1, 2009 the centrist

Republican candidate, Dede Scozzafava, decided to drop out of the special election in New York's 23rd congressional district and endorse the Democrat candidate, Bill Owens. Owens won the election in a district that had been Republican since 1872.

As the Healthcare debate heated up over summer and fall of 2009 it became clear that Republicans were intending to continue utilize their blocking coalition as long as possible to stymie Obama and the Democrats. Interestingly, some Democrats contributed to this opposition as well; in the health bill vote in the House in early November 2009, 219 Democrats with 1 Republican voted for the bill, while 176 Republicans and 39 "Blue Dog" Democrats voted against.[36] By December 19, Senator Bernie Sanders of Vermont, an independent who caucuses with the Democrats, as well as Democrat Senators Ben Nelson and Sherrod Brown, had agreed to a compromise bill. This brought the size of the coalition to the critical size of 60 votes, sufficient to force a decision in the Senate.[37] Finally on Christmas Eve, 2009, the health bill passed in the Senate, again by 60 votes with 39 Republicans opposed. However, the victory by Republican Scott Brown in the special Senate election in Massachusetts on January 19 deprived the Democrats of the 60 seat majority required to push through the legislation. On February 25, 2010, an attempt to reach a bipartisan compromise failed, and there was talk of using a manoeuvre known as "reconciliation" to force though a health bill using simple majority rule.[38] Finally, on March 25, after strenuous efforts by President Obama and House speaker, Nancy Pelosi, the House voted 220–207 to send a health care bill to the President. Republicans voted unanimously against the legislation, joined by 33 dissident Democrats. The Senate passed the bill by simple majority of 56 to 43, as required under reconciliation and the President signed a draft of the bill, the "Patient Protection and Affordable Care Act," on March 23, 2010 and an updated version of the bill on March 30, 2010.[39]

While it seemed that "gridlock" ensued over the health care legislation, several other major pieces of legislation passed with far less opposition. On February 22, 2010 and again on March 17, 2010 the Senate voted 62–30 and 68–29 respectively to implement two multi-billion-dollar "jobs creation" programs. Even though the vote to end debate on the Financial Regulation bill failed to obtain the required supra-majority on May 19, 2010, it eventually passed the Senate. On July 15, 2010 the Senate voted 60–39 for the Dodd–Frank Wall Street Reform and Consumer Protection Act, and this was signed into law by President Obama on July 21.

---

[36]On Saturday, November 21, the Senate voted 60 to 40, along partisan lines, to move to the final discussion on the health care bill.

[37]Cloture is a motion aimed at bringing debate to an end. It originally required a two-thirds majority, but since 1975 has required a super-majority of 60.

[38]Reconciliation is a measure whereby a bill can pass the Senate with a simple majority; the legislation must be shown to be budget neutral over a ten-year span in accordance with the Byrd rule.

[39]Contrary to expectations the Supreme Court upheld the constitutionality of the health care act by 5 to 4 on June 28, 2012.

Nearing the end of the 111th Congress in November, 2010, there remained four major bills to put through Congress: A Deficit Reduction Act, an Expanded Trade and Export Act, a Comprehensive Immigration Act, and an Energy Independence and Climate Change Act. Despite passage by the House on June 26, 2009, the Waxman-Markey climate change bill, formally called the American Clean Energy and Security Act (ACES), never reached action in the Senate. On July 22, 2010, the effort to push forward with the Climate Change Act collapsed due to Republican opposition to a carbon tax. A major problem also remained with regard to the Bush tax cuts of 2001 and 2003, which were due to expire at the end of 2010. If these bills, and the resolution of the tax cuts, were to prove impossible to enact because of Republican opposition, the electorate could blame either party or simply oppose any incumbent due to their lack of efficacy at passing legislation.

Given these uncertainties surrounding policy choices in the legislature, it is hardly surprising that voters in the United States doubt that government can be effective. Part of the problem would appear to be the degree of political polarization that results from the power of interest groups located in the opposed quadrants of the policy space.

4.1 Impact of the 'Citizens United' Decision in 2010

As a result of the Supreme Court decision, *Citizens United v. Federal Election Commission*, on January 21, 2010, which removed limits on campaign contributions, it is clear that the importance of activist contributions will only increase. In the November, 2010 mid-term election large amounts of money were funneled through nonprofit advocacy groups that can accept unlimited donations and are not required to disclose their donors. As of November 1, 2010, it was estimated that these groups had spent $280 million, 60 % from undisclosed donors. Three "super PAC" Republican activist groups, the US Chamber of Commerce, American Crossroads and the American Action Committee had spent $32.8 million, $26.6 million and $17 million respectively.[40]

In his State of the Union address in late January, President Obama said the court had "reversed a century of law that I believe will open the floodgates for special interests—including foreign corporations—to spend without limit in our elections."[41] Dworkin (2006) later called the Supreme Court decision "an unprincipled political act with terrible consequences for the nation."

In July, 2010, the Federal Election Commission had approved the creation of two "independent" campaign committees, one each from the left and right, expressly designed to take advantage of the lack of spending limits. One committee was set

[40]The pro-Democrat America's Families First Action Committee raised $7.1 million.

[41]Supreme Court Justice Samuel Alito, appointed by George W. Bush, broke from traditional judicial decorum at State of the Union speeches to shake his head in disagreement with the President, reportedly muttering the words "that's not true."

up by the Club for Growth, the conservative advocate for low taxes and less government. The other, called Commonsense Ten, with close ties to the Democrats, will raise money from individuals, corporations and unions. Both groups will be able to spend unlimited amounts, thanks to the *Citizens United* decision. A Democrat effort to impose new campaign finance regulations before the November congressional election was defeated on July 27 when all 41 Senate Republicans blocked a vote on a bill that would force special interest groups to disclose their donors when purchasing political advertisements. A second attempt at cloture on the bill failed by 59 to 39 in the Senate on September 23.

Former Bush advisors, Karl Rove and Ed Gillespie, first formed American Crossroads as a 527 independent-expenditure-only committee, but was required to disclose donors. They then formed Crossroads Grassroots Policy Strategies (GPS) as a 501(c)(4) social welfare nonprofit. This means it does not need to disclose donors, but is not supposed to be used for political purposes. GPS spent $17 million. The Chamber of Commerce is a 501(c)(6) nonprofit, but corporations that donate to the Chamber must disclose these contributions in their tax filings. These corporations include Dow Chemical, Goldman Sachs, Prudential Financial. The most highly publicized was a singular donation in excess of $1 million from Rupert Murdoch's News Corporation.

In addition to the external activist groups, South Carolina Senator, Jim DeMint, used the Senate Conservatives Fund as a PAC to funnel about $1 million to many of the most right-wing of the Tea Party candidates. Indeed, a key element of the successful Republican campaign was that these activist bodies were able to target House and Senate races where incumbent Democrats were weak.

In the 2010 election cycle total campaign spending was about $4 billion, with Republican spending somewhat higher than total Democrat spending. The extremely high level of expenditure (especially for a midterm election) is of particular interest because there is evidence that the policy positions of activists on the social axis have become more polarized over the last forty years (Layman et al. 2010). This polarization appears to have benefited the wealthy in society and may well account for the increase the inequality in income and wealth distribution that has occurred (Hacker and Pierson 2006, 2010; Pierson and Skocpol 2007; Reich 2010).

5 Implications of the 2010 Election

In the midterm elections the electorate blamed incumbents, particularly Democrats, for their economic woes. In November, 2010, the Democrats lost 63 seats in the House, leading to a Republican majority of 242 to 192. In the Senate the Democrats lost 6 seats but retained a majority of 51 to 46 (with 3 Independents).[42] Many of

[42]This was the backlash predicted by Bunch (2010). However, the Democrat losses may be due to the spending pattern. The *New York Times* analysis suggested that in 21 House districts where groups supporting Republican candidates spent about $2 million, they won 12.

the newly elected members of Congress received the backing of the Tea Party and vocally subscribed to extreme policy stances like abolishing the Federal Reserve, unemployment benefits, and even income taxes. Further, preliminary demographic studies of the Tea Party indicate that they are predominantly older, middle class suburban and rural white Americans.[43] This demographic make-up leads one to postulate that the Tea Party is a representation of a populist movement supported primarily by elites in the South and West. Although tea party supporters are opposed to deficit spending, they generally are supportive of social security and medicare, and want to reduce the deficit by cutting other programs. Perhaps most striking about the Tea Party is the immediate impact they had on Congress itself with the Republican House leadership creating a special leadership post for a Representative from the Tea Party wing.

Because of the plurality nature of the US electoral system, parties have to build a winning coalition of mobilized disaffected activists and current party activists Many of the Tea Party activists see themselves as conservative independents that are opposed to big business. This is despite the fact that large corporations and wealthy individuals heavily funded many of the Tea Party candidates campaigns. Even before the 112th Congress entered session the Republican Party stood up for the wealthy benefactors by insisting on blocking all legislation during the lame duck session until the wealthiest two percent of Americans received the same extension on their tax cuts that the other 98 percent were set to receive. This Republican measure included blocking discussion on repealing the "Don't Ask, Don't Tell" legislation, immigration reform legislation, a nuclear arms treaty and even legislation allocating funds to provide healthcare to September 11, 2001 first responders.

In an effort to close his career with parting advice about compromise, retiring Connecticut Senator Chris Dodd gave his valedictory speech on the Senate floor on November 30, 2010 with remarks including the following:

> From the moment of our founding, America has been engaged in an eternal and often pitched partisan debate. That's no weakness. In fact, it is at the core of our strength as a democracy, and success as a nation. Political bipartisanship is a goal, not a process. You don't begin the debate with bipartisanship—you arrive there. And you can do so only when determined partisans create consensus—and thus bipartisanship. In the end, the difference between a partisan brawl and a passionate, but ultimately productive, debate rests on the personal relationships between Senators.

Another elder statesman in the Senate, Indiana's Richard Lugar, clearly felt the same way as Senator Dodd after the 2010 election as he defied the Republican Party over their various demands. Senator Lugar has said that the environment in Washington was the most polarized he had seen since joining the Senate in 1977. John C. Danforth, the former Republican senator from Missouri, remarked that

[43]Skocpol and Williamson (2010) have been collecting survey and interview data on the Tea Party since its emergence and although their findings are only preliminary, all indications are that Tea Party members are a very specific demographic sub-group with traditional populist concerns. See also Rasmussen and Schoen (2010).

> If Dick Lugar, having served five terms in the US Senate and being the most respected person in the Senate and the leading authority on foreign policy, is seriously challenged by anybody in the Republican Party, we have gone so far overboard that we are beyond redemption.

In May of 2012 Senator Lugar lost a primary election to Tea Party candidate Richard Mourdock. Lugar was the first six-term Senator to lose a primarly election in 60 years.

Despite increased polarization, President Obama continued to press for any legislative accomplishment within reach, he eventually struck a deal to allow the tax cuts to be extended for all Americans (in exchange for an extension of unemployment benefits) despite the fact that even the most positive economic forecasts do not predict that these tax cuts to the wealthy will bring unemployment down by more than 0.1 percent over the two year lifespan of the tax cut extension. This compromise angered many in the liberal wings of Democratic Party as they saw compromise as a betrayal of President Obama's progressive values. In the wake of persistent attack by several prominent liberal Democrats, Obama invited former President Bill Clinton to give a White House press conference in support of the compromise. Involving the former President in this way can be seen as either an act of desperation or an attempt by the administration to harken back to the 1990's (or earlier) when compromise was an acceptable political tactic.[44]

On Monday December 13, 2010 the Republican bargaining ploy worked. The Senate voted to halt debate on the tax cut bill. Other provisions of the $858 billion bill would extend unemployment insurance benefits and grant tax breaks for schoolteachers, mass transit commuting expenses and landowners who invest in conservation techniques. The compromise bill overwhelmingly passed the Senate on December 15 by a vote of 81 to 19. Despite accusations by House Speaker, Nancy Pelosi, that Republicans were forcing Democrats "to pay a king's ransom in order to help the middle class" at midnight on December 16 the measure passed with 139 Democrats and 138 Republicans in favor and 112 Democrats and 36 Republicans opposed. President Obama signed the bill into law the next day.

After this initial compromise was struck, the logjam seemed to have broken as Congress began debate on repealing "Don't Ask, Don't Tell," on the passage of the nuclear arms treaty, and on temporary measures to continue funding the federal government into 2011. This step toward compromise and productivity irked Senators Jon Kyl (Republican from Arizona) and Jim DeMint (Republican from South Carolina) who criticized Majority Leader Harry Reid (Democrat from Nevada) for "disrespecting" the institution and the Christmas holiday by putting so much work on the Congressional docket that Senators might need to return to work during the week between Christmas and New Year. These statements by Senators Kyl and DeMint provide a stark reminder of the roadblocks to compromise in activist driven politics. House and Senate Republicans derailed a $1.2 trillion spending measure put forward by Senate Democrats, and promised to use their majority in the new House to

[44] It is worth noting that the Founding Fathers repeatedly cited the need for compromise as one of the greatest strengths of the US political system.

shrink government. On December 21 Congress did approve a temporary spending bill up until March 2011.

On December 18, the "Dream Act" to allow illegal immigrant students to become citizens failed on a Senate vote of 55–41, but the Senate did vote 65 to 31 to repeal the "Don't Ask, Don't Tell" legislation, making it possible for gays to serve openly in the military. The House had previously approved this repeal by 250 to 175.

On December 20, the Senate voted 59 to 37 to reject an amendment to the new arms control treaty, New Start, with Russia. The amendment would have killed the treaty because any change to the text would have required the United States and Russia to renegotiate the treaty. Two days later the Senate voted 71 to 26 for the treaty. This treaty was seen as the most tangible foreign policy achievement of President Obama's administration. Thirteen Republicans joined a unanimous Democratic caucus to vote in favor, exceeding the two-thirds majority required by the Constitution.

As Obama said:

> I think it's fair to say that this has been the most productive post-election period we've had in decades, and it comes on the heels of the most productive two years that we've had in generations. If there's any lesson to draw from these past few weeks, it's that we are not doomed to endless gridlock. We've shown in the wake of the November elections that we have the capacity not only to make progress, but to make progress together.

However, the Democrats in Congress increasingly represent the richest and the poorest constituencies, while the Republican Party is no longer the party of the wealthy but of the disillusioned middle class and the ultra-wealthy. Given the results of the 2010 elections, it is no surprise that a highly divided Congress and increasingly activist driven politics has resulted in escalating partisan conflict in the run up to the 2012 election.

5.1 Gridlock in the 112th Congress

One of the first moves by the House in the 112th Congress was to vote, on January 19, 2011, to repeal the Health Care Bill by a margin of 245 to 189. However, this repeal was not be able to pass the Democrat majority in the Senate and would obviously not be signed by President Obama.

In early April, 2011 a shutdown of the government was only just averted by a compromise that cut the budget by $38 billion. After much wrangling, the House passed legislation on April 14, to finance the federal government for the rest of the fiscal year. The final House vote was 260 to 167, with 59 members of the House Republican majority and more than half the Democratic minority voting against the legislation. The bill also passed the Senate, 81 to 19, again with many Republicans opposed. On April 15, the House voted 235 to 193 to approve the fiscal blueprint for 2012, drafted by Representative Paul D. Ryan, Republican of Wisconsin and chairman of the Budget Committee. The blueprint proposed a cut in expenditure of $5.8 trillion over the next decade.

By July, it seemed that the political system was again in gridlock with the parties completely polarized over the question of the US public debt. The debt ceiling was at \$14.3 trillion and the current US Treasury debt was \$14.29 trillion.[45] Republicans demanded a reduction in spending and the maintenance of tax cuts, while Democrats basically wanted the opposite, continued spending on social programs and tax increases on certain segments of the population.

The House on Friday July 29, finally approved a plan for a short-term increase in the debt ceiling and cuts in spending. The vote was 218–210, with 22 Republicans unwilling to support the efforts by House Speaker, John A. Boehner, to get a bill approved. This ended a week of intense fighting among Republicans. The game then shifted to the Senate which tabled the House proposal. On August 1 the House of Representatives passed a compromise bill, 269–161, supported by Democrats, increasing the debt ceiling by \$400 billion, with an additional \$500 billion through February, with spending caps of over \$900 billion. A newly designed joint committee was vested with the responsibility of determining future cuts of over \$1 trillion. The Senate passed the bill 74–26 on August 2 with 19 Republicans, and 6 Democrats and one independent voting against. President Obama immediately signed the bill into law. Despite the eventual compromise on the debt ceiling, on August 5, 2011 Standard and Poor, the credit rating agency, downgraded US Federal debt from AAA to AA+, and the Dow industrial index dropped about 20 % in the following days. However, demand for US Treasury Bonds increased.

On September 13, President Obama acted on the economic turmoil set off by the Debt Ceiling debate, Standard and Poor downgrade and continuing European debt crisis by sending a \$447 billion jobs bill to Congress. Initial reaction from Republicans indicated a willingness to accept some measures of the bill, coupled with an insistence on keeping tax cuts for the wealthiest and resistance to closing corporate loopholes. On November 21, however, the Joint Committee to reduce the deficit announced that it could not come to any agreement, but declared: "We remain hopeful that Congress can build on this committee's work and can find a way to tackle this issue in a way that works for the American people and our economy." The Dow closed down about 2 % for the day.

The debate over the jobs bill highlights the fact that, despite media attention to the contrary, Obama has attempted to attract and retain pro-business social liberals with his response to the economic crisis. In addition to naming General Electric CEO Jeffrey Immelt as Chairman of the President's Council on Jobs and Competitiveness, the President's second Chief of staff was former Commerce secretary and bank executive William Daley. These steps, along with his massive budget proposals providing relief to banks and other businesses in order to address the economic down-turn, has angered many in populist circles. Meanwhile, insistence on closing

[45]Of this \$6.2 trillion is held by the US government, \$2.7 trillion in the Social Security Trust Fund, \$1.9 trillion in other government agencies and \$1.6 trillion in the Federal Reserve. China and Hong Kong hold \$1.3 trillion, other countries hold \$3.2 trillion, the remaining \$3.6 trillion is held by pension funds etc.

corporate tax loopholes and the spectre of increased financial regulation, has eroded business support for the President.

This lack of support in both the populist and cosmopolitan quadrants leaves the President and his party vulnerable to attacks by traditionally conservative Republicans as well as to the more populist demands of the Tea Party. As a result of persistently high unemployment rates, populist anger has spiked and it is and even spawned a second, distinctly liberal-minded populist group, the "Occupy Wall Street" protesters. It is possible that the Republican Party will gain votes from the blue-collar voters who are suffering the most from the economic collapse. Should the Republican party cater to the traditional populist demands expressed by those in the Tea Party, they will be hearkening back to an era of old-style populism as expressed by William Jennings Bryan: anti-Wall Street, anti-banking, anti-Detroit, anti-immigration, and pro-evangelical religion. This will result in a party realignment to a situation where the socially liberal and economically conservative "cosmopolitan" Democrats are opposed to populist Republicans. That is, the Republican Party may begin to move to the lower left quadrant of the policy space, while some business interests in the upper right quadrant will switch to the Democrats.[46] Over the long term, the partisan cleavage line may rotate further in a clockwise direction.

6 Conclusion and 2012

Money has made US politics irrational. With legal barriers falling and money playing an increasingly large role in recent elections, this irrationality and non-convergence to the electoral center is likely to persist. The 2012 election cycle highlights the role of money and non-convergence. Early Republican Presidential frontrunners included Tea Party darlings Representative Michele Bachman, Representative Ron Paul, and Governor Rick Perry along with seasoned conservative ideologues former Senator Rick Santorum and former Speaker of the House Newt Gingrich. Comparing himself to the other Republican candidates, Former Governor Mitt Romney initially admitted to seeking a more centrist route to the nomination, but facing activist money such as the PAC "Make Us Great Again" which supported Rick Perry to the tune of $55 million and billionaire Sheldon Adelson who provided tens of millions in support of Newt Gingrich, Romney was forced to adopt increasingly conservative policy positions. By the end of the primary campaign, some Republican strategists were publicly declaring concern that Governor Romney had taken such radically conservative positions in the primaries that it might be hard for him to appeal to moderate voters in the general election. All the while, new legal precedent allowed the Federal Election Commission to turn a blind eye to the creation of candidate Super PACs, such as "Make Us Great Again" for Republican

[46]For example, on April 28, 2010 Arlen Specter, the Senator from Pennsylvania, shifted his allegiance from the Republican Party to the Democrats.

Rick Perry and "Restore Our Future" for Republican Mitt Romney. Even President Obama's PAC "Priorities USA" plans to raise $100 million for the 2012 election.

Utilizing the model we have presented, we contrast the current situation with the 1960s. After Kennedy was elected President in 1960 (by a very narrow margin of victory against Nixon), he delayed sending a Civil Rights Bill to Congress, precisely because of the possible effect on the South (Branch 1998). To push the Civil Rights Act through in 1964, Johnson effectively created, with Hubert Humphrey's support, an unstable coalition of liberal northern Democrats and moderate Republicans, with sufficient votes in the Senate to effect 'cloture', to block the southern Democratic filibusters.[47] This was the first time since Reconstruction that the Southern veto was overwhelmed. The danger for Johnson in the election of 1964 was that a Republican candidate could make use of the fact of Republican party support for civil rights to attract disaffected social liberals. Traditional Republican Party activists were thus in an electoral dilemma, but resolved it by choosing the southern social conservative, Goldwater. The present gridlock between the legislative and executive branchs is more extreme than in 1964 because there are now no moderate Republicans to join the social-liberal coalition. The electoral pivot line has rotated so that all Republicans are located in the socially conservative half of the policy space. In addition money has become more important and has made US politics "irrational". With money playing an increasingly large role in recent elections, this electoral irrationality and non-convergence to the electoral center is likely to persist. Moreover, powerful activist groups in the cosmopolitan and populist sectors have the potential to draw in politicians and shift the partisan cleavage line between parties. Were it not for the resources the activist groups provide it would be irrational for politicians to move toward these activist bases. Simply put, activists influence politicians so they adopt policies that would be electorally irrational, were it not for money.

Popper (2008) argued that plurality electoral systems, otherwise known as "first past the post" were to be preferred to proportional electoral systems because they gave voters a clear choice. As we have seen, the constitutional structure of the US polity, coupled with the influence of money has recently tended to gridlock. Although there is the appearance of choice for the voters, Government has been unable to come to grips with the severe quandaries briefly mentioned in the introduction. The absence of effective choice by the US increases uncertainty in policymaking thus creating a difficult situation for business and international leaders attempting to make long-term investments and policy decisions. Indeed, Posner and Vermeule (2011) argue that the United States needs to reconsider its constitutional separation of powers in the presence of such gridlock and uncertainty.

On the other hand, the recent European debt crisis has led to the fall of governments in the multiparty systems of Ireland (February, 2011) Finland (2011), Portugal (June 2011), Denmark (September, 2011), Slovakia (October 2011), Greece, Italy and Spain (November 2011). The model presented here and developed further

---

[47]Caro (2012: 568) describes the drama of the cloture vote of Jun 10, 1964 after a filibuster of 57 days with 27 Republicans and 44 Democrats voting aye. The bill passed on June 19 by 73 to 27. The voting Rights Act of 1965 passed again after a long fight by Johnston against Congress.

in Schofield and Gallego (2012) suggests that in fragmented or multiparty systems, based on proportional representation, small parties will adopt radical policies far from the electoral center, thus inducing coalition instability. This phenomenon coupled with a fragile fiscal system based on the euro also has created difficulties in dealing effectively with the fall-out from the recession of 2008–2009. At the time of writing this euro crisis has not been resolved.

A general perspective on recent events is provided by Lind (2012). He suggests that in order to maintain a post World War II international economic system to facilitate growth and oppose the Soviet Union the US maintained its hegemonic power by its willingness to accept mercantilistic trade strategies by its allies Germany, Japan. In the first 30 years until the oil crisis of the 1970's this system could be maintained without great cost. Indeed economic growth in the US was maintained. Although Nixon tried to limit this mercantilism by coming of the gold standard in 1973, Finance capital exerted pressure to sustain this system of US dominance. After the fall of the Soviet Union, it seemed attractive to allow China to institute trade mercantilism, allowing it to grow very rapidly. As Keynes saw back in 1945, such a system is inherently unstable. The resulting "globalization" (and increased trade flows) has led to the massive US trade deficits of the last thirty or forty years, and the loss of much of the manufacturing capacity of the US. While increased trade has contributed to an increase in global GDP, it has forced down unskilled wage rates in the US. It is for this reason that the US has become such an unequal economy (Stiglitz 2012), making the conflict between labor and capital more intense. High artificial savings by China and its willingness to fund US debt (both necessary components of its mercantilism) disguised the costs to the US, but also provided the financial basis for the extreme form of speculation that came to dominate the market. Capital benefited from globalization and was able to fund political support for the maintenance of this hegemonic system. Stiglitz adds that the current mode of oligopoly rent seeking in the US is consistent with the external pattern of hegemony and sustains both inequality and underprovision of social public goods such as innovation. Since the most important global public good is prevention of climate change, the severe costs of this potentially unstable political economic system will burden future generations.[48]

Acknowledgements This paper is based on work supported by NSF grant #0715929.

References

Abramowitz A (2010) The disappearing center. Yale University Press, New Haven

Abramowitz A, Saunders A (2005) Why can't we get along: the reality of polarized America. Forum 3(2):1–21. Article 1

[48] Israel (2012) has pointed out that the modern period since 1700 witnessed a conflict between a Radical Enlightenment espoused by Condorcet, Jefferson and Paine, in support of reason and equality and opposed to monarchy and hierarchical hegemony, and the compromising Moderate Enlightenment of Hamilton and Burke.

Acemoglu D, Robinson J (2008) Persistence of power, elites, and institutions. Am Econ Rev 98:267–293
Adams J (2001) Party competition and responsible party government. University of Michigan Press, Ann Arbor
Aldrich JH (1983) A Downsian spatial model with party activists. Am Polit Sci Rev 77(4):974–990
Allen FL (1994) Since yesterday: the 1930's in America. Borgo, New York
Alpert D, Hockett R, Roubini N (2011). The way forward. The new America foundation. www.newamerica.net
American national election studies. 2004, 2008
Ansolabehere S, Snyder JM, Stewart C (2001) Candidate positions in congressional elections. Am J Polit Sci 45:136–159
Aragones E, Palfrey T (2002) Mixed equilibrium in a Downsian model with a favored candidate. J Econ Theory 103:131–161
Ashworth S, Bueno de Mesquita E (2009) Elections with platform and valence competition. Games Econ Behav 67:191–216
Banks J, Duggan J (2005) Probabilistic voting in the spatial model of elections: the theory of office motivated candidates. In: Austen-Smith D, Duggan J (eds) Social choice and strategic decisions: essays in honor of Jeffrey Banks. Springer, Heidelberg
Branch T (1998) Pillar of fire. Simon and Schuster, New York
Buchanan P (2011) Suicide of a superpower. St. Matins Press, New York
Bunch W (2010) Backlash. Harper, New York
Calvert RL (1985) Robustness of the multidimensional voting model: candidates, motivations, uncertainty and convergence. Am J Polit Sci 29:69–85
Caro RA (2012) The passage of power. Knopf, New York
Chace J (2004) 1912: Wilson, Roosevelt, Taft and Debs. Simon and Schuster, New York
Clarke HD, Kornberg A, Scotto TJ (2009) Making political choices. Toronto University Press, Toronto
Clarke HD, Kornberg A, Scotto T, Reifler J, Sanders D, Stewart M, Whiteley P (2011) Yes we can! Valence politics and electoral choice in America 2008. Elect Stud 30:450–461
Clinton W (2011) Back to work. Knopf, New York
Coate S (2004) Political competition with campaign contributions and informative advertising. J Eur Econ Assoc 2:772–804
Crick F (1995) The astonishing hypothesis. Scribner, New York
Dawkins R (2011) The magic of reality. Free Press, New York
Downs A (1957) An economic theory of democracy. Harper and Row, New York
Duggan J (2006) Candidate objectives and electoral equilibrium. In: Weingast BR, Wittman D (eds) The Oxford handbook of political economy. Oxford University Press, Oxford
Duggan J, Fey M (2005) Electoral competition with policy-motivated candidates. Games Econ Behav 51:490–522
Dworkin R (2006) Is democracy possible here? Princeton University Press, Princeton
Enelow JM, Hinich M (1989) The location of American presidential candidates. Math Comput Model 12:417–435
Erikson RS, Romero DW (1990) Candidate equilibrium and the behavioral model of the vote. Am Polit Sci Rev 84:1103–1126
Field AJ (2003) The most technologically progressive decade of the century. Am Econ Rev 93:1399–1414
Fiorina M, Abrams SJ (2009) Disconnect: the breakdown of representation in American politics. University of Oklahoma Press, Norman
Fiorina M, Abrams SJ, Pope JC (2005) Culture war?: The myth of a polarized America. Pearson Longman, New York
Fisher I (1933) The debt-deflation theory of great depressions. Econometrica 1:337–357
Friedman T, Mandelbaum M (2011) That used to be us. Farrar, Straus and Giroux, New York
Galbraith JK (2008) The predator state. Free Press, New York
Gelman A (2009) Red state, blue state. Rich state, poor state. Princeton University Press, Princeton

Gould LL (2008) Four hats in the ring. University of Kansas Press, Lawrence
Graham J, Haidt J, Nosek B (2009) Liberals and conservatives rely on different moral foundations. J Pers Soc Psychol 96:1029–1046
Groseclose T (2001) A model of candidate location when one candidate has a valence advantage. Am J Polit Sci 45(4):862–886
Groseclose T, Snyder J (1996) Buying supermajorities. Am J Polit Sci 90:303–315
Grossman GM, Helpman E (1996) Electoral competition and special interest politics. Rev Econ Stud 63:265–286
Hacker JS, Pierson P (2006) Center: the republican revolution and the erosion of American democracy. Yale University Press, New Haven
Hacker JS, Pierson P (2010) Politics: how Washington made the rich richer—and turned its back on the middle class. Simon and Schuster, New York
Harvey D (2011) The enigma of capital and the crises of capitalism. Oxford University Press, Oxford
Herrera H, Levine D, Martinelli C (2008) Policy platforms, campaign spending and voter participation. J Public Econ 92:501–513
Hitchens C (2007) God is not great. Twelve, New York
Hotelling H (1929) Stability in competition. Econ J 39:41–57
Israel J (2012) Democratic enlightenment. Oxford University Press, Oxford
Kennedy DM (1999) Freedom from fear. Oxford University Press, Oxford
Keynes JM (1930a) A treatise on money. In: The pure theory of money, vol 1. Macmillan, London. Reprinted in Keynes, Collected Writings, vol 5
Keynes JM (1930b) A treatise on money. In: The applied theory of money, vol 2. Macmillan, London. Reprinted in Keynes, Collected Writings, vol 6
Keynes JM (1933) National self-sufficiency. Yale Rev 26:755–769
Keynes JM (1936) The general theory of employment, interest and money. Macmillan, London
Kramnick I (1990) Republicanism and bourgeois radicalism. Cornell University Press, Ithaca
Kramnick I (1992 [1968]) Bolingbroke and his circle. Cornell University Press, Ithaca
Layman GC et al (2010) Party polarization, party commitment and conflict extension among American party activists. Am Polit Sci Rev 104:324–346
Lessig L (2011) Republic, lost. Twelve, New York
Lind M (2012) Land of promise. Harper, New York
Livingston J (2011) Against thrift. Basic, New York
Madison J (1999 [1787]) Federalist X. In: Rakove J (ed) Madison: writings. Library Classics, New York
McCarty N, Poole K, Rosenthal H (2006) Polarized America. MIT Press, Cambridge
McKelvey RD, Patty J (2006) A theory of voting in large elections. Games Econ Behav 57:155–180
Meirowitz A (2008) Electoral contests, incumbency advantages and campaign finance. J Polit 70:681–699
Micklethwaite J, Wooldridge A (2004) The right nation. Penguin, New York
Milanovic B (2010) The haves and the have nots. Basic, New York
Miller G, Schofield N (2003) Activists and partisan realignment in the US. Am Polit Sci Rev 97:245–260
Minsky H (1986) Stabilizing an unstable economy. Yale University Press, New Haven
Mondak JJ, Hibbing MV, Canache D, Seligson MA (2010) Personality and civic engagement: an integrative framework for the study of trait effects on political behavior. Am Polit Sci Rev 104:85–110
Morgenson G, Rosner J (2011) Reckless endangerment. Holt, New York
Noah T (2012) The great divergence. Bloomsbury Press, New York
Olson M (1982) The rise and decline of nations. Yale University Press, New Haven
Patty J, Snyder JM, Ting M (2009) Two's company, three's an equilibrium: strategic voting and multicandidate elections. Q J Polit Sci 4:251–278
Penn E (2009) A model of far-sighted voting. Am J Polit Sci 53:36–54

Pierson P, Skocpol T (eds) (2007) The transformation of American politics: activist government and the rise of conservatism. Princeton University Press, Princeton
Popper K (1945) The open society and its enemies. Routledge and Kegan Paul, London
Popper K (2008) The open society and its enemies revisited. Economist 307:19–22
Posner EA, Vermeule A (2011) The executive unbound. Oxford University Press, Oxford
Putnam RD, Campbell DE (2010) American grace: how religion divides and unites us. Simon and Schuster, New York
Rachman G (2011) Zero-sum future. Simon and Schuster, New York
Rasmussen S, Schoen D (2010) Mad as hell: how the tea party movement is fundamentally remaking our two-party system. Harper, New York
Reich RB (2010) Aftershock: the next economy and America's future. Knopf, New York
Sachs JD (2011) The price of civilization: reawakening American virtue and prosperity. Random House, New York
Sanders D, Clarke HD, Stewart MC, Whiteley P (2011) Downs, stokes and the dynamics of electoral choice. Br J Polit Sci 41:287–314
Schofield N (2007) The mean voter theorem: necessary and sufficient conditions for convergent equilibrium. Rev Econ Stud 74(3):965–980
Schofield N, Gallego M (2012) Leadership or chaos. Springer, Berlin
Schofield N, Miller G (2007) Elections and activist coalitions in the US. Am J Polit Sci 51:518–531
Schofield N, Miller G, Martin A (2003) Critical elections and political realignments in the US: 1860–2000. Polit Stud 51:217–240
Schumpeter J (1942) Capitalism, socialism, and democracy. Harper, New York
Skocpol T, Williamson V (2010) The tea party and the re making of republican conservatism. Oxford University Press, Oxford
Smith H (2012) Who stole the American dream? Random House, New York
Steyn M (2011) After America. Regnery, New York
Stiglitz JE (2012) Price of inequality: how today's divided society endangers our future. Norton, New York
Stokes D (1963) Spatial models and party competition. Am Polit Sci Rev 57:368–377
Stokes D (1992) Valence politics. In: Kavanagh D (ed) Electoral politics. Clarendon Press, Oxford
Triffin R (1960) Gold and dollar crisis. Yale University Press, New Haven
Von Hayek F (1944) The road to serfdom. Routledge & Kegan Paul, London. [2007] The University of Chicago Press, Chicago
Von Mises L (1940) Nationalökonomie: Theorie Des Handelns und Wirtschaftens. Yale University Press, New Haven. [1949] Trans. as Human Action
Wittman D (1977) Candidates with policy preferences: a dynamic model. J Econ Theory 14:180–189

Sub-central Governments and Debt Crisis in Spain over the Period 2000–2011

Fernando Toboso

1 Introduction

Since the financial crisis erupted in the fall of 2008, the government borrowing sector has been in turmoil in almost all western developed countries. The present chapter focuses on the quantitative evolution of sub-central, as well as central, government borrowing in Spain, a country that is being experiencing serious problems at this respect. Because an intense process of political and fiscal decentralization has taken place in Spain since the mid eighties, the chapter examines whether this drive to decentralization has been paralleled by any fiscally undisciplined behavior on the part of sub-central governments over the periods 2000–2007 and 2008–2011. The empirical analysis will be based on the internationally comparable public finance provided by the OECD, the Eurostat and the Bank of Spain. As regards the breakdown by governmental subsectors, the National Accounts criteria[1] require the government sector to be broken down into four sub-sectors: central, state, local and social security funds. Concerning public debt, central governments usually are by far the most important debt holders, owing more than half of total debt in most cases, as we are going to see also in the case of Spain. Of course, Spain enjoys some singular organizational characteristics regarding intergovernmental relations

[1]S.N.A. 93 has recently been updated to S.N.A. 2009. These criteria are fully compatible with those of E.S.A. 95.

A previous version of this chapter was presented at the International Conference on Political Economy and Institutions held in May 2–4, 2012, Baiona, Spain. I thank participants in the conference, as well as anonymous referees, for helping me to concentrate on what we all consider to be the key issues.

F. Toboso (✉)
Faculty of Economics, Departamento de Economía Aplicada, University of Valencia,
Av. Tarongers s/n, 46022 Valencia, Spain
e-mail: Fernando.Toboso@uv.es
url: www.uv.es/ftoboso

N. Schofield et al. (eds.), *Advances in Political Economy*,
DOI 10.1007/978-3-642-35239-3_6, © Springer-Verlag Berlin Heidelberg 2013

and debt issues that will have to be addressed in the paper, including legal controls on borrowing by sub-central governments.

It is worthy to mention here also that Spain represents a country that has experienced both a relatively rapid economic growth till 2007 and a policy of significant political decentralization since democratic transition in 1978. Seventeen regional-state parliaments and executives were created from the outset in their own political and electoral processes from 1979 to 1982. Each regional-state government autonomously enjoys now even more public policy responsibilities than the Länder in a traditional federal country such as Germany.[2] Central-managed public expenditure went from 87 per cent of total expenditures in 1983 to about 45 per cent in 2011. Sub-central governments' share in public expenditures went from 13 per cent of total in 1983 to about 54 per cent in 2011. Concerning tax powers and other autonomous sources of income at sub-central governments' disposition, several reforms have also taken place to increase their financial autonomy, with intergovernmental grants already representing less than 40 per cent of total income for regional-state governments in 2011. A significant devolution of the power to tax, not just the centrally collected tax revenue, to each regional-state government has also taken place since the 1980s.[3] All these figures already indicate that Spain has become a politically and fiscally quite decentralized country. Particularly, regional-state governments are now key policy actors as their autonomous regulatory powers have also increased substantially and their share in sub-central expenditure already reached 70 per cent of total sub-central expenditures in 2010. That is why regional-state parliaments and executives are already treated as states are in federal countries, with their public finance figures being classified as such for the reasons already mentioned.

Of course, all these figures represent a rough estimate of political decentralization because they do not take into account many relevant qualitative aspects such us, for example, the degree of discretion governments have regarding each type of expenditure, or the exact degree of regulatory power each sub-central government enjoy. Some of these expenditures may be financed from conditional grants or earmarked grants, for example. But this is not an issue to be addressed in the present paper. The issue of how are figures internally consolidated among subsectors will not be addressed either because the impact of this aspect on global percentages is irrelevant for the research purpose at hand.[4] Local governments' public finances figures that will be used include the spending, revenue, debt, etc by municipal and provincial governments, as well as by other governmental agencies created by each municipality or related public enterprises, as it is typically done when elaborating National Accounts statistics.[5] The same comments apply to the central and regional-state levels of government. In the case of subsectors, debt issued by social security

[2]On this comparison see Toboso (2006a), (2006b) and (2010).

[3]On this see Toboso (2005), Toboso and Scorsone (2010).

[4]On these and other measuring problems see Martinez-Vazquez and Timofeev (2010), Toboso (2006a) and Toboso and Scorsone (2010).

[5]A different issue that will not be addressed in the paper is that in Spain as elsewhere there are several public services whose management has been externalized to private or public enterprises,

funds will appear included at the central level as it is the central government who decides upon this debt in Spain.[6] Figures referring to "all governments" are consolidated among subsectors, as it is done in National Accounts.

Therefore, to accomplish its purpose, the present chapter is organized as follows. Following introductory remarks, in Sect. 1 I briefly review some of these key general contributions to the topic being investigated in the present paper. In Sect. 2 an empirical analysis is conducted for the period 1996–2007 on the Spanish case using National Accounts multilevel public finance figures in order to show the evolution of sub-central as well as central debt before the world financial crash. In this section the paper emphasizes some singularities regarding key aspects of the multilevel organization of government that exists in Spain, including legal details in place over the period concerning the ability to incur in deficit and to issue debt by sub-central governments. In Sect. 3 the same is done as regards to the 2008–2011 period that followed the said financial crash. This section will show that Spain has experienced a considerable increase in public deficit and debt since 2007, mainly at the central level. It also points to the current economic recession and the initial counter-cyclical measures adopted by all governments, including the increase in public expenditure needed for bailouts in the financial sector, as key factors leading Spain to exceed during this second period the limits on public deficit settled in the European Stability and Growth Path. Section 4 concludes by emphasizing that economic conditions seem factors more relevant for explaining the evolution of central and sub-central debt in Spain than factors linked to political and fiscal decentralization arrangements. As stressed in Sects. 3 and 4, the above statement is not to claim that debt limits, as well as some other public sector regulatory details and behavioral political practices, are irrelevant. The chapter also leaves for future econometric research the task of assigning numbers to the relative magnitude in which each of these impact factors have influenced the evolution of debt at the different tiers of government.

2 What Are the Main Factors Influencing the Evolution of Sub-central Debt that Are Being Emphasized in the Literature?

Before examining what has happened with sub-central, as well as central, debt we need briefly investigate which are the main factors influencing this evolution that are often stressed in the literature. Rodden and others[7] have made outstanding contribu-

---

to mixed consortiums, to public-private partnerships, etc. When these organizations belong to the business sector their activities are not directly accounted as part of the "general government" activities (central-regional-local-social security funds) but indirectly following National Account rules.

[6]This is not the case regarding multilevel public finance statistics provided by the IMF. That is why the percentages that follow are not strictly comparable with IMF based percentages. The OECD databases do not provide desegregated figures for social security funds debt for all countries.

[7]See Rodden (2002), Rodden and Wibbels (2002), Rodden et al. (2003), Rodden (2006).

tions on these issues from a comparative institutional perspective. They have recurrently stressed that institutional details characterizing federal systems are key factors (not necessarily the only ones) for explaining differences in performance among federations. They consider these factors crucial in explaining why sub-central governments behave in a fiscally conservative manner in some countries while they rely on deficit financing in others thus generating unsustainable levels of debt. This means that institutional-legal arrangements, as well as informal social norms and values, matter in the economy as well as in the polity. The key question however is: which institutional arrangements are decisive in each situation if political, economic and social circumstances as well as participants differ so much from case to case?[8]

Political and fiscal decentralization per se does not necessarily weaken fiscal discipline of sub-central governments according to this strand of literature. A key aspect seems to be whether the institutional setting for multilevel government provides expectations for sub-central government leaders that there is a possibility to be bailed out, ceteris paribus. In those multi-tiered systems of government in which the commitment by central government to reject demands for bailout lack credibility, political agents at sub-central governments may have the incentive to overspend and incur greater deficits if they have unrestricted access to borrowing or borrowing limitations are not credibly enforced.[9]

The incentive may be particularly relevant if political agents controlling a sub-central government belong to a different political party or coalition than the party or coalition controlling the central parliament and executive. The said incentive usually results in strong efforts on the part of sub-central politicians to ensure re-election by finding local and regional opportunities for spending if external financial sources are available and no obligation to raising own taxes over regional constituents exists. This is also referred to as the common pool problem.[10] This bias may driven the behavior of all parties, lobby groups and the people in general in the region or state. The more you get for "the state-region" from the common pool, the better.

Using a sample of 43 countries over the period 1982–2000, Plekhanov and Singh (2006) point to similar aspects as key factors in many cases. These authors conclude that no single institutional arrangement seems superior under all circumstances for disciplining sub-central government spending. Specific institutional characteristics of the country, state or region, the existence of any bailout precedent, and the quality of fiscal reporting seem relevant factors for all these countries.

Among these arrangements, the effectiveness of debt and spending limits has received considerable attention too in the literature, as well as the balanced budget

[8]See North (2005) or Ostron (1990) and (2005).

[9]From a sample of 30 countries, Melo (2000) shows evidence indicating that intergovernmental fiscal relations are likely to result in a deficit bias in decentralized policy-making with soft budgets constrains.

[10]Besley and Coate (2003), Knight (2006, 2008), Inman and Rubinfeld (1997), Baqir (2002), or Baron and Ferejohn (2007, 2009) address these common tax-pool issues mainly referring to the USA Congress and Senate. All emphasize on how the incentives created by national financing of local public goods lead to individual congressmen or senators to try to expand own-district spending at the same time that they try to restrain aggregate spending.

rule. Studies made upon panel data do not show a sole conclusion as usual. However, in many occasions these limits seem to have lowered the spending rate of growth during the boom periods, particularly if limits are well defined technically and it is easy to detect non-compliance by independent management bodies. But this is not always the case, as with regards to the US states for example, several authors have detected no significant difference in expenditure or revenue growth between states with and without such limitations for several periods of time. Shadbegian (1996) uses panel data from the 1960s till the 1990s with such a conclusion. Kousser et al. (2008) investigates changes within a given state, not among states, following the adoption of such ceilings and again they find little impact over the subsequent years since.

Of course, sub-central governments with strict balanced budget rules or debt limits are less able to help central government in the attempt to implement countercyclical policies.[11] Though, again, many exceptions and particularities exist from country to country that have to be taken into account for an in depth analysis and sound assessment. It must not be forgotten that debt limits typically apply only to guaranteed debt, excluding debt issued by special public enterprises, as well as by some public commercial agencies that are out of the so called "general government" entities whose budgets are passed at all levels of government. Though this debt usually needs central authorization, it represents a way to evade the said ceiling rules if central government political leaders are likely to do so.

The consequences of economic cycles are also critical factors examined in the literature.[12] Recessions usually lead to deliberate countercyclical spending measures as a first reaction.[13] If we also consider impact on spending derived from the automatic increase in other expenditures and the negative impact on tax revenues that also results, there can be little doubt that recessions always produce a negative impact on public deficits and debt levels. Bloechliger et al. (2010a, 2010b) show that recessions often affect public investment more than current expenditures as the former is easier to curtail in the face of budget constraints, while current expenditures are politically more sensitive or mandated and, consequently, more difficult to be changed.[14] Poterba (1994), for example, showed how the economic downturns in US during the late 1980s significantly and negatively affected public deficits by the States. He also found that political factors seemed were relevant, particularly for explaining deficits adjustments in subsequent years. Adjustments were made faster when a single political party controls the governorship and the state house than when party control was divided.[15]

[11]See Levinson (1998), Fatás and Mihov (2006) and Rose (2006).

[12]Barro (1979) is a seminal, much cited, contribution on this line of research.

[13]Padoan (2009), for example, investigates the size and composition of the fiscal stimulus packages of the major economies that were implemented during 2008 in an attempt to cushion the decline on aggregate demand and growth that occurred as a result of the world financial crash.

[14]See also Wibbels and Rodden (2006).

[15]See also Allain-Dupré (2011).

Periods of economic growth just work on the opposite direction. On this line of research and based on the evolution registered in the Swiss cantons between 1984 and 2000, Freitag and Vatter (2008), for example, provide empirical results showing that in periods of economic growth multilevel organization of government has no relevant impact on debt. There are enough revenues for all governments to share. However, in phases of economic recession differences among Cantons as regards to political autonomy seem to affect the evolution of their debt. In these periods, suddenly spending needs appear greater than public incomes and Cantons enjoying greater political decentralization tend to implement more active budgetary policies than centralized Swiss cantons, then incurring in greater debt.

There must be no doubt that both organizational factors as well as factors linked to economic conditions are attracting the attention of scholars dealing with fiscal behavior by sub central governments. However, knowing the relative role played by specific formal and informal organizational details as compared to the role of the economic cycle in determining the level and change in debt burdens is not an easy task. Moreover, econometric exercises attempting to find the definitive factors that are valid are often contradicted or refuted with other similar attempts found in the published literature. The purpose of the present paper is quite different as indicated in the introductory section. This paper attempts to quantitatively investigate the evolution of sub-central, as well as central, public debt in Spain and see whether the turn in economic conditions is paralleled by a similar turn regarding the evolution of debt. For accomplishing this research purpose, the next section focuses on statistics for the 1996–2007 period.

3 The Evolution of Sub-central and Central Debt in Spain Before the World Financial Crash

As Spain experienced major changes in developing a new quasi-federal political system from 1978 to 1983, it seems a suitable case study for investigating whether this political and fiscal decentralization drive was paralleled by a negative evolution of public debt at sub-central levels of government. How has public debt evolved in Spain? Did the world financial crash and the sever recession initiated in 2008 cause any significant turning point as regards to sub-central or central public debt?

It is evident that public deficits and outstanding public debt were reduced at all levels of government in Spain over the 2000–2007 period here considered if properly measured as a percentage of GDP, as Table 1 reveals. Contrary to the case in some Latin-American countries for example,[16] no relevant macroeconomic distortion has been generated and no bailout problem has existed over the period. Moreover, Table 1 also shows that both regional and local governments have contributed to the total outstanding debt in very low proportion over the period. Roughly speaking,

[16]See Tanzi (2000) for an analysis of the potential macroeconomic problems. For an analysis of the bailout problem in the Argentina case, see Jones et al. (2000), Sanguinetti and Tomassi (2004) Tommasi et al. (2001) or Saiegh and Tommasi (1999).

Table 1 General government debt in Spain before the world financial crash broken down by levels (% of GDP and Millions of Euros. National Accounts). Source: OECD, Eurostat and Bank of Spain. Figures in the public domain

	2000	2004	2006	2007
Sub-central Governments	9.6	9.1	8.7	8.5
Regional Governments	6.3	6.2	5.9	5.7
Local Governments	3.3	2.9	2.8	2.8
Central Government	51.5	37.1	31.0	27.7
ALL GOVERNMENTS in Spain	61.1	46.2	39.7	36.1
EU AVERAGE (Euro zone)	69.9	69.8	68.5	66.3
Sub-central Govs Debt in Millions Euros	59267	76148	86639	90424
Central Gov Debt in Millions Euros	314766	312994	304416	291883
Sub-Central Govs Debt as % of Total Debt	15.84	19.56	22.15	23.65

the central government contributed about three times more than regional and local governments did to outstanding debt. Since the mid 1990s, outstanding debt by the regional governments has remained around 6 per cent of Spanish GDP and that one by local ones around 3 per cent. Total outstanding debt in Spain has always been lower than the EU average level over the period prior to the current financial crash, as Table 1 also indicates.

Graphically, this evolution of public debt broken down by levels of government can be observed in Fig. 1.[17] If we take into consideration that over those years, the process of political decentralization was very intense,[18] it can be stated that this political decentralization was not paralleled by any relevant fiscal or debt problem at sub-central or central levels of government. A different issue to be addressed in the next section is if this new multilevel political system will be able to effectively respond to the fiscal consolidation strategies required after the world financial crash.

Several explanations may help point towards what occurred in Spain during this period. It is well-known that, along the past two decades, many developed countries have significantly changed the context in which their fiscal policies operate, particularly by adopting fiscal rules containing explicit limits to the public deficit and/or the outstanding public debt. In some cases, explicit top ceiling to annual total expenditures have also been settled. If compared with countries where these fiscal rules are absent or not fully endorsed, the empirical evidence taken from the former ones

[17] All figures are made according to the European excessive-deficit protocol. Debt issued by Social Security Funds is included at the central level of government.

[18] Three years after the approval of the 1978 democratic Constitution, regional governments only managed 2.9 percent of total public expenditures. In 2006 they managed 33.1 percent. If we also take into account that total public expenditure in Spain has experienced a significant and rapid growth over those years (from 24.9 per cent of Spanish GDP in 1974 to about 40 percent on average over the 2000s.

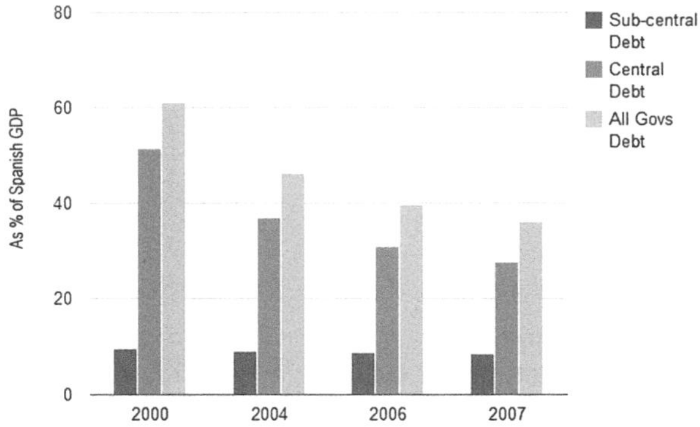

Fig. 1 General government debt in Spain before the world financial crash broken down by levels (% of the GDP and Millions of Euros. National Accounts). Source: Eurostat and Bank of Spain. Figures in the public domain

tend to show these rules as useful mechanisms in helping to maintain budgetary discipline, but mainly during periods with enough economic growth.[19] However, the specific design of limitations and controls greatly determines the effectiveness of these rules. Monitoring and enforcement aspects or the specific procedures settled for dealing with potential deviations seem also crucial aspects.

Moreover, some central legal rules for borrowing have always existed since democratic transition.[20] Therefore, they may have played a role in maintaining the fiscal discipline displayed by regional as well as by local governments over the period. However, these legal rules have not been sufficient controls once the financial crash and its associated economic recession started. Thought an increase in public debt measured in millions Euros was registered over the boom period, this did not cause any increase in the relative percentage of sub central debt in terms of GDP, which is the most relevant economic comparison. Controls and the economic cycle seemed to act to restrain relative debt burdens across levels of government.

Though these rules and controls have also been changed on several occasions, a written approval of the Central Finance Minister has always been required for regional governments to access long term credit and issue debt, and specific constraints and requirements were settled by Law for obtaining such a written authorization.[21] In particular, for regional governments to get long term credit (longer than a year), two requirement have always been in place. First, all credit must be dedicated to investment. And second, annual repayment (capital and interests) must not be higher than 25 % of each regional government annual current income. As regarding the legal rules framing financial sources at local governments' disposition, two Laws were passed in the Central Parliament since the very beginning of

[19]See Debrun and Kumar (2008).

[20]These Law initially passed in the central parliament were: Organic Law 8/1980 on Regional Governments Finances, Law 7/1985 and Law 38/1988 on local public finances. These laws have been reformed in several occasions since.

[21]In 2001, borrowing activities by Regional governments were also linked to the balanced budget principle, though some flexibility was introduced in the application of this principle in 2006, and latter on in 2009.

democratic transition, once the 1978 Constitution was in effect. These two initial legislation packages were Law 7/1985 and Law 38/1988. The second is known as the Regulatory Law of Local Public Finances (*Ley Reguladora de las Haciendas Locales—LRHL*). Several reforms have taken place since those years.[22] As a result of all these regulatory packages, local governments have been subject to similar obligations in regards to budgetary stability as those affecting regional governments, though some flexibility and exceptions are explicitly considered in case of recessions in such legislative measures. Plans to progressively eliminate public deficit deviations are also required. In all cases, authorizations to access credit and issue short term and long term debt may be denied by the Central Finance Minister if these plans are not fully implemented.[23]

Moreover, it seems evident that the spectacular increase registered in total public income on average over the growth period (both in total euros and as a percentage of GDP), did also help in reducing public deficits and, consequently, the outstanding public debt levels as shown in previous Table 1. An increasing amount of public income has been available for financing public policies at all levels of government. Attention must be paid to the fact that over this period, the Spanish GDP also grew significantly. The economic growth registered over the period provided regional governments with an increasing amount of financial resources. Most of this public income has come from the increase registered in the Spanish tax revenue in relation to GDP: an increase of about eighteen points in about thirty years (from 18.4 per cent of GDP in 1975 to 36.7 in 2006 according to the ministry of finance figures). Moreover, Spain has also been receiving, until 2001, on average about 1–1.2 percent of GDP more each year in net terms as public income from the European Union.[24] The economic cycle seems a key issue as we are going to emphasize in the next section. Therefore, the figures provided show that the significant drive to political federalism and fiscal decentralization has not been paralleled by a non-disciplined fiscal behavior on the part of sub-central governments over the period that ended in 2007. Sub-central debt levels were reduced significantly in percentage of GDP, as OECD figures show. Sub-central public deficit also went from −0.6 percent of GDP in 1996 to −0.4 in 2006.

[22]Two of these significant reforms regarding borrowing issues were implemented through Royal Decree 1463/2007 (which further develops basic principles settled in the General Law for Budgetary Stability already mentioned) and Royal Decree Law 5/2009 (which contained urgent and extraordinary measures to facilitate local governments to pay their providers if some obligations remained unpaid in 2008. Local government have had three months after the approval of the 2009 Royal Decree Law for documenting these obligations that could not be paid and exceptionally apply for extra credit authorizations that will have to be repaid in six years maximum, that is in 2013).

[23]An extra requirement exists for local governments to freely access short term credit (repaid along the year): the total amount obtained must not exceed 30 percent of current incomes in the previous year.

[24]Since 2002, this source of income is becoming less significant in terms of GDP, and has suffered a further reduction for the period 2007–2014 as the twelve new countries that entered the EU in 2004 and 2007 are obtaining most of the EU funds for the new period.

4 What Has Happened with Sub-central, as well as, Central Debt in Spain After the World Financial Crash?

The above analysis does not mean that the singularities regarding political and fiscal decentralization arrangements are irrelevant. However, after more than a decade leading up to a major financial bubble in developed countries, some dramatic events erupted around the fall of 2008. The severity of the economic recession generated and the initial counter-cyclical measures adopted by all governments, together with some other singular national factors, has lead to all European countries, in particular, to double or triplicate the public deficit levels they registered prior to the financial crash, then exceeding the limits established in the European Stability and Growth Pact (ESGP). Several other measures that are being taking necessarily imply more public spending as is the case of the financial sector reform and those measures implemented to reorganize and recapitalize banks and savings banks, with several banks already bailed-out.

In countries that were not able to significantly diminish public deficits and debt over the boom, the consequences of recession, bankruptcies and bailouts in the financial sector, to mention but a few events, have been more severe in terms of public deficit and debt. This has caused considerable uncertainty on the part of international investors over the ability of these governments to successfully issue new debt at reasonable interest rates and even to pay back bonds previously issued.

But this evolution of debt levels alone does not explain why Spain has experienced such a critical situation, particularly since the beginning of 2010. Japan, for example, has got a debt burden of near 200 per cent of GDP and has had no similar financial problems at international markets. Key issues in the case of Spain are the bad record regarding economic growth since 2008, the bubble in the building sector that has finally burst and seriously affected banks and saving banks, and also the many needs regarding current and expected levels of elderly populations having the right to get a public pension. The situation looks even worse if we consider the huge increase in unemployment that Fig. 2 shows. This reveals not only that internal demand has dropped and more and more public expenditures are needed, but also that no dynamic export sector has come as a substitute. As a result, a spectacular decrease in public revenue is taking place at all tiers of government. Regarding the balance of payments, the current account external trade deficit that Spain is registering, according to OECD figures (with no compensation from the financial account) transmit the idea to international investor that problems will not be solved in the near future. As higher is external debt (not just public external debt, but also external debt by households, enterprises and banks) the worse regarding expectations.

The importance of having or the lack thereof of effective fiscal rules and public deficit and debt controls increases, of course, in the case of countries belonging to monetary unions, as is the case of Spain. As the Euro zone case reveals since early 2010, the sharp increase in public debt registered in some countries is clearly producing significant negative impacts on other partners in the zone. This, in fact, was a main argument for introducing the well-known public deficit and debt top limits into the European Union Treaty at late 1980s. These shared consequences have also

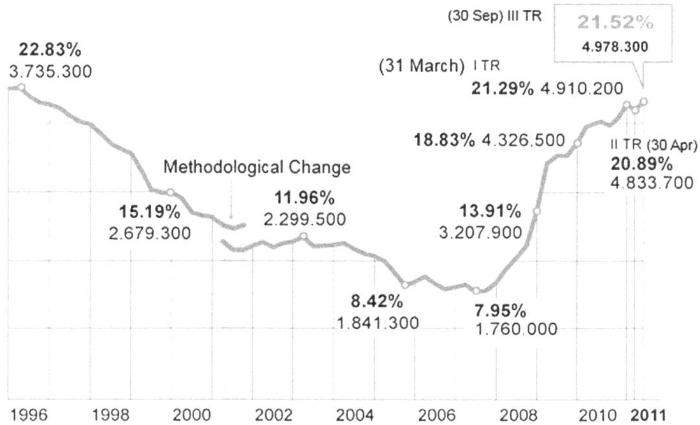

Fig. 2 Unemployment in Spain (percentage of active population and number of people unemployed). Source: Figures in the public domain from the Spanish National Institute of Statistics that are fully consistent with those provided by the OECD

lead to the several amendments of the already mentioned European Stability and Growth Pact (ESGP) that have taken place. They have finally been used also for justifying interventions or bailouts (Greece, Ireland, Portugal, and the bailout plan for the saving banks in Spain).

In all these countries, the extremely critical economic situation created since 2008, together with the particularities of the specific economic problems affecting each country, has resulted in spectacular increases in outstanding public debt levels in just four years. In the case of Spain, the total public debt has doubled in terms of the Spanish GDP if 2011 and 2007 years are compared, as Table 2 shows (from 36.1 per cent of GDP to 72.1 per cent). Sub-central governments' debt has also experienced a significant increase with about 68 thousand millions euros added to the stock of Spanish public debt in just four years, with regional governments as main contributors. However it has been at the central level of government where the drastic turning point in economic cycles that took place in 2008 has caused the greatest impact. Outstanding central public debt soared from 27.7 per cent of Spanish GDP in 2007 to 52.1 per cent in 2001, adding more than 267 thousand millions Euros (about 334 billions US dollars) to the total outstanding public debt in Spain over the said four years.

Graphically, this evolution of debt by levels of government over the 2007–2010 period is shown in Fig. 3, which includes also previous years for comparative purposes.

There must be no surprise that Moody's, Fitch and S&P, though they are very much contested agencies as they gave AAA to Leman Brothers in 2006,[25] recurrently downgrade the ratings for central and sub-central government debt in Spain,

[25]As well as to, for example, the four banks rescued in Ireland, which amounted the annual public deficit in the country to more than 30 per cent of GDP. Remember that the European Stability and

Table 2 General government debt in Spain after the world financial crash broken down by levels (% of GDP and Millions of Euros. National Accounts). Source: OECD, Eurostat and Bank of Spain. Figures in the public domain

	2007	2008	2009	2010	2011
Sub-central Governments	8.5	9.6	12.0	14.8	16.4
Regional Governments	5.7	6.7	8.7	11.4	13.1
Local Governments	2.8	2.9	3.3	3.4	3.3
Central Government	27.7	30.6	41.9	46.4	52.1
ALL GOVERNMENTS in Spain	36.1	40.2	53.9	61.2	72.1
EU AVERAGE (Euro zone)	66.3	70.0	79.5	85.3	87.2
Sub-central Govs Debt in Millions Euros	90424	114400	125662	154891	175502
Central Gov Debt in Millions Euros	291883	322584	439420	488245	559459
Sub-Central Govs Debt as % of Total Debt	23.65	26.17	22.23	24.08	23.87

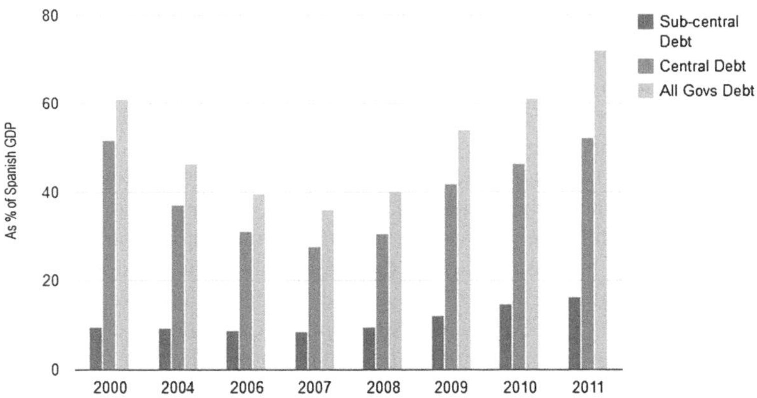

Fig. 3 General government debt in Spain before and after the world financial crash broken down by levels (% of the GDP). Source: Eurostat and Bank of Spain. Figures in the public domain

as well as in several other countries of course. Obviously, a main consequence of this downgrading is the increase in interest rates to be paid for issuing debt as downgrades imply greater estimated risk of default in repaying this debt, which negatively affects the purpose of reducing public deficits. There must be no surprise either that in the short term all austerity measures being implemented since 2010, particularly in several EU countries, represent contractive policy measures that have finally damaged the already weak economic recovery that seemed to have started at the last quarter of 2010, as Krugman and many other analysts recurrently called attention

Growth Pact required it to be under three per cent as a general rule, let aside the exceptions also settled.

to. With neither external demand nor internal consumption able to pull the Spanish economy and with all tiers of government cutting expenditures to reduce public deficits since 2010, it must be no surprise that the economy remains in contraction in 2011 and 2012, as preliminary figures already available reveal.

5 Concluding Remarks

Regarding the evolution of sub-central, as well as central, public debt in Spain over the period 2000–2011 the present investigation indicates that the impacts of economic conditions seem the key factors. The figures here provided show that a turning point took place in 2008 when the world financial crash started. This is not to say that the singularities regarding political and fiscal decentralization arrangements and public deficit and debt controls are irrelevant for the evolution of public debt. In fact, as the chapter stresses, it is a common ground in many published articles to state that if sub-central governments are left to their own devices and their borrowing activities are not centrally controlled, it is likely that these governments tend to borrow excessively as regards to the macroeconomic needs of the country, also entering the risk of default more easily than would be otherwise if strict regulations were settled and enforced, ceteris paribus.

In the Spanish case this undisciplined fiscal behavior has not taken place till 2007. The detailed formal limits on deficits and debt that have always existed have no doubt positively influenced this evolution of debt over the period, as mentioned in the chapter. The increase registered in tax revenue along the period played also a key role. As growth rates were higher in Spain than the EU average it is no surprise that debt levels in Spain experienced also greater reduction in terms of GDP till 2007, as the figures provided show. As regulations and controls regarding public deficits and debt were also in effect during 2008 and 2009, it seems straightforward that these regulations cannot be charged for the spectacular increase registered in public deficits and total debt after the world financial crash. Total public deficit in Spain reached (−) 4.5 per cent of GDP in 2008 and (−) 11.2 per cent in 2009, whereas in 2007 all governments had registered a surplus of (+) 1.9 per cent of GDP. And this has been also the case concerning many other European countries. The limits established in the European Stability and Growth Path could not be achieved by most EU countries. As regards to public debt, the chapter has stressed that in just four years total outstanding debt by all governments in Spain doubled (from 36.1 per cent in 2007 to 72.1 per cent in 2011). Therefore, it is evident that the extremely serious recession experienced since 2008 has been paralleled by a substantial increase in public deficits and debt levels in Spain even if no relevant change was introduced in the country regarding the basic rules characterizing political and fiscal decentralization as well as debt issuing controls.

Moreover, the analysis provided in the chapter also indicates that it has been at the central level of government where the debt has increased more in absolute terms since 2007, with 267 thousand millions euros (about 334 billions US dollars) being added to the stock of total public debt in Spain in just four years. In terms of GDP, central public debt has reached 52.1 per cent of Spanish GDP in 2011, whereas in 2007 this figure was 27.7 per cent. Regarding sub-central governments, the chapter shows that they have also registered a spectacular increase in debt since 2007, going from 8.5 per cent of Spanish GDP in 2007 to 16.4 per cent in 2011, then adding 85 thousand millions euros (about 106 billions US dollars) to the stock of total outstanding public debt. As previously stressed, the main reason for the higher amount of debt added by the central level of government relates again with the higher impact caused on central public finances by what most consider the worst financial crisis of the past century in the western world, and subsequent economic recession generated. As soon as the crisis was evident, central government in Spain, as well as in many other countries, engaged in stabilization policies in order to counteract the forces of the recession. In a period where tax revenues were drastically being reduced as a result of recession the increase registered in central public spending, including those public expenditures needed for first bailouts and restructuring in the financial sector, could lead to no other situation than the one mentioned above. Of course, in some countries public deficits and debt have increased more than in others, as mentioned in the paper.

As Spain has been highlighted as a main contributor, together with Greece, Portugal, Ireland and Italy, to the overall crisis in the Euro Zone, it is evident that Spain must suffer from singular problems. As mentioned in the chapter, the evolution of public debt alone cannot explain the serious problems experienced in the country since 2010 for successfully issuing new debt at reasonable interest rates. A key issue is again the extremely negative evolution registered in GDP since 2008, which has lead unemployment to reach 22 per cent of the active population after a bubble bursting taking place also in the building sector. The stock of private debt in the by households, banks and firms, as well as the expected levels of elderly population having the right to get a public pension, are also key aspects, though not among the research purposes of the present chapter. Finally, let me conclude by stating also that in no way did I attempt to extract any prediction for the future, nor did I attempt to examine the case of any specific regional government but their overall evolution regarding debt. Though the analysis provided in the chapter indicates that political and fiscal decentralization in Spain has not been paralleled by fiscally undisciplined behaviors on the part of sub-central governments, at least not till the financial crash started in 2008, there is nothing in the present chapter that excludes these undisciplined behaviors from happening in the future. Future political affairs cannot be predicted as we predict the result of chemical reactions.

References

Allain-Dupré D (2011) Multi-level governance of public investment: lessons from the crisis. OECD regional development working papers, No 5, OECD

Baqir R (2002) Districting and government overspending. J Polit Econ 110(6)1318–1354

Baron DP, Ferejohn J (2007) Bargaining and agenda formation in legislatures. Am Econ Rev 77(2):303–309

Baron DP, Ferejohn J (2009) Bargaining in legislatures. Am Polit Sci Rev 83(4):1181–1206
Barro R (1979) On the determination of the public debt. J Polit Econ 87:940–947
Besley T, Coate S (2003) Centralized versus decentralized provision of local public goods: a political economy analysis. J Public Econ 112:2611–2637
Bloechliger C et al (2010a) Fiscal policy across levels of government in times of crisis. OECD WP 12, 2010
Bloechliger C et al (2010b) Sub-central governments and the economic crisis: impact and policy responses. OECD economics department working paper, No 752
Debrun X, Kumar MS (2008) El papel de las instituciones fiscales en el fortalecimiento de la disciplina. Teoría y evidencia empírica. In: Salinas JV et al (eds) Economía política de las reglas e instituciones fiscales. Caja España
Fatás A, Mihov I (2006) The macroeconomic effects of fiscal rules in the US states. J Public Econ 90(1–2):101–117
Freitag M, Vatter A (2008) Decentralization and fiscal discipline in sub-national governments: evidence from the swiss federal system. Publius 38(2):272–294
Inman RP, Rubinfeld DL (1997) Rethinking federalism. J Econ Perspect 11(4):43–64
Jones MP, Sanguinetti P, Tomassi M (2000) Politics, institutions, and fiscal performance: an analysis of the Argentina provinces. J Econ Dev 61:305–333
Knight B (2006) Common tax pool problems in federal systems. In: Congleton R, Swedenborg B (eds), Democratic constitutional design and public policy: analysis and evidence. MIT Press, Cambridge
Knight B (2008) Legislative representation, bargaining power, and the distribution of federal funds: evidence from the US Congress. Econ J 118(532):1785–1803
Kousser T et al (2008) For whom the TEL tolls: can state tax and expenditure limits effectively reduce spending? State Politics Policy Q 8(4):331–361
Levinson A (1998) Balanced budgets and business cycles: evidence from the states. Natl Tax J 51(4):715–732
Martinez-Vazquez J, Timofeev A (2010) Decentralization measures revisited. Public Financ Manag 10(1):13–47
Melo RL (2000) Fiscal decentralization and intergovernmental fiscal relations: a cross-country analysis. World Dev 28(2):365–380
North DC (2005) Understanding the process of economic change. Princeton University Press, Princeton
Ostron E (1990) Governing the commons. The evolution of institutions for collective actions. Cambridge University Press, Cambridge
Ostron E (2005) A framework for institutional analysis. In: Ménard C, Shirley M (eds) Handbook of new institutional economics. Edwar Elgar, Cambridge
Padoan PC (2009) Fiscal policy in the crisis: impact, sustainability, and long-term implications. OECD ADBI working paper, No 178, December
Plekhanov AA, Singh RB (2006) How should subnational government borrowing be regulated? Some cross-country empirical evidence. IMF Staff Pap 53(3):426–452
Poterba J (1994) State responses to fiscal crises: the effects of budgetary institutions and politics. J Polit Econ 102:798–821
Rodden JA (2002) The dilemas of fiscal federalism: grants and fiscal performance around the world. Am J Polit Sci 43:6
Rodden JA (2006) Hamilton's paradox: the promise and peril of fiscal federalism. Cambridge University Press, Cambridge
Rodden J, Eskenland GS, Litvack J (eds) (2003) Decentralization and the challenge of hard budget constraints. MIT Press, Cambridge
Rodden JA, Wibbels E (2002) Beyond the fiction of federalism: macroeconomic management in multitiered systems. World Polit 54:494–531
Rose S (2006) Do fiscal rules dampen the political business cycle? Public Choice 128(3):407–431
Saiegh S, Tommasi M (1999) Why is Argentina's fiscal federalism so inefficient? Entering the labyrinth. J Appl Econ II(1):169–209

Sanguinetti P, Tomassi M (2004) Intergovernmental transfers and fiscal behavior. Insurance versus aggregate discipline. J Int Econ 62:149–170
Shadbegian RJ (1996) Do tax and expenditure limitations affect the size and growth of state government? Contemp Econ Policy 14(1):22–35
Tanzi V (2000) On fiscal federalism: issues to worry about. International monetary fund working paper. IMF, Washington, DC
Toboso F (2005) Institutional change and economic growth in Spain since democratic transition in 1978: regulating regional governments as a key factor. In: Oppenheimer M, Mercuro N (eds) Law and economics: alternative economic approaches to legal and regulatory issues. M.E. Sharpe, New York, pp 293–427. Chapter 16
Toboso F (2006a) Key organizational choices for financing regional governments in democratic Spain. Rev Anal Econ 2:61–82
Toboso F (2006b) Descentralización política y resultados económicos. Una análisis institutional del caso Español. Probl Desarro Rev Latinoam Econ 37(146):121–145
Toboso F (2010) La corresponsabilidad fiscal de los gobiernos autonómicos: evolución y perspectivas en tiempos de crisis. In: Antuñano I et al (eds) Crisis y transformación: ensayos en homenaje al profesor Emerit Bono. PUV, Valencia
Toboso F, Scorsone E (2010) How much power to tax do regional governments enjoy in democratic Spain? Reg Fed Stud 2:157–176
Tommasi M, Saiegh S, Sanguinetti P (2001) Fiscal federalism in Argentina: policies, politics, and institutional reform. Econ J Lat Am Caribb Econ Assoc 1:157–201
Wibbels E, Rodden J (2006) Business cycles and the political economy of decentralized finance: lessons for fiscal federalism in the EU. In: Wierts A et al (eds) Fiscal policy surveillance in Europe

Deciding How to Choose the Healthcare System

Olga Shvetsova and Katri K. Sieberg

1 Introduction

The continuing debate in the United States over the form of health care provision is illustrative as to how difficult that choice can be. The choice is further complicated by political activity—lobbyists with a vested interest in various formats—and a noticeable effect from path dependence—people are used to what they have and are afraid of change, and some groups actually stand to lose from change, at least in the short run. What might the decision have been in the absence of these effects? Our paper creates a model to explore this question. In particular, we appeal to insights from Buchanan and Tullock (1962), Rawls (1971) and Kornai and Eggleston (2001) to ask what type of health care provision would a polity choose from behind the veil of ignorance, and what type of mechanism—unanimity (constitutional) or majority (legislative) would they prefer to use to select it?

The selection of a health care system is a highly charged subject. Health care is a service that is expected to be used by everyone at least once in their lifetime, and because access to health care can make the difference between life and death, many argue that health care should be a right. However, the situation is complicated. Health care is expensive, and improvements in technology—while improving outcomes—also make it even more costly (Newhouse 1992). Thus, debates focus on which type of system would best provide health care at efficient costs, and what tradeoffs are associated with which systems. Many, including Pauly (1986), and

O. Shvetsova (✉)
Department of Political Science, Binghamton University, P.O. Box 6000, Binghamton, NY 13902, USA
e-mail: shvetsova@gmail.com

K.K. Sieberg
Department of North American Studies, University of Tampere 33104, Tampereen Yliopisto, Finland
e-mail: katri.sieberg@uta.fi

N. Schofield et al. (eds.), *Advances in Political Economy*,
DOI 10.1007/978-3-642-35239-3_7, © Springer-Verlag Berlin Heidelberg 2013

Klarman (1969) among others, assert that the market is the best way to induce efficiency in health care consumption. Here, cost control is the main objective. They appeal to the effect of prices to reduce surplus demand—noting that without this incentive, health provision will become overly costly. Klarman states,

> After considering several possible explanations, the hypothesis is advanced that health insurance may enhance one's taste for health services and permit one to indulge in it as the risk of large, unexpected, and unwanted bills is eliminated. (1969, 557)

Others (including Enthoven (1993); Fuchs 1996) argue for a highly regulated form of private insurance to avoid inherent problems in private provision—among these, lack of universal coverage. Hsaio (1994) and Sieberg and Shvetsova (2012) argue that if universal care is a goal, then private coverage will be more, not less costly.

Given the range of the debate among social scientists, it is interesting to consider what system would be chosen if given an opportunity to do so outside of the prior social context. Further, from an institutional perspective, we explore how the selection mechanism itself would affect that choice. Appealing to the logic of Buchanan and Tullock (1962) and Rawls (1971), we show that under unanimity, a polity would select an entitlement system of health care provision, and under majority rule, the same polity would opt for private provision. Behind the veil of ignorance, a polity would select unanimity as the selection mechanism in order to minimize overall cost to society.

One noteworthy aspect of our model is that although it is motivated by decision making over health care systems, it is not limited to that particular case. Instead, the model extends to apply to a certain case of collective actions problems. In typical collective action problems, society would be better off under cohesive support for one policy, but individual self-interest can lead to suboptimal provision. The twist for this particular set of problems is that this self-interest is bolstered by median voter awareness that 1. The polity is unwilling to allow the suboptimal outcome to occur, and 2. The median voter herself is unlikely to bear the added costs associated with choosing the suboptimal policy while nonetheless enjoying the benefits of the 'rescue' with regard to the outcome. In addition to the selection of health care systems, arrangements such as the Glass-Steagall Act (and the FDIC),[1] universal education provision, pollution control, among other issues, can be addressed through this analysis. We argue that in cases involving this particular version of the collective action problem, unanimity is the ex-ante preferred mechanism to make decisions.

1.1 Buchanan and Tullock

In *The Calculus of Consent* (1962), Buchanan and Tullock ask the same question as those debating the reorganization on healthcare in America are raising on both

[1] We are grateful to a reviewer for this suggestion.

sides of the controversy: "How shall the dividing line between collective action and private action be drawn?" (p. 5). Since, unlike the current debaters, Buchanan and Tullock offer a theory as their answer and not a prescription to cure all ills, their theory can be applied and we do so here.

Specifically, Buchanan and Tullock's theory of constitutional choice consists of two main components: they define a constitution as a delineation of which decision rule to apply to each policy area, and they propose to start with a premise that the constitution itself is arrived to by unanimity. Faced with healthcare as a policy area then, their approach is to: 1) unanimously choose which decision rule to put into the constitution for 2) making fundamental decisions on healthcare policy (we can suppose that the particulars of policy implementation can be delegated to the bureaucracy).

When it comes to defining a feasible set of decision rules, their approach is general, and they allow any fraction of the population to potentially be deemed decisive on an issue. While not claiming that they model any actual constitutional process, Buchanan and Tullock illustrate how various constitutional provisions are in actuality the decision rules of the format of "the fraction of the population." Of specific interest is their explanation of how one would model the Bill of Rights in this way: a right is a policy issue which can only be decided by unanimity, they say. Indeed, with any right, an individual is in a possession of her initial endowment of it (e.g., of free speech, or of property of some land). It is a matter of the society or some of its subsets wanting to expropriate that endowment that the constitution must address. So protecting the right means setting such a decision rule for that issue that expropriation can occur only with the consent of the person who possesses the initial endowment. Unanimity, with a blocking coalition of one, is the unique decision rule satisfying this requirement.

Another type of a decision rule common in constitutions is simple majority. Simple majority has the advantage of generating just one decisive coalition for each decision, whereas deciding by a specified-size minority has a potential for simultaneous existence of two or more decisive coalitions promulgating conflicting policies.[2] Realistically then minority decision rules fall in a category of federal or autonomy provisions, with *majoritarian* procedures, but instituted within constitutionally specified minorities.

In a constitution as it addresses the polity at large, then, options for deciding in policy areas range from simple majority, to super-majorities, and all the way to unanimity. To capture the constitutional process of Buchanan and Tullock, Fig. 1 takes just the extremes of the feasible set of decision rules and for a given policy issue sketches the sequence of decisions.

By backward induction, in order to know which decision rule would benefit her most, an individual at the unanimous constitutional stage needs to compare expected utilities from implementation of policy decisions which would be made under each

[2]Note however that majoritarian coalitions in representative bodies elected by majority in districts can reflect but a minority support in the electorate, in the extreme speaking for "50 percent of 50 percent."

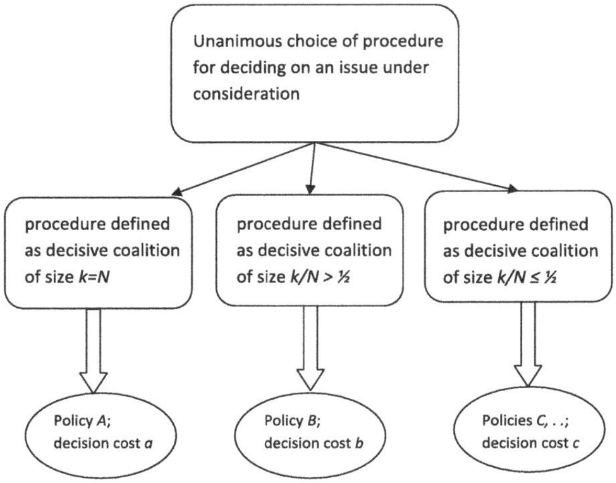

Fig. 1 Logistics of institutional choice according to Buchanan and Tullock (1962)

feasible procedure. This directly reflects the theory of Buchanan and Tullock: constitution is a unanimous choice of rules where we proceed from their expected consequences and select by backward induction.

1.2 Rawls

Unanimity, of course, is problematic because it can so easily lead to the inability to decide or, in Buchanan and Tullock's terms, to the cost of decision making becoming prohibitive. Indeed, under unanimity, each individual is a blocking coalition, and if they want different things, bargaining can be endless and even futile. Buchanan and Tullock suggest resolving the difficulty through agreeing on utility transfers and bargaining over the amounts of those transfers. That approach however works only in an ideal environment of perfect enforcement where one can be assured of receiving the utility transfer just as was promised at the bargaining stage. But in any realistic setting the commitment that the future winner from a policy would then (upon having won) share the benefits with the losers cannot be credible, and this knowledge would prevent the expected losers from entering any such contract. Promise of utility transfers made at a policy making stage might just as well be excluded from consideration once contract enforcement difficulties are taken into account. This makes unanimity as a decision rule impractical. Indeed, unanimity seems to work best when we want something *not* to happen, such as when we want a right not to be violated or entitlements withheld. But when it comes to reaching an active consensus, conflicting preferences present an insurmountable difficulty, which does not bode well for the constitutional stage as in Buchanan and Tullock (1962).

Rawls (1971) introduces an assumption which allows the unanimity rule to produce a Buchanan-Tullock style constitution successfully: in order for the individuals to be able to decide unanimously, they must decide as one. Literally, the decision-making process of each person must be exactly the same and incorporate identical inputs as everybody else's—we need a society to be comprised of individuals who are similarly uninformed about their positions in the future distributive processes which the constitution will regulate. In Rawlsian terms, at the meta-constitutional stage individuals decide behind the "veil of ignorance" and find it easy to think alike because they are in fact alike. Rawls makes de-facto additional assumptions about the risk-aversion of these individuals by invoking the maximin solution concept (thus his individuals are extremely risk-averse), but that assumption is needed only in order to lead to the specific constitutional outcome of interest to Rawls. If we keep an open mind with regard to what a constitution might be, his first, minimalist assumption that individuals are similarly uninformed about themselves, i.e., have identical beliefs, including about their risk-aversion, is sufficient for each individual to have the same preferences over institutional options and thus for the unanimity procedure to bear fruit.

If Rawls' framework can be accepted, then it could be argued that any individual, when properly deprived of identifying information, would know exactly what the decision rule should be for a particular policy area. Whether we see this theoretical construct as an appropriate approximation for the choice of the decision rule for a specific policy area depends very much on that policy area. On some issues it is easier to imagine that individuals do not know their type than on others. Things that will need to be weighed in when determining how far behind "the veil of ignorance" individuals remain with regard to their future gains or losses from the policy would include the issue-specific mechanisms by which the types of individuals become revealed, including the utility function and the technology of the provision of the good in question. We will return to the discussion of the Rawlsian assumption as it applies to healthcare when we describe the model below.

1.3 Kornai and Eggleston

Looking for the basis on which to ground the model's assumptions about the preferences of actors on the issue of interest—the safeguarding of health and life—what can one say about the social demand regarding healthcare outcomes? Can we discern at least some consensus for what could be viewed as a long-term social welfare function for healthcare? It turns out that the answer may be a very cautious "Yes." Kornai and Eggleston (2001) posit that, at the very least,

(1) people do not want a poor person to die from a disease from which a rich person would not have to die with standard medical treatment, and
(2) people do not believe that a sick person must pay more for basic necessary care than a healthy person (Kornai and Eggleston 2001, p. 50).

It is, of course, ultimately an empirical question whether or not individual preferences are aligned according to these assumptions. It is possible that different societies correspond to Kornai's postulates to different degrees. We adopt these two assumptions here, on the grounds of their theoretical appeal and based on the initial empirical validation in classroom experiments at the University of Tampere and Binghamton University in Fall 2010 and Fall 2012.

The two assumptions above sketch the popular consensus within the principal in favor of a social welfare function with the following characteristics:

- If it came to a life-threatening emergency, the principal will prefer to pay to apply accepted life-saving treatment, and
- The principal prefers not to withhold the public subsidy for the care of the more sick (whose care is more expensive) by the less sick (whose care is less expensive).

These presumably are the common preferences of every citizen in a society and thus are unanimously held at the constitutional stage. It is these preferences that designate our problem into the special class of collective action problems. Individual self-interest can lead to suboptimal provision under majority rule, and yet the polity is unwilling to let individuals suffer the consequences.

2 Actors: The "Society" and the "Patient"

Thinking about the process depicted in Fig. 1 above as a choice of a contractual mechanism where the society in some form functions as the principal, we observe that an individual—a patient—becomes the society's agent to whom the legislation assigns however many or few responsibilities for organizing her own healthcare financing.

Another observation to draw from Fig. 1 is that "society" is too general a term within this framework, because individuals who comprise it make decisions under different rules of aggregation at different junctions and experience changing levels of information as the process unfolds. We thus need to be more specific and identify the "society" in its varying incarnations as separate players. At the Rawlsian stylized "constitutional" stage, not knowing yet whether one will be rich or poor, healthy or sick, all individuals are as one and they share these preferences. If they were also maximin players (Rawls 1971), and so sought to avoid the worst possible turn of event, they would compare the alternative choice structures from the point of view of the most destitute member of the society. Thus when we assign payoffs for the ex-ante principal, we assign the minimal level of payoff achieved by any of the three principals. The payoffs of agent-patients may be even lower, but we ignore that in order to avoid building our argument on a tautology that the principal produces a certain policy because as an agent he would suffer the least under that policy.

This approach allows us to view the choice of the decision body which then chooses the healthcare policy as delegation to a sub-principal of the full principal, or, alternatively, as relying on a super-agent of the full principal. The principal's preferences over who to entrust with the drafting of the healthcare "contract" will then simply depend on the comparison of the implementation outcomes of the contracts which maximize the respective utility functions of the appointed sub-principal (super-agent) which acts on the society's behalf.

In addition to the Constitutional principal and the policy-setting principal, there is also the stage of implementation of the policy, and the contract enforcement at the implementation stage is also conducted by the principal or some authorized representative thereof. If, for example, a patient has no assets to cover a life saving or life extending treatment, it is up to the medical provider on site to deny her care if that is what the contract calls for, and a doctor or a hospital in that case unilaterally represents the societal principal.

In a sense, we have three different personifications of what colloquially is treated as the same actor in matters of welfare provision. Multiple personifications however imply separate actors with distinctive preferences and potentially conflicting interests. Our model exposes the implications of these conflicting interests within different institutional structures.

The three types of actors representing the societal principal are labeled below as EAP, IP, and PP. An Ex-ante Principal, EAP, acts at the constitutional stage. An Interim principal, IP, depending on the constitutional choice, can be either majoritarian or by unanimity (IPM or IPU). Notice that the by-unanimity interim principal is comprised of the same people but differs from the ex-ante principal by the level of information that members of the society have about their own types and the distribution of types in the population. Finally, at the implementation and enforcement stage, there is the Ex-Post Principal, PP.

All four (counting both IPM and IPU) actors representing the principal, we claim, share the basic preferences as postulated by Kornai and Eggleston (2001) which we discussed above.

2.1 The Ex-ante Rawlsian Principal

Rawls's premise and Kornai–Eggleston's assumptions have been historically appealing to scholars of political economy. Hayek has argued as far back as 1945 that:

> There is no reason why, in a society which has reached the general level of wealth ours has, the first kind of security should not be guaranteed to all without endangering general freedom; that is: some minimum of food, shelter and clothing, **sufficient to preserve health**. Nor is there any reason why the state should not help to organize a **comprehensive system of social insurance** in providing for those common hazards of life against which few can make adequate provision. (emphasis added, Matthews 2010)

Fuchs (1996, 16) also states that medical care meets Adam Smith's 1776 definition of a necessary—in that it is necessary to sustain life and that it is indecent for even the lowest people in society to be without it.

Insofar as the total (or average) cost of the policy is concerned, we assume that the constitutional principal, EAP, prefers it minimized as long as acceptable outcome is achieved with regard to care. Provision of healthcare at some level viewed as adequate is the first priority, while cost-minimization is secondary. We stay away from

Table 1 Utility functions of the four types of principals

	Minimal adequate care	Personal tax burden	Societal cost (average tax burden)
EAP	Yes		Yes
UIP	Yes	Yes	
MIP	Yes	Yes	
PP	Yes		

the discussion of whether it is possible to view as minimally adequate a level of care that the society cannot afford (there is research to suggest that the notion of what is adequate may vary, to a point with the societal wealth, see Attfield (1990), Blank and Burau (2006), Howell and McLaughlin (1989)). Also, given the Kornai–Eggleston assumption of lexicographic preference for basic care provision, we do not include in consideration any surplus care beyond what is minimally adequate and make no additional assumptions about individual and societal preferences for that.

Table 1 summarizes the composition of the EAP's utility function, and also highlights the distinctions in the utility functions of the actors-principals. We elaborate on these differences below.

2.2 Interim Principal—The Policy-Setting Body

Our interim principal is a coalition of individuals in the society of the size and composition as empowered by the constitution to be decisive on the fundamentals of the healthcare policy. It chooses the contract with the agent-patient which constitutes the healthcare policy. The choice of the contract/policy can take place anywhere from a constitutional body or a referendum to a legislative chamber or even the local government, depending on the rules in place. Importantly, only under unanimity, the set of members of the decisive coalition for policy is fixed at the outset as the entirety of the society. Under all other rules, the membership of the decisive coalition is endogenous to the policy choice and thus a pair: (specific policy choice; specific make-up of the decisive coalition) must be an equilibrium outcome of the interaction according to the rules of the decisive body.

In Fig. 2, we compare side by side the process of policy making and implementation where the venue for policy choice is a constitutional (unanimous) body versus a legislature with simple majority rule (the UIP or MIP respectively). Be it unanimous or majoritarian, the interim principal offers the patient/agent a contract of some sort. The contract might be: "we are going to automatically withhold a portion of yours and everyone else's earnings, and in return we assume the responsibility for taking care of your health." Something like that would effectively mean the entitlement single-payer system. Or a contract might read: "You can buy as much health coverage as you choose, either directly from providers at point of service, or by means of purchasing a specific amount and type of health insurance. You will be provided only with the services which either you or your health insurance can finance and

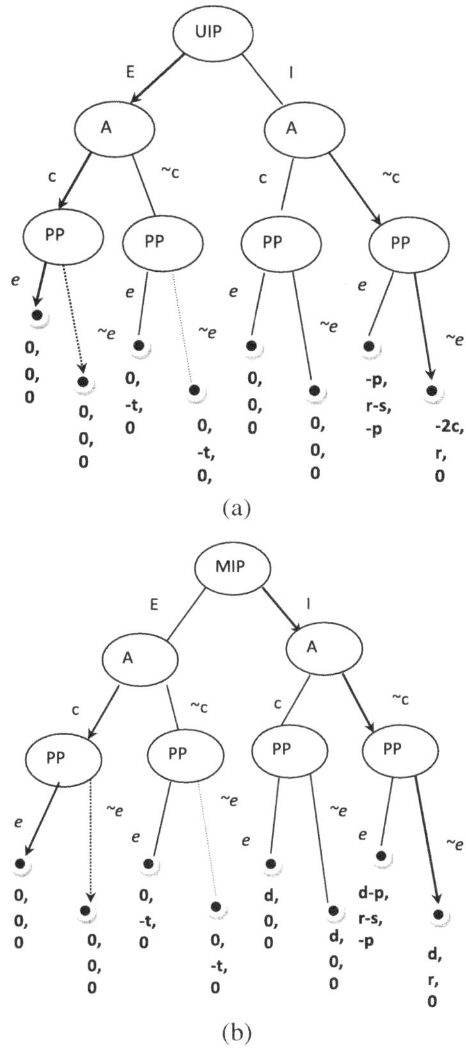

Fig. 2 (**a**) Decision by unanimity: Some members of the decisive coalition will have to finance the case of the individual non-compliance/public non-enforcement. (**b**) Decision by majority rule: Members of the decisive coalition are exempt from taxation to cover the costs in the case of the individual non-compliance/public non-enforcement

nothing beyond that, regardless of your health needs." This would be the contract behind an ideal type of a pure market private insurance system. In the model in Fig. 2 we limit ourselves with these two extreme types of policy choices, though in practice the full range of in-between options might also be available. While all contracts have their implementation issues, below we show that the latter is fundamentally non-enforceable, yet even knowing it to be non-enforceable, decision bodies of certain types would choose to adopt such a contract.

The utility function of a citizen as a member of an interim principal is more specific than that of the EAP in regards to which costs become the part of the calculation. Notice, that the contract/policy necessarily must include the a) the funding principle, b) the level of services (only covered or all that is necessary), and, c) also must stipulate the fallout provisions, as in what to do when there is a cost overrun. We claim that such provisions are indeed in place, through the access to the general state budget, and that they are implied within the broad constitutional framework of the state. We will thus assume that any shortfall which might arise from enforcement failure is made up from regular taxation, where the general tax burden is allocated via the majoritarian process. From that our actors who know what share of the tax burden they bear can form expectations about the share of the cost overrun that will fall on them if the enforcement of the contract/policy fails.

2.3 Ex-post Principal at the Contract Implementation Stage

At the time of enforcing the market-type contract/policy, the ex-post principal is a citizen in a position of authority who acts on the society's behalf, such as a doctor or administrator in an emergency room where an uninsured patient shows up. This individual then has to make a decision on whether or not to treat the patient who is in breach of a contract. It has been long claimed that at this stage the market-type contract goes unimplemented: though patients cannot pay and have failed to carry sufficient medical coverage, they receive the treatment which ought to be denied to them according to the rules, including treatment for not immediately life-threatening conditions. Providers thus incur costs which they cannot recoup from these patients, and such costs, in one way or another, are eventually transferred to be covered by the society at large, either by overcharging the paying patients or through infusions from state budget. This observation is consistent with our assumption that the principal adheres to Kornai and Eggleston's premises. Specifically, PP holds a preference to treat the patient and to not deny care to the poor which he would be able to offer to the rich. IP, in a position to sanction PP most severely, in turn prefers not to do that because the alternative outcome for the patient—her continued sickness or death—is considered even worse by the IP as well. This could be the last move in games in Figs. 2a and 2b, but we leave it unmodelled for it is redundant given the assumed preference of the principal. This redundant move by UIP or MIP is sufficient to justify the use of state budget to cover cost overrun. The last resort access to state budget follows logically from the Kornai–Eggleston assumptions.

In the model's terms, then, the ex-post principal, PP, has the choice at the last decision node to *enforce* or *not enforce* a contract (in the case of *Entitlement*, the contract is enforced via taxation, so there the move by PP that we show is redundant[3]). These choices, e versus $\sim e$, apply under *Insurance* health policy to enforcing the implied "no-care" policy for those without purchased adequate coverage and without sufficient private funds to cover the cost of treatment. Parameter $-p$ in the PP

[3]The choice to enforce or not to enforce the "no care" provision reappears where the entitlement is not universal, and might apply, for example, when the treatment of immigrants/non-citizens is concerned.

payoff captures this utility loss from having to deny a patient needed care because of his or her failure to pay or carry insurance. It captures Kornai's premises, and as it applies to every individual in the society, it is felt by the ex-post principal, but it is also present in utility functions of other actors-principals, EAP, UIP, and MIP. They all sustain loss if care is indeed refused to a patient.

The Agent (patient) values her health and wants to receive care if sick. But generally she does not like to bear the costs according to the contract/policy. In reality, the agent sometimes is financially unable, not just unwilling, to bear the cost of a serious treatment or of an insurance that would cover such treatment—but that consideration calls for a separate, normative argument, and so we do not include that possibility in our model. Here, the agent abides by the contract choosing between c (*comply*) and $\sim c$ (*not comply*). To *comply*, depending on a subgame, means either to pay the social tax or buy enough insurance (zero may be enough if no treatment is sought). To *not comply* in a single-payer system requires that the agent stays out of the workforce, and her payoffs reflect that. In a market-type system, *not complying* consists of two components: how much coverage one has purchased and how much care she is requesting. Thus, to *comply* means to ask for care in the amount the patient/agent has covered. To *not comply* means to ask for care in excess of what she can pay for.

The decision to not comply in the Entitlement case is strictly dominated for the agent since it equals non-participation in employment thus escaping universal tax. This is indicated in Fig. 2 by the utility loss of $-t$ due to the loss of wages. Generally, we stay away from the problem of enforcing tax collection, thus de-facto assuming that tax collection is enforced. The same, however, is not the case with *compliance* under the market-based policy. Not buying insurance does not by itself constitute non-compliance, and therefore cannot be punished or otherwise enforced. The contract can be enforced only at the point of service, when denying care to a sick uninsured patient who chose to request care. If the contract is enforced, the agent sustains a catastrophic utility loss from avoidably getting worse, a decline in the quality of life, or from dying. If on the other hand the contract is not enforced by the PP and care is provided, then no such utility loss to agent occurs while no contribution to financing the care is made by the agent-patient.

3 Health-Related Technology and Costs to Actors

3.1 Extra Cost of Delivering Health Care as Emergency Care

In Fig. 2, $c > 0$ captures the financial efficiency loss from substituting emergency care for preventative and regular care. Scholars of healthcare consider it a major objective to determine whether similar health outcomes can be reached with greater efficiency under some medical "technology" compared to others. Specifically, a substantial consensus has developed that investment in preventative measures generates much better returns than that in high-end life-saving medicine (see Halfon and

Hochstein 2002, among others). This effect is potentially explained by the fact that consistent preventative and regular care reduces the instances of having to save lives in emergencies (Institute of Medicine 2002).

If we accept the tradeoff in favor of preventative medicine as efficient, then logic dictates that the principal who is willing to pay for emergency procedures should be willing to pay for the cheaper preventative medicine as it replaces at a lower cost some of the eventual emergency medicine. Put plainly, since we are willing to pay (and are paying) for the latter, we should be willing to replace a part of that with "regular" care, since regular care is cheaper than treating the share of emergencies that it will prevent. There is even a possibility that regular and preventative care may boost the productive resources of the society (Bloom and Canning 2000) and generate a net surplus, thus paying for itself twice.

So combining the premise of preference for saving lives in an emergency with the technological fact that emergency care is more expensive than regular care as its substitute, we must conclude that the principal prefers the outcomes where regular and preventative care is consistently applied.

Summing up the discussion of the aspects of medical technology that affect the overall cost to the principal, we can conclude that the information that we have about the aims in the social welfare function and the cost structure in the medical field lead to the prediction that the overall cost to the principal is minimized when the outcome is that all have preventative and regular care, and when health is financed in a society-wide "insurance" or other redistributive pool.

3.2 Marginal Costs of Healthcare Are Increasing

Technology aspects bearing on the costs to agent/patient add further complexity. Having mentioned earlier the possibility of paying with private funds for care, we mentioned that such funds are unlikely to be available (with the exception of very few individuals) when it comes to urgent need for specialized and critical care. Here is the right place to elaborate why that is the case, and consequently why the financial transfers from the healthy to the sick are a present-day necessity. They are necessary, and it is pure luck that, according to Kornai and Eggleston (2001), the collective principal has preferences consistent with authorizing those transfers.

For almost any individual or family, as the costs of medical innovations and life-saving procedures rise, as is implied by the technological characteristics of medical innovations, the cost of treatment *if* one actually becomes very ill exceeds the ability to pay.

The distinctive nature of healthcare as a good, another technology-related aspect, accounts for the second-order market failure following the first-order market failure as described above. Where with any other good the financial markets would make the resources available, and the price of credit would be bolstered by the strength of the individual's demand for such credit, with financing health this approach fails. This is because in financing healthcare a lender would be financing the "investment" in the survival and the subsequent earning ability of a sick individual—the greater the demand for funding, the sicker the individual and, so to speak, the weaker the "collateral."

The view that individual savings can become a means of financing health care is similarly fallacious for related reasons. A large number of the sickest patients are sick because of genetic or related to genetic predispositions reasons and thus need expensive care when they are younger than the wage-earning age. Moreover, this view once again fails to account for the peculiarities of health as a good. The costlier variety of health care is demanded by the sickest individuals in a society—by precisely those who encounter additional difficulties in developing their earning capacity in the knowledge-based economy and present high risk as potential hires. And later in life, once an illness strikes, maintaining one's career can be near impossible even for high-earning individuals. Finally, almost a necessary precursor to high earnings in a modern economy is accumulation of massive debt—not savings—during the stage of professional education and early career development, which excludes a large portion of the demographics from the ability to accumulate savings of sufficient size to fund a serious treatment.

A combination of failure to purchase adequate amount of insurance, not having enough ready money, and getting sick and requiring treatment falls in our category of non-compliance with the market-type health contract/policy as in Fig. 2. In our abstract representation, it is up to an individual to decide how much insurance or care to purchase, as long as she does not attempt to receive anything beyond what she paid for. In other words, one can look at the situation from the following angle: *asking* for treatment for which you are not eligible under this form of the social contract is what constitutes non-compliance by the Agent (patient).

3.3 Is Consumption of Healthcare Peculiar?

The next question that we need to ask ourselves as we generate the payoff functions for our model is to what extent and when is the demand for healthcare elastic? Pauly (1986) revisits the application of the economic model of insurance to health care to argue that tax subsidies to health insurance create incentives to overuse health care. He argues that moral hazard plays a strong role in medical insurance. Here, moral hazard can either occur when the presence of health insurance causes the insured person to spend less on preventative care—i.e. to take greater risks because the of certainty of coverage in the event of an illness—or it occurs when the purchase of insurance causes a person to spend more to treat an illness than that person would have spent without the insurance. (1986, 640) As an example, Pauly cites data showing that people who are insured for only part of the year use ambulatory care twice as much while insured than while uninsured. (1986, 636). He assumes that the relative lack of care while uninsured indicates the true value of health care for this group—thus the care consumed while insured constitutes overconsumption.

The moral hazard notion has a number of critics. A RAND corporation experiment notes that high levels of co-pays for health insurance will induce people to use less health care, but not necessarily in an efficient way (Gladwell 2005). Many of the services they neglected were necessary and using them could have decreased, rather than increased, overall costs. In a popular article, Gladwell (2005) thus portrays the real-life choices many lower income people make in health care consumption:

> Steve uses less health care than he would if he had insurance, but that's not because he has defeated the scourge of moral hazard. It's because instead of getting a broken bone fixed he put a bandage on it.

Gladwell's numerous colorful examples show that, rather than revealing low utility for health care, many choose not to purchase health insurance because that purchase would make it impossible for them to purchase anything else. If this is the case, then we must be careful to not let concerns regarding misuse of medical care be inflated in assessing efficiency.

This elasticity, manifested in reduced demand below some basic level of necessary care due to agent's inability to pay, is contrary to the principal's preferences, and therefore a decrease in demand for these reasons decreases the principal's utility, costs notwithstanding. And it might not even reduce the costs: Currie and Gruber (1996) explore the effects from the extension of Medicaid services to a larger proportion of people. They note that, consistent with Pauly's findings, following the increased opportunity to use health services, a larger number of people made use of them. They also note that this use was beneficial—child mortality decreased significantly. In terms of efficiency, they argue that the cost per life saved was lower than the typical "value of a human life"—or that the benefits of the Medicaid extension were higher than the costs. This is consistent with the claim that access to regular care is less costly than reliance only on emergency care.

Another aspect of moral hazard with agents-patients arises when they do not put enough effort in preventative care and so eventually run up the cost of treatment by developing advanced diseases or acute problems. However, since they are unlikely to delay seeking treatment when they have coverage as compared to those who are uninsured, this possibility merely has the potential to wipe out some of the cost gains. Yet one more instance of moral hazard is when patients fail to select the cheaper and more efficient providers and treatments out of available alternatives. This can be addressed by incentive schemes in a straightforward way. To encourage the use of preventative care which may be personally costly in terms of time and effort, the principal may choose to reward desirable behavior of individuals. When it comes to encouraging economical use of health care resources, health care structures must provide incentives.

4 Health Policy Choice: Entitlement Versus Market (Insurance-)Based Contracts

We simplify the field of healthcare provision mechanisms to two stylized policy extremes between our policy makers who will be choosing using their constitutionally decided decision rule: the entitlement mechanism with automatic flat tax versus fully individualistic purchase (of either healthcare of health insurance). The Entitlement policy is the single payer guaranteed basic care provision funded with a universal tax on all workers (a system like the funding of Medicare and Social Security). The single payer system generally collects taxes from the population and uses that money to fund universal health care for its population. On the one hand, it maximizes the size of the risk pool, and on the other hand it requires making resource allocation decisions that would allow the resource expenditures over the entire population to fit within the budget constraint. Both of these aspects of the *Entitlement* policy choice are outside of our analytical framework here. We do not rely in our conclusions on assuming that population wide risk pool improves financial solvency of the system, nor do we address the decision by the principal of what healthcare services and under what circumstances must be provided to each person.[4]

4.1 The Model

Our model analyzes the choice of policy coverage using backward induction. In Fig. 2a, we depict the choices made using unanimity rule. In this situation, the UIP must decide between health care as an *entitlement*, E, or through private (*insurance*) purchase, I. Next, the Patient/agent, A, either *complies* (c) or not ($\sim c$) with the requirements of either coverage scheme. Finally, the PP chooses whether to *enforce* (e) or not ($\sim e$) the rules of the given coverage scheme at point of service.

Moving now to the stylized model of constitutional and policy choice, payoffs in Fig. 2 to all three actors-principals reflect their preferences for delivering health benefits according to Kornai and Eggleston (2001). The other model's necessary component is the allocation of costs within the principal, and payoffs to EAP, UIP, MIP, and PP reflect those costs as they are born by each particular type of a player. A contract that the principal chooses consists of a funding scheme and of the guarantee of the delivery of the good (healthcare), which may or may not be a function of the agent's contribution to funding. Due to the lexicographic preferences in the polity, the budget constraint within the health policy area is soft and provision does not have to cease when designated funding is depleted.[5] This is not an ad hoc assumption but follows from the presumed preferences of the PP and the nature of the enforcement process. In short, it is this assumption that identifies the particular case of collective action problems that we address.

In this essay we choose to treat the soft budget constraint in regard to health as an assumption, but it could be viewed a part of an equilibrium strategy of the principal who, among other things, could be asked to decide whether or not to hold the budget

[4]For arguments regarding the relative efficiencies of single payer versus private insurance systems, see Sieberg and Shvetsova (2012).

[5]As noted by a reviewer, the terms 'soft constraint' appears to be an oxymoron. We use the term here to distinguish between the intended constraint on health care spending determined by private purchase and the extra spending, that must covered by taxation, because the principal is unwilling in the end to let the people pay the price for their own decisions.

constraint as firm at a price of human lives or health. The source of additional funds presumably is the national budget, where the budget constraint is firm but one could allow for borrowing against the next period or redistributing from other spending areas.

Thus, to make up for the potential shortfall in the area of healthcare, in parallel, and in the background, there is a nesting policy of general taxation addressed in the extant literature discussed in the next section. General taxation to cover any care that was provided but not purchased, we here assume, is always decided by majority.[6] Thus we can fall back on the results on the median voter tax preferences.

Constitutional choice for policy procedure that we model applies only to the area of healthcare. But actors in their decisions are cognizant that it takes place under the expectations generated by majoritarian general taxation and this factors into their expected payoffs. We show that the majoritarian procedure leads to exploiting the state budget in lieu of designing an efficient policy-specific financing mechanism. The combined (health policy-designated budget, plus cost overruns covered from general taxation) funding mechanism will be more equitable if the decision is made by unanimity, and will end up more redistributive when the decisive coalition diminishes in size (e.g., under majority). This is because when the contract is designed by (ex-ante) unanimity (as in the case of UIP in Fig. 2a), there does not exist a minority outside the decisive coalition which could be legally obligated to disproportionately finance the policy (or as may be the case in the US, its cost overruns), so every person will have to agree to bear a part of the burden.

4.2 The Median Voter Theorem and Majoritarian Taxation

While the taxing decision is not included in the extensive form in Fig. 2, it is certainly implied and must be accounted for in the payoffs of the interim principals both in Figs. 2a and 2b. Under a private insurance system, individuals will purchase a certain amount of coverage, beyond which they should not get treatment. However, there is a contingency where the ex-post principal will not deny treatment in the case of need. If, ex-post, these unfunded expenses are covered from general taxation, agreed on by majority rule, then majority preference over healthcare policy that generates budget overruns will depend directly on how much of this excess burden is borne by the median voter.

Scholars of fiscal policy (see, e.g., Meltzer and Richard 1981, 1983) rely on the premise that median income is way below the mean of the income distribution and thus redistributive taxation by majority is enabled. The voluminous body of literature predicts it to be placing the chief burden of taxes on the wealthy minority. In a population with an income distribution that is skewed towards the left, the

[6]In general, taxes can be used to fund a host of services, projects, redistribution schemes, etc. To avoid complication, we merely address the issue of taxation to finance extra health care spending here.

median voter has a lower income than the mean voter. This voter, then, has more incentive to demand redistributive taxation (see Rosenthal and Eibner 2005, Nelson 1999) because she bears less of the burden. Holcombe and Caudill (1985) show that the median voter can bear no tax burden at all. In this case, the median voter prefers an insurance system in which she pays only for her own insurance, and wealthier voters pay for the care of those who need care beyond their level of coverage. If this holds, then a healthy median voter would pay less under an insurance scheme than with *Entitlement*; thus her payoff for *Insurance* is d which is greater than or equal to the baseline payoff of 0. This idea is consistent with other research on the link between the median voter's tax share and social spending. For example, Corcoran and Evans (2010) find that a reduction in the median voter's tax share induces higher local spending on public education. Thus the expectation of the majority coalition on the dimension of general taxation is zero personal contribution to paying for the cost overrun on healthcare.

4.3 Median Preferences on Healthcare Policy

The next step to identifying the payoff to MIP is to see what the median on healthcare dimension expects to pay and to receive. Adding the premise that the distribution of health is skewed similarly to that of wealth but in the substantively "opposite" direction, we assume that the mean "level of sickness" is above the population median, meaning that most healthcare costs (due to the costly specialized care and severe disability maintenance) are demanded by a relatively small minority of the population.

As an illustration, consider a hypothetical example with binary types in the population on each dimension. Suppose, to keep it simple, that individuals who comprise the principal at the interim stage know their health type as well as their wealth type, and the probabilities are .2 of the wealthy type on the dimension of wealth, and .2 of the sick type on the dimension of health. Then the joint distribution in the voting population deciding on healthcare policy given that cost overruns are made up from general taxation becomes as in Table 2.

Notice in the illustration in Table 2 that in this rather extreme case 64 percent of the electorate will not need to pay anything for their own healthcare AND are not going to be in the fiscal pool for general taxation. Relatively to the baseline payoff from *Entitlement* policy, with its uniform tax, they are thus saving some positive amount d, as reflected in the payoffs to the MIP in Fig. 3.

In real circumstances, the distributions of health and/or of wealth might be relatively more centered, yet the coalition with preference for *Insurance* might still

Table 2 A hypothetical distribution of types in the electorate

	Poor	Wealthy
Sick	.16	.04
Healthy	.64	.16

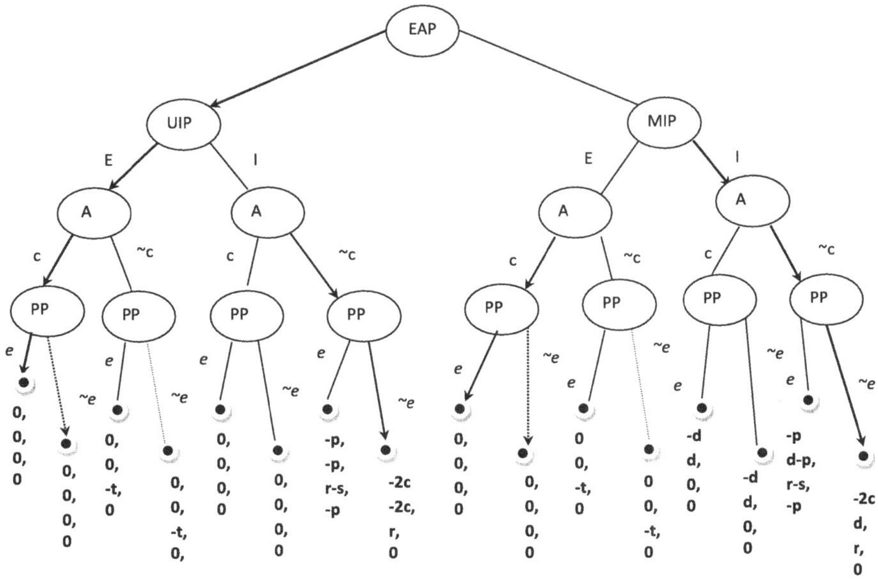

Fig. 3 Choice of the decision rule for Healthcare policy at the constitutional (Rawlsian) stage (the payoff of the ex-ante principal (EAP) is the first payoff)

exceed majority—due to those groups that are exempt from participation in the policy but can vote on its adoption.

5 Analysis

We can now apply backward induction to the game with the payoffs generated from the above discussion. In the subgame starting with the move by UIP on the left hand side of the tree in Fig. 3, if *Insurance* is the policy, the PP obtains a negative payoff of $-p$ if he *Enforces* the rules and does not treat a patient who has not purchased sufficient coverage. Given that preference of PP, the Agent knows that she can safely *not comply*, because she does not risk the payoff $r\text{–}s$, and instead she can obtain the positive payoff r.

If the policy is *Entitlement*, the PP has no difference in payoffs due to his choice, because all citizens are covered under *Entitlement* and so he has to provide care under both *enforce* and *not enforce*. The Agent, in this case does better by *complying*—and obtaining the baseline payoff of 0 than by *not complying* and obtaining $-t$ if she stays out of the workforce (which is what it takes to *not comply*).

At the top of the subgame, then, the UIP knows that it faces a choice between the baseline payoff, 0 and covering emergency care, $-c$, so the UIP will opt for *Entitlement*.

In the subgame on the right hand side starting with the move by MIP, however, the situation differs. Here, the left hand side of the tree is identical to that in the UIP subgame, with Agent complying. And on the right hand side, the PP will still opt not to enforce the rules. Given the choice by PP, the Agent, similarly, knows that she can safely *not comply*.

But the MIP's preferences are different from the UIP's and so with the same expectation with regard to the outcomes, he makes a different move. The median voter, at most, pays only for her own insurance. And she is also exempt from the general tax which will be used to cover the care of those who will *not comply*. This lower personal cost to the median voter results in a higher utility than the baseline payoff, thus, the MIP will opt for *Insurance*.

The move by EAP in Fig. 3 shows the decision at the Rawlsian "veiled" stage. Our EAP, anticipating the outcomes in the Unanimity and Majoritarian subgames and their respective consequences, will opt for *Unanimity*, thus avoiding a lower payoff, $-2c$, from paying for emergency care instead of regular care.

6 Alternate Coalitions

To this point, we have not considered the possibility that emergency health care is inferior to regular care not just in its cost, but in the health outcomes as well. Introducing that assumption now allows us to suggest the potential for other coalitions that could arise with regards to health care coverage systems. In particular, if we assume that the value of emergency care is less than that of regular care (or, more generally, that the expected utility from emergency care is lower than that from regular care) then the poor and unhealthy are less likely to be as satisfied with the emergency care as their sole health care option as they would be with access to regular care. If a poor person pi's utility from care that she would receive under Entitlement, R, minus her uniform tax that she would pay, T_{pi}, were higher than her utility from emergency care, E, i.e. if

$$U_{pi}(R - T_{pi}) > U_{pi}(E)$$

then pi would prefer the Entitlement option.

Similarly, if a wealthy person, rj, pays lower taxes under *Entitlement* than her own health premiums and other payments under *Insurance*, d_{rj}, combined with her burden of funding the emergency care of the sick poor, IT_{rj}, then she would also prefer *Entitlement*, as long as the following holds (where I is health care from *Insurance* while R is health care from *Entitlement*):

$$U_{rj}(R - T_{rj}) > U_{rj}(I - d_{rj} - IT_{rj}).$$

If the combined population in the two above groups is large enough to constitute a majority, then these groups can form a coalition and adopt Entitlement even at the legislative stage.[7]

[7] If, in addition to differences in values of emergency versus regular care, we include high enough uncertainty as to one's own health status, we have the potential for everyone to opt for Entitlement.

7 Conclusion

Organization and financing of healthcare is characterized by an apparent general preference for something that, at least in the US, the legitimate and democratic political process is not quite able to supply—some sort of a fair single-payer system. This makes healthcare one in a class of issues for which the established political process seems to be a "wrong" decision structure. There are other issues with similar manifested qualities which linger unresolved or unaddressed possibly for similar reasons—maternity and parental leave and pay policies, and societal support for childcare, pollution control, and banking regulation come to mind. All of these situations are among the special case of collective action problems described above. Among the developed democracies, so similar in so many other regards, some seem to have much easier time grappling with such issues than others, suggesting that the theoretical story to explain the variation might involve institutional differences. We here suggest that those institutional differences are to be found at the constitutional level.

We claim that these "hung" issues are so problematic because the decision-making rule applied in their attempted resolution is "suboptimal", given the distribution of preferences and the technology of the good provision. In the tradition of Buchanan and Tullock (1962), we show that, given the preference distribution, *for that issue*, the society would have preferred a different decision rule if it were possible for it to revert to the ex-ante, rules-choosing, constitutional stage and to pick rules for one issue at a time.

Our conclusions here are two-fold. First, with regard to the healthcare policy, or any policy in this set of collective action problems, we show that the socially preferred rule for producing such policy is not majoritarian. We tentatively suggest that it approximates the unanimity given our assumptions. This means that the socially preferred approach to healthcare given the modern state of technology of that industry is to treat the issue as (quasi-)constitutional, rather than to relegate it to the on-going legislative process. In practice, this could manifest in giving it the status of a positive right or an entitlement and fixing its funding principle outside of the ebb and flow of the policy process, much as is done in the US with Social Security.

Second, on a grander scale, our findings lead us to argue that reliance on the policy process to address all issues, including those that significantly evolve and transform and those that newly emerge, is fraught with efficiency losses. Health care is but one example where access to the "constitutionalization" of an issue could be of benefit. Rigid and impervious to amendment, constitutions which evolve mostly by interpretation may engender political environments that are particularly unfit to take up such issues.

There are numerous arguments in favor of single-payer entitlement health care systems ranging from assertions that it reduces health care risks for citizens and avoid inequities (Blumenthal and Hsaio 2005) to that it is more socially efficient than private insurance systems (Sieberg and Shvetsova 2012). Regardless of their benefits, single payer systems may fail to be implemented if the decision procedure itself is not selected carefully. Our model shows that the legislature is not necessarily the best venue to decide ALL issues of importance for the society at large. Some majority choices, while understandably best for their particular coalition, are particularly costly to society overall. Behind the veil of ignorance, the ex-ante principal would have recognized this potential and opt to have these matters decided as constitutional.

References

Attfield R (1990) The global distribution of health care resources. J Med Ethics 16(3):153–156

Blank R, Burau V (2006) Setting health priorities across nations: more convergence than divergence? J Public Health Policy 27(3):265–281

Bloom DE, Canning D (2000) The health and wealth of nations. Science 287(5456):1207–1209

Blumenthal D, Hsaio W (2005) Privatization and its discontents—the evolving Chinese health care system. N Engl J Med 333(11):1165–1170

Buchanan JM, Tullock G (1962) The calculus of consent: logical foundations of constitutional democracy. University of Michigan Press, Ann Arbor

Corcoran S, Evans WN (2010) Income inequality, the median voter, and the support for public education. NBER working paper No 16097

Currie J, Gruber J (1996) Health insurance eligibility, utilization of medical care, and child health. Q J Econ 111.2:431–466

Enthoven AC (1993) The history and principles of managed competition. Health Aff 12(Suppl 1): 24–48

Fuchs VR (1996) Economics, values, and health care reform. Am Econ Rev 86(1):1–24

Gladwell M (2005) The moral-hazard myth: the bad idea behind our failed health-care system. The New Yorker, August 29

Howell JD, McLaughlin CG (1989) Regional variation in 1917 health care expenditures. Med Care 27(8):772–788

Halfon N, Hochstein M (2002) Life course health development: an integrated framework for developing health, policy, and research. Milbank Q 80(3):433–479

Holcombe RG, Caudill SB (1985) Tax shares and government spending in a median voter model. Public Choice 46:197–206

Hsaio WC (1994) 'Marketization'—the illusory magic pill. Health Econ 3:351–357

Institute of Medicine (2002) Care without coverage: too little, too late, committee on the consequences of uninsurance, board of health care services. National Academy Press, Washington

Kornai J, Eggleston K (2001) Welfare, choice, and solidarity in transition: reforming the health sector in Eastern Europe. Cambridge University Press, Cambridge

Klarman HE (1969) Reimbursing the hospital the differences the third party makes. J Risk Insur 36(5):553–566

Matthews D (2010) Hayek on social insurance. The Washington Post, 9 July

Meltzer AH, Richard SF (1981) A rational theory of the size of government. J Polit Econ 89:914–927

Meltzer AH, Richard SF (1983) Tests of a rational theory of the size of government. Public Choice 41:403–418

Nelson P (1999) Redistribution and the income of the median voter. Public Choice 98:187–194

Newhouse JP (1992) Medical care costs: how much welfare loss? J Econ Perspect 6(3):3–21

Pauly MV (1986) Taxation, health insurance, and market failure in the medical economy. J Econ Lit 24(2):629–675

Rawls J (1971) A theory of justice. Harvard University Press, Cambridge

Rosenthal H, Eibner C (2005) Immigration and the median Voter's incentive to redistribute income in the United States. Paper presented at the annual meeting of the society for the advancement of socio-economics, "What counts? Calculation, representation, association," Budapest, Hungary. June 30–July 2

Sieberg KK, Shvetsova O (2012) Kustannustehokkuuden ja kattavuuden ongelmat Yhdysvaltain terveydenhuollossa (Efficiency and coverage problems in United States' Healthcare) Puheenvuoro. Hallinon Tutkimus, Administrative Studies (forthcoming)

Part II
Modelling

Challenges to the Standard Euclidean Spatial Model

Jon X. Eguia

1 Introduction

Spatial models are useful to represent political competition over policy issues. If the feasible policies over a given policy issue are endowed with a natural left/right or low/high order, we can represent the set of feasible policies by a subset of the real line. Many policy issues are indeed easily ordered: tax rates can vary from 0 % to 100 %; any budgeted policy item can receive a lower or higher budget; criminal law can specify lighter or harsher sentences; etc. It is standard to assume that agents have a unique ideal policy and that given two policies below the agent's ideal policy, or given two policies above the agent's ideal policy, the agent prefers the policy closer to the agent's ideal. Preferences satisfying this assumption are *single-peaked*. If agents' preferences are single peaked over the real line, simple majority rule is transitive (Black 1948); furthermore, the median ideal policy among all the agents' ideal policies defeats any other policy if the number of agents is odd and it cannot be defeated by any other policy when preferences are aggregated by majority rule (Black 1958). Since the median policy cannot be defeated by any other, electoral competition between two candidates leads to policy convergence: both candidates choose the median policy (Downs 1957, building on Hotelling's (1929)), even if the candidates have diverging policy preferences (Wittman 1983; Calvert 1985).

Political competition usually involves multiple policy issues. Candidates propose policy bundles with one policy per issue. Multidimensional spatial models represent preferences over policy bundles: each dimension corresponds to a given issue. Starting with Davis et al. (1972), the standard approach is to assume that agents have a

This working paper is meant to be published as a chapter in the volume "Advances in Political Economy", edited by G. Caballero, D. Kselman and N. Schofield. I thank Scott Tyson for suggestions. Comments to ammend errors or to provide updates to the working paper are welcome even after the publication of the volume.

J.X. Eguia (✉)
Department of Politics, New York University, 19 West 4th, 2nd floor, New York, NY 10012, USA
e-mail: eguia@nyu.edu

N. Schofield et al. (eds.), *Advances in Political Economy*,
DOI 10.1007/978-3-642-35239-3_8, © Springer-Verlag Berlin Heidelberg 2013

most preferred alternative in the policy space, and utilities that are decreasing in the Euclidean distance to this point, typically with a linear (Kramer 1977; Wittman 1977; Patty et al. 2009; Degan and Merlo 2009; or Eguia 2012), quadratic (Feddersen 1992; Clinton et al. 2004; Schofield and Sened 2006; or Schofield 2007b,a) or exponential (Poole and Rosenthal 1985) loss function.[1] Other theories allow for more general utility functions, but they preserve the circular Euclidean shape of indifference curves (McKelvey 1976), or they relax the assumption of circular indifference curves but maintain the restrictions that utility functions be differentiable (Plott 1967; Schofield 1978; Duggan 2007; or Duggan and Kalandrakis 2012), quasiconcave (Banks and Duggan 2008), or differentiable and quasiconcave (Kramer 1973).

I present a series of theoretical and empirical results that challenge the assumption that preferences over multiple issues can be adequately represented by utility functions that are linear, quadratic or exponential Euclidean in a multidimensional space. More generally, I present results that call into question whether preferences can be represented by differentiable or quasiconcave utility functions, let alone with Euclidean or weighted Euclidean utility functions.

I divide these theoretical and empirical challenges to standard assumptions in three classes:

I. Concerns about the concavity of the loss function, accepting the Euclidean shape of the indifference curves.
II. Concerns about the shape of indifference curves: convexity, and different weights for different dimensions.
III. Concerns about the shape of indifference curves: separability across issues.

2 Concerns About the Loss Function

Circular indifference curves are a common assumption on preferences in multidimensional spatial models. Circular indifference curves are such that two policy points which are at identical distances from an agent's ideal point are valued identically, i.e. the 'direction' of the perturbation from the agent's ideal point is inconsequential for his or her utility. This is a standard assumption on indifference curves. However, no similar consensus exists on a standard or default assumption on the loss function associated with these indifference curves. Linear or quadratic loss functions are the most commonly used (McCarty and Meirowitz 2007, Sect. 2.5). As noted in the Introduction, exponential functions are also used (Poole and Rosenthal 1985).[2] The choice of the functional form of the utility function in the various theories in the literature appears motivated by convenience or simplicity.

The choice of loss functions is consequential: important results rely crucially on the concavity of the loss function. For instance, in a probabilistic voting model of

[1] D'Agostino and Dardanoni (2009) provide an axiomatization of the Euclidean distance; Azrieli (2011) provides an axiomatization of Euclidean utilities with a quasilinear additive valence term.

[2] In support of their assumption of exponential utility functions, Poole and Rosenthal (1997) argue that (standard) concave utility functions do not fit the data well.

electoral competition with two candidates, Kamada and Kojima (2010) show that in equilibrium candidates converge to the median if voters' utility functions are concave, but candidates diverge if voters' utility functions are sufficiently convex.

Osborne (1995) warns that "*the assumption of concavity is often adopted, first because it is associated with 'risk aversion' and second because it makes easier to show that an equilibrium exists. However, [...] it is not clear that evidence that people are risk averse in economic decision-making has any relevance here. I conclude that in the absence of any convincing empirical evidence, it is not clear which of the assumptions is more appropriate.*"

Seeking to test voters' risk attitude, Berinsky and Lewis (2007) assume that utility functions take the form $u_i(x, x_k) = -d(x, x_i^*)^\alpha$, where $d(x, x_i^*)$ is a weighted Euclidean distance and α is a parameter to be estimated. They find that the estimate that provides a best fit for voter choices in US presidential elections is $\hat{\alpha} \approx 1$, suggesting that it is appropriate to assume that voters' utilities are linear weighted Euclidean. They interpret this finding as evidence that voters are risk neutral, but Eguia (2009) casts axiomatic doubt on this interpretation: linear Euclidean utilities do not satisfy additive separability, so the preferences over lotteries on a given issue and hence the risk attitude of a voter with a linear Euclidean utility function depend on outcomes on other issues. In other words, voters with multi-dimensional linear Euclidean utilities are not risk neutral. With utilities that decrease in weighted Euclidean distances, additive separability (i.e. independence of preferences over lotteries on one issue with outcomes on other issues) requires that the loss function be quadratic (Eguia 2011b). The only way to reconcile additive separability (which under Euclidean indifference curves requires a quadratic loss function) with Berinski and Lewis's (2007) finding (with Euclidean indifference curves a linear loss function provides the best fit) is to discard the assumption of Euclidean indifference curves, and to check if under different shapes of the indifference curves, we obtain a best fit with a parameter for the loss function that is consistent with additive separability. This leads us to the second class of concerns: concerns about the shape of the indifference curves.

3 Concerns About Convexity of Preferences

A first concern about the assumption of utility functions that depend on the Euclidean distance is that some issues may be more important than others, and hence utilities ought to be weighted, generating elliptical (rather than circular) indifference curves in the case with two dimensions. If all voters assign the same weights to these dimensions, the problem is trivially solved, and Euclidean circles reinstated, by rescaling the units of measure of each dimension according to its weight. If different groups of voters assign different relative weights to the various dimensions, then it is not possible to rescale the dimensions so as to use unweighted Euclidean utilities, and we must instead use weighted Euclidean utilities with different weights for different voters (Miller and Schofield 2003).

A deeper concern is that preferences may not be representable by weighted Euclidean utility functions: indifference curves may have shapes that are not elliptical. Weighted Euclidean utilities represent a particular class of convex preferences. Preferences are (strictly) convex if the upper contour set defined by each indifference curve is (strictly) convex; that is, if the set of policies preferable to policy x is convex, for any x. Representable (strictly) convex preferences are representable by (strictly) quasiconcave utility functions. If preferences are not strictly convex, they cannot be represented by Euclidean utility functions, neither unweighted nor weighted ones. The curvature imposed by Euclidean utilities is simply not adequate to represent the preferences.

An alternative assumption to Euclidean preferences is city-block preferences, which define square indifference curves (with squares tilted at a 45 degree angle relative to the axes of coordinates), and are representable by utility functions that are decreasing in the l_1 distance $\|x - x^*\|_1 = \sum_{k=1}^{K} |x_k - x_k^*|$, where x_k is the policy on issue $k \in \{1, \ldots, K\}$. That is, agents with city block preferences calculate the distance between two points by adding up the distance dimension by dimension, as if traveling on a grid (that is why the l_1 or city block distance is sometimes called "Manhattan distance"), and they prefer points closer to their ideal according to this notion of distance. If preferences are city block, their utility representation is not strictly quasiconcave, and it is not differentiable. Classic results on the instability of simple majority rule (Plott 1967; McKelvey 1976) do not apply if agents have city block preferences. In fact, the core of simple majority rule is not empty under more general conditions if agents have city-block preferences (Rae and Taylor 1971; Wendell and Thorson 1974; McKelvey and Wendell 1976; Humphreys and Laver 2009).

Humphreys and Laver (2009) invoke results from psychology and cognitive sciences (Shepard 1987; Arabie 1991) to argue that agents measure distance to objects with separable attributes by adding up the distance in each attribute, which implies that if the object under consideration is a policy bundle on separable issues, agents measure distance according to the city block function.

Grynaviski and Corrigan (2006) find that a model that assumes voters have city block preferences provides a better fit of vote choice in US presidential elections than an alternative model that assumes voters have linear Euclidean preferences. Westholm (1997) finds that a model with city block preferences outperforms a model with quadratic Euclidean preferences, when aiming to predict vote choice in Norwegian elections. However, a binary comparison between city block utilities based on the l_1 metric $\|x - x^*\|_1 = \sum_{k=1}^{K} |x_k - x_k^*|$ and the linear Euclidean utilities based on the l_2 metric $\|x - x^*\|_2 = (\sum_{k=1}^{K} (x_k - x_k^*)^2)^{\frac{1}{2}}$ is unnecessarily restrictive: l_1 and l_2 are special cases of the Minkowski (1886) family of metric functions, which parameterized by δ, gives the distance between x and x^* as:

$$\|x - x^*\|_\delta = \left(\sum_{k=1}^{K} (x_k - x_k^*)^\delta\right)^{\frac{1}{\delta}}. \tag{1}$$

Rather than comparing $\delta = 1$ (linear city block) and $\delta = 2$ (linear Euclidean), it appears more fruitful to estimate parameter δ. Rivero (2011) estimates δ for several Spanish regional elections and finds that $\hat{\delta} \in (0.92, 1.17)$; none of the estimates is significantly different from $\delta = 1$, and they are all significantly different from $\delta = 2$. These tests support the use of linear city block over linear Euclidean utility functions.

Utility functions that are linearly decreasing in expression (1) are not additively separable unless $\delta = 1$. To satisfy additive separability, the utility function must be linearly decreasing in the δ power of $\|x - x^*\|_\delta$, so that

$$u(x, x^*) = -\sum_{k=1}^{K} (x_k - x_k^*)^\delta, \tag{2}$$

with linear city block utilities corresponding to $\delta = 1$, and quadratic Euclidean to $\delta = 2$. Notice that any parameter $\delta > 1$ results in strictly convex preferences and strictly quasiconcave and differentiable utility functions, while $\delta < 1$ results on preferences that are not convex, and utility functions that are neither strictly quasiconcave, nor differentiable. Ye et al. (2011) estimate parameter δ using the utility function (2) and voting data from the American National Election Studies corresponding to the 2000, 2004 and 2008 Presidential elections. However, their results are inconclusive, obtaining estimates that vary greatly across elections and, most puzzlingly, across candidates.

Further empirical work appears necessary to establish which utility functions provide a better fit, and whether the standard assumption of convex preferences is justified.

Most of the literature, and all of the discussion above, considers the set of alternatives as exogenously given: there is a subset $X \subseteq \mathbb{R}^K$ that is given, and agents have preferences over X. In this view, the question on the adequate assumption on the shape of the utility functions (Euclidean, city block, Minkowski with parameter δ) is a question on what primitive preferences over alternatives do we believe that agents have on $X \subseteq \mathbb{R}^K$.

However, the spatial representation of the set of feasible policies is itself a representation used for convenience, just as the utility functions are representations of underlying preferences. If, for instance, there are three policies x, y and z and agent i prefers x to y to z, and agent i is indifferent between y and a fair lottery between x and z, then we can map the three policies to the real line using a mapping $f : \{x, y, z\} \rightarrow \mathbb{R}$ such that $f(x) = 0$, $f(y) = 0.5$ and $f(z) = 1$ and then we can say that the agent has a linear utility function over $[0, 1]$ with ideal point at 0. But we can represent the same underlying preferences using a mapping $g : \{x, y, z\} \rightarrow \mathbb{R}$ such that $f(x) = 0$, $f(y) = \sqrt{\frac{1}{2}}$ and $f(z) = 1$ and say that the agent has a quadratic utility function over $[0, 1]$ with ideal point at 0. Under this perspective, we see that the shape of the utility function is an object of choice for the theorist who wishes to study an individual: using a different mapping of the set of alternatives into a vector space leads to indifference curves of different shapes. The spatial representation of the set of alternatives and the utility function we use in this space jointly determine the assumptions we make on the underlying preferences of the agent.

Once we recognize that the spatial representation of the set of alternatives is an endogenous choice made by the theorist who wishes to model preferences, we can ask new questions: can all preferences over policies be represented by Euclidean utility functions *in some space?* if not, what preferences can be represented by Euclidean utility functions? If we accept a spatial representation with great dimensionality, we obtain a positive result: any preference profile with N agents can be represented by utility functions that are Euclidean for all N agents if we let the mapping of the set of alternatives X into $\mathbb{R}^K$ contain $K \geq N$ dimensions (Bogomolnaia and Laslier 2007). If we care for the number of dimensions in our spatial representation, we do not obtain such a positive result. Suppose the policy issues are exogenously given, and we want to use no more than one dimension per issue in our spatial representation. In this case, while we can represent any single-peaked, separable preference relation of a single individual using quadratic Euclidean utility functions over an appropriately chosen spatial representation of the set of alternatives, we cannot represent the preferences of all N individuals with quadratic Euclidean utility functions in any spatial representation unless the underlying preference profile satisfies very restrictive conditions (Eguia 2011a).[3]

For any single-peaked preference profile with separable preferences, we can map the set of alternatives into $\mathbb{R}^K$ so as to represent the preferences of a given agent by quasiconcave utility functions over the chosen map. However, depending on the preference profile, any mapping that achieves this may be such that the utility representations of the preferences of other agents violate quasiconcavity and/or differentiability. Whether preference profiles in any given application are such that the preferences of all agents can be represented in some map with quasiconcave utility functions is an open empirical question.

4 Concerns About Separability of Preferences

Expressions (1) or (2) above, or variations with weights for each dimension, allow us to relax the assumption that indifference curves have circular or elliptical curvature. We are free to assume any degree of curvature, including preferences that are not convex by choosing $\delta < 1$. These generalizations of the standard model from $\delta = 2$ to any $\delta > 0$ preserve the assumption that preferences are separable across issues: ordinal preferences over alternatives on a given issue do not depend on the realized outcome on other issues.

Milyo (2000b) and (2000a) notes that preferences over multiple dimensions of public spending cannot possibly be separable. Suppose a fixed unit of national income is to be allocated between public spending on policy one, public spending on

[3]Calvo et al. (2012) analyze an additional complication: agents may not agree on which alternative is to the right or left of another on a given issue. If so, we cannot use a unique spatial representation; rather, we must have subjective maps of the set of the set of alternatives, one for each agent.

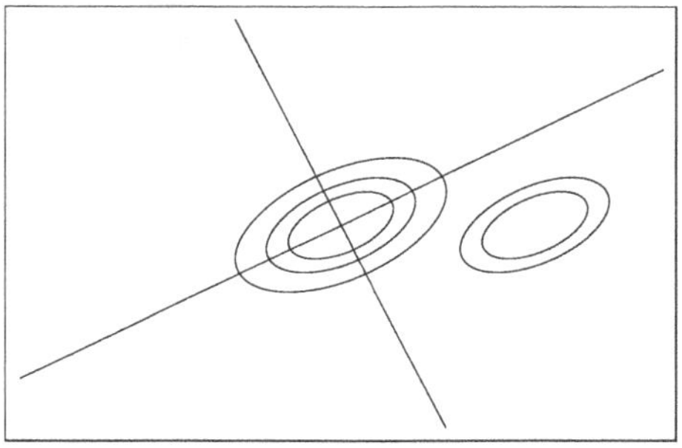

Fig. 1 Obtaining separability by using a new basis of vectors

policy two, and private consumption. Decreasing marginal utility over consumption of public goods means that as public spending on policy one increases, the opportunity cost of spending on issue two also increases, so the ideal amount of expenditures on issue two must decrease with the amount spent on issue one. Preferences over public spending on issues one and two cannot be separable. This problem is easily solved by redefining the policy dimensions over which we assume that agents have separable preferences: let the first dimension be total public spending, and let the second dimension be the fraction of public spending devoted to issue one. Preferences may well be separable under this representation of the set of issues, and in any case they escape Milyo's (2000b) and (2000a) critique.

A more insidious difficulty arises if preferences are truly non-separable, not due to budgetary concerns, but because agents' ideal values on a given issue actually depend on the outcomes on other issues. For instance, it is possible that agents have non-separable preferences about immigration policy and the social safety net, preferring a more generous safety net if immigration policy is restrictive so redistributive policies benefit only natives, than if immigration policy is lax so redistributive policies would in part favor immigrants. Lacy (2001a,b, 2012) uncovers evidence of such non-separability across various pairs of issues.

If agents have non-separable preferences, but the correlation between issues is the same for all agents, then the problem is addressed by considering new, endogenous policy dimensions over which agents have separable preferences. Suppose that there are two complementary issues, such that for any agent i,

$$u(x_1, x_2) = -\left(x_1 - x_1^i\right)^2 - \left(x_2 - x_2^i\right)^2 + \left(x_1 - x_1^i\right)\left(x_2 - x_2^i\right).$$

These utility functions, depicted for two arbitrary agents in Fig. 1, are not separable over the two issues. However, if we use a different basis of vectors, as depicted in Fig. 1, and consider the new two dimensional vector space given by the two tilted axes of coordinates in Fig. 1, then agents have separable preferences over the new, endogenous dimensions.

This solution fails if agents have non-separable preferences and the correlation between preferences on different issues is heterogeneous across agents. In this case, we cannot create dimensions to make all agents separable over our newly defined dimensions. For instance, returning to non-separability between immigration and social safety net, if some agents prefer a larger safety net to help needy immigrants when immigration policy is lax, while other agents prefer a smaller safety net to not spend money on immigrants when immigration policy is lax, then we can redraw the axes to make the preferences of one group of agents separable, but in doing so, the preferences of the other group of agents remain non-separable. In very non-technical terms, agents have non-separable preferences if their indifference curves are tilted; if all agents have curves equally tilted, we can tilt the whole map to return to a standard model over newly defined dimensions.

If, on the contrary, different agents have preferences tilted in different directions, we cannot correct this problem by tilting the whole map. We need instead to introduce parameters to accommodate the correlation across issues. This is a considerable setback, similar to the problem of agents who assign different relative weights to the various dimensions -but more damaging, because we need more parameters to fix it. In order to accurately represent the preferences of agents who disagree on the weights they assign to the different dimensions we need to add one parameter per dimension per agent or group of agents who disagree on these weights, for a maximum of $(K-1)(N-1)$ new parameters if there are N agents and K dimensions. In order to represent the preferences of agents who disagree on the correlation in preferences between issues, we must add one correlation parameter per possible pair of issues and per agent or group of agents who disagree, for a maximum of $\frac{K(K-1)}{2}N$ new parameters.

While violations of separability do not affect classic results on the instability of simple majority rule as long as preferences are smooth (Plott 1967; McKelvey 1979), they affect how we can interpret and use common spatial models. Consider the structured-induced equilibrium theory (Shepsle and Weingast 1981), which proposes that the instability is solved by choosing policy dimension by dimension. In the standard structured-induced equilibrium theory, the order in which the legislature considers the various policy dimensions is irrelevant, because preferences are separable. With non-separable preferences, the order in which each policy dimension is considered affects the chosen policy outcome. For a second example, consider the ideal point estimation literature (Poole and Rosenthal 1985; Clinton et al. 2004): if preferences are not separable, estimating the ideal point of each legislator is not enough to predict vote choice.

5 Discussion

Theoretical and empirical work questions not only the standard assumption of Euclidean utility functions in multidimensional spatial models, but the more general assumptions of separable, convex and/or smooth preferences.

Standard spatial models suffer from limitations that I have not considered here. For instance, an increasing body of literature argues that we must add a candidate valence term to capture the actual preferences of voters about candidates. Valence is any quality that all voters agree is good, and makes the candidate who possesses more of it more attractive to all voters. Current research on valence seeks to endogenize it and to analyze its relation to the candidate's spatial location (Ashworth and Bueno de Mesquita 2009; Zakharov 2009; Serra 2010 and 2012; Krasa and Polborn 2010, 2012; or Schofield et al. 2011). In this chapter I analyze concerns about a basic pillar of the spatial model: the assumption that agents have preferences over a vector space that represents the set of feasible policies, preferences that can be represented by analytically convenient utility functions. Valence, dynamics, uncertainty, bounded rationality, other-regarding preferences or other improvements can be added to the basic spatial model to generate richer theories, but any theory with a spatial component must address the challenges posed in this chapter about the appropriate formalization of spatial preferences in the theory.

Further empirical work is necessary to establish whether agents have convex preferences over policy bundles with multiple policy issues. Assuming the functional form (1) or, if we want to satisfy additive separability, functional form (2) for the utility functions, empirical work must estimate parameter δ. If the estimated parameter $\hat{\delta}$ is less than 1, the consequences for theoretical work are dramatic: Preferences are not convex, and hence utility functions are neither quasiconcave, nor differentiable. Standard results in the literature that rely on these assumptions, most notably the instability of majority rule (Plott 1967; McKelvey 1976; Schofield 1978), would not apply. Whereas, results that rely on city block preferences (Humphreys and Laver 2009) or on non-differentiable utility functions (Kamada and Kojima 2010) would become more relevant, and further theoretical work would be needed to establish what results in the literature obtained under assumptions of quasiconcavity or differentiability of preferences are robust and apply in environments with agents whose preferences are not representable by quasiconcave or differentiable utility functions.

If the estimated parameter $\hat{\delta}$ is consistently greater than 1, even if it is not near 2, much of the theoretical literature will be validated. The main impact of obtaining a better estimate of δ in utility functions of the form (2) that is $\hat{\delta} \neq 2$ but $\hat{\delta} > 1$ will be to improve the fit of further empirical work on ideal point estimation models (Clinton et al. 2004; Poole and Rosenthal 1985), or vote choice models, by assuming that agents have utility functions with the curvature corresponding to the best estimate of δ within the parameterized family of utility functions (2), instead of assuming that agents have utility functions with parameter $\delta = 2$ even though parameter $\delta = 2$ provides a poorer fit for the model.

With regard to separability, violations of the assumption typically do not affect equilibrium existence or convergence results on models of electoral competition or policy choice. However, application of spatial models to specific real world polities or electorates should take into account existence evidence on non-separability across various pairs of issues (Lacy 2001a,b, 2012), so that if the models explicitly include such issues, utility functions are not assumed to be separable over them. Many spatial models do not include many issues; rather, they collapse the list of all issues onto two dimensions, one that groups economic issues (from left/pro-state to right/pro-market) and another that includes all cultural issues (from left/progressive to right/conservative). It is more difficult to determine whether preferences are separable or not over such dimensions, which are not precisely defined. Nevertheless, if future empirical work reveals evidence of a systematic correlation between preferences across economic and cultural issues, models should either seek to define new dimensions (new ways of bundling or weighing the issues) in such a way that preferences are separable over the new dimensions, or else, if this cannot be achieved, then it may be necessary to allow for non-separable preferences, estimating not only an ideal point, but also a degree of correlation between dimensions for each agent or group of agents.

Euclidean preferences have been an extremely useful tool in the development of multidimensional spatial models that can explain electoral competition, government formation and legislative policy-making. Generalizations that show that several theoretical results are robust if preferences are not Euclidean but are convex and smooth allowed us to conjecture that Euclidean preferences are only a simplifying shortcut with limited effect on our ability to understand the political processes we model. Nevertheless, we lack convincing empirical evidence that preferences are convex and smooth. If preferences are not convex and smooth, nor separable, and our theoretical models assume that they are, we are impaired in our ability to understand and predict the political processes we study.

Future empirical work shall establish whether preferences are convex and smooth, and whether we can find systematic evidence of differentiated non-separability over pairs of issues, or systematic differences in the weights assigned to different dimensions, across different groups of voters or legislators. Future (better) theories must make assumptions that are consistent with these future empirical findings.

References

Arabie P (1991) Was Euclid and unnecessarily sophisticated psychologist? Psychometrika 56(4):567–587

Ashworth S, Bueno de Mesquita E (2009) Elections with platform and valence competition. Games Econ Behav 67(1):191–216

Azrieli Y (2011) Axioms for Euclidean preferences with a valence dimension. J Math Econ 47(4–5):545–553

Banks JS, Duggan J (2008) A dynamic model of democratic elections in multidimensional policy spaces. Q J Polit Sci 3:269–299

Berinsky AJ, Lewis JB (2007) An estimate of risk aversion in the U.S. electorate. Q J Polit Sci 2:139–154

Black D (1948) On the rationale of group decision-making. J Polit Econ 56(1):23–34

Black D (1958) The theory of committees and elections. Cambridge University Press, Cambridge

Bogomolnaia A, Laslier J-F (2007) Euclidean preferences. J Math Econ 43:87–98

Calvert R (1985) Robustness of the multidimensional voting model: candidate motivations, uncertainty and convergence. Am J Polit Sci 29:69–95

Calvo E, Hellwig T, Chang K (2012) The eye of the beholder: ideological lensing, information effects, and the vote. In: Fundacion Juan March conference on contemporary applications of the spatial model

Clinton JD, Jackman SD, Rivers D (2004) The statistical analysis of roll call data: a unified approach. Am Polit Sci Rev 98:355–370

D'Agostino M, Dardanoni V (2009) What's so special about Euclidean distance? Soc Choice Welf 33(2):211–233
Davis OA, DeGroot MH, Hinich MJ (1972) Social preference orderings and majority rule. Econometrica 40(1):147–157
Degan A, Merlo A (2009) Do voters vote ideologically? J Econ Theory 144(5):1868–1894
Downs A (1957) An economic theory of political action in a democracy. J Polit Econ 65(2):135–150
Duggan J (2007) Equilibrium existence for zero-sum games and spatial models of elections. Games Econ Behav 60:52–74
Duggan J, Kalandrakis T (2012) Dynamic legislative policy bargaining. J Econ Theory
Eguia JX (2009) Utility representations of risk neutral preferences in multiple dimensions. Q J Polit Sci 4(4):379–385
Eguia JX (2011a) On the spatial representation of preference profiles. Econ Theory (accepted for publication)
Eguia JX (2011b) Foundations of spatial preferences. J Math Econ 47(2):200–205
Eguia JX (2012) A spatial theory of party formation. Econ Theory 49(3):549–570
Feddersen TJ (1992) A voting model implying Duverger's law and positive turnout. Am J Polit Sci 36(4):938–962
Grynaviski JD, Corrigan BE (2006) Specification issues in proximity models of candidate evaluation (with issue importance). Polit Anal 14:393–420
Hotelling H (1929) Stability in competition. Econ J 39(153):41–57
Humphreys M, Laver M (2009) Spatial models, cognitive metrics and majority rule equilibria. Br J Polit Sci 40(1):11–30
Kamada Y, Kojima F (2010) Voter preferences, polarization and electoral policies. Working paper
Kramer GH (1973) On a class of economic conditions for majority rule. Econometrica 41(2):285–297
Kramer GH (1977) A dynamical model of political equilibrium. J Econ Theory 16(2):310–334
Krasa S, Polborn M (2010) Competition between specialized candidates. Am Polit Sci Rev 104(4):745–765
Krasa S, Polborn M (2012) Political competition between differentiated candidates. Games Econ Behav 76(1):249–271
Lacy D (2001a) A theory of nonseparable preferences in survey responses. Am J Polit Sci 45(2):239–258
Lacy D (2001b) Nonseparable preferences, measurement error, and unstable survey responses. Polit Anal 9(2):1–21
Lacy D (2012) Nonseparable preferences, issue voting, and issue packaging in elections. In: Fundacion Juan March conference on contemporary applications of the spatial model
McCarty N, Meirowitz A (2007) Political game theory. Cambridge University Press, Cambridge
McKelvey RD (1976) Intransitivities in multidimensional voting models and some implications for agenda control. J Econ Theory 12:472–482
McKelvey RD (1979) General conditions for global intransitivities in formal voting models. Econometrica 47(5):1085–1112
McKelvey RD, Wendell RE (1976) Voting equilibria in multidimensional choice spaces. Math Oper Res 1(2):144–158
Miller G, Schofield N (2003) Activists and partisan realignment in the United States. Am Polit Sci Rev 97(2):245–260
Milyo J (2000a) A problem with Euclidean preferences in spatial models of politics. Econ Lett 66(2):179–182
Milyo J (2000b) Logical deficiencies in spatial models: a constructive critique. Public Choice 105(3–4):273–289
Minkowski H (1886) Geometrie der Zahlen. Teubner, Leipzig
Osborne M (1995) Spatial models of political competition under plurality rule: a survey of some explanations of the number of candidates and the positions they take. Can J Econ 28(2):261–301

Patty JW, Snyder JM, Ting MM (2009) Two's company, three's an equilibrium: strategic voting and multicandidate elections. Q J Polit Sci 4(3):251–278
Plott CR (1967) A notion of equilibrium and its possibility under majority rule. Am Econ Rev 57(4):331–347
Poole K, Rosenthal H (1985) A spatial model for roll call analysis. Am J Polit Sci 29:331–347
Poole KT, Rosenthal H (1997) Congress: a political-economic history of roll call voting. Oxford University Press, London
Rae DW, Taylor M (1971) Decision rules and policy outcomes. Br J Polit Sci 1:71–90
Rivero G (2011) Integrality and separability in multidimensional voting models: ideology and nationalism in Spanish regional elections. Center for Advanced Study in the Social Sciences, Fundacion Juan March, 2011/265, December
Schofield N (1978) Instability of simple dynamic games. Rev Econ Stud 40(3):575–594
Schofield N (2007a) Political equilibria with electoral uncertainty. Soc Choice Welf 28:461–490
Schofield N (2007b) The mean voter theorem: necessary and sufficient conditions for convergent equilibrium. Rev Econ Stud 74:965–980
Schofield N, Claassen C, Gallego M, Ozdemir U (2011) Empirical and formal models of the United States presidential elections in 2000 and 2004. In: Schofield N, Caballero G (eds) Political economy of institutions, democracy and voting. Springer, Heidelberg
Schofield N, Sened I (2006) Multiparty democracy. Cambridge University Press, Cambridge
Serra G (2010) Polarization of what? A model of elections with endogenous valence. J Polit 72(2):426–437
Serra G (2012) Does charisma discourage experience? an election with two types of valence. ICOPEAI II conference paper
Shepard RN (1987) Toward a universal law of generalization for psychological science. Science 237:1317–1323
Shepsle KA, Weingast BR (1981) Structure-induced equilibrium and legislative choice. Public Choice 37(3):503–519
Wendell RE, Thorson SJ (1974) Some generalizations of social decisions under majority rule. Econometrica 42:893–912
Westholm A (1997) Distance versus direction: the illusory defeat of the proximity theory of electoral choice. Am Polit Sci Rev 91(4):865–883
Wittman D (1977) Candidates with policy preferences: a dynamic model. J Econ Theory 14(1):180–189
Wittman D (1983) Candidate motivation: a synthesis of alternatives. Am Polit Sci Rev 77(1):142–157
Ye M, Li Q, Leiker KW (2011) Evaluating voter-candidate proximity in a non-Euclidean space. J Elect Public Opin Parties 4:497–521
Zakharov A (2009) A model of candidate location with endogenous valence. Public Choice 138:347–366

A Non-existence Theorem for Clientelism in Spatial Models

Daniel Kselman

1 Introduction

In spatial models of political competition, political parties typically announce positions on one or more issue dimensions; voters then choose from among these parties according to their preferences over the same issue dimensions. Put otherwise, spatial models typically analyze *programmatic* elections in which the link between voter choice and elite behavior is consummated indirectly, via collectively applicable policy issues.[1] In contrast, a growing body of research in comparative politics and comparative political-economy investigates *clientelistic* linkages between citizens and elected officials. Such linkages are grounded not in national-level public policy debates, but rather in a direct and contingent exchange of votes (or other forms of political participation...) for tangible material or professional rewards. These inducements take many forms: jobs in the public sector, access to the electric grid, washing machines, alcohol, fuel, etc. In such contexts, in addition to evaluating political parties' policy stances on one or more programmatic issues, voters choose based on parties' ability to provide targeted inducements.

A series of recent papers, reviewed in Sect. 2 below, has analyzed clientelism in a game theoretic setting. While all make valuable contributions to the literature on contingent electoral exchange, none explicitly introduces clientelistic concerns into the traditional spatial model, which has for decades been the work-horse in formal political theory. This paper develops a spatial model in which political parties strategically choose: (1) their programmatic policy position, (2) the effort they

[1] A similar accountability mechanism underpins the 'Responsible Party Government' model, which dates at least to Lipset and Rokkan (1967), and sees ties between political parties and voters as grounded in campaign and governance strategies on issues of national-level public policy.

D. Kselman (✉)
Center for Advanced Studies in the Social Sciences, Juan March Institute, C/Castelló 77, 28006 Madrid, Spain
e-mail: dkselman@march.es

N. Schofield et al. (eds.), *Advances in Political Economy*,
DOI 10.1007/978-3-642-35239-3_9,

devote to clientelism as opposed to the promotion of their programmatic position, and (3) the set of voters who are targeted to receive clientelistic benefits. Section 3 presents the model's actors, their utility functions, and the actions which comprise their choice sets. Section 4 then demonstrates that, absent stronger restrictions on candidate behavior, there will never exist Nash Equilibria with positive clientelistic effort: given some clientelistic proposal by their opponent, candidates can always propose a slightly 'narrower' set of recipients and win an electoral plurality.

This is not to say that the game in its most general form is always characterized by instability. On the contrary, if voter responsiveness to clientelistic resources is sufficiently low, then the game's Nash Equilibrium will be for all candidates to choose the median voter's ideal point, and to devote 100 % of their campaign effort to promoting this platform. Thus, the game in its most general form yields either traditional median voter convergence or theoretical instability. Section 5 relates this general result to past literature on instability in coalition formation processes. It also discusses a set of necessary conditions for the emergence of Nash Equilibria with positive levels of clientelism. One condition is that parties have differential abilities to target distinct subsets of voters. A second condition is that political parties face a *binding turnout constraint*. When turnout is not a given and parties have differential abilities to target distinct subsets of voters, the need to balance one's interest in courting the electoral median with that in maintaining the support of one's ideological base leads, at times, to the adoption of positive equilibrium levels of clientelism.

2 Theories of Clientelism

So as to highlight this paper's specific contributions, here I briefly outline recent theoretical research on the causes of clientelism. In the Introduction to their edited volume, Kitschelt and Wilkinson (2007) present an argument to explain the mix of clientelistic and programmatic appeals in politicians' vote production functions. Driving this mix is the interaction between economic development and electoral competitiveness.[2] At low levels of economic development politics is heavily clientelistic, and increasingly so as competitiveness increases. At high levels of economic development, politics is heavily programmatic and increasingly so as competitiveness increases. Finally, it is at intermediate levels of development that politicians invest more equitably in both forms of linkage. To complement these basic comparative statics, the authors also highlight the role of a publicly controlled political-economy and formal political institutions in conditioning the mix of linkage strategies.

[2]Competitiveness is a notably tricky concept to precisely define and operationalize. Different authors have assigned the concept different empirical referents. Kitschelt and Wilkinson (2007) define competitive elections as those in which "...elections are close between rival blocs of parties... and there is a market of uncommitted voters sufficiently large to tip the balance in favor of one or another bloc." (p. 28)

In the same volume Magaloni et al. (2007) develop a decision-theoretic model to consider an incumbent politician's decision to generate public as opposed to clientelistic goods. Public goods offer the ability to target a large number of voters, but are risky insofar as voters' response to public good proposals is uncertain. On the other hand, clientelistic goods allow politicians to gain smaller blocs of voter support with certainty. The optimal allocation of clientelistic effort thus increases in: (a) voters' relative preferences for small-scale targeted policy goods (for which economic development should be a reasonable proxy); (b) the relative uncertainty of vote returns to public good provision; and (c) politicians' risk aversion.

These papers emphasize the role of economic development, electoral competitiveness, and incumbents' risk profile in conditioning politicians' optimal mix of clientelistic and programmatic electoral appeals. They do not, however, investigate the relationship between clientelistic appeals and the relative extremism or moderation of political parties' programmatic stances; nor the processes by which candidates choose which segments of the electorate to target with clientelistic goods. Finally, they do not embed the linkage decision in a strategic context such that parties' electoral strategies are an explicit function of their competitors' decisions.

Stokes (2005) analyzes an infinitely-repeated prisoner's dilemma played between an incumbent politician and a potential supporter, where the incumbent decides between providing a benefit 'B' and the potential supporter decides to vote for the incumbent or a challenger candidate. In equilibrium, clientelistic relationships of vote targeting are more likely to arise when: (a) the benefit B is large; (b) voters are 'moderate' supporters of the incumbent, i.e. not heavily biased for or against the incumbent's programmatic policy stances; and (c) when the ideological distance between the incumbent party and her competitor shrinks. Nichter (2008) analyzes a similar model with one major distinction: the game is played between an incumbent politician and a potential voter whose basic decision is not who to choose but whether or not to turnout. Rather than targeting 'moderate' supporters, politicians who use clientelism to increase turnout are more likely to do so among 'strong' ideological supporters. As well, the likelihood of clientelism effectively inducing turnout is no longer a function of the ideological distance separating incumbent and challenger candidates.

This first set of game theoretic papers has made valuable contributions to research on the nature of parties' clientelistic constituencies, i.e. the particular voters or subsets of voters to which parties' devote their clientelistic efforts. However, it does not address the question asked by Kitschelt and Wilkinson (2007) and Magaloni et al. (2007), namely "What is politicians' optimal mix between clientelistic and programmatic campaign strategies?" Furthermore, it does not address the relationship between a party's linkage strategies and the relative extremism of its programmatic stances. Indeed, models by Stokes (2005) and Nichter (2008) stipulate political parties' spatial positions as exogenously fixed, and from these fixed positions identify the subsets of 'moderate' and 'strong' party supporters. In model derived below the choice of programmatic stances is explicit, such that the identity of 'moderate' and 'strong' party ideological supporters arises as an endogenous outcome of strategic competition.

Keefer and Vlaicu (2008) adapt a particular political-economic model (Persson and Tabellini 2000) to the comparative study of fiscal policy under alternative credibility environments. Politicians in their model choose: (a) a level of public good provision; (b) a level of targeted good provision; (c) the set of districts to which targeted goods will be allocated; and (d) rent extraction levels. Not unlike Stokes (2005), the authors find that clientelism will be targeted to electoral districts with low levels of ideological bias, i.e. those districts in which voters are more effectively swayed by targeted policy appeals. They also find that a 'broader' segment of the electorate will be targeted as parties devote more overall effort to clientelistic appeals, i.e. targeting becomes more 'inclusive' as clientelistic effort increases. Finally, they argue that such appeals will be more prevalent in systems where national-level politicians lack credibility on matters of economic governance; and that they will tend to open the door to rent-seeking by public officials.[3] Keefer and Vlaicu (2008) come closest to addressing the set of questions tackled in the proceeding sections. That said, as with the above reviewed research, parties in their model do not choose explicit programmatic positions, which in turn implies an exogenous stipulation of electoral districts which are 'more' or 'less' ideologically biased. In the model developed below clientelistic coalitions' relative 'inclusiveness' and parties' programmatic choices emerge simultaneously in equilibrium.

3 Actors and Utility Functions

The game contains two types of actors: candidates and voters. Label candidates with the marker P and assume throughout that only two candidates compete, such that $P \in \{1, 2\}$. Candidates' decision processes are interdependent, i.e. candidate 1's optimal action is contingent on candidate 2's campaign strategy and vice versa. In contrast voters are non-strategic: they simply choose the candidate whose campaign platform they find most attractive. In the spatial model, campaign platforms consist of what I will label *programmatic* policy proposals. Consider a simple unidimensional policy continuum $x \in [0, 1]$ such that the policy $x = 0$ is the most 'left' policy available to candidates and the policy $x = 1$ is the political spectrum's most 'right' policy option. Candidates' action-set in spatial models consists of a platform choice x_P somewhere in the continuum $x \in [0, 1]$. Having chosen campaign platforms, voters then choose based on their evaluation of candidates' policy proposals.

To embed clientelistic linkage strategies in the traditional spatial model, assume that both candidates must divide *expendable political effort* between promoting and implementing their proposals on issues of national-level public policy, and providing targeted goods to individuals and small social groups. More particularly assume

[3]However they also note that it is not patron-client ties themselves that generate less than ideal fiscal policy, but rather national officials' lack of credibility. Indeed, in a world without such credibility the presence of local patrons actually *improves* voter welfare as compared to one without such local intermediaries.

that both candidates have a *single unit* of campaign effort which they must divide between promoting their programmatic stances (labeled G_P) and providing clientelistic benefits (labeled C_P). This implies the effort constraint $G_P + C_P = 1$. They must thus choose not only a spatial position x_P, but also the effort levels G_P and C_P which they will devote to two distinct modes of vote-seeking. As we will see below, to the extent that candidates engage in clientelistic campaign strategies voters will discount their national-level policy proposals, and vice versa.

An additional question which candidates must answer in devising a comprehensive campaign strategy is "To whom shall I target my clientelistic effort?" In other words, beyond choosing the overall level of effort to be expended on clientelism C_P, candidates must also choose the subset of voters who will benefit from C_P. This subset may, at least in the abstract, range anywhere from the entire electorate all the way down to a single voter.[4] To make this more concrete, consider our model of the electorate. Voters are defined first and foremost by their *ideal point*, i.e. their most-preferred policy on the continuum $x \in [0, 1]$. Define x_i as voter i's ideal point such that, roughly speaking, a voter i with ideal point $x_i < .5$ ($x_i > .5$) most prefers a policy on the political 'left' ('right'). For simplicity, assume throughout that ideal points are distributed uniformly in the policy space $x \in [0, 1]$ (i.e. $x_i \sim$ uniform$[0, 1]$), such that both the *mean* and *median* of the voter preference distribution are located at $x_m = .5$.

Electoral candidates must choose from this distribution of voters those which they will target with clientelistic inducements. For example, a candidate might target all voters on the political 'left', i.e. whose most-preferred policy is $x_i < .5$; or only the most 'leftist' quartile of voters in the range $x_i \in [0, 1/4]$; or all voters from the political center in the range $x_i \in [1/4, 3/4]$; and so on. Define $\underline{x}_P$ ($\overline{x}_P$) as the most left-leaning (right-leaning) voter targeted by candidate P. We make the following assumptions as to the nature of clientelistic vote-seeking:

Assumption 1 The target set Θ_P must be *continuous* in $x \in [0, 1]$.

Assumption 2 Clientelistic effort C_P is *evenly distributed* among all members of the target set Θ_P.

The first assumption prohibits candidates from choosing a target set with 'breaks' in the distribution of voter preferences. For example, it precludes a strategy in which P targets *both* ideologues on the right in the range $x_i \in [3/4, 1]$ and those on the left in the range $x_i \in [0, 1/4]$. Similarly it precludes a strategy in which P targets ideologues on the right from the range $x_i \in [3/4, 1]$ and 'moderates' on the left in the range $x_i \in [1/4, 1/2]$. On the other hand, it does not prevent P from choosing a target set which contains both 'left' and 'right' voters, so long as these voters come

[4]These extremes, however, are unlikely to be observed in the empirical world, where politicians tend to target more than a single citizen but less than the entire citizenry with clientelistic inducements.

from a continuous range of the preference distribution $x \in [0, 1]$ (as when the target set includes all 'moderates' in the range $x_i \in [1/4, 3/4]$). The second assumption precludes candidates from providing more clientelistic goods to certain members of their target set than to others. All voter types who find themselves contained within a candidate's target set are assumed to receive an equal amount of the benefits resulting from C_P.[5] Define the set of voters targeted by P as the this party's *target set*, denoted $\Theta_P \in [\underline{x}_P, \overline{x}_P]$.

Let $\mathbf{v}_P = \{x_P, G_P, \underline{x}_P, \overline{x}_P\}$ represent a *strategy* for candidate P. Candidates thus choose a platform x_P, a level of effort G_P devoted to promoting this platform, and the endpoints of the target set to which the remaining $C_P = 1 - G_P$ will be targeted clientelistically. Compared to the traditional spatial approach, this model substantially expands the set of campaign strategies available to electoral candidates. On the other hand, I adopt the Downsian assumption that candidates are exclusively *office-seeking*, i.e. their only goal in devising campaigns is political incumbency, implying the following utility function: $U_P = \pi_P \cdot \beta$. The marker π_P represents P's probability of winning the election, and will emerge endogenously as a function of both candidates' campaign strategies (by construction $\pi_1 = 1 - \pi_2$). The marker $\beta > 0$ represents the value candidates attach to winning office.[6]

Just as candidates may employ both forms of electoral linkage, voters too have preferences over both programmatic policy issues and targeted material, professional, or personal inducements. Begin with the natural assumption that holding all else constant a voter with ideal point x_i would prefer that P choose a policy $x_P = x_i$ rather than a policy further removed from her ideal point. We will also assume that voters discount candidates' programmatic policy stances to the extent that candidates engage in clientelistic linkage strategies. For example, even if P chooses the policy $x_P = x_i$, voter i will attribute little or no value to this policy when G_P is very low and C_P is very high. Put simply, if candidates exert little effort in promoting and/or implementing their programmatic policy stances, voters will discount these stances accordingly. To operationalize this notion, consider the following specification of a voter's *programmatic utility* for P:

$$u_{i,P}(\text{prog}) = G_P \cdot \big(1 - abs[x_P - x_i]\big). \tag{1}$$

The term $abs[\cdot]$ denotes the absolute value function such that, holding G_P constant, as x_P moves further from x_i voter i's programmatic utility for P decreases. Simi-

[5]Both assumptions are primarily technical, and simplify the model immensely. As well, both are plausible: it seems quite natural to eliminate the possibility of an electoral strategy in which parties attempt to include extremists from both sides of the political spectrum in their target set. That said, Assumptions 1 and 2 do eliminate from candidates' action sets a series of campaign strategies which may, at least in theory, be observed empirically. In future iterations I will examine the consequences of relaxing both assumptions.

[6]The purely office-seeking assumption is the simplest of all candidate preference models. More recent research has extended the traditional spatial model to situations in which candidates also care about the policies which are implemented as a result of democratic elections (e.g. Wittman 1983; Calvert 1985). Strom (1990) represents an early attempt to explain why some candidates might be primarily office- and/or vote-seeking while others might be primarily policy-seeking.

larly, holding x_P constant, as G_P decreases so does voter i's programmatic utility for P.[7] As a result of this functional form, the maximum programmatic utility that any voter will have for candidate P is '1'; this occurs when $G_P = 1$ and $x_i = x_P$.

In expressing voter i's *clientelistic utility* for candidate P, it is important to first distinguish between voters who are in P's target set and those who are not. We will assume that voters who are not targeted by a particular candidate simply receive a clientelistic utility of '0' from that candidate's policies. So, if candidate 1 chooses the target set $\Theta_1 = [1/4, 1/2]$, then all voters with ideal points $x_i < 1/4$ or $x_i > 1/2$ will receive a clientelistic utility of '0' from 1's campaign. What about voters who find themselves within a candidate's target set? Consider the following functional form:

$$\forall[i : x_i \in \Theta_P], \quad u_{i,P}(\text{client}) = \left\{ \frac{C_P^{\eta}}{\delta + \Theta_P} \right\}. \tag{2}$$

Beginning with (2)'s numerator, the parameter η is an exponent which we will assume to be $\eta \leq 1$. While voter i's utility will always increase with C_P, his or her marginal utility for a unit of additional clientelistic effort (weakly...) decreases as clientelistic effort increases. The notion that citizens' marginal utility for targeted policy benefits is decreasing with the extent of targeting appears frequently in political-economic models (e.g. Keefer and Vlaicu 2008). Operationally, it implies that the provision of targeted goods becomes less efficient in extremely large amounts.

Moving to (2)'s denominator, we have already defined Θ_P as candidate P's target set. Since Θ_P appears in the denominator, holding C_P constant voter i's clientelistic utility $u_{i,P}(\text{client})$ will always decrease with the size of P's target set. As candidates target more and more voters the effort level C_P must be distributed among a larger and larger population, thus reducing the *per capita* clientelistic consumption of all beneficiaries. The exogenous parameter δ represents the rate at which voters *discount* clientelistic appeals. When the discount rate δ is large, members of P's target set will receive little utility from clientelistic benefits, *even if* these benefits are extensive and narrowly targeted. When δ is small, members of P's target set may receive substantial utility from clientelistic benefits, *even if* the effort C_P is minimal and broadly targeted.

Voters' 'elasticity' to clientelistic appeals has many possible empirical determinants, including but not limited to one's income, profession, and cultural environ-

[7] The functional form in (1) implies that voters' programmatic utility for P will always be increasing in G_P. In the current model, the dimension x_P is a public good continuum; differing ideal points on x_P represent distinct preferences as to the ideal nature of public goods. Some voters may prefer national security, some environmental protection, and others free access to social services. That said, voters benefit from increased public good provision even when the nature of the good provided is not their most-preferred. Voters who prefer national security to environmental protection will nonetheless, all else held constant, benefit from reduced pollution. Formal models of public good provision often assume that voters are risk averse; if we were to assume that higher levels of G_P reduce the uncertainty surrounding parties' ability to implement national-level policies, voters' programmatic utility for P would again increase with G_P. As a result, (2) captures the type of programmatic utility of interest to this paper.

ment. As a first cut, in this paper we will assume that δ is invariant across voters, i.e. that all voters in an electorate are similarly responsive to clientelistic appeals.[8] Also as a first cut we assume δ to be exogenous to the game itself.[9] Ultimately, translating the theoretical framework developed here into an empirical framework for the study of democratic accountability will require a careful treatment of δ's endogenous and exogenous determinants, as well as its potential for subnational variation. Nonetheless, the assumption of an invariant and exogenous δ allows us to identify a first set of comparative static arguments which differentiate between national electorates based on their *median voter's responsiveness to clientelistic campaigns*. We can thus exhaustively express a voter i's utility for party P as follows:

$$u_{i,P}(\mathbf{v}_P) = \begin{cases} G_P \cdot (1 - abs[x_i - x_P]) + \left\{\frac{C_P^{\eta}}{\delta + \Theta_P}\right\} & \text{if } x_i \in \Theta_P, \\ G_P \cdot (1 - abs[x_i - x_P]) & \text{if } x_i \notin \Theta_P. \end{cases} \tag{3}$$

Voter i will choose the candidate whose policies yield the highest utility according to (3). If candidates adopt strategies that yield i identical payoffs, then i will randomize in an unbiased way (i.e. choose each candidate with a probability of $1/2$). Built into this model of voter preferences is a tradeoff between clientelistic and programmatic targeting. To see this note that $G_P = (1 - C_P)$: any and all effort not expended on programmatic campaign appeals will be allocated to clientelism. In a model without rent-seeking in which politicians receive utility only from gaining political incumbency, all effort will be spent on vote-seeking (i.e. the effort constraint will be binding). Every additional increment of effort devoted to programmatic linkage formation is thus, by definition, taken away from a candidate's clientelistic effort, and vice versa.

While our approach to modeling campaign strategies and voter preferences is substantially more complex than that found in the traditional spatial model, the game sequence itself is not. In a first stage both candidates choose a set of actions $\mathbf{v}_P = \{x_P, G_P, \underline{x}_P, \overline{x}_P\}$ so as to maximize their utility $U_P = \pi_P \cdot \beta$. In a second stage voters evaluate these actions and choose the candidate whose policies maximize their utility. For $P, \sim P \in \{1, 2\}$, given $\mathbf{v}_P$ and $\mathbf{v}_{\sim P}$ define α_P as the proportion of voters who choose P, i.e. the proportion of voters for whom either $u_{i,P}(\mathbf{v}_P) > u_{i,\sim P}(\mathbf{v}_{\sim P})$, or for whom $u_{i,P}(\mathbf{v}_P) = u_{i,\sim P}(\mathbf{v}_{\sim P})$ but whose random choice lands on P (in which case α_P is an 'expected' vote share). The election is conducted under plurality rule.

[8]Of course, empirically this is unlikely to be the case: voters within a given electorate will likely exhibit some degree of differentiation according to their socio-economic and cultural status.

[9]The model may eventually be extended to situations in which δ is endogenously determined by the set of candidate campaign strategies and voter choices. For example, one might envision δ as assuming high values among moderate voters when both parties choose extremist policies in $x_i \in [0, 1]$: the alienation which arises from political extremism may make moderates particularly susceptible to more 'cynical' electoral appeals.

4 Clientelistic Instability

Define $\mathbf{v}_P^*$ as a *Nash Equilibrium* strategy and $\mathbf{v}_m = \{x_m, 1, \emptyset, \emptyset\}$ as the *median-voter programmatic* strategy. The latter is a strategy which essentially replicates the equilibrium choice made in Downs' original model (Downs 1957), i.e. to choose the median voter's most-preferred policy position without any effort devoted to clientelistic appeals. Begin with a situation in which candidates can target any continuous subset of voters. Although constrained by Assumptions 1 and 2 from above, this allows both candidates a good deal of freedom in choosing Θ_P.

Lemma 1 *When candidates can choose any continuous range of voter ideal points as a potential target set, in any Nash Equilibrium each candidate must win with probability* $1/2$ (*i.e. in any Nash Equilibrium* $\pi_1 = \pi_2 = 1/2$).

The proof of Lemma 1 is straight-forward. Consider a case in which some candidate has a greater than $1/2$ probability of winning, implying that the opposing candidate has a less than $1/2$ probability of winning. In such a case, the lower probability candidate will always have an optimal deviation: they can improve their chances of winning to $1/2$ by simply choosing a strategy identical to that of their opponent, in which case all voters are indifferent between the two parties and election is decided by a coin flip. As such, as long as candidates are unrestricted in choosing target sets, Lemma 1 obtains.

I now demonstrate the impossibility of Nash Equilibria with positive levels clientelism in these unconstrained environments.

Theorem 1 *When candidates can choose any continuous range of voter ideal points as a target set, there* ***never*** *exists a Nash Equilibrium in which* $C_P > 0$ *for either party.*

Proof of Theorem 1 Consider a situation in which P chooses a strategy $\mathbf{v}_P = \{x_P, G_P, \underline{x}_P, \overline{x}_P\}$ with $G_P < 1$ (such that $C_P > 0$) and target set $\Theta_P = [\underline{x}_P, \overline{x}_P]$. By Lemma 1, we know that any strategy vector which makes $\pi_P < .5$ or $\pi_P > .5$ will induce defection by whichever party is less likely to win the election.

What about a situation in which P chooses $\mathbf{v}_P = \{x_P, G_P, \underline{x}_P, \overline{x}_P\}$ with $G_P < 1$ and target set $\Theta_P = [\underline{x}_P, \overline{x}_P]$, and at which $\pi_P = 1/2$? In this case P's opponent $\sim P$ could choose an identical level of clientelistic effort $C_{\sim P} = C_P = 1 - G_P$, an identical policy position $x_{\sim P} = x_P$, and a nearly identical but slightly narrower target set $\Theta_{\sim P} = [\underline{x}_P, (\overline{x}_P - \varepsilon)]$ where $\varepsilon \to 0$. In so doing, P's opponent will win the support of all voters in $\Theta_{\sim P}$ (since $C_{\sim P}$ will be distributed over a slightly narrower target set than C_P). As well, all voters not in either target set will randomize, since both parties choose identical platforms and programmatic effort levels. Trivially, this implies $\pi_{\sim P} > 1/2$. Put otherwise, anytime P chooses $\mathbf{v}_P = \{x_P, G_P, \underline{x}_P, \overline{x}_P\}$ with $G_P < 1$ at which $\pi_P = 1/2$, $\sim P$ can choose $\mathbf{v}_{\sim P} = \{x_P, G_P, \underline{x}_P, \overline{x}_P - \varepsilon\}$ and increase her probability of winning.

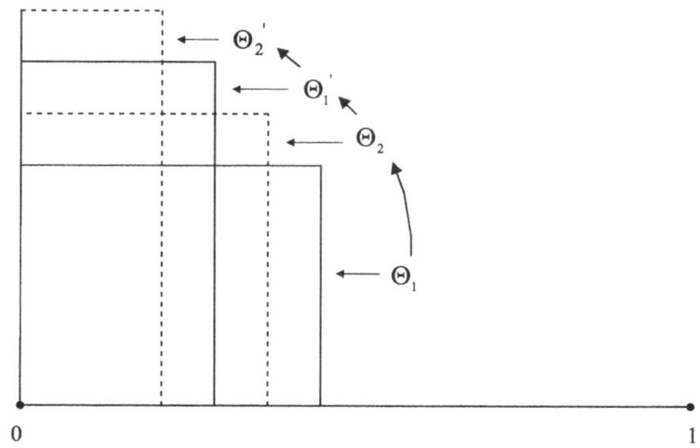

Fig. 1 Clientelistic instability

What about a strategy $\mathbf{v}_P = \{x_P, G_P, \underline{x}_P, \overline{x}_P\}$ with $G_P < 1$ and target set $\Theta_P = x_i$ (i.e. a target with only one voter type) at which $\pi_P = 1/2$. In this case P's opponent $\sim P$ could choose $\mathbf{v}_{\sim P} = \{x_P, 1, \emptyset, \emptyset\}$ and win the election with certainty: since only one voter is contained in Θ_P, all remaining voters will choose based on their programmatic utility for the respective parties. If $\sim P$ chooses $\mathbf{v}_{\sim P} = \{x_P, 1, \emptyset, \emptyset\}$, then all voters will have a higher programmatic utility for $\sim P$, since she chooses an identical platform but devotes more effort to promoting and implementing that platform (since $G_P = 1$). As such, all but the single voter in P's target set choose $\sim P$.

Taken together, these arguments demonstrate that there is no Nash Equilibrium with positive levels of clientelism when parties can choose any continuous range of voter ideal points as a potential target set. □

In words, when both candidates can target any continuous subset of voters, any choice of $C_P > 0$ induces a string of deviations in which candidates choose overlapping but slightly narrower target sets; each of these deviations leads to an increase in the deviating candidate's probability of winning. The process is displayed in Fig. 1.

Such jockeying for ever smaller target sets may continue until only the voter x_i is contained in candidates' target sets. At this point, either candidate will have the incentive to deviate and win the remaining voters' support on programmatic grounds.

Theorem 1 does not necessarily imply that the game in its most general form has no Nash Equilibrium; just that it has no clientelistic Nash Equilibrium. For sufficiently high levels of δ the game's unique Nash Equilibrium will be $\mathbf{v}_1^* = \mathbf{v}_2^* = \mathbf{v}_m$, i.e. the traditional median-voter convergence without clientelism. As an example I now derive the conditions under which $\mathbf{v}_1^* = \mathbf{v}_2^* = \mathbf{v}_m$ when $\eta = 1$. At the strategy vector $\mathbf{v}_1 = \mathbf{v}_2 = \mathbf{v}_m$ both candidates win with probability 50 %, so a deviation from this strategy vector will only be optimal if it yields the deviating candidate a greater than 50 % probability of winning. By definition any such deviation would require the deviating candidate P to choose $G_P < 1$: as long as her opponent $\sim P$ chooses $\mathbf{v}_{\sim P} = \mathbf{v}_m$, any deviation which involves choosing a different policy position without clientelist targeting costs P the election (Downs 1957).

To identify whether or not a deviation from $\mathbf{v}_m$ to some $\mathbf{v}_P = \{x_P, G_P, \underline{x}_P, \overline{x}_P\}$ will yield P a value of $\pi_P > 50\ \%$, I adopt the following procedure: I first identify, for any level of $G_P < 1$, the accompanying policy platform and target set deviations which would represent the *necessary condition* deviations, denoted as $\hat{x}_P(G_P)$, $\hat{\underline{x}}_P(G_P)$, and $\hat{\overline{x}}_P(G_P)$. To elaborate, note that as long as voters value clientelism enough (i.e. δ is small enough), there may be many deviations from $\mathbf{v}_m$ which yield $\pi_P > 50\ \%$. Necessary condition deviations are defined here as follows: for any level of $G_P < 1$, if deviating to the choices $\hat{x}_P(G_P)$, $\hat{\underline{x}}_P(G_P)$, and $\hat{\overline{x}}_P(G_P)$ *does not* yield the deviating candidate P a probability of winning $\pi_P > 50\ \%$, then for that level of $G_P < 1$ *there does not exist* a set of choices which yields $\pi_P > 50\ \%$. Denote $\hat{\Theta} = [\hat{\underline{x}}_P(G_P), \hat{\overline{x}}_P(G_P)]$. The following lemma establishes $\hat{x}_P(G_P)$, $\hat{\underline{x}}_P(G_P)$, and $\hat{\overline{x}}_P(G_P)$ for all values of $G_P < 1$:

Lemma 2 *When $\eta = 1$, for any deviation from $\mathbf{v}_m$ to a value $G_P < 1$, the accompanying necessary condition parameters are $\hat{x}_P(G_P) = x_m$ and a target set that includes any bare plurality of voters (any Θ such that $\overline{x}_P - \underline{x}_P = .5 + \varepsilon$, where $\varepsilon \to 0$).*

So, the most flexible deviation from $\mathbf{v}_m$ actually involves maintaining x_m as a platform, and targeting C to any bare plurality of voters. Lemma 2 (proof in the Appendix) establishes that, for any deviation from $\mathbf{v}_m$, if the accompanying choice $\hat{x}_P(G_P) = x_m$ and *any* bare plurality target set *does not* yield the deviating candidate P a probability of winning $\pi_P > 50\ \%$, then for that level of $G_P < 1$ *there does not exist* a set of accompanying choices which yields $\pi_P > 50\ \%$. Consider the case in which $\delta = 0$, and in which P chooses a deviation to $G_P = .4$. Clearly, in this case adopting the necessary condition strategies would allow P to win the election with certainty: all voters in the bare majority target set would receive $u_{i,P}(\text{client}) = .6/.5 = 1.2$. Of all voters in this target set, the median voter will be the hardest to win over, because she receives $u_{i,\sim P}(\text{prog}) = 1$ from $\sim P$ (since $\mathbf{v}_{\sim P} = \mathbf{v}_m$). Since $1.2 > 1$, the median voter and all voters in the target set would choose P on the basis of clientelist utility alone, making $\pi_P = 1$.

However, if $\delta = 0$ then P could also deviate to the strategy $\mathbf{v}_P = \{.4, .4, 0, .6\}$ and win the election with certainty. By choosing the platform $x_P = .4$ and allocating $C_P = .6$ to the target set $\Theta_p = [0, .6]$, all voters in the target set receive $u_{i,P}(\text{client}) = 1$. Of all voters in this target set, the median voter will be the hardest to win over, because she receives $u_{i,\sim P}(\text{prog}) = 1$ from $\sim P$ (since $\mathbf{v}_{\sim P} = \mathbf{v}_m$). The median voter receives $u_{i,P}(\text{prog}) = .4 \times .9 = .36$ from the strategy $\mathbf{v}_P = \{.4, .6, 0, .6\}$, and as such receives total utility $1 + .36 > 1$, so she will vote for the deviating candidate P. A similar comparison demonstrates that all additional voters in the target set $\Theta_p = [0, .6]$ will also prefer P's new strategy, such that a deviation to $\mathbf{v}_P = \{.4, .6, 0, .6\}$ to allows P to win the election with certainty against an opponent at $\mathbf{v}_{\sim P} = \mathbf{v}_m$.

Thus, when $\delta = 0$, for any value of G_P there will be a *large set of deviations* from $\mathbf{v}_1 = \mathbf{v}_2 = \mathbf{v}_m$ which allow the deviating candidate to win the election with certainty. Lemma 2 doesn't tell us, in equilibrium, which of these deviations would be adopted; indeed, the candidate in question will be indifferent between any set of deviations which increases her probability of winning to 100 %. What Lemma 2 tells is that, for any value of $G_P < 1$, if the deviation from $\mathbf{v}_m$ to $\hat{x}_P(G_P) = x_m$ and a bare plurality target set does not increase P's probability of winning, then there does not exist an payoff-improving deviation for that level G_P. This leads to the following result:

Proposition 1 *When $\eta = 1$, if $\delta \geq 1/2$ then $\mathbf{v}_1^* = \mathbf{v}_2^* = \mathbf{v}_m$, and if $\delta < 1/2$ then the game has no Nash equilibrium.*

The Appendix contains the proof. For any value of $\delta < 1/2$ at least one deviation exists which grants the deviating party $\pi_P > 50$ %. For any value of $\delta \geq 1/2$ no such deviation exists. If a deviation does exist (i.e. if $\delta < 1/2$) this sets in motion the strategic dynamic uncovered in Theorem 1, by which both parties continually cut into one another's target sets, until both parties eventually end up back at the median-voter programmatic strategy vector $\mathbf{v}_m$. This in turn sets in motion another series of deviations, and so on *ad infinitum*. As such, when $\delta < 1/2$ the two parties cycle infinitely between the competing linkage strategies, and the game has no Nash Equilibrium. While numerically different, the same qualitative implications obtain regardless of the value of η: at high levels of δ the game's Nash Equilibrium will be $\mathbf{v}_1^* = \mathbf{v}_2^* = \mathbf{v}_m$, and at lower levels the game will have no Nash Equilibrium.

5 Discussion

The absence of Nash Equilibria with positive levels of clientelism in the most general model arises from the fact that candidates can continually usurp their opponent's clientelistic supporters by adopting overlapping but distinct target sets. This result is related to general instability results in non-cooperative models of coalition formation (see Humphreys 2008 for an excellent review). Early research on the subject came primarily in the form of cooperative game theory (Nash 1953), and among other things tended to uncover the potential for theoretical instability and cycling in coalitional processes. While non-cooperative approaches initially generated greater theoretical stability (though often Nash equilibria were not unique), recent work introducing sequential bargaining strategies has once again uncovered the possibility for theoretical instability in coalition processes. Both the existence of stable equilibria and the properties of stable coalitions depend, crucially, on the assumptions one makes regarding the set of 'allowable' coalitions; and in turn this set of allowable coalitions is dependent on the commitment technologies with which one endows strategic actors (Humphreys 2008, p. 377).

With regards to the model above, the notion of 'allowable' coalitions can be thought of as the set of voters we allow electoral candidates to target with clientelistic goods. Assumptions 1 and 2, which are primarily technical, serve as preliminary restrictions on the set of allowable clientelistic coalitions which can form. However, Theorem 1 above demonstrates that, without additional restrictions, no set of clientelistic coalitions is stable in equilibrium. I am now experimenting with additional constraints which allow for equilibria with positive levels of clientelism. While I reserve these extensions for future research, here I report on a series of results which emerge when we assume that each candidate can only effectively target voters on one side of the political spectrum, i.e. that one candidate can only target voters on the 'right' and the other can only target voters on the 'left', such that the only voter potentially in both parties' target sets is the median voter. Interestingly, in a simple game in which this additional restriction is added to Assumptions 1 and 2, we once again end with an instability result: any deviation from the median-voter programmatic outcome leads to an infinite cycle of competitive vote jockeying for the median voter's clientelistic loyalties.

For example, suppose for argument's sake that P has an optimal deviation from the strategy vector $\mathbf{v}_1 = \mathbf{v}_2 = \mathbf{v}_m$ characterized by an effort allocation of $G_P = .8$ (such that $C_P = .2$), a policy position $x_P = .7$, and a target set $\Theta_P = [.5, .7]$. In response to this deviation P's opponent $\sim P$ could choose an identical allocation effort $G_{\sim P} = .8$ and $C_{\sim P} = .2$, a policy position $x_{\sim P} = .3$, and a target set $\Theta_{\sim P} = [(.3 + \varepsilon), x_m]$, where $\varepsilon \to 0$. By doing so, $\sim P$ will win the median voter's support since its effort $C_{\sim P}$ is distributed over a slightly narrower target set than P's effort C_P. In turn, P can respond similarly, and so on such that both parties pursue the median voter's support by continually shrinking the target set of which this median voter is a part. Such jockeying proceeds until both candidates include only the median voter in their target sets, at which point either party can deviate to the median voter programmatic strategy vector $\mathbf{v}_m$ and win the election with probability 1. The cycle then recommences.

This instability arises due to the fact that competitive parties can continually alter their campaign strategy so as to concentrate greater and greater emphasis on the median-voter's desires, without having to concern themselves with the turnout of more ideological voters. I have now established that, by combining the above restriction on allowable target sets with a *binding turnout constraint*, it is possible to generate Nash equilibria with positive levels of clientelism. Define μ as a voter's *reservation utility*, such that voters whose utility for both candidates is less than μ choose not to vote in the election. When $\mu > .5$ the game's turnout constraint becomes 'binding', insofar as some subset of voters on the ideological extremes will abstain from the election when $\mathbf{v}_1 = \mathbf{v}_2 = \mathbf{v}_m$. This stricter turnout constraint implies that policies which cater too closely to the median voter's interests may alienate extremist voters whose participation is uncertain. If candidates can only target voters on one side of the political spectrum and $\mu > .5$, then the need to balance one's interest in courting the electoral median with that in maintaining the support of one's ideological base leads at times to the adoption of positive equilibrium levels of clientelism.

Based on preliminary results which employ these additional constraints, we can begin to examine the comparative static consequences of moving from high to low values of δ. Begin with a hypothesis which caries a grain of counter-intuition: the model's equilibrium level of clientelistic targeting is *not* monotonically related to the size of δ. In fact, overall levels of clientelism are higher when δ assumes intermediate values than when δ assumes extremely low values. Put otherwise, higher voter susceptibility to targeted goods does not always lead to higher overall levels of clientelistic effort. The intuition behind this result is as follows: when δ is very small, the median voter's high responsiveness to targeting increases her preference that candidates announce *small target sets*.

Indeed, the equilibrium with extremely small δ is characterized by much smaller target sets than those which emerge when δ is intermediate. In the latter, parties target clientelist effort to all voters on their respective sides of the political spectrum; in the former parties cater only to a small set of centrist supporters at or near the electoral median. When target sets are small, in order to win the election candidates must ensure that some subset of voters not included in their target set nonetheless provides them with electoral support. In equilibrium this forces candidates to choose significant levels of G_P. It also forces them adopt increasingly polarized policy positions: since only centrists are included in parties' target sets, extremists must be placated in order to gain their votes.

Not only does the equilibrium when δ is small represent the paper's first in which parties choose programmatic positions other than the median voter's ideal point; it is a highly polarized equilibrium in which both parties occupy ideological positions well-removed from the electoral median. When δ is sufficiently small the median voter will prefer that candidates keep their target sets narrow, *even if* it means devoting less overall effort to clientelistic targeting and choosing more polarized programmatic stances. Embedded in this logic are a series of curvilinear intuitions. Firstly, as already noted, the extent of a political system's clientelist linkage efforts display a 'hump-shaped' relationship with δ, such that programmatic policy appeals are most prevalent at very high and very low levels of δ. Similarly, ideological polarization should display a 'hump-shaped' relationship with the extent of a political system's clientelist linkage efforts: parties' programmatic positions should approximate the median voter's ideal point at both very low and very high levels of clientelist effort, and should be more polarized at intermediate levels of clientelist effort. Finally, the 'inclusiveness' of parties' target set should bear a 'quasi U-shaped' relationship to clientelist effort. At very low levels of clientelist effort policy is purely programmatic and centrist, i.e. parties have no target sets ($\Theta_P = \emptyset$); at intermediate levels of clientelist effort parties have narrow target sets concentrated near the electoral median; and at high levels of clientelism parties have broad target sets which cater to all voters of their ideological orientation.

These hypotheses constitute, perhaps, the paper's most empirically relevant theoretical results. Information collected via an Expert Survey on Citizen-Politician Linkages (ESCPL), developed and administered by Duke University political scientists with World Bank support, provides data on a number of the above model's basic parameters in a contemporary cross-section of 88 world democracies. First of all, the ESCPL will allow us to estimate the intensity of efforts that parties expend on clientelism vis-à-vis programmatic competition. Secondly, it provides data on the relative moderation or extremism of political parties' programmatic positions. Finally, it also provides data about the target sets of clientelistic parties: expert respondents in all countries were asked to identify the interest groups parties target with clientelist goods (profession, religion, socioeconomic status etc) as well as whether targeted goods are distributed to party loyalists or swing voters.

Although this newly emerging data set may permit empirical testing of the paper's main claims, it must be admitted that the above results are limited in their empirical applicability in a number of important ways. Firstly, the equilibrium results above all come in the form *symmetric* strategy profiles. The symmetry of parties' policy decisions arises from the symmetry of their strategic situations: both parties face identical budget constraints, have access to equally-sized target sets, and face an ideologically unbiased electorate. Ideally, future work will extend the current model to situations in which parties have distinct strategic options, which in turn might lead to equilibria in which one party is clientelistic while the other is not; one party is extreme while the other is not, etc. Furthermore, the model contains only two political parties, which endows the median voter with a pivotal role in establishing the game's equilibrium outcomes. Whether the above comparative static hypotheses are robust to multi-party situations in which the median voter's role is reduced is a question left to future research.

Beyond the paper's empirical implications, its results carry implications for the normative debate on clientelism's viability as a democratic linkage mechanism. It is not unusual to hear arguments in both academic and policy circles which criticize clientelism as a flawed form of accountability with perverse consequences for political governance, economic growth, and the consolidation of democratic norms and practices. There is undoubtedly much to this position. However, a growing current in studies of clientelism offers a more nuanced normative appraisal of clientelistic linkage. Keefer and Vlaicu (2008) note that the presence of local patrons, who are capable of serving as intermediaries between average citizens and elected officials, often improves aggregate social welfare in environments without credible elected officials. Fernandez and Pierskalla (2009) find that clientelism's political-economic consequences are not as clear cut as we might have expected; clientelist countries in fact outperform their counterparts on select dimensions of economic and human development (e.g. infant mortality and literacy). Finally, my own work on the governance consequences of electoral institutions (Kselman 2008) suggests that, in the absence of an exogenous legal and bureaucratic infrastructure capable of constraining self-interested politicians, electoral rules associated with personalistic politics actually *improve* governance when compared to less personalistic rules. Stated another way, in countries where public institutions are insufficient to constrain political rent-seeking, personalistic accountability is, while certainly imperfect, better than the total *absence* of accountability.

Though in different contexts, these papers share the undercurrent that at times clientelistic linkage may serve as a 'second-best' option when the exogenous environment is not conducive to more normatively palatable forms governance and accountability. Highly clientelistic systems in this model are also associated with ideological moderation and political inclusiveness, values which many consider laudable in and of themselves. On the other hand, systems with intermediate levels of clientelism tend to generate extremism and 'exclusiveness', which many consider perilous for democracy. Thus, not only will future empirical analysis of this model's predictions serve to identify its predictive capacity; as well it will provide information germane to the debate on clientelism's normative status.

Theoretical Appendix

6.1 Proof of Lemma 2 for the Case $G_P \leq 1/2$

If $G_P \leq 1/2$ and P's opponent $\sim P$ chooses $\mathbf{v}_m$, it will be impossible to for P to persuade any voters on programmatic grounds. To see this note that, when $G_P \leq 1/2$, no voter will have a purely programmatic utility for P greater than $1/2$ (i.e. $u_{i,P}(\text{prog}) \leq 1/2$ for all voters). As well, note that all voters have a programmatic utility of at least $1/2$ for any candidate $\sim P$ who chooses $\mathbf{v}_m$: the voters least satisfied with this platform are those with ideal points $x_i = 1$ and $x_i = 0$, and for these voters $u_{i,\sim P}(\text{prog}) = 1/2$ for any party $\sim P$ which chooses the median voter programmatic vector $\mathbf{v}_m$.

As a result, when $G_P \leq 1/2$ and P's opponent $\sim P$ chooses $\mathbf{v}_m$, P will only gain the support of voters who are in its target set. In turn, any deviation from the outcome $\mathbf{v}_1 = \mathbf{v}_2 = \mathbf{v}_m$ will need to involve a target set of at least half the electorate in order to give P a chance of winning. Furthermore, any target set greater than a bare plurality contains more voters than necessary to win the election, and thus will not represent the necessary condition choices $\hat{\underline{x}}_P(G_P)$, and $\hat{\overline{x}}_P(G_P)$ (recall above definition of necessity).

By Assumption 1 above, this bare plurality target set will include the median voter. The median voter will be the voter from this target set whose allegiance will be most difficult to gain, since the opposing party $\sim P$ chooses the median voter's ideal point at $\mathbf{v}_m$. It follows that $\hat{x}_P(G_P) = x_m$.

6.2 Lemma 3 and the Ideological Swing Voter

When $G_P > 1/2$ and P's opponent $\sim P$ chooses $\mathbf{v}_m$, it may be *possible* to for P to persuade some voters on programmatic grounds. In turn, there may exist payoff-enhancing deviations for P which do not involve choosing a bare plurality target set. Lemma 3 establishes the necessary condition strategy for a payoff-enhancing deviation which does not involve a bare plurality target set. Put otherwise, if the strategy identified in Lemma 3 leads does not lead to $\pi_P > 1/2$, then no deviation without a bare plurality target set is payoff-enhancing. Lemma 3 establishes the necessary condition strategy for a payoff-enhancing deviation on the political right; a symmetric condition applies on the political right.

Lemma 3 *For any $G_P > 1/2$, the necessary condition strategy without a bare plurality target set on the political right is $\hat{x}_P(G_P) = 3/2 - G_P$ and $\hat{\Theta}_P(G_P) = [x_m, (3/2 - G_P)]$.*

This lemma, tells us that for any $G_P > 1/2$ the necessary condition strategy for payoff-enhancing deviation on the political right involves the platform $\hat{x}_P(G_P) =$

($3/2 - G_P$) and the target set $\Theta_P = [x_m, (3/2 - G_P)]$. For example, if $G_P = .8$ then $\hat{x}_P(.8) = .7$ and the $C_P = .2$ units of clientelistic effort will be targeted to voters in the range $\hat{\Theta}_P = [.5, .7]$.

Proof of Lemma 3 When one party $\sim P$ chooses the median-voter programmatic strategy vector $\mathbf{v}_m$ and her opponent P chooses x_P and $G_P > 1/2$, define x_S as the swing ideological voter, a voter whose programmatic utility for party P is the same as his or her programmatic for party $\sim P$:

$$u_{S,P}(\text{prog}) = u_{S,\sim P}(\text{prog}) \quad \Rightarrow \quad G_P \cdot \left(1 - abs[x_P - x_S]\right) = 1 - abs[x_m - x_S]. \tag{A.1}$$

We will now identify, for any $G_P > 1/2$, the swing ideological voter x_S when $\sim P$ chooses $\mathbf{v}_m$ and P chooses $x_P > 1/2$, i.e. when P chooses an ideological deviation on the political right. An identical process applies for deviations on the political left. Note first that swing ideological voters may exist both in the range $[1/2, x_P]$ and in the range $[x_P, 1]$, i.e. both voters to the left and to the right of x_P may be indifferent between the parties' respective programmatic stances.[10]

Define $\underline{x}_S$ as a swing ideological voter in the range $[1/2, x_P]$. Given our specification of programmatic utility $u_{i,P}(\text{prog})$, for any $G_P > 1/2$ the following expression implicitly defines $\underline{x}_S$ when $\sim P$ chooses $\mathbf{v}_m$ and P chooses $x_P > 1/2$:

$$1 - (\underline{x}_S - 1/2) = G_P \cdot \left\{1 - (x_P - \underline{x}_S)\right\}. \tag{A.2}$$

This can be rewritten as:

$$\underline{x}_S = \frac{3/2 - \{G_P \cdot (1 - x_P)\}}{1 + G_P}. \tag{A.3}$$

Based on (A.3) I establish the following Sub-lemma:

Sub-lemma 1 *For any $G_P > 1/2$, when $\sim P$ chooses $\mathbf{v}_m$ and P chooses $x_P > 1/2$, there is no swing voter ideological voter $\underline{x}_S$ in the range $[1/2, x_P]$ for values of $x_P < 3/2 - G_P$.*

Proof of Sub-lemma 1 We are looking for swing ideological voters in the range $[1/2, x_P]$. As such, if (A.3) generates a value $\underline{x}_S > x_P$, then there is no swing ideological voter $\underline{x}_S$ in the range $[1/2, x_P]$. To see this, note that (A.2) above applies only to voters in the range $[1/2, x_P]$. In turn, if (A.3) generates a value $\underline{x}_S > x_P$, we know that the indifference conditions for a swing voter in the range $[1/2, x_P]$ are not satisfied for voters in the applicable range, such that there is no swing voter ideological voter $\underline{x}_S$ in the range $[1/2, x_P]$. It is then straightforward to establish that (algebra omitted), for any $G_P > 1/2$:

[10]Voters with ideal points $x_i < 1/2$ will all have a higher programmatic utility for $\sim P$ than for P since: (a) they are located closer to $\sim P$ in policy space, and (b) $G_{\sim P} = 1 > G_P$.

$$\underline{x}_S = \frac{3/2 - \{G_P \cdot (1 - x_P)\}}{1 + G_P} > x_P \quad \text{if and only if} \quad x_P < 3/2 - G_P.$$

□

In turn, for any $G_P > 1/2$ Sub-lemma 1 allows to express $\underline{x}_S$ as follows:

$$\underline{x}_S = \begin{cases} \emptyset & \text{if } 1/2 < x_P < 3/2 - G_P, \\ \frac{3/2 - \{G_P \cdot (1 - x_P)\}}{1 + G_P} & \text{if } x_P > 3/2 - G_P. \end{cases} \tag{A.4}$$

We now move to identifying ideological swing voters $\overline{x}_S$ in the range $[x_P, 1]$. Given our specification of programmatic utility $u_{i,P}(\text{prog})$, for any $G_P > 1/2$ the following expression implicitly defines $\overline{x}_S$ when $\sim P$ chooses $\mathbf{v}_m$ and P chooses $x_P > 1/2$:

$$1 - (\overline{x}_S - 1/2) = G_P \cdot \{1 - (\overline{x}_S - x_P)\}. \tag{A.5}$$

This can be rewritten as:

$$\overline{x}_S = \frac{3/2 - \{G_P \cdot (1 + x_P)\}}{1 - G_P}. \tag{A.6}$$

Based on (A.6) we can establish the following Sub-lemmas:

Sub-lemma 2 *For any $G_P > 1/2$, when $\sim P$ chooses $\mathbf{v}_m$ and P chooses $x_P > 1/2$, there is no swing voter ideological voter $\overline{x}_S$ in the range $[x_P, 1]$ for values of $x_P < 1/2G_P$.*

Sub-lemma 3 *For any $G_P > 1/2$, when $\sim P$ chooses $\mathbf{v}_m$ and P chooses $x_P > 1/2$, there is no swing voter ideological voter $\overline{x}_S$ in the range $[x_P, 1]$ for values of $x_P > 3/2 - G_P$.*

Proof of Sub-lemma 2 We are looking for swing ideological voters in the range $[x_P, 1]$. By definition, if (A.6) generates a value $\overline{x}_S > 1$, then there is no swing ideological voter $\overline{x}_S$ in the range $[x_P, 1]$: no voters in the applicable range satisfy the indifference condition in (A.6). It is then straightforward to establish that (algebra omitted):

$$\overline{x}_S = \frac{3/2 - \{G_P \cdot (1 + x_P)\}}{1 - G_P} > 1 \quad \text{if and only if} \quad x_P < 1/2G_P.$$ □

Proof of Sub-lemma 3 We are looking for swing ideological voters in the range $[x_P, 1]$. By definition, if (A.6) generates a value $\overline{x}_S < x_P$, then there is no swing ideological voter $\overline{x}_S$ in the range $[x_P, 1]$: no voters in the applicable range satisfy the indifference condition in (A.6). It is then straightforward to establish that (algebra omitted),

$$\overline{x}_S = \frac{3/2 - \{G_P \cdot (1 + x_P)\}}{1 - G_P} < x_P \quad \text{if and only if} \quad x_P > 3/2 - G_P.$$ □

Sub-lemmas 2 and 3 allow us to express $\overline{x}_S$ as follows:

$$\overline{x}_S = \begin{cases} \emptyset & \text{if } 1/2 < x_P < 1/2G_P, \\ \frac{3/2 - \{G_P \cdot (1 - x_P)\}}{1 + G_P} & \text{if } 1/2G_P < x_P < 3/2 - G_P, \\ \emptyset & \text{if } x_P > 3/2 - G_P. \end{cases} \tag{A.7}$$

Taken together, expressions (A.4) and (A.7) tell us that, for any $G_P > 1/2$, when $\sim P$ chooses $\mathbf{v}_m$ and P chooses $x_P > 1/2$ the game never has more than one swing voter, i.e. the existence conditions stipulated in Sub-lemmas 1, 2, and 3 are never simultaneously satisfied for both $\underline{x}_S$ and $\overline{x}_S$. Furthermore, they allow us to precisely identify the swing ideological voter for any $G_P > 1/2$ and $x_P > 1/2$:

$$x_S = \begin{cases} \emptyset & \text{if } 1/2 < x_P < 1/2G_P, \\ \overline{x}_S & \text{if } 1/2G_P < x_P < 3/2 - G_P, \\ \underline{x}_S & \text{if } x_P > 3/2 - G_P. \end{cases} \tag{A.8}$$

In words, when $1/2 < x_P < 1/2G_P$ the game has no swing ideological voters. At such moderate values of x_P, all voters have a higher programmatic utility for party $\sim P$ than for party P, because the latter has not sufficiently distinguished her programmatic stance from the median voter policy adopted by $\sim P$. In contrast, at intermediate values of x_P ($1/2G_P < x_P < 3/2 - G_P$) the game's swing ideological voter will be $\overline{x}_S \in [x_P, 1]$, and the subset of extremist voters in the range $[\overline{x}_S, 1]$ will have a higher programmatic utility for P than for $\sim P$ despite the fact that $G_{\sim P} = 1 > G_P$. Finally, at more extreme values of $x_P > 3/2 - G_P$, the game's swing ideological voter will be $\underline{x}_S \in [1/2, x_P]$, and all voters in the range $[\underline{x}_S, 1]$ will have a higher programmatic utility for P than for $\sim P$ despite the fact that $G_{\sim P} = 1 > G_P$.

Note from the above swing voter analysis that, for any value of $x_P > 1/2G_P$, voters with ideal points in the range $[x_S, 1]$ have a higher programmatic utility for party P than for party $\sim P$. It follows immediately from (A.8) that, for any $G_P > 1/2$, the programmatic position $x_P = 3/2 - G_P$ is the position which maximizes the range of $[x_S, 1]$, i.e. maximizes the number of voters who prefer P on purely programmatic grounds. For any $G_P > 1/2$ and $x_P > 1/2$, P will only target clientelistic goods to some subset of voters with ideal points $x_i < x_S$, since those with ideal points $x_i > x_S$ can be counted on to choose P on purely programmatic grounds. It follows that the necessary condition strategy given some $G_P > 1/2$ includes the platform $\hat{x}_P(G_P) = 3/2 - G_P$: this is the policy position which maximizes the number of P's ideological supporters, and in turn minimizes the size of Θ_P to which P's clientelistic efforts will need to be targeted so as to secure a bare majority.

When P chooses $\hat{x}_P(G_P) = 3/2 - G_P$, it is straightforward to see from (A.8) above that the game's swing ideological voter has ideal point $x_S = 3/2 - G_P$, i.e. that the swing ideological voter is the voter whose ideal point is identical to P's programmatic position. All voters with ideal points $x_i < 3/2 - G_P$ prefer $\sim P$ to P on purely programmatic grounds, and vice versa for voters with ideal points $x_i > 3/2 - G_P$. In turn, given that $\hat{x}_P(G_P) = 3/2 - G_P$ we know that $\hat{\Theta}_P = [x_m, (3/2 - G_P)]$, i.e. that target set most conducive to securing a bare majority victory, is that which targets all voters between the median ideal point and the swing voter $x_S = \hat{x}_P(G_P) = 3/2 - G_P$. □

6.3 Proof of Lemma 2 for the Case $G_P > 1/2$

The median voter receives a utility of '1' from the set of actions $\mathbf{v}_m$. On the other hand, Lemma 2 tells us that, when $\eta = 1$, the median voter's utility for necessary condition deviations when $G_P < 1/2$ will be:

$$u_{m,P}\big(\hat{x}(G_P,), \hat{\Theta}_P(G_P)\big) = G_P + \left(\frac{1 - G_P}{\delta + 1/2}\right). \tag{A.9}$$

When $G_P > 1/2$, party P can consider both locally optimal deviations with a bare majority is target set and the median policy stance (Lemma 2), or deviations to the political right or left (Lemma 3). If the former, the median voter's utility when $\eta = 1$ will be (A.9). If the latter, the median voter's utility for locally optimal deviations when $\eta = 1$ will be:

$$u_{m,P}\big(\hat{x}(G_P,), \hat{\Theta}_P(G_P)\big) = (G_P)^2 + \left(\frac{1 - G_P}{\delta + 1 - G_P}\right). \tag{A.10}$$

To prove Lemma 2, I first establish that, for any $G_P > 1/2$, the median voter will always receive a higher utility from the deviation stipulated in Lemma 2 than that stipulated in Lemma 3: (A.9) > (A.10) (algebra omitted). This in turn implies that the strategy identified Lemma 2 is more likely to yield payoff-enhancing deviations than is that identified in Lemma 3, i.e. if the strategy from Lemma 2 yields a payoff-enhancing deviation then so does the strategy in Lemma 3, but not vice versa. This establishes Lemma 2 in the text, i.e. that for any value of $G_P < 1$ Lemma 2 identifies the necessary condition strategy for payoff-enhancing deviations.

6.4 Proof of Proposition 1

When $\eta = 1$, as long as $\delta > 1/2$ there *does not* exist a payoff-improving deviation from $\mathbf{v}_m$ to a value $G_P < 1$, and conversely as long $\delta < 1/2$ there *does* exist a payoff-improving deviation from $\mathbf{v}_m$ to a value $G_P < 1$.

Given a deviation from $\mathbf{v}_m$ to the necessary condition strategy, it is straightforward to see that, as long as the median voter prefers the deviating candidate P to the her opponent $\sim P$, then do all other voters in P's target set. The median voter receives a utility of '1' from the set of actions $\mathbf{v}_m$. On the other hand, when $\eta = 1$, the median voter's utility for the necessary condition strategy when $G_P < 1$ will be:

$$u_{m,P}\big(\hat{x}(G_P,), \hat{\Theta}_P\big) = G_P + \left(\frac{1 - G_P}{\delta + 1/2}\right). \tag{A.11}$$

In turn it is straightforward to see that, for values of $G_P < 1$, the function $G_P + (\frac{1-G_P}{\delta+1/2})$ can only be greater than '1' if $\delta > 1/2$ (algebra omitted).

References

Calvert RL (1985) Robustness of the multi-dimensional voting model: candidate motivations, uncertainty, and convergence. Am J Polit Sci 29:69–95

Downs A (1957) An economic theory of democracy. Harper and Row, New York

Fernandez M, Pierskalla J (2009) Partisan strategies and political economic performance. Do modes of democratic accountability affect economic fortunes? Paper presented at the 2009 annual meeting of the American political science association, Toronto, Canada, September 3rd–6th

Humphreys M (2008) Coalitions. Annu Rev Pol Sci 11:351–386

Keefer P, Vlaicu R (2008) Credibility, clientelism and democracy. J Law Econ Organ 24(2):371–406

Kitschelt H, Wilkinson S (2007) Citizen-politician linkages: an introduction. In: Kitschelt H, Wilkinson S (eds) Patrons, clients, and policies. Patterns of democratic accountability and political competition. Cambridge University Press, Cambridge

Kselman D (2008) Governance and intra-party choice. Economics masters thesis, Duke University Department of Economics

Lipset SM, Rokkan S (eds) (1967) Party systems and voter alignments. A cross-national perspective. Free Press, Toronto

Magaloni B Diaz-Cayeros A et al (2007) Clientelism and portfolio diversification: a model of electoral investment with applications to Mexico. In: Kitschelt H, Wilkinson S (eds) Patrons, clients, and policies. Patterns of democratic accountability and political competition. Cambridge University Press, Cambridge

Nash JF (1953) Two-person cooperative games. Econometrica 21:128–140

Nichter S (2008) Vote buying or turnout buying? Machine politics and the secret ballot. Am Polit Sci Rev 102(01):19–31

Persson T, Tabellini G (2000) Political economics. Explaining economic policy. MIT Press, Cambridge

Stokes SC (2005) Perverse accountability: a formal model of machine politics with evidence from Argentina. Am Polit Sci Rev 99(03):315–325

Strom K (1990) A behavioral theory of competitive political parties. Am J Polit Sci 34:565–598

Wittman D (1983) Candidate motivations: a synthesis of alternative theories. Am Polit Sci Rev 77:142–157

Nonseparable Preferences and Issue Packaging in Elections

Dean Lacy and Emerson M.S. Niou

1 Introduction

Suppose a candidate in a two-candidate plurality rule election faces an opponent who has adopted the policy position of the median voter. We know from work by Hotelling (1929), Black (1948), and Downs (1957), that in a one dimensional policy space the best the challenging candidate can do is to also adopt the policy position of the median voter, yielding a tied election. Suppose further that the candidates are restricted from moving freely in the policy space, perhaps due to party reputations on the issue or to voters penalizing the candidates for changing positions. A candidate who is pinned to a losing position in a one-dimensional policy space has no recourse but to accept defeat.

In this chapter we ask: what strategies are available to a candidate facing an opponent who is unbeatable in the current policy space? As Schattschneider (1960) observed, losers in a political conflict may benefit from expanding the scope of the conflict. Schattschneider originally conceived of this strategy as bringing new groups into the conflict. But his observation extends to bringing new issues into the election. Losing candidates can potentially win elections by introducing new issues.

Whether the strategy of introducing new issues into an election will succeed depends on the structure of voter preferences on the original policy space and the new

---

The National Science Foundation provided financial support for this research through Grant No. SES-0242255.

Presented at the Conference on Contemporary Applications of the Spatial Model, The Juan March Institute, Madrid, Spain, April 27–28, 2012.

D. Lacy (✉)
Department of Government, Dartmouth College, HB 6108, Hanover, NH 03755, USA
e-mail: dean.lacy@dartmouth.edu

E.M.S. Niou
Department of Political Science, Duke University, Durham, NC 27708-0204, USA
e-mail: niou@duke.edu

N. Schofield et al. (eds.), *Advances in Political Economy*,
DOI 10.1007/978-3-642-35239-3_10, © Springer-Verlag Berlin Heidelberg 2013

issues. In particular, candidates can gain an advantage in an election by introducing issues over which voter preferences are nonseparable. When a voter has nonseparable preferences across issues, her preference for a candidate's position on one issue depends on the candidate's position on other, related issues. For example, a voter may prefer a candidate who promises to cut taxes only if that candidate also pledges to cut specific government spending programs. Or a voter may prefer a candidate who opposes abortion only if the candidate also pledges to increase federal assistance to single mothers and their children. When voters have nonseparable preferences, packages of issues carry greater weight in the voting booth than each issue separately. Conversely, a voter with separable preferences evaluates a candidate's position on each issue separately from the candidate's positions on other issues.

Nonseparable voter preferences open opportunities for candidates to package issues strategically in elections. We present a model of spatial competition between two candidates. The candidates begin competing on single issue on which candidates' positions are fixed and one candidate has an advantage. We show that the disadvantaged candidate can introduce a new issue and take a position that her opponent cannot beat, but only if some voters have nonseparable preferences for the issues. If all voters have separable preferences for the issues, then the disadvantaged candidate cannot find a position to beat her opponent. We then show that nonseparable preferences are more than a theoretical curiosity. Results from a 2004 election survey demonstrate that nonseparable preferences are held by a substantial portion of the voting public on a variety of issues. The complexity of public preferences on important policy issues can profoundly influence the logic of candidate competition.

2 Spatial Competition and the Number of Issues

Most of the research on electoral competition has been a search for electoral equilibria (Black 1948; Downs 1957; Plott 1967; Davis et al. 1970; McKelvey 1976; Schofield 1978; Enelow and Hinich 1984). This body of literature offers clear theoretical results. Two candidates in a single-winner plurality election compete for votes by seeking the position of the median voter when the policy space is one-dimensional, voter preferences are single-peaked, and candidates can move freely in the policy space (Hotelling 1929; Black 1948; Downs 1957). The result is that candidates converge to the position of the median voter, resulting in a tie. However, this *candidate convergence* prediction rarely fits reality. In most two-candidate elections, the candidates adopt distinct positions. Policy-motivated candidates, uncertain voters, probabilistic voting, and the need for candidates to appeal to activists for campaign contributions all create incentives for candidates to diverge. Probably the most interesting and realistic variant on the median voter model is a multi-dimensional policy space.

As voters and candidates take positions on more than one issue, the dimensionality of the issue space expands and an equilibrium position for candidates will not generally exist. Only in the rare case in which the distribution of voter ideal points produces a median in all directions will there be an equilibrium (Plott 1967; Davis et al. 1972). In the absence of an equilibrium, candidates can adopt positions to beat their opponents in an almost endless cycle (McKelvey 1976; Schofield 1978). In multiple dimensions when a Condorcet winner does not exist, dislodging a winning candidate is easy since there is always another position in the issue space that will defeat any given position. However, a challenger who adopts a new position to defeat her opponent can also then be defeated by a new position that her opponent adopts. Although candidates can dance around the policy space to find new winning positions, no position is unbeatable except under the rare condition that it splits the voters exactly in half in every possible direction (Enelow and Hinich 1984).

The median voter result in one dimension and the general instability result in multiple dimensions form the foundation of research on electoral competition. Both results require that candidates can move freely in the policy space. In real elections, unrestricted candidate movement may not be plausible. Parties and their affiliated candidates develop reputations on issues that are difficult to change (Petrocik 1996). Activists and party leaders may confine a candidate to a position on an issue (Aldrich 1983). Voters may penalize candidates for "flip-flopping" on issues. All of these restrictions on candidate movement are substantively meaningful and empirically plausible. Yet little research to date has explored variations on the multidimensional model in which candidates are restricted in the policy positions they can adopt.

When candidates are constrained in their ability to change positions on the issues in an election, introducing a new issue or issues can help a candidate defeat a well-positioned opponent (Schattschneider 1960; Riker 1982, 1986). The conventional wisdom on expanding the issue space has been that candidates should try to split the support of their opponents (Riker 1982). A classic example in American politics is the Republican party's adoption in the 1850s and 1860s of a platform to halt the expansion of slavery. The Republicans' position on economic development mimicked the Whigs', but their position on restricting slavery differentiated them from both the Whigs and Democrats, pulled voters away from the Whigs, and swept the Whig party from the American electoral landscape (Riker 1982).

As we will show, the introduction of new issues in an election can be a successful strategy depending on whether voter preferences are nonseparable across the issues. Much of the research in voting behavior and electoral competition assumes that voters have separable preferences across issues of public policy. The importance of nonseparable preferences was identified in the public choice literature years ago (Kadane 1972; Kramer 1972; McKelvey 1976; Schwartz 1977; Enelow and Hinich 1984). Little work since then has examined the implications of nonseparable preferences for candidate strategies or the extent of nonseparable preferences in the voting public. In this chapter we show that nonseparable voter preferences create opportunities for candidates to package new issues with old issues for electoral gain.

3 The Strategy of Issue Packaging

We present a model of issue packaging based on a spatial competition game between two candidates. Each candidate (or party) adopts a vector of issue positions in n-dimensional Euclidean space. For purposes of illustration and without loss of generality, we restrict attention to two issues, X and Y. Candidates A and B adopt positions $A = \{X_A, Y_A\}$ and $B = \{X_B, Y_B\}$, respectively.

At the start of the election, $\{X_A, X_B\} \in \Re^1 \equiv X$, and $X_A \neq X_B$. Candidate A is in a winning position since a majority of voters are closer to A than to B. Candidate B then announces a position on a new issue, Y. Candidate A can then announce a position on issue Y. Candidates cannot change their positions on X as they adopt a position on Y.

A set of $M \geq 3$ voters each has ideal point $\theta_i \in \Re^n$ and a quasiconcave utility function. When confronted with a choice across two or more alternatives, a voter compares the generalized Euclidean distance (GED) from her ideal point to each of the alternatives and prefers the one that is closest to her (Enelow and Hinich 1984).

Separable preferences are indicated by indifference contours that are concentric circles or ellipses whose axes are parallel to the axes of the space. *Nonseparable preferences* are indicated by indifference contours whose axes are not parallel to axes of the space. Nonseparable preferences imply interdependence among issues, or that a person's preference on one issue depends on the choices available or the outcome on another issue.[1] Issues can be related to each other as either positive or negative complements. Positive complements are issues that are positively related to each other: a person wants more on one dimension as she receives more on another dimension (Black and Newing 1951).

Negative complements are issues on which a person wants less out of one dimension as she gets more on the other dimension. For issues with clear "directions" such as increases or decreases in taxes or education spending, the distinction between positive and negative complements is meaningful. For issues without a clear direction, such as privatizing Social Security or allowing same-sex marriage, the direction of complementarity in the issues is arbitrary.

If a voter has nonseparable preferences, her evaluation of a candidate's position depends on the candidate's stance on other issues. For example, a voter may initially approve of a candidate's announced position against abortion. But if the candidate also promises to end welfare support for unwed teenage mothers, the voter may disapprove of the candidate's position on abortion. Or, a voter may disapprove of a candidate's proposal to cut funding for education unless the candidate also promises to cut taxes.

We label voter ideal points by the voter number, $1, 2, \ldots, m$. Define voter i's induced ideal point z_i as the point of tangency of her indifference contours on the line $\overline{AB}$ containing the candidates' positions. A voter votes for the candidate closest to her ideal point measured in generalized Euclidean distance. Therefore, voter i votes for the candidate whose position on $\overline{AB}$ is closest to the voter's induced ideal point, z_i. A cutpoint, $\frac{A+B}{2}$ at the midpoint between A and B on $\overline{AB}$, divides the voters into those closer to A, who vote for A, and those closer to B, who vote for B.

[1] Any pair of issues could be completely nonseparable or partially nonseparable. Partially nonseparable preferences occur when, for instance, issue 1 is nonseparable from 2 while 2 is separable from 1 (Lacy and Niou 2000; Lacy 2001).

Each voter chooses the candidate whose position falls on the indifference contour closest to her ideal point.

The model includes two additional assumptions. First, candidates cannot change their positions on the initial issue, X. Either the candidate positions are given exogenously on the issue due to constraints such as party reputation or activist demands, or voters penalize candidates for changing positions. Either way, candidate positions on issue X remain fixed. Second, we assume that one candidate, arbitrarily labeled A, has an advantage on issue X. Candidate A could be at the position of the median voter on X or closer to the median voter than candidate B. The purpose of both assumptions is to capture a realistic scenario in which one candidate has an advantage on an issue that the other candidate cannot overcome. Even if candidate B can move freely on issue X and confronts an opponent who has staked out the position of the median voter, the best that candidate B can do is to adopt A's position and end up in a tie. But, candidate B can do better by introducing a new issue.

Proposition *In a two candidate plurality election, if a candidate is winning on one issue on which candidate positions are fixed, then that candidate can be defeated only if new issues are introduced over which some voters have nonseparable preferences.*

If a candidate is winning in a one dimensional issue space, then there is no way to beat that candidate when voter and candidate positions are fixed. If the winning candidate has adopted the position of the median voter, a more rigid assumption, then there is no way a challenging candidate can do any better than a tie even if the challenger can choose any position on the issue. When confronting a candidate who has staked out a winning position in a one dimensional issue space, the only recourse for a challenger is to introduce a new issue.

The strategy of introducing a new issue hinges critically on whether voter preferences are separable or nonseparable. Suppose that all voters have separable preferences across the original issue, X, and any new issue, Y, that a candidate can introduce. In Fig. 1, voters are labeled by their ideal points, 1, 2, and 3, with induced ideal points on X labeled, respectively, z_1, z_2, and z_3. There is no equilibrium in this election if candidates can move freely since the distribution of voter ideal points does not produce a median in all directions (Davis et al. 1972). At the start of the election, X is the only issue, candidate positions are given by A and B, and candidate A is positioned at the ideal point (induced on issue X) of the median voter, z_2. The other voters have induced ideal points z_1 and z_3 on the candidate space $\overline{AB}$. The candidates are constrained by their positions on X and can move only along the vertical dashed lines anchored by their positions on X.

Candidate B introduces issue Y and can take any position. Suppose B takes position B'. The new candidate space is then $\overline{AB'}$, with new cutpoint $\frac{A+B'}{2}$. Voter 2's induced ideal point may well switch to B's side of the cutpoint, in which case B wins. However, A can "mimic" B's position on Y by adopting a position A' that matches B' on Y. Since all voters have separable preferences, their induced ideal points, $z_i' \in \overline{A'B'}$, are orthogonal projections of their induced ideal points, $z_i \in \overline{AB}$,

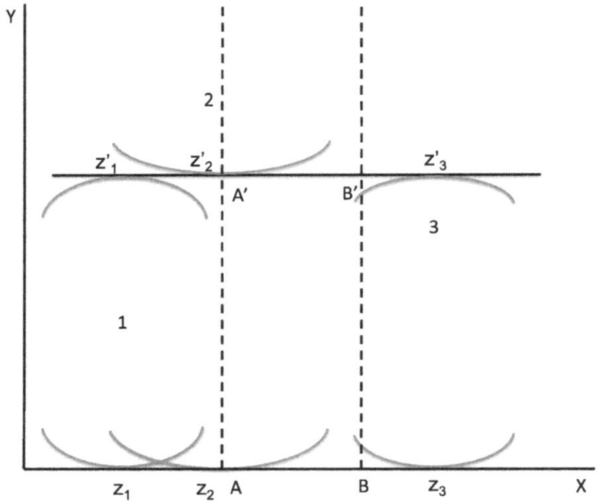

Fig. 1 All voters have separable preferences. Voters 1 and 2 are closer to Candidate A's position; voter 3 is closer to Candidate B's position. After B moves to B', A can find another position, A', that maintains her advantage on the distribution of induced ideal points, z_i'

and thus preserve the positions of the voters relative to the candidates. Candidate A is closer to a majority of voters on $\overline{A'B'}$ just as she was on $\overline{AB}$. When all voters have separable preferences, candidate A can always adopt candidate B's position on the new issue and maintain the electoral advantage she had on the original issue. There is no position for B that can guarantee a victory over A when all voters have separable preferences.

When some voters have nonseparable preferences, then B can find a position that A cannot beat with any position on the new issue. In Fig. 2, voters 1 and 2 are closer to candidate A's position on issue X. When candidate B adopts position B', voters 1 and 2 are closer to B' than to A. Voter 1's preferences are separable across the two issues, but voter 2's preferences are nonseparable. Candidate A cannot adopt a position on the vertical dotted line at A that allows her to win voters 1 and 2. For instance, voters 1 and 2 both prefer B' to A' since A' is outside of the voters' indifference contours that include B'. There is no position A can adopt that is closer to voters 1 and 2 than B' in generalized Euclidean distance. The positions for A that could beat B' are in the areas in which the indifference contours of any two voters overlap. But these areas are out of reach for A due to her position on X.

Voter 3 could be positioned anywhere in the issue space to the right of voter 2 and have preferences that are either separable or nonseparable as long as she prefers B' to any point on the dotted line at A. It is also noteworthy that B begins with a position on issue X that is more extreme than any voter's position. Candidate B is outside of the distribution of voter preferences on issue X but wins by finding a new issue over which voter 2 has nonseparable preferences. Candidate A loses the election and cannot adopt any position on Y that will allow her to win.

The example does not require that the median voter have nonseparable preferences. Similar examples are possible when a moderate voter 2 has separable pref-

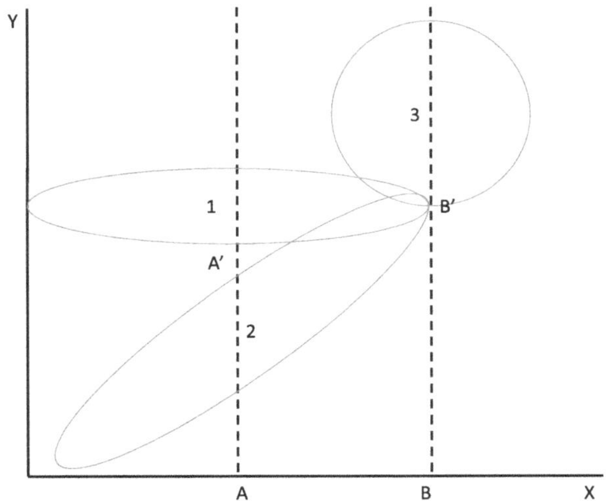

Fig. 2 A pivotal voter has nonseparable preferences. Voters 1 and 2 are closer to *A* than to *B* on issue *X*. Voters 1 and 2 switch to supporting candidate B after she moves to *B′*. Candidate A cannot find a position on issue *Y* to win back both voters 1 and 2 given her position on issue *X*

erences while a more extreme voter 1 has nonseparable preferences. Candidate A does not have to be located at the position of the median voter on *X* as long as she is closer to the median voter than B. Candidate B does not have to adopt the position of the median voter on issue *Y*.

Figure 2 illustrates that a candidate can move from a losing position to a winning position by introducing an issue on which voter preferences are nonseparable from the original issues in the election. Only one of three voters in the example has nonseparable preferences. There is not a critical number of voters who must have nonseparable preferences in order for the result to hold. The one pivotal voter with nonseparable preferences gives candidate B an opportunity to find a winning position.

Political candidates frequently present voters with packages of issues. Ronald Reagan in 1980 told American voters that if they agreed with him on any issue of taxing, spending, national defense, and deficit reduction, then they agreed with him on the whole set of issues. Bill Clinton and Tony Blair advocated a "Third Way" of free trade combined with job training and social insurance programs to aid workers whose jobs disappeared due to globalization. The Republican party during the 1850s and 1860s quickly rose from a minor party to one of the two major parties on a platform of restricting the Westward expansion of slavery while promoting infrastructure development that would help Western farmers ship their products to markets in the East. The combination of opposition to slavery and support for internal improvements linked the interests of voters in the North and West, giving the Republicans a national electoral majority for decades. Candidates' strategies are made richer by the possibility of exploiting voters' nonseparable preferences to engineer packages of issues that appeal to voters when the issues individually might not.

4 Do Voters Have Nonseparable Preferences?

Are nonseparable preferences a theoretical curiosity or empirical reality? Few public opinion surveys include questions designed to measure whether voter preferences are nonseparable across issues. Questions designed to detect nonseparable preferences appeared on a 2004 survey of US citizens.[2] The survey contained questions about twelve different issues that figured prominently in candidate debates and commentary about the election. Although each of the twelve issues could be nonseparable from all of the remaining issues for some voters, detecting nonseparable preferences across all combinations of issues would have been impossible in a 20-minute survey. To make the survey manageable, questions paired each issue with only one other issue—some obviously related, some not—to uncover nonseparable preferences. For instance, taxes and education spending were paired. For the issue of taxes, respondents first answered a question similar to existing surveys. We label this type of question "unconditional" since it asks a respondent's opinion on an issue in isolation, without reference to the outcome of other issues. Later in the survey respondents answered two "conditional" questions to detect whether preferences on taxes are nonseparable from spending on education. The questions were:

(unconditional) Do you want the amount of money that people pay in taxes to the US government to

go up a lot, say to 50 % more than we spend now
go up somewhat, say to 25 % more than we spend now
go up a little, say to 10 % more than we spend now
remain at current levels
go down a little, say to 10 % less than we spend now
go down somewhat, say to 25 % less than we spend now
go down a lot, say to 50 % less than we spend now

(conditional) If the government reduces the amount of money it spends on education to 25 percent less than it spends now, then would you want the amount of money that people pay in taxes to the US government to

go up a lot, say to 50 % more than we spend now
go up somewhat, say to 25 % more than we spend now
go up a little, say to 10 % more than we spend now

[2] Knowledge Networks recruited over 50,000 subjects nationwide to participate in surveys administered by WebTV. The computer format of the survey allows respondents to complete surveys at their leisure, and often results in more reliable and valid responses than telephone interviews (Chang and Krosnick 2009). A random sample of the Knowledge Networks panel was chosen to participate in a three-wave survey, with Wave 1 conducted April 27–May 31 (N = 1308); Wave 2, September 17–October 7 (N = 947); and Wave 3, November 19–December 3, 2004 (N = 717). A sample of 211 new respondents also completed interviews in Wave 3. Completion rates were 76 percent in Wave 1, 85 percent in Wave 2, and 77 percent in Wave 3.

remain at current levels
go down a little, say to 10 % less than we spend now
go down somewhat, say to 25 % less than we spend now
go down a lot, say to 50 % less than we spend now

(conditional) If the government increases the amount of money it spends on education to 25 percent more than it spends now, then would you want the amount of money that people pay in taxes to the US government to

go up a lot, say to 50 % more than we spend now
go up somewhat, say to 25 % more than we spend now
go up a little, say to 10 % more than we spend now
remain at current levels
go down a little, say to 10 % less than we spend now
go down somewhat, say to 25 % less than we spend now
go down a lot, say to 50 % less than we spend now

Similar questions appeared on the survey for education spending conditional on different levels of taxes. The two conditional questions reveal whether preferences are separable or nonseparable. In a crosstabulation of responses to the conditional questions, all responses on the diagonal do not change on the issue of taxes depending on the level of education spending. Responses above the diagonal indicate nonseparable positive complements: a person wants taxes to increase as education spending increases but wants taxes to decrease as education spending decreases. Responses below the diagonal indicate nonseparable negative complements: as education spending increases, a person wants taxes to decrease; as education spending decreases, a person wants taxes to increase. In a split-half sample, some respondents answered the two conditional questions before the unconditional question, others answered the questions in reverse order.

While nonseparable preferences should be expected for taxing and spending issues, many other issues are nonseparable to some people. Respondents answered questions that paired defense spending and health care spending, Social Security and free trade, same sex marriage and same sex adoption, immigration and a national health insurance plan, and, in wave 2 only, background checks for gun owners and a ban on assault weapons.

Table 1 shows the percentage of respondents with nonseparable preferences (both positive and negative complements) for all twelve issues in the survey. The remaining percentages of responses are separable. The issues are ordered from the largest to the smallest combined percentage of nonseparable preferences. For half or more of the issues, at least 20 percent of respondents have nonseparable preferences. Issues such as taxes, education spending, Medicare, defense spending, trade, and imigration all show significant percentages of potential voters with nonseparable preferences. Recall that even a small percentage of voters with

Table 1 Percentages of respondents with nonseparable preferences. Source: 2004 panel survey of nonseparable preferences

Issue	Conditional on	N	Positive complements	Negative complements
		May 2004, N = 735		
Taxes	Education spending	623	46.7 %	7.2 %
Education spending	Taxes	620	42.2	8.2
Medicare spending	Defense spending	621	18.5	17.6
Defense spending	Medicare spending	622	12.2	22.3
Immigration	National health care	628	8.6	16.2
Free Trade	Privatize Social Security	623	14.8	8.7
National health care	Immigration	622	2.3	15.8
Assault weapons ban	Background checks	448*	4.2	9.5
Privatize Social Security	Free Trade	617	6.3	3.6
Adoption	Marriage	626	6.8	2.1
Marriage	Adoption	621	3.8	0.8
Background Checks	Assault weapons ban	451*	1.6	1.6

*Questions from wave 2, N = 462

nonseparable preferences create opportunities for candidates to package issues strategically.[3]

Table 2 shows the percentage of respondents who have nonseparable preferences broken down by the voter's self-placement on a standard seven-point ideological scale. Voters who described themselves as ideological moderates, at the midpoint of the scale, are more likely to have nonseparable preferences on most issues than voters who are more ideologically extreme. This finding suggests that the example in Fig. 2 may not be far off from real elections where voters in the middle of the issue space are the ones who have nonseparable preferences. In a one dimensional issue space or a multidimensional space in which all voters have separable preferences, the ideal points of moderate voters always remain in the middle of the space. But in a multidimensional space, moderate voters who have nonseparable preferences may have induced ideal points that make them more extreme on bundles of issues.

The results may also explain evidence of the disappearing center in electoral politics. Much has been written about the rise in polarization among voters and elected officials (Abramowitz 2010). But other evidence suggests that most voters remain moderate on most issues and that voter preferences are normally distributed rather than bimodal (Fiorina 2005). As Fig. 2 shows, moderate voters with nonseparable preferences over issues can have induced ideal points that are more extreme.

[3]The percentages of respondents with nonseparable preferences for taxes conditional on education does not have to match the percentage with nonseparable preferences for education spending conditional on taxes since voters may have partially nonseparable preferences (Lacy 2001).

Table 2 Percentages of respondents with nonseparable preferences. Source: 2004 panel survey of nonseparable preferences

Issue	Conditional on	Ideological moderates	Ideological non-moderates
Taxes	Education spending	59.5 %	48.5 %
Education spending	Taxes	54.8	47.1
Medicare spending	Defense spending	40.1	31.7
Defense spending	Medicare spending	37.1	32.8
Immigration	National health care	24.2	26.0
Free Trade	Privatize Social Security	23.9	23.0
National health care	Immigration	19.1	16.7
Assault weapons ban	Background checks	13.0	14.2
Privatize Social Security	Free Trade	11.5	8.0
Adoption	Marriage	9.0	8.6
Marriage	Adoption	7.5	2.4
Background Checks	Assault weapons ban	3.0	3.3

Voter 2, for instance, has an ideal point on issue X that makes him the median voter on X. But when issue Y is introduced, he supports candidate B's extreme position on X. Even though voter 2's ideal point may be moderate on X, his induced ideal point given the constraints of the options before him—candidate positions A and B'—is extreme. Debates about whether voters are extreme or moderate, polarized or centrist, are based on interpreting the distribution of voter ideal points issue by issue (Fiorina 2005; Abramowitz 2010). We need more information about voter preferences across issues to draw conclusions about whether voters are moderate or extreme. Nonseparable preferences may make moderate voters appear extremist or extremist voters appear moderate depending on the constraints imposed by other issues or the candidates' positions.

5 Conclusion

As E.E. Schattschneider wrote, "Political strategy deals… with the inclusion and exclusion of contestants because it is never true that the balance remains the same if the number is changed" (1957, 941). The same may be said of political issues as contestants. Changing the issues can tip the balance of a close election. We already know that moving from one issue to multiple issues fundamentally alters the nature of elections. As we show in this chapter, moving to a multi-dimensional issue space can be a strategic choice in an election. Introducing new issues may be a candidate's only hope of unseating an entrenched opponent. But simply introducing a new issue is not alone a path to victory. For a disadvantaged candidate to have any hope of winning an election by introducing new issues, some voters must see the issues as linked.

In the one dimensional spatial model, two competing candidates will converge to the position of the median voter. This theoretical result does not fit reality, primarily because politics is multidimensional. In a multidimensional model with two candidates, an equilibrium will not generally exist and candidates will change positions on issues in a never-ending quest for an electoral advantage. This prediction also does not appear to fit real elections. Imposing some additional realistic structure on the multidimensional spatial model of electoral competition produces new and surprising results.

When candidates have fixed positions in an issue space, a candidate can take a position on a new issue in order to beat an advantaged opponent. Instead of changing positions on existing issues, a potentially costly strategy if voters penalize "flip-floppers," candidates can compete by expanding the scope of conflict to include new issues. But only when some voters have nonseparable preferences will the strategy of introducing a new issue prove beneficial for a disadvantaged candidate. Issue packaging is a fundamental strategy of electoral politics, part of what William Riker called "heresthetics," or the art of political manipulation (Riker 1986).

References

Abramowitz A (2010) The disappearing center: engaged citizens, polarization, and American democracy. Yale University Press, New Haven

Aldrich JH (1983) A Downsian spatial model with party activism. Am Polit Sci Rev 77(4):974–990

Black D (1948) On the rationale of group decision-making. J Polit Econ 56(1):23–24

Black D, Newing RA (1951) Committee decisions with complementary valuation. William Hodge and Company, London

Chang L, Krosnick JA (2009) National surveys via RDD telephone interviewing versus the internet: comparing sample representativeness and response quality. Public Opin Q 73(4):641–678

Davis OA, DeGroot MH, Hinich MJ (1972) Social preference orderings and majority rule. Econometrica 40(1):147–157

Davis OA, Hinich MJ, Ordeshook PC (1970) Social preference orderings and majority rule. Am Polit Sci Rev 64(2):426–448

Downs A (1957) An economic theory of democracy. Harper and Row, New York

Enelow JM, Hinich MJ (1984) The spatial theory of voting: an introduction. Cambridge University Press, New York

Fiorina MP (2005) Culture war? The myth of a polarized America. Longman, New York

Hotelling H (1929) Stability in competition. Econ J 39:41–57

Kadane J (1972) On division of the question. Public Choice 13:47–54

Kramer GH (1972) Sophisticated voting over multidimensional choice spaces. J Math Sociol 2:165–180

Lacy D (2001) A theory of nonseparable preferences in survey responses. Am J Polit Sci 45(2):239–258

Lacy D, Niou EMS (2000) A problem with referendums. J Theor Polit 12(1):5–31

McKelvey RD (1976) Intransitivities in multidimensional voting models and some implications for agenda control. J Econ Theory 12:472–482

Petrocik JR (1996) Issue ownership in presidential elections, with a 1980 case study. Am J Polit Sci 40(3):825–850

Plott CR (1967) A notion of equilibrium and its possibility under majority rule. Am Econ Rev 57(4):787–806

Riker WH (1982) Liberalism against populism: a confrontation between the theory of democracy and the theory of social choice. Waveland Press, Prospect Heights
Riker WH (1986) The art of political manipulation. Yale University Press, New Haven
Schattschneider EE (1957) Intensity, visibility, direction, and scope. Am Polit Sci Rev 51(4):933–942
Schattschneider EE (1960) The semisovereign people. Holt, Rinehart, and Winston, New York
Schofield N (1978) Instability of simple dynamic games. Rev Econ Stud 45(3):575–594
Schwartz T (1977) Collective choice, separation of issues and vote trading. Am Polit Sci Rev 71:999–1010

When Will Incumbents Avoid a Primary Challenge? Aggregation of Partial Information About Candidates' Valence

Gilles Serra

1 Introduction

Incumbents and other insiders tend to enjoy a comfortable position within their parties. In particular, they frequently have an advantage to secure their party's nomination for a future election. Outsiders who do not necessarily belong to the dominant faction in the party have a much harder time getting their name on the ballot. They are disadvantaged in at least two ways: they might be less well-known than the party grandees they are competing with; and there might not even be a fair competition such as a primary election for them to prove themselves. A question of interest is why parties allow well-known insiders to have such and advantage over lesser-known outsiders. We would imagine an ambitious party that wishes to win elections to find mechanisms for identifying and selecting the best possible candidate, regardless of that candidate's previous standing in the party. One option would be to democratize the nomination process to let fresh outsiders join an open competition where they can display their true campaigning skills. This option is widely available to political parties around the world, though it is not always used. In this paper I explore the conditions under which candidate-selection is democratized, and I show that rational parties who wish to find the most talented candidate may nevertheless shut down the possibility of unknown hopefuls coming forward to display their talents.

Indeed, a political party can use a variety of methods to nominate those who will later compete for office at a given election. Broadly speaking, a candidate-selection method (CSM) can fall in two categories. On one hand, the method could be *open* (or *democratic*) by allowing the participation of all the members, activists and sympathizers of the party in the nomination of candidates. Of all the selection methods that parties can use, the most open and democratic one is the *primary election*. By

G. Serra (✉)
Department of Political Science, Center for Economics Research and Teaching (CIDE), Carretera México-Toluca 3655, Lomas de Santa Fe, Mexico City 01210, Mexico
e-mail: gilles.serra@cide.edu

N. Schofield et al. (eds.), *Advances in Political Economy*,
DOI 10.1007/978-3-642-35239-3_11,

primary election, I refer to the organized competition among aspiring candidates within the same party that culminates in the democratic vote of all party members. On the other hand, the nomination method could be *closed* (or *undemocratic*), consisting of a closed-door decision at the elite level of the party. For example, the nominee for an upcoming presidential or gubernatorial election could be chosen by a handful of party bosses at a private meeting. As argued throughout this paper, the choice matters for the party in terms of its prospects of winning the election; but it also matters for citizens in terms of the quality of candidates they are offered.

Party leaders are for the most part responsible for the way their parties nominate candidates. In most presidential systems, political parties have leeway in choosing their CSM, and it is usually *not* the case that primaries are exogenously imposed on them by the government. In fact, it is common for political parties to have serious deliberations on what CSM to adopt before even discussing which candidates to select. Their adoption of primary elections is most often *voluntary* rather than mandated by law. Throughout Latin America we repeatedly see party elites debating whether to open the nomination process or not. Actually, it is not uncommon for parties to go back and forth between primaries and other CSMs in recurrent elections, which clearly indicates the strategic nature of that choice. In the United States, party elites also have a strong say in choosing whether their nomination will be open and inclusive, or closed and exclusive. They do so by choosing whether to endorse a favored candidate or not. If party leaders decide to rally behind a well-known insider, they will provide her with public endorsements, strategic advice and large amounts of funding to overwhelm any challenger. On the other hand, if party leaders do not identify an insider candidate that satisfies them, they will withhold or divide their endorsements such that a competitive race among several hopefuls takes place. Thus, while parties are "officially" holding a primary election, in practice that primary can be competitive or uncompetitive. In effect, this is equivalent to choosing between a democratic and an undemocratic CSM. Hence, I claim the explanation for the use of primaries around the world lies in the strategic calculations of party leaders

This paper postulates a benefit to party leaders that helps explain why they occasionally allow the use of primary elections within their parties. To be concrete, I claim that primary elections have a practical advantage over elite-centered nominations: *they reveal information about candidates' appeal to voters*. My premise is that a candidate nominated through a primary election can be expected to have higher campaigning skills than a candidate nominated through an elite appointment. This happens because the primary campaigns reveal valuable information about the contenders. Indeed, there is much uncertainty surrounding the individuals seeking to become a party's candidate, often called *pre-candidates*. Their future vote-getting effectiveness is never known for sure. A primary can serve as a "trial" election *within* a party that shares many of the features of the subsequent general election *between* the parties. Pre-candidates must participate in debates, broadcast television advertisements, manage a campaign, and so forth. Thus primaries can reveal how effective the pre-candidates would be in the general election. In that sense, my model provides an "information rationale" for the existence of primary elections.

On the other hand, as mentioned above, primaries might carry several costs to party leaders. In this paper I focus on one oft-mentioned cost: primary elections might push candidates to adopt policies far from the leaders' preferences. Indeed, the party bosses know that primary voters may not quite share their ideology. They might be too extremist or too moderate to be trusted with the selection of the party's candidate. The main point is that party leaders face a trade-off between the costs and benefits of a primary election. The results in this paper reveal that the party leaders' decision is not trivial

On that basis, I build a spatial voting model that includes a party's choice between a competitive primary election and an elite-centered nomination. The main question is: When does the informational benefit of primaries outweigh the cost of losing control of the candidates' platforms? As the results will indicate, the answer depends on several fundamental variables: the ideology of parties, the ideology of primary voters, the intensity of the primary election, and the quality of insider and outsider candidates.

This model is a continuation of the research in Serra (2011). The main contribution with respect to that research is analyzing the revelation of *partial* information rather than *full* information, by which I mean that primary elections only reveal part of the information needed to assess a contender, but his or her ability to perform well in the general election would still not be known in full. To be concrete, I assume the contenders' performances within the party are interpreted as "noisy signals" that can be interpreted as forecasts of their performance if they were nominated to compete against another party. In this sense, the model falls in the tradition of modeling voting as a process to *aggregate* information—a tradition initiated by Condorcet (1785), Austen-Smith and Banks (1996), Feddersen and Pesendorfer (1998).

Several new results are found with this modeling choice. Two new variables can be studied more precisely. The ability of primaries to reveal valuable information, which I call the *quality* of primaries; and the reputation of the insider candidate as proficient vote-getter, which I call the *prior belief* about the insider's skill. Regarding the quality of primaries, I find that a party can benefit from stiff competition in its primary election. This result stands in contrast with an oft-mentioned view that parties should ensure their primaries are light and cordial. Regarding the prior belief held about the skill of candidates, I find that an insider might have a good enough reputation to prevent a primary election altogether. This result would help explain why many incumbents are able to be re-nominated for a subsequent election without being opposed inside their parties. Both results are new in the literature on primary elections as far as I can tell.

In addition to these new results, many of the previous results in Serra (2011) are corroborated. In particular, this paper also finds that primaries are more likely when there is congruence between the elite and the mass membership of the party; and primaries are more appealing to the party that is most disadvantaged given its valence and policies.

The rest of the paper is developed as follows: Sect. 2 briefly summarizes the theoretical literature that relates to my model. Section 3 introduces a spatial voting model between two parties that will serve to study the general election. It is a variant of the Downsian voting model, with an additional dimension corresponding to the candidates' valence. In Sect. 4, I take a step back in the electoral process, and I study the nomination that takes place inside a party before the general election. Section 5 develops a signaling mechanism for primary voters to update their beliefs about pre-candidates based on their performance in the primary campaigns. Section 6 introduces a cost of adopting primaries based on the lack of congruence between the elite and the mass in the party. In Sect. 7, I derive a number of conditions for a party to hold a competitive primary election, which is the purpose of this paper. Finally, Sect. 8 discusses the main results and suggests some interpretations of relevance to democratic theory. The Appendix contains all the proofs of the results in this paper.

2 Previous Theories of the Adoption of Primary Elections

The paper adds to the formal literature on primary elections. Most authors have studied the consequences of primaries, rather than their causes. Several papers in that literature share common aspects with this one, especially those comparing different candidate-selection methods (CSM). Owen and Grofman (2006) compare primaries with different degrees of divergence between the party mean and the population mean. Jackson et al. (2007) study three different nomination processes: an arbitrary appointment by a party leader, a primary election, and a spending competition between candidates. In Castanheira et al. (2010), parties select their internal organization possibly including intra-party competition. Cho and Kang (2008) compare open and closed primary elections.

Another set of papers that relate to my model, are those that have paid attention to informational aspects of primaries. In Caillaud and Tirole (2002) and Castanheira et al. (2010), the use of primaries provides information about the credibility and trustworthiness of the party. In Meirowitz (2005), primaries allow candidates to acquire information about voters' preferences. Then there is a set of papers where primaries reveal information about the valence of primary contenders.

For instance, Adams and Merrill (2008) postulate that primary elections may allow a party to identify a high-quality nominee. The authors find, as I do, that weak parties benefit from primaries more than strong parties do. In spite of those similarities, our models have important differences because the focus of their paper is the candidates' choice of platforms, while the focus of my paper is the parties' choice of candidates.

Another closely related paper is Snyder and Ting (2011) who also studies a party's decision to hold a primary election or not. As in my model, parties compete both in terms of ideology and valence. Snyder and Ting also assume that primaries increase the expected valence of the nominee. A main difference is the alternative CSM. If a party does not hold a primary, Snyder and Ting assume that the nominee will be chosen at random among all the willing pre-candidates. In contrast, I assume the party elite will choose an insider candidate in a smoke-filled room. Another difference is that both parties are bound to use the same CSM by state law, whereas in my model parties can have different CSMs.

Kselman (2012) develops a model where aspirants must compete in a primary election to obtain their party's nomination. In his model, candidates enjoy a type of valence that serves as a bonus for parties that are office-seeking. Interestingly, this type of valence is particularistic in the sense that only a subset of voters benefit from it.

Finally, this paper is related to the literature on *endogenous valence*. Some other papers have also allowed the agents in their models to affect the valence parameter are Ashworth and de Mesquita (2009), Schofield and Sened (2005), Schofield (2007), Carrillo and Castanheira (2008), Callander (2008), Meirowitz (2008), Schofield et al. (2008).

The model in this paper is one of the few that combines both literatures, the one on valence and the one on primaries. As in Adams and Merrill (2008), Snyder and Ting (2011), and Serra (2011), the premise here is that primaries help parties by revealing the valence of their candidates. Unlike those papers, however, this paper develops a signaling mechanism to reveal partial rather than full information.

3 General Election Between the Two Parties

In this section I focus on the competition between two parties without any reference to primary elections. In essence, this corresponds to the "general election" that occurs after all parties have already completed their nomination cycle. This will be a *valence-policy model*, meaning that it will have two dimensions. First, the election occurs in a left-right policy spectrum. I denote by x the policy implemented, with $x \in \mathbb{R}$. Second, there is a dimension corresponding to valence, which is described in detail below. The valence dimension is denoted by v, with $v \in \mathbb{R}_+$. The model I present here is an application of the more general model developed in Serra (2010).

3.1 Parties

There are two parties competing in this election, labeled party L and party R. Following the Wittman-Calvert-Roemer tradition, I assume that parties are *policy-motivated*, meaning that they care about the policy implemented after the election (Wittman 1973; Calvert 1985; Roemer 2001). Parties L and R have ideal policy points X_L and X_R, respectively. The two parties have distinct ideologies so that $X_L \neq X_R$. I normalize the ideal point of the median voter in the general election to zero, and without much loss of generality I assume $X_L < 0 < X_R$. The utility functions of L and R are

$$U_R(x) = -|X_R - x|$$

$$U_L(x) = -|X_L - x|$$

In later sections I will specify two separate groups within party R with different ideal points X_{RE} and X_{RM}. For this section, however, it is sufficient to think of X_R as the generic ideal point of R. At this stage it is useful to define a few concepts. By a party's *extremism* I will mean how far its ideal point is from the median voter's ideal point. Concretely, party R's extremism will be measured by $|X_R|$, and party L's extremism will be measured by $|X_L|$.[1]

Finally, parties formulate policy platforms to compete in the election, and they do so strategically in order to maximize their expected utility. I call those platforms x_L and x_R, with $x_L, x_R \in \mathbb{R}$.

3.2 Candidates

All candidates are characterized by a parameter v denoting how appealing their non-policy attributes are to voters in that election. Parameters such as v have been called "valence parameters" and can be given many interpretations (for an overview see Schofield (2007) and Adams et al. (2009)). In the context of this paper, v is best interpreted as the candidate's *campaigning skill*. It can take two values: a low value normalized to zero corresponding to a low-skilled candidate, and a high value of V corresponding to a high-skilled candidate. Hence $v \in \{0, V\}$. I label v_L and v_R the skills of candidates in parties L and R, respectively. To focus on the interesting cases, I will assume that valence is sufficiently salient to make a difference in the election; technically I will assume that the valence of a high-skilled candidate is strictly larger than the extremism of both parties, meaning that $|X_L|$, $|X_R| < V$.[2] Indeed, for smaller values of V, the valence dimension loses influence in the election and the results become trivial. I report these results in footnotes, and I refer the reader to Serra (2011) for a fuller analysis of a lower salience of valence.

In this model, candidates do not have policy preferences of their own. Rather, they will adopt the policy preferences of their party. To be exact, the candidate will behave as if having the exact utility function of the party that nominated her. She will announce the platform designed by her party during the campaigns, and she will implement such platform in case she wins the election.

[1]Of course, note that $|X_R| = X_R$ and $|X_L| = -X_L$.

[2]This is equivalent to assuming that $-V < X_L$ and $X_R < V$.

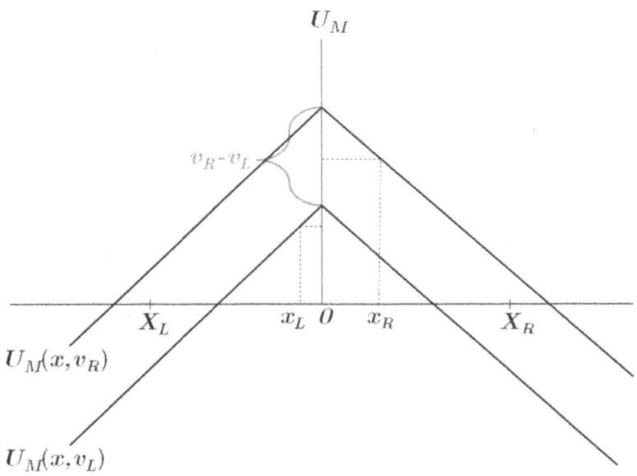

Fig. 1 The effect of a valence advantage for R over L

3.3 *The General Electorate*

The electorate cares about the policy implemented after the election. To simplify the analysis, I will assume that there is a median voter, which I call M, whose preferences are decisive in the election. I normalize her ideal point to zero.

In addition to the policy implemented x, the electorate also cares about the skill v of the winning candidate. The utility function of M is given by

$$U_M(x, v) = -|x| + v$$

M will vote for the party whose candidate maximizes her utility. I make the following indifference assumptions. If M is indifferent between the two parties, she will vote for the one whose candidate has the highest skill. If both candidates have the same skill, she will randomize equally between the two.

It is worth looking more closely at how the median voter makes her decision in this kind of model. As elaborated in Serra (2010), M's appreciation for a candidate decreases with the distance between her ideal point and that candidate's platform, and increases with the candidate's valence. In essence, the valence parameter v "shifts up" the utility function of M. An example of how M evaluates R and L is illustrated in Fig. 1, where it is assumed that $v_L < v_R$ and $|x_L| < |x_R|$. In the case depicted in this figure, candidate R is strictly preferred to candidate L in spite of having a more extremist platform. Candidate R is able to win the election because her higher score in the valence dimension more than compensates her extremism in the policy dimension.

3.4 *Timing and Solution Concept*

The timing of this election is the following:

1. **Assessment of the candidates' skills**: Parties announce their candidates who start campaigning. The candidates' campaigning skills v_L and v_R are observed.

2. **Assessment of the policy platforms**: Candidates announce their platforms x_L and x_R.
3. **The general-election vote**: The median voter elects L or R.

Stage 1 does not involve any decision: the candidates are revealed to voters, along with their valence attributes. The first decision is made in Stage 2 where each candidate must announce and promote her platform taking the other candidate's platform into account. In Stage 3, once candidates' skills, v_L, v_R, and platforms, x_L, x_R, have been observed and assessed, the median voter elects L or R to office. All this information is common knowledge. The game must be solved by backward induction and the solution concept is subgame-perfect equilibrium (SPE) in pure strategies. It will be important to recall that a SPE requires that all strategies form a Nash equilibrium (NE) in every subgame.

3.5 Results of the General Election

Before stating the main results of this section, some important variables should be defined. I call Δv the difference in skill between R's candidate and L's candidate. To be concrete, $\Delta v \equiv v_R - v_L$. Note that Δv can take three values: $\Delta v \in \{-V, 0, V\}$. I call x_L^* and x_R^* the equilibrium strategies of parties L and R, and x^* the winning platform. These parameters will determine the results of the general election, as indicated in the main theorem on this section. It must be remember that valence was assumed to be salient enough that $|X_L|$ and $|X_R|$ are smaller than V, which implies that $-V < X_L$ and $X_R < V$.

Theorem 1 *The equilibrium strategies and equilibrium outcomes of this election for given values of* v_L, v_R, V, X_L *and* X_R *are given in Table* 1, *where* $\Delta v \equiv v_R - v_L$.

There are several comments to make about Table 1.[3] First note the results when $\Delta v = 0$, that is, when there is no skill difference between the candidates. Both par-

Table 1 Equilibrium outcomes of the general election

Value of Δv	Equilibrium platforms x_R^* and x_L^*	Winning platform x^*	Winning party
V	$x_R^* = X_R$ $x_L^* \in \mathbb{R}$	X_R	R
0	$x_R^* = 0$ $x_L^* = 0$	0	R or L with equal probability
$-V$	$x_R^* \in \mathbb{R}$ $x_L^* = X_L$	X_L	L

[3]The proofs of all the results come in the Appendix.

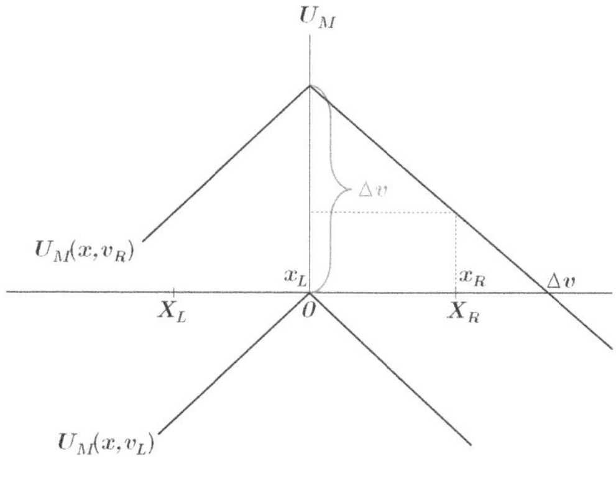

Fig. 2 Equilibrium platforms x_L^* and x_R^* when there is a valence advantage for R over L

ties converge completely to the median voter's ideal point. However, when $\Delta v \neq 0$ the candidate with highest skill is able to diverge from the median voter toward the ideal point of her party, and still win the election based on her superior skill. So the policy implemented is biased toward R when $\Delta v > 0$, biased toward L when $\Delta v < 0$, and unbiased when $\Delta v = 0$. In fact, given the assumption that valence is salient enough, the party with the highest-skilled candidate is able to pull policy all the way to its ideal point.[4] Such equilibrium is illustrated in Fig. 2, which depicts the case where $0 < X_R < \Delta v$.

4 The Nomination Process

In this section, I take a step back in the election process to study the nomination of candidates within a party. At this stage, the identity of each party's candidate is still unknown. Consequently, the exact values of the candidates' campaigning skills are uncertain. However, there exist some prior beliefs about these skills based on some information about parties and their potential candidates. According to that information, the probabilities that L's candidate and R's candidate will be high-skilled are π_L and π_R respectively, with $\pi_L, \pi_R \in (0, 1)$. In other words, $\pi_L \equiv P(v_L = V)$ and $\pi_R \equiv P(v_R = V)$. Those prior beliefs before the election campaigns are common knowledge among voters and parties.

The rest of this paper seeks to study the ability of party R to increase π_R by choosing a CSM over another. Indeed, choosing to hold a primary election could affect π_R positively under circumstances specified below. There could be a cost, however, in terms of the policy implemented by the candidate after a primary. Solving party R's cost-benefit analysis is the final goal of this research. I eschew in

[4]This ideal point depends on which group controls policy within the party. In this section we have called X_L and X_R the generic ideal points of parties L and R. In later sections, however, party R's ideal point will be given by $X_R = X_{RE}$ if the leaders control policy, or $X_R = X_{RM}$ if the members control policy. In other words, what we mean by "party" will vary according to the CSM.

this paper the parallel decision of party L who might also be pondering whether to choose a primary election. Such analysis is being done in a separate paper, and here I simply assume that party L has already chosen a candidate by any method. In other words, π_L is taken as an exogenous parameter. In any case, remember that the actual campaigning skills of L and R's candidates are revealed when they start campaigning to win the election. Thus v_L and v_R are fully known when voters decide who to vote for.

4.1 Party Members Versus Party Leaders

Party R consists of an "elite" (or "leadership") and a "membership" (or "rank and file"). The elite of R will be referred to as RE. This leadership is policy-motivated and has an ideal policy point X_{RE}, with $X_{RE} > 0$. The utility function of R's elite is

$$U_{RE}(x) = -|X_{RE} - x|$$

The rank and file (RAF) of R is also policy-motivated. To simplify the analysis, I will assume that the RAF has a median member whose preferences are decisive in the primary election. I call RM the median member of R and I call X_{RM} her ideal point, with $X_{RM} > 0$. The utility function of RM is

$$U_{RM}(x) = -|X_{RM} - x|$$

In general, we will have $X_{RE} \neq X_{RM}$, so there will be a tension between the policy preferences of a party's leadership and its RAF. It will be useful to measure the divergence, if any, between a party's establishment and its primary voters. With that purpose, I define d_R as the *internal divergence* in party R, where $d_R \equiv |X_{RM} - X_{RE}|$. An interesting interpretation of d_R is as the *congruence* (or lack thereof) between R's elite and mass membership. Higher levels of the internal divergence d_R indicate a lower elite-mass congruence inside the party. Note that d_R can take any non-negative value: $d_R \geq 0$.

Parties are also responsible for formulating policy platforms to compete in the election. More precisely, parties are in charge of indicating the policy platforms they wish their candidates to follow in each circumstance. If party R uses a leadership selection, then its leaders formulate the policy strategies to be followed by its candidate. If, instead, party R uses a primary election, then its candidate will follow the policy strategies desired by the RAF. Note that both the leadership and the RAF think strategically. This implies that they would not passively impose their ideal points on the candidate, but rather, they will design a strategy that maximizes their expected utility taking into account the behavior of the rival party in the general election.

Table 2 The objective of party R's candidate

After an elite selection:	$\max_{x_R} U_{RE}(x) = -\lvert X_{RE} - x \rvert$
After a primary election:	$\max_{x_R} U_{RM}(x) = -\lvert X_{RM} - x \rvert$

4.2 Primary Election Versus Elite Endorsement

Before selecting a candidate, the leadership of party R needs to choose a candidate-selection method (CSM). There exist two methods: an elite endorsement or a primary election. The default CSM would be for the leadership to directly nominate or endorse an insider candidate. Alternatively, it could hold a competitive primary election where an outsider candidate has a chance to run, and the decision to choose the nominee is delegated to the party's rank and file. I call m_R the method that R's leaders choose, with $m_R \in \{elite, primary\}$. Following standard language in the party-politics literature, I will call *selectorate* the group in charge of selecting a party's candidate. If $m_R = elite$, the selectorate is the party's leadership. If $m_R = primary$, the selectorate is the party's RAF. In the former case, $X_R = X_{RE}$. In the latter case, $X_R = X_{RM}$.

Candidates adopt the policy preferences of their selectorate. In other words, they behave as perfect agents of whichever group inside their party nominated them. Therefore, depending on whether the CSM is a primary election or an elite endorsement, the nominee will inherit the preferences of either *RM* or *RE*, respectively. This is summarized in Table 2.

The interpretation is that in striving to win the nomination, the pre-candidates are forced to cater to the wishes of those selecting them. In exchange for having their names on the ticket, they have to yield on policy by making concrete commitments to those in charge if the nomination. Those commitments are credible because parties have effective ways of enforcing their candidates' promises.

4.3 Insiders Versus Outsiders

An important difference across nomination rules is the number of aspirants who have a realistic chance of getting their party's nomination. When a party elite chooses to endorse someone without further consultation, it is usually because there is a trusted insider who has previously emerged as the natural nominee. In contrast, when a party decides to allow a truly competitive primary election, it is opening the door to outside aspirants who might have previously been unknown or ignored. This empirical observation motivates the following assumptions.

Any individual who is officially contesting the party's nomination will be referred to as a *pre-candidate*. If $m_R = elite$ then party R has only one pre-candidate to choose from, which I call the *insider* and I denote by *RI*. If $m_R = primary$ then party R has two pre-candidates to choose from, which consist of the insider, *RI*, and an outsider denoted by *RO*. Hence, by adopting a primary, the party is expanding the pool of candidates that it can choose from.

I call v_{RI} and v_{RO} the campaigning skills of *RI* and *RO* respectively, and I call v_R the campaigning skill of the candidate who is finally nominated by R. As I mentioned before, a candidate's skill can take two values, 0 or V. However, the exact values of the pre-candidates' campaigning skills are uncertain ex-ante. The party has some prior information about the probability that its insider candidate, *RI*, is high-skilled or low-skilled. That information could come from previous performance in office, from past elections, or from polls. According to that information, *RI* has a probability π_{RI} of being high-skilled, with $\pi_{RI} \in (0, 1)$. On the other hand, the party has *no* prior information about the outsider candidate. The party believes that the outsider candidate *RO* has a probability of one-half of being high-skilled, hence $\pi_{RO} = \frac{1}{2}$.

4.4 Timing

The timing of the nomination is the following:

1. **The selection of the candidate-selection method**: The leaders of party R choose a nomination process.
2. **The nomination contest**: If the CSM is a primary election, the pre-candidates commit to pursuing the policy interests of *RM* and some information about their skills is revealed. If the CSM is an elite endorsement, the pre-candidates commit to pursuing the policy interests of *RE* and no information is revealed.
3. **The nomination decision**: Party R selects its candidate.

After this nomination, the game is played exactly as described in the previous section, i.e. the three stages of the nomination are followed by the three stages of the general election. All this information is common knowledge.

5 The Benefit of Primary Elections

In this section, I develop a model of primary elections as a means to acquire some information about the campaigning skills of aspirants. Primaries reveal partial information through a system of noisy signals sent by candidates and processed by primary voters using Bayes rule. This informational mechanism is the main innovation with respect to Adams and Merrill (2008), Serra (2011), Snyder and Ting (2011) and other models postulating that primaries reveal information about candidates. In those models information is *fully* revealed in the primary election, and there is no additional information in the general election. In contrast, in this model the information is only *partially* revealed in the primary, and there is additional information in the general election. As I will show, this realistic assumption leads to new insights about the adoption of primary elections, in particular the possibility that a high-skilled insider might prevent such primaries.

A later section describes a cost of primaries. This will allow studying, in the final section of the paper, the cost-benefit analysis carried out by party leaders when deciding whether to hold a primary election or stick to an elite selection.

5.1 Primaries as a Mechanism to Reveal Information

Here I formalize the informational incentive to adopt primary elections. For party leaders, the benefit is to increase the expected campaigning skill of their nominee. I will call that increase the "primary skill bonus". Primaries achieve this in two ways. (1) The pool of potential nominees is expanded. Concretely, primaries open the door to untested or non-mainstream contenders who can register as pre-candidates hoping to display their skills during the primary campaign. Those outsiders might have a large appeal to voters but would not come to the party's attention through an inside-track elite nomination. And (2) useful information about those pre-candidates is revealed. Specifically, primaries can reveal valuable information about the pre-candidates' assets and resources. Indeed, during the primary campaigns the pre-candidates are tested on how they raise funds, manage a team of supporters, debate other candidates, design political advertisements and give interviews to journalists. So primaries serve as a testing ground for the subsequent general election. In that sense this paper provides an information rationale for democratizing a political party.

Given these differences, each method will have different probabilities of nominating a high-skilled candidate. The value that party leaders are seeking to maximize is $\pi_R \equiv P(v_R = V)$. To do so, they calculate which candidate-selection method m_R maximizes $P(v_R = V|m_R)$, with $m_R \in \{primary, elite\}$.

To calculate $P(v_R = V|elite)$ note that if party leaders choose to select the candidate themselves they would directly nominate *RI*. The probability of nominating a high-skilled candidate would simply be π_{RI}. Hence $P(v_R = V|elite) = \pi_{RI}$.

If, however, they choose to hold a competitive primary election, the candidate *RO* would join the race and the nomination will be delegated to the party's RAF who will decide between *RI* and *RO*. Hence the probability of nominating a high-skilled candidate, $P(v_R = V|primary)$, would depend on the actual skills of these candidates, which are ex-ante uncertain except for the prior beliefs.

The premise in this paper is that primaries will reveal some information about the actual skills of their pre-candidates. This information subsequently helps the party choose the most skilled one. To be more precise, if there is a primary election, a candidate's performance in the primary can itself reflect high skill or low skill. Party members interpret the performance of a candidate in the primary-election campaign as a *forecast* of how well she would perform in the general-election campaign against the other party. Those forecasts are imperfect, however, because the information is "noisy." Hence I assume that the true skills of candidates v_{RI} and v_{RO} are revealed only *partially* if there is a primary election.

To be concrete, I denote by s_j the performance of candidate j in the primary, with $j = RI, RO$. I say that $s_j = high$ if j's performance showed high skill, and $s_j = low$

if j's performance showed low skill. I assume that a candidate's performance in the primary has a probability q of accurately forecasting the performance she would have in the general election, with $q \in (\frac{1}{2}, 1)$. In other words, s_{RI} and s_{RO} have probability q of "being correct". We can interpret s_j as a noisy signal of candidate j's skill, and we can interpret q as the quality of this signal. More broadly, q is a measure of the effectiveness of primary elections as an information-revelation method.

In sum, the pre-candidates' performances, s_{RI} and s_{RO}, are independently-distributed random variables whose distribution depend on v_{RI} and v_{RO} in the following way:

$$P(s_j = high | v_j = 1) = P(s_j = low | v_j = 0) = q$$
$$P(s_j = high | v_j = 0) = P(s_j = low | v_j = 1) = 1 - q$$
$$j = RI, RO$$

Once the party members observe the candidates' performances, they can update their prior beliefs about *RI*'s and *RO*'s skills using Bayes rule. This approach to voting based on updated beliefs following a noisy signal has its roots in Condorcet (1785), Austen-Smith and Banks (1996), and Feddersen and Pesendorfer (1998).

The candidates' performances are public, and therefore the values of s_{RI} and s_{RO} are common knowledge. In particular, all the RAF members observe the same s_{RI} and s_{RO}, and hence they update their beliefs based on the same information. Given its interest in winning the general election, the RAF will vote for the candidate who is believed to have the highest skill. When a party member is indifferent between *RI* and *RO*, I assume she will vote for the one whose prior probability of being high-skilled was largest. If both have the same prior, she will randomize equally.

5.2 Primary Voters Update Their Beliefs

These elements allow studying the behavior of primary voters. When $s_{RI} \neq s_{RO}$, I say that a member of party R's rank and file will "vote according to the signals" if her strategy is to vote for the pre-candidate whose signal was highest, meaning, whose performance was best in the primary campaign. On the other hand, if her strategy does not depend on the signals sent during the primary, meaning that performance in the primary is irrelevant, I say that a member of party R will "ignore the signals".

These concepts can be used to describe the RAF's behavior during a primary. As it turns out, their behavior will depend crucially on their prior belief about the insider candidate's valence, π_{RI}. In all the results below, the symbols $\underline{\pi}$ and $\overline{\pi}$ refer to two constants whose values are $\underline{\pi} \equiv \frac{(1-q)^2}{1-2q+2q^2}$ and $\overline{\pi} \equiv \frac{q^2}{1-2q+2q^2}$.

Lemma 1 *In a primary election, for each value of* π_{RI}*, the rank-and-file members of party R will*

- *if* $\pi_{RI} \in (0, \underline{\pi}]$, *ignore the signals and always vote for RO*
- *if* $\pi_{RI} \in (\underline{\pi}, \frac{1}{2})$, *vote according to the signals if* $s_{RI} \neq s_{RO}$, *and vote for RO if* $s_{RI} = s_{RO}$
- *if* $\pi_{RI} = \frac{1}{2}$, *vote according to the signals if* $s_{RI} \neq s_{RO}$, *and randomize between RI and RO if* $s_{RI} = s_{RO}$
- *if* $\pi_{RI} \in (\frac{1}{2}, \overline{\pi})$, *vote according to the signals if* $s_{RI} \neq s_{RO}$, *and vote for RI if* $s_{RI} = s_{RO}$
- *if* $\pi_{RI} \in [\overline{\pi}, 1)$, *ignore the signals and always vote for RI.*

There are several noteworthy features of this result, the first one being how influential the prior beliefs are: given that each member of R is assumed to be rational and to use all information available to make her decision, she will combine the prior beliefs about the candidates with the new information coming from their performance. However, the prior beliefs might be so compelling that even a Bayesian party member will choose to disregard the candidates' performances. In particular, for high enough values of π_{RI} the RAF will *always* vote for *RI* even if it receives strong indications of the insider's low skill compared with the outsider's high skill. Primary voters will simply not trust that such performances will carry through to the general election. Hence the insider candidate *RI* is immune against an open contest with the outsider *RO*; he will be nominated regardless of their performances. This result is significant as it opens the possibility that any information revealed during the primary election will be useless: primary voters might vote according to preexisting information while completely ignoring the new information.

On the other hand, the results for intermediate values of π_{RI} go in the expected direction: primary voters will take the signals into account, and will vote for the candidate whose performance in the primary campaigns was best. Hence the insider candidate I will indeed be vulnerable to being beaten by the outsider O in an open contest.

Our next task is to quantify the benefit of holding a primary instead of a leadership selection. As I derive below, the bonus of using a primary election is to increase the expected skill of the party's nominee. Hence the value I am looking to find is the difference between $E(v_R|primary)$ and $E(v_R|elite)$.[5] It is easy to see that such difference is given by

$$E(v_R|primary) - E(v_R|elite) = V \cdot S$$
$$\text{with } S \equiv P(v_R = V|primary) - P(v_R = V|elite)$$

The important value is S, which represents the extra probability of having a high-skilled candidate that a primary brings above an elite selection. I call it the *skill bonus* of a primary. Studying S, how large it is and how it changes, is the main task now. Rather than giving the exact value of S, which comes in the Appendix,

[5]We should keep in mind that, even though the actual value of v_R is discreet, the expected value $E(v_R)$ is continuous.

I will focus on the key properties that will buttress the rest of the paper. I start by rephrasing the previous considerations in terms of π_R, which is the variable that party R is seeking to maximize.

Theorem 2 *The probability that R's nominee will be high-skilled, π_R, given R's nomination process, m_R, is given by*

$$\pi_R \equiv P(v_R = V|m_R) = \begin{cases} \pi_{RI} & \text{if } m_R = elite \\ \pi_{RI} + S & \text{if } m_R = primary \end{cases}$$

where S is called the primary skill bonus and is given by $S \equiv P(v_R = V|primary) - P(v_R = V|elite)$.

This demonstrates how the information revealed in primary campaigns is translated into a better nominee in terms of valence. Holding an internal contest will increase the probability of nominating a high-skilled candidate in the amount S. Is that a small or a large benefit? I answer that question in the next subsection.

5.3 What Makes Primaries More Appealing?

I begin by establishing whether primaries have a benefit to party leaders.[6]

Lemma 2 *The primary skill bonus S is strictly positive for $\pi_{RI} \in (0, \overline{\pi})$ and zero for $\pi_{RI} \in [\overline{\pi}, 1)$.*

Primaries therefore do bring a benefit for small enough priors about the insider's skill. When the insider candidate is weak, meaning that π_{RI} is below a certain threshold, forcing her to compete with an outsider candidate increases the excepted skill of the nominee by a strictly positive amount. The reason is that for $\pi_{RI} \in (0, \overline{\pi})$ party members will take a serious look at the outsider candidate's performance in the primary to decide whether she is more convincing than the party insider. This result was expected as it conforms with previous findings in Serra (2011).

The surprising result comes from high priors about the insider's skill: in such case a primary election might not bring any benefit whatsoever. When the insider candidate is strong, meaning that π_{RI} is above a certain threshold, forcing her to compete with an outsider candidate does not increase the expected skill of the nominee at all. The reason is that for $\pi_{RI} \in [\overline{\pi}, 1)$ party members find the insider candidate so compelling that they will vote for her regardless of the outsider candidate's performance in the primary. This result is new with respect to the papers about primaries that I am aware of.

---

[6] As mentioned before, the symbols $\underline{\pi}$ and $\overline{\pi}$ refer to two constants whose values are $\underline{\pi} \equiv \frac{(1-q)^2}{1-2q+2q^2}$ and $\overline{\pi} \equiv \frac{q^2}{1-2q+2q^2}$.

Fig. 3 The primary skill bonus S as a function of the insider's probability of being high-skilled π_{RI}

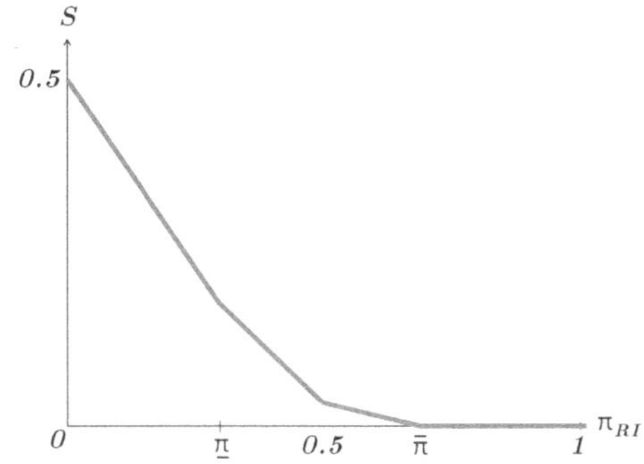

It is now turn to study how S changes with a change in its two main determinants: the prior about the insider candidate's skill, π_{RI}, and the accuracy of the candidates' performances q. Do they make primaries more or less attractive? I first describe the comparative statics with respect to π_{RI}.

Lemma 3 *The primary skill bonus S is strictly decreasing with* π_{RI} *for* $\pi_{RI} \in (0, \overline{\pi})$, *and constant (equal to zero) to any increase in* π_{RI} *for* $\pi_{RI} \in [\overline{\pi}, 1)$.

Several insights about S can come from the lemma above, most notably that it decreases with π_{RI}. This makes intuitive sense, because the benefit of primaries is to improve upon the skill of the candidate that would be nominated through an elite selection, namely the insider candidate. As the skill of the insider candidate is expected to be higher, it becomes less likely that a primary will improve upon it. In fact, as mentioned before, this electoral advantage reaches zero once the insider candidate's appeal to voters exceeds a certain threshold labeled $\overline{\pi}$.

The message is that the electoral advantage brought by primaries is larger the less appealing the insider candidate is to begin with. This is clearly seen in Fig. 3, which depicts the value of S as a function π_{RI}.

I can turn now to studying how S changes with q. Remember that we can interpret q as the *quality* of primary elections as an information-revelation method. To be exact, an increase in q improves the accuracy of the performances s_{RI} and s_{RO} as forecasts of future performances in the general election. This improvement could occur because the primary campaigns became longer, or because the media paid more attention to them, or because they included more challenges like debates on television and so on. In essence, a larger q implies that the primary performance is a better *forecast* of the candidate's campaigning ability in the general election. Intuition would suggest that any improvement in the primaries' technology would make those primaries more attractive. Surprisingly, as the following result shows, this intuition is only correct under certain circumstances.

Lemma 4 *The effect on the primary skill bonus S of a marginal increase in q is strictly positive for* $\pi_{RI} \in [\underline{\pi}, \overline{\pi}]$, *but is null for* $(0, \underline{\pi})$ *and* $(\overline{\pi}, 1)$.

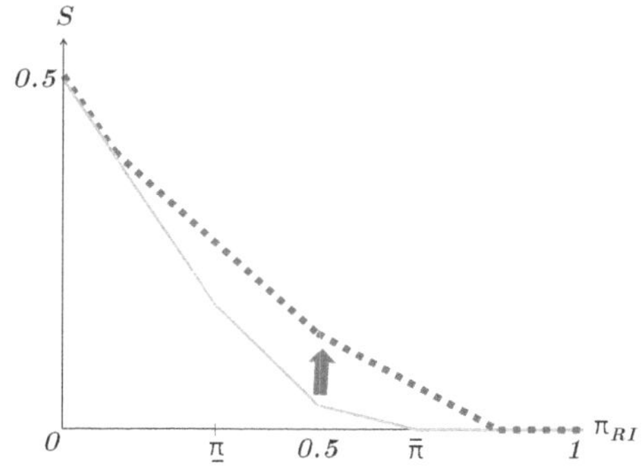

Fig. 4 The effect of increasing the quality of signals q on the primary skill bonus S

The result goes in the expected direction for moderate priors about the insider candidate's skill. For intermediate values of the prior π_{RI}, marginal increases in q will indeed increase S. The reason is that primary voters are unsure about the relative merits of the insider candidate compared to the unknown outsider that will join the race. They will pay close attention to the primary campaigns to nominate the candidate with a better performance. A higher quality of the information revealed will increase the probability of making the right nomination choice. Such an increasing effect is depicted in Fig. 4.

However, for other priors, the quality of a primary elections will bear no impact on its benefit. When the insider candidate is expected to be overwhelmingly competent in the general election, she will be nominated even if her performance in the primary is appalling. Primary voters will trust that her performance in the primary was due to bad luck. On the other hand, when the insider candidate is expected to be overwhelmingly unqualified, she will lose to the outsider candidate even if her performance was better. Primary voters will believe her performance was just a fluke that does not justify giving her a chance in the general election. In sum, for extremely high or extremely low values of π_{RI}, primary voters quickly make up their minds, either to nominate *RI* for sure or to nominate *RO* for sure, regardless of any campaign events that may occur. Improving the quality of primaries by marginally increasing q will have no effect on this decision.

In sum, primaries have two potential benefits: (1) allowing primary voters to replace the insider candidate with an outsider candidate whose prospect are believed to be superior; and (2) using new information revealed during the primary campaigns to discriminate between both candidates. As it turns out, whether those benefits actually occur depends crucially on the prior beliefs about the campaigning skill of the insider candidate. This finding is qualitatively summarized in Table 3.

To summarize this section, the benefit, when there is one, of primary elections is a larger probability of nominating a candidate with a high campaigning skill. I called that extra probability the primary skill bonus. Primaries might carry a cost however, in terms of the policy that candidates are induced to adopt. That cost is described in detail in the following section. As a consequence, the party leadership needs to carry out a cost-benefit analysis when choosing whether to hold a primary election or not.

Table 3 The two potential benefits of a primary election as a function of π_{RI}

Expectation that *RI* is high-skilled, π_{RI}	Benefit of primaries		
	Replacing *RI* with *RO*	Using the information revealed during the primary	Skill bonus of a primary *S*
Low	Yes, for sure	No, information ignored	High
Intermediate	Yes, probably	Yes, taken into account	Low
High	No, never	No, information ignored	Zero

6 The Cost of Primary Elections

As we just saw, the benefit to party leaders of adopting a competitive primary election is to increase the expected skill of their nominee. However, primaries might carry a cost in terms of the policy that candidates are induced to adopt. To be precise, a primary election has two differences with respect to an elite endorsement: first, the probability that *R*'s nominee is high-skilled increases from π_{RI} to $\pi_{RI} + S$. And second, it would be *RM* and not *RE* that *R*'s candidate would have made policy commitments to; and thus it would be the RAF's preferences rather than the leadership's preferences which would determine *R*'s policy platform.

By glancing at Table 4, we can readily see the trade-off that *R*'s leadership faces in choosing a primary election over an elite endorsement. As a benefit, using a primary increases the probability of nominating a high-skilled candidate (due to the primary skill bonus *S*). As a cost, the payoff from having the highest skilled candidate decreases (due to the internal divergence $X_{RM} - X_{RE}$). Put differently, *a primary makes losing less likely but makes winning less attractive.*

The goal now is to find expressions for the expected utility of *R*'s leadership by choosing either a primary election or an elite selection. I call $EU_{RE}(m_R)$ the expected utility of *R*'s leadership from adopting m_R as its CSM. It can be derived from Theorem 1, which gives the outcomes of the election depending on the value $\Delta v \equiv v_R - v_L$. If *L*'s candidate has a skill advantage, she will announce the platform X_L and she will win the election. If *R*'s candidate has a skill advantage, she will announce the platform X_{RE} if she was nominated by an elite appointment or she will announce X_{RM} if she was nominated by a primary election; and either way she will win the election. If *L*'s candidate and *R*'s candidate have the same skill, they will both announce the platform 0 and they will tie in the election. These considerations lead to the following expressions for $EU_{RE}(m_R)$.

Table 4 The trade-off faced by party *R*'s elite

	Probability that *R* wins the election	Utility of *RE* if *R* wins the election
Elite selection	π_{RI}	0
Primary election	$\pi_{RI} + S$	$-\lvert X_{RE} - X_{RM}\rvert$

Lemma 5 *The expected utility of R's leadership for each value of* m_R *is*

$$\begin{aligned} EU_{RE}(m_R = elite) = & -(X_{RE} - X_L)\pi_L(1 - \pi_{RI}) \\ & -(X_{RE} - 0)\big[\pi_L\pi_{RI} + (1 - \pi_{RI})\big] \\ & -(X_{RE} - X_{RE})(1 - \pi_L)\pi_{RI} \\ EU_{RE}(m_R = primary) = & -(X_{RE} - X_L)\pi_L\big(1 - (\pi_{RI} + S)\big) \\ & -(X_{RE} - 0)\big[\pi_L(\pi_{RI} + S) + (1 - \pi_L)\big(1 - (\pi_{RI} + S)\big)\big] \\ & -|X_{RE} - X_{RM}|(1 - \pi_L)(\pi_{RI} + S) \end{aligned}$$

Armed with these results, the leadership in party R can measure the consequences of choosing one CSM over the other.

7 The Optimal Selection of a CSM

The leadership in party R will choose the optimal rule m_R by comparing $EU_{RE}(m_R = elite)$ and $EU_{RE}(m_R = primary)$. It will choose the CSM that yields the highest expected utility, and if it is indifferent, I assume that it will choose an elite selection. A primary will be adopted if and only if $EU_{RE}(m_R = elite) < EU_{RE}(m_R = primary)$. That condition leads to the following result, recalling that $d_R \equiv |X_{RM} - X_{RE}|$.

Theorem 3 *The leadership of party R will adopt a primary election if and only if*

$$d_R < T$$

with $T \equiv \frac{S[X_{RE}(1-\pi_L) - X_L\pi_L]}{(1-\pi_L)(\pi_{RI}+S)}$.

The intuition behind this result is that R's leadership will delegate the nomination if and only if the RAF's ideology is close enough to its own. In other words, internal party democratization will only ensue from enough elite-mass congruence. How close do primary voters need to be to the party elite? It depends on a certain threshold, T, introduced in the theorem. If the preferences of the elite and the mass of party R are so incongruent that $T \leq d_R$ then the leadership will not adopt a primary election. This could happen for two reasons. On one hand, the RAF could be so far on the right of the leadership that $X_{RE} + T \leq X_{RM}$. In that case the leadership will not adopt a primary election because the primary voters are too *extremist*. On the other hand, the RAF could be so far on the left of the leadership that $X_{RM} \leq X_{RE} - T$. In that case the leadership will not adopt a primary election because the primary voters are too *centrist*.

As it turns out, the first reason (that primary voters might be too extreme) is frequently found in some way or another in scholarly comments about primary elections. Yet the second reason (that primary voters might be too moderate) is equally

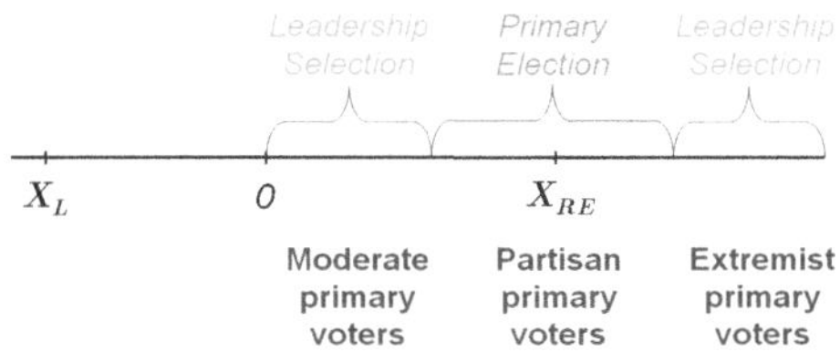

Fig. 5 The candidate-selection method as a function of the ideal point of the median primary voter, X_{RM}

intuitive but is seldom mentioned in the existing literature. The same intuition can be obtained from Fig. 5. For low values of X_{RM} (which I label "moderate primary voters") the party will endorse an insider candidate. For intermediate values of X_{RM} (which I label "partisan primary voters") the party will hold a competitive primary election. For high values of X_{RM} (which I label "extremist primary voters") the party will endorse an insider candidate. Consequently, the CSM has a non-monotonic relationship with the ideal point of the median primary voter.

From the results above it is clear that the threshold T determines how likely primary elections are. The interval $(X_{RE} - T, X_{RE} + T)$ corresponds to the values that X_{RM} should take for the nomination to be delegated to party members. Such interval can therefore be interpreted as the *likelihood that R will adopt a primary*. For a larger T it is more "likely" that the internal divergence between R's establishment and RAF will be lead to a primary. Then a way of phrasing the previous theorem is that *the likelihood of opening the CSM decreases with the internal divergence between the party's leadership and the primary voters.*

7.1 Comparative Statics

We would like to gain insight on what makes the adoption of primary elections more likely. According to the previous theorem, the likelihood of adopting a primary is given by T. Hence, I study how T changes with the parameters in the model. As it turns out, the results will crucially depend on the value of π_{RI}. To be specific, I need to divide two cases. The first case is $\pi_{RI} \in (0, \overline{\pi})$ corresponding to low and intermediate priors, and the second case is $\pi_{RI} \in [\overline{\pi}, 1)$ corresponding to high priors. Recall that $\underline{\pi}$ and $\overline{\pi}$ refer to two constants whose values are $\underline{\pi} \equiv \frac{(1-q)^2}{1-2q+2q^2}$ and $\overline{\pi} \equiv \frac{q^2}{1-2q+2q^2}$.

I start with low and intermediate prior beliefs about the skill of the insider candidate, which corresponds to the situation where primaries are most attractive.

Theorem 4 *Suppose the initial expectation that RI is high-skilled,* π_{RI}, *is such that* $\pi_{RI} \in (0, \overline{\pi})$. *Then the threshold* T, *which determines the likelihood of primaries, is:*

1. *Strictly positive*
2. *Strictly increasing with S*

3. *Strictly decreasing with* π_{RI}
4. *Strictly increasing with* q *if* $\pi_{RI} \in [\underline{\pi}, \overline{\pi})$, *and insensitive to* q *otherwise*
5. *Strictly increasing with* π_L
6. *Strictly decreasing with* X_L
7. *Strictly increasing with* X_{RE}.

The first two results of this theorem corroborate the benefit of primaries. First, I find that $T > 0$. Hence there will always exist a certain distance with the RAF that party leaders can tolerate for delegating it the nomination decision. Second, this threshold increases with the primary skill bonus. The larger the primary skill bonus S, the more likely it is that the elite will forgo appointing the insider in a smoke-filled room.

The third and fourth results decompose the effect of S in its two components, π_{RI} and q. The effect of the expected competence of the insider candidate is intuitive: the more competent the insider candidate is, the less likely that a primary will identify a better candidate, and hence the less attractive primaries are. This effect can be observed in Fig. 6 which depicts how the likelihood of adopting a primary decreases with the prior belief about the insider. The comes from Lemma 3 which established the negative effect of π_{RI} on S, and hence on T.

The effect of q is also intuitive though more complex. As I mentioned, an increase in q can be interpreted as an improvement in the information-revelation feature of primaries. For intermediate values of π_{RI}, an increase in q will increase S as we know from Lemma 3, which in turn will increase T. In other words, a primary election is more attractive for party leaders when its ability to reveal information is larger. This effect can be observed in Fig. 7 which depicts how the likelihood of adopting a primary increases when the quality of primaries increase.

This result contradicts a certain view of primaries in the literature. It is sometimes advised that primary elections should be short and smooth to avoid candidates draining their energy and resources (see for example Ezra (2001)). The theorem above provides a different perspective. A party can actually benefit from having long and challenging primaries, as this would increase the amount of information revealed about pre-candidates (namely q). This result is new in the literature about

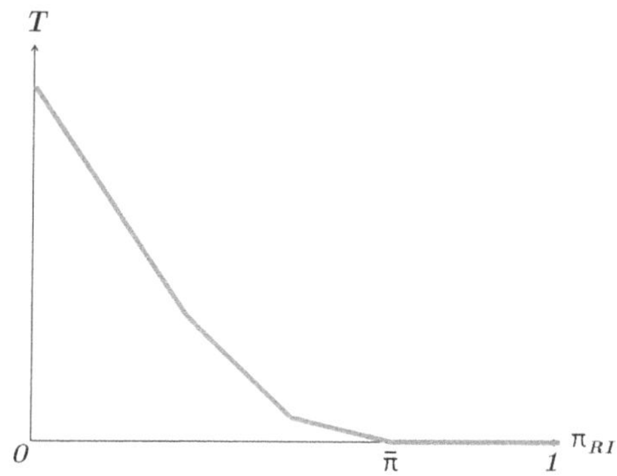

Fig. 6 The likelihood of adopting a primary as a function of the insider's probability of being high-skilled π_{RI} (all things equal)

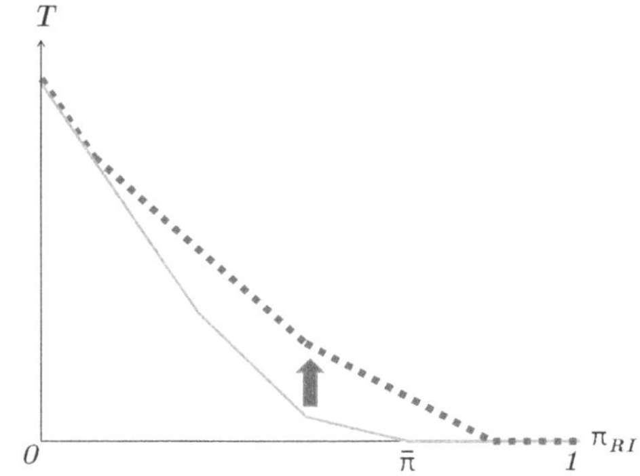

Fig. 7 The effect of increasing the quality of signals q (all things equal) on the likelihood to adopt a primary

primaries, as it could only be obtained by making the realistic assumption that primaries can only reveal information *partially* rather than *fully*.

The last part of the result is more surprising. For low values of π_{RI}, an increase in q will not have any effect on T. The reason is that candidates' performances in the primary would actually being ignored. Primary voters have already made up their minds in favor of an outsider candidates irrespective of her eventual performance in the primary. So increasing or decreasing the amount of information will not alter the nomination decision and consequently will not make primaries more or less attractive.

The fourth, fifth and sixth results broadly indicate that disadvantaged parties are more likely to adopt primaries than advantaged parties. They were all previously found in Serra (2011) so I do not elaborate on them here. Rather I focus on the importance of π_{RI} which is a new contribution.

In particular, the following result departs from previous research as it provides conditions for an insider candidate to avoid a primary challenge. As it turns out, an insider might have a good enough reputation that party leaders will *inevitably* nominate her by not opening the competition to outsiders under *any* circumstance.

Theorem 5 *Suppose the initial expectation that RI is high-skilled,* π_{RI}*, is such that* $\pi_{RI} \in [\overline{\pi}, 1)$*. Then the threshold* T*, which determines the likelihood of primaries, is zero and primaries will never be adopted under any value of the other parameters.*

In other words, the insider's reputation could be so good that leaders will inexorably appoint her. This type or reputation could be enjoyed, for example, by an incumbent who has already won a previous election. Strikingly, a primary election will be eschewed even if primaries reveal a maximum amount of information; even is there is perfect congruence between the elite and the membership of the party; and even if party R has important weaknesses with respect to L. There exists a threshold above which π_{RI} will prevent the use of primary elections for all values of q, X_{RM}, X_{RE}, X_L and π_L.

Hence this result provides an explanation for the empirical observation that many incumbents get re-nominated in their parties without a primary challenge. The reason is that for sufficiently high expectations about the insider candidate's skill, primaries do not bring any advantage at all: both the RAF and the elite are sure to nominate the same candidate. This comes from Lemma 2. Given that primaries do not bring a benefit, any amount of elite-mass incongruence is enough to deter party democratization. S is equal to zero and hence T is equal to zero, which means that any value of d_R is intolerable for party leaders.

8 Conclusions and Discussion

When can an incumbent or any well-known insider feel safe against a challenge for the nomination of a future election? When can he or she be confident that party leaders will directly appoint her rather than holding a competitive primary election? Primary elections are a frequent method used by political parties around the world to select their candidates—and increasingly so. The premise in this paper is that primary elections can serve as a mechanism to reveal information about the candidates' personal appeal to voters. In particular, by forcing candidates to run a primary campaign before the general election campaign, the candidates reveal their campaigning skills and the primary voters can select them accordingly.

An implication of those two features is that a primary election will increase the expected valence of the party's nominee. Such benefit has been modeled previously, for example in Adams and Merrill (2008), Serra (2011), Snyder and Ting (2011), and indeed the findings in this paper corroborates some of the findings in that previous literature (for example that primaries are most beneficial to the weakest parties as found by Adams and Merrill (2008), Serra (2011)).

However those models assume that primaries reveal information fully, meaning that candidates' performance in the primary are a perfect forecast of their performance in the general election. In contrast, this paper assumes that primaries only reveal information partially, meaning that candidate's performance in the primary are a noisy and imperfect forecast of their performance in the general election.

Making this realistic assumption led to new insights. The prior reputation of the party insider (the parameter π_{RI}) turns out to play a crucial role in deterring the use of primaries. Primaries are less appealing to party leaders the better the insider candidate is believed to be. In fact, if the party insider has a good enough reputation for winning votes, for example by virtue of being an incumbent who won a previous election, then a primary election will be eschewed altogether. The paper thus provides an explanation for the empirical fact that many incumbents get re-nominated by their parties without a primary challenge.

This new setup also allowed studying the behavior of primary voters more precisely. As expected, primary voters may use the information provided by primary campaigns to select the pre-candidate with a most impressive performance. However, as it turns out they will only do so for moderate expectation about the ability of the insider candidate. If, on the other hand, the insider is believed to be extremely competent or extremely incompetent, primary voters will actually ignore the contenders' performance in the primary campaigns and vote exclusively according to their preexisting priors. In other words, primary voters will completely disregard the information provided to them.

I finish with a prescriptive note. If we believe that democratization should occur in any representative institution, we should care about when and why political parties become internally democratic. A question for reformers, then, is how to make competitive primary elections more prevalent. This paper provides several suggestions, but the most direct one is to improve the revelation of information during the primary cycle (the parameter q). Political parties and the general public can benefit from improving the design of primaries to test the pre-candidates' campaigning skills thoroughly enough. For example, parties could include more debates, make campaigns longer, and allow tough critiques among contenders. In other words, the more challenging primaries are, the more information they will reveal about the pre-candidates. A recent example is the competition between Hillary Clinton and Barack Obama during the Democratic primary election. Several Democratic supporters complained that the competition between Clinton and Obama was too long and too severe. Those Democrats worried about the possible costs to their party's prospects in the general election. I do not deny that such costs existed: the potential drawbacks of a competitive primary election include division and resentment among the party base, among other possible costs. But this paper points to a benefit that was seldom mentioned during the 2008 primary. Observers claimed that too much information was being revealed about Clinton and Obama—information which could later be misused by the Republicans. My premise, however, is that such information would have been revealed anyway in the course of the general-election campaign. As a consequence, it was beneficial for the Democratic sympathizers to acquire that information beforehand to help them select their nominee wisely. According to this paper, the length and intensity of the primary campaign are not necessarily a curse for the party, but could actually be a blessing.

Appendix with the Proofs

A.1 Proof of Theorem 1

Table 1 here is a particular case of Table 1 in Theorem 1 of Serra (2011).

A.2 Proof of Lemma 1

If there is a primary election, Party R's RAF will vote for the candidate that it believes to have highest probability of being high-skilled. The beliefs it holds about each candidate's skill depend on two pieces of information: its prior beliefs, and the information acquired throughout the primary campaign. Given that the RAF members are rational, they will update their prior beliefs based on the performances s_{RI} and s_{RO} to form a couple of posterior beliefs about the probabilities that *RI* and *RO* are high-skilled. If the RAF uses Bayes Rule to update its prior beliefs after receiving a given estimate, its posterior beliefs will be given by

$$P(v_{RI}=1|s_{RI}=low)=\frac{(1-q)\pi_{RI}}{(1-q)\pi_{RI}+q(1-\pi_{RI})}$$

$$P(v_{RI}=1|s_{RI}=high)=\frac{q\pi_{RI}}{q\pi_{RI}+(1-q)(1-\pi_{RI})}$$

$$P(v_{RO}=1|s_{RO}=low)=1-q$$

$$P(v_{RO}=1|s_{RO}=high)=q$$

There are four couple of performances (s_{RI}, s_{RO}) that the RAF could observe, which are $(0,0)$, $(1,1)$, $(0,1)$ and $(1,0)$, I study each of them in turn, along with the decision that the RAF makes upon receiving those couples of estimates.

- If the RAF observes $s_{RI}=low$ and $s_{RO}=low$:

The RAF will vote for *RI* if $P(v_{RO}=1|s_{RO}=low)<P(v_{RI}=1|s_{RI}=low)$ which is equivalent (after some algebra) to $\frac{1}{2}<\pi_{RI}$. Then, given my indifference assumption, the RAF will vote for *RO* if $\pi_{RI}<\frac{1}{2}$, will vote for *RI* if $\frac{1}{2}<\pi_{RI}$, and will randomize equally if $\pi_{RI}=\frac{1}{2}$.

- If the RAF observes $s_{RI}=high$ and $s_{RO}=high$:

The RAF will vote for *RI* if $P(v_{RO}=1|s_{RO}=high)<P(v_{RI}=1|s_{RI}=high)$ which is equivalent (after some algebra) to $\frac{1}{2}<\pi_{RI}$. Then, given my indifference assumption, the RAF will vote for *RO* if $\pi_{RI}<\frac{1}{2}$, will vote for *RI* if $\frac{1}{2}<\pi_{RI}$, and will randomize equally if $\pi_{RI}=\frac{1}{2}$.

- If the RAF observes $s_{RI}=low$ and $s_{RO}=high$:

The RAF will vote for *RI* (in other words, disregard the candidates' performance) if $P(v_{RO}=1|s_{RO}=high)<P(v_{RI}=1|s_{RI}=low)$ which is equivalent (after some algebra, and noting that $1-2q+2q^2>0$) to $\frac{q^2}{1-2q+2q^2}<\pi_{RI}$. Then, given my indifference assumption (and noting that $\frac{1}{2}<\frac{q^2}{1-2q+2q^2}$), the RAF will vote for *RI* if and only $\overline{\pi}\leq\pi_{RI}$, with $\overline{\pi}\equiv\frac{q^2}{1-2q+2q^2}$.

- If the RAF observes $s_{RI}=high$ and $s_{RO}=low$:

The RAF will vote for *RO* (in other words, disregard the candidates' performance) if $P(v_{RO}=1|s_{RO}=low)<P(v_{RI}=1|s_{RI}=high)$ which is equivalent (after some algebra, and noting that $1-2q+2q^2>0$) to $\pi_{RI}<\frac{(1-q)^2}{1-2q+2q^2}$. Then, given

Table A.1 The primary vote as a function of the signals

	$s_{RI} = low$ $s_{RO} = low$	$s_{RI} = high$ $s_{RO} = high$	$s_{RI} = low$ $s_{RO} = high$	$s_{RI} = high$ $s_{RO} = low$
if $\pi_{RI} \in (0, \underline{\pi}]$	Vote for *RO*	Vote for *RO*	Vote for *RO*	Vote for *RO*
if $\pi_{RI} \in (\underline{\pi}, \frac{1}{2})$	Vote for *RO*	Vote for *RO*	Vote for *RO*	Vote for *RI*
if $\pi_{RI} = \frac{1}{2}$	Randomize	Randomize	Vote for *RO*	Vote for *RI*
if $\pi_{RI} \in (\frac{1}{2}, \overline{\pi})$	Vote for *RI*	Vote for *RI*	Vote for *RO*	Vote for *RI*
if $\pi_{RI} \in [\overline{\pi}, 1)$	Vote for *RI*	Vote for *RI*	Vote for *RI*	Vote for *RI*

my indifference assumption (and noting that $\frac{(1-q)^2}{1-2q+2q^2} < \frac{1}{2}$), the RAF will vote for *RO* if and only $\pi_{RI} \leq \underline{\pi}$, with $\underline{\pi} \equiv \frac{(1-q)^2}{1-2q+2q^2}$.

Table A.1 summarizes these results. Which is what the lemma claims.

A.3 *Proof of Theorem 2*

This conclusion comes directly from two observations: (1) With an elite selection, the party will directly appoint *RI*, and thus $P(v_R = V|m_R = elite) = \pi_{RI}$. And (2) with a primary election the probability of nominating a high-skilled candidate will increase by S by definition, such that $P(v_R = V|m_R = primary) = \pi_{RI} + S$.

A.4 *Proof of Lemma 2*

I start by calculating the exact value of S. All its properties are derived from this value. We can use the RAF's behavior described in the previous lemma. For that, I first need to calculate $P(v_R = V|primary)$. We can do so by noting that

$$P(v_R = V|primary) = \sum_{v_{RI}, v_{RO}} \sum_{s_{RI}, s_{RO}} P(v_R = V|primary, s_{RI}, s_{RO}; v_{RI}, v_{RO}) \cdot P(s_{RI}, s_{RO}|v_{RI}, v_{RO}) \cdot P(v_{RI}, v_{RO})$$

which uses the definition of conditional probability twice.

Each summand in that expression is straightforward to calculate. $P(v_{RI}, v_{RO})$ depends only on the prior probabilities that v_{RI} and v_{RO} are high-skilled, which are π_{RI} for the insider and $\frac{1}{2}$ for the outsider. $P(s_{RI}, s_{RO}|v_{RI}, v_{RO})$ depends only on the accuracy of the signals, which is q. And $P(v_R = V|primary; s_{RI}, s_{RO}; v_{RI}, v_{RO})$ depends on how the RAF will vote given the candidates' performances, which I just computed in the table above. Multiplying and adding those probabilities is easy but too long to develop here (the detailed calculations are reported in previous versions of this paper). With the appropriate algebra we find that

$$P(v_R = V|primary) = \begin{cases} \frac{1}{2} & \text{if } \pi_{RI} \in (0, \underline{\pi}] \\ \pi_{RI}q^2 + q - \frac{1}{2}q^2 - \pi_{RI}q + \frac{1}{2}\pi_{RI} & \text{if } \pi_{RI} \in (\underline{\pi}, \frac{1}{2}) \\ \frac{1}{2}q + \frac{1}{4} & \text{if } \pi_{RI} = \frac{1}{2} \\ \pi_{RI}q - \pi_{RI}q^2 + \frac{1}{2}q^2 + \frac{1}{2}\pi_{RI} & \text{if } \pi_{RI} \in (\frac{1}{2}, \overline{\pi}) \\ \pi_{RI} & \text{if } \pi_{RI} \in [\overline{\pi}, 1) \end{cases}$$

I can now calculate the value of interest, S. The values above are used to calculate $S \equiv P(v_R = V|primary) - P(v_R = V|leadership)$, remembering that $P(v_R = V|leadership) = \pi_{RI}$. With some algebra and noting the continuity of S at $\pi_{RI} = \underline{\pi}$, $\pi_{RI} = \frac{1}{2}$ and $\pi_{RI} = \overline{\pi}$, we find that

$$S = \begin{cases} \frac{1}{2} - \pi_{RI} & \text{for } \pi_{RI} \in (0, \underline{\pi}] \\ \pi_{RI}q^2 - \pi_{RI}q - \frac{1}{2}q^2 - \frac{1}{2}\pi_{RI} + q & \text{for } \pi_{RI} \in [\underline{\pi}, \frac{1}{2}] \\ -\pi_{RI}q^2 + \pi_{RI}q + \frac{1}{2}q^2 - \frac{1}{2}\pi_{RI} & \text{for } \pi_{RI} \in [\frac{1}{2}, \overline{\pi}] \\ 0 & \text{for } \pi_{RI} \in [\overline{\pi}, 1) \end{cases}$$

which are the values we were looking for.

Now we need to analyze the sign of S. If $\pi_{RI} \in (0, \underline{\pi}]$ we have that $S = \frac{1}{2} - \pi_{RI} > 0 \Leftrightarrow \pi_{RI} < \frac{1}{2}$, but that is satisfied because $\pi_{RI} \leq \underline{\pi}$ and I have already noted that $\underline{\pi} < \frac{1}{2}$. If $\pi_{RI} \in [\underline{\pi}, \frac{1}{2}]$ we have that $S = \pi_{RI}q^2 - \pi_{RI}q - \frac{1}{2}q^2 - \frac{1}{2}\pi_{RI} + q > 0 \Leftrightarrow \pi_{RI} < \frac{2q-q^2}{1+2q-2q^2}$ (noting that $1 + 2q - 2q^2 > 0$) which is satisfied because $\frac{1}{2} < \frac{2q-q^2}{1+2q-2q^2}$. If $\pi_{RI} \in [\frac{1}{2}, \overline{\pi})$ we have that $S = -\pi_{RI}q^2 + \pi_{RI}q + \frac{1}{2}q^2 - \frac{1}{2}\pi_{RI} > 0 \Leftrightarrow \pi_{RI} < \frac{q^2}{1-2q+2q^2}$ which is satisfied because $\overline{\pi} = \frac{q^2}{1-2q+2q^2}$. And finally if $\pi_{RI} \in [\overline{\pi}, 1)$ we have $S = 0$. So we have indeed $S > 0$ for $\pi_{RI} \in (0, \underline{\pi}] \cup [\underline{\pi}, \frac{1}{2}] \cup [\frac{1}{2}, \overline{\pi})$ and $S = 0$ for $\pi_{RI} \in [\overline{\pi}, 1)$, as the lemma claims.

A.5 Proof of Lemma 3

I calculate the differential of S with respect to π_{RI} and check its sign. If $\pi_{RI} \in (0, \underline{\pi})$, $\frac{\partial S}{\partial \pi_{RI}} = -1$ which is strictly negative. If $\pi_{RI} \in (\underline{\pi}, \frac{1}{2})$, $\frac{\partial S}{\partial \pi_{RI}} = q^2 - q - \frac{1}{2}$ which is strictly negative for $q \in (\frac{1}{2}, 1)$. If $\pi_{RI} \in (\frac{1}{2}, \overline{\pi})$, $\frac{\partial S}{\partial \pi_{RI}} = -q^2 + 2q - 1$ which is strictly negative for $q \in (\frac{1}{2}, 1)$. So S is decreasing with π_{RI} in all those intervals. S is non-differentiable at $\pi_{RI} = \underline{\pi}$ and $\pi_{RI} = \frac{1}{2}$, but is continuous at both points, and is therefore decreasing just like their neighboring points. Hence S decreases with π_{RI} when $\pi_{RI} \in (0, \underline{\pi}) \cup \{\underline{\pi}\} \cup (\underline{\pi}, \frac{1}{2}) \cup \{\frac{1}{2}\} \cup (\frac{1}{2}, \overline{\pi})$.

If $\pi_{RI} \in [\overline{\pi}, 1)$, S is constant for all values of π_{RI} (and equal to zero), so an increase in π_{RI} will not affect it.

A.6 *Proof of Lemma 4*

I calculate the differential of S with respect to q and check its sign, remembering that the values of $\underline{\pi}$ and $\overline{\pi}$ are $\underline{\pi} = \frac{(1-q)^2}{1-2q+2q^2}$ and $\overline{\pi} = \frac{q^2}{1-2q+2q^2}$. According to the values of S in Theorem 1, if $\pi \in (0, \underline{\pi})$, $\frac{\partial S}{\partial q} = 0$; similarly if $\pi \in (\overline{\pi}, 1)$, $\frac{\partial S}{\partial q} = 0$. So in those intervals, S is unresponsive to marginal changes in q.

However, if $\pi \in (\underline{\pi}, \frac{1}{2})$, $\frac{\partial S}{\partial q} = 2\pi q - \pi + 1 - q$ which is strictly positive; if $\pi = \frac{1}{2}$, $\frac{\partial S}{\partial q} = \frac{1}{2}$ which is strictly positive; if $\pi \in (\frac{1}{2}, \overline{\pi})$, $\frac{\partial S}{\partial q} = -2\pi q + \pi + q$ which is strictly positive. So in those intervals, S is strictly increasing with marginal increases in q.

To analyze the cases where $\pi = \underline{\pi}$ and $\pi = \overline{\pi}$, note that $\frac{\partial}{\partial q}(\frac{(1-q)^2}{1-2q+2q^2}) < 0$, so with a marginal increase in q, $\underline{\pi}$ remains in the interval $[\frac{(1-q)^2}{1-2q+2q^2}, \frac{1}{2}]$ where I just proved that S is increasing with q. Similarly note that $\frac{\partial}{\partial q}(\frac{q^2}{1-2q+2q^2}) > 0$, so with a marginal increase in q, $\overline{\pi}$ remains in the interval $[\frac{1}{2}, \frac{q^2}{1-2q+2q^2}]$ where I just proved that S is increasing with q.

To summarize, S is unresponsive to marginal changes in q for $\pi \in (0, \underline{\pi}) \cup (\overline{\pi}, 1)$, and is strictly increasing with q for $\pi \in \{\underline{\pi}\} \cup (\underline{\pi}, \frac{1}{2}) \cup \{\frac{1}{2}\} \cup (\frac{1}{2}, \overline{\pi}) \cup \{\overline{\pi}\}$.

A.7 *Proof of Lemma 5*

See the proof of Lemma 1 in Serra (2011).

A.8 *Proof of Theorem 3*

See the proof of Theorem 2 in Serra (2011).

A.9 *Proof of Theorem 4*

For points 1, 2, 5, 6 and 7, see the proof of points 1, 2, 6, 7 and 8 of Theorem 4 in Serra (2011), respectively.

To study the effect of q (point 3 in the theorem), we note that it only has an indirect effect on T through its effect on S. I proved in Lemma 5 that q has a strictly positive effect on S whenever for $\pi_{RI} \in [\underline{\pi}, \overline{\pi}]$. And I have proved (in point 2 of the theorem) that S has a strictly positive effect on T. Therefore, combining both partial derivatives, I prove that q has a strictly positive effect on T whenever for $\pi_{RI} \in [\underline{\pi}, \overline{\pi}]$.

To study the effect of π_{RI} we must note that it has two effects on T: a direct effect, and an indirect effect through its effect on S. In total, we have that $\frac{dT}{d\pi_{RI}} = \frac{\partial T}{\partial \pi_{RI}} + \frac{\partial T}{\partial S}\frac{\partial S}{\partial \pi_{RI}}$. It is easy to calculate that $\frac{\partial T}{\partial \pi_{RI}} = \frac{-S[X_{RE}(1-\pi_L)-X_L\pi_L]}{(1-\pi_L)(\pi_{RI}+S)^2}$ which is strictly negative. On the other hand I just calculated that $\frac{\partial T}{\partial S}$ is strictly positive, and we know from Lemma 4 that $\frac{\partial S}{\partial \pi_{RI}}$ is non-positive. We therefore have that $\frac{dT}{d\pi_{RI}} < 0$ and T is strictly decreasing with π_{RI}.

A.10 Proof of Theorem 5

Note from Lemma 2 that $S = 0$ when $\pi_{RI} \in [\overline{\pi}, 1)$. And remember that $T \equiv \frac{S[X_{RE}(1-\pi_L)-X_L\pi_L]}{(1-\pi_L)(\pi_{RI}+S)}$. Hence, when $\pi_{RI} \in [\overline{\pi}, 1)$ we have that $T = 0$ for any value of the other parameters.

References

Adams J, Merrill S III (2008) Candidate and party strategies in two-stage elections beginning with a primary. Am J Polit Sci 52(2):344–359

Adams J, Merrill S III, Stone WJ, Simas EN (2009) When candidates value good government: a spatial model with applications to congressional elections. Manuscript

Ashworth S, de Mesquita EB (2009) Elections with platform and valence competition. Games Econ Behav 67(1):191–216

Austen-Smith D, Banks JS (1996) Information aggregation, rationality, and the Condorcet jury theorem. Am Polit Sci Rev 90(1):34–45. 1996

Caillaud B, Tirole J (2002) Parties as political intermediaries. Q J Econ 117(4):1453–1489

Callander S (2008) Political motivations. Rev Econ Stud 75:671–697

Calvert RL (1985) Robustness of the multidimensional voting model: candidate motivations, uncertainty, and convergence. Am J Polit Sci 29:69–95

Carrillo J, Castanheira M (2008) Information and strategic political polarisation. Econ J 118(530):845–874

Castanheira M, Crutzen BSY, Sahuguet N (2010) Party organization and electoral competition. J Law Econ Organ 26(2):212–242

Cho S-J, Kang I (2008) Open primaries and crossover voting. Paper presented at the annual national conference of the Midwest Political Science Association

Condorcet M de [1785](1994) Essai sur l'application de l'analyse a la probabilite des decisions rendues a la pluralite des voix. McLean I and Hewitt F (trans) Paris

Ezra M (2001) The benefits and burdens of congressional primary elections. In: Galderisi PF, Ezra M, Lyons M (eds) Congressional primaries and the politics of representation. Rowman & Littlefield, New York

Feddersen T, Pesendorfer W (1998) Convicting the innocent: the inferiority of unanimous jury verdicts under strategic voting. Am Polit Sci Rev 92(1):23–35. 1998

Jackson MO, Mathevet L, Mattes K (2007) Nomination processes and policy outcomes. Q J Polit Sci 2(1):67–94

Kselman D (2012) Median-activists or median-voters? A spatial model with intra-party competition. Manuscript, Juan March Institute

Meirowitz A (2005) Informational party primaries and strategic ambiguity. J Theor Polit 17(1):107–136
Meirowitz A (2008) Electoral contests, incumbency advantages, and campaign finance. J Polit 70(03):681–699
Owen G, Grofman B (2006) Two-stage electoral competition in two-party contests: persistent divergence of party positions. Soc Choice Welf 26(3):547. Heidelberg
Roemer JE (2001) Political competition: theory and applications. Harvard University Press, Cambridge
Schofield N (2007) The mean voter theorem: necessary and sufficient conditions for convergent equilibrium. Rev Econ Stud 74:965–980
Schofield N, Claassen C, Ozdemir U, Schnidman E, Zakharov AV (2008) Party positioning under proportional representation and plurality rule. Center in Political Economy, Washington University. Typescript
Schofield N, Sened I (2005) Multiparty competition in Israel, 1988–1996. Br J Polit Sci 35:635–663
Serra G (2010) Polarization of what? A model of elections with endogenous valence. J Polit 72(2):426–437
Serra G (2011) Why primaries? The party's trade-off between policy and valence. J Theor Polit 23(1):21–51
Snyder JM Jr, Ting MM (2011) Electoral selection with parties and primaries. Am J Polit Sci 55(4):781–795
Wittman D (1973) Parties as utility maximizers. Am Polit Sci Rev 67:490–498

Measuring the Latent Quality of Precedent: Scoring Vertices in a Network

John W. Patty, Elizabeth Maggie Penn, and Keith E. Schnakenberg

Examples of network data in political science are ubiquitous, and include records of legislative co-sponsorship, alliances between countries, social relationships, and judicial citations.[1] Numerical estimates of the *influence* of each node (*e.g.* legislator, country, citizen, opinion), defined in terms of its propensity to form a relationship with another node, are often of interest to an analyst in each of these examples. In this chapter we present a new approach to solving a common problem in the social sciences—that of estimating the influence of vertices in a network. Our approach assumes that observed levels of influence relate to an underlying latent "quality" of the vertices.[2] Although common methods for measuring influence in networks assume that each vertex has the potential to influence every other vertex, many networks reflect temporal, spatial, or other practical constraints that make this assumption implausible. We present a scoring method that is appropriate for measuring influ-

[1]The networks literature in political science is large and growing. Recent comprehensive reviews include Lazer (2011) and Ward et al. (2011). In addition, Fowler et al. (2011) summarize and discuss methodological issues with inference of causality in networks.

[2]The word "quality" is simply a placeholder, though one that is roughly descriptive (at least in common parlance) of the characteristic that our method is estimating. While one might be precise and use a term such as "citability," we note the traditional issues of scope and space constraints and, setting this larger issue to the side, default to the use of a real word to refer to the latent construct our method is attempting to detect and estimate.

This research was supported by NIH Grant # 1RC4LM010958-01.

J.W. Patty (✉) · E.M. Penn · K.E. Schnakenberg
Center in Political Economy, Washington University in Saint Louis, 1 Brookings Drive, Saint Louis, MO 63130, USA
e-mail: jpatty@wustl.edu

E.M. Penn
e-mail: penn@wustl.edu

K.E. Schnakenberg
e-mail: keith.schnakenberg@gmail.com

N. Schofield et al. (eds.), *Advances in Political Economy*,
DOI 10.1007/978-3-642-35239-3_12,

ence in networks where (1) some vertices cannot form an edge with certain vertices for reasons that are unrelated to their underlying "quality" and (2) each vertex may be influenced by a different number of other vertices, so that some edges reveal different amounts of information about the latent "quality" of the influencing vertices.

As an example, we rate the "quality" of Supreme Court decisions, which we define as the likelihood that the decision will be cited in a future decision. These decisions are readily analyzed by our method due to their connectedness—the Supreme Court's explicit usage of previous decisions as precedent for current and future decisions generates a network structure. The network data enable us to assess some instances when a given decision "succeeded" (*i.e.*, was cited in a later opinion) or "failed" (*i.e.*, was not cited in a later opinion). However, because later decisions cannot be cited by earlier opinions, the data do not allow us to observe whether a given opinion *would have been cited* by an earlier opinion. Our network structure is necessarily incomplete.

The method we describe and employ in this chapter is intended to deal explicitly with this problem of incompleteness. The method, developed and explored in more detail by Schnakenberg and Penn (2012), is founded on a simple (axiomatic) theoretical model that identifies each opinion's latent quality in an (unobserved) world in which every object has the potential to succeed or fail. The theoretical model identifies the relative quality of the objects under consideration by presuming that the observed successes are generated in accordance with the independence of irrelevant alternatives (IIA) choice axiom as described by Luce (1958). In a nutshell, the power of this axiom for our purposes is the ability to generate scores for alternatives that are not directly compared in the data. Substantively, these scores locate all opinions on a common scale.

1 Inferring Quality from Network Data

We conceive of our data as a network in this chapter. Accordingly we first lay out some preliminaries and then discuss how one applies the method to general network data. We represent the observed network data by a graph denoted by $G = (V, E)$, where $V = \{1, 2, \dots, n\}$ is a set of n vertices and E is a set of directed edges, where for any $v, w \in V$, $(v, w) \in E$ indicates that there is an edge *from* v *to* w.[3] We define a *community* to be a subset of vertices, $C \subseteq V$, with a *community structure* $\mathcal{C} = (C_1, \dots, C_n)$ being a set of subsets of V, and C_i being the community of vertex i.

Underlying our model is an assumption that each vertex j in a community C_i has the potential to influence vertex i. To define this formally, let $\tilde{E}$ be a set of *potential interactions*, with $E \subseteq \tilde{E}$. If $(i, j) \in E$ then we know that i and j interacted with j influencing i, and so it is known that they had the *potential* to interact: it is known that $j \in C_i$. On the other hand, of course, $(i, k) \notin E$ need not imply that i could not

[3] In general network settings, we interpret a connection from v to w as implying that w "influences" or "is greater than" v. What is key for our purposes is that the notion of influence be conceptually tied to the notion of quality, as we have discussed earlier.

have been connected to k. Rather, it may be the case that opinion that i could have been connected to k, but the link was not created for some reason (possibly because k was not of high enough quality to influence i, possibly because k and i never had an opportunity to interact, or for some other independent factor(s)). Our community structure is designed to accommodate this fact, and in particular we assume that $k \in C_i$ implies that $(i, k) \in \tilde{E}$. Thus, k being in community C_i implies that k had the potential to influence i (*i.e.*, i had the opportunity to link to k), regardless of whether k may or may not have succeeded (*i.e.*, regardless of whether an edge between i and k is observed).

The second assumption of our model is that each vertex can be placed on a common scale representing the vertex's quality. We assume that vertices with higher latent qualities are more likely to have had successful (*i.e.*, influential) interactions with vertices that they had the potential to interact with. Thus, the higher latent quality of vertex i, the more likely that, for any given vertex $j \in V$, $(j, i) \in \tilde{E}$ implies that $(j, i) \in E$.

Our goal is to estimate each vertex's "latent quality" score subject to a network G and an observed or estimated community structure, $\mathcal{C}$. We conceive of our network and community structure as generating a collection of "contests" in which some vertices were influential, some had the potential to be influential but were not, and others had no potential to influence. These contests are represented by the set $\mathcal{S} = \{s \in V : (s, v) \in E \text{ for some } v \in V\}$. Thus, every vertex that was influenced represents the outcome of a contest.

Let $x = (x_1, \ldots, x_n) \in \mathbf{R}^n$ represent each vertex's latent quality. Then for each $i \in \mathcal{S}$ we let the expected influence of vertex k in contest i (*i.e.*, probability of i connecting to k), which we denote by $E(i, k)$, equal 0 if $(i, k) \notin \tilde{E}$. Thus, k's expected influence in contest i is zero because in this opinion we assume that $k \notin C_i$, and thus k had no potential to influence i (*i.e.*, there is no chance that i will connect to k). Otherwise,

$$E(i, k) = \frac{x_k}{\sum_{j \in C_i} x_j}.$$

In words, the expected share of influence of k in a contest in which k has the potential to influence i is k's share of latent influence relative to the total latent influence of the vertices that can potentially influence i.

Similarly, we can calculate the share of *actual* influence of k in i, or $A(i, k)$, by looking at the total set of vertices that actually influenced i in the network described by G. This set is $W_i = \{w : (i, w) \in E\} \subseteq C_i$, and (without any additional information such as edge weights), k's share is $\frac{1}{|W_i|}$ if $k \in W_i$ and 0 otherwise. We can now utilize our network and community structure to estimate x subject to an unbiasedness constraint that is conditional on the community structure. The constraint is that

$$\sum_{s \in \mathcal{S}} E(s, i) = \sum_{s \in \mathcal{S}} A(s, i) \quad \text{for all } i,$$

or that each vertex's total actual score equals their total expected score. Satisfaction of this constraint implies, given a correct community structure, that no vertex is estimated to be more or less influential than it actually was. Schnakenberg and Penn (2012) prove that, subject to a minimal connectedness condition, there exists a vector $x^* = (x_1^*, \ldots, x_n^*)$ that solves the above system of equations and that is unique up to scalar multiplication.[4] Viewed substantively, this vector represents the relative qualities/influences of the different nodes. In particular, as x^* is uniquely identified up to scalar multiplication, the ratio of any two nodes' qualities,

$$\rho_j^i \equiv \frac{x_i}{x_j},$$

is uniquely identified. This ratio ρ_j^i represents the hypothetical relative frequency of selection/influence by node i versus that by node j in a future contest in which both nodes i and j compete (*i.e.*, for any future node that both i and j have the ability to exert influence on).

2 Measuring the Quality of Precedent

The use of judicial precedent by Supreme Court Justices—and, in particular, a focus on citations as an indication of this usage—has attracted sustained attention from legal and political science scholars for over 60 years.[5] Unsurprisingly, given the breadth of the topic, scholars have adopted various approaches to the study of precedent, but most have focused on the determinants of citation: in a nutshell, what factor or factors of an opinion augur revisitation of the opinion in future opinions?

Because our model imputes unobserved relationships between objects, it is particularly well-suited to analyzing networks in which certain links are impossible to observe. These types of networks could, for example, arise in situations in which vertices are indexed by time and a later vertex is incapable of influencing a vertex that preceded it.

We utilize a data set consisting of the collection of citations by United States Supreme Court majority opinions to Supreme Court majority opinions from 1791 to 2002. Thus, viewed in the theoretical framework presented above in Sect. 1, the vertices of our network are Supreme Court majority opinions, and if majority opinion i cites majority opinion j, we include the edge $(i, j) \in E$.

Before moving on, it is important to note what we are explicitly abstracting from in our operationalization of the judicial citation/precedent network. Most importantly, we omit consideration of all opinions other than the majority opinion. Both

---

[4]For reasons of space, we refer the interested reader to Schnakenberg and Penn (2012) for more details on the method.

[5]Seminal offerings include Merryman (1954) and Landes and Posner (1976), while more recent, book-length analyses include Hansford and Spriggs II (2006) and Gerhardt (2008). Other relevant citations are provided where appropriate in our discussion.

dissenting and concurring opinions are relevant for understanding both the bargaining processes at work in constructing the majority opinion and inferring the role and quality of precedent (*e.g.*, Carrubba et al. (2011)).[6] In addition, our approach ignores the citing opinion's treatment of the cited opinion (*e.g.*, favorable, critical, or distinguishing).[7,8] We leave each of these for future work.

Differentiating Cases: Community Structure As discussed earlier, the method we employ allows us to compare/score objects that have not been directly compared. Accordingly, it offers an analyst the freedom to "break up" the data in the sense of estimating (or, perhaps, observing) communities of objects that are less likely to be directly compared with one another. For the purposes of this chapter, we take into account only the temporal bias discussed earlier—later opinions cannot be cited by earlier opinions—and presume that each opinion is eligible (*i.e.*, "in competition") for citation by every subsequently rendered opinion.[9]

Thus we construct the community C_i for a given opinion i as follows. Letting $\text{Year}(i)$ be the year in which opinion i was heard, we assume that for any pair of vertices (*i.e.*, majority opinions), i, j,

$$\text{Year}(i) > \text{Year}(j) \quad \Leftrightarrow \quad j \in C_i.$$

In words, an opinion can be influenced by any and only opinions that strictly predate it.

Data We apply our method to Fowler and Jeon's Supreme Court majority opinion citation data (Fowler et al. (2007), Fowler and Jeon (2008)). There are a number of ways one might approach this data when considering the question of the quality or influence of each opinion. The most straightforward approach would rank all of the opinions that have been cited at least once (any opinion that is not cited by any other opinion in the database cannot be ranked). In this approach, every opinion is a *contest*, and each opinion that is cited at least once is a *contestant*.

Practical constraints prohibit us from ranking all of the opinions. Fortunately, our approach implies that we can examine any subset of the data and recover relative rankings that are (in theory) identical to the rankings that would be estimated from

[6] In addition, there are many interesting theoretical and empirical questions regarding how one should conceive of the relationship between opinions and opinions (*e.g.*, Bommarito et al. (2009)) that the data we employ here do not allow us to explore more fully.

[7] Practically speaking, there are a number of ways that scholars have developed and employed to consider this aspect of how Justices cite earlier opinions. For recent examples, see Clark and Lauderdale (2010), Spriggs II et al. (2011).

[8] We are not aware of any recent work that has differentiated citations by the number of times the citation occurs in the citing opinion.

[9] Note that, for simplicity, we approximate this "later than" relation in the sense that we presume (unrealistically) that, in any year, the Court cannot cite one opinion that is decided in that year in another opinion that is decided in that same year. Given the number of years that we consider, this approximation affects a *very* small proportion of the number of potential citations we consider.

the entire data set. Accordingly, we restrict our attention to the 100 most frequently cited opinions between 1946 and 2002. In graph theoretic terms, we examine the smallest subgraph containing all edges beginning or ending (or both) with an opinion whose *in degree* (number of times cited) ranks among the top 100 among the opinions rendered between 1946 and 2002. This graph contains many more than 100 opinions (3674, to be exact). After these opinions, and their incident edges, are selected, they are then used for our community detection algorithm, which we now describe.

Using the years of the opinions to create the communities as described earlier, we then solve for the influence scores of the opinions (*i.e.*, contestants) as follows. First, we choose the contestants in turn and, for each majority opinion (*i.e.*, contest) that was subsequent to an opinion and cited at least one member of the contestant's community, we count the contestant as having been participant (*i.e.*, available for citation) in that majority opinion/contest. If the contestant was cited in (*i.e.*, won) that contest, the contestant is awarded $1/|W|$ points, where W is the set of opinions (contestants) cited in that majority opinion (contest). Otherwise, the contestant is awarded 0 points in that contest. With this vector of scores for each contestant in each contest, it is then possible to directly apply the method developed by Schnakenberg and Penn (2012) to generate the latent influence scores of each majority opinion, $\hat{x} = (\hat{x}_1, \dots, \hat{x}_n)$.

These latent influence scores represent, in essence, the appeal of each majority opinion as a potential citation in any subsequent majority opinion. What this appeal represents in substantive terms is not unambiguous, of course. It might proxy for the degree to which the opinion is easily understood, the degree to which its conclusions are broadly applicable,[10] or perhaps the likelihood that the policy implications of the opinion support policies that are supported by a majority of justices in a typical opinion. Obviously, further study is necessary before offering a conclusion on the micro-level foundations of these scores. Such research will require inclusion of observed and estimated covariates distinguishing the various opinions and majority opinions.

3 Results

We now present the results of three related analyses. We first present our results for the 100 most-cited opinions rendered between 1946 and 2002.[11] Following that, we present the results for the 100 most-cited opinions since 1800.[12] Finally, we consider the 204 most-cited opinions since 1800 with an eye toward comparing the ranking

[10]Note that this is true *despite* the presumption that an opinion might have been feasible only in a subset of observed and subsequent majority opinions.

[11]This time period includes all cases in the Fowler and Jeon data for which Spaeth's rich descriptive data (Spaeth 2012) are also available.

[12]This time period includes all cases in the Fowler and Jeon data.

Table 1 Descriptive correlations with scores. Sample: Top 100 most-cited cases since 1946

Correlation (Age, Score):	−0.461
Correlation (# Cites, Score):	0.496
Correlation (# Cite/Year, Score):	0.787

of the 100 most-cited opinions since 1946 with the ranking of those cases when all opinions that have been cited at least as many times as these 100 are considered.

3.1 Top 100 Opinions Since 1946

Table 2 presents the opinions with the top 36 estimated latent quality scores for this period. This is the set of opinions for which the estimated quality score is greater than 1, which is by construction the average estimated quality score for the 100 cases.

This ranking is interesting in a number of ways. The top two majority opinions score significantly higher than all of the others.[13] The top-scoring opinion, *Chevron*, is a well-known case in administrative law with broad implications for the judicial review of bureaucratic decision-making. The second-ranked opinion, *Gregg*, clarified the constitutionality of the death penalty in the United States. Of course, the third highest scoring opinion is the famous *Miranda* decision in which the Court clarified the procedural rights of detained individuals.

Space prevents us from a full-throated treatment of the scores, but a few simple correlations are of interest. Table 1 presents three Pearson correlation coefficients relating the opinions' scores with, respectively, the age of the opinion, the number of subsequent opinions citing the opinion, and the number of subsequent opinions citing the opinion divided by the age of the opinion.

The negative correlation between the age of an opinion and its score is broadly in line with previous work on the depreciation of the precedential value (or, at least, usage) of judicial opinions.[14] It is important to note, however, that this effect is *potentially* at odds with the IIA axiom on which the scoring algorithm is based. We partially return to this question below when we expand the sample of opinions.

That the correlation between the opinions' scores and the number of times each opinion has been cited by a subsequent Supreme Court majority opinion is positive is not surprising: the score of an opinion is obviously positively responsive to the number of times that an opinion has been cited, *ceteris paribus*. Accordingly, the interesting aspect of the correlation is not that it is positive but, rather, that it is not closer to 1. Indeed, inspection of Table 2 indicates, *a fortiori*, that the rank-

[13]Note that the estimated scores for the top 100 opinions sum to 100, so these two opinions account for over 1/8th of the sum of the estimated scores. In other words, any opinion that cites exactly one of these 100 cases is predicted to cite either *Chevron* or *Gregg* almost 13 % of the time.

[14]See, for example, Black and Spriggs II (2010).

Table 2 The 36 highest scoring opinions. Sample: Top 100 most-cited cases since 1946

Rank	Name	Year	Score	# Cites	Cites/Year
1	Chevron, USA, Inc. v. NRDC, Inc.	1984	7.52	129	6.8
2	Gregg v. Georgia	1976	5.14	266	9.9
3	Miranda v. Arizona	1966	2.72	225	6.1
4	Cannon v. University of Chicago	1979	2.62	73	3
5	Younger v. Harris	1971	1.89	129	4
6	Strickland v. Wash.	1984	1.74	68	3.6
7	Edelman v. Jordan	1974	1.65	92	3.2
8	Reynolds v. Sims	1964	1.62	144	3.7
9	Monell v. Dep't of Soc. Servs.	1978	1.58	78	3.1
10	Dandridge v. Williams	1970	1.5	132	4
11	Arlington Heights v. Metro. Hous. Dev. Corp.	1977	1.5	74	2.8
12	Mathews v. Eldridge	1976	1.49	100	3.7
13	Buckley v. Valeo	1976	1.49	100	3.7
14	In re Winship	1970	1.47	131	4
15	Eddings v. Okla.	1982	1.4	91	4.3
16	New York Times Co. v. Sullivan	1964	1.38	161	4.1
17	Baker v. Carr	1962	1.34	149	3.6
18	Gideon v. Wainwright	1963	1.28	207	5.2
19	Miller v. California	1973	1.27	131	4.4
20	Lockett v. Ohio	1978	1.26	104	4.2
21	Brown v. Board of Education	1954	1.25	155	3.2
22	Bivens v. Six Unknown Named Agents…	1971	1.21	96	3
23	Monroe v. Pape	1961	1.18	134	3.2
24	Craig v. Boren	1976	1.17	70	2.6
25	S.D. Bldg. Trades Council v. Garmon	1959	1.15	89	2
26	Furman v. Georgia	1972	1.12	118	3.8
27	Terry v. Ohio	1968	1.1	97	2.8
28	Warth v. Seldin	1975	1.1	72	2.6
29	Roe v. Wade	1973	1.08	91	3
30	Textile Workers Union v. Lincoln Mills	1957	1.08	80	1.7
31	Wainwright v. Sykes	1977	1.07	71	2.7
32	Katz v. United States	1967	1.06	127	3.5
33	Roth v. United States	1957	1.05	155	3.4
34	Benton v. Maryland	1969	1.04	75	2.2
35	Stone v. Powell	1976	1.01	80	3
36	Woodson v. North Carolina	1976	1.01	97	3.6

ings of the opinions with respect to the number of citations they have received and with respect to their scores are not identical. Put another way: the scores are measuring something different than the opinions' citation counts or, as it is commonly known in network analysis, the *degree centralities* of the opinions in the citation network.

Finally, the correlation between the score and the average number of times per year the opinion has been cited since it was handed down is strongly positive. This highlights the fact that the scores control for the fact that an opinion cannot cite an opinion that is rendered subsequently. Again, though, it is important to note that the ranking of the opinions generated by our scores differs from that generated by the number of citations per year. It is useful to consider the origins of this difference. Specifically, the distinction arises because of the fact that the IIA axiom on which the method is based implies that an opinion's "reward" (or score) for being cited by a subsequent opinion is inversely proportional to the number of other opinions cited by that opinion. At the extreme, for example, a hypothetical opinion that cited every previous opinion would compress the scores of the opinions in the sense that the scores of all opinions that initially had lower than average scores would increase as a result of the citation by the hypothetical opinion, whereas the scores of all of those opinions with above average scores prior to the hypothetical opinion would decrease.[15]

3.2 *Top 100 Opinions Since 1800*

We now present our results for the top 100 most-cited opinions rendered between 1800 and 2002. Table 3 presents the opinions with the top 38 estimated latent quality scores for this period. As with the previous analysis for the period between 1946 and 2002, this is the set of opinions for which the estimated quality score is greater than 1.

Comparing these scores with those in Table 2, it is perhaps surprising how similar the two sets of scores are. In particular, the top three majority opinions are identical and have very similar scores in the two analyses. Things get interesting at the fourth highest-scoring position. First, the majority opinion ranked fourth-highest in the 1946–2002 analysis reported in Table 2, *Cannon v. University of Chicago*, is not among the top 100 most-cited majority opinions since 1819.[16] The fourth highest-scoring opinion among the 100 most-cited majority opinions since 1819 is *Miller v. California*, in which the Court affirmed and clarified the power of state and local governments to place limits on obscenity. This opinion is, of course, among the top

[15] Recall that the scores are identified only up to multiplication by a positive scalar, implying that they inherently relative scores.

[16] In that case, the majority opinion affirmed an individual's right to sue recipients of federal financial support for gender discrimination under Title IX, which calls for gender equity in higher education.

Table 3 The 38 most influential cases among the top 100 most-cited cases since 1800

Rank	Name	Year	Score	# Cites	Cites/Year
1	Chevron, USA, Inc. v. NRDC, Inc.	1984	7.21	129	6.8
2	Gregg v. Georgia	1976	5.82	266	9.9
3	Miranda v. Arizona	1966	3.28	225	6.1
4	Miller v. California	1973	2.04	131	4.4
5	Younger v. Harris	1971	2.03	129	4
6	Erie R.R. v. Tompkins	1938	1.92	189	2.9
7	Reynolds v. Sims	1964	1.89	144	3.7
8	Mathews v. Eldridge	1976	1.84	100	3.7
9	In re Winship	1970	1.78	131	4
10	Dandridge v. Williams	1970	1.76	132	4
11	Baker v. Carr	1962	1.73	149	3.6
12	Buckley v. Valeo	1976	1.58	100	3.7
13	Monroe v. Pape	1961	1.57	134	3.2
14	Brown v. Board of Education	1954	1.54	155	3.2
15	Edelman v. Jordan	1974	1.51	92	3.2
16	Gideon v. Wainwright	1963	1.5	207	5.2
17	New York Times Co. v. Sullivan	1964	1.48	161	4.1
18	Eddings v. Okla.	1982	1.44	91	4.3
19	Bivens v. Six Unknown Named Agents...	1971	1.41	96	3
20	Chapman v. California	1967	1.39	130	3.6
21	Lockett v. Ohio	1978	1.38	104	4.2
22	Furman v. Georgia	1972	1.36	118	3.8
23	Paris Adult Theatre I v. Slaton	1973	1.33	103	3.4
24	Morrissey v. Brewer	1972	1.32	94	3
25	San Diego Bldg. Trades Council v. Garmon	1959	1.29	89	2
26	Duncan v. Louisiana	1968	1.26	107	3.1
27	Roth v. United States	1957	1.25	155	3.4
28	Katz v. United States	1967	1.25	127	3.5
29	Terry v. Ohio	1968	1.22	97	2.8
30	United States v. Socony-Vacuum Oil Co.	1940	1.2	113	1.8
31	Red Lion Broadcasting Co. v. FCC	1969	1.17	87	2.6
32	Roe v. Wade	1973	1.16	91	3
33	Goldberg v. Kelly	1970	1.14	97	2.9
34	Woodson v. North Carolina	1976	1.13	97	3.6
35	Johnson v. Zerbst	1938	1.07	159	2.4
36	NAACP v. Alabama ex rel. Patterson	1958	1.05	153	3.4
37	Ashwander v. Tennessee Valley Authority	1936	1.03	180	2.7
38	Phelps Dodge Corp. v. NLRB	1941	1.02	88	1.4

Table 4 Descriptive correlations with scores. Sample: Top 100 most-cited cases since 1800

Correlation (Age, Score):	−0.466
Correlation (# Cites, Score):	0.425
Correlation (# Cite/Year, Score):	0.849

Table 5 Intersample correlations of scores. Sample: Top 100 most-cited cases since 1946

Spearman's Rank Correlation:	0.981
Pearson's Correlation Coefficient:	0.995

100 most-cited rendered since 1946, yet ranks only 19th in the scores reported in Table 2. This point highlights a feature of the scores in both tables: after the top 3 or 4, there is a relatively large "plateau" of scores.

Beyond visual inspection, it is useful to reconsider the correlations analogous to those reported in Table 1. These are displayed in Table 4 and closely conform to the conclusions drawn in the discussion of the correlations reported in Table 1: older opinions tend to have lower scores, and scores are positively associated with both number of subsequent citations as well as the average annual rate of subsequent citation.

3.3 Probing IIA: Top 204 Opinions Since 1800

We calculated the scores for the top 204 most-cited majority opinions since 1819. This is the smallest set of most-cited opinions for the entire time period that contains the top 100 most-cited opinions rendered since 1946. Each opinion rendered after 1946 is accompanied by two scores and two ranks: the "Post '46" values are identical to those reported in Table 2. The "Full" values, presented in Table 6, correspond to the rank of that opinion's score from the analysis of the 204 most-cited opinions since 1800 *relative to the analogous scores for the opinions rendered after 1946*. The IIA axiom underpinning the scoring method implies that the relative ranking of the opinions should be invariant to including additional opinions, as the scoring of the 204 most-cited opinions does. Inspection indicates a strong similarity between the two rankings. Most telling are the following two correlations between, respectively, the (relative) ranks of the 100 post-1946 opinions in the two samples and the scores of these cases in the two samples in Table 5.

Each of these correlations indicate a *very* strong agreement between the (relative) ranks and scores, respectively, for the top 100 most-cited opinions since 1946. This agreement provides support for the supposition of IIA that identifies the method.

4 Conclusion

In this chapter we score all Supreme Court majority opinions since 1800 on the basis of their "quality" (measured as influence or citability), using network citation data.

Table 6 Comparing scores of post 1946 cases (full sample: 204 most-cited opinions since 1800)

Rank		Name	Year	Score	
Full	Post'46			Full	Post'46
1	1	Chevron, USA, Inc. v. NRDC, Inc.	1984	5.67	7.52
2	2	Gregg v. Georgia	1976	4.23	5.14
3	4	Cannon v. University of Chicago	1979	2.04	2.62
4	3	Miranda v. Arizona	1966	2.03	2.72
5	8	Reynolds v. Sims	1964	1.34	1.62
6	5	Younger v. Harris	1971	1.31	1.89
...	...	Erie R.R. v. Tompkins	1938	1.29	...
7	6	Strickland v. Wash.	1984	1.19	1.74
8	10	Dandridge v. Williams	1970	1.17	1.50
9	14	In re Winship	1970	1.14	1.47
10	9	Monell v. Dep't of Soc. Servs.	1978	1.14	1.58
11	15	Eddings v. Okla.	1982	1.13	1.40
12	12	Mathews v. Eldridge	1976	1.13	1.49
13	11	Arlington Heights v. Metro. Hous. Dev. Corp.	1977	1.11	1.50
14	20	Lockett v. Ohio	1978	1.04	1.26
15	19	Miller v. California	1973	1.03	1.27
16	7	Edelman v. Jordan	1974	1.02	1.65
17	16	New York Times Co. v. Sullivan	1964	1.00	1.38
18	17	Baker v. Carr	1962	0.99	1.34
19	13	Buckley v. Valeo	1976	0.98	1.49
20	26	Furman v. Georgia	1972	0.94	1.12
21	21	Brown v. Board of Educ.	1954	0.93	1.25
22	18	Gideon v. Wainwright	1963	0.90	1.28
23	34	Benton v. Maryland	1969	0.88	1.04
24	22	Bivens v. Six Unknown Named Agents...	1971	0.87	1.21
25	23	Monroe v. Pape	1961	0.86	1.18
26	25	San Diego Bldg. Trades Council v. Garmon	1959	0.84	1.15
27	24	Craig v. Boren	1976	0.83	1.17
28	31	Wainwright v. Sykes	1977	0.82	1.07
29	36	Woodson v. North Carolina	1976	0.82	1.01
30	33	Roth v. United States	1957	0.82	1.05
31	39	North Carolina v. Pearce	1969	0.81	0.98
32	42	Universal Camera Corp. v. NLRB	1951	0.80	0.95
33	27	Terry v. Ohio	1968	0.80	1.10
34	30	Textile Workers Union v. Lincoln Mills	1957	0.79	1.08
35	32	Katz v. United States	1967	0.78	1.06
36	29	Roe v. Wade	1973	0.77	1.08

Table 6 (Continued)

Rank		Name	Year	Score	
Full	Post'46			Full	Post'46
37	38	Morrissey v. Brewer	1972	0.77	0.98
38	43	Paris Adult Theatre I v. Slaton	1973	0.76	0.93
39	45	Cohen v. Beneficial Industrial Loan Corp.	1949	0.75	0.91
40	28	Warth v. Seldin	1975	0.75	1.10
41	35	Stone v. Powell	1976	0.74	1.01

In placing all such opinions on a common scale we are faced with the problem that majority opinions cite heterogeneous numbers of other opinions and that an opinion cannot be cited by a different opinion that predates it—our network is necessarily incomplete. To deal with the incomplete nature of our data we utilize an axiomatic scoring method that is designed to compare objects that have never been directly compared in the data.

The scores calculated by this method are analogous to measures of network influence—specifically, it is a *vertex metric*. As such, it fundamentally differs from other centrality measures for partially connected networks such as eigenvector centrality and degree centrality. One difference is that our measure does not utilize the score of s in computing the contribution of link (s, v) to v's score (as in eigenvector centrality); instead our score utilizes the scores of the other w that could have potentially influenced s, or $\{w : (s, w) \in \tilde{E}\}$. In generating estimates of the x_i using observed network and community data we impute "influence relationships" between vertices that did not have the potential to interact. This leads to the following interpretation of our scores: if there were a hypothetical vertex with a community equal to the set of all possible vertices, then our scores represent the expected influence of each vertex on that hypothetical vertex.

The analysis presented in this chapter is preliminary, with an obvious shortcoming being the fact that we assume that the community of a case i, or collection of cases that could potentially influence i, consists of all of the cases that predate it. In future work we intend to allow community structure to be determined not only by the year in which a case was considered but also by the topic of the case. Additionally, we hope to apply our scoring method to other types of incomplete network data as we believe it provides a useful new measure of node centrality that generalizes the concept of in-degree centrality.

References

Black RC, Spriggs JF II (2010) The depreciation of US Supreme Court precedent. Working paper, Washington University in Saint Louis

Bommarito MJ II, Katz D, Zelner J (2009) Law as a seamless web? Comparison of various network representations of the United States Supreme Court corpus (1791–2005). In: Proceedings of the

12th international conference on artificial intelligence and law, ICAIL'09. ACM, New York, pp 234–235
Carrubba C, Friedman B, Martin AD, Vanberg G (2011) Who controls the content of Supreme Court opinions? Am J Polit Sci 56(2):400–412
Clark TS, Lauderdale B (2010) Locating Supreme Court opinions in doctrine space. Am J Polit Sci 54(4):871–890
Fowler JH, Heaney MT, Nickerson DW, Padgett JF, Sinclair B (2011) Causality in political networks. Am Polit Res 39(2):437–480
Fowler JH, Jeon S (2008) The authority of Supreme Court precedent. Soc Netw 30(1):16–30
Fowler JH, Johnson TR, Spriggs JF II, Jeon S, Wahlbeck PJ (2007) Network analysis and the law: measuring the legal importance of Supreme Court precedents. Polit Anal 15(3):324–346
Gerhardt MJ (2008) The power of precedent. Oxford University Press, New York
Hansford TG, Spriggs JF II (2006) The politics of precedent on the US Supreme Court. Princeton University Press, Princeton
Landes WM, Posner RA (1976) Legal precedent: a theoretical and empirical analysis. J Law Econ 19(2):249–307
Lazer D (2011) Networks in political science: back to the future. PS Polit Sci Polit 44(1):61
Luce RD (1958) Individual choice behavior. John Wiley, New York
Merryman JH (1954) The authority of authority: what the California Supreme Court cited in 1950. Stanford Law Rev 6(4):613–673
Schnakenberg K, Penn EM (2012) Scoring from contests. Working paper, Washington University in Saint Louis
Spaeth HJ (2012) The United States Supreme Court database. Center for the Empirical Research in the Law, Washington University in Saint Louis
Spriggs J II, Hansford T, Stenger A (2011) The information dynamics of vertical stare decisis. Working paper, Washington University in Saint Louis
Ward MD, Stovel K, Sacks A (2011) Network analysis and political science. Annu Rev Pol Sci 14:245–264

Part III
Empirical Analysis

The Politics of Austerity: Modeling British Attitudes Towards Public Spending Cuts

Harold D. Clarke, Walter Borges, Marianne C. Stewart, David Sanders, and Paul Whiteley

Are there no prisons?... And the union workhouses, are they still in operation?
Ebenezer Scrooge to Charity Collector, 1851

Beginning in 2008 financial crises and ensuing economic turbulence have prompted acrimonious national debates in many Western democracies over the need for substantial budget cuts and debt reductions. Among economic and political elites there is broad agreement that substantial public sector budget cuts are necessary to address unsustainable sovereign debt loads and establish long-term fiscal integrity. Many ordinary citizens see things differently—proposed austerity measures threaten programs that aid the disadvantaged while challenging longstanding public commitments to education, health and personal security that constitute the foundation of the modern welfare state. Coming close on the heels of massive, widely publicized bailouts of major banks, investment firms and manufacturing companies, the pro-

H.D. Clarke (✉) · M.C. Stewart
School of Economic, Political and Policy Sciences, University of Texas at Dallas, PO Box 830688, Richardson, TX 75083-0688, USA
e-mail: clarke475@msn.com

M.C. Stewart
e-mail: mcmstewart@gmail.com

W. Borges
Division of Liberal Arts and Life Sciences, University of North Texas-Dallas, 7300 University Blvd., Dallas, TX 75241, USA
e-mail: Walter.Borges@unt.edu

H.D. Clarke · D. Sanders · P. Whiteley
Department of Government, University of Essex, Colchester C043SQ, UK

D. Sanders
e-mail: sanders@essex.ac.uk

P. Whiteley
e-mail: whiteley@essex.ac.uk

N. Schofield et al. (eds.), *Advances in Political Economy*,
DOI 10.1007/978-3-642-35239-3_13,

posed reductions in public sector spending threaten to overturn the distributional policy consensus in contemporary mature democracies.

As of this writing, several countries—*inter alia*, Ireland, Italy, Greece, Portugal, Spain, the United States and the United Kingdom—either have implemented or are seriously contemplating large-scale budget cuts that will necessitate painful reductions in public services and benefits. Perhaps the best known case is Greece where the European Union and the International Monetary Fund have dictated draconian financial policies to remedy the country's sovereign debt crisis. The result has been widespread, oftentimes violent, public protests and ongoing political turmoil. In the United Kingdom, proposed public-sector cuts have prompted civil unrest and charges that the Conservative-led Coalition government accords higher priority to enacting a neo-Thatcherite ideological agenda of small government and re-privatization than the provision of effective health care and education for its citizens.

This study focuses on the British experience. Confronted with a pernicious combination of rising public debt and growing unemployment when his coalition government of Conservatives and Liberal Democrats assumed power in May 2010, Prime Minister David Cameron and his Chancellor of the Exchequer, George Osborne, proposed to cut an average of 20 percent from government spending over the next four years (Burns 2011). The plan was to reduce the budget by £83 billion by eliminating 490,000 government jobs, curtailing benefits, and chopping a broad range of "unnecessary" programs (BBC 2011). Public employee pay was frozen for two years, with the prospect of one percent annual raises offered for the following two years. Reductions in the government workforce would be mitigated by increased participation by civic-minded volunteers who would provide public services *pro bono*—a devolution-of-power and responsibility that Cameron and his advisors termed "the Big Society".

Progress towards these goals has been slow—by the end of 2011, the UK inflation rate was nearly five percent and unemployment exceeded eight percent (Burns). Economic growth has been less than projected and Chancellor George Osborne now anticipates that the public sector cuts will take seven years to clear the deficit (Werdigier 2011). The projected level of spending reductions is now fully £123 billion. A sense that the cuts are "too far, too fast" is increasingly widespread, being enunciated both in the news media (Bloomberg 2011) and, as will be documented below, in public opinion surveys.

Nothing has prompted more resistance than the Coalition Government's attempt to devolve management and ownership of the National Health Service, its hospitals and other facilities to physicians and private investors. Public skepticism about the benefits of such moves has been compounded by criticism by medical professionals. Fearing the political repercussions of such negative reactions to his plans for the NHS, Cameron and his Health Secretary, Andrew Lansley, have excluded professional groups representing physicians, nurses and midwives from recent conferences on how to implement the reforms.

Models incorporating demographic, attitudinal and evaluative variables are staples in analyses of public support for political parties and their leaders, and here we develop similar models for policy preferences. We first investigate the nature of public attitudes towards the budget cuts using cross-sectional data from the British Election Study's 2011 Alternative Vote (AV) Referendum Survey. Then, we specify a multivariate model of these attitudes. The model incorporates demographics, attitudinal/policy beliefs and economic evaluations. We also use data from the monthly BES Continuous Monitoring Surveys (CMS) to analyze the dynamics of public opinion about the likelihood of economic recovery since the failure of Lehman Brothers Bank in September 2008 dramatized the onset of the financial crisis.

The proposed budget cuts pose pressing political questions. Will citizens in modern welfare states accept their leaders' assertions that public spending reductions are necessary? If the answer is "no", will governing parties and leaders that propose and try to implement such cuts face major losses of electoral support? To answer these questions in the British context, we examine public attitudes towards the proposed cuts and assess how these attitudes affect support for the Conservatives and Prime Minister David Cameron. As part of this analysis, we estimate rival vote intention models to determine the relative importance of attitudes towards the cuts as an explanatory factor. Do voters place more weight on economic conditions, attitudes towards the spending cuts, or do they focus more heavily on the overall performance of parties and their leaders? We also investigate the dynamics public opinion about the likelihood of solving the financial crisis. This analysis begins in October 2008, the month after the failure of Lehman Brothers. Monthly survey data are used to track the dynamics of opinions about solving the crisis and factors that account for these dynamics.

1 Theoretical Perspectives

We distinguish our study from previous work that analyzes the formation and persistence of values that undergird the modern welfare state. We investigate factors affecting policy evaluations and policy preferences and the political impacts of those evaluations and preferences. Borre and Viegas (1995) have observed that there is only a weak connection between attitudes that support general government intervention in the national economy and the specifics of that response. In this study, we focus on a specific response—attitudes towards cuts in government spending on services and benefits—rather than on the general ideological and belief-system framework that provides the political cultural context for responses to government intervention.

Earlier research has raised questions about whether an individual's overall level of support for the welfare state is determined by careful weighing of the benefits and services provided and the tax burden that must be assumed to sustain those benefits and services. Over 50 years ago, Downs (1960) speculated that there may be a large gap between citizens' evaluations of policy inputs and outputs because people cannot see direct relationships between what they contribute and what they receive. In markets, there is a direct relationship between cost and benefits; in governments, there is not. Downs suggested that this disconnect may reduce support for government spending among ordinary citizens. Subsequent studies focused not on the disconnect, but rather on the idea that the tax burdens of the welfare state are recognized by citizens, but are underestimated. Survey questions that "price" the benefits by reminding respondents of the connection between social spending and taxation often show lower support for spending (Winter and Mouritzen 2001), even while general policy preferences remain largely the same (Confalonieri and Newton 1995).

In a recent review, Kumlin (2007) suggests that responses to the individual-level consequences of welfare state programs may affect political attitudes and behavior. He notes that this runs counter to stylized facts in the economic voting literature, in which sociotropic economic evaluations, i.e., retrospective, contemporaneous and prospective evaluations of the national economy, have stronger effects on political attitudes and voting behavior than do egocentric evaluations (e.g., Lewis-Beck 1988; Clarke et al. 2004).

Moreover, it bears emphasis that we are studying support for spending cuts in a crisis context. Over a decade ago Pierson (1993) pointed out that many countries are finding it difficult to fund previous commitments to the social safety net and the welfare state, and were entering a period of what he called "permanent austerity". The current situation may accentuate this long-term general condition, but this study addresses the imposition of crisis-induced austerity measures through a specific policy approach—the "shock therapy" of immediate, large-scale cuts in public spending.

Models of political support in mature and emerging democracies usually focus on three phenomena—support for the political community as a whole, for the political regime and its institutions, and for specific authorities embodied as individual officeholders or incumbent governments (Easton 1965; Kornberg and Clarke 1992). When analyzing public reactions to budget cuts in the United Kingdom, we concentrate instead on attitudes towards a set of government policies—the spending cuts instituted in 2010–2011 by the Conservative-led Coalition Government of Prime Minister David Cameron. Extending electorally oriented models to analyze support for policies is appropriate because, as Kornberg and Clarke (1992) have observed, governments and political systems in mature democracies are expected to help improve the quality of citizens' lives, provide a safety net to ensure basic needs are met, while at the same time mitigating the impact of individual- and group-level variations in economic conditions that can significantly affect personal well-being and life chances. This is the essence of the political-economic settlement that has defined the contours of mainstream political discourse in Western democracies since the Great Depression of the 1930s.

When delineating factors that affect public attitudes towards the spending cuts proposed by Mr. Cameron's Government, it is plausible that economic evaluations will be prime determinants of those attitudes. *Circa* early 2012, the British economy is on the verge of a "double-dip" recession as are the economies of many of its trading partners. Citizens are exercised that massive debt has been amassed and are unsure who to blame. For their part, the Conservatives and their coalition partners, the Liberal Democrats, contend that the problem is attributable to the profligate practices of the previous New Labour governments of Tony Blair and Gordon Brown. Other, more radical, voices on the right blame an influx foreign workers and growing numbers of immigrants and miscellaneous miscreants who exploit the benefit system at the expense of hardworking Britons. Still others argue that, despite its best intentions, no 21st century British government can afford the commitments made over half a century ago for a comprehensive social safety net in an era when the percentage of elderly people is rapidly expanding and attendant health care costs are exploding. All of these arguments are being made in a context of simmering public anger over the bailout of British banks that worsened the debt and the deficits.

Students of economic voting long have argued that the economy and related valence issues typically dominate the electoral agenda in mature democracies. The economy is fundamental; it provides a simple, extremely useful guide for deciding how to cast one's ballot. A strong economy indicates that the government is performing well, whereas a weak economy is a clear signal of incompetence. Voters make responsibility attributions and when the economy is in trouble incumbent parties and their leaders are in trouble as well. Of course, the economy is not of a piece, and there have been protracted debates about which aspects of economic performance matter most for political support (see, e.g., Lewis-Beck 1988; Clarke et al. 2004). In this regard, Lewis-Beck and Stegmaier (2000; see also Bartels 2008), have contended that rising income equality and enhanced financial insecurity may become increasingly important components of the "economic vote" in contemporary mature democracies.

Conjectures about the significance of income inequality, financial insecurity and "fair shares" hearken back to longstanding arguments concerning the significance, indeed dominance, of social class in British electoral politics (e.g., Butler and Stokes 1969). Although the growing weakness of social class as a predictor of party support in Britain is well established (Clarke et al. 2004, 2009b), it is possible that the political relevance of class divisions will be reinvigorated by the current economic crisis and the austerity policies being pursued by the Coalition government. In this regard, Dalton (2006) has argued that social class no longer matters much in most elections, but economics does. Increasingly, voters are focusing on economic issues to satisfy individual interests, not to show solidarity with a social class to which they belong.

Cutler (2002) is among the more recent voices stating the case for including social class and other demographic variables in party support models. In studies of Canadian elections, he finds that even the best informed voters who might be expected to make electoral choices on the basis of policy considerations instead fall back on simple, observable similarities and differences among parties and their support coalitions. Cutler also argues that demographic effects undercut models of voter choice that emphasize partisan and leader image heuristics.

The latter argument is problematic since there is an enormous volume of research testifying that party identification is one of the most powerful factors cuing electoral choice and orientations towards candidates and issues (e.g., Campbell et al. 1960; Clarke et al. 2004, 2009b; Lewis-Beck et al. 2008). In the present study, the pertinent question is whether partisan and leader heuristics provide meaningful explanations of people's attitudes towards budget cuts. Other heuristics may be at work as well. In this regard, general risk acceptance/aversion orientations may be relevant to attitudes towards government cuts that are being justified as "short-term pain for long-term gain". *Ceteris paribus*, risk acceptant people will be willing to bet that the cuts will have beneficial effects going forward, whereas risk averse individuals will be unwilling to take the wager.

Long ago St. Thomas Aquinas warned to beware the man of one book. Political economists also should beware the researcher of one model. Composite models incorporating different explanations of political behavior are routinely used in major election studies (e.g., Lewis-Beck et al. 2008) and in the British context the statistical justification for such models has been demonstrated by Clarke et al. (2004, 2009b). This is the approach we take in this study, assembling variables from competing models of electoral choice to specify a composite model of attitudes towards the spending cuts and voting intentions. We draw from socio-demographic models rooted in the voting studies of Lazarsfeld, Berelson and the Columbia school in the 1940s and 1950s (Lazarsfeld et al. 1944; Berelson et al. 1954), from the models of *The American Voter* (Campbell et al. 1960) and from models that posit economic evaluations (both cognitive and emotional) as the most important components of political choice (e.g., Fiorina 1981; Lewis-Beck 1988).

In particular, we are interested in valence politics models of party support. The model draws on Stokes' concept of valence issues (1963, 1992). Unlike positional issues such as taxation-social spending trade-offs, the desirability of participating in the Iraq War or electoral system reform that divide public opinion, valence issues manifest a strong opinion consensus—voters share a common ideal point. The canonical valence issue is the economy, with overwhelming numbers of people preferring low rates of inflation and unemployment coupled with vigorous, sustainable economic growth. However, there are other important valence issues as well, with massive majorities favoring affordable, effective health care and educational systems, a clean environment and policies that promote national and personal security. *Pace* Downs (1957) and the many advocates of spatial models of party competition whom he inspired (see Adams et al. 2005), Stokes contended that valence, not positional, issues typically dominate the political agenda. Voter's assessments of parties' demonstrated and expected performance on such issues do much to drive electoral choice.

The valence politics model as articulated by Clarke et al. (2004, 2009b; see also Clarke et al. 2009a; Lewis-Beck et al. 2011) adds two other major explanatory variables—partisanship and party leader images. Unlike the venerable Michigan model that stressed the stability of party identification (Campbell et al. 1960), in the valence politics model partisanship has dynamic properties (Clarke et al. 2004; Clarke and McCutcheon 2009; see also Fiorina 1981; Achen 1992; Franklin 1992). However, like its Ann Arbor ancestor, at any point in time valence partisanship provides a powerful and accessible voting cue (Sniderman et al. 1991). Leader images are similar in that they serve as influential heuristic devices for voters who lack information about parties' policy preferences and, more important, their ability to deliver desired policy outcomes (Clarke et al. 2004, 2009a; Lupia and McCubbins 1998). Together with assessments of party performance on valence issues, partisanship and leader images provide a powerful and parsimonious explanation of electoral choice.

Data Sources The British Election Study (BES)'s AV Ballot Referendum Survey was conducted in April and May 2011, with fieldwork being carried out by YouGov. Two survey waves were administered to a representative national internet panel, with 22,124 respondents completing the pre-referendum wave and 18,556 completing the post-referendum wave. The BES also conducts a regular monthly internet survey—the Continuous Monitoring Survey (CMS)—measuring the political attitudes, beliefs and opinion of approximately 1,000 Britons. Both sources of data are used for the analyses presented below.

2 Model Specification

2.1 Public Support for the Cuts

The principal dependent variable for the analyses—attitudes towards the budget cuts—was constructed using responses to five questions. In three of the questions, a five-point agree-disagree scale was used to measure responses.[1] The fourth question asked respondents to choose between two statements about the cuts, one stating that the cuts would strengthen Britain economically, and one stating that the cuts would

[1] The question format for the first three components of the dependent variable was as follows:
Please indicate how far you agree or disagree with each of the following statements:

- The Government's cuts in public expenditure are essential for the long-term health of the UK economy.
- The cuts in public expenditure that the Government proposes are likely to cause serious financial difficulties for me and my family.
- Excessive public spending is the main cause of Britain's debt.

Respondents could choose between Strongly approve, Approve, Neither approve nor disapprove, Disapprove, Strongly disapprove or Don't know.

The fourth question stated:

Which of the following statements come closest to your view about the overall impact of the proposed public expenditure cuts?
- The public expenditure cuts will strengthen Britain's economic growth and international competitiveness.
- The public expenditure cuts will damage Britain's economy by pushing it further into recession.
- Don't know.

The fifth question was worded thus:

Which of the following statements comes closest to your view?
- The government should do less to provide publicly funded services and do more to encourage people to provide services for themselves.
- Good public services can be provided only by the government.
- Don't know.

push the UK into recession. A middle category allowed respondents to say they did not know which option to choose. A fifth question asked respondents about whether they favored more or fewer services from the government, with a "don't know" option as well. Responses to the five questions were rescaled to produce high scores when the respondent thought that cuts were needed to solve the UK's economic problems, whereas low scores indicated that the respondent believed that the cuts would be harmful. A principal components exploratory factor analysis indicated that a single factor structures answers to the five questions, and we use factor scores produced by this analysis as the dependent variable. Given the continuous nature of the dependent variable, our model of attitudes towards the cuts was estimated with ordinary least squares regression.

Predictor variables included demographic measures for gender, age, ethnicity, education and income bands. Gender was a 0–1 dummy variable and age was measured in years. We expected that men, who traditionally have less responsibility for child and family care, would be more likely to favor the cuts. For age, we entertained two possibilities; older people might be more conservative and favor the cuts, or they might recognize the vulnerability of old age and oppose them. We also computed a new variable, the square of a respondent's age, in an effort to capture possible curvilinear effects of age. Ethnicity was dichotomized into "white British" and other ethnicity and race identifications, with minorities scored as 1 and "white British" as 0. As a vulnerable social group, we expected non-whites to be opposed to the cuts. Income was measured in 14 bands. As income increased, we anticipated that support for the cuts to increase, but education proved to be a trickier prediction. Education often correlates with income, but the more highly educated also might be more sympathetic to the need for an extensive set of publicly funded social programs.

The model also included dummy variables for Scotland and Wales to determine if regional differences emerged. Scotland in particular is considered to be considerably more left in its ideological proclivities than is the UK as a whole, and we hypothesized that being a resident of Scotland would produce a negative coefficient in the multivariate analysis. We made no such prediction for Wales.

We also included a dummy variable to evaluate the effects of workforce status and vulnerability, combining short- and long-term unemployed into a single category with the permanently disabled and ill and those with long-term caregiver responsibilities. We predicted that those who were unemployed would find the public spending cuts harsh, both because benefits were reduced and because spending cuts meant fewer opportunities for job seekers. Similarly we predicted that the sick, disabled and caregivers would manifest less support for the cuts than would other people.

As elsewhere, the economy is a major concern for most citizens of the UK. Our model of attitudes towards the cuts contains a predictor variable measuring cognitive evaluations of national and personal economic evaluations, constructed via an exploratory factor analysis. The BES routinely measures economic evaluations with four questions on five-point Likert scales. The questions elicit sociotropic and egocentric evaluations both retrospectively and prospectively. The factor analysis of these items indicates that a single economic evaluation factor structures responses. Emotional reactions towards the economy were also elicited, using a question in which respondents were asked to describe their feelings about the general economic situation. Respondents could select up to four words from a field of eight that was divided equally between positive and negative labels. Respondents then were scored by computing the number of positive answers minus the negative ones. The resulting index ranges from -4 to $+4$, with -4 representing a very negative emotional response and 4 representing a very positive view of the economy. For both economic variables we predicted that increasingly positive scores would be associated with greater support for the cuts.

The model also includes several variables drawn from valence models of electoral choice described above. We created dummy party identification variables for the coalition-leading Conservative Party, the coalition minority partner Liberal Democrats and the principal opposition Labour Party. Identifiers with various minor parties were placed in a single dummy variable. Non-identifiers served as the reference party identification category. Because the coalition proposed and enacted the cuts, we predicted positive correlations between the Conservative and Liberal Democrat identification and support for the cuts and a negative coefficient for the Labour Party. We did not predict the direction of the other party identification effects. We did not include the party leader images in this model since feelings about leaders are likely both cause and consequence of major policy initiatives such as public sector spending cuts.

Risk acceptance/aversion, left-right ideology, attitudes towards EU membership and attitudes towards political reform also were included in the model. The risk variable was measured on an 11-point scale where 0 indicated a person really disliked taking risks and 10 indicated a person really liked taking them. The data indicated that Britons on the average are slightly risk adverse, with a mean of 4.3 on the scale. Left-right ideology often is measured on an 11-point scale using increased taxation and spending and tax cuts as the opposing anchors, but this variable incorporated policy preferences intertwined with other attitude variables, which led us to opt for alternative measures of ideology. In this regard, the BES surveys ask respondents to choose placement on a similar 11-point scale that contrasts giving priority to fighting crime as opposed to protecting the rights of the accused, and this was employed as a proxy measure of general ideological conservatism. We also included a variable that measured a respondent's approval or disapproval of membership in the European Union, with the expectation that those opposing EU membership are conservative individuals who would be more likely to support the cuts. Attitudes towards reform were measured using seven questions in the AV referendum post-wave survey and one in the pre-wave.[2] Factor analysis indicated three factors were in play, which we designated as support for electoral reforms, support for traditional

[2]Respondents were asked to evaluate seven statement on five-point Likert scales:

- The House of Commons should be reduced to 600 members.
- The electoral system should be changed to proportional representation.
- Local governments should have more authority.

British institutions, and general support for the devolution of government power away from Westminster. We anticipated that support for traditional institutions and devolution of power would correlate with support for the cuts, whereas support for electoral reforms proxied a progressive "left" orientation which would be associated with diminished support for the cuts.

3 Voting Intentions and Feelings About David Cameron

For the Conservative voting intentions model, the dependent variable was dichotomized in terms of a respondent's intention to vote for the Conservatives or another party. Feelings about Conservative Leader David Cameron were measured using an 11-point scale ranging from 0 "really dislike" to 10 "really like". We also included another predictor variable from the valence politics model, evaluations of which party was best on the most important issue facing the country. This variable was measured as four 0–1 dummies for the Conservatives, Labour, Liberal Democrats and miscellaneous other parties. Persons saying "no party" was best or that they "didn't know which party was best" constituted the reference category. The Cameron affect model was estimated with OLS regression.

We also estimated a series of rival models of voting intention for the Conservatives, Labour, Liberal Democrats and other parties. Our purpose here was to determine which models best explain voting intentions. The sociodemographic model included the age, education ethnicity, gender, income, region and vulnerability variables described above. The economic conditions model comprised variables measuring cognitive evaluations of and emotional reactions to the economy. The political beliefs model included attitudes towards political reform, as well as the variables measuring left-right ideology and support/opposition to EU membership. Attitudes towards the cuts—the dependent variable in the spending cuts regression analysis described above—becomes an explanatory variable in a separate model in the voting intention models. Given its pro-con quality, it constitutes a concrete manifestation of more abstract issue-proximity variables typically employed in Downsian-type spatial models (e.g., Adams et al. 2005). Finally, as per the discussion above, the valence politics model incorporates variables measuring feelings about the leaders of the three major parties (David Cameron, Ed Miliband and Nick Clegg) as well as

---

- The Monarchy should be abolished.
- The Church of England should keep its status.
- The United Kingdom needs more referendums to decide important issues.
- MPs who vote against the party manifesto should resign and run again for their seats.

The pre-wave question asked the respondents to designate which statement was more important:

- That one party get more than half the vote so it can govern on its own.
- That every party's percentage of seats in Parliament is the same as their percentage of the vote.
- Don't know.

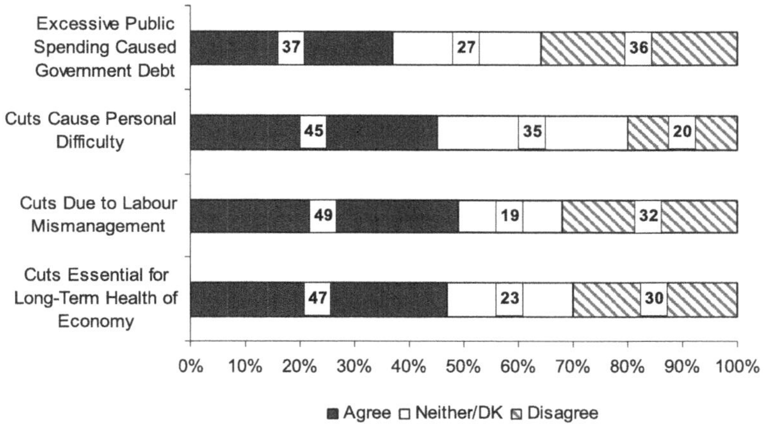

Fig. 1 Opinions about cuts in public expenditure. Source: 2010 BES-CMS AV referendum survey

the several dummy variables measuring party identification and party deemed best on the most important issue facing the country.

The Conservative versus all other parties voting intention models were estimated using binomial logit procedures. Voting intentions for Labour, Liberal Democrats and "other parties" were estimated using multinomial logit models with Conservative voting intentions serving as the base category. Since we were interested in the explanatory power of various competing model specifications described above, we calculated McFadden and McKelvey R^2's, Akaike Information Criteria (AIC) and the percentage of voting intentions correctly predicted by each model.

Of particular interest in the model comparisons is whether attitudes towards the cuts largely account for the political preferences of voters, or whether the valence politics model provides greater explanatory power. Our hypothesis is that, even in times of economic crisis, voters' reactions to policies designed to address such a crisis are a substantial, but secondary, element in the calculus of electoral choice. Accordingly, we hypothesize that the valence politics model incorporating party performance on a range of valence issues, partisan identifications and leader images will outperform a pure 'cuts model' and other rivals. In addition, based on previous research, we expect that a composite model incorporating the predictor variables from all five individual models will perform better than any individual model.

4 Public Reactions to the Budget Cuts

The May 2011 BES survey data shows that many Britons are not sanguine about the conditions facing the country. They also are divided about the cause of the crisis and the policy path to recovery. Specifically, as Fig. 1 illustrates, almost half of the respondents (49 percent) attribute the necessity for spending cuts to mismanagement by the Labour Party during its tenure in office, with 32 percent disagreeing

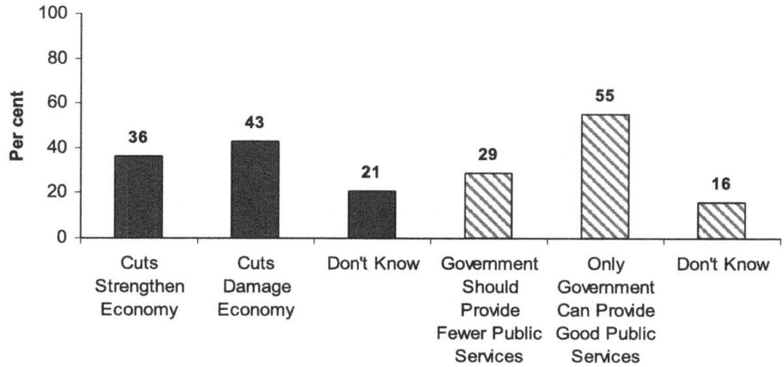

Fig. 2 Opinions about budget cuts and public services. Source: 2010 BES-CMS AV referendum survey

that Labour policies caused the cuts. Almost as many (47 percent) agreed that cuts were essential to preserve the long-term health of the economy. Forty-five percent believed that the policies of the Cameron Government would cause difficulties for their households whereas only 20 percent disagreed. Thirty-five percent said they did not know what the personal impact of the cuts would be.

Regarding assessments of the cause of Britain's public debt, there were lower levels of agreement on whether public excessive spending was the cause. Specifically, 37 percent agreed that public spending was the cause of the debt, but 36 percent disagreed, and 27 were uncertain. A possible explanation for this division in opinion may be widespread anger over massive bailouts provided by the government to stabilize British banks. News stories persist about the anger of Britons towards their banks, as manifested in recent controversies over bonuses for bank executives who presided over speculative investments and the credit crunch that followed the meltdown of major financial institutions.

Figure 2 summarizes data on attitudes towards expenditure cuts and the philosophical balance between government provision of services and personal responsibility. Thirty-six percent of Britons believe the spending cuts will strengthen the economy and 43 percent believe the cuts will damage it. But a majority of respondents were skeptical of the proposition that the government should provide fewer services and rely on individuals to fend for themselves—55 percent said only the government can provide good public services, compared to 29 percent who would opt for fewer government services.

Tracing the dynamics of these opinions over time was accomplished using identical questions contained in the monthly Continuous Monitoring Study surveys conducted between June 2010 and January 2012. During this time frame, the percentage agreeing that the cuts are essential to Britain's economic health has fallen from 68 percent to the high 50s (see Fig. 3). In contrast, agreement that the cuts are likely to cause serious personal difficulties has risen from 41 to 54 percent, while disagreement has fallen from 26 to 19 percent. Whether excessive public spending was the cause of Britain's debt produces is a contentious proposition; public agreement and

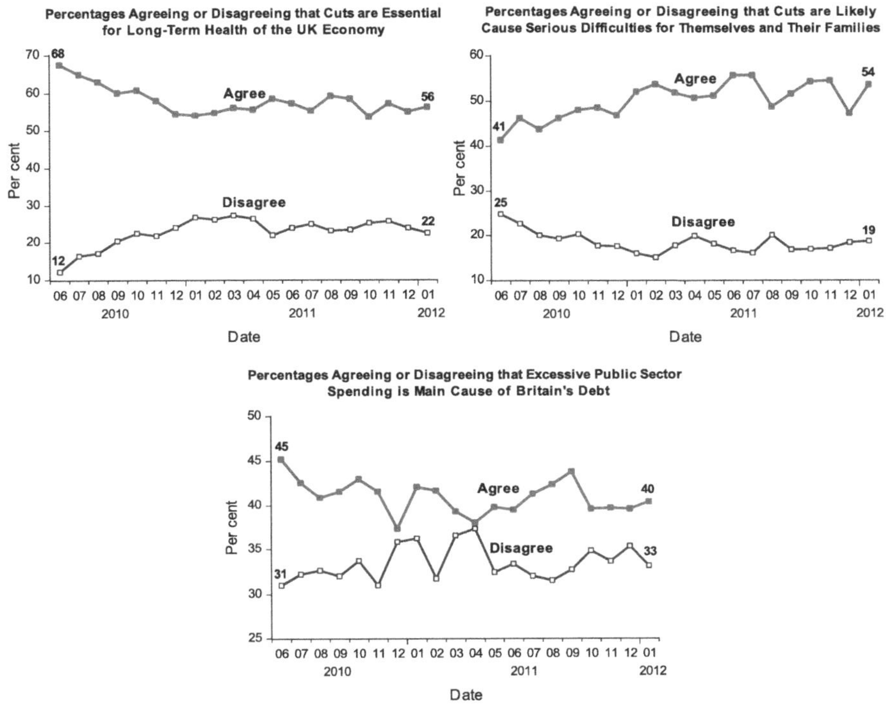

Fig. 3 Dynamics of public opinion about cuts in public expenditure October 2008–January 2012. Source: June 2010–January 2012 BES-CMS surveys

disagreement has fluctuated across a 10 point range for agreement and a seven-point range for disagreement, but more people continue to think that excessive spending is the main cause of the British debt than disagree.

5 Analyzing Attitudes Towards the Budget Cuts

The multivariate model of attitudes towards the cuts specifies 21 predictor variables, of which 18 are statistically significant ($p \leq .05$) (Table 1). The model accounts for 51 percent of the variation in the dependent variable. As expected, party identification proved to be a powerful predictor of support, with the Conservative identifiers (B = 0.58) supporting the cuts. Identifiers with the Liberal Democrats, the Conservatives' occasionally balky coalition partner, showed more modest support (B = 0.17). Labour identifiers were strongly against the cuts, with a coefficient of −0.52.

Most socio-demographic variables were statistically significant and correctly signed. Higher income and education, and male gender, produced positive support for the cuts, but vulnerability (i.e., unemployed, disabled, caregiver), residing in Scotland and advanced age decreased support for the cuts. The negative coefficient

Table 1 Multivariate model of opinions about cuts in public expenditure, May 2010 BES-AV survey (OLS estimates)

Predictor variable	B	s.e.
Party Identification:		
Labour	$-.518^{***}$	.015
Conservative	$.581^{***}$	.016
Liberal Democrat	$.174^{***}$	.021
Other Party	$-.007$	.020
Economic Evaluations	$.264^{***}$	.007
Emotional Reactions Economic Conditions	$.074^{***}$	.004
Ideological/Policy Beliefs:		
Attitudes Towards Reform:		
Electoral System	$-.986^{***}$	.006
Devolution of Power	$.063^{***}$	.006
Traditional Institutions	$.091^{***}$	.006
Crime v. Rights of Accused	$-.023^{***}$	.002
EU Membership	$-.073^{***}$	.005
Risk Orientation	$.012^{***}$	.002
Vulnerability Status†	$-.061^{**}$	.019
Age	$-.004^{*}$	.002
Age Squared	9.334E-05***	2.406E-05
Education	$.018^{***}$	.004
Ethnicity	.009	.024
Gender	$.067^{***}$	.011
Income	$.022^{***}$	.002
Scotland	$-.032^{*}$	.019
Wales	$-.009$	.238
Constant	.045	.061

Adjusted $R^2 = .51$
$N = 18{,}556$
$^{***}p \leq .001$; $^{**}p \leq .01$; $^{*}p \leq .05$, one-tailed test
†Unemployed, disabled, care-giver

for age suggests that the elderly do indeed perceive threats to their security from the cuts.

Similarly, most attitudinal variables tapping left-right political orientations of various kinds performed as expected. Thus, people who support EU membership and those who emphasize the rights of the accused were less likely to support the cuts than were those calling for Britain to sever its EU ties and prioritize crime fighting. The three dimensions of attitudes towards institutional reform also produced the hypothesized results. The greater is one's support for traditional institutions—the church, monarchy and Parliament—the greater is the likelihood of supporting the public spending cuts. The same relationship obtains for those who support devolving more government power to local governments and individuals, a key component of Mr. Cameron's "Big Society" vision. Again, as also expected, support for reform of the electoral system is associated with opposition to the cuts. Finally, there is evidence that more general personality characteristics are relevant, with heightened risk acceptance being correlated with increased support for the cuts.

6 Analyzing Support for the Conservatives and David Cameron

Table 2 reports the results of estimating composite models of Conservative vote intentions and feelings about Prime Minister Cameron, the chief proponent (with Chancellor George Osborne) of the public spending cuts. After party identification and the judgment that a Conservatives are best on the most important issue, support for public spending cuts is the strongest predictor of affect for Cameron. The composite model explains 62 percent in the variance in feelings about the prime minister, and estimates of coefficients for 17 of 24 predictor variables are statistically significant. All party identification terms are significant predictors, as are all of the judgments on which party is best able to handle the most important issue.

As noted above, we estimate the effects of factors affecting Conservative vote intentions using a binomial logit model. This composite model correctly classifies 93.4 percent of the vote intentions and generates a McKelvey R^2 of .87. To provide intuition about the strength of the effects of various independent variables, we also estimated changes in probability of voting Conservative as statistically significant predictors were varied over their range while holding other predictors at their mean values in the case of continuous variables or zero in the case of dummy variables. This procedure showed that the predicted probability of voting Conservative would increase by .44 as attitudes towards the cuts shifted from their lowest to their highest value (see Fig. 4). Other powerful predictors are feelings about Cameron (.79 increase in probability of voting Conservative) and Conservative Party identification (.38 increase). Support for electoral reform produces a $-.45$ decrease in the probability of voting Conservative. Other strong predictors include judgments that Liberal Democrats ($-.33$ decrease) or Labour ($-.31$ decrease) are best on the most important issue.

The analysis of the performance of rival models for voting intentions is summarized in Table 3. Among the five competing specific models, the valence politics model best predicts voting intention for Conservatives and for various opposition parties. By every diagnostic measure, the valence politics model does significantly better than its competitors. The other model of interest here, the "pure cuts model", outperforms all of the remaining rivals. Echoing earlier research, Table 3 also documents that the composite model does better than any of the specific models. However, as measured by the various summary statistics presented in the table, its per-

Table 2 Multivariate models of Conservative vote intentions and feelings about Prime Minister David Cameron, May 2010 BES-AV survey

Predictor variables	Conservative vote intentions†		Feelings about David Cameron‡	
	B	s.e.	B	s.e.
Opinions About Public Expenditure Cuts	*.604******	*.059*	*.974******	*.021*
Feelings About:				
David Cameron	.516***	.025	–	–
Ed Miliband	−.152***	.021	–	–
Nick Clegg	−.140***	.022	–	–
Party Identification:				
Labour	−1.776***	.134	−.573***	.046
Conservative	2.065***	.110	1.351***	.050
Liberal Democrat	−1.774***	.140	.356***	.061
Other Party	−1.628***	.129	−.222***	.057
Party Best Most Important Issue:				
Labour	−1.867***	.255	−.709***	.046
Conservative	.887***	.099	1.204***	.046
Liberal Democrat	−2.098***	.412	.216*	.093
Other Party	−1.088***	.129	−.287***	.052
Economic Evaluations	.079	.051	.166***	.019
Emotional Reactions to Economic Conditions	.022	.030	.206***	.011
Ideological/Policy Beliefs:				
Attitudes Towards Reform:				
Electoral System	−.479***	.044	−.089***	.016
Devolution of Power	−.053	.045	.005	.015
Traditional Institutions	.115**	.047	.309***	.016
Crime v. Rights of Accused	−.020	.019	−.003	.007
EU Membership	−.091*	.040	.027*	.014
Vulnerability Status	−.004	.152	−.067	.051
Age	−.012***	.003	.006***	.001
Education	−.080**	.032	−.007	.011
Ethnicity	.235	.183	.033	.064
Gender	−.358***	.083	−.187***	.029
Income	.027*	.017	.003	.005
Scotland	−.704***	.157	−.010	.051
Wales	−.685***	.191	.153**	.065
Constant	−.968***	.310	4.161***	.097
			Adjusted $R^2 = .62$	

McKelvey $R^2 = .87$
Percentage Correctly Classified = 93.4
$N = 18{,}556$
– Variable not included in model
*** $p \leq .001$; ** $p \leq .01$; * $p \leq .05$, one-tailed test
†Binomial logit model
‡OLS regression model

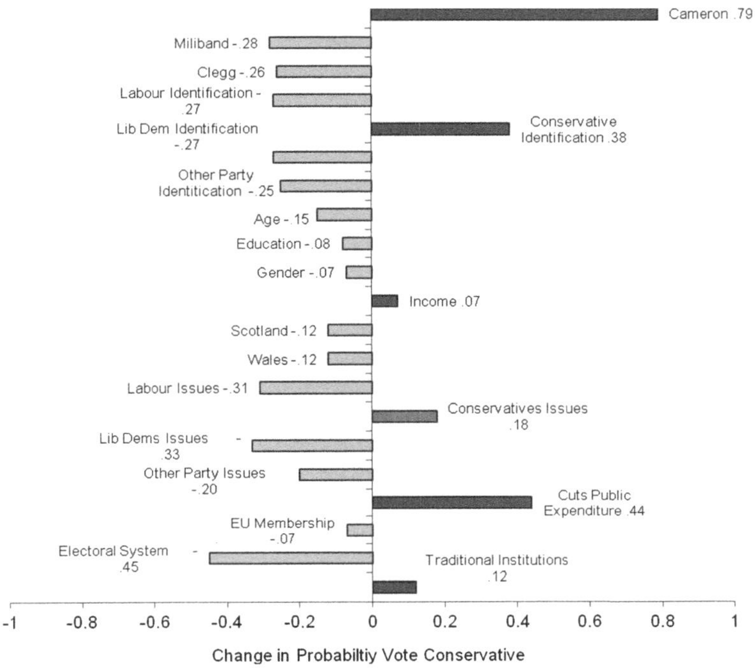

Fig. 4 Change in probability of intending to vote Conservative associated with statistically significant predictors in binomial logit model

formance is only marginally better than the valence politics model. This finding underscores the point that valence politics considerations are the principal proximate drivers of vote intentions.

7 Why Are There so Many Bears in Britain?

The failure of Lehman Brothers on September 15th 2008 symbolized the growing financial crisis and signaled the onset of the most serious global economic downturn since the great depression of the 1930s. Starting in October 2008, the BES team began asking respondents in monthly Continuous Monitoring Surveys (CMS) to use a 0–10 scale with 0 meaning "very unlikely" and 10 meaning "very likely" to forecast the likelihood that the crisis would be resolved over the year ahead. From the outset, CMS respondents were quite bearish, with their average score being 4.0 on the scale. Moreover, as illustrated in Fig. 5, their pessimism has grown over time, such that the average score in January 2012, is only 2.1. Since the Conservative-Liberal Democrat Coalition took office, the average score has never exceeded 3.0.

What are the sources of this pessimism? A simple answer to this question is: "It's reality!—people are bearish because the economy is in terrible shape and shows lit-

Table 3 Rival models of voting intentions, May 2011 CMS survey

Panel A. Conservative voting intentions (binomial logit model)

Model	McFadden R^2	McKelvey R^2	Percent correctly classified	AIC†
Socio-demographics	.04	.06	64.6	19052.93
Economic Conditions	.10	.17	69.0	17708.06
Political Beliefs	.17	.29	72.3	16479.42
Attitudes-Cuts	*.38*	*.54*	*80.9*	*12309.00*
Valence Politics‡	.76	.86	93.8	4829.82
Composite	.77	.87	94.4	4506.15

Panel B. Labour, Liberal Democrat and other party voting intentions (multinomial logit model)

Model	McFadden R^2	McKelvey R^2	Percent correctly classified	AIC†
Socio-demographics	.04	–	44.7	36445.06
Economic Conditions	.07	–	51.6	35014.82
Political Beliefs	.14	–	53.8	32513.98
Attitudes-Cuts	*.25*	–	*66.7*	*28238.60*
Valence Politics‡	.70	–	87.2	11344.86
Composite	.72	–	88.2	10634.37

– Not defined for multinomial logit model

†Akaike Information Criterion; smaller values indicate better model performance (Burnham and Anderson, 2002)

‡leader images, party identification, party best on most important issue

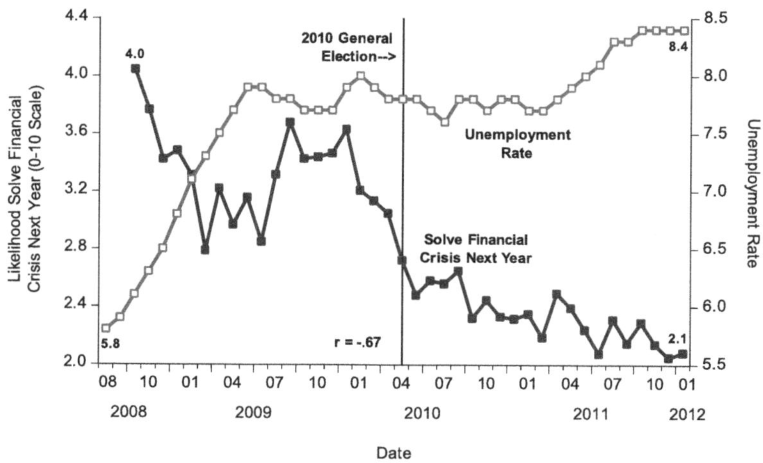

Fig. 5 Likelihood of solving financial crisis next year and unemployment rate, August 2008—January 2012. Source: August 2008–January 2012 BES-CMS surveys and ONS unemployment data

tle, if any, sign of reviving". Given a continuing barrage of bad news about economic conditions, it is not surprising that many people are less than sanguine about that the crisis will be resolved anytime soon. In this regard, perhaps no single indicator carries as much weight in the public mind as the unemployment rate—it is effectively an operational definition of how hard times are. In this regard, Fig. 5 documents that UK unemployment has risen from 5.8 percent in October 2008 to 8.4 percent in January 2012, with modest decreases in the run-up to the 2010 election being followed by upward movements throughout much of 2011. The correlation between expectations of solving the crisis and the unemployment rate is strongly negative ($r = -.67$).

If, in fact, people typically use unemployment as the "big heuristic" for assessing the present state and future prospects of the economy, then we should be able to model the relationship between forecasts for solving the crisis and the jobless rate as an error correction process. Other factors may have transient relevance for explaining variation in these forecasts, but over the long run, they should evolve in dynamic equilibrium with movements in the length of lines at Jobs Centers. Here, we specify three such factors. The first is Chancellor George Osborne's annual budget speeches in 2009, 2010 and 2011 which have delivered a largely unrelieved litany of bad news about the need for varying mixtures of spending cuts and tax hikes. Second is the March 2009 announcement by the former Labour government of a massive and unprecedented quantitative easing program to jump start the faltering economy. Third is the presence since May 2010 of the Conservative-Liberal Democrat Coalition Government. Prime Minister Cameron and Chancellor of the Exchequer, George Osborne, have made the ailing economy and an attendant need for austerity the touchstone of virtually every policy proposal advanced by the Coalition Government. As a result, most of what passes for daily political news includes a reminder that times are indeed tough. And, for their part, Labour Leader, Ed Miliband, and his Shadow Chancellor, Ed Balls, have countered by claiming that the hard times are worse than need be because their opposite numbers insist on pursuing an ill-advised neo-Thatcherite economic agenda. In their view, privileging Hayek over Keynes is a recipe that risks rehearsing the 1930s.

The resulting model of public forecasts for whether the economic crisis will be resolved over the forthcoming year is:

$$\begin{aligned}(1-L)\mathrm{RESOLVE}(t) &= b_0 + b_1 * (1-L)\mathrm{UN}(t-i) - \alpha_1 * \big(\mathrm{RESOLVE}(t-1) \\ &\quad - \lambda_1 * \mathrm{UN}(t-1)\big) + b_2 * \mathrm{BUDGET}(t-i) \\ &\quad + b_3 * \mathrm{QE}(t-i) + b_4 * \mathrm{COAL}(t-i) + \varepsilon(t) \qquad (1)\end{aligned}$$

where: RESOLVE = forecast for resolving the economic crisis; UN = unemployment rate; BUDGET = annual budgets; QE = quantitative easing; COAL = Coalition government; ε_t = stochastic error term ($N(0, \sigma^2)$, t is time, and α, b and λ are parameters to be estimated. Given the structure of the model, its parameters are estimated using nonlinear least squares.

Table 4 Error correction model of dynamics of opinions whether the financial crisis will be resolved in year ahead, October 2008–January 2012

Predictor variables	B	s.e.
Change in Unemployment Rate ($t-1$)	$-.954^{***}$	.022
Error Correction Mechanism	$-.743^{***}$	.103
Unemployment Rate ($t-1$)- ECM	$-.289^{***}$	.071
2009–2011 Budget Statements	$-.146^{*}$	.087
2009 Quantitative Easing	$-.426^{**}$	.149
2010 General Election	$-.712^{***}$	.102
Constant	4.172^{***}	.744

Adjusted $R^2 = .64$
$N = 39$
Residual Diagnostics:
Autocorrelation: LBQ = 9.967, df = 12, p = .619
ARCH: LBQ = 7.339, df = 12, p = .834
Normality: Jarque-Bera = .573, df = 1, p = .751
Heteroskedasticity: $\chi^2 = 5.119$, df = 6, p = .529
$^{***}p \leq .001$; $^{**}p \leq .01$; $^{*}p \leq .05$, one-tailed test

Results of analyzing the model using data for the October 2008–January 2012 period are displayed in Table 4. As shown, the model can account for a large percentage of the variation in public forecasts for resolving the economic crisis (adjusted $R^2 = .64$) and all parameters are statistically significant and properly signed. Indicative of the power of the error correction mechanism between these forecasts and monthly unemployment, the adjustment parameter is $-.74$, $p < .001$. This signifies that a shock to the system, from whatever source, is eroded at a rate of nearly 75 percent in each subsequent month by the error correction relationship between forecasts for resolving the crisis and the unemployment rate. Unemployment also has large short-term effects, with a one per cent increase in joblessness being sufficient to lower forecasts by nearly one full point ($-.95$) on the 0–10 scale.

Other factors are in play as well. As expected, annual budgets, the March 2009 round of quantitative easing, and the replacement of Labour by the Coalition all worked to lower public forecasts of the likelihood that the economic crisis would be resolved over the next year. The impact of the presence of the Coalition government is especially noteworthy. Specified as a (thus far) permanent effect, the presence of the Coalition has worked (ceteris paribus) to reduce economic forecasts by $-.71$ points each month. Effects of annual budget statements and quantitative easing are smaller, $-.15$ and $-.43$, respectively, but statistically significant ($p < .001$).

Overall, the model provides a parsimonious account of public forecasts about the future course of the economic crisis. As hypothesized, unemployment is the key heuristic, with forecasts and joblessness defining a powerful error correction process. Since the autumn of 2008, that process has adjusted the effects of various political economic shocks, the largest being the replacement of Labour by the Conservative-Liberal Democrat coalition at Westminster.

8 Conclusion: Economic Crisis and Performance Politics

David Cameron and his Coalition colleagues have chosen to ride the tiger of the poor economic times while attempting to enact public spending cuts that trade pain today with the promise of gain tomorrow. As the anti-Wimpy (Popeye's sidekick sought a hamburger today for payment tomorrow), the prime minister demands payment today and promises a hamburger tomorrow. To date, Cameron has successfully tapped British public opinion that acknowledges the seriousness of budgetary and sovereign debt difficulties and the need to address endemic fiscal problems. Support for the Coalition's budget cuts is tied to party identification, economic evaluations and reactions, and demographic factors that indicate self-sufficiency. But factors that suggest economic vulnerability—unemployment, aging and lack of education and income—mitigate the willingness to jump head first into schemes to shrink government.

Although there is a strong partisan divide in attitudes toward the cuts, Mr. Cameron and his friends on the government benches face mounting skepticism on several fronts. First, there is substantial fear that the cuts could damage the economy instead of curing it, and that the cuts could cripple government infrastructure required to provide public services effectively. Second, the uncertainty of policy outcomes and a changing economic environment mean the cuts, however well conceived in 2010 and 2011, may not be seen as effective policy going forward and will prove to be a political liability in the run-up to the next general election. Open-ended responses to the question in the BES AV referendum survey about the most important issue facing the country are suggestive with regard to the latter possibility. Many of these responses acknowledge the need of fiscal restraint, but others reject the present program as "too far, too fast". Still others raise equity-fairness concerns which could gain traction in the face of disappearing benefits and services and continuing economic malaise.

A third, more pointed, element of skepticism recently has been enunciated as medical professionals, interest groups and concerned patients attempt to rein in government plans to restructure the cherished National Health Service. Since the Conservative-Liberal Democrat Coalition came to power, commentators in the British press have asked whether a single-minded pursuit of deep spending cuts is the right policy at the right time. Now they are asking if Prime Minister Cameron and his much maligned Health Secretary Andrew Lansley are privileging a Thatcherite ideological agenda at the expense of effective health care delivery.

Analyses of CMS time series data suggest that public support for the cuts eventually may be undermined by a lack of visible results in the real economy. Although cuts currently are widely perceived as essential for Britain's long-term economic health, an upward trending view that slashing public services will cause serious difficulties for families may lead many people to say enough is enough. Sustained high levels of unemployment propelled by public sector job cuts put mounting pressure on relief programs and are unlikely to be regarded kindly by either frustrated job seekers or those who used to be served by the fired employees. Furthermore, confidence in the nation's ability to solve the economic crisis has been falling as unemployment continues to rise. At some point, public spending cuts may seem an inappropriate, unjust and harsh response to a problem that is increasingly viewed as intractable to short-term solutions.

Finally, the fact that valence politics variables do much to drive the composite vote intention model indicates that attitudes toward the spending cuts will not be the sole drivers of party support in the next general election. Rather than respond directly and reflexively to the conditions around them, British voters place economic hardships and policy in broader context with images of party leaders, partisan attachments and more global assessments of party performance. Differing attitudes about the harsh austerity measures are exerting substantial effects on party support, but these attitudes have not negated the force of valence politics considerations. Rather, reactions to the evolving state of the economy coupled with mutable partisan attachments and the more general evaluations of party and leader performance that voters are making can be expected to animate the model in predictable ways in the years ahead. Performance politics remains important for understanding electoral choice in Britain and other mature democracies as the present era of economic hardship and austerity policies unfolds.

References

Achen CH (1992) Social psychology, demographic variables, and linear regression: breaking the iron triangle in voting research. Polit Behav 14(3):195–211

Adams J, Merrill S III, Grofman B (2005) A unified theory of party competition. Cambridge University Press, Cambridge

Bartels L (2008) Unequal democracy: the political economy of the new gilded age. Princeton University Press, Princeton

Berelson BR, Lazarsfeld PF, McPhee WN (1954) Voting. University of Chicago Press, Chicago

Bloomberg.com (2011) U.K. needs Cameron's austerity, but perhaps not so quickly: view. Dec 11: http://www.bloomberg.com/news/2011-12-07/u-k-needs-cameron-s-austerity-program-but-perhaps-not-so-quickly-view.html. Accessed 24 Feb 2012

Borre O, Viegas JM (1995) Government intervention in the economy. In: Borre O, Scarbrough E (eds) The scope of government. Oxford University Press, Oxford, pp 234–280

British Election Study (2011) AV Ballot referendum study. University of Essex, Colchester

Burns JF (2011) British leader pushes for 'can-do optimism' and faith in austerity path. NY Times Oct 6:A10

Butler D, Stokes DE (1969) Political change in Britain. St. Martin's, New York

Campbell A, Converse PE, Miller WE, Stokes DE (1960) The American voter. Wiley, New York

Clarke HD, Kornberg A, Scotto TJ (2009a) Making political choices: Canada and the United States. University of Toronto Press, Toronto

Clarke HD, McCutcheon A (2009) The dynamics of party identification revisited. Public Opin Q 73:704–728

Clarke HD, Sanders D, Stewart MC, Whiteley P (2004) Political choice in Britain. Oxford University Press, Oxford

Clarke HD, Sanders D, Stewart MC, Whiteley P (2009b) Performance politics and the British voter. Cambridge University Press, Cambridge

Confalonieri MA, Newton K (1995) Taxing and spending: tax revolt or tax protest. In: Borre O, Scarbrough E (eds) The scope of government. Oxford University Press, Oxford, pp 121–148

Cutler F (2002) The simplest shortcut of all: sociodemographic characteristics and electoral choice. J Polit 64:466–490

Dalton RJ (2006) Citizen politics, 4th edn. CQ Press, Washington
Downs A (1957) An economic theory of democracy. Harper and Row, New York
Downs A (1960) Why the government budget is too small in a democracy. World Polit 12(4):541–563
Easton D (1965) A systems analysis of political life. Wiley, New York
Fiorina MP (1981) Retrospective voting in American national elections. Yale University Press, New Haven
Franklin C (1992) Measurement and the dynamics of party identification. Polit Behav 14:297–309
Kornberg A, Clarke HD (1992) Citizens and community: political support in a representative democracy. Cambridge University Press, Cambridge
Kumlin S (2007) The Welfare state: values, policy preferences, and performance evaluations. In: The Oxford handbook of political behavior. Oxford University Press, Oxford
Lazarsfeld PF, Berelson B, Gaudet H (1944) In: The people's choice. Duell, Sloan and Pearce, New York
Lewis-Beck MS (1988) Economics and elections: the major western democracies. University of Michigan Press, Ann Arbor
Lewis-Beck MS, Nadeau R, Bélanger E (2011) French presidential elections. Palgrave Macmillan, London
Lewis-Beck MS, Stegmaier M (2000) Economic determinants of electoral outcomes. Annu Rev Pol Sci 3:183–219
Lewis-Beck MS, Jacoby WG, Norpoth H, Weisberg HF (2008) The American voter revisited. University of Michigan Press, Ann Arbor
Lupia A, McCubbins MD (1998) The democratic dilemma: can citizens learn what they need to know? Cambridge University Press, New York
Pierson P (ed) (1993) The new politics of the Welfare state. Oxford University Press, Oxford
Sniderman PM, Brody RA, Tetlock P (1991) Reasoning and choice: explorations in political psychology. Cambridge University Press, Cambridge
Stokes DE (1963) Spatial models of party competition. Am Polit Sci Rev 57(2):368–377
Stokes DE (1992) Valence politics. In: Kavanagh D (ed) Electoral politics. Clarendon, Oxford
Werdigier J (2011) Its growth slowing, Britain extends austerity measures. NY Times Nov 30:B8
Winter S, Mouritzen PE (2001) Why people want something for nothing: the role of asymmetrical illusions. Eur J Polit Res 39:109–143

Modeling Elections with Varying Party Bundles: Applications to the 2004 Canadian Election

Kevin McAlister, Jee Seon Jeon, and Norman Schofield

1 Introduction

Early work in formal political theory focused on the relationship between constituencies and parties in two-party systems. It generally showed that in these cases, parties had strong incentive to converge to the electoral median (Hotelling 1929; Downs 1957; Riker and Ordeshook 1973). These models assumed a one-dimensional policy space and non-stochastic policy choice, meaning that voters would certainly vote for a party. These models showed that there exists a Condorcet point at the electoral median. However, when extended into spaces with more than one dimension, these two-party pure-strategy Nash equilibria generally do not exist. While attempts were made to reconcile this difference, the conditions necessary to assure that there is a pure-strategy Nash equilibrium at the electoral median were strong and unrealistic with regards to actual electoral systems (Caplin and Nalebuff 1991).

Instead of pure-strategy Nash equilibria (PNE) there often exist mixed strategy Nash equilibria, which lie in the subset of the policy space called the uncovered set (Kramer 1978). Many times, this uncovered set includes the electoral mean, thus giving some credence to the median voter theorem in multiple dimensions (Poole and Rosenthal 1984; Adams and Merrill 1999; Merrill and Grofman 1999; Adams

K. McAlister (✉) · J.S. Jeon
Center in Political Economy, Washington University in Saint Louis, 1 Brookings Drive, Saint Louis, MO 63130, USA
e-mail: kevinmcalister@wustl.edu

J.S. Jeon
e-mail: jsjeon@wustl.edu

N. Schofield
Weidenbaum Center, Washington University in St. Louis, Seigle Hall, Campus Box 1027, One Brookings Drive, St. Louis, MO 63130-4899, USA
e-mail: schofield.norman@gmail.com

N. Schofield et al. (eds.), *Advances in Political Economy*,
DOI 10.1007/978-3-642-35239-3_14,

2001). However, this seems at odds with the chaos theorems which apply to multidimensional policy spaces.

The contrast between the instability theorems and the stability theorems suggest that a model in which the individual vote is not deterministic is most appropriate (Schofield et al. 1998; Quinn et al. 1999). This kind of stochastic model states that the voter has a vector of probabilities corresponding to the choices available in the election. This insinuates that if the voter went to the polls for the same election multiple times, he might not make the same vote every time. This model is in line with multiple theories of voter behavior and still yields the desirable property of showing that rational parties will converge to the electoral mean given the simple spatial framework.

Using this framework, Schofield (2007) shows that convergence to the mean need not occur given that valence asymmetries are accounted for. In this context, valence is taken to mean any sorts of quality that a candidates has that is independent of his location within a policy space. In general, valence is linked to the revealed ability of a party to govern in the past or the predicted ability of a party to govern well in the future. In recent years, models with a valence measure have been developed and utilized in studies of this sort. Schofield extends upon these models and demonstrates a necessary and sufficient condition for convergence to the mean, meaning that the joint electoral mean is a local pure-strategy Nash equilibrium (LNE) in the stochastic model with valence.

Valence can generally be divided into two types of valence: aggregate valence (or character valence) and individual valence (or sociodemographic valence). Both types of valence are exogenous to the position that a party takes in an election, meaning that these valence measures rely on some other underlying characteristic. Aggregate valence is a measure of valence which is common to all members in an electorate, and can be interpreted as the average perceived governing ability of a party for all members of an electorate (Penn 2003). Individual valence is a bit more specific, where this kind of valence depends upon the characteristics of a voter. This kind of valence differs from individual to individual. For example, in United States elections, African-American voters are very much more likely to vote for the Democratic candidate than they are to vote for the Republican candidate. Thus, it can be said that the Democratic candidate is of higher valence among African-American voters than the Republican candidate is. Both kinds of valence can be important in determining the outcomes of elections and are necessary to consider when building models of this sort.

Recent empirical work on the stochastic vote model has relied upon the assumption of Type-I extreme value distributed errors (Dow and Endersby 2004). These errors, commonly associated with microeconometric models, are typical of models that deal with individual choice, where individual utility is determined by the valence terms and the individual's distance from the party in the policy space. This distance is weighted by β, a constant that is determined by the average weight that individuals give to their respective distances from the parties. The workhorse of individual choice models is the multinomial logit distribution, which is an extension of the dichotomous response logit distribution. This distribution assumes that the probability that an individual votes for a party follows the Type-I extreme value distribution, thus matching the assumed distribution of the stochastic voting model. This creates a natural empirical partner for the stochastic vote model.

Using this statistical framework and the assumption that individual choice follows this distribution, Schofield (2007) introduced the idea of the convergence coefficient, c, which is a measure of attraction to the electoral mean in an electoral system. This coefficient is unitless, thus it can be compared across models. Low values of this value indicate strong attraction to the electoral mean, meaning that the electoral mean is a local pure-strategy Nash equilibrium (Patty 2005, 2007). High values indicate the opposite. He also lays out a necessary and a sufficient condition for convergence to the electoral mean with regards to the convergence coefficient:

1. When the dimension of the policy space is 2, then the sufficient condition for convergence to the electoral mean is $c < 1$.
2. The necessary condition for convergence is if $c < w$, where w is the number of dimensions of the policy space of interest.

When the necessary condition fails, at least one party will adopt a position away from the electoral mean in equilibrium, meaning that a LNE does not exist at the electoral mean. As a LNE must exist for the point to be a pure strategy equilibrium, this implies non-existence of a PNE at the center. Given the definition of the convergence coefficient, the general conclusion is that the smaller β is, the smaller the valence differences are among candidates, and the lower the variance of the electoral distribution is, the more likely there is to be a LNE at the electoral center.

However, this only answers the question where the local Nash equilibria are in the simplest case of having one electoral mean that parties are responding to. This problem can quickly become more complicated. Imagine a country with five parties and two different regions. Four of the parties run in both regions, and are thus attempting to appeal to voters in both regions. However, one of these parties only runs in one of the regions and is only trying to appeal to the voters of this region. Thus, it would be unreasonable for it to position itself with regards to the electoral mean for the entire electorate. Rather, it wants to maximize its vote share within in the region in which it runs. Parties can choose to run in select regions for a variety of reasons. They may run for historical reasons or responsive reasons or even choose not to run in regions where they know they will not do well at all. As parties have limited resources, sometimes this kind of decision must be made.

In order to assess convergence to the electoral mean in this case, one must take into account the electoral centers that parties are responding to. In the above example, convergence to the electoral mean would mean that the first four parties converge to the overall electoral mean, or the mean of all voters in the electorate, while the fifth party would converge to the electoral mean of those individuals in its respective region. Thus, the convergence coefficient would no longer be appropriate, as it is proven only when the position for all parties is equal to zero on all dimensions. Similarly, when there are parties which run in different combinations of regions, the typical multinomial logit model is no longer appropriate because the underlying assumption of "independence of irrelevant alternatives" (IIA) is no longer met (Train 2003). Given that there are problems with estimation of parameters from the currently utilized empirical methodology and problems with the underlying theoretical mechanism that drives the reasoning behind the convergence coefficient, we are left without the useful information gained about party tendencies in the stochastic model. Under the current framework, researchers can only analyze convergence, valence, and spatial adherence within specific regions. However, in this paper we propose a method for handling more structurally complex electorates.

In this chapter, we introduce methods for analyzing the stochastic vote model in electorates where individuals do not all vote for the same party bundle. First, this chapter will demonstrate that the convergence coefficient first defined by Schofield can be adjusted to handle any vector of party positions. We will determine the first and second order conditions necessary to show that a vector of policy positions is a local Nash equilibrium (LNE). From this, we will show that the convergence coefficient for a more complex electorate can be derived in a similar manner to that used previously. We will also show the necessary and sufficient conditions for convergence. Secondly, we will introduce a method that can be used to estimate the parameters necessary to find equilibria in the model. This empirical model, an extension of the mixed logit model, will utilize the same Type-I extreme value distribution assumptions used previously, but will not rely upon the IIA assumption necessary to use the basic multinomial logit model. This varying choice set logit (VCL: see Yamamoto 2011) will allow for aggregate estimation of parameters to occur while also allowing regional parameters to be estimated. This method of estimation along with the notions of convergence that will allow analysis of the stochastic voting model in more complex situations.

Finally, to illustrate these methods, we will analyze the Canadian elections in 2004. Canada has a regional party which only runs in one region of the country, however, in 2004, the regional party gained seats in the Parliament. As this election is an ideal testing point for these new methods, they can tell us whether or not these new methods give logical results. From this analysis, some insight can be gained as to the way in which parties can organize themselves to maximize the number of votes received.

2 The Formal Stochastic Model

The data in the spatial model is distributed $x_i \in X$ where $i \in N$ represents a member of the electorates's ideal point and n is the number of members in the sample. We assume that X is an open convex subset of Euclidian space, $\mathbb{R}^w$, where w is finite and corresponds to the number of dimensions selected to represent the policy space.

Each of the parties, $j \in P$, where $P = \{1, \dots, j, \dots, p\}$ chooses a policy, $z_j \in X$, to declare to the electorate prior to the election. Let $\mathbf{z} = (z_1, z_2, \dots, z_p)$ be the vector of party positions. Given $\mathbf{z}$, each voter i is described by a vector:

$$u_i(x_i, \mathbf{z}) = \big(u_{i1}(x_i, z_1), u_{i2}(x_i, z_2), \ldots, u_{ip}(x_i, z_p)\big)$$
$$\text{where } u_{ij}(x_i, z_j) = u^*_{ij}(x_i, z_j) + \epsilon_{ij}$$
$$\text{and } u^*_{ij}(x_i, z_j) = \lambda_j - \beta\|z_j - x_i\|^2 + \alpha_{ij}$$

Here, $u^*_{ij}(x_i, z_j)$ is the observable utility for i, associated with party j. λ_j is an exogenous valence term for agent j which is common throughout all members of a population (i.e. party quality).[1] β is a positive constant and $\|.\|$ is the Euclidian distance between individual i and party j.[2] α_{ij} is an exogenous sociodemographic valence term, meaning that this term can be viewed as the average assessment of a party's governing ability to the members of a specific group.[3] The error term, ϵ_{ij} is assumed to be commonly distributed among individuals. In particular, we assume that the cumulative distribution of the errors follows a Type-I extreme value distribution. This is not only the norm in individual choices, it also allows the theoretical model to match the corresponding empirical model, making the transition between the two easier.

Given the stochastic assumption of the model, the probability that i votes for j given z, $\rho_{ij}(z)$ is equal to:

$$\rho_{ij}(\mathbf{z}) = Pr\big[u_{ij}(x_i, z_j) > u_{il}(x_i, z_l),\ \forall l \neq j\big]$$

In turn, we assume that the expected vote share for agent j given $\mathbf{z}$, is $V_j(\mathbf{z})$ where:

$$V_j(\mathbf{z}) = \frac{1}{n} \sum_{\forall i \in N} \rho_{ij}(\mathbf{z})$$

We assume in this model that agent j chooses z_j to maximize $V_j(\mathbf{z})$ given the positions of the other parties. We seek equilibria of the model where each of the parties attempts to maximize vote share.

For the purposes of this paper, when we talk about an equilibria, we refer to a local Nash equilibria (LNE). This definition of equilibrium relies on maximizing the expected vote share gained by a party given the positions of the other parties. A vector of positions, $\mathbf{z}^*$, is said the be a LNE if $\forall j$, z^*_j is a critical point of the

---

[1]This can be conceptualized as an average assessment of the parties quality to govern among all members of the electorate, regardless of sociodemographic identity.

[2]To match up with the empirical applications later in the paper, the utility individual i gains from having party j in office is compared to a base party, $j = 1$. As is normal, we assume this party has a utility of zero and the other utilities are compared to this party. Thus, the utility gained by i by voting for j can also be seen as $u^*_{ij}(x_i, z_j) = \lambda_j - \beta(\sum_{m=1}^{w}((x_{jm} - x_{im})^2 - (x_1m - x_{im})^2)) + \alpha_{ij}$ where the summation is of the Euclidian distances for each dimension of the policy space. This places our model in line with the latent utility models that are commonly used in microeconometric theory and bridges the gap between our theoretical model and the corresponding empirical model.

[3]In this paper, we assume that this term is common among all members of a specific sociodemographic group. However, we can set up these terms to represent individuals with individual level random effects.

vote function and the Hessian matrix of second derivatives is non-positive, meaning that the eigenvalues are all non positive. More simply put, a vector, $\mathbf{z}^*$, is a LNE if each party locates itself at a local maximum in its respective vote function. This means, that given the opportunity to make moves in the policy space and relocate its platform, no vote-maximizing party would choose to move. We assume that parties can estimate how their vote shares would change if they marginally move their policy position. The local Nash equilibrium is that vector z of party positions so that no party may shift position by a small amount to increase its vote share. More formally a LNE is a vector $\mathbf{z} = (z_1, \ldots, z_j, \ldots, z_p)$ such that each $V_j(\mathbf{z})$ is weakly locally maximized at the position z_j. To avoid problems with zero eigenvalues we also define a strict local Nash equilibrium (SLNE) to be a vector that strictly locally maximizes $V_j(\mathbf{z})$. We typically denote an LNE by $\mathbf{z}(K)$ where K refers to the model we consider. Using the estimated MNL coefficients we simulate these models and then relate any vector of party positions, $\mathbf{z}$, to a vector of vote share functions $V(\mathbf{z}) = (V_1(\mathbf{z}), \ldots, V_p(\mathbf{z}))$, predicted by the particular model with p parties.

Given that we have defined the errors as cumulatively coming from a Type-I extreme value distribution, the probability $\rho_{ij}(z)$ has a multinomial logit specification and can be estimated. For each voter i and party j the probability that i votes for j given z is given by:

$$\rho_{ij}(\mathbf{z}) = \frac{\exp(u^*_{ij}(x_i, z_j))}{\sum_{k=1}^{p} \exp(u^*_{il}(x_i, z_k))}$$

$$= \left[1 + \sum_{k \neq j}^{p} \exp(f_k) \right]^{-1}$$

$$\text{where } f_k = \sum_{k=1}^{p} \big(u^*_{il}(x_i, z_k) \big) - \big(u^*_{ij}(x_i, z_j) \big).$$

$$\text{Thus} \quad \frac{d\rho_j(\mathbf{z})}{dz_j} = 2\beta(z_j - x_i) \left[1 \times \left[1 + \sum_{k \neq j}^{p} \exp(f_k) \right] \right]^{-2} \left[\left[\sum_{k \neq j}^{p} \exp(f_k) \right] \right]$$

$$= 2\beta(z_j - x_i) \times \big[\rho_{ij}(\mathbf{z})\big]\big[1 - \rho_{ij}(\mathbf{z})\big]$$

in region k, with population, N_k, of size n_k the first order condition becomes

$$\left.\frac{dV_{jk}(\mathbf{z}_k)}{dz_j}\right|_{z_{-j}=z} = \frac{1}{n_k} 2\beta_k \sum\nolimits_{i \in N_k} \rho_{ijk}(1 - \rho_{ijk})(z_j - x_i) = 0, \tag{1}$$

$$\text{so } z_j = \sum\nolimits_{i \in N_k} w_{ij} x_i, \tag{2}$$

$$\text{where } w_{ij} = \frac{\rho_{ijk}(1 - \rho_{ijk})}{\sum_{k=1} \rho_{ijk}(1 - \rho_{ijk})}. \tag{3}$$

In order to show that points are LNE, we need to show that given $\mathbf{z}$, all agents are located at a critical point of their respective vote functions, $V_j(\mathbf{z})$. Thus, we need to show that the first derivative of the vote function, given $\mathbf{z}$, is equal to zero. Then we need to show the Hessian matrices at these points and compute their eigenvalues.

In this paper, we make two key departures from previous papers that have used this stochastic vote model. First, and certainly the most important departure, we intend to assess convergence in a model where the position vector of interest does not have all of the parties at the joint aggregate electoral origin. As explained before, in cases where there are regional parties that do not run in all parts of an electorate, there is no incentive for these agents to locate at the overall electoral mean. Rather, in line with other median voter results, these parties have incentives to locate at their respective electoral means, meaning that they position themselves on the ideal point of the average voter that actually has the choice to vote for that party. Thus, should we find that parties in an electoral system converge to the electoral mean in equilibrium, we should find that parties that run in all regions of an electorate converge to the joint electoral mean and regional parties converge to their respective regional electoral means. Previous papers have adjusted the scale of the policy space such that the electoral mean corresponds to the origin of the policy space and this allowed for some convenient cancelation to occur in proofs. For the purposes of this paper, though, we cannot make those cancelations and, thus, we are assessing convergence for a general vector of party positions rather than a zero vector. Second, we assume a second kind of valence, an individual valence, that was not previously included in utility equation. We intend to assess convergence to the mean given these individual valence measures as well, showing proofs including these variables.

The first derivative of $V_j(z)$ with respect to one dimension of the policy space is:

$$\frac{dV_j(\mathbf{z})}{dz_j} = \frac{2\beta}{n}\sum_{i=1}^{n}(z_j - x_i)\rho_{ij}(1-\rho_{ij})$$

Of course, a LNE has to be at a critical point, so all the set of possible LNE can be obtained by setting this equation to 0. Note that this derivative is somewhat different than that from earlier works as we do not assume that ρ_{ij} equals ρ_j (being independent of i). This is due to the fact that we do not assume that all parties are located at the electoral mean.

This result is important in a couple of ways. First, we see that the first derivative does not rely on λ_j or α_{ij} in any way aside from the calculation of the probability, ρ_{ij}, that an individual i votes for party j. This is an encouraging result because any resulting measures that assess convergence (i.e. the convergence coefficient) will not depend on the individual level valences. Previously, Schofield (2007) only showed that the convergence coefficient could be calculated when we assume a common valence for agent j across all members of an electorate. This finding allows us to expand the convergence coefficient notion to include these individual level valences as long as they are exogenous of a voter's ideal point. Second, after doing some simple algebra, it is easy to see that when a party locates at its respective electoral mean, the equation always equals zero, meaning that it is always at a critical point. This is also a good result, because it gives further support to the idea that the electoral mean is always a possible LNE.

To test if a critical point is a local maximum in the vote function, thus a LNE, we need a second order condition. The Hessian matrix of second derivatives is a $w \times w$ matrix defined as follows:

- Let $v_t = (x_{1t}, x_{2t}, \ldots, x_{nt})$ be the vector of the tth coordinates of the positions of the n voters and let. Let $z_j = (z_{1j}, z_{2j}, \ldots, z_{tj})$ and $\langle v_t - z_{tj}, v_s - z_{sj} \rangle$ be the scalar product, with $\Delta_0 = [\langle v_t - 0, v_s - 0 \rangle]$ the electoral covariance matrix about the origin.Then diagonal entries of the Hessian for candidate j have the following form:

$$\frac{1}{n}\sum_{i=1}^{n} 2\beta(\rho_{ij})(1-\rho_{ij})\big(2\beta(x_{it}-z_{tj})^2(1-2\rho_{ij})-1\big)$$

- The off diagonal elements have the following form:

$$\frac{1}{n}\sum_{i=1}^{n} 4\beta^2(x_{is}-z_{sj})(x_{is}-z_{tj})\rho_{ij}(1-\rho_{ij})(1-2\rho_{ij})$$

- where $s \neq t$, and $s = 1, \ldots, w$, and $t = 1, \ldots, w$.

Given this matrix, if all w eigenvalues of the Hessian are negative given $\mathbf{z}$, then we can say that the position of interest is a LNE.

Unlike previous models of this sort, there is no characteristic matrix that the Hessian can be reduced to in order to assess whether or not a point is a local Nash equilibria. Thus, for the proper second order test, the eigenvalues of the Hessian must be found. However, as in earlier works, a reduced equation can be used to find a convergence coefficient, a unitless measure of how quickly the second derivative is changing at a given point. This convergence coefficient can be viewed substantively as a measure of how much a rational, vote-optimizing party is attracted to a certain position. As the coefficient becomes large, the party is repelled from the position.

We know that the trace of the Hessian is equal to the sum of the eigenvalues associated with the matrix. In order to be a local maximum, and thus a LNE, the eigenvalues have to all be negative. Thus, the trace of the Hessian must be negative as well in order for the point to be a local maximum. Given the equation for the main diagonal elements, we can see that it relies on β, $\rho_i j$, and the squared distance between the individual's ideal point on one dimension and the party's position on the same dimension. As β and $\rho_i j$ are necessarily positive, the only way in which the second derivative can be negative is if $2\beta(x_i - z_i)^2(1 - 2\rho_{ij})$ is greater than 1. Thus, this is the value of interest when trying to assess whether or not a point is a local maximum. This value can be viewed as the measure of how fast the probability that voter i votes for party j changes as the party makes small moves. We reason that the mean of $2\beta(x_i - z_i)^2(1 - 2\rho_{ij})$ over all voters is an equivalent concept to the convergence coefficient that does not rely on parties being positioned at the electoral origin. However, this is only for one dimension, so the full definition of the convergence coefficient is:

$$c(\mathbf{z}) = \frac{1}{n}\sum_{i=1}^{w}\sum_{i=1}^{n} 2\beta(x_{it} - z_{tj})^2(1 - 2\rho_{ij})$$

In words, the convergence coefficient is equal to the sum of mean values of

$$2\beta(x_i - z_i)^2(1 - 2\rho_{ij})$$

over all individuals in the electorate for each dimension of the policy space. This notion is supported by the fact that when all parties do locate at the electoral origin, this definition of the convergence coefficient is equivalent to the definition provided in Schofield (2007).

Given this definition of the convergence coefficient, we can derive necessary and sufficient conditions for convergence to a given vector of party positions. Given a vector of party positions, a sufficient condition for the vector being a local Nash equilibrium is that $c(\mathbf{z}) < 1$. If $c(\mathbf{z})$ is less than 1, then we can guarantee that the second derivatives with respect to each dimension are less than 0. This eliminates the possibility that the party is located at a saddle point. A *necessary* condition for convergence to the vector of interest is that $c(\mathbf{z}) < w$. However, for the position to be a LNE, each second derivative has to be negative. Thus, each constituent part of $c(\mathbf{z})$ must be less than 1.

It is important to note that a convergence coefficient can be calculated for each party in the electoral system. Previously, given that all of the parties have been attempting to optimize over the same population, an assumption could be made that the highest convergence coefficient would belong to the party which had the lowest exogenous valence. However, with the slight restructuring of the model to include individual level valences and parties which run in singular regions, as ρ_j can no longer be reduced down to a difference of valences, we can no longer make the assumption that the lowest valence party will be the first to move away from the mean should that be equilibrium behavior. In fact, given that there are multiple definitions of valence in the equation and multiple values of these valences for each region, a notion of lowest valence party becomes very difficult to define. Thus, the convergence coefficient should be calculated for each party to ensure a complete analysis of convergence behavior. Then the party with the highest convergence coefficient represents the electoral behavior of the system. Thus, for an electoral system, the convergence coefficient is:

$$c(\mathbf{z}) = \arg_p c_p(z)$$

In summary, the method for assessing whether or not a vector of party positions is a LNE is as follows:

1. Define z*, or the vector of party positions in the policy space.
2. Check that each party position meets the first order condition given the other party positions:

$$\frac{dV_j(z)}{dz_j} = \frac{2\beta}{n}\sum_{t=1}^{w}\sum_{i=1}^{n}(x_i - z_j)\rho_{ij}(1-\rho_{ij}) = 0$$

   - Note that each party's respective electoral mean is a position that is always a critical point in the vote function.

3. Define the Hessian, $C_j(\mathbf{z})$ for each party position as follows:
   - diagonal entries are

$$\frac{1}{n}\sum_{i=1}^{n} 2\beta(\rho_{ij})(1-\rho_{ij})\big(2\beta(x_{it} - z_{tj})^2(1-2\rho_{ij}) - 1\big)$$

   where $t = 1, \dots, w$.
   - The off diagonal elements have the following form

$$\frac{1}{n}\sum_{i=1}^{n} 4\beta^2(x_{is} - z_{js})(x_{it} - z_{jt})\rho_{ij}(1-\rho_{ij})(1-2\rho_{ij})$$

4. Check the eigenvalues for each Hessian. If all of the eigenvalues are negative, the vector of positions is a local Nash equilibrium.
5. The necessary condition that the eigenvalues all be negative is that trace$(C_j(\mathbf{z})) < 0$. Since $\beta(\rho_{ij})(1-\rho_{ij}) > 0$ this reduces to: $\sum_{t=1}^{w}\sum_{i=1}^{n} 2\beta(\rho_{ij})(1-2\rho_{ij})(x_{itw} - z_{tj})^2 < w$.
6. In two dimensions, the further sufficient condition is that det$(C_j(\mathbf{z})) > 0$, which is equivalent to the condition that $\sum_{t=1}^{w}\sum_{i=1}^{n} 2\beta(\rho_{ij})(1-2\rho_{ij})(x_{itw} - z_{iw})^2 < 1$.
7. Calculate the convergence coefficient for each party,

$$c_j(\mathbf{z}) = \frac{1}{n}\sum_{i=1}^{w}\sum_{i=1}^{n} 2\beta(\rho_{ij})(1-2\rho_{ij})(x_{itw} - z_{iw})^2$$

   The convergence coefficient, labelled $c(\mathbf{z})$, represents the electoral system.
   - If $c(\mathbf{z}) > w$, then we cannot have convergence. If, however $c(\mathbf{z}) < 1$, then the sufficient condition is satisfied, and the system converges to the vector of interest. If $c(\mathbf{z}) \leq w$, check the components of $c_j(z)$ in dimension w, if all are less than 1, then the system converges to $\mathbf{z}$.
   - To compare this general model with the one presented in Schofield (2007), suppose that all parties adopt the same position at the electoral mean $\mathbf{z} = 0$. Then ρ_{ij} is independent of i. We let Δ_0 be the w by w electoral covariance matrix about the origin. Then

- $$C_j(\mathbf{z}) = (\rho_j)(1-\rho_j)4\beta^2(1-2\rho_j)\Delta_0(1-2\beta I)$$

where I is the w by w identity matrix. Since $(\rho_j)(1-\rho_j)(2\beta) > 0$, we can identify the Hessian with the matrix

$$C_j^*(\mathbf{z}) = \left[2\beta(1-2\rho_j)\Delta_0 - I\right]$$

Thus the eigenvalues are determined by the necessary condition trace$(C_j^*(\mathbf{z})) \leq w$, which we can write as

$$\mathbf{c} = 2\beta(1-2\rho_j)\,\mathrm{trace}(\Delta_0) \leq w$$

It can also be shown that the sufficient condition for convergence, in two dimensions, is given by $\mathbf{c} = 2\beta(1-2\rho_j)\,\mathrm{trace}(\Delta_0) < 1$.

3 Estimation Strategies Given Varying Party Bundles

In order to utilize the stochastic election model proposed above, we need to have measures of valence, both aggregate and individual, for each party in the system, and an estimation of β along with the data in order to analyze equilibrium positions within the system. Typically, given the assumptions of the model, it is an easy translation of data to conditional logit model to equilibrium analysis. However, this is only true when all of the voters exist in one region. In other words, this only works when all voters vote with the same bundle of alternatives on the ballot. However, as shown in the beginning, when there are regional parties in a country which only run in one region, and are thus on the ballot for only a fraction of members of an electorate, the situation quickly becomes more complicated.

The reason that a new method is necessary is that multinomial logit models are reliant upon the assumption of independence of irrelevant alternatives. Simply put, IIA is a statement that requires that all odds ratios be preserved from group to group, even if the choice sets are different.

1. When IIA is violated, the multinomial logit specification is incorrect if we want to do any estimation procedures with this data.

Yamamoto (2011) proposed an appropriate model, called the *varying choice set logit model* (VCL). This model, which follows the same specification as the typical multinomial logit model when Type-I extreme value errors are assumed, is the same as used above to derive the convergence coefficient, that is:

$$\rho_{ij}(\mathbf{z}) = \frac{\exp(u_{ij}^*(x_i, z_j))}{\sum_{k=1}^{p}\exp(u_{ik}^*(x_i, z_k))}$$

Thus the framework of the formal model and the empirical model still match, allowing easy transition from empirical estimations of parameters to analyzing the equilibria of the system given the parameters.

The VCL differs from typical logistic regression models, though, by not relying on the IIA assumption. This is done by allowing there to be individual logistic regression models for each choice set type then aggregating these estimates to make an aggregate estimate of valence for the entire electorate. In this case, each choice set type is seen as a region, as each region has a different bundle of parties offered to voters. In these models, we can assume that parameters are common to all regions in an electorate or that the parameters have values that are region specific. For example, in our model, we assume that β is common to all members of the electorate regardless of region. On the other hand, we assume that both types of valence are individual specific; the VCL is able to accommodate parameters of both types by using a random effects hierarchical structure, meaning that the parameters estimated for each region are assumed to come from some probability distribution, generally a normal distribution. This method of estimation is best done utilizing random effects.

The VCL model uses random effects for the individual choice set types, meaning that for each individual type of choice set in an electorate, we estimate the parameters of interest for the individuals within that choice set. Then, using these estimates, we assume that these individual estimates come from their own distribution, and we use that to determine the best aggregate estimate for a parameter within the model. For our model, we assume the following specification for the observed utility gained by voter i from voting for party j:

$$u_{ij}^*(x_i, z_j) = \lambda_j + \beta \|z_j - x_i\| + \mu_{jr} + \xi_{jrs}$$

where λ_j is the aggregate estimate of the exogenous valence of party j and β and Euclidian distance between voter and party has the same interpretation as within the formal model. μ_{jr} is the added utility over the aggregate valence that the average individual from region r get for voting for party j and ξ_{jrs} is the added utility over μ_{jr} that the average member from sociodemographic group s gets from voting for party j. This clearly hierarchical specification of valence lends itself very well to the VCL model. As with typical logit models, the probability that voter i votes for party j follows the typical logit specification, which states that the probability that the voter votes for party j is the ratio of the exponentiated utility of voting for j to the sum of the utility gained for voting for each party. This model clearly lines up with the formal model specified before and makes the VCL a very attractive choice when attempting to estimate parameters from an electorate with a clear regional structure.

Using the VCL, however, places a few light assumptions on the model, as any estimation procedure does. First, given the structure of the utility equation, we assume that β is common over all members of the electorate, regardless of region or sociodemographic group. This is not a departure from previous papers which have utilized this assumption. This simply means that individuals only differ in how they view each of the parties and not how much weight they apply to the differences between their ideal points and the parties' ideal points. Second, by virtue of the usage of random effects, this model assumes that each of the regional and sociodemographic group random effects are orthogonal to the other covariates in the model. Simply put, we assume that these random effects for each person are independent of one's position within the policy space. Third, by virtue of our usage of the VCL model, we assume that a party's decision to run in a specific region is exogenous of its perceived success within that region. This assumption can be troublesome in some electoral systems where parties frequently do not remain on the same ballots from year to year. However, many electoral systems with regional parties have parties which are historically bound to one region or another. Thus, when we assume that parties historically choose to run in a region, this model is appropriate. When all three of these assumptions are met by the electorate of interest the VCL is a flexible choice of estimation procedure.

The reason that the varying choice set logit (VCL) is the superior method when handling electorates with multiple regions is that it relaxes the IIA assumption while also providing us with the most information from the model. VCL relaxes IIA by allowing each of the parameters to be estimated within each group and allowing these parameters to derive the aggregate estimation of parameters through the notion of partial pooling. Partial pooling is best achieved through hierarchical modeling and through the use of random effects. VCL can be viewed as a specific kind of mixed logit model, meaning that the mixed logit model can be used to achieve the same aggregate results. However, given the structure of VCL, parameter estimates can be achieved for each choice set type (i.e. region) rather than for each individual, demonstrating a significant efficiency gain over the standard mixed logit model. Similarly, mixed logit does not allow the researcher to estimate choice set specific values of parameters, thus VCL is more efficient and informative. Another alternative is the multinomial probit model, which does not rely on the IIA assumption either. However, the multinomial probit model does not allow the researched to estimate parameters at the level of the individual choice set, as the errors are absorbed in the error matrix and, thus, the IIA itself is absorbed. However, as with the mixed logit, the individual regional values are often of as much interest as the parameter values, so the mixed probit is essentially discarding information that the researcher may find useful. Thus, we opt to use the VCL method when examining the behavior of parties in an electorate with party choice sets that vary over the electorate.

The structure of the VCL lends itself to Bayesian estimation methods very easily. While random effects can be estimated in a frequentist manner, as is demonstrated with Yamamoto's (2011) expectation-maximization algorithm for estimation using the VCL, the implementation of the estimation procedure is much easier in a Bayesian hierarchical setting. Assuming that each of the parameters of interest (both random effects and fixed effects) come from commonly used statistical distributions, generally those within the Gamma family, a Gibbs sampler is easily set up and can be utilized to garner estimates of the parameters of interest.

For applications to this model, we make a few assumptions about the underlying distributions of the parameters of interest. We assume that β, λ_j, and the random effects all have underlying normal distributions. Further, we assume that all of these distributions are independent of one another. This assumption follows from our assumptions that the variables, and thus the draws in the Gibbs sampler, are all orthogonal. We could easily assume that each level of the hierarchy (aggregate, region, sociodemographic) comes from a multivariate normal within itself. However, time spent with this model has shown that this assumption is taxing computationally, adding to the amount of time it takes the Gibbs sampler to converge and yielding results that are virtually indiscernible from those garnered when independence is assumed. However, it is unreasonable to assume that the orthogonality assumption is perfectly met. For example, in some cases, region and location within the policy space are correlated (as in Canada). This assumption violation will lead to biased estimators. While the bias is not large, it is certainly a cause for some concern. However, this problem is easily fixed.

Gelman et al. (2008) utilize a method to rid random effects of the collinearity which causes the estimates to be biased. They propose that the problem is solved very simply by adding the mean of the covariate of interest as a predictor a level lower in the hierarchy than the random effect of interest. In this case, given a specific party, the mean of its regional level random effects and the mean of its sociodemographic level random effects are indeed situated at the respective mean of the difference of Euclidian differences between the party of interest and the base party. Given that this is the covariate that will theoretically be correlated with sociodemographic group and region, this is the mean that we need to include as a predictor in the random effects. In doing this, the researcher controls for the discrepancy as if it is an omitted variable and allows the random effect to take care of its own correlation. The normal priors in this case can still be diffuse, but the mean needs to be at the specified value to fix the problem.

One practical note is necessary regarding the time necessary to achieve convergence within the model. Convergence of the VCL can be quite slow given a large number of choice set types and individual observations. Similarly, as random effects are estimated for each party, the number of parties and the number of sociodemographic groups can slow down the rate at which samples are derived from the Gibbs sampler. Though it is a time consuming method, the sheer amount of information gained from the VCL is, thus, the best choice when it is necessary to use a discrete choice model which does not rely on IIA.

4 Application to Canadian Elections

In recent history, Canadians have elected at least three different parties to the Federal legislature and 2004 was no different. However, the 2004 election in Canada was significant because it yielded the first minority government for Canada since 1979. The Liberal Party gained the most seats (135 seats) and the largest percentage of the vote (36.7 percent), however it failed to gain a majority of the seats in Parliament and needed to form a coalition government in order to control the legislature. Paul Martin and the Liberals initially formed a coalition with the New Democratic Party (NDP), a liberal party whose support increased from the 2000 elections, in

Table 1 Actual and sample vote percentages

	Actual	Sample—All	Sample—Quebec
Liberal	36.71	34.34	25.13
NDP	15.65	18.45	8.02
Conservative	29.66	31.55	9.01
Green	4.29	3.71	2.68
BQ	12.42	11.95	55.08

order to control government (19 seats, 15.7 percent). The Liberal Party's main opponent was the newly formed Conservative Party of Canada, the party formed by the merger of the Alliance Party and the Progressive Conservative party, which significantly chipped into the Liberal's vote share. After splitting support in the 2000 elections, the merger of the two parties gave the Conservative Party hope of controlling the Canadian government. Given exposure of scandal within the Liberal Party, the Conservative Party and the Liberal Party were neck and neck in the weeks leading up to the elections. However, the relative inexperience of the new party led to key mistakes prior to the elections and the Conservative Party was not able to garner a seat majority and was not able to form a coalition to control government.

Perhaps the most interesting aspect of the 2004 Canadian elections was Quebec's regional party, Bloc Quebecois (BQ). The BQ only ran in Quebec and, thus, was only on the ballot for approximately twenty percent of Canadians. However, their support within the region was overwhelming, with nearly fifty percent of Quebec voters voting for the party. This strong showing put quite a dent in the Liberal Party's showing within the region and made the BQ a significant player in the Canadian parliament (54 seats, 12.4 percent). Similarly, while not quite on the scale of the BQ, the Green Party was another small party which undoubtedly played a part in reducing the vote share of the Liberal Party. Though support for the party increased in the 2004 elections, its small initial voter base kept it from receiving any seats within parliament. However, it did gain a significant portion of votes in the election (0 seats, 4.3 percent).

To study the 2004 Canadian election we used the survey data for Canada collected by Blais et al. (2006). Table 1 shows vote shares within the sample and the overall vote shares. The similarity between these two sets of shares suggests that the sample is fairly representative of the Canadian electorate. Table 1 also has columns for those voters within Quebec, as Bloc Quebecois only ran within Quebec.

The factor analysis performed on the voters' responses in the survey questions led us to conclude that there were two factors or policy dimensions: one "social," the other "decentralization." The social dimension is a weighted combination of voters' attitudes towards (1) the gap between poor and rich, (2) helping women, (3) gun control, (4) the war in Iraq and (5) their position the left-right scale. We coded the social dimension such that lower values imply higher interest in social programs so as to have a left-right scale along this axis. The decentralization dimension included voters' attitudes towards (1) the welfare state, (2) their standard of living, (3) inter-jurisdictional job mobility, (4) helping Quebec and (5) the influence of

Table 2 Survey items

Inequality	How much to you think should be done to reduce the gap between the rich and the poor in Canada? (1) much more—(5) much less
Women	How much do you think should be done for women? (1) much more—(5) much less
Gun Only police/military	Only the police and the military should be allowed to have guns. (1) strongly agree—(4) strongly disagree
Iraq War	As you may know, Canada decided not to participate in the war against Iraq. Do you think this was a good decision or a bad decision? (1) good decision (2) bad decision
Left-Right	In politics, people sometimes talk of left and right. Where would you place yourself on the scale below? (0) left—(11) right
Welfare	The welfare state makes people less willing to look after themselves. (1) strongly disagree—(4) strongly agree
Standard of Living	The government should see to it that everyone has a decent standard of living. (1) leave people behind (2) Don't leave people
Quebec	How much do you think should be done for Quebec? (1) much more—(5) much less
Moving Cross Region	If people can't find work in the region where they live, they should move to where the jobs are? (1) strongly disagree—(4) strongly agree
Federal-provincial	In general, which government looks after your interests better? (1) provincial (2) no difference (3) federal

Federal versus Provincial governments in their lives. A greater desire for decentralization implies higher values on this axis. The questions used in the factor analysis can be found in Table 2.

Using the factor loadings given in Table 3, we computed the value for each voter along the social and decentralization dimensions. The mean and median values of voters' positions along these two dimensions in Canada are at the electoral origin, (0; 0). To illustrate, a voter who thinks that more should be done to reduce the gap between rich and poor would tend to be on the left of the Social axis (x axis), while a voter who believes that the federal government does a better job of looking after peoples' interests would have a negative position on the D axis (y axis), and could be regarded as opposed to decentralization.

The survey asked voters which party they would be voting for, so we estimated party positions as the mean of voters for that party. The party positions in the policy space are given by the vector:

Table 3 Weighting coefficients for Canada

Components	Social	Decentralization
Inequality	0.36	−0.03
Women	0.35	0.07
Gun only police/military	0.20	0.52
Iraq War	0.30	0.20
Left-Right	0.38	−0.06
Welfare	0.37	−0.17
Standard of Living	0.38	−0.05
Quebec	−0.35	0.00
Moving cross region	0.27	−0.48
Federal-provincial	−0.09	−0.65
SD ($\sqrt{var}$)	1.67	1.07
% Var	28	11
Cumulative % Var	28	39

$$z^* = \begin{bmatrix} & Lib. & Con. & NDP & Grn. & BQU \\ S & -0.17 & 1.27 & -0.78 & -0.63 & -1.48 \\ D & -0.38 & 0.32 & 0.05 & -0.13 & 0.23 \end{bmatrix}$$

These party positions correspond closely with those estimated by Benoit and Laver (2006), obtained using expert opinions in 2000. As with these estimates, the Liberal Party locates to the left on the social access while the Conservative party lies in the upper right quadrant, as shown in Fig. 1. Figure 1 also shows the distribution of voters in Canada. From this, we see that most voters have a moderately leftist view on social issues and are fairly evenly split on decentralization issues, with most voters lying right in the middle. In Fig. 1, the "Q" represents the electoral mean within Quebec, which is noticeably left of the overall electoral mean. Figure 2 shows the voter distribution for Quebec only. The majority of voters in Quebec advocate more liberal social policies than the average voter in Canada. Similarly, voters in Quebec tend to want more decentralization of government, as Quebec has a strong regional identity and wants to maintain its somewhat independent state. This, along with the differences that are easily seen from the two plots, are evidence that the two regions have strong regional identities.

The survey also collected sociodemographic data. For each respondent, sex, age, and education level were recorded. Age was divided into four categories: 18–29, 30–49, 50–65, 65 and older. Education was divided into three categories: No High School Diploma, High School Diploma but No Bachelors, Bachelors or Higher. Due to the structure of the VCL and the underlying random effects model, sociodemographics are viewed as categorical so that groups can be made. As noted previously, parsimony is very important in the VCL model as the time to convergence and the time necessary to run the Gibbs sampler can be long (each sociodemographic group

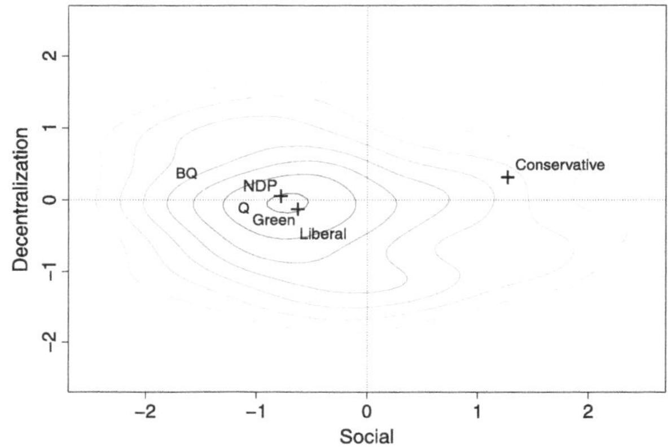

Fig. 1 Distribution of voters and party positions for Canada in 2004

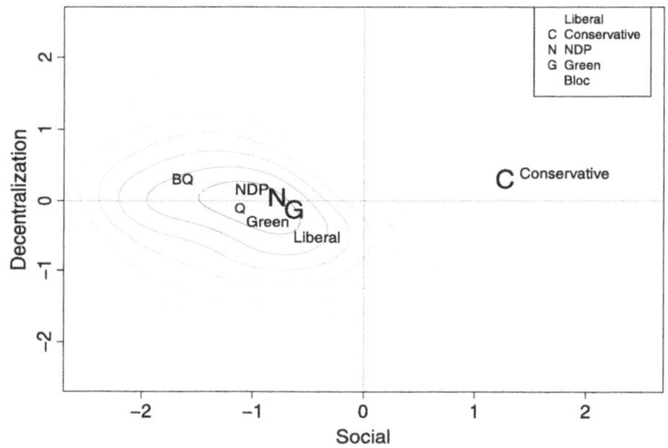

Fig. 2 Distribution of voters and party positions for Quebec in 2004

has a random effect for each region being considered), thus it is always a good idea to examine the relationships between the variables and see if it makes sense to keep them all in the model. In this case, after toying with the model for some time, it seemed that the relationship between sex and vote was yielded spurious by age and education. Thus, to preserve time and allow the Gibbs sampler to run efficiently, our model does not include sex as a variable.

Using the varying choice set logit proposed earlier, we estimate β and the valences for a model with sociodemographics. For the model, given some correlation between the random effects of interest and the independent variable of Euclidian difference, we use the random effects correction procedure proposed earlier. We include the mean difference for each party in each region's respective random effects by setting the mean of the normal priors to the random effects at this value. To assist in convergence of the VCL, we create a diffuse gamma hyperprior for the variance of each prior. As stated before, this model does take a while to converge, so it is necessary to let the Gibbs sampler for this model run a while. We ran each Gibbs sampler for around 100,000 iterations and received nice normal distributions for each of the parameters of interest. Similarly, allowing the Gibbs sampler to run this long reduces the effects of the inherent autocorrelation that occurs in the sampler.

The results of the VCL are shown in Table 4. We show the VCL estimates of the parameter values and the corresponding 95 percent credible intervals. In this example, we use the Liberal Party as the base group, thus their valence is always restricted at 0. For the model, we report β and the aggregate valences first. We then report the regional effect for each party. While the sociodemographic random effect values may be of substantive interest sometimes, they are included simply as controls in this case, thus we do not report these values. We also report the deviance information criterion (DIC), which is a hierarchical model analogue to AIC or BIC. When the posterior distribution is assumed to be multivariate normal (as it is in this case), the DIC functions as a measure of model quality rewarding a model with a small number of parameters, but penalizing a model that does not fit the data well. The DIC can be seen as a measure of the log-likelihood of the posterior density. Lower values of DIC are preferred.

From this model, we can see a number of things. First, as would have been predicted before running the model, the Liberal Party is the highest valence party in Canada outside of Quebec. However, the Conservative Party is almost equivalent in valence level. By simply adding the aggregate valence to the Non-Quebec regional random effect, we can see that the two are almost equivalent in valence outside of Quebec. However, this model shows that the BQ is, in fact, the highest valence party in Canada. This makes sense, given that of the people that could actually vote for the party, nearly 50 percent of them did. This exemplifies one of the strengths of this model, which is that it accurately specifies this party as the highest valence party, even though it is only available to around 25 percent of the electorate. Thus, if we view parties as entities that look down and see a uniform electorate of members without specific regional affiliation or sociodemographic groups, then they would estimate that BQ is the highest valence party.

Outside of Quebec, as mentioned before, the Conservative Party and the Liberal Party are the highest valence parties, with almost equivalent valence. The NDP is of somewhat lower valence as the party simply does not have the same presence as its larger Liberal counterpart. However, its valence and positioning in the preference space of Canada allows it to be a significant competitor outside of Quebec. The lowest valence party outside of Quebec is the Green Party, which makes plenty of sense as it is was (and is still) more of a one-issue dimension party and fails to have mass appeal to the electorate.

Inside Quebec, BQ is the highest valence party, with an even larger valence than that estimated by the aggregate valence measure. The Liberal Party also has a strong presence in Quebec; however, given that BQ and the Liberal Party are in similar areas of the preference space, they compete for many of the same voters and BQ simply has a stronger presence in Quebec. The Conservative Party is of somewhat lower valence within Quebec, as it fails to draw voters that instead choose to vote for BQ. The lowest valence party in Quebec is also the Green Party.

Recall that we are interested in finding where the parties will locate in the policy space in order to maximize their vote share. Because the outcome of the election

Table 4 2004 Canada VCL model given sociodemographics (LPC base)

	NDP		Conservatives		Greens		BQ	
β				0.2598 (0.2234, 0.2976)				
λ_j	−0.5883 (−1.678, 0.4625)		−0.0864 (−1.057, 1.107)		−1.826 (−3.446, 0.2405)		0.4525 (−0.9229, 2.322)	
	NQ	Q	NQ	Q	NQ	Q	NQ	Q
μ_{rj}	0.0341	−0.6085	0.0655	−0.1827	−0.4038	−0.4915	–	0.1797
	(−1.014, 1.127)	(−1.778, 0.4704)	(−1.135, 1.04)	(−1.465, 0.8110)	(−2.493, 1.217)	(−2.720, 1.062)	–	(−1.67, 1.565)
DIC				2029.291				

depends on these vote shares, we assume that parties use polls and other information at their disposal to form an idea of the anticipated election outcome and then use this information to find their most preferred position taking into account their estimates of where other parties will locate.

One possibility is that all parties will locate at their respective electoral means, meaning that $\mathbf{z}^*$ is as follows:

$$\mathbf{z}^* = \begin{bmatrix} & Lib. & Con. & NDP & Grn. & BQU \\ S & 0 & 0 & 0 & 0 & -1.11 \\ D & 0 & 0 & 0 & 0 & -0.08 \end{bmatrix}$$

Notice that this means that BQ will not locate at the same position as the other parties as it only runs in Quebec, so its regional mean is at the mean of voters in Quebec. Given this vector of party positions and the information about the voter ideal points, we can calculate the Hessian of the vote function for each party as well as the convergence coefficient, $c(\mathbf{z}^*)$ for each party. For the Hessians, we are interested in the eigenvalues associated with the Hessians for each party; if they are both negative, then the Hessian is negative definite and the party location is at a local maximum. Given $\mathbf{z}^*$, if any of the Hessians are not negative definite, then one of the parties will not choose to locate at this position in equilibrium. Similarly, we can check the convergence coefficients to see if they meet the necessary condition for convergence. Given that any of these conditions fail, the party for which they fail will choose to move elsewhere in the policy space at equilibrium and. Given that the Green Party is the lowest valence party in both regions, as well as at the aggregate level, we can assume that if a party is going to move, it will be the Green Party. We now examine the Hessians and $c(\mathbf{z}^*)$ for each party.

$$\mathcal{H}_{Lib} = \begin{bmatrix} -0.0365 & -0.0004 \\ -0.0004 & -0.0705 \end{bmatrix}; \quad \mathcal{H}_{NDP} = \begin{bmatrix} 0.0021 & 0.0012 \\ 0.0012 & -0.0362 \end{bmatrix}$$

$$\mathcal{H}_{Con} = \begin{bmatrix} -0.0326 & -0.0002 \\ -0.0002 & -0.0676 \end{bmatrix}; \quad \mathcal{H}_{GPC} = \begin{bmatrix} 0.0085 & 0.0085 \\ 0.0085 & -0.0091 \end{bmatrix}$$

$$\mathcal{H}_{BQ} = \begin{bmatrix} -0.1194 & 0.0034 \\ 0.0034 & -0.1286 \end{bmatrix}$$

$$eigen(\mathcal{H}|z^*) = \begin{bmatrix} & Lib. & NDP & Con. & Grn. & BQ \\ Eigen1 & -0.0365 & 0.0021 & -0.0326 & 0.0085 & -0.1183 \\ Eigen2 & -0.0705 & -0.0361 & -0.0676 & -0.0092 & -0.1297 \end{bmatrix}$$

$$c_j(\mathbf{z}^*) = \begin{bmatrix} & Lib. & NDP & Con. & Grn. & BQ \\ c(\mathbf{z}^*) & 1.031 & 1.518 & 1.071 & 1.945 & -0.5921 \end{bmatrix}$$

From the Hessian's and their corresponding eigenvalues, we can see that two parties will diverge from the vector of electoral means. The NDP and the Green Party both have positive eigenvalues, meaning that $\mathbf{z}^*$ is not a vote maximizing position for them and, thus, not a LNE. It is interesting to note that both of these parties $\mathbf{z}^*$ is a saddle point. Thus, when they choose a better position, it will still be on the mean of the decentralization axis as the second eigenvalue represents that axis.

We can also utilize the test of convergence coefficients to assess convergence to the vector of interest. Here, we see that all of the convergence coefficients, except for BQ's, are greater than one but less than w (which in this case is 2),[4] thus we need to check the largest one to see if it indicates convergence to the mean vector. The largest convergence coefficient belongs to the Green Party and examination of the constituent portions of its $c(\mathbf{z}^*)$ shows:

$$c_{GPC}(\mathbf{z}^*) = 1.379 + 0.5657$$

where 1.379 corresponds to the social axis. This means that the Green Party is not maximizing its vote share at the mean social position. These values indicate that the Green Party is also located at a saddle point when given the mean vector, just as the Hessian test did.

However, taken as they are, we do not know if these two tests actually match the vote maximizing tendencies of the parties. Thus, in order to give validity to the proposed tests, we need to use optimization methods to show that the vote maximizing positions for parties are not located on the mean vector. In a Gibbs sampling style of optimizer, we create an optimization method in which each party optimizes its vote share given the positions of the other parties. If we do this for each party in rotation beginning at some arbitrary starting values, the parties should eventually converge on the equilibrium set of positions where no party can do any better by moving given the positions of the other party. This method is necessary given that each party can potentially be optimizing over a different portion of the electorate. In this case, while the other four parties are attempting to optimize their respective vote shares over all of Canada, BQ is only trying to optimize its vote share among those voters in Quebec. Thus, this style of optimizer is necessary for finding the optimizing positions in Canada.

Figure 3 shows the vote optimizing positions for each party in Canada, which are as follows:

$$z^*_{opt} = \begin{bmatrix} & \mathit{Lib.} & \mathit{Con.} & \mathit{NDP} & \mathit{Grn.} & \mathit{BQ} \\ S & 0.0524 & 0.0649 & 1.099 & 2.337 & -1.069 \\ D & -0.0259 & -0.0264 & 0.0266 & 0.2281 & -0.1290 \end{bmatrix}$$

Fortunately for our measures, the vote optimizing positions echo what we were told by the convergence coefficients: the NDP and the Green Party have incentive to move away from the electoral mean while the other parties want to stay there. Given that these two parties are of relatively low valence, their relocation has little effect on the maximizing positions for the largest three parties. However, in accordance with

[4] It is interesting to note that the convergence coefficient need not be positive, as is the case with $c_{BQ}(z^*)$. This simple indicates a particularly strong desire to stay in the given position. A negative convergence coefficient indicates a quickly changing local maximum, meaning that a small departure from this position would result in a large decrease in vote share.

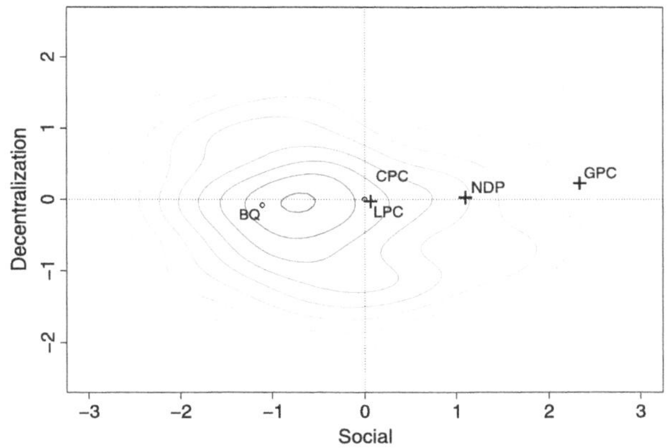

Fig. 3 Vote maximizing positions in Canada 2004

Table 5 Vote shares given various z^*s

	Current	Mean	Optimal
LPC	36.71	33.42	33.43
CPC	29.66	33.34	33.29
NDP	15.65	17.89	16.96
GPC	4.29	3.55	3.80
BQ	12.42	11.79	12.52

the equilibrium theory of proposed by Schofield (2007), the parties locate along the same axis, with distances away from their electoral means proportional to their respective perceived valence differences.

This begs the question, though, how much better can the parties do at these positions than they did at their current positions? Table 5 shows the vote shares in the sample for each party at their current positions, at the electoral mean, and at the vote maximizing positions determined by the optimization routine. These vote shares are predicted using the actual valences from each region (i.e. the aggregate valences plus the regional random effects).

This table strengthens our notion that the vector of means is not a LNE as the Green Party, the BQ, and the Liberals all do better when the Green Party and the NDP locate away from the mean. As the Green Party is one of the parties that is dissatisfied with the electoral mean, it can choose to move to a more extreme position and do better. The NDP is forced to adapt and do worse than it would if the parties all located at their respective electoral means.

5 Conclusion

In this paper, we proposed a method for examining the vote maximizing positions of parties in electoral systems with parties that do not run in every region. When parties do not run in every region, different voters have different party bundles at the polls and existing theories of valence and empirical methods for estimating valence are no longer appropriate. We proposed a more generalized notion of the convergence coefficient which is able to handle any generalized vector of party positions and tell us whether or not these positions are a local Nash equilibrium for the given electoral system. We also proposed a new method for estimating the parameters necessary to utilize the convergence coefficient that does not rely on the IIA assumption. Though methods of doing so already exist, the sheer amount of information gained from the Varying Choice Set Logit makes it the ideal model to run when examining voting tendencies within complex electorates that have clear hierarchical structures.

Using these methods, we examined the 2004 Canadian elections. Using the new empirical methods, we found that even though it only ran in Quebec, a region that makes up around 25 percent of Canada's population, the Bloc Quebecois was the highest valence party in Canada in the 2004 elections. Using these empirical findings, we found that parties were not able to maximize their respective vote shares by locating at the joint electoral mean, which included BQ locating at the mean of voters in Quebec and not at the join electoral mean. Rather, the lower valence parties were able to maximize vote shares by taking more extreme positions within the policy space. This finding is in direct contrast of widely accepted theories that political actors can always maximize their vote shares by taking positions at the electoral center.

Given the accurate outcomes of these methods, there are a number of more complex situations in which these methods can be used. First, this type of model is not limited to the two region case and can be applied to cases where there are numerous "party bundles" which arise in a nation's electorate. A region, in this case, is equivalent to a party bundle; thus, a region can be a combination of many regions (the case when a party runs in two out of three regions, for example). Similarly, in further uses of this model, it is possible to examine equilibria where parties have perfect information about each of the voters, meaning that parties know each voter's region, sociodemographic group, and ideal point. Given this information, new equilibria can be computed and differences can be examined. This further demonstrates the general nature of the new definition of the convergence coefficient and its ability to handle an even wider variety of electorate types than previously.

Appendix

This appendix gives the algorithm for the Gibbs sampling.

```
model{

for(i in 1:N) {
for(k in 1:K) {
v[i,k] <- alpha[k] + beta[1]*(d[(N*(k-1))+i]-d[i]) +
```

```
m[region[i],k] + ed[region[i], education[i], k] +
ag[region[i],education[i],age[i],k]

expv[i,k] <- exp(v[i,k])
pv[i,k] <- expv[i,k]/sum(expv[i,1:K])
vote[i]  ~ dcat(pv[i, 1:K])
}}

beta[1] ~ dnorm(0,taub[1])I(-5,5)

alpha[1] <- 0
alpha[2] ~ dnorm(0,taua[2])
alpha[3] ~ dnorm(0,taua[3])
alpha[4] ~ dnorm(0,taua[4])
alpha[5] ~ dnorm(0,taua[5])

m[1,1] <- 0
m[1,2] ~ dnorm(0,taum[1,2])
m[1,3] ~ dnorm(0,taum[1,3])
m[1,4] ~ dnorm(0,taum[1,4])
m[1,5] <- -100000
m[2,1] <- 0
m[2,2] ~ dnorm(0,taum[2,2])
m[2,3] ~ dnorm(0,taum[2,3])
m[2,4] ~ dnorm(0,taum[2,4])
m[2,5] ~ dnorm(0,taum[2,5])

taub[1] ~ dgamma(.1,.1)I(.1,10)
taua[2] ~ dgamma(.1,.1)I(.1,10)
taua[3] ~ dgamma(.1,.1)I(.1,10)
taua[4] ~ dgamma(.1,.1)I(.1,10)
taua[5] ~ dgamma(.1,.1)I(.1,10)
taum[1,2]~dgamma(.1,.1)I(.1,10)
taum[1,3]~dgamma(.1,.1)I(.1,10)
taum[1,4]~dgamma(.1,.1)I(.1,10)
taum[2,2]~dgamma(.1,.1)I(.1,10)
taum[2,3]~dgamma(.1,.1)I(.1,10)
taum[2,4]~dgamma(.1,.1)I(.1,10)
taum[2,5]~dgamma(.1,.1)I(.1,10)

for(f in 1:e){
ed[1,f,5] <- -10000
}

for(f in 1:e){
for(z in 1:4){
ed[1,f,z] ~ dnorm(0,taued[1,f,z])
taued[1,f,z] ~ dgamma(.01,.01)I(.01,10)
}}
```

```
for(f in 1:e){
for(z in 1:5){
ed[2,f,z] ~ dnorm(0,taued[2,f,z])
taued[2,f,z] ~ dgamma(.01,.01)I(.01,10)
}}

for(f in 1:e){
for(w in 1:a){
ag[1,f,w,5] <- -10000
}}

for(f in 1:e){
for(z in 1:4){
for(w in 1:a){
ag[1,f,w,z] ~ dnorm(0,tauag[1,f,w,z])
tauag[1,f,w,z] ~ dgamma(.01,.01)I(.01,10)
}}}

for(f in 1:e){
for(z in 1:5){
for(w in 1:a){
ag[2,f,w,z] ~ dnorm(0,tauag[2,f,w,z])
tauag[2,f,w,z] ~ dgamma(.01,.01)I(.01,10)
}}}

for(f in 1:e){
for(z in 1:4){
for(w in 1:a){
tot[1,f,w,z] <- alpha[z] + m[1,z] + ed[1,f,z] + ag[1,f,w,z]
}}}

for(f in 1:e){
for(z in 1:5){
for(w in 1:a){
tot[2,f,w,z] <- alpha[z] + m[2,z] + ed[2,f,z] + ag[2,f,w,z]
}}}
}
```

References

Adams J (2001) Party competition and responsible party government. University of Michigan Press, Ann Arbor

Adams J, Merrill S III (1999) Modeling party strategies and policy representation in multiparty elections: why are strategies so extreme? Am J Polit Sci 43:765–781

Benoit K, Laver M (2006) Party policy in modern democracies. Routledge, London

Blais A, Fournier P, Gidengil E, Nevitte N, Everitt J (2006) Election 2006: how big were the changes... really? Working paper, Universite de Montreal

Caplin A, Nalebuff B (1991) Aggregation and social choice: a mean voter theorem. Econometrica 59:1–23
Dow JK, Endersby J (2004) Multinomial logit and multinomial probit: a comparison of choice models for voting research. Elect Stud 23:107–122
Downs A (1957) An economic theory of democracy. Harper and Row, New York
Gelman A, Park D, Shor B, Bafumi J, Cortina J (2008) Red state, blue state, rich state, poor state: why Americans vote the way they do. Princeton University Press, Princeton
Hotelling H (1929) Stability in competition. Econ J 39:41–57
Kramer G (1978) Existence of electoral equilibrium. In: Ordeshook P (ed) Game theory and political science. New York University Press, New York, pp 375–389
Merrill S, Grofman B (1999) A united theory of voting. Cambridge University Press, Cambridge
Patty JW (2005) Local equilibrium equivalence in probabilistic voting models. Games Econ Behav 51:523–536
Patty JW (2007) Generic difference of expected vote share and probability of victory maximization in simple plurality elections with probabilistic voters. Soc Choice Welf 29:149–173
Penn E (2003) A model of far-sighted voting. Unpublished paper, Harvard University
Poole K, Rosenthal H (1984) US presidential elections 1968–1980. Am J Polit Sci 28:283–312
Quinn K, Martin A, Whitford A (1999) Voter choice in multiparty democracies. Am J Polit Sci 43:1231–1247
Riker WH, Ordeshook PC (1973) An introduction to positive political theory. Prentice-Hall, Englewood Cliffs
Schofield N (2007) The mean voter theorem: necessary and sufficient conditions for convergent equilibrium. Rev Econ Stud 74:965–980
Schofield N, Martin A, Quinn K, Whitford A (1998) Multiparty electoral competition in the Netherlands and Germany: a model based on multinomial probit. Public Choice 97:257–293
Train K (2003) Discrete choice methods for simulation. Cambridge University Press, Cambridge
Yamamoto T (2011) A multinomial response model for varying choice sets, with application to partially contested multiparty elections. Working paper

Spatial Model of Elections in Turkey: Tracing Changes in the Party System in the 2000s

Norman Schofield and Betul Demirkaya

1 Introduction

During the first decade of the 21st century, electoral politics in Turkey underwent significant changes in terms of both the number and the ideological positions of political parties. The 1990s were marked by a historically high degree of fragmentation with the effective number of parties rising to 4.3 in 1995 elections and 4.8 in 1999 elections (Ozbudun 2000; Kalaycioglu 2008). This was partly due to a decrease in the vote share of the center-right and center-left parties and a concurrent rise in the vote share of the nationalist and Islamist parties. The 1999 elections resulted in a parliament with five parties, each with seat shares ranging between 15 % and 25 %.[1] A coalition government was formed by the center-left Democratic Left Party (DSP), the Nationalist Action Party (MHP) and the center-right Motherland Party (ANAP). The 2001 financial crisis was followed by an early election in 2002, in which none of the parties from the previous parliament were able to pass the electoral threshold.[2] The new parliament was formed by the members of the Justice and Development Party (AKP)—a new conservative party founded by the former members of Islamist parties—and the Republican People's Party (CHP)—

[1] See Tables 1 and 2 for vote and seat shares of parties in the last four elections.

[2] According to the electoral law of 1983, a political party needs to win at least 10 % of the national vote in order to win seats in the parliament.

N. Schofield (✉)
Weidenbaum Center, Washington University in St. Louis, Seigle Hall, Campus Box 1027, One Brookings Drive, St. Louis, MO 63130-4899, USA
e-mail: schofield.norman@gmail.com

B. Demirkaya
Center in Political Economy, Washington University in Saint Louis, 1 Brookings Drive, Saint Louis, MO 63130, USA
e-mail: betul.demirkaya@wustl.edu

N. Schofield et al. (eds.), *Advances in Political Economy*,
DOI 10.1007/978-3-642-35239-3_15,

Table 1 Vote shares (%)—1999–2011. Source: www.ysk.gov.tr; www.resmigazete.gov.tr

Party name		Vote shares			
		1999	2002	2007	2011
Justice and Development Party	AKP	–	34.28	46.58	49.80
Republican People's Party	CHP	8.71	19.39	20.88	25.98
Nationalist Action Party	MHP	17.98	8.36	14.27	13.02
Felicity Party	SP[a]	–	2.49	2.34	1.26
Virtue Party	FP	15.41	–	–	–
Democrat Party	DP		–	5.42[b]	0.65
Democratic Left Party	DSP	22.19	1.22	–[c]	0.25
True Path Party	DYP	12.01	9.54	–	0.15
Motherland Party	ANAP	13.22	5.13	–[d]	–
Genc Party	GP	–	7.25	3.04	–
People's Democracy Party	HADEP	4.75	–	–	
Democratic People Party	DEHAP[e]	–	6.22	–	–
Independents		0.87	1.00	5.24[f]	6.59[g]
Others		4.86	5.13	2.25	2.29
Total		100.00	100.00	100.00	100.00
Turnout		87.09	79.14	84.25	83.16

[a]Felicity Party is the successor to Virtue Party, which was banned by the Constitutional Court
[b]DYP changed its name to Democrat Party in a failed attempt to merge with ANAP
[c]The candidates of DSP entered the elections in the CHP lists
[d]ANAP withdrew from elections and asked their supporters to vote for DP
[e]Democratic People Party is the successor to People's Democracy Party, which was banned by the Constitutional Court
[f]Majority of independent candidates are supported by Democratic Society Party (DTP), which is the successor to DEHAP
[g]Majority of independent candidates are supported by Democratic Society Party (DTP), which is the successor to DEHAP

a party with a strong emphasis on a secularist agenda. In the 2007 elections, AKP consolidated their power by receiving 46.6 % of the votes while CHP increased their share of the vote by only 1.5 percentage points to 20.9 %. In addition, the Nationalist Action Party (MHP) and independent candidates supported by the pro-Kurdish Democratic Society Party (DTP) were able to win seats in the 2007 elections.

The changes in electoral politics brought about several important questions: What are the main issues that shape political debate? How can we describe the position of AKP and other parties on issues that are relevant for voters? How can we explain the voters' preferences in this new electoral landscape? The characterization of political parties and voters along a left-right continuum has been widely-used and helpful in making comparisons across political systems. However, the reduction of political views to a single dimension may conceal the diversity of issues that may

Table 2 Seats—1999–2011. Source: www.ysk.gov.tr; www.resmigazete.gov.tr

Party name		1999	2002	2007	2011
Justice and Development Party	AKP	–	363 (66)	341 (59.56)	327 (59.45)
Republican People's Party	CHP	–	178 (32.36)	112 (20.4)	135 (24.55)
Nationalist Action Party	MHP	129 (23.45)	–	70 (12.75)	53 (9.64)
Felicity Party	SP	–	–	–	–
Virtue Party	FP	111 (20.18)	–	–	–
Democrat Party	DP	–	–	–	–
Democratic Left Party	DSP	136 (24.73)	–	–	–
True Path Party	DYP	85 (15.45)	–	–	–
Motherland Party	ANAP	86 (15.64)	–	–	–
People's Democracy Party	HADEP	–	–	–	–
Independents		3 (0.55)	9 (1.64)	26 (4.74)	35 (6.36)
Others		–			–
Total		550 (100.00)	550 (100.00)	549 (100.00)	550 (100.00)

cut across each other. Moreover, the substantive content of the left-right continuum may change across countries and over time. It has been discussed that economic and social issues that define the political space in advanced industrial democracies were not sufficient in describing the electoral politics in Turkey in 2000s (Onis 2009). Self-placement of voters on a left-right continuum is explained by ethnic and sectarian differences rather than socioeconomic characteristics (Carkoglu 2007). Religion and nationalism emerge as the primary dimensions that separate voters and political parties in the spatial analyses of 1999 and 2002 elections. AKP is located on the right on the religion axis albeit closer to the electoral mean than the Islamist parties while CHP is located on the left. On the nationalism axis, there is pro-Kurdish DTP on the one end and Turkish nationalist MHP on the other end with other parties placed in between (Carkoglu and Hinich 2006; Schofield et al. 2011). In this paper, we apply the spatial model described in the following section to the 2007 elections in order to trace the changes in the position of voters and parties.

2 Spatial Model of Elections

We start our analysis with a pure spatial model $\mathbb{M}(\lambda, \beta)$ which includes the distance between the position of the voters and the political parties and the *exogeneous* valence (Schofield 2008). The valence term refers to the voters' perceptions of political leaders that are independent from their policy positions (Stokes 1963). In the model, the utility that voter i with position x_i gets from voting for party j with position z_j equals

$$u_{ij}(x_i, z_j) = \lambda_j - \beta \|x_i - z_j\|^2 + \epsilon_j$$

In the equation, $\|x_i - z_j\|$ denotes the Euclidian distance between the voter i's ideal point and the party j's policy position. ϵ_j is an error vector with a type I extreme value distribution. The intercept term λ_j gives the exogeneous valence of party j. The valence is exogeneous in the sense that it is not determined by the characteristics of the voter. We use a multinomial logit model to estimate the coefficients.

We continue our analysis with the calculation of convergence coefficient c which gives information about whether or not the position of the mean voter would be an Local Nash Equilibrium (LNE) given the spatial coefficient and the relative valence terms in the model. Schofield (2007) proves that $c < 1$ is a sufficient and $c < \omega$ is a necessary condition for electoral mean to be a LNE, where ω is the number of dimensions. By simulation, we search for a LNE and see whether the small parties have any incentive to diverge from the center given the spatial coefficient and the relative valence terms.

Finally, we incorporate the demographic characteristics of voters into the spatial model. In the joint model $\mathbb{M}(\lambda, \beta, \theta)$, the utility of voter x_i from voting for party z_j equals

$$u_{ij}(x_i, z_j) = \lambda_j + (\theta_j \cdot \eta_i) - \beta \|x_i - z_j\|^2 + \epsilon_j$$

where $(\theta_j \cdot \eta_i)$ refers to the sociodemographic valence of voter i for party j (Schofield 2007).

3 2007 Elections in Turkey

We analyze 2007 elections based on World Values Survey (WVS) conducted on a nationally representative sample in 2007.[3] We limit our analysis to the voters who indicated that they would vote for a political party in the following elections and answered all the questions used in the factor analysis.[4,5] We use factor analysis to

[3]World Values Survey 1981–2008 official aggregate v.20090901 (2009). World Values Survey Association (www.worldvaluessurvey.org). Aggregate File Producer: ASEP/JDS, Madrid.

[4]Due to low levels of response to survey questions used to measure the position of voters, DTP voters are underrepresented in the sample compared to the election results, which may have a deflating influence on the valence term for DTP.

[5]We excluded the voters of Felicity Party, Young Party and Democratic Left Party from our analysis. The vote shares for Felicity Party and Young Party were below 5 % in the 2007 elections (see Table 1). As explained in Table 1, after a failed attempt to merge with ANAP, DYP changed its name to DP in the 2007 elections. ANAP withdrew from the elections but their leader recommended that their voters vote for DYP. We decided to include these two parties separately in our analysis because at the time survey was conducted and until the elections, they were two distinct parties with different voter profiles.

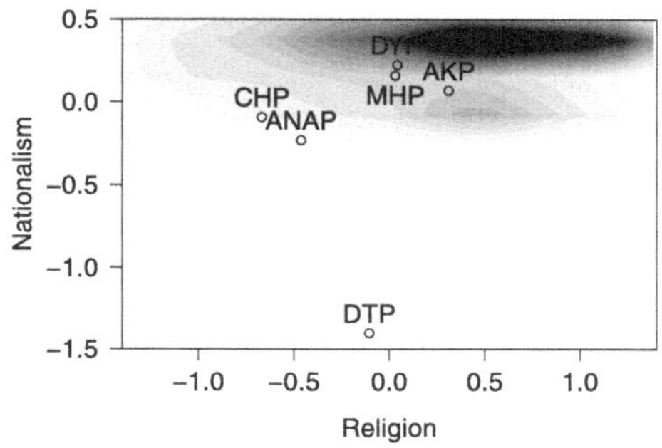

Fig. 1 Voter distribution and party positions in the 2007 election

identify the issues that differentiate voters from each other. We start with a long list of questions about the attitudes of voters toward religion and nationalism as well as economic and social issues.[6] Similar to previous studies, our analysis shows that religion and nationalism are principal dimensions that characterize the ideological position of Turkish voters.[7]

Figure 1 shows the position of voters with the x axis corresponding to the religion dimension and the y axis corresponding to the nationalism dimension. A movement from left to right on the x axis indicates a view that favors an increasing role of religion in private and public life. A movement from south to north on the y axis indicates an increasing association with Turkish nationalism. The variance on the x axis is 0.729 while the variance on the y axis is 0.498. The covariance between the two axes is 0.073. Thus the voter covariance matrix is the 2×2 matrix:

$$\nabla = \begin{bmatrix} 0.729 & 0.073 \\ 0.073 & 0.498 \end{bmatrix}$$

with $\text{trace}(\nabla) = 1.227$. The covariance matrix reveals two important points that differ from the analysis of previous elections.[8] First, the variance on the nationalism dimension is considerably smaller. The majority of voters are concentrated on the northern part of Fig. 1 with higher levels of association with Turkish nationalism. There is another group of voters concentrated on the southern part of the figure, most of whom are the voters of the pro-Kurdish DTP. Second, the covariance between the two axes is considerably smaller, which implies that the attitudes toward nationalism are not related very strongly to the attitudes toward religion.

The position of parties is calculated by taking the mean position of its voters on the religion and nationalism dimensions respectively. The party positions are given by the following matrix:

---

[6]The questions used in the factor analysis and the model are listed in Appendix 1.

[7]The factor loadings of the analysis are given in Appendix 2 (Table 6).

[8]See Carkoglu and Hinich (2006) and Schofield et al. (2011) for a spatial analysis of 1999 and 2002 elections in Turkey.

Table 3 Pure spatial model for 2007 elections. Normalized with respect to MHP

Party name		λ	Std. error	|t-value|
Justice and Development Party	AKP	1.413*	0.129	10.93
Republican People's Party	CHP	0.623*	0.151	4.138
Nationalist Action Party	MHP	–	–	–
Democratic Society Party	DTP	−1.688*	0.36	−4.684
True Path Party	DYP	−1.479*	0.269	−5.507
Motherland Party	ANAP	−1.676*	0.302	−5.551
Spatial Coefficient β		0.658*	0.061	−10.758
Convergence Coefficient		1.537		

n = 558; Log likelihood = −603.57; McFadden $R^2 = 0.114$
*Significant with probability <0.001

$$z^* = \begin{bmatrix} Party & AKP & CHP & MHP & DTP & DYP & ANAP \\ x\text{: } religion & 0.31 & -0.67 & 0.03 & -0.1 & 0.04 & -0.46 \\ y\text{: } nationalism & 0.07 & -0.09 & 0.16 & -1.4 & 0.22 & -0.23 \end{bmatrix}$$

The position of parties is similar to the previous elections with relatively minor differences. On the religion axis, CHP and AKP are located at the opposite ends with all the other parties located in between. Although position of AKP on the religion dimension is closer to the center compared to the position of pro-Islamist parties in previous elections, it is located to the right of the electoral mean. On the nationalism axis, there is a polarization between the pro-Kurdish DTP on the one hand, and all the other parties on the other hand. As discussed above, the position of parties other than DTP are very close to each other on this dimension. We are cautious, however, to interpret this as a change in the position of parties since we used questions that are different from the previous analyses. Due to the lack of questions related to policies on issues such as language, we used questions that measure association with Turkish nationalism. Interestingly, and unlike the previous years, the nationalist MHP is closer to the center on this dimension than DYP; however, this may be related to the small number of DYP supporters both in the population in 2007 elections and in our sample.

We use the pure spatial model $\mathbb{M}(\lambda, \beta)$ to estimate the relationship between the ideological position and valence of political parties, and their electoral success. The results are summarized in Table 3. The spatial coefficient β is 0.658 and statistically significant. The valence terms are calculated with respect to MHP. The vector of relative valences is

$$(\lambda_{AKP}, \lambda_{CHP}, \lambda_{MHP}, \lambda_{DTP}, \lambda_{DYP}, \lambda_{ANAP})$$
$$= (1.413, 0.623, 0, -1.688, -1.479, -1.676)$$

The party with the lowest valence is DTP with $\lambda_{DTP} = -1.688$. According to the model, when all parties are located at the electoral mean, the probability that a voter chooses DTP is

$$\begin{aligned}
&\rho_{DTP}\\
&= \frac{\exp(-1.688)}{\exp(1.413) + \exp(0.623) + \exp(0.0) + \exp(-1.688) + \exp(-1.479) + \exp(-1.676)}\\
&= \big[\exp(3.101) + \exp(2.311) + \exp(1.688) + \exp(0) + \exp(0.209) + \exp(0.012)\big]^{-1}\\
&= [22.225 + 10.084 + 5.409 + 1 + 1.232 + 1.012]^{-1}\\
&= 0.024
\end{aligned}$$

The standard error for λ_{DTP} is 0.36. Accordingly, the 95 % confidence interval for λ_{DTP} is $[-2.398, -0.978]$ and the 95 % confidence interval for ρ_{DTP} is $[0.01, 0.05]$. As explained above, DTP did not participate in the 2007 elections but supported independent candidates; therefore, it is difficult to assess the vote share of DTP in 2007. Table 1 shows that the independent candidates received 5.24 % of the votes; however, this includes candidates that were not supported by DTP as well. The respondents that indicated that they would vote for DTP constitute 2.5 % of our sample.

Schofield (2007) shows that the Hessian of the DTP is governed by the convergence coefficient of the pure spatial model, which is given by:

$$\begin{aligned}
c &= 2\beta(1 - 2\rho_{DTP})\,\mathrm{trace}(\nabla)\\
&= 2 \times 0.658 \times (1 - 2 \times 0.024) \times 1.227\\
&= 1.537
\end{aligned}$$

Schofield (2007) further shows that if $c < 1$, than the Hessian will have negative eigenvalues, giving a local equilibrium at the origin. In addition a necessary condition for this convergence is that $c < 2$. We calculate a conservative confidence interval for the convergence coefficient using the upper bound of the β coefficient and the lower bound of ρ_{DTP} and vice versa. The standard error for β is 0.061 so the 95 % confidence interval for β is $[0.538, 0.778]$. Thus, the 95 % confidence interval for the convergence coefficient is $[1.188, 1.871]$. The confidence interval for the convergence coefficient satisfies the necessary condition for the electoral mean to be an LNE since the upper bound is smaller than 2. It does not, however, satisfy the sufficient condition since the lower bound is greater than 1.

The Hessian, or the characteristic matrix of DTP:

$$\begin{aligned}
C_{DTP} &= 2\beta(1 - 2\rho_{DTP})\nabla - I\\
&= 2 \times 0.658 \times (1 - 2 \times 0.024)\nabla - I\\
&= 1.253\begin{bmatrix} 0.729 & 0.073\\ 0.073 & 0.498 \end{bmatrix} - I\\
&= \begin{bmatrix} -0.087 & 0.091\\ 0.091 & -0.376 \end{bmatrix}
\end{aligned}$$

The eigenvalues of the characteristic matrix are -0.06 with the eigenvector $(-0.961, -0.278)$ and -0.403 with the eigenvector $(-0.278, 0.961)$. We calculate a confidence interval for the Hessian using the upper bound of the β coefficient and the lower bound of ρ_{DTP} and vice versa.

$$\begin{aligned}
C_{DTP} &= 2\beta(1 - 2\rho_{DTP})\nabla - I \\
&= 2 \times 0.538 \times (1 - 2 \times 0.05)\nabla - I, 2 \times 0.778 \times (1 - 2 \times 0.01)\nabla - I \\
&= 0.968 \begin{bmatrix} 0.729 & 0.073 \\ 0.073 & 0.498 \end{bmatrix} - I, 1.525 \begin{bmatrix} 0.729 & 0.073 \\ 0.073 & 0.498 \end{bmatrix} - I \\
&= \begin{bmatrix} -0.294 & 0.071 \\ 0.071 & -0.518 \end{bmatrix}, \begin{bmatrix} 0.112 & 0.111 \\ 0.111 & -0.241 \end{bmatrix}
\end{aligned}$$

The eigenvalues of the lower bound for the characteristic matrix are -0.273 with the eigenvector $(-0.96, -0.279)$ and -0.539 with the eigenvector $(-0.279, 0.96)$. The eigenvalues of the upper bound for the characteristic matrix are 0.144 with the eigenvector $(-0.961, -0.277)$ and -0.273 with the eigenvector $(-0.277, 0.961)$.

As mentioned above, Schofield (2007) shows that a necessary and sufficient condition for the electoral mean to be LNE is that the eigenvalues of the characteristic matrix are both negative. As we see above, the point estimate and the lower bound for the characteristic matrix have negative eigenvalues, which implies that the electoral mean should be LNE. The upper bound for the characteristic matrix has one positive and one negative eigenvalue, and a negative determinant (-0.15). Hence, the upper bound gives a saddle point.

By simulation based on the point estimates of the spatial coefficients and the valence terms, we can verify that the electoral mean is an LNE in our case. When all the parties are located at the electoral mean their predicted vote shares were calculated as:

$$\begin{aligned}
\rho^{z_0} &= \left(\rho^{z_0}_{AKP}, \rho^{z_0}_{CHP}, \rho^{z_0}_{MHP}, \rho^{z_0}_{DTP}, \rho^{z_0}_{DYP}, \rho^{z_0}_{ANAP}\right) \\
&= (0.543, 0.246, 0.132, 0.024, 0.03, 0.025)
\end{aligned}$$

We compare this to votes shares in our sample:

$$\begin{aligned}
&(s_{AKP}, s_{CHP}, s_{MHP}, s_{DTP}, s_{DYP}, s_{ANAP}) \\
&\quad = (0.556, 0.231, 0.134, 0.025, 0.03, 0.023)
\end{aligned}$$

This comparison is important as it tells us about whether the low valence parties have any incentive to move to the electoral mean. Schofield and Gallego (2011, 190) call an equilibrium at position z a *stable attractor* when the lower 95 % bound of predicted vote shares of low valence parties at the equilibrium are higher than their actual vote shares. If an equilibrium is not a stable attractor than the party activists would have more incentive to pull the party from the electoral mean to z^*. As we see in the vectors, the equilibrium at the electoral mean is not a stable attractor for DTP or DYP.

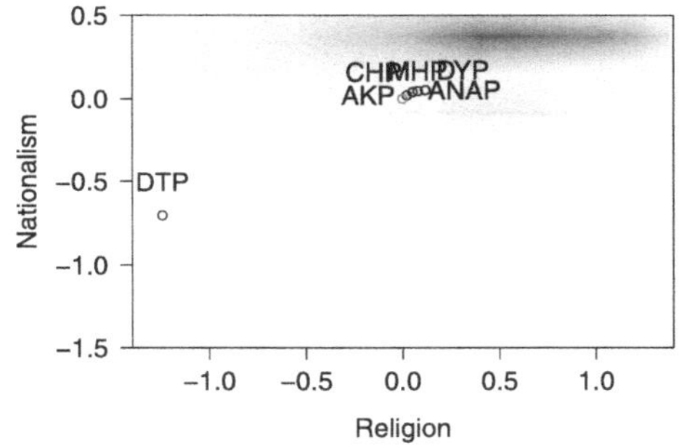

Fig. 2 Local Nash equilibrium

By using simulation, we found another LNE with the following party positions:

$$z_1 = \begin{bmatrix} Party & AKP & CHP & MHP & DTP & DYP & ANAP \\ x\text{: } religion & 0.02 & 0.05 & 0.08 & -1.24 & 0.12 & 0.12 \\ y\text{: } nationalism & 0.02 & 0.04 & 0.05 & -0.7 & 0.05 & 0.05 \end{bmatrix}$$

As can be seen in Fig. 2, all the parties other than DTP are concentrated around the electoral mean and DTP is on the southwest of the graph. The difference between the initial party positions and the party positions at the equilibrium is given by the following matrix:

$$z^* - z_1 = \begin{bmatrix} Party & AKP & CHP & MHP & DTP & DYP & ANAP \\ x\text{: } religion & 0.29 & -0.72 & -0.05 & 1.14 & -0.08 & -0.58 \\ y\text{: } nationalism & 0.05 & -0.13 & 0.11 & -0.7 & 0.17 & -0.29 \end{bmatrix}$$

This matrix shows how much and in which direction the parties are pulled from the equilibrium point by the party activists. The most obvious differences are seen in the positions of CHP and DTP. The former takes a position far to the left of the equilibrium position on the religion axis and the latter takes a position far to the south of the equilibrium position on the nationalism axis. The predicted vote shares at the equilibrium were calculated as:

$$\begin{aligned} \rho^{z_1} &= \left(\rho^{z_1}_{AKP}, \rho^{z_1}_{CHP}, \rho^{z_1}_{MHP}, \rho^{z_1}_{DTP}, \rho^{z_1}_{DYP}, \rho^{z_1}_{ANAP}\right) \\ &= (0.539, 0.245, 0.131, 0.03, 0.03, 0.025) \end{aligned}$$

Compared to the sample vote shares the equilibrium provides a higher predicted vote share for CHP, DTP and ANAP.

Finally, we supplement the spatial model with the demographic characteristics of voters. Following previous studies, we include age, education, ethnicity and socio-economic status as independent variables. We measure ethnicity by the primary language that the respondents speak at home and construct it as a dummy variable that takes the value 1 for Zaza and Kurdish, and 0 for Turkish and all other languages.[9]

[9]See Appendix 2 for the list of questions used to measure demographic characteristics.

Table 4 Joint model for 2007 elections. Normalized with respect to MHP

Variable	Party	Coefficient	Std. error	|t-value|
Spatial Coefficient β		0.603***	0.066	−9.167
Relative Valence λ_k	AKP	−0.694	1.228	−0.565
	CHP	−1.171	1.625	−0.72
	DTP	−5.183*	2.229	−2.326
	DYP	11.571	3083.355	0.004
	ANAP	11.583	4329.811	0.003
Age	AKP	0.025*	0.012	2.205
	CHP	0.032*	0.013	2.411
	DTP	0.004	0.032	0.109
	DYP	0.063**	0.019	3.266
	ANAP	0.025	0.025	0.995
Education	AKP	−0.227*	0.095	−2.392
	CHP	0.118	0.107	1.104
	DTP	−0.285	0.288	−0.988
	DYP	−0.228	0.193	−1.181
	ANAP	−0.113	0.209	−0.542
Kurdish	AKP	1.486	1.045	1.423
	CHP	−0.359	1.441	−0.249
	DTP	4.653***	1.245	3.738
	DYP	−14.527	3083.354	−0.005
	ANAP	−14.965	4329.811	−0.003
Socio-economic Status	AKP	0.314*	0.145	2.164
	CHP	0.288	0.174	1.651
	DTP	−0.36	0.484	−0.744
	DYP	0.252	0.305	0.826
	ANAP	0.541	0.36	1.503

n = 558; Log likelihood = −565.6; McFadden $R^2 = 0.17$
***Significant with probability <0.001
**Significant with probability <0.01
*Significant with probability <0.05

Previous studies point to a relationship between religious sect and vote choice. More specifically, Alevi voters were more likely to vote for CHP compared to other parties (Schofield et al. 2011). We were not able to include religious sect in our analysis because the question was not asked to the respondents.

In the joint model, which is summarized in Table 4, the spatial coefficient is smaller than the pure spatial model but it is still statistically significant. However, none of the valence terms except the one for DTP are statistically significant. Among the demographic characteristics, the only one that is both substantively and statistically significant is ethnicity. Not surprisingly, Kurdish speakers are more likely to vote for DTP compared to the baseline, which is the nationalist MHP. If we compare the McFadden R^2 of the pure model to the joint model, we see that the joint model provides a better fit.

4 Comparison with Previous Elections

A comparison of our results with previous analyses of 1999 and 2002 elections enables us to trace the change in electoral politics in Turkey during the last decade. In order to facilitate comparison, we rerun the model by using DYP as the baseline and summarized the results in Table 5.[10] The considerable increase in the relative valence of the three parties in the parliament compared to DYP points to the culmination of the decline of center-right parties. The valence of AKP increased compared to both CHP and MHP. This can be explained by the good performance of AKP's economic policies.[11] It is important to note, however, that it is practical rather than ideological considerations about economic policy that effect voters' preferences. Our factor analysis did not detect any coherent attitudes toward economic policy that explain the variance among voters. Economic policy can be thought as part of the valence term to the extent it is perceived as the competence of the party leaders. The positive valence terms for all three parties—AKP, CHP and MHP—can also partly be explained by the role party activists in providing financial and organizational resources.

One of the critical findings of our comparison is the decrease in the convergence coefficient from 5.9 in 2002 to 1.5 in 2007, which implies an increas-

Table 5 Comparison with previous years.[a] Normalized with respect to DYP

Party name	1999	2002	2007
Justice and Development Party	–	0.78*	2.893*
Republican People's Party	0.734*	1.33*	2.102*
Nationalist Action Party	0.666*	−0.12	1.479*
Democratic Society Party	−0.071	0.43	−0.209
Motherland Party	0.336	−0.31	−0.197
Democratic Left Party	0.724*	–	–
Spatial Coefficient β	0.375*	1.52*	0.659*
Convergence Coefficient	1.49*	5.94*	1.54*

[a]The entries for 1999 and 2002 are the results of the analysis in Schofield et al. (2011)

[10]In the previous section, we use MHP as the baseline because the small number of DYP supporters in our sample result in large standard errors in the joint model.

[11]In an analysis of 2007 elections, Kalaycioglu (2010) points that economic satisfaction is the primary determinant of both party identification and party preference for AKP voters.

ing likelihood of convergence to the electoral mean. By using simulation, we verified that electoral mean gives an LNE in 2007 elections.We also found another LNE with all parties except DTP aligned close to the electoral mean and DTP located in the southwest of the ideological space. We argue that the electoral strength of AKP pulls the equilibrium point to the right of electoral mean on the religion axis. The initial position of all parties except DTP and AKP are to the left of the equilibrium. The initial positions of parties except DTP on the nationalism axis got closer to each other compared to 2002 elections. DTP takes a position that is to the south of the equilibrium point. None of the parties except DTP diverge from the electoral mean on this axis in the equilibrium.

Appendix 1: Survey Questions

The analysis of 2007 elections in this paper is based on World Values Survey (WVS).[12] The survey was conducted between January and March 2007, that is three—six months before the 2007 elections. The questions used in our analysis are the following:

Vote Choice

If there were a national election tomorrow, for which party on this list would you vote?

Secularism

(1) How strongly do you agree or disagree with each of the following statements? Strongly Agree, Agree, Neither Agree Nor Disagree, Disagree, Strongly Disagree
  (a) Politicians who do not believe in God are unfit for public office.
  (b) It would be better for Turkey if more people with strong religious beliefs held public office.
(2) For each of the following, indicate how important it is in your life. Would you say it is Very important, Rather important, Not very important, Not at all important? Religion

[12]World Values Survey 1981–2008 official aggregate v.20090901 (2009). World Values Survey Association (www.worldvaluessurvey.org). Aggregate File Producer: ASEP/JDS, Madrid.

Nationalism

(1) How proud are you to be Turkish? Very Proud, Quite Proud, Not Very Proud, Not At All Proud
(2) People have different views about themselves and how they relate to the world. Using this card, would you tell me how strongly you agree or disagree with each of the following statements about how you see yourself? I see myself as part of the Turkish nation. Strongly Agree, Agree, Disagree, Strongly Disagree

Demographic Characteristics

(1) Age: Can you tell me your year of birth, please? This means you are … years old.
(2) Education: What is the highest educational level that you have attained? 1—No Formal Education, 9—University Level Education—With Degree
(3) Language: What language do you normally speak at home?
(4) Socio-economic Status: People sometimes describe themselves as belonging to the working class, the middle class, or the upper or lower class. Would you describe yourself as belonging to the: 1 Upper class, 2 Upper middle class, 3 Lower middle class, 4 Working class, 5 Lower class?

Appendix 2: Factor Loadings

Table 6 Factor loadings

n = 588	Religion	Nationalism
Politicians' belief in god	0.738	0.092
People with strong beliefs in public office	0.748	0.064
Religion important in life	0.478	0.246
Proud of nationality	0.071	0.656
Part of the nation	0.106	0.405
Variance	0.270	0.133
Cumulative Variance	0.270	0.403

References

Carkoglu A (2007) The nature of left-right ideological self-placement in the Turkish context. Turk Stud 8(2):253–271

Carkoglu A, Hinich MJ (2006) A spatial analysis of Turkish party preferences. Elect Stud 25(2):369–392

Kalaycioglu E (2008) Attitudinal orientation to party organizations in Turkey in the 2000s. Turk Stud 9(2):297–316

Kalaycioglu E (2010) Justice and development party at the Helm: resurgence of Islam or restitution of the right-of-center predominant party? Turk Stud 11(1):29–44

Onis Z (2009) Conservative globalism at the crossroads: the justice and development party and the thorny path to democratic consolidation in Turkey. Mediterr Polit 14(1):21–40

Ozbudun E (2000) Contemporary Turkish politics: challenges to democratic consolidation. Lynne Rienner Publishers, Boulder

Schofield N (2007) The mean voter theorem: necessary and sufficient conditions for convergent equilibrium. Rev Econ Stud 74(3):965–980

Schofield N (2008) The spatial model of politics. Routledge, New York

Schofield N, Gallego M (2011) Leadership or chaos: the heart and soul of politics. Springer, Berlin

Schofield N, Gallego M, Ozdemir U, Zakharov A (2011) Competition for popular support: a valence model of elections in Turkey. Soc Choice Welf 36(3):451–482

Stokes DE (1963) Spatial models of party competition. Am Polit Sci Rev 57(2):368–377

World Values Survey 1981–2008 official aggregate v.20090901 (2009) World Values Survey Association. www.worldvaluessurvey.org. Aggregate File Producer: ASEP/JDS, Madrid

Do Competitive Districts Necessarily Produce Centrist Politicians?

James Adams, Thomas L. Brunell, Bernard Grofman, and Samuel Merrill III

1 Evaluating Conventional Wisdom About the Effects of District Composition on Party Convergence Among the Members of the U.S. Congress

We have come a long way from the simplistic portrait of two-party plurality competition resulting in tweeedledum-tweedledee politics that is commonly attributed

We are indebted to Keith Poole for making available to us Poole-Rosenthal DW-NOMINATE data for the House for the period of interest, and to Dan Butler for helpful comments on a previous version of the manuscript. We also owe special thanks to Clark Bensen of POLIDATA who routinely provides us with high quality aggregate election data. We are indebted to Clover Behrend-Gethard and Sue Ludeman for bibliographic assistance. The listing of authors is alphabetical. Work on this project by the third-named author was supported by SSHRCC research grant #410-2007-2153 (co-PIs Stanley Winer and J. Stephen Ferris) and by the Jack W. Peltason (Bren Foundation) Chair, University of California, Irvine.

J. Adams (✉)
Department of Political Science, University of California, Davis, Davis, CA 95616, USA
e-mail: jfadams@ucdavis.edu

T.L. Brunell
School of Economic, Political and Policy Sciences, University of Texas at Dallas, 800 W. Campbell Road, Richardson, TX 75080, USA

B. Grofman
Department of Political Science and Center for the Study of Democracy, University of California, Irvine, Irvine, CA 92697-5100, USA
e-mail: bgtravel@uci.edu

S. Merrill III
Department of Mathematics and Computer Science, Wilkes University, Wilkes-Barre, PA 18766, USA
e-mail: sammerrill3@comcast.net

N. Schofield et al. (eds.), *Advances in Political Economy*,
DOI 10.1007/978-3-642-35239-3_16, © Springer-Verlag Berlin Heidelberg 2013

to Downs (1957).[1] Two key modifications are the recognition that (1) paralleling Downsian pressures for party convergence, there are strong competing incentives for party divergence; and, (2) that the existence of multiple legislative constituencies in which competition occurs affects the standard Downsian logic.

For example, we now recognize the theoretical potential for divergence due to politicians' sincere policy motivations,[2] candidate nomination rules,[3] party activists, voters' partisan loyalties, the threat of abstention due to alienation, and a host of other factors.[4] Theoretical research also suggests that the consequences of multi-constituency competition for party convergence are expected to be larger (a) the more diverse the locations of the median voter across different districts, (b) the greater the extent to which candidates/elected officials have the leeway to modify their policy platforms/legislative behavior to accommodate the median voter in their own district,[5] and (c) the greater the difference in variance in the support bases of the two parties.[6] Neo-Downsian models of the type pioneered by Adams and Merrill (2003), Butler (2009), Miller and Schofield (2003) demonstrate that, under certain empirically plausible circumstances, candidates maximize support in general elections not by appeal to the median voter position but by mobilizing their own partisan supporters (i.e., what we think of as the party's "base").

There is also extensive empirical support for party divergence in two party competition in the United States, including work on the ideological differences between Senators of the same state from rival parties (e.g., Poole and Rosenthal 1984; Grofman et al. 1990), work that tests hypotheses about the extent to which primary voting rules affects party divergence (Gerber and Morton 1998; Grofman and Brunell 2001), and a body of work dating back as least as far as Froman (1963) looking at the degree to which newly elected members of congress resemble their predecessors in voting behavior and at the degree to which members of Congress are responsive to the ideology of their constituents. For example, Schmidt et al. (1996) test the hypothesis that candidates derive electoral benefits in general elections from appealing on policy grounds to their partisan constituencies. In a study of U.S. Senate elections from 1962–1990, they conclude that incumbent Senators were more likely to win reelection when their voting records coincided with their state party's platform

[1]Downs' own (1957) views of party convergence are, however, far less simplistic than often painted, see, e.g., Grofman (2004).

[2]See e.g., Wittman (1983); Groseclose (2001).

[3]Gerber and Morton (1998); Burden (2001, 2004); Grofman and Brunell (2001); Owen and Grofman (2006); Adams and Merrill (2008).

[4]See Grofman (2004) for a recent review of the theoretical literature on party divergence in plurality elections.

[5]Winer et al. (2008); see also Snyder (1994).

[6]Grofman et al. (1999) report analyses suggesting that the policy preferences of state-level Democratic partisan constituencies are substantially more heterogeneous than are the policy preferences of state-level Republican constituencies, and that this difference is not an artifact of the fact that Democratic partisans from the South hold substantially more conservative views than do Democrats from the rest of the country.

than when their voting records reflected the median state voter's position, and, furthermore, that senators who appealed to their state party constituencies were more likely to run for reelection.[7]

Griffin (2006) argues that district competitiveness promotes responsiveness. Griffin's analysis, however, does not address our main question of how the policy differential between Democratic and Republican office-holders in similar districts varies between competitive districts on the one hand and uncompetitive ones on the other. What Griffin shows, instead, is that the average ideology of representatives (rather than the differential between parties) varies *across districts* as the median voter ideology varies, and that this relation is more pronounced among generally moderate districts than among uncompetitive districts.[8] Griffin, however, does not compare Democratic positions with Republican positions in similar districts.

In this essay we show that theoretically expected patterns of candidate positioning are reflected in the empirical record of the ideological locations of those individuals who become members of Congress. In particular, we look at the implications of presidential voting patterns at the district/state level—which we view as a surrogate for district/state ideology—for the degree of ideological similarity among Democratic and Republican officeholders, as reflected in their legislative voting records. We analyze data for the U.S. House and Senate over the period 1956–2004. We take support levels for Democratic presidential nominees as our measure of the underlying ideological predisposition in the district, and we use the first dimension of DW-NOMINATE scores as our measure of the policy positions taken by officeholders. Our focus is empirical and descriptive rather than theoretical (although, as we discuss below, our findings have important implications for theory-based models of candidate competition).[9]

Exactly as expected, we find that representatives from opposite parties who are elected from districts of similar ideology display sharply different legislative voting records, such that, for any given level of Democratic presidential support, Democrats elected from such districts are, on average, considerably more liberal than Republicans elected from such districts. Moreover, we also find the expected constituency-specific effects that pull office holders toward the views of their own constituency, so that the greater the support for Democratic presidential nominees

[7]In a study of postwar presidential elections, however, Kenny and Lotfinia (2005) report mixed results, i.e. they report that in some sets of analyses the presidential nominees who were closer to their party's ideological position fared better in general elections, while other sets of analyses suggest that the nominees who were closer to the median voter appeared to be electorally advantaged.

[8]In particular, Griffin finds that the slope over districts relating average representative ideology to (normalized) presidential vote is steeper for competitive (moderate) districts than for lop-sided districts. He further finds that within districts legislators are more likely to adjust to changing voter ideology over time in competitive rather than uncompetitive districts.

[9]Our evidence does not speak to a current lively debate over issue ownership and dialogue in political campaigns, which revolves around whether rival candidates emphasize the same policy issue areas, not whether the candidates take similar positions on these issues (see, e.g., Sigelman and Buell 2004; Petrocik 1996; Kaplan et al. 2006).

in the district, the more liberal are both Democratic and Republican officeholders from such districts.

We look more closely at the degree of ideological similarity among officeholders of the two parties as a function of presidential voting in the district. We also consider differences found across different time periods and offer evidence from both Houses of Congress. In particular, rather than looking at each party separately, we look at whether the degree of closeness/competitiveness in the underlying partisan characteristics of a district lead to differences in the ideological *gap* between representatives of the two different parties elected from districts of that type.

Our primary purpose is to investigate the theoretical expectations derived from the modeling of Adams et al. (2005), Butler (2009), and Adams et al. (2010), that policy convergence between vote-seeking Democratic and Republican candidates need not be maximized in districts with balanced partisan compositions, i.e., where there are approximately equal proportions of Democratic and Republican partisans. Indeed, Adams et al. (2010), who account for voters' partisan loyalties and abstention due to alienation, advance the opposite argument, that, *ceteris paribus*, districts with balanced partisan compositions will motivate maximal policy *divergence* between Democratic and Republican candidates. Figure 1 in Adams et al. (2010) depicts the expected pattern, i.e., ideological divergence is greatest when partisans are equally balanced. Although the arguments of Adams et al. and Butler[10] apply to the degree of policy divergence between rival candidates (one of whom must lose), while our analyses consider only winning candidates, these authors' arguments imply that when comparing the ideological positions of winning candidates from different parties, these differences should be at least as large in competitive districts as in non-competitive districts.

We focus on winners because we recognize that idiosyncratic factors may drive the locations of the candidate of the minority party in uncompetitive seats, and our interest is about how different from the location of the median voter a candidate can be and still be able to win the district. We treat idiosyncratic candidate characteristics and incumbency advantages as effectively washing out when we compare the set of Democratic and Republican winners from districts with the same ideological characteristics (as inferred from presidential election outcomes). Under these assumptions, we evaluate the hypothesis that the difference in policy positioning between Democratic and Republican *winners* should be at least as large in districts where the presidential outcome is competitive as in districts where the presidential outcome is non-competitive.

In the recent theoretical models, unlike the standard Downsian model, being in a potentially competitive seat does not necessarily imply that winners are closer to the median voter in the district. This is because, in such competitive settings, candidates have various strategic options to seek to improve their election chances, such as gaining financial support from an activist and interest-group base and using the money and publicity it buys to appeal to less ideologically-oriented voters (see

[10]Using district-level estimates of the voter distribution, Butler (2009) explains polarization among candidates in terms of the location and size of candidates' bases and proportion of swing voters.

e.g., Schofield and Miller 2007). Such an appeal can result from emphasizing one's own competence or likeability, by attacking the opponent, or by appealing to one's own party base and trying to further mobilize it. When candidates in a potentially competitive district seek support from potential activists—who are typically more polarized than the general electorate—they move *further* away from the median voter in that district. Candidates can compensate for being more distant from the median voter than their opponent by increasing turnout and activism[11] among their own party faithful.

To gain intuition about why candidates might be most dispersed when the election is most competitive, Adams et al. (2010) first consider the *least* competitive election context, namely that in which all citizens in the electorate identify with the same party. If, say, all citizens are Democratic partisans, then both candidates will appeal on policy grounds to these partisans, since there are no others. Therefore—even while courting citizens to vote and activists to contribute—margin-maximizing candidates will converge to identical positions in this "perfectly" uncompetitive scenario, and, by extension, they can be expected to converge to similar positions for partisan contexts that strongly favor one party over the other.

By contrast, in competitive districts, each candidate is motivated to appeal in large part to his/her own partisan constituency, which motivates increased divergence of the candidates' positions. To see intuitively why this might be true, Adams et al. (2010) consider another extreme situation where voters' partisan biases are so strong that they invariably prefer their party's candidate to the rival party's candidate, regardless of the candidates' positions, but where partisan voters are also prone to abstain from voting and/or activism, so that they participate only if they approve of their preferred candidate's policy position. Because, in this scenario, each candidate influences decisions to participate by the members of only her own partisan constituency—and neither candidate can attract support from the rival party's partisans—each candidate is motivated to give weight to the policy preferences of her own partisan constituency (along with the preferences of any independent voters in the electorate), while ignoring the policy preferences of the rival party's partisan constituency.[12]

Our empirical analyses support this expectation that candidates may be most dispersed when the election is most competitive. We find that, contrary to the intuition

---

[11] In competitive House elections, even if the positions of the House candidates do not greatly affect actual turnout, they may affect the decision to vote in the House contest and will likely affect the efforts of potential activists (cf. Schofield and Miller 2007).

[12] More generally, using a conditional logit model, Adams et al. (2010) argue that the more uncommitted a voter's decision to vote for a candidate, the more the candidate will take the voter's preferences into account (Erikson and Romero 1990, p. 1107). In a two-candidate election where voters have nonzero probabilities of abstaining, the higher of the voter's probabilities of voting for one or the other of the candidates must be the one nearer 0.5, and hence the voter is most marginal with respect to the candidate that she is most likely to support. Given that partisan voters are more likely to vote for their party's candidate than for the opposition party's candidate, candidates attach greater weight to the policy preferences of the members of their own partisan constituency than to the preferences of the members of the rival candidate's constituency.

that competitive districts should pull candidates of opposite parties closer together toward the median voter in that district, the ideological difference between the winners from the two parties is typically as great or greater in districts that, in presidential support terms, are the most competitive. *Simply put, in election contexts that one might think give candidates the strongest possible incentives to maximize their electoral support, the winning candidates tend to present the most* radical policies *relative to the center of district opinion.* Note that this finding does not imply that the most competitive districts elect the most extremist members of Congress. Rather it indicates that Democrats and Republicans elected in competitive districts are at least as polarized *relative* to each other—but not necessarily more extreme—than those elected in lopsided districts.

We believe empirical research on the policy extremism of candidates contesting competitive districts is relevant not only to the theoretical models of Butler (2009) and Adams et al. (2005) discussed above, but also to the more general question: Do candidates believe they maximize their support by converging towards the center of district opinion, or by presenting noncentrist positions that may be more appealing to their base and also to special interest groups?

As we noted above the basic Downsian model provides a strong intuition that, all other factors being equal, candidates and parties enhance their support by moving to the center of constituency opinion. However subsequent theoretical and empirical research has developed several reasons why other factors are *not* equal, and may reward candidates for presenting noncentrist positions. These include motivating turnout among party supporters who hold noncentrist viewpoints; energizing party activists to work on the candidate's campaign;[13] motivating special interest groups to finance the campaign;[14] and, convincing voters that the candidate is of superior character because her announced noncentrist positions demonstrate that she is not "pandering" to voters in the district.[15] Given these theoretical considerations it is not obvious whether, in real-world elections, candidates enhance their electoral prospects by positioning themselves near the center of the district electorate, or by presenting noncentrist positions that appeal to their partisans, to party activists, and to special interest groups. The empirical findings we present below that the winning candidates in more competitive districts present more radical policies suggest that the candidates themselves believe there are electoral advantages to noncentrist positioning. We believe this finding is important.

Our analysis is also consistent with the empirical findings of Ansolabehere et al. (2001), who find little support for the claim that winners of competitive races are more ideologically centrist than members of that same party elected from safe seats. Ansolabehere et al. (2001) look at the degree of divergence between winners and losers.

Unlike these and most other authors, we define competition in a national (i.e., presidential) rather than a House/Senate contest-specific way. Here, because DW-

[13]See, Schofield and Sened (2006).

[14]See Baron (1994) and Moon (2004).

[15]See Callander and Wilkie (2007).

NOMINATE scores are generally available for winners but not for losers, we look only at the positions of winners. But, of course, it is the winners who matter most. There are advantages and disadvantages to both approaches—i.e., defining competition in a national or a contest-specific way—and they should be seen as complementary. When Ansolabehere et al. (2001) and others define competition in terms of contests for House seats, they look directly at the competitiveness of the election in which a given officeholder is elected. On the other hand, any given House contest involves idiosyncratic features such as the backgrounds and campaign skills of the two candidates (and controlling for incumbency only partly controls for these other effects). This problem is exacerbated by the fact that there are only a few data sets that contain the ideological locations of both challengers and candidates. In contrast, by using presidential level data for all districts we provide more comparable data on the underlying partisan predispositions of the districts and we have comparable data over a larger number of districts over a much longer time period. In addition, potential statistical problems arise if we substitute votes in the House/Senate elections themselves for the presidential vote shares. Specifically, if we regress DW-NOMINATE scores on vote shares in House/Senate elections, this regression introduces an endogeneity problem because the Democratic proportion of the vote in each election is in part dependent on the ideological positions of the Congressional candidates, which biases estimates of the regression parameters.[16] Thus, there are good reasons to believe that the kind of data which we analyze in this paper is informative about pressures for ideological divergence.

2 Ideological Extremism in the U.S. House, 1956–2004, by Party and by Democratic Presidential Vote in the District

We begin by analyzing the relationship between candidate extremism and district competitiveness, using data for U.S. House districts over the 1956–2004 period. Taking DW-NOMINATE scores as our measure of a member's ideology for data pooled for the House elections from 1956 through 2004,[17] we have plotted member

[16]In fact for an extreme case in which vote-share is completely determined by spatial factors—namely the candidates' relative proximities to the median voter—the slope for each party would be decidedly positive rather than negative, i.e., more liberal Democratic candidate positioning would be associated with lower Democratic vote shares (and vice versa for Republicans). To see why regressing against vote shares in House districts biases toward positive slopes, consider a scenario in which the voters are uniformly distributed on the interval from –0.5 to 0.5 (the center half of the Left-Right scale from—restricted and, on average, less liberal). This leads to a positive slope when spatial position is regressed against Democratic vote-share. So endogeneity can seriously bias inferences from data that relate spatial position to Democratic vote-share in district House races. Regressions of DW-NOMINATE scores against House vote-shares that we have done give lines that are essentially flat. We take this as evidence of significant endogeneity effects (data omitted for space reasons).

[17]As explained in the website http://polisci.ucsd.edu/faculty/poole.htm, the average DW-NOMINATE coordinate for every legislator is constrained to lie within the unit hypersphere, with +1

DW-NOMINATE scores against the (district-specific) normalized Democratic vote share in the district in the contemporaneous Presidential election,[18] which we use as an estimate of district ideology. We label this variable the *normalized district Democratic vote proportion for president,* or *district ideology* for short.

Plots for pooled data over the period 1956–2004 are presented in Fig. 1; plots broken down by time period are shown in Fig. 2. Areas of the figure to the left of the vertical line represent Republican districts, i.e., those in which the district Democratic presidential vote was less than the national Democratic vote, while the areas to the right of it represent Democratic districts. Each curve, one for each party, represents a quadratic regression for that party, in which we regressed the representatives' DW-NOMINATE scores on the normalized district Democratic vote proportion, which we take as a measure of district ideology, *and* on the square of the district ideology; we also included a dummy variable for districts from the South.[19] Thus for each party our specification was:

$$\begin{aligned}\text{DW-NOMINATE score}_j = b_1 &+ b_2[\text{District ideology}_j] \\ &+ b_3[\text{District ideology}_j]^2 + b_4[\mathit{South}], \qquad (1)\end{aligned}$$

where

DW-NOMINATE score$_j$ = representative j's DW-NOMINATE score, based on j's legislative voting record in the two years preceding the election,

District ideology$_j$ = normalized presidential vote in j's district, as defined in footnote 18,

[District ideology$_j$]^2 = the square of the normalized presidential vote in j's district,

South = 1 if the district was located in the South, and zero otherwise.

---

interpretable as the most conservative score and -1 interpreted as the most liberal score. However, some members may have large linear terms so that for some Congresses their coordinates can be greater than $+1/-1$. In our data, there are 12 data points for which the DW-NOMINATE scores are beyond the range of -1 or 1.

[18]Specifically, the normalized Democratic vote proportion for president is equal to district presidential vote share minus the national presidential vote share. For example, if a presidential candidate gets 65 percent in a district, and 60 percent nationally, then the normalized district percent is $65 - 60 = +5$ percent, reflecting the fact that the presidential candidate ran five percentage points ahead of his national average in that district. If the presidential vote share in the district is the same as the national vote, then the normalized district vote is zero percent. Centering the district vote on zero is necessary, as explained in footnote 20 below, in order for the quadratic regressions (described below) to generate informative parameter estimates. Because the mean of the national Democratic presidential vote over the period of the study (49.9 %) is almost exactly 50 percent, we may interpret the zero point of the normalized Democratic vote proportion for president as representing either the mean national presidential vote or as zero deviation from a 50–50 district.

[19]We define the south as Arkansas, Alabama, Florida, Georgia, Louisiana, Mississippi, North Carolina, South Carolina, Texas, and Virginia.

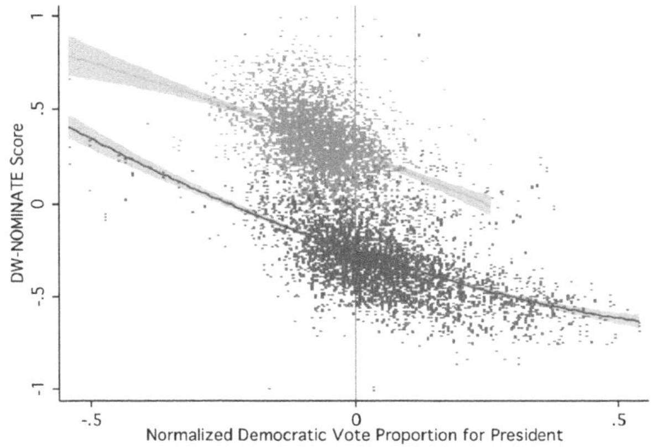

Fig. 1 House quadratic relation of DW-NOMINATE scores and partisan distribution by district: 1956–2004. Notes: The plot presents quadratic regression curves for DW-NOMINATE scores versus the normalized Democratic vote proportion for president in the House member's district, which is equal to district Democratic presidential vote share minus the national Democratic presidential vote share (see footnote 12). These regression lines were plotted using the full set of House members' DW-NOMINATE scores over the period 1956–2004; the sample sizes for the regression models are 4,613 for Republicans and 6,161 for Democrats. The *vertical line* at 0.0 represents identical Democratic presidential vote shares at the national and district level. The *shaded regions* around the lines represent 95 percent confidence intervals

Inclusion of the term $[\text{District ideology}_j]^2$ in (1) allows us to investigate the possibility of nonlinear effects of district ideology on the House member's DW-NOMINATE score, and to estimate how the degree of ideological dispersion between Republican and Democratic representatives varies with district competitiveness.[20] Table 1 reports these regression coefficients for the U.S. House, and the shaded regions in the figures represent the 95 percent confidence regions for the regressions.[21] As expected, the parameter estimates reported in Table 1 and illustrated in Figs. 1–2 support the expectation that representatives' ideological positions respond to the position of the median voter by district, so that the fitted curve for each party slopes downward (party responsiveness), both for the 1956–2004 period as a

[20]To see why it is necessary to employ a measure of district ideology that is centered on zero in order to estimate informative parameters in (1), note that in a quadratic regression, parameter estimates reflect behavior around the zero point of the independent variable. If we use the actual district vote as our measure of district ideology, then the zero point of this independent variable corresponds to a district where the Democratic candidate received zero percent of the presidential vote, which is outside the range of interest. Under this parameterization, estimates would reflect behavior over an unrealistic region. Using the normalized Democratic vote proportion for president, on the other hand, places the zero value of the independent variable at a district whose presidential vote matches the national presidential vote, focusing attention on behavior around competitive electorates.

[21]For simplicity, the party-specific regression curves and their confidence intervals in the figures are based on the full data set without the breakdown by region.

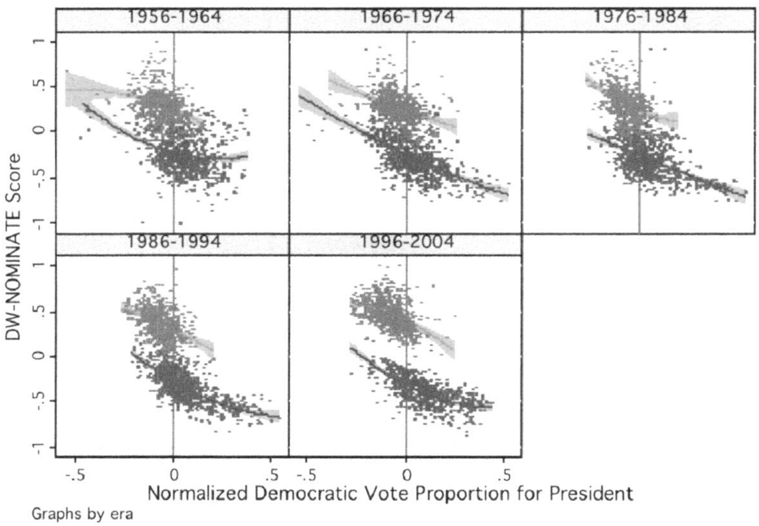

Fig. 2 Quadratic regression for the presidential vote share and ideology for U.S. House members with data separated by time periods. Notes: These plots present quadratic regression curves for DW-NOMINATE scores versus the normalized Democratic vote proportion for president in the House member's district, which is equal to district Democratic presidential vote share minus the national Democratic presidential vote share (see footnote 12). The data are the same as in Fig. 1, just separated by the eras noted in the figure. The *vertical line* at 0.0 represents identical Democratic presidential vote shares at the national and district level. The *shaded regions* around the lines represent 95 percent confidence intervals

whole (Fig. 1) and for each of the time periods 1956–1964, 1966–1974, 1976–1984, 1986–1994, and 1996–2004 (Fig. 2). All of these downward slopes—for the full period (as well as for each subperiod) and for each party—are statistically significant at the 0.001 level. In addition, note that the downward slopes of these regression lines for both Democrats and Republicans are substantial, suggesting mean *within-party* ideology does vary substantially as a function of the presidential voting patterns in the district. For the analyses pooled over the entire 1956–2004 time period, the estimated parameters on the linear coefficient reported in Table 1 are −0.75 for Democratic representatives and −1.03 for Republican representatives, indicating a downward trend in the DW-NOMINATE score of about one tenth of a unit for each increase of ten percent in the Democratic proportion of the district vote.[22]

On the other hand, if we look at the gap between the two curves, which reflects differences *across party lines*, we find very substantial differences between the win-

[22]These estimates apply to marginal changes in district presidential vote when the Democratic vote share in the district is similar to the national vote (so that the normalized measure of district ideology is near zero), in which case the value of the squared district ideology variable in (1) is negligible. In this range of values the predicted effect of district ideology on representatives' DW-NOMINATE scores is approximately linear.

Table 1 Regression of DW-NOMINATE scores versus partisan distribution of the district: House of representatives

Period	Regression coefficients							
	Democrats				Republicans			
	Intercept	South	Ideology	$[\text{Ideology}]^2$	Intercept	South	Ideology	$[\text{Ideology}]^2$
1956–2004	-0.32^{***}	0.19^{***}	-0.75^{***}	0.13^{*}	0.27^{***}	0.06^{***}	-1.03^{***}	-0.54^{*}
(full period)	(0.01)	(0.01)	(0.02)	(0.06)	(0.01)	(0.01)	(0.04)	(0.24)
1956–1964	-0.33^{***}	0.30^{***}	-0.36^{***}	0.33^{*}	0.24^{***}	0.06^{*}	-0.91^{***}	-1.11^{**}
	(0.01)	(0.01)	(0.03)	(0.14)	(0.01)	(0.03)	(0.09)	(0.44)
1966–1974	-0.32^{***}	0.24^{***}	-0.64^{***}	–0.22	0.23^{***}	0.01	-0.76^{***}	0.12
	(0.01)	(0.01)	(0.04)	(0.13)	(0.01)	(0.02)	(0.07)	(0.46)
1976–1984	-0.32^{***}	0.21^{***}	-0.86^{***}	0.34	0.20^{***}	0.10^{***}	-1.02^{***}	1.21
	(0.01)	(0.01)	(0.06)	(0.19)	(0.01)	(0.01)	(0.12)	(0.68)
1986–1994	-0.30^{***}	0.07^{***}	-1.17^{***}	0.83^{***}	0.29^{***}	0.03^{**}	-1.03^{***}	–0.56
	(0.01)	(0.01)	(0.05)	(0.17)	(0.01)	(0.01)	(0.10)	(0.61)
1996–2004	-0.33^{***}	0.05^{***}	-1.06^{***}	1.16^{***}	0.39^{***}	0.02	-1.03^{***}	-1.30^{**}
	(0.01)	(0.01)	(0.05)	(0.17)	(0.01)	(0.01)	(0.10)	(0.45)

* Significance at the 0.05 level; ** Significance at the 0.01 level; *** Significance at the 0.001 level. Significance levels are 2-sided

The definitions of the independent variables are given in the text. Curvature in the expected direction (i.e., convex for Democrats and concave for Republicans) is significant for both parties for the full period and for the earliest and latest subperiods. Thus, the data offer evidence that the curves either bow outward or may be straight, but the coefficients are never significant in the other direction, i.e., the data offer no significant evidence that any of the partisan curves bow inward. N's for the analyses are as follows: Full period (1956–2004): Democrats 6158, Republicans 4616; 1956–1964 period: Democrats 1304, Republicans 843; 1966–1974 period: Democrats 1254, Republicans 873; 1976–1984 period: Democrats 1323, Republicans 843; 1986–1994 period: Democrats 1243, Republicans 932; 1996–2004 period: Democrats 1034, Republicans 1125 ners from the two parties; for instance the pooled data in Fig. 1 suggests that, on average, a Republican Congressperson from even a 70 percent Democratic district can be expected to be more conservative than a Democratic member from a 30 percent Democratic district. The difference in regression intercepts between Democrats and Republicans indicates the typical difference between the DW-NOMINATE scores of House members of the two major parties when the partisan composition of the district is 50–50. As reported in Table 1, these differences range from 0.52–0.57 DW-NOMINATE units in each of the first three subperiods to 0.72 units in the most recent subperiod 1996–2004, reflecting the increased polarization in the House.[23] Clearly, party has a huge effect relative to that of district ideology.[24] Finally, the positive coefficient estimates on the South dummy variable suggest that—particularly in the earlier time periods—representatives tended to compile more conservative legislative voting records when they were elected from Southern districts, compared to when they were elected from non-Southern districts with similar presidential voting patterns.

So far we have considered what our data implies about House members' responsiveness to district ideology, along with the ideological differences between Democratic and Republican representatives. However our most interesting findings concern how district ideology is related to *partisan divergence*, i.e., the degree of ideological divergence between House members from different parties. As noted above, the conventional wisdom is that partisan divergence will be greatest when the election is not competitive, because in a lopsided district the candidate from the dominant party can move away from either the national or district median and expect to win anyway. Given that districts with highly unequal partisanship are likely to be less competitive in terms of presidential voting, this conventional wisdom implies that we should observe the largest ideological gap between Republican and Democratic representatives in districts that feature lopsided presidential vote margins.

However the curves in Fig. 1, which are fitted to the full 1956–2004 data, do not conform to this pattern: instead they bow out slightly away from each other in the middle of the partisan distribution scale.[25] Note that neither for the full period (1956–2004) nor for any of the five breakdown periods is there evidence that the curve for either party is significantly bowed *inward* at the 0.05 level. By contrast,

[23]The partisan gaps reported above apply to the reference category, non-South. For the category South, the estimated intercept and parameter estimate for the variable South must be combined, so that the partisan gap in the South ranges from 0.32–0.33 in the first two subperiods to 0.69 in the most recent subperiod.

[24]We note that Ono (2005) obtains similar plots for two Congresses (1969–1970 and 2003–2004) and observes the increasing polarization of the parties in Congress. Similarly, Clinton (2006), using samples that aggregate to over 100,000 voters, finds systematic differences in Republican and Democratic voting behavior in the 106th House (1999–2000) that cannot be entirely accounted for by same-party constituency preferences.

[25]Figure 4 in Butler (2009) appears to suggest this same convexity for Democrats and concavity for Republicans.

positive coefficients on the quadratic term for the Democrats and negative coefficients for the Republicans indicate significant *outward* bowing for both parties for the overall period and for the earliest (1956–1964) and the latest (1996–2004) periods, each at the 0.05 level or better (see Table 1 and Fig. 2).[26] In other words, Republican and Democratic House winners are as different or more so in ideology in the most competitive districts than in un-competitive ones. The outward bowing of the curves is not pronounced; what is remarkable is that the curves do not bow inward, as we would expect if the partisan gap narrowed in competitive districts.

Related plots are obtained by Erikson and Wright (2000). In particular, using the NES seven-point scale for both axes, these authors plot the mean perception of the ideology of incumbent House members during the 1980s against constituency ideology, obtaining as we do a sharp separation between Democrats and Republicans and trends reflecting party responsiveness (Erikson and Wright 2000, Fig. 8.6). The authors' scatter plots for each party appear to show curvature that bows out between the parties, but this possible effect is not noted.[27]

3 Ideological Extremism in the U.S. Senate, 1956–2004, by Party and by Presidential Vote in the State

We replicate the analyses on the House of Representatives, reported above, for the U.S. Senate. We use the vote for president for each quadrennial election as a measure of the underlying partisan support for each state (both for that particular election as well as the midterm election that follows it),[28] and the DW-NOMINATE scores for all senators as a measure of senatorial ideology from each congress. The plots for the regressions are depicted in Fig. 3 (which presents results for the entire 1956–2004 period) and Fig. 4 (which depicts results for the same subperiods used for the

[26]One explanation for convex curvature of the Democratic scores in the earlier part of the period under study may be that a number of conservative Southern Democrats won uncontested races, causing the quadratic regression curves for Democrats to turn up on the right side of the scale. But controlling for districts in the South as we have done should reduce this effect and, in any event, it cannot explain the pronounced convex curvature for the Democrats in the most recent subperiod.

[27]Erikson and Wright (2000, Fig. 8.1) also plot roll-call ideology based on the ADA/ACA indices for the 1980s against presidential vote, obtaining similar patterns; linear regression results are reported for the period 1976–1996. The authors note that "Districts in the middle are generally represented by relatively moderate Republicans or relatively moderate Democrats," but these authors do not assess the size of the ideologically *gap* between Republicans and Democrats as a function of district ideology. The fact that representatives from competitive districts tend to be more moderate than those from lopsided districts does not imply that the partisan gap between the sets of Republican and Democratic winners in moderate districts is smaller than the corresponding gap for more extreme districts.

[28]As with our analyses of House districts (see footnote 18), for the Senate-based analyses our measure of ideology was the difference between the state's Democratic presidential vote and the national Democratic presidential vote, a measure that is centered on zero.

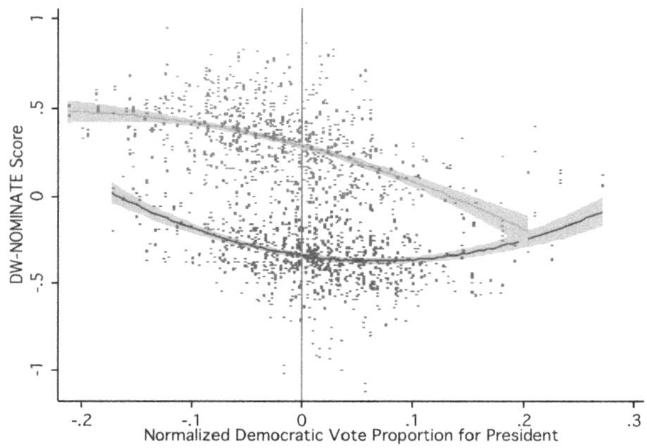

Fig. 3 Senate quadratic relation of DW-NOMINATE scores and partisan distribution by district: 1956–2004. Notes: The plot presents quadratic regression curves for DW-NOMINATE scores versus the normalized Democratic vote proportion for president in the Senator's state, which is equal to state Democratic presidential vote share minus the national Democratic presidential vote share (see footnote 12). These regression lines were plotted using the full set of Senators' DW-NOMINATE scores over the period 1956–2004; the sample sizes for the regression models are 1335 for Republicans and 1353 for Democrats. The *vertical line* at 0.0 represents identical Democratic presidential vote shares at the national and state level. The *shaded regions* around the lines represent 95 percent confidence intervals

House). Table 2 reports the regression coefficients for the Senate, and the shaded regions in the figures again represent the 95 percent confidence intervals for each regression.

The patterns we estimate for the Senate data are similar to those for the House data. As was the case for the House data, all of the downward, linear slopes—for the full period (as well as for each subperiod) and for each party—are statistically significant, at the 0.05 level; in fact, all except those for the subperiod 1956–1964 are also significant at the 0.001 level. Furthermore, the difference in regression intercepts between Democrats and Republicans, which indicates the typical difference between the DW-NOMINATE scores of Senate members of opposing parties when the partisan composition of the state is competitive, reflects the increasing partisan polarization in the Senate over time: these differences increase from 0.66 DW-NOMINATE units in the first subperiod 1956–1964, to 0.80 units in the most recent subperiod 1996–2004 (see Table 2).

Finally, our estimates on the Senate data again support the proposition that the differences between Democratic and Republican senators' voting records are as great or greater in states that are evenly divided, in partisan terms, than in states that are overwhelmingly democratic or republican: The curves in Fig. 3, which are fitted to the 1956–2004 data, again bow out away from each other in the middle of the state ideology scale, i.e., in states where the presidential vote mirrors the national vote, indicating that Republican and Democratic Senate winners are *as different* (and if anything more different) in ideology in the most competitive states. The evidence for outward bowing is significant at the 0.05 level for both

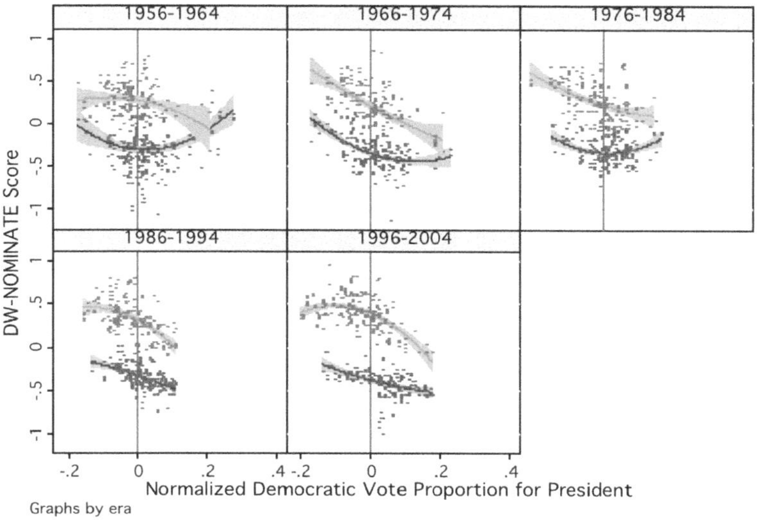

Fig. 4 Quadratic regression for the presidential vote share and ideology for Senators with data separated by time periods. Notes: These plots present quadratic regression curves for DW-NOMINATE scores versus the normalized Democratic vote proportion for president in the Senator's state, which is equal to state Democratic presidential vote share minus the national Democratic presidential vote share (see footnote 12). The data are the same as in Fig. 3, just separated by the eras noted in the figure. The *vertical line* at 0.0 represents identical Democratic presidential vote shares at the national and state level. The *shaded regions* around the lines represent 95 percent confidence intervals

parties for the full period and for the earliest and latest periods—the same periods that exhibited outward bowing in the House; whereas no curve for either party for either the full period or for any of the breakdown periods bows significantly inward.

4 Discussion

Our findings cast considerable doubt on any simplistic claim that more evenly balanced electoral competition in a district prompts candidate convergence across party lines. Moreover, our substantive conclusions are consistent across the House and Senate, and they largely generalize across time periods. Our findings concerning the partisan ideological gap and party responsiveness to constituency views are, of course, well known, and have been identified using alternative measures of legislative ideology.[29] In particular, we find the expected evidence that elected officials' legislative voting records respond to district ideology, and that Democratic repre-

[29]Restriction of the data to open-seat races changes the pattern only very marginally, with a slight tendency for Republicans to be more moderate in competitive districts. Furthermore, the patterns

Table 2 Regression of DW-NOMINATE scores versus partisan distribution of the State: results for the U.S. Senate

Period	Regression coefficients							
	Democrats				Republicans			
	Intercept	South	Ideology	$[\text{Ideology}]^2$	Intercept	South	Ideology	$[\text{Ideology}]^2$
1956–2004	-0.39^{***}	0.26^{***}	-0.66^{***}	4.29^{***}	0.26^{***}	0.16^{***}	-1.57^{***}	-2.30^{**}
(full period)	(0.01)	(0.01)	(0.07)	(0.54)	(0.01)	(0.02)	(0.09)	(0.81)
1956–1964	-0.39^{***}	0.39^{***}	-0.49^{*}	3.08^{*}	0.27^{***}	0.26^{**}	-0.72^{**}	-5.02^{*}
	(0.03)	(0.03)	(0.22)	(1.32)	(0.02)	(0.10)	(0.26)	(2.50)
1966–1974	-0.38^{***}	0.23^{***}	-0.62^{***}	2.18^{*}	0.19^{***}	0.19^{***}	-2.05^{***}	1.22
	(0.01)	(0.03)	(0.15)	(1.08)	(0.02)	(0.05)	(0.22)	(2.04)
1976–1984	-0.37^{***}	0.23^{***}	-0.67^{***}	5.50^{***}	0.17^{***}	0.28^{***}	-1.59^{***}	2.86
	(0.01)	(0.02)	(0.11)	(1.14)	(0.02)	(0.03)	(0.21)	(1.80)
1986–1994	-0.36^{***}	0.13^{***}	-1.05^{***}	0.47	0.29^{***}	0.09^{**}	-1.94^{***}	-5.56^{*}
	(0.01)	(0.02)	(0.12)	(1.77)	(0.02)	(0.03)	(0.21)	(2.61)
1996–2004	-0.42^{***}	0.16^{***}	-0.95^{***}	3.45^{**}	0.38^{***}	0.04	-1.63^{***}	-7.48^{***}
	(0.01)	(0.02)	(0.12)	(1.23)	(0.01)	(0.02)	(0.15)	(1.16)

*Significance at the 0.05 level; **Significance at the 0.01 level; ***Significance at the 0.001 level. Significance levels are 2-sided

The definitions of the independent variables are given in the text. Curvature in the expected direction is significant for both parties for the full period and for the earliest and latest subperiods. Thus, as for the House, the data offer evidence that the curves either bow outward or may be straight, but the coefficients are never significant in the other direction, i.e., there is no evidence that any of the partisan curves bow inward. N's for the analyses are as follows: Full period (1956–2004): Democrats 1353, Republicans 1135; 1956–1964 period: Democrats 314, Republicans 187; 1966–1974 period: Democrats 270, Republicans 205; 1976–1984 period: Democrats 263, Republicans 242; 1986–1994 period: Democrats 272, Republicans 234; 1996–2004 period: Democrats 234, Republicans 267 sentatives are more liberal than Republicans when controlling for district ideology. *But* we find no evidence that the degree of ideological polarization between Democratic and Republican representatives is smallest in the most competitive districts—in fact, if anything, the data suggests the opposite pattern, that over the past fifty years partisan polarization has tended to be as *great or greater* in districts that are most competitive. This latter finding, which we label the *competitive polarization result*, is contrary to the intuition that political competition exerts maximal pressures on politicians to moderate their positions when this competition is most intense, i.e., in highly competitive districts.

Our findings have theoretical, empirical, and practical implications. The practical implication of the competitive polarization result is that it casts doubt on whether using redistricting to draw more competitive districts for members of the House will bring the politics of moderation to Congress. Indeed, our results suggest that Democratic and Republican representatives elected from competitive districts, in terms of the presidential vote, may be even more ideologically polarized relative to each other than when they are elected from districts that are lopsidedly Democratic (or Republican) at the presidential level. We emphasize, however, that our results do not imply that the redesigning of districts to be more competitive would necessarily increase overall polarization in Congress. On the contrary, Democratic and Republican members of Congress in competitive districts, while sharply different from each other, would in most cases be less extremist than those that would have been elected in more lopsided districts, as can be seen in Figs. 1 and 3. Thus, redistricting to produce competitive districts might reduce, not increase, overall polarization.

Theoretically, our competitive polarization result squares with the recent spatial modeling-based arguments of Butler (2009) and Adams et al. (2010), which take account of voters' partisan loyalties and abstention due to alienation. These arguments conclude that, *ceteris paribus*, districts with balanced partisan compositions will motivate maximal policy *divergence* between Democratic and Republican candidates. And, as we have noted above additional theoretical arguments developed by Schofield and Sened (2006), Moon (2004), and Baron (1994) present reasons why candidates who present noncentrist policies that appeal to party supporters, activists, and special interest groups may derive electoral benefits that surpass the benefits that accrue to candidates who appeal to the center of public opinion in their constituency.

Finally, our analyses are relevant to the lively current debate over how political diversity mediates the impact of numerous variables that influence election outcomes, roll call voting, and candidate positioning (e.g., Bond et al. 2001; Koetzle 1998; Jones 2003). With respect to senators' roll call votes on free trade, for instance, Bailey and Brady (1998) find that in demographically homogeneous states

---

observed are not likely the result of the particular measure (DW-NOMINATE scores) of ideological voting in the House that we have used. Lee et al. (2004) plot legislative voting records as assessed by NOMINATE scores and by each of fifteen monitoring associations ranging from the liberal American for Democratic Action (ADA) to the conservative League of Conservative Voters (LCV) (against the Democratic vote share in the House election by district). These plots show internal consistency among many different measures of ideological voting in Congress.

constituent preferences are the only factor that exerts statistically significant influences on roll-call votes, while in heterogeneous states constituent preferences are but one of several influences. To the extent that heterogeneous states tend to be more electorally competitive at the presidential level, the Bailey and Brady findings imply that we will observe equal or greater divergence between Democrats' and Republicans' roll-call records in competitive states, than in non-competitive states—a pattern that fits our empirical finding that partisan polarization tends to be as large or larger in competitive districts. And with respect to candidate positioning, Bishin et al. (2006) report empirical analyses that the ideological positions of senate candidates from rival parties were no more similar when these candidates faced off in an election held in a heterogeneous state, than when the election was held in a homogeneous state.[30] This finding is again consistent with our results.

In sum, in this paper we have analyzed how the degree of ideological polarization between the parties in the House and the Senate varies as a function of district ideology, defined in terms of Democratic presidential support in the district. Consistent with previous research, we find that representatives' roll-call voting records reflect their district and their party. However, and we believe of greatest interest, we also find that as great or greater ideological difference between the winners of the two parties occurs in districts that, in presidential support terms, are the most competitive.

References

Adams J, Brunell T, Grofman B, Merrill S (2010) Why candidate divergence should be expected to be just as great (or even greater) in competitive seats as in non-competitive ones. Public Choice 145(3–4):417–433

Adams J, Merrill S (2003) Voter turnout and candidate strategies in American elections. J Polit 65(1):161–189

Adams J, Merrill S (2008) Candidate and party strategies in two-stage elections beginning with a primary. Am J Polit Sci 52(2):344–359

Adams J, Merrill S, Grofman B (2005) A unified theory of party competition: a cross-national analysis integrating spatial and behavioral factors. Cambridge University Press, Cambridge

Ansolabehere S, Snyder J, Stewart C (2001) Candidate positioning in U.S. House elections. Am J Polit Sci 45:136–159

Bailey M, Brady D (1998) Heterogeneity and representation: the Senate and free trade. Am J Polit Sci 42:524–544

Baron D (1994) Electoral competition with informed and uninformed voters. Am Polit Sci Rev 88(1):33–47

Bishin B, Dow JK, Adams J (2006) Issue representation and diversity in Senate elections. Public Choice 129(2):201–215

Bond JR, Campbell K, Cottrill JB (2001) The puzzle of constituency diversity revisited: conditional effects of district diversity in congressional elections. Manuscript, Texas A&M University

[30]Bishin et al. find that this conclusion holds regardless of whether the state electorate's diversity was measured in terms of demographic characteristics (using the Sullivan index) or in terms of ideological diversity.

Burden B (2001) The polarizing effects of congressional elections. In: Galderisi PF (ed) Congressional primaries and the politics of representation. Rowman and Littlefield, New York
Burden B (2004) Candidate positioning in US congressional elections. Br J Polit Sci 34:211–227
Butler DM (2009) The effect of the size of voting blocs on incumbents' roll-call voting and the asymmetric polarization of Congress. Legis Stud Q 34(3):297–318
Callander S, Wilkie S (2007) Lies, damned lies, and political campaigns, with Simon Wilkie. Games Econ Behav 60(2):262–286
Clinton J (2006) Representation in Congress: constituents and roll calls in the 106th House. J Polit 68(2):397–409
Downs A (1957) An economic theory of democracy. Harper and Row, New York
Erikson R, Romero D (1990) Candidate equilibrium and the behavioral model of the vote. Am Polit Sci Rev 84:1103–1126
Erikson R, Wright G (2000) Representation of constituency ideology in Congress. In: Brady D, Cogan J, Fiorina M (eds) Continuity and change in House elections. Stanford University Press, Stanford, pp 149–177
Froman LA (1963) Congressmen and their constituencies. Rand McNally, Chicago
Gerber E, Morton RB (1998) Primary election systems and representation. J Law Econ Organ 11(2):304–324
Griffin JD (2006) Electoral competition and democratic responsiveness: a defense of the marginality hypothesis. J Polit 68(4):911–921
Grofman B (2004) Downs and two-party convergence. Annu Rev Pol Sci 7:25–46. Polsby N (ed)
Grofman B, Brunell T (2001) Explaining the ideological differences between the two U.S. senators elected from the same state: an institutional effects model. In: Galderisi PF (ed) Congressional primaries and the politics of representation. Rowman and Littlefield, New York, pp 132–142
Grofman B, Griffin R, Glazer A (1990) Identical geography, different party: a natural experiment on the magnitude of party differences in the U.S. Senate, 1960–1984. In: Johnston RJ, Shelley FM, Taylor PJ (eds) Developments in electoral geography. Routledge, London, pp 207–217
Grofman B, Merrill S, Brunell TL, Koetzle W (1999) The potential electoral disadvantages of a Catch-All party: ideological variance among republicans and democrats in the 50 U.S. states. Party Polit 5(2):199–210
Groseclose T (2001) A model of candidate location when one candidate has a valence advantage. Am J Polit Sci 45(4):862–886
Jones DR (2003) Position-taking and position avoidance in the U.S. Senate. J Polit 65(3):851–863
Kaplan N, Park D, Ridout T (2006) Dialogue in U.S. Senate campaigns? An examination of issue discussion in candidate television advertising. Am J Polit Sci 50(3):724–736
Kenny L, Lotfinia B (2005) Evidence on the importance of spatial models in presidential nominations and elections. Public Choice 123(3):439–462
Koetzle W (1998) The impact of constituency diversity on the competitiveness of U.S. House elections, 1962–1996. Legis Stud Q 23:561–573
Lee DS, Moretti E, Butler MJ (2004) Do voters affect or elect policies? Evidence from the U.S. House. Q J Econ 119(3):807–859
Miller G, Schofield N (2003) Activists and partisan realignment in the United States. Am Polit Sci Rev 97:245–260
Moon W (2004) Party activists, campaign resources, and candidate position taking: theory, tests, and applications. Br J Polit Sci 34(4):611–633
Ono K (2005) Electoral origins of partisan polarization in Congress: debunking the myth. Extensions (Fall):15–20
Owen G, Grofman B (2006) Two-stage electoral competition in two-party contests: persistent divergence of party positions. Soc Choice Welf 26:547–569
Petrocik JR (1996) Issue ownership in presidential elections, with a 1980 case study. Am J Polit Sci 40(3):825–850
Poole KT, Rosenthal H (1984) The polarization of American politics. J Polit 46:1061–1079
Schmidt A, Kenny L, Morton R (1996) Evidence of electoral accountability in the U.S. Senate: are unfaithful agents really punished? Econ Enquiry 34:545–567

Schofield N, Miller G (2007) Elections and activist coalitions in the United States. Am J Polit Sci 51(3):518–531

Schofield N, Sened I (2006) Multiparty democracy: elections and legislative politics. Cambridge University Press, Cambridge

Sigelman L, Buell EH Jr (2004) Avoidance or engagement? Issue convergence in U.S. presidential campaigns, 1960–2000. Am J Polit Sci 48(4):650–661

Snyder J (1994) Safe seats, marginal seats, and party platforms: the logic of platform differentiation. Econ Polit 6:201–214

Winer S, Kenny L, Grofman B (2008) Explaining variation in the degree of electoral competition in a mature democracy: U.S. Senate elections, 1922–2004. Presented at the annual meeting of the Public Choice Society, San Antonio, March

Wittman D (1983) Candidate motivation: a synthesis of alternatives. Am Polit Sci Rev 77:142–157

A Heteroscedastic Spatial Model of the Vote: A Model with Application to the United States

Ernesto Calvo, Timothy Hellwig, and Kiyoung Chang

1 Introduction

How do candidate policy positions affect the citizen's vote choice? For over 50 years scholars in political science have built on the standard spatial model inherited from Black (1958) and Downs (1957), where voters assess the relative distance between their own preferred policies and the expected policies to be implemented by competing candidates. The greater the difference between the preferences of the voter and policies of the candidates, the lower the utility the voter derives from selecting them at the polls.

The building blocks of all spatial models of voting are similar: firstly, voters *know* their preferred polices. It may be the case that such preferences are misguided and lead to suboptimal outcomes. But voters know what they want and can compare said policy preferences to those of each of the candidates. Secondly, voters *know* the revealed policy preferences of the candidates. They may use informational shortcuts to assess candidate preferences; they may have imperfect information about likely

For helpful comments and suggestions, the authors thank Jim Adams, Johanna Birnir, Bernie Grofman, Dan Kselman, Noam Lupu, Sam Merrill, Richard Moore, Vicky Murillo, Bernhard Weßels, and participants at conferences at the Juan March Institute and the Social Science Research Center Berlin (WZB).

E. Calvo (✉) · K. Chang
Government and Politics, University of Maryland, 3144F Tydings Hall, College Park, MD 20742, USA
e-mail: ecalvo@umd.edu

K. Chang
e-mail: kychang@umd.edu

T. Hellwig
Department of Political Science, Indiana University, Woodburn Hall 210, 1100 E Seventh Street, Bloomington, IN 47405-7110, USA
e-mail: thellwig@indiana.edu

N. Schofield et al. (eds.), *Advances in Political Economy*,
DOI 10.1007/978-3-642-35239-3_17, © Springer-Verlag Berlin Heidelberg 2013

policy choices; and they may even have very biased views of the policies that different candidates will eventually implement. But voters nonetheless make rational decisions by comparing their perceived distance to the candidates using the available information. And thirdly, preferences are assumed to be transitive and single-peaked, allowing our models to produce sensible theoretical social choice results. While not made explicit in most research, single-peaked preferences are drawn with the assumption that the metric of distances in the policy space are identical for all actors involved. That is, if two parties in the same policy location move, say, to the left a given distance, voters use the same metric to measure this change for both parties.

But what if voters have different perceptions of the movement of parties in the policy space? What if when two parties move, say, to the left in the policy space voters perceive a more dramatic change in one compared to the other? In other words, what if voters have different metrics when assessing their relative distance to different parties? In this chapter we will relax this fundamental assumption of standard spatial models of voting and allow voters to *stretch* or *compress* the policy space measuring the distance from their preferred policy location to that of different parties and candidates. To this end, we propose here a *heteroscedastic spatial model of voting*, where the perceived distance from voters to parties is systematically altered by information effects.

Our emphasis on informational biases is directed at observed inadequacies in the existing research on spatial models of the vote. Previous research has shown that "voters may misestimate the policy platforms of candidates or parties either out of ignorance or in a fashion which reflects systematic bias" (Merrill et al. 2001, 200). In particular, respondents tend to overstate the reported proximity to parties which they intend to vote for as well as the distance between themselves and parties which they will not vote for (Granberg and Brent 1980; Granberg and Jenks 1977; Haddock 2003). These biases are not trivial and in many cases contribute adversely to the predictive accuracy of spatial models. Empirical tests of proximity voting often find smaller than expected statistical effects and yield attenuated parameter magnitudes, even if most analysis validate the general tenants of the theory. Furthermore, equilibrium positions for parties are often attenuated, resulting in models that overestimate centrist positions of parties and candidates. Attenuation biases give rise to theoretical problems when trying to ascertain the "correct" location of candidates in policy space and, hence, when testing spatial models of voting under *misreported* proximity. Attenuated proximity estimates and centripetal biases are but one of many puzzles confronting scholars in recent years, as more extensive empirical testing falsifies the theoretical validity of spatial models of voting (e.g., Adams and Merrill 1999; Iversen 1994; Rabinowitz and McDonald 1989).

Attempts have been made to address the problem. Adams et al. (2005), for example, propose a "discount" model in which a weight is assigned to recalibrate the effect of proximity. Others have augmented existing spatial model to include behavioral factors (Erikson and Romero 1990) and information in regards to the candidates' non-policy appeals (Sanders et al. 2011). Scholars also have looked to the effect of political institutions, suggesting that centripetal biases are moderated through the consideration of the distribution of power across party actors (Kedar 2009). Electoral rules have also been shown to alter the incentives facing political parties (Calvo and Hellwig 2011) and the voter's perception of party locations (Dahlberg 2012). More fundamentally, others posit alternative non-proximity models for how party and candidate policy positions enter the vote calculus (Macdonald et al. 2001). Many argue that these solutions improve on traditional proximity models. Yet others have used experimental designs to show that proximity voting rules are, in fact, more commonly employed than discounting or directional models (Tomz and van Houweling 2008; see also Lacy and Paolino 2010).

In this chapter our goal is to confront the observed systematic biases in the reported locations of parties and candidates. Working within the standard spatial model of Black and Downs, our emphasis is how information biases contort voter perceptions. The solution we propose allows the analyst to model *how information biases alter the shape of the policy space used by voters to assess their proximity to candidates.* Our model *allows us to alter the perceived distance between the voter and the candidate, allowing the policy space to contract or expand as a function of a variety of covariates.*

The chapter proceeds as follows. The next section elaborates on information biases and how they are reflected in how voters place candidates in policy space. We use data from the 1992, 1996, and 2008 American presidential elections to illustrate the magnitude of these information biases. As a motivating example, we draw from the field of optics and conceive of these biases in terms of ideological lensing, or *magnification*. We provide a naïve estimate of the degree of magnification in the voters' perceived ideological distance from themselves to the candidate. Finally, we propose a heteroscedastic proximity model of voting where magnification is estimated as a function of behavioral and candidate specific covariates. Section 4 reports results of estimating the effect of ideological proximity on vote choice—with and without correcting for magnification—using data from three U.S. presidential elections. Section 5 concludes.

2 Voting with Biased Perceptions of Candidate Positions

Despite decades of research, the literature on how voters decide remains divided by a conceptual gulf. On the one hand, researchers have developed a rich set of models to explain how rational voters make decisions by measuring their relative *proximity* to the policies proposed by candidates and parties. On the other hand, a large body of research shows that voters are ignorant—rationally or not—about politics and, more to the point, the preferences of political candidates running for office.

Contending models of voting differ in important ways. Spatial proximity models assume that voters select among candidates by minimizing the distance from their ideal policy outcome to that proposed by each candidate (Downs 1957; Enelow and Hinich 1984). A competing school argues that voters are motivated by conviction and prefer candidates that take on more extreme positions (Rabinowitz and McDonald 1989). Finally, a third group of scholars argue that voters also make decisions based on valence-issues, with candidates or parties building a reputation for performance rather than positions (Stokes 1963). Each of these approaches assumes that voters know something about the characteristics of competing candidates for office—be it in terms of policy positions, policy extremity, competence/reputation, or some combination thereof.

The research on political knowledge and voter choice naturally calls into question the validity of said proximity based models of vote choice. Indeed, there is a vast American and comparative literature documenting information deficits and political naïveté among voters. Describing voters' abilities to assimilate candidate positions in summary terms, Converse (1964) succinctly argued that Americans are "ideologically innocent." He showed that very few people could meet the criteria of voting on the basis of a liberal-conservative (or left-right) scale. In his seminar work on public opinion formation, Zaller (1992) largely echoed Converse's view. While the typical voter may know something about politics, such knowledge tends to be shallow and ephemeral. As Zaller (1992, 16) puts it, "a majority pays enough attention to public affairs to learn something about it. But even so, it is easy to underestimate how little typical Americans know about even the most prominent political events—and also how quickly they forget what for a time they do understand." This view certainly calls into question the average American's ability to cast a vote based on candidate positions on one or a set of issues.[1]

There is much evidence in existing survey data to support this more pessimistic view of voters' ability to discern and correctly use information about parties and candidates when making their decisions. Survey respondents differ in predictable ways when reporting the location of parties in the ideological space. Respondents with very different political leanings consistently overestimate their distance to parties with which they do not identify as well as the ideological distance to parties they do not expect to vote for (Adams et al. 2005; Bartels 1988; Page 1976).

As an example of this phenomenon, consider voter choice in the 1980, 1996, and 2008 U.S. presidential elections. In Fig. 1 we plot respondent placements of the two major party candidates in each of these elections. The graphs illustrate how respondents' self-placements affect their view of where the candidate is located in policy space. Take as example the task of placing the Democratic Party's candidate in 2008, Barack Obama. When asked in to place Obama on the 1–7 liberal-conservative scale, a self-identified "extremely conservative" respondent (scored 7 on the scale) places Obama around 6 (5.8) on the scale if she intends to vote for Obama. A similarly conservative respondent places Obama at less than 2 (1.7) if she instead planned to support another candidate. This can be taken

[1]The authors of *The American Voter* (Campbell et al. 1960) laid out such criteria for voting according to issue position. These include the ability to cognicize the issue in some form (generally interpreted as have an opinion on the issue), to perceive where the candidates stand on it, and to see a difference between them. To this list, Abramson et al. (2009) add that voters must see the positions of the relevant parties or candidates (approximately) correctly if they are to make reasonable decisions.

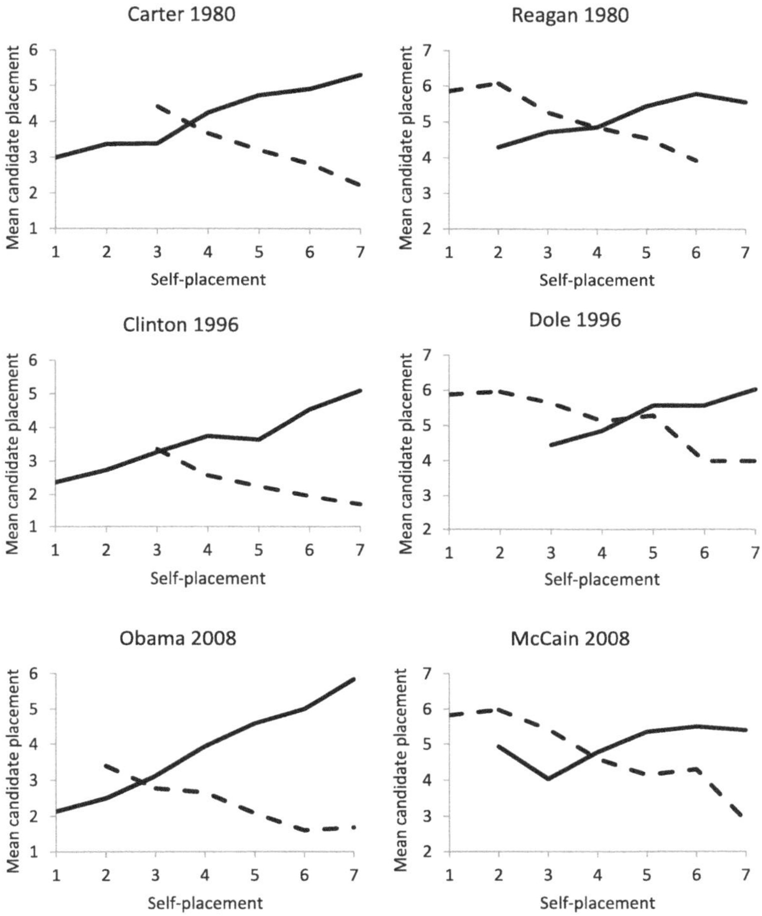

Fig. 1 Mean candidate placements versus self-placements, U.S. 1980, 1996, 2008. Notes: *Solid lines* report mean candidate placements among candidate supporters, *dashed lines* report mean candidate placements among non-supporters. Means with 10 or fewer respondents not reported. Source: American National Election Studies

as strong evidence of projection effects: party supporters systematically locate the party closer to their own ideal point, while non-supporters place the party further away.[2]

---

[2]These biases are not strictly an American phenomenon. For example, British election studies data from 2005 show that when asked to place the Conservative Party on the left-right scale, a voter located on the far-right of the left-right scale identify the Party as very conservative, at approximately 9 (8.9) 0–10 point scale if she voted for one of its candidates. A similarly conservative voter will perceive the Tories as very liberal—at 2.2—if she voted against the party (see Calvo et al. 2012). See also Adams et al.'s (2005, Chap. 10) analysis of survey data from France, Norway, and Britain.

We might surmise that such biases due to assimilation and contrast effects shape how voters make use of candidates' placements when making their decision (Adams et al. 2005; Granberg and Brent 1980; Granberg and Jenks 1977; Merrill et al. 2001). As we show in the next section, this picture implies that individual, candidate, and contextual factors may *stretch* or *compress* the policy space, altering the perceived distance between the voter and the candidates. Our contribution in this chapter is to provide a means to model and assess the factors that contribute to what we term *magnification*: the curving of the policy space in response to information. In the next section we propose a novel way to incorporate assimilation and contrasting biases into a spatial model of candidate choice.

3 A Motivating Example to Describe *Magnification* (Assimilation and Contrast) in Policy Distances

Let us begin with a motivating example for our heteroscedastic spatial model of voting. The intuition comes from the field of physics, which has developed an extensive literature on *gravitational lensing*: i.e., the effect that matter exerts on a beam of light from a background source as it travels across the space towards an observer. The curving of a beam of light passing through a lens alters the perceived location of the background source while revealing information about the distribution of matter in space. Such altered perceptions apply to politics as well. When it comes to elite-mass communications, the perceived policy position of a political representative is shaped by the location of the observer—the observer here being the voter. Drawing from an extensive literature on information bias, we describe similar lensing effects in the perceived location of parties in the ideological space.

Let us assume that all voters see the location of a party through a *convex* lens that projects an "image" of the location of the party that differs from its actual location. While we expect all voters to observe the party in a single "true" location in the ideological space, spherical aberration[3] shifts the view of observers so that the image of the party appears closer or further away from its true location. When voting **for** a party, the *focal point* of the object (party or candidate) falls *behind* the object, which appears closer than it should. When voting **against** the party, the *focal* point appears ahead of the object, which is projected further away than it should. We might think of the first of these cases as one where the voter is farsighted (unable to focus at a distance); in the second case the voter is nearsighted.

Just as individuals correct their eyesight with lenses, we can speculate that there is a graduation of this lens which explains the degree of optical aberration in ideological distances. The curvature of this lens can be approximated by a large number

[3] A convex lens suffers from spherical aberration when light transmitted through the lens fails to converge to a single point. This is known in optics as hyperopia or, more commonly, as farsightedness.

of different functions, but for the sake of our example we can use a simple parabola (e.g. a quadratic approximation) estimating the convexity of lenses or the projection of a ray of light on a parabolic mirror.

As an illustrating example, let us use the case of the Republican Party in the U.S. In the model L_{iR} describes the reported location of the Republican Party by respondent i. The self-reported ideological position of the same respondent is given by x_i. The quadratic approximation is thus

$$L_{iR} = a + bx_i + cx_i^2. \tag{1}$$

We can center the convex lens of the Republican Party at its projected axis; that is, where there exists an individual x_i^* that observes the "true" location of the Republican Party, designated L_{iR}^*, from a position perpendicular to the principal ideological axis on which the N respondents—each with a different image of R's position—are arrayed. This allows us to set $L_{iR}^* = x_i^*$. With this equality, we can use (1) to solve for x_i^*. The solution is

$$L_{iR}^* = x_i^* = -\frac{1}{2}\frac{-1 + b + \sqrt{1 - 2b + b^2 - 4ca}}{c}. \tag{2}$$

When voting for the party, all respondents $x_i \neq x_i^*$ observe images that are either closer to or further away from $L_{iR} \neq L_{iD}^*$ for every $x_i \neq x_i^*$, e.g. magnification.

We can describe this *magnification* (M) of the mirror that i attaches to R as:

$$M_{iR} = \frac{(x_i - L_{iR})^2}{(x_i - L_{iR}^*)^2}. \tag{3}$$

Note that magnification is defined as the ratio of two quadratic (Euclidian) distances: the distance from the voter's position and her perception of the candidate's position, and the distance from the voter's position to the "true" location of the party. We can think of the first of these as "reported distance" and the second as "true distance." Thus, when $M > 1$ we have a lens that *stretches* ideological, distance and when $M < 1$ the effect of the lens is to *compress* ideological distance. Moreover, if we had information to explain the degree of magnification in reported data, we could also estimate the "true" rather than the reported distance from the voters to the candidates.

$$\left(x_i - L_{iR}^*\right)^2 = \frac{(x_i - L_{iR})^2}{M_{iR}}. \tag{4}$$

While there are many different functional forms that can be used to estimate biases in the perceived location of parties, the previous example serves two purposes. First, it provides the intuition for how we might link lessons from physics to models of voter choice. And second, it provides a point of departure to estimate assimilation and contrast in proximity models of voting.

4 A Heteroscedastic Proximity Voting Model

The existing literature on assimilation and contrast has shown that reported proximity to parties is different for respondents that expect to vote for or against a party. We can go one step further and argue that a number of covariates will explain assimilation and contrast, compressing and stretching ideological distances as described in (4). Indeed, let us assume that magnification is the result of information processes that can be explicitly modeled with covariates.

As it is commonly done when estimating heteroscedastic discrete models (e.g., models in which the variance component is explained by covariates such as heteroscedastic probit models, negative binomial, etc.), we can assume that the level of magnification in ideological proximity can also be itself a function of other covariates. We can therefore use a placeholder parameter θ_{iR} in lieu of our magnification term, which will be used to assess the effect of variables that induce magnification:

$$\mathrm{U(V_R)} = -\alpha\frac{(x_i - L_{iR})^2}{\exp(\theta_{iR})} + \mathbf{BZ}. \tag{5}$$

In (5) we have substituted the angular magnification estimate with the exponentiated parameter θ_{iR}, so that $\log(\theta_{iR}) \sim N(\mu_\theta, \sigma_\theta^2)$. Notice that if all covariates for the magnification equation have no effect, the $\exp(0) = 1$, and (5) will be reduced to the standard proximity model.

As in the case of a heteroscedastic choice model (Alvarez and Brehm 1995), the expression in (5) has the desirable feature of allowing us to model the variance as a linear function of a set of covariates. Yet different from a heteroscedastic model, the variance is only rescaling the ideological proximity measure. The second component of the model, **BZ**, is a vector of individual-specific controls which are unaffected by the covariates for the magnification. Since the variance applies only to distance, we label this a *heteroscedastic proximity model*.

By explicitly modeling the magnification in the ideological scale, (5) provides a means for testing arguments about which factors, both individual and systemic, shape the voter's capacity to "see clearly." In particular, this representation provides a novel way to bring in different candidate and voter attributes into the spatial model of the vote and, hence, gives us a strategy for incorporating those factors discussed in the introduction: non-proximal (directional) spatial components, candidates' valence characteristics, and voter attributions. Let's consider each of these in turn.

First, take directional effects. Directional models provide an alternative conception of how voters incorporate information on party positions. First proposed by Rabinowitz and McDonald (1989), the directional model has long been the chief rival to the proximity model from *within* the spatial modeling tradition. Like the Downsian proximity model, the directional model posits that voters obtain utility from candidates' positions on the issues. This utility is not gained by minimizing proximity but is a positive function of the candidate's distance from the voter. Specifically, when candidates are on opposite sides of the neutral point, N, directional voters prefer the candidate who advocates their side. In the context of American politics, voters select the larger from $(x_i - N)(L_{iR} - N)$ and $(x_i - N)(L_{iD} - N)$.

The explanatory power of directional models relative to the Downsian proximity model has been much contested, and with mixed results.[4] Tests of the two models, however, have compared them directly, with each component affecting voter utility directly and in additive fashion. Conclusions in favor of one or the other often hinge on how analysts measure voter utility or on which modeling assumptions are relaxed (see Lewis and King 1999). Mixed findings aside, directional and proximity effects are typically pitted against one another within the context of a mean model. Tests between rival models are thus on the order of a horse race between variables as analysts discern whether proximity of directional components carry greater weight. Our approach is different. It uses information on the extremity of where respondents place candidates as shaping the degree of angular magnification, rather than on affecting directly the choice model.

Next, consider valence. Our model of ideological lensing provides a new strategy for incorporating candidates' non-policy appeals. A great deal of recent scholarship has emphasized the importance of parties' non-positional related reputations with respect to competence, integrity, charisma, and the like (Adams et al. 2005; Clarke et al. 2009; Schofield and Sened 2006). These studies demonstrate that the inclusion of non-proximity components into the random utility model yields more complete models for understanding election outcomes and how party strategies respond to voter preferences. We build on this insight. However, rather than incorporating party valence advantages additively, we explore whether valence evaluations bias voters' perceptions of where the party is positioned in ideological space. We know from previous work that valence advantages allow parties to attain larger shares of the vote than they would as predicted solely by spatial considerations.[5] But voters' assessment of a party's location in policy space, on the one hand, and its valence (dis)advantage, on the other hand, are typically assumed to be unrelated to one another.[6] Further, the spatial modeling literature generally assumes that parties' valence advantages are identical across voters.

We relax these assumptions. We model the degree of bias in voter assessments of party positions as a function of the voter's perception of the party's valence appeals. We maintain that if a voter i views the image of a party R as proximally closer to her than R's actual location, then the degree of magnification, M, should decrease. With reference to (4), this makes it likely that $(x_i - L^*_{iR})^2 > (x_i - L_{iR})^2$. To the extent that reputational considerations are built on familiarity, this claim finds support in work on voter choice out of the behavioral tradition which shows that voters dislike

[4]Recent research, however, has used experimental designs to get around previous measurement problems and finds stronger support for the proximity view (Tomz and van Houweling 2008; Lacy and Paolino 2010). We take this as instructive evidence for using direction extremity to modify ideological lensing arising from proximity models, rather than the other way around.

[5]See especially Adams et al.'s (2005) unified model; also see Wittman (1983), Groseclose (2001), Calvo and Hellwig (2011).

[6]Something of an exception is Sanders et al. (2011) who model valence as a function of voter-party issue proximity, thus positing that spatial effects shape utility indirectly, through valence characteristics.

uncertainty and resist supporting parties they know little about (even if they share the party's policy preferences).[7] Parties who voters view as being more competent, trustworthy, charismatic, and the like, should receive a biased evaluation by the voter in positional terms (that is, the distance between x_i and L_{iR} is small). Lastly, the heteroscedastic proximity model provides a way to model how the effect of voter perceptions of candidate location on the vote is altered by the individual's acquisition of information about politics. As noted above, there exists a large and generally uncontested literature highlighting the dearth of Americans' objective knowledge about political institutions and affairs (Converse 1964; Delli Carpini and Keeter 1996). More contested among scholars is whether such information discrepancies matter for voter choice and, by extension, election outcomes. Perhaps not surprisingly, researchers have sought out different pathways through which information effects are present (Gomez and Wilson 2001; Zaller 2004). Using our heteroscedastic proximity model, we examine whether exposure to information about politics matters for voter choice by sharpening, or "clarifying," the influence of ideological distance.

With this information, the heteroscedastic proximity model is as shown in (5) with desirable feature of allowing us to model the variance, θ_{iR}, specified as a linear function of policy extremism, valence, and political information, expressed as

$$\theta_{iR} = \gamma_1 D_{iR} + \gamma_2 T_{iR} + \gamma_3 I_i. \tag{6}$$

In (6), D_{iR} represents voter i's perception of the extremity of R's policy preferences, T_{iR} is i's assessment of R's non-positional qualities, or valence characteristics, I_i represents i's exposure to political information, and the γs are parameters to be estimated. The directional effect, D_{iR}, is scored 1 if the voter places the candidate as more extreme but on the same side of the neutral point as herself, and 0 otherwise. Valence, T_{iR}, is coded +1 if the respondent likes anything about the presidential candidate's party, −1 if she dislikes anything about the party, and 0 otherwise.[8] The political information variable, I_i, is a subjective measure of how much attention the respondent pays to news about government and politics.[9] Finally, note that we control for the respondent's partisan dispositions using the standard ANES seven-point scale for party identification. This is entered into the specification in (5) as part of **BZ**, the vector of controls.

We estimate a set of heteroscedastic proximity models—one each for U.S. presidential elections in 1980, 1996, and 2008—using the Markov Chain Monte

[7] See, among others, Alvarez (1997) and Bartels (1996). Enelow and Hinich's (1981) formal model yields consistent predictions.

[8] Specifically, the American National Election Studies surveys ask respondents to identify whether there is anything they like about the Democratic and Republican Parties. This is followed by an item asking whether there is anything they dislike about the two main parties. With responses to these two binary choice items, we construct a three-point scale scored −1 dislike only, 0 for neither like nor dislike, or both like and dislike, and +1 for like only.

[9] The measure is coded 1 = "don't pay much attention," 2 = "pay some attention," 3 = "pay a great deal of attention."

Table 1 Heteroscedastic proximity models. Source: American National Election Studies

	1 1980	2 1980	3 1996	4 1996	5 2008	6 2008
Choice Model						
Ideological Distance	–0.068	–0.067	–0.065	–0.190	–0.056	–0.039
	(0.746)	(0.018)***	(0.302)	(0.033)***	(0.060)	(0.010)***
Party Identification	0.029	0.040	0.071	0.094	0.096	0.099
	(0.009)**	(0.009)***	(0.008)***	(0.009)***	(0.008)***	(0.011)***
Constant	–0.290		–0.750		–0.594	
	(10.973)		(4.656)		(1.080)	
Ideological Variance Model						
Directional Effect		–0.811		–0.398		–0.028
		(0.171)***		(0.118)**		(0.198)
Party Valence		0.747		0.698		1.252
		(0.092)***		(0.101)***		(0.132)***
Attention to News		–0.088		0.078		–0.210
		(0.099)		(0.046)+		(0.067)**
LogLik	–1102.1	–998.7	–1389.2	–1075.8	–1717.4	–753.1
N	1838	1736	2570	2076	3064	1418

*** $p < 0.001$, ** $p < 0.01$, * $p < 0.05$, + $p < 0.1$, two-tailed tests
Cells report coefficients and standard errors from estimating heteroscedastic proximity model described in the text

Carlo (MCMC) engine in WinBUGS (Spiegelhalter et al. 2003). We estimate two equations—one for the choice model and the other for the variance component. The choice model is further split between the vector of exogenous controls (party identification), **BZ**, and the ideological distance component, $(x_i - L_{iR})^2$.

Table 1 presents the model results: the choice model includes the estimated effect of ideological distance on the likelihood the respondent selects the candidate. The choice-specific coefficients for partisanship are positively signed and precisely estimated in each case. Our interest, however, lies with the results for ideological distance. Here, we observe differences in the effect of positional proximity in models that do model the variance as a function of ideological extremity, valence, and information (Models 2, 4, 6) and those that do not (Models 1, 3, 5). When the variance model is left unspecified, parameter estimates on *Ideological Distance*, while negatively signed, are imprecisely estimated. However, when we do specify the variance, these estimates in the choice model attain statistical significance. This finding holds across the 1980, 1996, and 2008 elections. The remaining covariates pertaining to directional, valence, and information effects are specified to account for *variations* about the voter's decision with respect to ideological proximity. We consider each in turn.

4.1 Explaining the Effect of Candidate Extremity on Proximity Voting

First consider the influence of directional effects. The heteroscedastic specification implies that the ideological space is stretched so that candidates' distance to voters differs as they move to the extreme or to the center of the ideological space. A positively signed coefficient on the directional term would indicate ideological distance matters less when that when the candidate is more extreme than the voter, and on the same side of N, than otherwise. A negative sign, on the other hand, means that the penalty attached to the non-proximal candidates is greater. That is, while the proximity model attaches a penalty to candidate R when L_{iR} is far from x_i, the magnitude of that penalty is greater if $\gamma_1 < 0$. Table 1 shows that this is in fact the case for the 1980 and 1996 elections. In these cases, voters who viewed the candidate as more extreme than themselves put greater (negative) weight on ideological distance than voters who did not. In terms of ideological lensing, the directional effect *stretches* the distance between the voter and the candidates. This story does not apply, however, to the 2008 election. In this case, γ_1 is indistinguishable from zero, meaning that extremely placed candidates receive no penalty on policy terms.

These results suggest that in 1980, a typical voter i was less and less likely to support Ronald Reagan or Jimmy Carter for president as a function of how extreme he viewed the particular candidate's ideology to be. In 1980 the large and precisely estimated coefficient on *Directional Effect* indicates that she assigns a relatively heavy penalty on extreme position-taking candidates. The same story applies to 1996. The negatively signed coefficient on the directional term in the variance equation implies that proximity voters punished the candidates, Bob Dole and Bill Clinton, for taking what they perceived as extreme positions. However, the "extremity penalty" confronting Dole and Clinton in 1996 was less than that facing Reagan and Carter in 1980, as evinced by the relative sizes of the coefficients. And by 2008, this penalty had altogether disappeared: taking extreme positions (on the preferred side of the neutral point) had no adverse effect on proximity voting. We can infer from this result that the candidates in 2008, John McCain and Barack Obama, did not suffer from coming across as either too conservative or too liberal or conservative the way their predecessors did.

4.2 Explaining the Effect of Valence on Proximity Voting

Next consider valence effects. Unlike the directional effect, coefficients estimated for the valence parameters are consistent across elections: in 1980, 1996, and 2008, the estimate on *Party Valence* is positively signed and statistically significant. In terms of the heteroscedastic model, this means that as valence increases, the voter's perceived ideological distance, $(x_i - L_{iR})^2$, shrinks. Put differently, as the distance between the voter's preferred policy location and that of the party increases, higher valence makes the distance smaller and the disutility smaller. As a party's valence advantage goes up, the effect of ideological distance on the vote becomes smaller. In the extreme, if valence is sufficiently high, a voter will perceive that the candidate

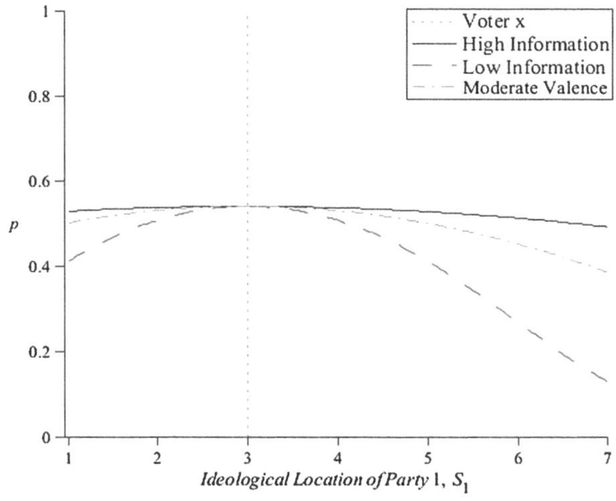

Fig. 2 The effect of party valence in the heteroscedastic proximity model. Notes: Figure displays the probability voter i intends to vote for a candidate as the candidate moves in policy space. Voter i is located at 3 on the 1–7 ideology scale. The other candidate (not shown) is located at position 5. The figure indicates how the candidate's position as perceived by i (*horizontal axis*) and i's perceived valence of the candidate's party (*solid and dashed lines*) affect the probability i supports the candidate. Simulated probabilities are based on parameter estimates from Table 1 Model 6 for the 2008 U.S. presidential election

is "right next to her," irrespective of the policy proposed, and the utility of spatial proximity voting will remain constant. In effect, *as a candidate's valence advantage approaches its maximum, he becomes spatially closer to each and every voter in the population.*

Figure 2 illustrates this effect for a moderately liberal voter (located at 3 on 1–7 scale) using parameter estimates from Model 6 in Table 1 for the 2008 election. If the candidate is also located at 3, then i prefers the candidate with equally high probability (∼0.63) regardless of its valence level.[10] But as the candidate moves away from i's preferred location, it loses less utility if it is deemed to have high valence (solid line) than if it has low valence (dashed line). Notice that this interpretation shows that the effect of high valence is to "drown out" spatial proximity as a determinant of voting. By contrast, as valence declines, the effect of spatial proximity becomes more pronounced.

The intuition is straightforward and surprising: voters will perceive low valence parties as ideological and high valence parties as pragmatic, irrespective of their actual policy location. In other words, voters who attach high valence marks to their party will see them close to themselves and pragmatic, while parties with low valence will appear further removed and much more ideological. Again, this trait remains constant in all model results.

[10] In this illustration, the other candidate in the two-candidate race is placed at 5 on the 1–7 scale.

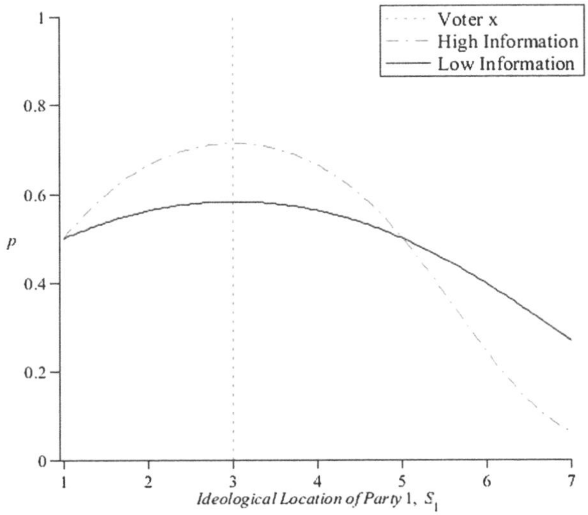

Fig. 3 The effect of information (attention to news) in the heteroscedastic proximity model. Notes: Figure displays the probability voter i intends to vote for a candidate as the candidate moves in policy space. Voter i is located at 3 on the 1–7 ideology scale. The other candidate (not shown) is located at position 5. The figure indicates how the candidate's position as perceived by i (*horizontal axis*) and i's level of attention to news (*solid and dashed lines*) affect the probability i supports the candidate. Simulated probabilities are based on parameter estimates from Table 1 Model 6 for the 2008 U.S. presidential election

4.3 Attention to News and Ideological Distance

Finally, consider information effects, captured in our models as attention to political news. Many researchers have sought to ascertain the influence of political information on an individual's voting behavior. We examine what effect, if any, information acquisition has on ideological lensing. The same logic applies as above: a positive coefficient on the information variable in the variance component implies that ideological distance is *compressed*, or that ideology matters for voter utility among informed individuals. A negative coefficient, on the other hand, implies that the politically informed are more likely to use ideological proximity to inform their vote—in this case, information *stretches* distance. Results show that our information measure, *Attention to News*, does not exert the same general effect across the three elections. In the 1980 and 1996 polls, attention to news had no biasing effect on *Ideological Distance*. In 2008, however, the coefficient on *Attention to News* is precisely estimated and negatively signed. This means that *among those located proximally close* to a candidate (say Barack Obama), the utility of voting for Obama was greater as information levels increased. This utility, however declines rapidly among the informed as the candidate moves away from the voter, i.e., as $(x_i - L_{iR})^2$ increases. Among the less informed ideology matters less: the gains from proximally located candidates are lower but so are the losses incurred by moving further away on the ideological continuum. Figure 3 illustrates this dynamic, again using parameter estimates from the 2008 election. We again set $x_i = 3$.

Taken together, the results of these heteroscedastic proximity models provide insights into American presidential politics. Voters in the United States do select candidates to the office of president based policy (ideological) considerations. The voter's view of the candidates' policy positions, however, is highly biased, particularly but not exclusively among those at self-identify at the extreme positions on the liberal-conservative scale (see Fig. 1). And once we model the "shape" of this lensing effect, ideological distance becomes a stronger predictor of voter utility (Table 1). Yet perhaps of greatest interest to students of American politics come from when we model the lensing effects via the heteroscedastic proximity model of voter utility. Comparing the voter's calculus in the 1980, 1996, and 2008 elections, we uncover a mix of continuity and change. Not surprisingly, partisanship and ideology matter, and do so consistently. Candidates' non-positional valence appeals, with respect to competence, integrity, and the like, also matter across elections—yet we provide a novel means for showing how valence blunts the proximity effect.

5 Concluding Remarks

The assumptions undergirding spatial models of voting are by now familiar: 1) voters *know* their preferred polices; 2) voters *know* the revealed policy preferences of candidates; and 3) voter preferences are transitive and single-peaked. Employing a novel *heteroscedastic proximity model*, we are able to relax these assumptions. In particular, we allow voters to use different metrics when measuring their relative proximity to parties. Furthermore, we show that information effects *stretch* and *compress* the policy space in systematic ways. While we have not been the first to acknowledge this perceptual bias in the voters' perceptions, our work offers a more cogent and theoretically informed way (a) to measure ideological lensing and (b) to correct for it.

By allowing spatial distances to vary in response to changes in information, our *heteroscedastic proximity* approach is able to explain attenuation biases in current proximity models of voting. Drawing on insights from physics, this research sheds new light on the problems of—and offer solutions to—ideological lensing in elections. Borrowing from lens models in optics, we assume that individuals observe the image of a party located in the ideological space rather than the actual location of a party.

In this chapter, we applied the heteroscedastic proximity model to three presidential elections in the United States. As a means to correct for—or make adjustments to—ideological aberration, we model the level of angular magnification in proximity voting via a trio of non-proximity covariates. Our model of magnification includes a directional component, a valence component, and an information component. Using this *heteroscedastic* proximity model, we show that the directional component and the information component both vary across electoral contests. Regarding direction, our three-period analysis shows that the penalty of candidates' taking extreme positions as declined over time. Indeed, the size of the coefficient on the directional effect, D_{iR}, is half as great in 1996 as in 1980, and by 2008 is essentially zero. This trend suggests that while presidential candidates used to be penalized by taking extreme positions on the issues, such penalties have declined with time. This tendency comports with a general sentiment that American politics has become polarized and that such polarization is electorally sustainable (McCarty et al. 2005). As for political information, our results imply that in earlier periods, access to information had no effect in terms of enhancing (stretching) or blunting (compressing) the effects of voter and candidate policy positions. However, in the recent 2008 election, proximity voting was stronger among the more politically informed. Both of these changes comport with common characterizations of the changing, increasingly volatile nature of presidential politics in the United States.

Future work on elections in the U.S. and elsewhere should might extend and improve upon the framework we have provided. For example, extrapolating from current trends, it might be the case that the heteroscedastic proximity model applied to the 2012 U.S. election would yield a positive coefficient on the directional parameter, indicating that proximity voting is *greater* among those perceiving candidates as more extreme. Future work might also distinguish among different sources of political information. Are viewers of more politically charged news outlets like Fox News or MSNBC more likely to vote on the basis of ideological proximity than those receiving information from other sources? In short, our contribution has provided a tool for systematically comparing these effects across elections and, in turn, a means for deepening our understanding about how voters decide.

References

Abramson PR, Aldrich J, Rohde DW (2009) Change and continuity in the 2008 elections. CQ Press, Washington

Adams J, Merrill S III (1999) Modeling party strategies and policy representation in multiparty elections: why are strategies so extreme? Am J Polit Sci 43:765–791

Adams J, Merrill S III, Grofman B (2005) A unified theory of party competition. Cambridge University Press, New York

Alvarez RM (1997) Information and elections. University of Michigan Press, Ann Arbor

Alvarez RM, Brehm J (1995) American ambivalence towards abortion policy: development of a heteroskedastic probit model of competing values. Am J Polit Sci 39(4):1055–1082

Bartels L (1988) Presidential primaries and the dynamics of public choice. Princeton University Press, Princeton

Bartels L (1996) Uninformed votes: information effects in presidential elections. Am J Polit Sci 40:194–220

Black D (1958) The theory of committees and elections. Cambridge University Press, New York

Calvo E, Hellwig T (2011) Centripetal and centrifugal incentives under different electoral systems. Am J Polit Sci 55(1):27–41

Calvo E, Hellwig T, Chang K (2012) The eye of the beholder: ideological lensing, information effects, and the vote. Paper presented and prepared for the conference "Contemporary Applications of the Spatial Model". Instituto Juan March, 27 April 2012

Campbell A, Converse P, Miller W, Stokes D (1960) The American voter. Wiley, New York

Clarke HD, Sanders D, Stewart MC, Whiteley PF (2009) Performance politics and the British voter. Cambridge University Press, Cambridge
Converse P (1964) The nature of belief systems in mass publics. In: Apter D (ed) Ideology and discontent. Free Press, New York, pp 206–261
Dahlberg S (2012) Does context matter? The impact of electoral systems, political parties and individual characteristics on voters' perceptions of party positions. Unpublished manuscript, University of Gothenburg
Delli Carpini M, Keeter S (1996) What Americans know about politics and why it matters. Yale University Press, New Haven
Downs A (1957) An economic theory of democracy. Harper and Row, New York
Enelow JM, Hinich MJ (1981) A new approach to voter uncertainty in the Downsian spatial model. Am J Polit Sci 25(3):483–493
Enelow JM, Hinich MJ (1984) The spatial theory of voting: an introduction. Cambridge University Press, New York
Erikson R, Romero D (1990) Candidate equilibrium and the behavioral model of the vote. Am Polit Sci Rev 84:1103–1126
Granberg D, Brent E (1980) Perceptions of issue positions of presidential candidates: candidates are often perceived by their supporters as holding positions on the issues that are closer to the supporters' views than they really are. Am Sci 68(6):617–625
Granberg D, Jenks R (1977) Assimilation and contrast effects in the 1972 election. Hum Relat 30(7):623–640
Gomez BT, Wilson JM (2001) Political sophistication and economic voting in the American electorate: a theory of heterogeneous attribution. Am J Polit Sci 45(4):899–914
Groseclose T (2001) A model of candidate location when one candidate has a valence advantage. Am J Polit Sci 45(4):862–886
Haddock G (2003) Making a party leader less of a party member: the impact of ambivalence on assimilation and contrast effects in political party attitudes. Polit Psychol 24(4):769–780
Iversen T (1994) Political leadership and representation in Western European democracies: a test of three models of voting. Am J Polit Sci 38:45–74
Kedar O (2009) Voting for policy, not parties. Cambridge University Press, New York
Lacy D, Paolino P (2010) Testing proximity versus directional voting using experiments. Elect Stud 29(3):460–471
Lewis JB, King G (1999) No evidence on directional vs. proximity voting. Polit Anal 8(1):21–33
Macdonald SE, Rabinowitz G, Listhaug O (2001) Sophistry versus science: on further efforts to rehabilitate the proximity model. J Polit 63(2):482–500
McCarty N, Poole K, Rosenthal H (2005) Polarized America: the dance of ideology and unequal riches. MIT Press, Cambridge
Merrill S III, Grofman B, Adams J (2001) Assimilation and contrast effects in voter projections of party locations: evidence from Norway, France and the USA. Eur J Polit Res 40(2):199–221
Page BI (1976) The theory of political ambiguity. Am Polit Sci Rev 70(3):742–752
Rabinowitz G, McDonald SE (1989) A directional theory of issue voting. Am Polit Sci Rev 83:93–121
Sanders D, Clarke HD, Stewart MC, Whiteley P (2011) Downs, stokes, and the dynamics of electoral choice. Br J Polit Sci 41(3):287–314
Schofield N, Sened I (2006) Multiparty democracy: elections and legislative politics. Cambridge University Press, New York
Spiegelhalter D, Thomas A, Best N, Lunn D (2003) WinBUGS user manual 1.4, Cambridge, UK. http://www.mrc-bsu.cam.ac.uk/bugs
Stokes D (1963) Spatial models of party competition. Am Polit Sci Rev 57:368–377
Tomz M, van Houweling RP (2008) Candidate positioning and voter choice. Am Polit Sci Rev 102(3):303–318
Wittman D (1983) Candidate motivation: a synthesis. Am Polit Sci Rev 77:142–157

Zaller JR (1992) The nature and origins of mass opinion. Cambridge University Press, New York

Zaller JR (2004) Floating voters in U.S. presidential elections, 1948–2000. In: Saris WE, Sniderman PM (eds) Studies in public opinion: attitudes, nonattitudes, measurement error, and change. Princeton University Press, Princeton

Inferring Ideological Ambiguity from Survey Data

Arturas Rozenas

Keywords Ideological placement · Ambiguity · Bayesian · Latent variables · Missing data

1 Introduction

It has become conventional wisdom to think of electoral competition in terms of parties taking positions on policy issues and voters choosing their representatives based on those positions. Quite often, however, instead of communicating clear platforms, politicians make contradicting policy statements, remain ambiguous about details or avoid talking about issues altogether. For example, Mitt Romney, a presidential candidate in the U.S. 2012 elections, has been constantly accused of remaining too vague on key policy issues.[1] In the 2008 presidential campaign, Barack Obama promised to withdraw the U.S. troops from Iraq within 16 months whereas John McCain proposed far more ambiguous plan to remain in Iraq for "up to 100 years."[2]

To explain ideological ambiguity, spatial theorists have referred to risk-attitudes of the voters (Shepsle 1972), the desire of politicians to avoid divisive issues (Page 1976), context-dependence of voting decisions (Callander and Wilson 2008), uncertainty of the candidates(Glazer 1990), or strategic benefits of not committing to a certain platform (Alesina and Cukierman 1990; Aldrich 1995). Empirical research, on the other hand, focused mostly on voting behavior finding that accounting for ideological ambiguity improves predictions of the standard spatial voting models (Alvarez 1997; Bartels 1986; Campbell 1983a,b; Tomz and van Houweling 2009).

These examples suggest theoretical and empirical reasons to treat policy platforms not as points but as probability distributions over policy space. Indeed, the

[1] For example, "Where are Mitt Romney's details?", by Scott Lehigh, *Boston Globe*, June 27, 2012.

[2] 'Obama Fuels Pullout Debate With Remarks', *New York Times*, July 4, 2008.

I am grateful to John Aldrich, Scott Desposato, Jeremy Reiter, Fan Li, Mitchell Seligson, and James Stimson for comments and suggestions.

A. Rozenas (✉)
ISM University of Management and Economics, LT-01129, Vilnius, Lithuania
e-mail: arturasro@gmail.com

N. Schofield et al. (eds.), *Advances in Political Economy*,
DOI 10.1007/978-3-642-35239-3_18,

notion of policy platforms as points has a very limited reach. For example, it cannot be applied to study policy positions of decentralized political parties involving a variety of activists with diverse policy preferences (Aldrich 1983; Miller and Schofield 2003). Another case concerns developing democracies, where, for many reasons, parties are known to lack defined ideological positions (Evans and Whitefield 2000; Kitschelt et al. 1999; Mainwaring 1995; Scully 1995). If policy positions are defined as points, it is not clear what it means for a party or a candidate not to have a position. Conceptualizing policy position as a probability distribution provides a more general approach to empirical study of party competition: a "no position" platform can be described by a highly dispersed distribution whereas a platform as a point can be defined as a distribution with a vanishingly small dispersion.

Although there are multiple reasons to study ideological ambiguity, efficient tools to measure this quantity are lacking. The existing scholarship on the measurement of policy positions operates under the assumption that these positions are points, often even referred to as 'ideal points' (Ansolabehere et al. 2001; Clinton et al. 2004; Laver et al. 2003; Martin and Quinn 2002). This paper presents a statistical model to estimate ideological ambiguity from survey data (e.g., opinion polls or expert surveys)—the kind of data that is widely available in terms of temporal depth and geographical width.

2 Survey Data and Ambiguity Measurement

The existing literature offers two approaches for measuring ideological ambiguity. The first approach uses direct measures by asking respondents to report their uncertainty about the position of a given candidate (Alvarez 1997) or by asking them to place political actors on a scale in a form of an interval rather than a point (Tomz and van Houweling 2009). Unfortunately, such surveys are rare making it difficult to use these approaches for a systematic study of ideological ambiguity, especially in a cross-national context.

Another approach is to use indirect methods where ambiguity is inferred either from disagreement among the respondents (Campbell 1983a,b) or from the patterns in the missing survey data (Bartels 1986). These indirect methods can be applied to many data sets, which ask citizens or political experts to place political parties on a policy scale. However, a naive application of these approaches is wanting, as I discuss now.

2.1 Interpreting Respondent Disagreement

Every survey where respondents are asked to place political candidates on issue scales generates variation in judgments. It appears intuitive to use the sample standard deviation of the placements $\hat{\sigma}$ as an estimate of a party's ideological ambiguity as suggested by Campbell (1983a,b). However, the intuition is flawed on several levels. First, a high degree of disagreement between the respondents (and hence high $\hat{\sigma}$)

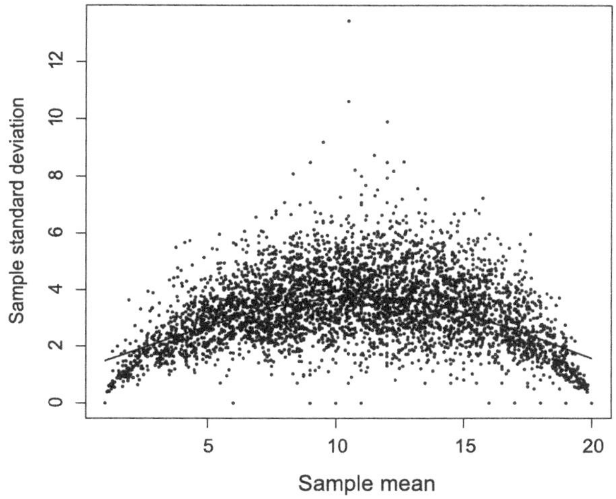

Fig. 1 Sample mean and standard deviation in Benoit and Laver (2006) expert data

may indicate the lack of information on the part of respondents (Marks et al. 2007) or an intrinsic ambiguity of a party's policy position Campbell (1983a,b). Thus, to correctly estimate ideological ambiguity, we have to disentangle the respondent-level and party-level effects on the observed respondent disagreement.

Second, respondent disagreement might occur due to the scale-heterogeneity effect: even if a party is not ambiguous and respondents are well-informed, they might provide conflicting placements due to different interpretation of the measurement scale. Treating disagreement among respondents without proper adjustments for the scaling effects can result in faulty inference about ideological ambiguity.

The third flaw of $\hat{\sigma}$ as the estimator of ideological ambiguity stems from the ordinal nature of placement scales. Since the respondents are almost universally required to place parties on an ordinal scale, the measurement procedure induces dependence between the sample mean, $\hat{\mu}$, and the sample standard deviation, $\hat{\sigma}$. It is easily demonstrated that for an M category measurement scale, $\hat{\sigma} \leq \sqrt{\hat{\mu}(M - \hat{\mu})}$. Therefore, parties with extreme positions will necessarily be evaluated as less ambiguous simply due to the mathematical properties of the estimators $\hat{\mu}$ and $\hat{\sigma}$. Indeed, this pattern is well represented in the real data on party positions in Fig. 1. The quadratic pattern in Fig. 1 could represent the 'true' relationship between positions of candidates and their ambiguity, or it can merely be an artifact of the measurement model; if we use $\hat{\sigma}$ as our estimate of ambiguity, we simply cannot evaluate which is the case.

2.2 Interpreting Missing Values

A different approach to ambiguity measurement is offered by Bartels (1986), who suggests that respondents are more likely not to place a party on a policy scale if they are uncertain about its platform. In Bartels' model, the source of uncertainty is

Table 1 An example of missing data pattern from Benoit and Laver (2006) expert survey

Expert/Party	PAD	PBDNJ	PD	PDr	*PLL*	PR	PS	PSD
1	NA	9	12	13	14	13	7	8
2	18	19	14	17	NA	16	11	10
3	18	13	16	15	NA	19	3	1
4	NA	2	2	2	NA	2	2	2
5	NA	14	14	14	NA	14	14	14
6	NA	NA	12	NA	NA	NA	9	NA
7	NA	10	14	16	NA	13	8	4
8	NA	8	17	13	18	16	3	7
9	7	10	9	12	NA	5	2	NA
10	8	3	14	12	NA	15	5	7
11	NA	8	12	NA	NA	18	5	16
12	NA	12	15	16	NA	16	9	11
13	NA	3	6	10	NA	6	7	4
14	NA	6	15	16	NA	18	3	5
15	NA	5	5	5	NA	7	4	3
16	NA	5	15	15	NA	15	3	3

respondents' personal characteristics like education or exposure to media. One can extend this idea further and argue that the uncertainty about platforms may have to do not only with the respondent-level knowledge but also with the ambiguity of the platform that is being evaluated.

Table 1 shows an excerpt of expert-data on Albanian political parties from the expert survey in Benoit and Laver (2006). Evidently, there are party-specific and expert-specific effects in the non-response rates: PAD and PLL are the two parties with high non-response rates and experts 6 and 11 appear to be the least knowledgeable. It is reasonable to assume that PAD and PLL have such high non-response rates because they are ambiguous about the given policy—the parties either did not make any public statements on the policy or the statements they made varied greatly in their content.

In sum, the discussion suggests that a proper method for estimating ideological ambiguity should (1) adjust for the scale-heterogeneity effects, (2) separate the respondent- and party-level effects on observed respondent disagreement, and (3) exploit the patterns in missing data as an additional source of information on ideological ambiguity.

3 A Model

Suppose that data provided by respondents $i = 1, \dots, N$ on parties $j = 1, \dots, J$ are generated in a two-step process. In the first stage, respondents perceive a 'true' position of each party on some given issue-scale. Since we define party positions to be probability distributions, we treat each such perception as a random draw from that probability distribution.[3]

In the second stage, the respondent has to report his/her observed value on some ordinal measurement scale. The key issue here is that respondents might differ in their interpretation of the measurement scale. To account for that, I follow the framework by Aldrich and Mckelvey (1977) and assume that each respondent's reported placement is an affine transformation of his/her latent perception. Formally, suppose that the measurement scale has M points and let $C = \{c_m : m = 1, \dots, M\}$ be an ordered set of cut-off points with $c_1 = -\infty$ and $c_M = \infty$. Let z^*_{ij} denote unobserved latent perception of party's j platform by respondent i. The latent policy positions are defined as Gaussian probability distribution functions:

$$z^*_{ij} \sim \mathcal{N}(\mu_j, \sigma^2_j), \tag{1}$$

$$y_{ij} = m \quad \text{iff } c_m < \psi_i z^*_j + \tau_i \leq c_{m+1} \tag{2}$$

where τ_i and ψ_i are expert-specific location and scale parameters accounting for scale heterogeneity. A respondent with a low ψ_i tends to place parties closer to each other than a respondent with high ψ_i. Similarly, a respondent with a high τ_i tends to place parties on the right side of the scale relative to a respondent with low τ_i.

Alternatively, one could specify a common location and scale parameter and allow each respondent to have an idiosyncratic cut-off point, similar to Johnson and Albert (1999) and Clinton and Lewis (2007). For an M point scale, this alternative approach introduces $N(M - 1)$ respondent-level parameters. In comparison, the model in (5)–(6) has only $2N$ respondent-level parameters. Given that the number of parties in any survey is typically small and M is large, a more parsimonious model is preferred.

The model in (1)–(2) can be seen as an extension of some widely used ordinal data models. It represents cross-classified (rather than nested) hierarchical model (Zaslavsky 2003, p. 341). When $\psi_i = 1$ and $\sigma_j = 1$ for all i and j, we would have the usual random-effects linear model coupled with ordinal data. For $\sigma^2_j = \sigma$ for all j, the model results in the scaling model by Aldrich and Mckelvey (1977).[4] Finally, when $\sigma^2_j = 1$ for each j, the model resembles the multiple-rater model as presented in Johnson and Albert (1999, Chap. 5) and applied to expert data by Clinton and Lewis (2007). In contrast to these alternatives, we allow σ_j's and ψ_i's to vary across parties and respondents respectively.

Since the policy space is defined only up to an affine transformation, Aldrich and Mckelvey (1977) suggest to constrain the estimates of μ to have zero mean and unit

[3]For example, such interpretation of respondent opinions has been used in the risk analysis literature (Huyse and Thacker 2004).

[4]Palfrey and Poole (1987) analyzed how assumption of heterogeneous variance affects inference about μ but did not address how σ should be estimated.

standard deviation. These constraints turn out to be insufficient to identify the model in (1)–(2). The following restrictions are imposed instead:

$$\mu_j \in [c_1 - \delta, c_{M-1} + \delta] \quad \text{for } j = 1, \ldots, J, \tag{3}$$

$$\sum_{i=1}^{N} \tau_i = 0 \quad \text{and} \quad \sum_{i=1}^{N} \psi_i^2 = 1 \quad \text{for } i = 1, \ldots, N. \tag{4}$$

Here, δ is a hyper-parameter estimated in the model. Finally, we assume that the cut-off points are fixed at equal intervals between -1 and 1 (any other interval would do as well). Since policy space is defined only up to affine transformation, these constraints do not result in loss of information.

3.1 Model for Missing Data

The model can be extended to exploit the patterns in the missing data (NA responses) as an additional source of information about the ideological ambiguity. In particular, I assume that if a party is perceived to be very ambiguous and/or if a respondent is not knowledgeable, one is more likely to observe an NA answer. Thus, in the terminology of Little and Rubin (1987), we assume that the missing data are non-ignorable. For convenience, let $z_{ij} = \psi_i z_j^* + \tau_i$. Also let $r_{ij} = 1$ if data entry y_{ij} is missing and $r_{ij} = 0$ otherwise. The model for the observed data can be written as

$$z_{ij} \sim \mathcal{N}(\psi_i \mu_j + \tau_i, \psi_i^2 \sigma_j^2), \tag{5}$$

$$y_{ij} = \begin{cases} m & \text{if } c_m < z_{ij} \le c_{m+1} \text{ and } r_{ij} = 0 \\ \text{NA} & \text{if } r_{ij} = 1, \end{cases} \tag{6}$$

$$\Pr(r_{ij} = 1) = \Phi(\alpha_0 + \alpha_1 \sigma_j \psi_i). \tag{7}$$

Notice, first, that if a respondent is not highly knowledgeable (high ψ_i) or a party is ambiguous (high σ_j), or both, the answers will exhibit high variation. Second, z_{ij}'s that are drawn from distributions with low standard deviation (low $\psi_i \sigma_j$) are less likely to be reported as NA's, as implied by the missingness model in (7). Here, Φ is a standard normal distribution function, resulting in a probit model. By making missingness dependent both on σ_j and ψ_i we allow for data distributions where some parties and/or some respondents tend to have more missing values than others. Parameter α_1 measures how much missingness in the data depends on the respondent-level scale ψ_i and party-level ambiguity σ_j.

3.2 Prior Distributions

The model is completed by specifying prior distributions If a cross-national survey is used, one can specify hierarchical priors where some party-level parameters depend upon country-level hyper-parameters. Let $k = 1, \ldots, K$ denote a country in which the survey is taken. The mean ideological positions μ_{jk} are assumed *a priori* to follow truncated normal distributions so that

$$\mu_{jk}|\delta \sim \mathcal{N}(0, \eta_\mu)\mathbb{1}\big[\mu_{jk} \in (c_1 - \delta, c_{M-1} + \delta)\big], \tag{8}$$

$$\ln(\delta) \sim \mathcal{N}(c_{i+1} - c_i, v_\delta). \tag{9}$$

We set $\eta_\mu = 100$ resulting in a vague but proper prior distribution. The hyper-parameter δ is *a priori* set to have a log-normal distribution with mean equal to the distance between any two cut-off points. We set $v_\delta = 1$, resulting in identifiable and yet highly flexible model: under this specification, we have 0.44 prior probability that the most extreme party is two units (one-fifth of the scale) away from the smallest or largest cut-off point. For the remaining parameters, we set

$$\sigma^2_{jk}|b_k \sim \text{Inv-Gamma}\big(a, (a-1)b_k\big), \tag{10}$$

$$b_k \sim \text{Gamma}(\epsilon, \epsilon), \tag{11}$$

$$\psi_{ik} \sim \mathcal{U}\big(\tfrac{1}{2}, 2\big), \tag{12}$$

$$\tau_{ik} \sim \mathcal{N}(0, 1). \tag{13}$$

In (10), the shape and scale of the inverse gamma distribution is fixed so that the $\mathbb{E}(\sigma^2_{jk}) = b_k$. Setting $a = 4$ yields a priori variance of $b^2_k/2$. Letting ϵ be a small number (e.g., 0.1), yields a prior on b_k with large variance; thus, the priors end up having a negligible effect on the estimates. The hierarchical priors induce adaptive shrinkage: the estimates of ideological ambiguity in a country k are shrunken towards the common mean b_k. The statistical advantages of the hierarchical shrinkage are well-documented in the literature (Gelman et al. 2003).

Further, under priors in (12), each respondent can expand or shrink the perceptual space at most by a factor of two. Notice that as $\psi_i \to 0$, the distribution of z_{ij} collapses to a degenerate distribution with the mass at τ_i. This implies that, for ψ_i near zero, a respondent would place all parties on the same point. Similarly, if ψ_i is very large, a respondent places all parties on the opposite extremes of the scale. Since both of these alternatives are not common, we constraint ψ_i's to the specified interval.

Relative to the scale of cut-off points, the prior distribution of τ_i in (13) also allows sizable idiosyncratic location shifts. Lastly, the selection model parameters α_0 and α_1 are assumed to follow normal distributions with 0 mean and variance of 100 (a higher variance reduces the speed of convergence without affecting the results).

4 Parameter Estimation

The model is estimated using Markov Chain Monte Carlo (MCMC) methods using Gibbs sampling approach (Gelfand and Smith 1990). Let N_k and J_k denote the number of respondents and number of parties in country k respectively. Let N_{jk} denote the set of respondents in country k who have placed party j on the scale ($N_k - N_{jk}$ is the number of NA answers for party j in country k). Let $\boldsymbol{y} = (\boldsymbol{y}_{obs}, \boldsymbol{y}_{mis})$, where $\boldsymbol{y}_{obs}$ is observed and $\boldsymbol{y}_{mis}$ is missing data respectively and let $\boldsymbol{z}$ and $\boldsymbol{r}$ denote a vector of latent perceptions z_{ijk} and missing data indicators r_{ijk} respectively. For brevity, let θ denote all parameters of the model. The joint distribution of $\boldsymbol{y}$, $\boldsymbol{z}$ and $\boldsymbol{r}$ is

$$\pi(\boldsymbol{y}, \boldsymbol{z}, \boldsymbol{r}|\theta) = \pi(\boldsymbol{y}_{obs}, \boldsymbol{y}_{mis}, \boldsymbol{z}|\boldsymbol{r}, \theta)\pi(\boldsymbol{r}|\theta). \tag{14}$$

This factorizations yields a pattern-mixture model with shared parameters (Little 1993). In this model, there is a set of common parameters affecting both the distribution of data $\boldsymbol{y}$ and missingness pattern in $\boldsymbol{r}$. In the model of missingness given in (7), the distribution of $\boldsymbol{r}$ depends on the vectors of ambiguity and uncertainty parameters $\boldsymbol{\sigma}$ and $\boldsymbol{\psi}$ and the coefficient vector $\boldsymbol{\alpha} = (\alpha_0, \alpha_1)$. Note that this model differs from selection models of missing data where the distribution of $\boldsymbol{r}$ depends on $\boldsymbol{y}_{obs}$ and $\boldsymbol{y}_{mis}$ but not on the data model parameters. The model for the observed data is derived by integrating out the missing data from the complete data model, so that

$$\begin{aligned}\pi(\boldsymbol{y}_{obs}, \boldsymbol{z}, \boldsymbol{r}|\theta) &= \int \pi(\boldsymbol{y}_{obs}, \boldsymbol{y}_{mis}, \boldsymbol{z}|\boldsymbol{r}, \boldsymbol{\mu}, \boldsymbol{\sigma}, \boldsymbol{\tau}, \boldsymbol{\psi})\pi(\boldsymbol{r}|\boldsymbol{\sigma}, \boldsymbol{\psi}, \boldsymbol{\alpha})d\boldsymbol{y}_{mis} \\ &= \pi(\boldsymbol{y}_{obs}|\boldsymbol{r}, \boldsymbol{\mu}, \boldsymbol{\sigma}, \boldsymbol{\tau}, \boldsymbol{\psi})\pi(\boldsymbol{r}|\boldsymbol{\sigma}, \boldsymbol{\psi}, \boldsymbol{\alpha}).\end{aligned} \tag{15}$$

This yields the complete data likelihood, which is a product of two likelihoods—one for observed data and one for missing data:

$$\begin{aligned}L(y, z, r; \theta) \propto &\prod_{k=1}^{K} \prod_{i \in N_{jk}} \prod_{j=1}^{J_k} \pi(y_{ijk}, z_{ijk}|\mu_{jk}, \tau_{ik}, \sigma_{jk}, \psi_{ik}) \\ &\times \prod_{k=1}^{K} \prod_{i=1}^{N_k} \prod_{j=1}^{J_k} \pi(r_{ijk}|\sigma_{jk}, \psi_{ik}, \boldsymbol{\alpha}).\end{aligned} \tag{16}$$

Using previously specified prior distributions, the full conditionals for most of the parameters in the model have known distributional form. Specifically, the Gibbs sampler iterates between the following blocks:

1. Sample latent perceptions z_{ijk} conditional on the observed data y_{ijk} and all parameters of the model:

$$z_{ijk}|y_{ijk}, \cdot \sim \mathcal{N}\left(\mu_{jk}\psi_{ik} + \tau_{ik}, \psi_{ik}^2\sigma_{jk}^2\right) \mathbb{1}(c_{y_{ijk}} < z_{ijk} \leq c_{y_{ijk}+1}).$$

2. Given the latent variables $\boldsymbol{z}$, the remaining full conditionals do not depend on the ordinal data $\boldsymbol{y}$. The means of the platforms are sampled as follows:

$$\mu_{jk}|\boldsymbol{z}_{jk}, \cdot \sim \mathcal{N}\left(S_{jk}/D_{jk}, \sigma_{jk}^2/D_{jk}\right)\mathbb{1}(c_1 - \delta < \mu_{jk} < c_{M-1} + \delta),$$

where $S_{jk} = \sum_{ik}(z_{ijk} - \tau_{ik})/\psi_{ik}$ and $D_{jk} = N_{jk} + \sigma^2_{jk}/\eta_\mu$. The respondent location parameters are sampled as follows:

$$\tau_{ik}|\cdot \sim \mathcal{N}\left(\frac{\sum_j (z_{ijk} - \psi_{ik}\mu_{jk})/\sigma^2_{jk}}{\sum_{jk}\sigma^{-2}_{jk} + \psi^2_{ik}}, \frac{\psi^2_{ik}}{\sum_{jk}\sigma^{-2}_{jk} + \psi^2_{ik}}\right).$$

3. Full conditionals for $\boldsymbol{\sigma}$ and $\boldsymbol{\psi}$ do not have a recognizable form, thus Metropolis-Hastings algorithm is employed. The log-posterior of σ^2_j is proportional to

$$\ln \pi\left(\sigma^2_j | z, \mu, \tau, \psi, a_k, \alpha\right) \propto -(N_{jk}/2 + 3)\ln \sigma^2_{jk} - \sigma^{-2}_{jk}\left(S_{jk}/2\psi^2_{ik} + b_k\right)$$
$$+ \sum_{i \in N_k} r_{ijk} \ln p_{ijk} + (1 - r_{ijk})\ln(1 - p_{ijk}),$$

where $p_{ijk} = \Phi(\alpha_0 + \alpha_1 \phi_{jk}\sigma_{jk})$ and $S_{jk} = \sum_{i \in N_{jk}}(z_{ijk} - \psi_{ik}\mu_{jk} - \tau_{ik})^2$. The log-posterior for $\boldsymbol{\psi}^2$ has a similar form:

$$\ln \pi\left(\psi^2_{ik} | z, \mu, \sigma, \tau\right) \propto -(J_{ik}/2 + 1/2)\ln \psi^2_{ik} + S_1/\psi^2_{ik} - S_2/\psi_{ik}$$
$$+ \sum_{i \in N_k} r_{ijk} \ln p_{ijk} + (1 - r_{ijk})\ln(1 - p_{ijk}),$$

where $S_1 = .5\sum_{jk}(z_{ijk} - \tau_{ik})^2\sigma^{-2}_{jk}$ and $S_2 = \sum_{jk}(z_{ijk} - \tau_{ik})\mu_{jk}\sigma^{-2}_{jk}$. Proposal values $\sigma^{2(t)}_{jk}$ are sampled from the inverse gamma with shape λ and scale $(\lambda - 1)\sigma^{2(t-1)}_{jk}$. Here, λ is the tuning parameter that set to achieve an acceptance rate between 30 and 50 %.
4. $\ln(\delta)$ is sampled from the left-truncated normal distribution with mean $c_{i+1} - c_i$, unit variance and lower bound equal to $\ln(\max\{\mu_{jk}\} - c_{M-1})$. The conditional distribution for the hyper-parameter b_k is gamma with scale $2J_k + \epsilon$ and rate $(a - 1)\sum_j \sigma^{-2}_j + 1/\epsilon$.
5. The coefficients in the missing data model, α_0 and α_1, are sampled using the standard data augmentation method by Albert and Chib (1993).

To implement the identification constraints in (4), after each block of iterations, each ψ_{ik} is divided by the country average of ψ_{ik}'s; similarly, from each τ_{ik} the country average of τ_{ik}'s is subtracted. This procedure is similar to hierarchical centering by "sweeping" and is known to improve the convergence of MCMC algorithms in weakly identified models (Robert and Casella 2004, p. 397). The convergence can be monitored using the standard tools, as, for example, Geweke (1992) or Heidelberger and Welch (1983) diagnostics.

5 Application: Ideological Ambiguity and Electoral Performance

We apply our model to the expert data by Benoit and Laver (2006). The survey was conducted in 48 countries with about 8 parties and 30 experts per country on average. The analyzed dataset contains 10,603 entries with about 9 % of missing values, 364 parties, and 1493 experts. Our goal is to investigate whether a party's ambiguity on the issue of taxation and provision of public services is related to its ideological extremism and vote-share in the last elections.

In the survey, the experts were asked to place political parties on the 20 point scale with the end-points defined as follows:

[1] Party promotes raising taxes to increase public services.
[20] Party promotes cutting public services to cut taxes.

The posterior estimates of σ from the proposed model are very different from the naive sample standard deviation, with correlation of only 36 percent. The posterior mean of the missing data mechanism parameter α_1 is 0.245 with the standard deviation of 0.014 indicating that the missingness of the data is related to the ambiguity of party positions and the uncertainty of experts. Together this serves as the evidence that (1) the sample standard deviation would yield an incorrect measure of ideological ambiguity *if the assumed data generating model is valid* and that (2) the patterns in missing data do provide additional information about the ideological ambiguity and respondent uncertainty.

Using direct measures of ideological ambiguity and voters' uncertainty, the previous literature has found that ambiguity is related to voting behavior (Alvarez 1997; Tomz and van Houweling 2009). Therefore, ideological ambiguity should also be also related to a party's electoral performance. In case the model provides correct estimates of ideological ambiguity, one should observe *a* relationship between the posterior estimates of ideological ambiguity and vote-shares of political parties. Furthermore, if the sample standard deviation $\hat{\sigma}$ is not a valid measure of ideological ambiguity (as was suggested earlier), the correlation between $\hat{\sigma}$ and the parties' electoral performance should be low.

After computing the posterior distributions of σ_{jk}'s for all parties in the dataset, the following model is estimated:

$$T(v_{jk}) = \beta_0 + \beta_1|\mu_{jk} - \overline{\mu}| + \beta_2\frac{1}{1+\sigma_{jk}} + \epsilon_{jk}, \tag{17}$$

where v_{jk} is a vote-share of party j in country k, $T(\cdot)$ is a Box-Cox transformation, and $\overline{\mu}$ is the estimated empirical center of party platforms. The coefficients β_1 and β_2 represent the effect of ideological extremism and ideological precision (the inverse of the ideological ambiguity) respectively.

The model in (17) is estimated in three settings. In the first setting, I use the sample mean $\hat{\mu}$ and standard deviation $\hat{\sigma}$ in place of μ and σ in (17). In the second setting, the mean posterior estimates $\mathbb{E}(\mu|y)$ and $\mathbb{E}(\sigma|y)$ derived from the latent hierarchical model are used in place of $\hat{\mu}$ and $\hat{\sigma}$. Both of the above models do not take into account the fact that the covariates $(\hat{\mu}, \hat{\sigma})$ and $(\mathbb{E}(\mu|y), \mathbb{E}(\sigma|y))$ are only estimates that are measured with error, not fixed values. Ignoring, the presence of the measurement error in the covariates might lead to invalid inference about the regression parameters in model (17).

Table 2 Ideological ambiguity and electoral performance of parties

	No measurement error[a]		With measurement error[b]
	$\hat{\mu}, \hat{\sigma}$	$\mathbb{E}(\mu\|y), \mathbb{E}(\sigma\|y)$	$\mathbb{E}(\mu\|y), \mathbb{E}(\sigma\|y)$
Intercept	-2.32^{**}	-3.125^{***}	-3.823[c]
	(0.115)	(0.156)	[−4.393, −3.275][d]
Extremism:	−0.01	-0.073^{*}	−0.049
$\|\mu_{jk} - \overline{\mu}\|$	(0.03)	(0.042)	[−0.137, 0.030]
Ideological precision:	0.039	2.875^{***}	3.860
$1/(1 + \sigma_{jk})$	(0.612)	(0.413)	[2.486, 5.126]
RMSE	1.126	1.057	
R^2	0.1-e4	0.12	
AIC	1124	1078	
$F(2, 361)$	0.062	24.5	
N	364	364	

$^{*}p < 0.1$, $^{**}p < 0.05$, $^{***}p < 0.001$

[a]Frequentist regression ignoring the measurement error in the covariates. Standard errors in the parentheses

[b]Bayesian regression with flat priors accounting for the measurement error

[c]Posterior mean

[d]95 % highest posterior density interval

Therefore, in the third setting, the linear regression with measurement error is fit to the data. This is accomplished easily by adding a step in the Gibbs sampling algorithm. Assuming uniform priors over the coefficients $\boldsymbol{\beta}$ and regression error s^2—$\pi(\boldsymbol{\beta}, s^2) \propto 1/s^2$—one can sample $\boldsymbol{\beta}$ from the multivariate normal distribution with mean $(\boldsymbol{X}'\boldsymbol{X})^{-1}\boldsymbol{X}'T(\boldsymbol{v})$ and covariance matrix $s^2(\boldsymbol{X}'\boldsymbol{X})^{-1}$, where $\boldsymbol{X}$ is the design matrix for model in (17) and $\boldsymbol{v}$ is the vector of vote-shares. At each iteration, the columns of $\boldsymbol{X}$ representing μ and σ are replaced with a draw from the posterior $\pi(\mu|y)$ and $\pi(\sigma|y)$ respectively. Finally, s^2 is sampled from the inverse gamma distribution with shape $J/2$ (where J is the overall number of parties in the analysis) and scale $(T(\boldsymbol{v}) - \boldsymbol{X}'\boldsymbol{\beta})'(T(\boldsymbol{v}) - \boldsymbol{X}'\boldsymbol{\beta})/2$.

Results of the three analyses are reported in Table 2. First, let us compare the two frequentists regressions that use the naive sample estimates and the average posterior estimates from the proposed model. Evidently, there are stark differences: If the sample estimates of μ and σ are used, there is no statistically tractable relationship between the electoral performance of a party and its ideological ambiguity or extremism. None of the coefficients are significant at conventional levels and the overall fit of the model is extremely poor, as indicated by low R^2 and F statistics. Both of these results are counter-intuitive as existing theories and evidence would suggest that ideological extremism is rarely rewarded by voters and that ideological ambiguity *does* affect voters' behavior.

In contrast, if one uses the measures of μ and σ derived from the proposed latent hierarchical model, the model fit increases dramatically as indicated by lower root mean squared error (RMSE), higher R^2 and F statistics and substantially lower Aikaike's Information Criterion (AIC). In this model, increasing ideological ambiguity and extremism are both statistically associated with worse electoral performance. Since this empirical pattern is closer to the theoretical expectations, this suggests that the measure σ derived from the latent hierarchical model does improve upon the naive estimator.

Finally, the third model which takes into account the measurement error in μ and σ, shows qualitatively similar results, albeit, with some important deviations. First, the effect of ideological extremism is now lower and the 95 % credible now covers zero (though 90 % credible interval does not cover zero, however). Second, the effect of ideological precision increases by about 1/3 when the measurement error is taken into account. Fitting the model with the measurement error is more appropriate given the nature of the problem and it is advisable to use this approach as a standard practice.

It is important to note that we do *not* claim to have found any causal effect of ideological ambiguity on the electoral performance. It might well be the case that smaller political parties have fewer means to communicate their policy positions and there is nothing in the design of our analysis that would allow us to circumvent this problem. Instead, the nature of this exercise was merely to show that these two quantities are associated—as we should expect them to be—and that the sample estimates of ideological ambiguity would (perhaps erroneously) lead us to believe otherwise.

6 Discussion

The goal of this study was to construct and evaluate a model that allows to estimate ideological ambiguity from survey data. The proposed model focused on synthesizing two distinct approaches previously used by political methodologists—one approach focused on disagreement among the respondents while another approach attempted to infer the degree of ideological ambiguity from the patterns of missing data. This study demonstrated how these two approaches can be synthesized into a single inferential framework yielding more accurate and more informative measures of ideological ambiguity than what is offered by focusing on naive sample standard deviations. The greater accuracy results from the fact that the latent hierarchical model exploits the rich informational structure of the survey data and allows to represent policy positions of parties in terms of probability distributions rather than points.

Although the proposed method of inferring ideological ambiguity is promising, there are several issues that should be further studied. First, the model relies heavily on the assumption that the patterns of data missingness are related to underlying ideological ambiguity. The estimates of the model will be biased to the extent that this assumption is violated. A survey experiment where, in placing parties, some respondents use the interval scales (e.g. Tomz and van Houweling 2009) while others place them on the standard single-point scales could evaluate the empirical plausibility of this assumption. Second, external validation analyses using direct measures of ideological ambiguity as benchmarks could also elicit potential strengths and weaknesses of the proposed model.

References

Albert JH, Chib S (1993) Bayesian analysis of binary and polychotomous response data. J Am Stat Assoc 88(442):669–679

Aldrich J (1983) A spatial model with party activists: implications for electoral dynamics. Public Choice 41(1):63–100

Aldrich J (1995) Why parties?: The origin and transformation of political parties in America. University of Chicago Press, Chicago

Aldrich J, Mckelvey R (1977) A method of scaling with applications to the 1968 and 1972 presidential elections. Am Polit Sci Rev 71(1):111–130

Alesina A, Cukierman A (1990) The politics of ambiguity. Q J Econ 105(4):829–850

Alvarez MR (1997) Information and elections. University of Michigan Press, Ann Arbor

Ansolabehere S, Snyder JM Jr, Stewart CS III (2001) Candidate positioning in US house elections. Am J Polit Sci 45(1):136–159

Bartels L (1986) Issue voting under uncertainty: an empirical test. Am J Polit Sci 30:709–728

Benoit K, Laver M (2006) Party policy in modern democracies. Routledge, London

Callander S, Wilson CH (2008) Context-dependent voting and political ambiguity. J Public Econ 92(3–4):565–581

Campbell JE (1983a) Ambiguity in the issue positions of presidential candidates: a causal analysis. Am J Polit Sci 27(2):284–293

Campbell JE (1983b) The electoral consequences of issue ambiguity: an examination of the presidential candidates' issue positions from 1968 to 1980. Polit Behav 5(3):277–291

Clinton JD, Jackman S, Rivers D (2004) The statistical analysis of roll call data. Am Polit Sci Rev 98:355–370

Clinton JD, Lewis DE (2007) Expert opinion, agency characteristics, and agency preferences. Polit Anal 16(1):3–20

Evans G, Whitefield S (2000) Explaining the formation of electoral cleavages in post-communist democracies. In: Klingemann HD (ed) Elections in central and eastern Europe. The first wave, Edition Sigma, Berlin

Gelfand AE, Smith AFM (1990) Sampling-based approaches to calculating marginal densities. J Am Stat Assoc 85(410):398–409

Gelman A, Carlin JB, Stern HB, Rubin DB (2003) Bayesian data analysis, 2nd edn. Chapman and Hall, London

Geweke J (1992) Evaluating the accuracy of sampling-based approaches to calculating posterior moments. In: Bernado JM, Berger JO, Dawid AP, Smith AFM (eds) Bayesian statistics, 4th edn. Clarendon, Oxford

Glazer A (1990) The strategy of candidate ambiguity. Am Polit Sci Rev 84(1):237–241

Heidelberger P, Welch PD (1983) Simulation run length control in the presence of an initial transient. Oper Res 31:1109–1144

Huyse L, Thacker BH (2004) Decision making under uncertainty on the basis of expert opinion. In manuscript

Johnson VE, Albert JH (1999) Ordinal data modeling. Springer, New York

Kitschelt H, Mansfeldova Z, Markowski R, Toka G (1999) Post-communist party systems. Cambridge University Press, Cambridge

Laver M, Benoit K, Garry J (2003) Extracting policy positions from political texts using words as data. Am Polit Sci Rev 97(2):311–331
Little RJA (1993) Pattern-mixture models for multivariate incomplete data. J Am Stat Assoc 88(421):125–134
Little RJA, Rubin D (1987) Statistical analysis with missing data. Wiley, New York
Mainwaring S (1995) Brazil: weak parties, feckless democracy. In: Mainwaring S, Scully T (eds) Building democratic institutions. Stanford University Press, Stanford
Marks G, Hooghe L, Steenbergen MR, Bakker R (2007) Crossvalidating data on party positioning on European integration. Elect Stud 26(1):23–38
Martin AD, Quinn KM (2002) Dynamic ideal point estimation via Markov chain Monte Carlo for the U.S. supreme court, 1953–1999. Polit Anal 10(2):134–153
Miller G, Schofield N (2003) Activists and partisan realignment in the United States. Am Polit Sci Rev 97(2):245–260
Page BI (1976) The theory of political ambiguity. Am Polit Sci Rev 70(3):742–752
Palfrey TR, Poole KT (1987) The relationship between information, ideology, and voting behavior. Am Polit Sci Rev 31(3):511–539
Robert CP, Casella G (2004) Monte Carlo statistical methods, 2nd ed. Springer, New York
Scully T (1995) Reconstituting party politics in Chile. In: Mainwaring S, Scully T (eds) Building Democratic Institutions. Stanford University Press, Stanford
Shepsle KA (1972) The strategy of ambiguity: uncertainty and electoral competition. Am Polit Sci Rev 66(2):555–568
Tomz M, van Houweling RP (2009) The electoral implications of candidate Ambiguity. Am Polit Sci Rev 103(1):83–98
Zaslavsky A (2003) Hierarchical bayesian modeling. In: Press JS (ed) Subjective and objective bayesian statistics. Principles, models, and applications. Wiley, New York

Biographies

1 Editors' Biographies

Norman Schofield was the Director of the Center in Political Economy at Washington University in Saint Louis from 1992 until 2012. He is currently the William R. Taussig Professor of Political Economy, and Professor in the Departments of Economics and Political Science. He has Ph.D.'s in both government and economics from Essex University, a LittD from Liverpool University and a doctorat d'etat from the University of Caen. He is currently working on topics in the theory of social choice, political economy, and democracy. He has written several books, including *Multiparty Government* (with Michael Laver, in 1990), *Social Choice and Democracy* (Springer, 1985), and edited or co-edited ten volumes, including *The Political Economy of Institutions, Democracy and Voting*, (co-edited with Gonzalo Caballero, Springer, 2011). His book, *Mathematical Methods in Economics and Social Choice*, was published by Springer in 2003. In 2006 he published *Architects of Political Change* as well as *Multiparty Democracy* (with Itai Sened) both with Cambridge University Press. His book, *The Spatial Model of Politics* was published by Routledge in 2008, followed by *The Political Economy of Democracy and Tyranny* in 2009 with Oldenbourg (Munich). He has just completed a book, *Leadership or Chaos* (co-authored with Maria Gallego, published by Springer in 2011). He has been the recipient of a number of NSF awards, most recently one on electoral politics and regime change. In 2003 he was the Fulbright distinguished professor at Humboldt University and, in 2007 and 2008, visiting fellow at ICER in Turin. In Spring 2008 he was the visiting Leitner Professor at Yale University and was a National Fellow at the Hoover Institution in summers 2009 and 2010. He was recipient of the Riker prize for contributions to political theory in 2002, and was elected to the American Academy of Arts and Sciences in 2005.
schofield.norman@gmail.com

Gonzalo Caballero is an Associate Professor of Economics at the University of Vigo, Spain. He received his Ph.D. and a B.Sc. in Economics with Honors from the University of Vigo, and he received a MPhil in Contemporaneous Political Studies

DOI 10.1007/978-3-642-35239-3, © Springer-Verlag Berlin Heidelberg 2013

from the University of Santiago de Compostela. He has been a Visiting Scholar at the Center for New Institutional Social Sciences, Washington University in St. Louis, the Center for Advanced Study in the Social Sciences in Madrid, the University of California in Santa Barbara and the University of California in Berkeley. He taught a course on "Economics of Institutions" at Charles University in Prague, at Comenius University in Bratislava and at the University Roma Tre. He has published many papers on institutional analysis in various journals, including *Economic Modelling*, *Journal of Institutional Economics*, *Ocean & Coastal Management*, *Marine Policy*, *Environmetrics*, *El Trimestre Económico*, *Brazilian Journal of Political Economy*, *Política y Gobierno*, *Revista Española de Investigaciones Sociológicas*, *Revista de Estudios Políticos* and *Revista Española de Ciencia Política*. He has written several books and co-edited a volume on the Great Recession.
gcaballerom@yahoo.com

Daniel Kselman is a Research Fellow at the Center for Advanced Studies in the Social Sciences, Juan March Institute (Madrid). His research employs both game theoretic and econometric modelling to study the impact if political institutions and political party organizations on a variety of contemporary political phenomena, including but not limited political corruption, legislative instability, and democratic accountability. He is also a student of modern Turkish politics, and has written on Turkish political institutions and party organizations.
dkselman@march.es

2 Biographies of Contributors

James Adams is Professor of Political Science at the University of California at Davis. He studies voting behavior, parties' election strategies, and political representation in Western Europe and the United States. His research, which encompasses both spatial models of party competition and empirical analyses of parties' policy programmes, has appeared in *the American Political Science Review*, *the American Journal of Political Science*, *the Journal of Politics*, *Political Analysis*, and *Public Choice*.
jfadams@ucdavis.edu

Luz Marina Arias received her Ph.D. in Economics from Stanford University. Her research focuses on the political economy of economic and political development, and in particular on the mechanisms behind institutional change and continuity. Her work has centered on the indigenous origins of colonial labor in the Americas, and on the origins of centralized fiscal capacity in Latin America. She has received fellowship positions from the Center for U.S.-Mexican Studies at the University ofCalifornia in San Diego and the Center on Democracy, Development and the Rule of Law at Stanford University. Luz Marina was born and raised in Mexico City and completed her undergraduate studies in Economics at ITAM, Mexico City.
larias@march.es

Xosé Carlos Arias is Professor of Economics and Economic Policy at the University of Vigo (Spain). In recent years, he actively worked in the analysis of the financial crisis in the world economy and the development of the research program of Transaction Cost Politics. He recently published the book *La torre de la arrogancia. Políticas y mercados después de la tormenta*, (Ariel, Barcelona, 2011), jointly with Antón Costas. He also co-edited *Organización de gobiernos y mercados*, (PUV, Valencia). He has published several papers on different topics in journals such as *Desarrollo Económico*, *Revista de Economía Aplicada*, *Revista Española de Ciencia Política* and *Revista de Economía Institucional*, among others.
xcarias@uvigo.es

Walter Borges obtained his Ph.D. from the University of Texas at Dallas in 2008 and is currently an assistant professor of Political Science at the University of North Texas-Dallas. His research focuses on public support for governments and parties, and the short- and long-term effects of austerity measures in industrialized democracies. He has also written on the economic policies of the Obama administration. In his first career as a journalist, he wrote extensively about electoral politics, judicial politics and judicial decision-making in Texas.
Walter.Borges@unt.edu

Thomas L. Brunell is a professor of Political Science at the University of Texas at Dallas. His teaching and research interests revolve around elections, representation, political parties and the U.S. Congress. He received his Ph.D. from the University of California, Irvine in 1997. His book "*Representation and Redistricting: Why Competitive Elections are Bad for America*" was published in 2008. He is currently working on a book about partisan gerrymandering.
tlb056000@utdallas.edu

Ernesto Calvo (Ph.D. Northwestern) is an Associate Professor of Political Science at the University of Maryland. His research focuses on issues of political representation, elections and Congresses. His research, which has received awards from the Representation and the Comparative Politics sections of the American Political Science Association, has been published in U.S., European, and Latin American journals such as the *American Journal of Political Science*, *the Journal of Politics*, *World Politics*, *The British Journal of Political Science*, *Comparative Political Studies*, *Electoral Studies*, *Política y Gobierno* (Mexico), *Desarrollo Económico* (Argentina), *Opiniao Publica* (Brazil), and the *Revista de Ciencia Politica* (Chile).
ecalvo@umd.edu

Kiyoung Chang is a Ph.D. Student in Government and Politics at the University of Maryland. His research interests include the diffusion of terrorism, bargaining in civil war, domestic audience costs, and U.N. voting.
Kiyoung Chang@gmail.com

Harold D. Clarke (Ph.D. Duke University) is Ashbel Smith Professor, School of Economic, Political and Policy Sciences, University of Texas at Dallas, and Adjunct Professor, Department of Government, University of Essex. He also is editor of

Electoral Studies. Clarke's research on electoral choice and the political economy of party support in Great Britain, the United States and Canada has been supported by the National Science Foundation (U.S.), the Economics and Social Research Council (U.K.), and the Social Sciences and Humanities Research Council (Canada). He is currently a principal investigator for the 2009/10 British Election Study and the 2008 Political Support in America Study. Other current research projects include the 2009 Political Support in Germany Study, and the 2008 Political Support in Canada Study. He is the author of numerous articles published in journals such as the *American Journal of Political Science, the American Political Science Review, the British Journal of Political Science*, the *Journal of Politics and Political Analysis*. His most recent books are *Performance Politics and the British Voter* (Cambridge: Cambridge University Press, 2009), *Making Political Choices: Voting in Canada and the United States* (Toronto: University of Toronto Press), and *Political Choice in Britain* (Oxford: Oxford University Press, 2004). Clarke's teaching interests focus on public opinion, voting and elections and research methods. He regularly teaches advanced time series analysis at the Essex Summer School in Data Collection and Analysis and the Concordia University Spring School.

hclarke@utdallas.edu

Betul Demirkaya is a graduate student in political science at Washington University in Saint Louis.

betul.demirkaya@wustl.edu

Leandro De Magalhães studied Economics at the University of Brasilia and received his Ph.D. from Bocconi University. For two years during his Ph.D. he was a visiting student at the University of Pennsylvania. He is currently an Assistant Professor at Bristol University. He has worked on the size of government in the American states, on Brazilian politics, and is currently working on war financing and political transitions.

leandro.magalhaes@bristol.ac.uk

Jon X. Eguia is an assistant professor in the Department of Politics and affiliated to the Department of Economics at New York University. He obtained his Ph.D. from the California Institute of Technology in 2007. His fields of specialization are political economy, formal political theory, social choice and public economics. His work on party formation, voting and elections, and the spatial model of policy preferences has been published in leading political science journals such as the *American Journal of Political Science* and the *Quarterly Journal of Political Science* and in economic theory journals such as *Social Choice and Welfare*, *Games and Economic Behavior*, *Economic Theory* and the *Journal of Mathematical Economics* among others.

equia@nyu.edu

Bernard Grofman is the Jack W. Peltason (Bren Foundation) Endowed Chair at University of California at Irvine (UCI), and Professor of Political Science and

Director of the UCI Center for the Study of Democracy His research deals with topics such as voting rights and theories of representation and electoral rules. He is co-author of 4 books (published by Cambridge University Press), and co-editor of 21 other books; with 250 research single and co-authored articles and book chapters, including ten in the American Political Science Review. He has been a visiting faculty member at nearly a dozen universities in the U.S. and Europe. He is a Fellow of the American Academy of Arts and Sciences, and has an Honorary Doctorate in Political Science from the University of Copenhagen.

bgrofman@uci.edu

Timothy Hellwig is an associate professor of political science at Indiana University. His research interests focus on the political economy of advanced industrial societies. He is currently completing a book manuscript on economic globalization and electoral politics. His work on globalization, economic voting, and party politics appears in the *American Journal of Political Science*, *The British Journal of Political Science*, *The Journal of Politics*, among other outlets.

thellwig@indiana.edu

JeeSeong Jeon is a graduate student in political science, at Washington University in Saint Louis. She has published papers in the *Journal of Elections, Public Opinion and Politics*, and *Electoral Studies*.

jsjeon@wustl.edu

Dean Lacy is Professor of Government and Director of the Program in Politics and Law at Dartmouth College. His Ph.D. in Political Science is from Duke University.

Dean.P.Lacy@dartmouth.edu

Kevin McCalister is a graduate student in political science, at Washington University in Saint Louis.

kevinmcalister@wustl.edu

Samuel Merrill III is Professor Emeritus of Mathematics and Computer Science at Wilkes University. He received his Ph.D. in mathematics from Yale University. His current research involves mathematical and statistical modelling, particularly in political science. He is the author of *A Unified Theory of Party Competition* (Cambridge University Press 2005; with James Adams and Bernard Grofman), *A Unified Theory of Voting* (Cambridge University Press 2005; with Bernard Grofman), and *Making Multicandidate Elections More Democratic* (Princeton University Press 1988). He has published in a number of journals, including the *American Political Science Review*, the *American Journal of Political Science*, and the *British Journal of Political Science*. He has been a Visiting Professor at Yale University and a visiting scholar at the University of Washington.

sammerrill3@comcast.net

Katja Michalak is reader of political science and public administration at the Department of Public Management and Governance at Zeppelin University. She holds a Master's degree in political science with a focus on democratization in Eastern Europe and a Master's degree in psychology with a focus on political psychology and organizational psychology. She received her doctorate (Ph.D.) in the field of 'Comparative Institutions' from Ohio State University with a thesis on 'Civil Service Reform and the Quality of Governance in Eastern Europe'. Her research interests include comparative politics, political governance, bureaucracy, political institutions, democratization, and political psychology.

katja.michalak@zu.de

Emerson Niou (Ph.D., U. of Texas at Austin, 1987), Professor of Political Science, specializes in Formal Theory, International Relations, Political Economy, and East Asian Politics. He is the co-author of *The Balance of Power*, (Cambridge University Press, 1989). His publications in the field of international relations include: "Less Filling, Tastes Great: The Realist-Neoliberal Debate," coauthored with P.C. Ordeshook, *World Politics*, January 1994 and "Alliances in Anarchic International Systems," coauthored with P.C. Ordeshook, *International Studies Quarterly*, June 1994. In the field of East Asian politics, his recent publications include: "An Analysis of Dr. Sun Yet-sen's Self-Assessment Scheme for Land Policy," with G. Tan, *Public Choice*, December 1993; "Seat Bonuses under the Single Non-Transferable Vote for Large Parties: Evidence from Japan and Taiwan," with G. Cox, *Comparative Politics*, January 1994; and "Police Patrol vs. Self-Policing: A Comparative Analysis of the Control Systems Used in the Ex-Soviet Union and the Communist China," with John Brehm, *Journal of Theoretical Politics*, 1996. His current projects include studies of local self-government in China and alliance politics in anarchic international systems. Professor Niou is Director of the Program in Asian Security Studies at Duke University.

niou@duke.edu

John Patty is a formal political theorist whose research focuses on political institutions. He regularly teaches undergraduate courses on Congress and the federal bureaucracy as well as graduate courses on game theory and formal models of political institutions, at Washington University in Saint Louis. His work has been published in *American Journal of Political Science*, *Annual Review of Political Science*, *Economics & Politics*, *Electoral Studies*, *Games & Economic Behavior*, *Journal of Politics*, *Journal of Theoretical Politics*, *Mathematical & Computer Modelling*, *Politics, Philosophy, & Economics*, *Public Choice*, *Quarterly Journal of Political Science*, and *Social Choice & Welfare*. In addition to serving as an Associate Editor of the *American Journal of Political Science*, he currently serves on the editorial boards of *Political Analysis* and *Journal of Theoretical Politics*. He received his Ph.D. in Social Sciences from the California Institute of Technology in 2001. Prior to coming to Washington University, he was Assistant Professor of Political Economy and Decision Sciences at Carnegie Mellon University and Assistant Professor of Government at Harvard University. His

book *Learning While Governing: Expertise and Accountability in the Executive Branch* (with Sean Gaillmard) will appear with the University of Chicago Press in 2013.
jwpatty@gmail.com

Gerald Pech is associate professor of economics at KIMEP University. He received his Ph.D. from Ruhr-University Bochum in Germany in 1995. Since then he has held teaching and research positions at the Graduate School Bochum and Dortmund, the University of St Andrews, the National University of Ireland in Galway, the American University in Bulgaria and the University of Mainz. His areas of research are collective decision making and economic and political institutions.
gp@geraldpech.net

Elizabeth Maggie Penn is a formal political theorist whose work focuses on social choice theory and political institutions. She regularly teaches undergraduate courses on electoral systems and agent-based modelling as well as graduate courses on positive political theory, at Washington University in Saint Louis. Her work has been published in the *American Journal of Political Science*, *Journal of Politics*, *Journal of Theoretical Politics*, *Mathematical & Computer Modelling*, *Public Choice*, *Social Choice & Welfare*, and *Complexity*. Professor Penn received her Ph.D. in Social Sciences from the California Institute of Technology in 2003 and her B.A. from the University of California at Berkeley in 1999. Previously, she was Assistant Professor of Political Economy and Decision Sciences at Carnegie Mellon University (2003–2005) and Assistant Professor of Government at Harvard University (2005–2009).
elizabeth.m.penn@gmail.com

Arturas Rozenas holds Ph.D. in Political Science and M.S. in Statistical and Decision Sciences, both from Duke University. His research focuses on game-theoretic and statistical models of democratic and non-democratic elections and Bayesian statistics. Currently, he is teaching at the ISM University of Management and Economics in Vilnius, Lithuania. In the fall of 2013, he will be joining the Department of Politics at New York University.
arturasro@gmail.com

David Sanders is a Professor of Government and Pro-Vice-Chancellor (Research) at the University of Essex, where he has taught politics since 1975. He is author of numerous books and articles on various aspects of U.K. and comparative politics. He has been a Fellow of the British Academy since 2005, and was joint editor of the *British Journal of Political Science* from 1990 to 2008. He is the author of *Patterns of Political Instability* (1981); *Lawmaking and Co-operation in International Politics* (1986); *Losing an Empire; Finding a Role: British Foreign Policy Since 1945* (1990), and co-author of *On Message* (1998); *Political Choice in Britain* (2004); *Performance Politics* (2009). His current research is on the British Election

Study, as well as political participation; election forecasting; the politics of the U.K. public sector; measuring and assessing European citizenship.

sanders@essex.ac.uk

Keith Schnakenberg is a Ph.D. student in political science at Washington University in Saint Louis.

keith.schnakenberg@gmail.com

Evan Schnidman obtained his AB and AM in political economy from Washington University in Saint Louis. He is currently a graduate student in the Department of Government, Harvard University.

evan.schnidman@gmail.com

Gilles Serra graduated with a Ph.D. in Political Economy and Government from Harvard University in 2007. He won a fellowship to do post-doctoral research at Nuffield College at the University of Oxford until 2010, and he is currently an assistant professor at the Center for Economics Research and Teaching (CIDE) in Mexico City. Dr. Serra uses formal theory to study political parties, elections, campaigns, and congressional reforms. His main regions of interest are Latin America and the United States. His publications have appeared in respected academic journals such as the *Journal of Politics*, the *Journal of Theoretical Politics*, and *Política y Gobierno*. This research has been presented in several universities in the United States, Europe, Latin America and Canada.

gilles.serra@cide.edu

Olga Shvetsova is an associate professor of political science and economics at Binghamton University, USA. She studies political mechanisms as they are shaped by institutional choices. Her long-term research focus is on incentives to political elites and how those can lead to amelioration of societal conflict. She publishes in the fields of political economy of federalism and determinants of party system stability and change in democracies. She co-authored *Designing Federalism: A Theory of Self-Sustainable Federal Institutions* (with Mikhail Filippov and Peter C. Ordeshook, Cambridge University Press, 2004) and is now working on *Parties and Party System Change in Legislatures Worldwide* (with Carol Mershon).

shvetsova@gmail.com

Katri Sieberg is the Erkko Professor of North American Studies in the School of Social Sciences and Humanities at the University of Tampere in Finland. Her research combines approaches from economics and political science to address the issues of how and why things work—or don't work. To that end, her research uses social choice theory to address how people make decisions, policy analysis to assess the effect of these decisions, and experimental analysis to evaluate the underlying theories. One of her key interests is welfare state institutions, with a recent focus on health care structures.

katri.sieberg@uta.fi

Marianne C. Stewart (Ph.D. Political Science, Duke University) is a Professor, and Co-Director of The Survey Center for Opinion Research and Elections, in the School of Economic, Political and Policy Sciences at the University of Texas at Dallas. She also has been Executive Vice-Dean, Acting Dean, Graduate Studies Director, and Political Science Program Director in the School at UTD, and on the faculties of Virginia Polytechnic Institute and State University and Rutgers University. She has been Editor of *The American Journal of Political Science*, Associate Editor of *International Studies Quarterly*, Assistant Editor of *The Journal of Politics*, and Political Science Program Director in the Division of Social and Economic Sciences of the National Science Foundation.

She conducts research and teaches in the areas of electoral politics, political behavior, and research methodology. She has been co-investigator of the British Election Study (2001, 2005, 2009–2010), and funded by the National Science Foundation and the Economic and Social Research Council (U.K.). Her articles have been published in *The American Journal of Political Science, The American Political Science Review, The British Journal of Political Science, The Journal of Politics, Political Analysis*, and other major research journals. Her recent books are *Political Choice in Britain* (Oxford University Press, 2004) and *Performance Politics and the British Voter* (Cambridge University Press, 2009).

mstewart@utdallas.edu

Fernando Toboso is Senior Lecturer at the Department of Applied Economics, University of Valencia, Spain. His research interests are in methodological and epistemological issues in economic analysis as well as the organization of policy tasks and public services provision, with an emphasis on the new Spanish federalism. He has contributed to several edited volumes on these topics and has published in various academic journals including the *Cambridge Journal of Economics, Regional and Federal Studies, European Journal of Law and Economics, Journal of Interdisciplinary Economics, Hacienda Pública Española, El Trimestre Económico*, and *Presupuesto y Gasto Público*. He has been a visiting scholar at the Public Choice Center, George Mason University, Leeds University, and the University of Bologna, Italy. He has also served as invited editor and author for a special issue published in the *Chilean Revista de Análisis Económico*, and has recently co-edited a book on economics and institutions.

Fernando.Toboso@uv.es

Paul Whitely is the author of *The Labour Party in Crisis*; *Political Control of the Macroeconomy* and co-author of *Advanced Statistical Methods in the Social Sciences*; *Pressure for the Poor—The Poverty Lobby and Policy-Making*; *How Voters Change: The 1987 British General Election Campaign in Perspective*; *Controversies in Political Economy—Canada, Great Britain and the United States*; *Labour's Grassroots—The Politics of Party Membership*; *True Blues: The Politics of Conservative Party Membership*; *High Intensity Participation—The Dynamics of the Party Activism in Britain*; *New Labour's Grassroots: The Transformation of the Labour*

Party Membership; *Political Choice in Britain: Citizenship in Britain: Values, Participation and Democracy*; *Third Force Politics: Liberal Democrats at the Grassroots*; *Performance Politics and the British Voter*. Author or co-author of more than fifty articles on: political economy; electoral behavior; political parties; British politics, citizenship, social capital and quantitative methods in political science. He was Director of the Economic and Social Research Council Research Programme on Democracy and Participation, 1998–2003 and co-director of the ESRC funded British Election Study.

whiteley@essex.ac.uk